ISBN: 9781313725675

Published by:
HardPress Publishing
8345 NW 66TH ST #2561
MIAMI FL 33166-2626

Email: info@hardpress.net
Web: http://www.hardpress.net

HISTORICAL COMMENTARIES

ON THE

STATE OF CHRISTIANITY

DURING THE FIRST THREE HUNDRED AND TWENTY-FIVE YEARS

FROM

THE CHRISTIAN ERA:

BEING

A TRANSLATION OF

"THE COMMENTARIES ON THE AFFAIRS OF THE CHRISTIANS BEFORE THE TIME OF CONSTANTINE THE GREAT,"

BY JOHN LAURENCE VON MOSHEIM, D. D.

LATE CHANCELLOR OF THE UNIVERSITY OF GOTTENGEN.

In two Volumes.
VOL. I.

VOLUME I. TRANSLATED FROM THE ORIGINAL LATIN,

BY

ROBERT STUDLEY VIDAL, Esq. F. S. A.

VOLUME II. TRANSLATED, AND BOTH VOLUMES EDITED,

BY

JAMES MURDOCK, D. D.

NEW-YORK:

PUBLISHED BY S. CONVERSE.

1852.

D. FANSHAW, Printer and Stereotyper,
35 Ann, corner of Nassau-street.

ADVERTISEMENT BY THE EDITOR.

This first volume of Dr. Mosheim's Historical Commentaries is a reprint of Robert Studley Vidal's translation, published in London, 1813, in two small volumes 8vo. The Editor has aimed to give Vidal's translation unaltered, except by the correction of typographical errors. But he has taken the liberty to arrange the notes, as in the original Latin, in solid masses, subjoined to the several sections. He has likewise altered the running titles or headings of the pages, and the location of the contents of each section; and has abridged Vidal's general Table of Contents, prefixed to the volume. He has, moreover, inserted, in the outer edges of the pages, the bracketed paging of the original, to enable the reader to find readily in this translation, the pages cited or referred to by the many writers who refer to the original Latin work. These alterations in the volume translated by Vidal, will render it similar in form to the subsequent volume translated by the Editor.

J. MURDOCK

New-Haven, May 1st, 1851.

PREFACE

BY THE EDITOR OF THE FIRST VOLUME AND TRANSLATOR
OF THE SECOND.

These very profound and learned Commentaries on the early history of the Church, were composed not long before the author's death, and, of course, contain his most matured thoughts and opinions on the important and interesting topics discussed. In this work he aims not only to give a good general History of the period over which the work extends, but also to embrace a thorough and candid Discussion, conducted on sound historical principles, of all the obscure and difficult points in this portion of ecclesiastical history. The general History he includes in his text, which is broke into short sections or paragraphs: the Discussion follows, in the form of notes or commentaries, constituting much the larger part of the work, and that in which he cites or refers to all the material testimonies of the ancients, and fully discusses their import and value, according to his maturest judgment.

Subsequent writers, especially within the last fifty years, while going over the same ground, have subjected Mosheim's opinions and reasonings to fresh examination; and, being aided by the discovery of some new authorities, and by the general advances of human knowledge, they have undoubtedly detected some errors of judgment in our author, and have cast some additional light on the obscure and difficult subjects he examines. But still these learned commentaries continue to be regarded as a standard work, by all Protestant ecclesiastical writers, and they are often quoted as being of high authority, and as models of profound and courteous historical discussion.

The original Latin work was printed in 1753, in a vol. of 988 pages, small 4to; and, having been long out of print, it is exceedingly difficult to be obtained. This induced a very competent English layman, Robert Studley Vidal, Esq. F. S. A. several years ago, to undertake an English translation of the work. From the year 1813 to the year 1837, he published three small volumes, embracing about three-fifths of the whole work, and bringing the history some distance into the third century. He is not known to have proceeded any further in translating, and nothing has been published by him during the last 14 years.

Vidal's translation is very faithful and true: but it has a fault not uncommon with the English writers; that of a too great fulness of expression, or the needless multiplication of words. Of the extent to which this fault prevails, the reader may form some judgment, by comparing the two volumes here presented to the public. In the first volume 447 pages of the Latin original make 536 pages in Vidal's translation; while, in the second volume, 542 pages of Latin make only 487 pages in our translation; that is, he expands the same amount of Latin into *four* pages, as we express adequately and fully in about *three* pages.— Vidal also erred, as we think, in changing the form or arrangement of the book; for he stretched the text along the tops of all the pages, and threw the commentary into notes at the bottom, which not only embarrassed the reading of the text, but often rendered it difficult to trace the connexion between the text and the notes. This error is avoided in both the volumes of this edition.

The translation of this second volume was undertaken nearly three years ago, by advice of several learned gentlemen, and at the particular request of Professor Frederic Huidekoper, of Meadville, Pennsylvania, who has most liberally patronised the work. At first it was proposed to translate only that large portion of the original which Vidal had left untouched. But, it being found advisable to issue the work in *two* volumes, the *first* embracing the first and second centuries, and the *second* including the third and fourth, it was deemed advisable to re-translate that minor part of the third century, which Vidal had translated in his verbose manner, so that each volume might preserve, throughout, a uniformity of style, or bear the impress of a single translator.

The editor of the first, and translator of the second of these volumes, has no higher aim in bringing the work before the public, than to present to the English reader the learned commentaries of Mosheim just as they are; with no enlargement, abridgement, or alteration. He has not gone into a re-examination of the topics discussed, or attempted to improve the original work, by adding to it the results of more recent investigations; nor has he criticised the arguments of his author, in any learned additional notes. He is content to be a mere editor and translator.

Some gentlemen advised the introduction of such improvements and criticisms as would make the work reflect the light thrown on several of the subjects by the writers who have written since the publication of the original work. But this would require about as much labor as to compose a new book; and it would either not preserve the work of Mosheim entire, or would greatly swell its bulk, and make it an undigested mass of diverging opinions and views.—Others recommended the insertion of an English translation of all the Greek and Latin quotations occurring in the work. But this would add much to its bulk, would enhance the price, and would make it less acceptable to the well educated readers.—For these reasons, the course adopted by Vidal has been followed, and Mosheim's Commentaries are here given to the public, with no modifications except the translation of the Latin original into English. And, perhaps, it may be the most satisfactory to many readers, to have the high authority of Mosheim standing alone, that they may examine and compare him for themselves, with those who have ventured to differ from him, on certain obscure and dubious points in the early history of the church.

The copious Tables of Contents which Vidal prefixed to his small volumes, have been combined, abridged, and prefixed to the first volume; and a similar table has been composed for the second volume. The Tables, it is believed, constitute an important addition to the original work.—And, as the Commentaries will be found to be most frequently referred to by the paging of the original Latin work, that paging has been inserted in brackets, at the outer ends of the lines of the translation, throughout both volumes: and a Table of the coincidences of that paging with ours, has been subjoined to the second volume.—The General Index to the whole work has been retained, translated into English, and annexed to the same volume. But the Index of authors quoted, and that of Passages of Scripture illustrated, have been omitted.

For the publication of the work in so elegant a style, and at so moderate a price, the reading community are indebted to Sherman Converse, Esq., who will be remembered as the very enterprising publisher, a few years ago, of extensive and learned works: and who, while laboring under severe bodily infirmities, has ventured upon an enterprise which promises lasting benefit to the learned world, although it may fail to repair materially his pecuniary misfortunes, as well as to remunerate adequately the editor and translator.

JAMES MURDOCK.

New-Haven, May, 1851.

THE

AUTHOR'S PREFACE.

THE work which I here offer to the public, owes its origin rather to a fortuitous concurrence of circumstances, than to any regular premeditated design. My *Institutes of Christian History* having met with such a rapid sale, that every copy was disposed of within four years; the worthy person at whose expense they were printed, urged me to publish an enlarged and improved edition of them. In compliance with his wishes, I sat down to a revision of the work; and having compared its contents with the original ancient authorities, together with what else was to be met with on the subject in the writings of the learned, and also with such notes and observations as a daily course of reading and reflection had enabled me to make, I perceived, or rather my attention was again caught by what for many years before I had perceived to be the case, that in the history of Christian affairs, some things had been almost entirely omitted, others not properly represented, and not a few, either from negligence, a partial view of the subject, or the placing of too great a reliance on the industry of others, altogether misconceived.

Whatever remarks of this kind presented themselves, were carefully minuted down, with a view to render the proposed fourth edition of my book both more complete and of greater utility than the preceding ones. Proceeding constantly in this way, my collection of notes at length acquired no inconsiderable degree of bulk; and the more frequently I considered them, the more disposed I felt, (for we naturally conceive a regard for what has cost us some pains,) to believe them not wholly unworthy of being preserved. In the course of time, a thought suggested itself to me of writing a set of Commentaries on Christian affairs, upon a different scale; reducing my observations within a narrower compass on such topics as had been sufficiently treated of by others, and at the same time, giving a more copious and satisfactory discussion of those matters which a long course of study and attention had rendered more particularly familiar to me, and respecting which I had obtained a precise and accurate knowledge. I mentioned this idea to the person above spoken of, who had submitted to me the proposal of publishing an enlarged edition of my former small work, and it met with his approbation : but, as the undertaking was of some magnitude, we agreed that the work should be published in separate parts; taking care, however, that each division might be so far complete in itself as not to have the appearance of being disjointed, or awkwardly torn off from the rest. The work was accordingly taken up by me without delay; and I have now to express my hope, that what is here offered to the public as the first part, (but which may be considered as forming a work of itself,) may be productive of the wished-for beneficial effects. If the Supreme Disposer of human affairs prolong my days, and grant me a continuance of my health and faculties, the others will follow in regular succession. Indeed the next, consisting of *Commentaries on the affairs of the Christians under the family of Constantine,* may be expected within a very short period : the materials have been long since collected and arranged, and only wait for the printer.

Since the subject of the following work has been treated of by many before me, it is impossible but that my book should contain several things in common with theirs; but notwithstanding this, it will be found, both in respect of the matter, as well as of the manner of handling it, to differ considerably from other works of a similar kind. With regard to the form or order of narration, I have endeavoured to steer a middle course, having neither arranged my materials after the plan of annals, nor yet according to that which I followed in my smaller history, and which many prefer, of distributing the transactions of each century under certain general titles. Each of these modes has its advantages: the latter, however, is attended with this inconvenience, that it frequently separates things the most closely connected; and by thus interrupting the chain of history, renders it difficult for the reader to trace the progress of events from their beginning to their close, or to connect some of the great revolutions and changes with the causes which produced them. My object, therefore, has been to unite, as far as possible, the advantages of both these methods, by managing my subject so as that, whilst every proper attention was paid to the order of time, a due regard should likewise be had to the connecting of events with their causes, and the keeping distinct things which had no relation to each other. I trust that both the memory and the judgment of the reader may be assisted by this mode of arrangement, and that it will be found instrumental in developing the more remote causes of those changes which have occasionally taken place in the Christian commonwealth.

For the matter which forms the basis of this work, I have principally depended on such original monuments of antiquity as have escaped the ravages of time. I have not, indeed, neglected to avail myself of whatever assistance could be drawn from those writers of a more recent date, whose merits have given them an authority with the public, and stamped a celebrity of character on their works; but, at the same time it has been my care to follow none of them without consulting, and, as far as I was able, examining with attention and assiduity the original sources themselves from whence the authors derived, or appeared to have derived, their information. That the reader may the more readily judge of my caution and fidelity in this respect, I have, in every case where doubts might arise on a point of any moment, subjoined the testimony of these ancient writers in their own words. I have not occupied myself in discussing the merits of the different opinions, explanations, and conjectures that are to be met with in the writings of the learned, unless through necessity, or where the antiquity and weight of the opinions themselves, or the abilities and high reputation of the authors by whom they were maintained, appeared to demand it. In treating of Christian affairs, it has been my study rather to recount what, upon the faith of ancient writers, I consider as the simple fact, than to entangle myself with any particular opinions that may have been entertained on the subject.

I have intentionally avoided entering into any discussion respecting matters of a minute and trifling kind; such, for instance, as the birth-place of Simon, Valentine, and others, the particular year in which any sect sprung up, the exact situation of places, obsolete and obscure words and phrases, and the like. For, not to say any thing of the uncertainty with which things of this sort must, in a great measure, remain enveloped, in spite of every endeavour that might be used to extricate them, it would neither be consistent with propriety, nor attended with the promise of any sort of benefit, to occupy the attention with them in a history like the present, of the practical species, or that which applies itself to the immediate and most important purposes of life; although, in another place, the consideration of them might probably be productive both of pleasure and utility. Besides, there are many works already extant, in which those who have a taste for disquisitions of this kind may meet with the most ample gratification.

In the following Commentaries the history of the first century will be found less copious than that of the succeeding ones: indeed, in some instances the reader will meet with scarcely anything more than a mere summary notice of the facts. To account for this it need only be known that an enlarged edition of my *Institutes of the Ecclesiastical History of the First Age* is already before the public, in which, whoever shall be desirous of obtaining further information on any topic which is but slightly noticed in the present work, may find it treated of expressly and more at large. I could not by any means, consistently with the plan of these Commentaries, entirely pass over the first century, since it was my design that they should comprehend an universal history of ecclesiastical affairs, from the commencement of the Christian era to the time of Constantine the Great, written upon a different scale from that of my former work, and disposed after a new method: but, on the other hand, common justice appeared to demand that I should not wholly disregard the interests of those who had purchased my above-mentioned enlarged Elementary History of the First Age; nor could I in any shape reconcile it with the principles of fairness and honesty, to send out into the world a mere transcript or repetition of what was already before it, under a different title. I therefore determined to follow a middle line of conduct, confining my account of the transactions of the first century within much narrower limits than I had prescribed to myself in my former work, but, at the same time, availing myself of the present opportunity to make several corrections in the history of that period, and also to enrich it with some additional matter. In fact, the two works will be found to assist and reflect mutual light on each other. The enlarged edition of my Institutes will supply the reader with a more ample and minute investigation of such particulars, relating to the history of the first century, as are but briefly touched on in the following work; whilst, on the other hand, by a reference to these Commentaries, light will be obtained on such matters as are not treated of with sufficient perspicuity in the Institutes, some partial omissions in that work will be supplied, and the means be furnished for correcting some inaccuracies which found their way into it through inadvertence, or want of better information. If, in the following work, any particulars hitherto unknown be brought to light; their due weight be given to any circumstances hitherto passed over without proper attention; any points, hitherto but imperfectly supported by proofs, or not explained with sufficient perspicuity, be substantiated and rendered easy of apprehension, (and unless I have been led to form too favourable an estimate of my reading, my memory, and my judgment, the book will be found to have some pretensions of this sort,) it will better accord with my feelings to leave these things to be noticed by the intelligent reader in the course of his progress, than for me to anticipate his discernment, by pointing them out in this place.

Göttingen, Sep. 6, A. D. 1753.

THE

TRANSLATOR'S PREFACE.

THE name of Dr. Mosheim ranks so deservedly high in the republic of Letters, that no additional recommendation, it is presumed, can be wanting to ensure the attention of the learned to any work that may come forth under its sanction. As a writer of Ecclesiastical History, this profound and judicious scholar may be said to stand without a competitor. The subject was congenial to his mind, and, whether we consider the talents he possessed, or the peculiar judgment and felicity with which he applied them to the elucidation of this department of literature, his merit is alike conspicuous, and can never be too highly appreciated or extolled.

Amongst other works of acknowledged ingenuity and erudition, which he published on this interesting and important subject, the one which we now venture to submit to the public, for the first time, in an English translation, appears to have engaged a very considerable portion of his attention and pains.

That vast fund of curious and important matter, which, in the shape of Notes, will be found to constitute its chief bulk, could not possibly have been within the reach of any common degree of exertion: on the contrary, we offer it; with no small confidence, to the intelligent reader, as an illustrious memorial of those laborious and extensive researches, and that severe course of study to which it is well known that Dr. Mosheim devoted himself, for the purpose of illustrating the history of Christianity, and bringing it more within the grasp of ordinary diligence and apprehension.

The masterly and highly valuable disquisitions which are to be met with in these Notes, respecting many abstruse and intricate points connected with the rise and first establishment of Christianity, appear to have been founded on a most comprehensive and deliberate re-examination of the Ecclesiastical History of the first ages, originally undertaken by the learned author with a view to an enlarged edition of his Elements of Christian History, a work of high and established reputation, and of which the English reader long since received a translation from the pen of the late learned Dr. Archibald Maclaine.* But, as the nature and design of that work could not well be brought to admit of any thing like a detailed examination, or satisfactory discussion, of several topics on which the curiosity of an intelligent and inquisitive reader might very naturally be excited, the illustrious author appears to have conceived that it would be yielding no unacceptable service to the literary world for him to write a set of Commentaries on a plan which, touching but lightly on subjects that had been previously well illustrated, should have an express reference to the investigation of such interesting particulars as had not been satisfactorily discussed either in his own Institutes or in the works of any other writer.

* And more faithfully translated, and much enlarged with notes, by James Murdock, D. D. and entitled: "Institutes of Ecclesiastical History, Ancient and Modern," in four books. The second edition is now published by Stanford and Swords, New-York.—ED.

Of these projected Commentaries, it is to be lamented that Dr. Mosheim lived only to publish a portion; but it will, we presume, be productive of no small degree of satisfaction to the reader, to be apprised that the work is complete as far as it goes, and embraces the entire history of somewhat more than the first three centuries; a period, perhaps, beyond all others, replete with matter of the highest import to the right understanding of the genuine, unsophisticated principles of the Christian Religion.

Of the motives by which the translator was induced to undertake the rendering of this Work into English, it can be necessary to say but little. It will probably be though sufficient for him to remark, that the original Work, having been long held in the highest estimation by those the best qualified to judge of its merits,* it was imagined that an attempt to extend,

---

* Amongst the more recent testimonies in favour of this Work, the Public will, we are persuaded, attach no inconsiderable degree of weight to that of the Rev. Henry Kett, B. D. senior Fellow of Trinity College, Oxford; who includes these Commentaries in the List of Books recommended at the end of his "Elements of General Knowledge," (vol. ii. p. 31.) and adds, "It is much to be regretted, that this excellent Work has never been translated into English, as it would so well fill up the defective account of the three first centuries in the Ecclesiastical History."

In addition to the very respectable testimony of the Rev. Henry Kett, the translator feels considerable gratification in being permitted to lay before the reader the following extract from a letter addressed to him by his much-respected friend, Charles Butler, Esq. of Lincoln's Inn, with the depth and extent of whose researches in Ecclesiastical and Civil History, the learned world has not now to be brought acquainted.

"I am rejoiced at your intention of favouring us with a publication of your translation of Mosheim's Commentaries. The original work is quite familiar to me. Some years ago I read the whole of it attentively, and committed to paper the observations which occurred to me in the perusal of it. I have since

ın some measure, the sphere of its utility through the medium
of an English translation, would at least be viewed with indulgence, and might possibly be rewarded with approbation by a
liberal and enlightened Public.—It may, however, farther be
observed, that the Book had become exceedingly scarce, insomuch that, although it was not unfrequently sought after with
the most eager assiduity, a copy was rarely to be procured, even
for any price.

In what manner the undertaking has been executed, it will
be for others to determine; and he will, therefore, as to this
point, content himself with merely stating that he has, throughout the whole Work, endeavoured to exhibit the sense of his
original with the most scrupulous fidelity, but at the same time
without so closely pursuing that object as to sink the spirit of
his Author in a tame and servile translation.

In submitting this translation to the judgment of the public,
it would be unbecoming for him not to feel a considerable degree
of diffidence, if not of apprehension.—He has endeavoured, indeed, to render it as perfect as he was able, but he is not so
much the dupe of vain conceit as to imagine that it will be
found altogether free from inaccuracies, or unblemished by mistakes.   There is a proper confidence, however, which belongs to

very frequently consulted it.   There can be no doubt of its being a work of
profound and extensive erudition, and that it contains much learning, both in
respect to fact and deduction, which is no where else to be met with.   It also
abounds with historical and literary anecdote.   In every sense, it is a distinct
work from the Ecclesiastical History; so that it may be deemed as necessary
to the possessors of that work, as if that work had never been written.—I think
your style very clear, and well suited to the work; and have no doubt but that
your translation of the Commentaries will be quite as popular as Maclaine's of
the General History."

every one who, in making an attempt like the present, is not conscious of having undertaken that to which he ought to have known himself to be unequal; and the translator trusts, that it will not be thought exceeding the just limits of that confidence, for him to express a hope that his labours will not be pronounced either discreditable to himself or injurious to the reputation of that illustrious author, to whom it has been throughout his most anxious wish and intention to do justice.

ROBERT STUDLEY VIDAL.

Nov. 17th, 1812.

N. B. The translator had it at one time in contemplation to have subjoined, as he went on, a few remarks of his own on certain points that either appeared to solicit further investigation, or on which additional light has been thrown since the time when Dr. Mosheim wrote; but on further consideration (and more particularly on account of the very great extent to which the page is already occupied with annotation,) he has been induced to abandon that design, and to reserve what observations he may have to offer of his own until the conclusion of the work; when, should the public appear disposed to regard his labours with an indulgent eye, and other circumstances not wear a discouraging aspect, it is his intention to bring them forward in a supplemental volume, accompanied with a Life of Mosheim, a Catalogue of his numerous Publications, and a Translation of some of his most approved Dissertations and smaller pieces.——To pledge himself to any thing beyond this at present, might, perhaps, be thought to savour somewhat of presumption; but he trusts that he shall not incur the imputation of arrogance, by adding, that there is one other undertaking, in the way of translation, to which he has occasionally ventured to direct his attention, and which, should it ever be in his power to accomplish, will put the English reader in possession of a work that, in the original Latin, has long been considered as an inestimable appendage to one of the noblest productions of the human mind: he alludes to Dr. Mosheim's Notes on Cudworth's Intellectual System of the Universe.

Testimonials prefixed to Vidal's Third Vol. printed A. D. 1837.

" Whether the Theologian or the general scholar be employed in ascertaining the nature of Christianity, including both doctrine and discipline, it is of the greatest moment to investigate the state and condition of the Christian church, previously to its union with the civil power, or its patronage by the emperors of the world. The period, therefore, which the history now before us embraces, ought to be minutely investigated; and we are surprised that the work of Mosheim, entitled *De Rebus Christianorum ante Constantinum Magnum*, and which especially details the epoch in question, was not long ago translated. At last this desideratum is supplied, and we congratulate the public on the execution of the task.——To the excellence, indeed, of the performance, which has been the object of Mr. Vidal's labours, testimonies without end, and such as are of the greatest weight, might be adduced; for scarcely has any writer of eminence had occasion to refer to it who does not pronounce its encomium : a matter of no wonder, when we bear in mind the importance of the subject, the judgment and discrimination which the author displays in treating it, the vast information which the work imparts, and the luminous and fair manner in which it is given.——No person who makes pretensions to liberal and enlarged knowledge can dispense with the diligent study of it."

" We cannot take our leave of this masterly performance without acknowledging the obligations under which we conceive Mr. Vidal has laid the public by giving it in an agreeable English dress."—*Monthly Review.*

" From the value that we attach to these Commentaries, we feel greatly indebted to Mr. Vidal for the pains which he has taken to render them accessible to the English student. Compared with Dr. Maclaine he will appear to great advantage. That learned person acknowledges he took 'considerable liberties with his author, and often added a few sentences.' Mr. Vidal seems to have indulged in no such liberties. He has faithfully preserved the sense and character of the original, without any sacrifice of the genius or idiom of the English tongue."— *Eclectic Review.*

CONTENTS OF VOL. I.

~~~~~~~~~~~~~~~~

INTRODUCTION

It appears to me desirable, (and the opinion is not, I think, built upon slight grounds,) that before we enter on the history of the origin and progress of Christianity, a summary view should be taken of the age in which the Gospel Dispensation had its commencement. For in no other way than by a reference to the manners and opinions of those times, can we obtain any insight into the reasons and causes of many things which happened to the early Christians, or form a proper judgment of several of their primary regulations and institutions; nor can we know justly how to appreciate the great extent of those benefits which Christ hath procured for mankind, unless we previously acquaint ourselves with the forlorn and miserable condition of the human race before the Redeemer's advent. By way of introduction, therefore, to the following work, we shall, in the first place, present the reader with a sketch of the general state of the world at the time of our Saviour's birth; and then call his attention particularly to the civil and religious economy of the Jewish nation at the same interesting period.

STATE OF THE WORLD.

CHAPTER I.

Of the Civil, Religious, and Literary State of the World in general, at the Time of Christ's Birth.[p. 2.]

I. State of the Roman Empire. At the time when the SON OF GOD, having taken upon himself our nature, was born in the land of Judea, the greatest part of the habitable earth was subject to the senate and people of Rome, who usually committed the care and administration of those provinces which were removed to any considerable distance from the imperial city, to temporary governors or presidents sent from Rome; or if in any of them the ancient form of government was permitted to be retained, gave it such a modification, and clothed it with so many restrictions, as effectually secured to the Roman state a supreme and controling dominion. Although the appearance, or rather the shadow of freedom and dignity yet remained with the senate and people of Rome, the reality had long been lost to them; all power having centred in the one CÆSAR AUGUSTUS, who was graced with the titles of Emperor, High Priest, Censor, Tribune of the People, and Proconsul, and invested with every office of the state that carried with it any thing either of majesty or authority.(')

(1.) Augustin. Campianus, *de Officio et Potestate Magistratuum Romanorum, et Jurisdictione*, lib. i. cap. i. § 2, p. 3. Edit. Genev. 1725, in 4to.

II. Defects of the Roman Government. Were we to form [p. 3.] our judgment of the Roman government from the principles of its constitution, or the nature of its laws, we must consider it as mild and moderate.(') But whatever promise of happiness the equitable spirit of the original system might hold out to the people, it was constantly checked and counteracted by a variety of causes, and particularly by the rapacity and dishonesty of the publicans to whom the collection of the public revenue was entrusted;(²) the unbounded avarice of the governors of provinces to increase their private wealth; and the insatiable cupidity of the people at large, which displayed

itself not merely in the tenacity with which they maintained
every part of their conquests, but also in a constant readiness to seize all opportunities of extending the bounds of the
empire. Whilst, on the one hand, this incessant thirst after
dominion gave rise to continual wars, and rendered it necessary
constantly to burthen the inhabitants of the provinces with the
maintenance of a formidable military force, a thing in itself
doubtless sufficiently grievous, the greedy publicans and governors were, on the other hand, fleecing the people of the residue
of their property by the most shameful and iniquitous pecuniary exactions.

(1.) See a discourse by the very ingenious Mr. Walter Moyle, entitled, *An
Essay upon the Constitution of the Roman Government*, published amongst his
posthumous works, vol. i, p. 1–48. Lond. 1726. 8vo. Petri Giannone, *Histoire Civile du Royaume de Naples*, vol. i, p. 3, 4, et seq. Scip. Maffei, *Verona
Illustrata*, lib. ii. p. 65.

(2.) See Pet. Burmannus, *de Vectigalibus Populi Romani*, cap. ix. p. 123, et seq.

III. **Benefits arising out of the Roman government.** It must not,
however, be overlooked, that the bringing of so many nations
into subjection under one people, or rather under one man, was
productive of many and great advantages. For, 1st, by means
of this, the people of various regions, alike strangers to each
other's language, manners, and laws, were associated together in
the bond of amity, and invited to reciprocal intercourse. 2dly,
By Roman munificence, which shrank from no expense to render the public ways commodious, an easy and ready access was
given to parts the most distant and remote.(') 3dly, Men that
had hitherto known no other rules of action, no other modes of
life, than those of savage and uncultivated nature, had now the
model of a polished nation set before their eyes, and were gradually instructed by their conquerors to form themselves after
it. 4thly, Literature and the arts, with the study of humanity
and philosophy, became generally diffused, and the cultivation
of them extended even to countries that previously had formed
no other scale by which to estimate the dignity of man, than
that of corporeal vigor, or muscular strength.

Since all these things materially contributed to facilitate the
propagation of the gospel by our Saviour's apostles, and enabled

them the more easily to impress mens minds with the doctrines of the true religion, we cannot but readily accord in opinion with those who maintain, that the Son of God could not have revealed himself to mankind at a more favorable or auspicious season.(*)

(1.) See a learned work of Nicol. Bergier concerning the Roman pub- [p. 4.] lic ways, entitled, *Histoire des grands Chemins de l' Empire Romain*, Brussels, 1728, in 4to. Also a treatise by the learned Everard Otto, *de Tutela Viarum publicarum*, lib. ii. p. 314. Many other highly respectable authors have also either professedly, or incidentally, treated of this subject, and pointed out the great care and industry of the Romans to render the channels of communication both by sea and land, throughout every part of the empire, safe, easy, and expeditious.

(2.) Amongst the early fathers of Christianity we may refer to Origen, who particularly notices this circumstance in the second book of his reply to Celsus, p. 79, edit. Cantab. In after-times we find it adverted to by several of those who have entered the lists against the adversaries of revealed religion.

IV. **Peace prevails nearly throughout the world.** Those intestine discords, by which the Roman state had long been distracted and ravaged, were terminated in the acquisition of the sovereign power by Augustus; and the wars with foreign states continued no longer to be undertaken with the accustomed precipitancy, or prosecuted with that degree of ardor by which they had been formerly characterised. Although, therefore, we cannot subscribe to the opinion of those writers, who, being led into a mistake by Orosius, have asserted, that at the time of our Saviour's birth the temple of Janus was shut, (¹) and every part of the Roman empire wrapt in a profound peace, it must nevertheless unquestionably be admitted, that if the period of which we are speaking, be brought into comparison with antecedent times, it may justly be termed the age of peace and tranquillity. Indeed, had not such been the state of things, it would have been almost impossible, (as St. Paul pretty plainly intimates, 1 Tim. ii. 2,) for our Saviour's apostles to have executed, with effect, the important commission to mankind with which they were entrusted.

(1.) Masson has given us a very masterly examination of the ancient opinion respecting the temple of Janus, in his *Templum Jani Christo nascente reseratum*, published at Roterdam, 1706, in 8vo.

V. **State of other nations.** Our knowledge of the state of any of those nations which were situated beyond the confines of the

Roman empire, is of necessity very imperfect and obscure, owing to the paucity of their historical monuments and writers. We obtain, however, light sufficient to perceive that the eastern nations were distinguished by a low and servile spirit, prone to slavery and every other species of abject humiliation, whilst those towards the north prided themselves in cherishing a warlike and savage disposition, that scorned even the restraint of a fixed habitation, and placed its chief gratification in the liberty of roaming at large through scenes of devastation, blood, and slaughter. A soft and feeble constitution both of body and mind, with powers barely adequate to the cultivation of the arts of peace, and chiefly exercised in ministering at the shrine of voluptuous gratification, may be considered as the characteristic [p. 5,] trait of the former; a robust and vigorous corporeal frame, animated with a glowing spirit, that looked with contempt on life, and every thing by which its cares are soothed, and the calamities to which it is obnoxious alleviated, that of the latter.(1)

(1.) *Fere itaque imperia penes eos fuere populos, qui mitiore cœlo utuntur: in frigora, septemtrionemque vergentibus immansueta ingenia sunt, ut ait poeta, suaque fimillima cœlo,* Seneca, *de Ira,* lib. ii. cap. xvi. p. 36. tom. i. opp. edit. Gronov.

VI. **All devoted to superstition and polytheism.** The minds of the people inhabiting these various countries were fettered and held in melancholy bondage by superstitions of the most abominable and degrading nature. At the command of their priests, who were invested with an authority bordering on despotism, these deluded beings shrank from no species of mental debasement whatever, but were ready to plunge headlong into every extravagance of the most absurd and monstrous credulity. In saying this, we would not be understood to mean that the sense of a supreme deity, from whom all things had their origin, and whose decrees regulate the universe, had become entirely extinct; but, that the number of those who endeavoured by meditation and prayer to elevate their minds to a just conception of his nature and attributes, and to worship him in spirit and in truth, was comparatively insignificant, and of no account. Throughout every nation, a general belief prevailed, that all things were subordinate to an association of powerful spirits, who were called Gods, and whom it was incumbent on every one who wished for a happy and prosperous course of life to worship and conciliate. One of these gods was supposed to excel the rest in dignity, and to possess a supereminent authority, by which the tasks or offices of the inferior ones were allotted, and the whole of the assembly, in a certain degree, directed and governed. His rule, however, was not conceived to be by any means arbitrary; neither was it imagined that he could so far invade the provinces of the others as to interfere with their particular functions; and hence it was deemed necessary for those who would secure the favor of Heaven, religiously to cultivate the patronage of every separate deity, and assiduously to pay that homage to each of them which was respectively their due.

VII. **The same deities, however, not worshipped by all.** Every nation, however, worshipped not the same gods, but each had its peculiar deities, differing from those of other countries, not only in their names, but in their nature, their attributes, their actions, and many other respects; and it is an highly erroneous supposition which some have adopted, that the gods of Greece and Rome were the same with those which were worshipped by the Germans, the Syrians, the Arabians, the Persians, the Egyptians, and others.([1]) Pride and ignorance, amongst other motives, and possibly something of a similarity, which might be perceptible between their own statues and images, and those which they [p. 6.] found in other countries, induced the Greeks and Romans to pretend that the gods which they acknowledged were equally reverenced in every other part of the world. In support of this identity, they accustomed themselves to apply the names of their own divinities to those of foreign states; and the opinion of its existence having found abettors in every succeeding age, even down to our own times, the press has swarmed with an host of idle disquisitions on the subject, by which the history of ancient religions, instead of being elucidated, has been involved in a degree of uncertainty, confusion, and obscurity, that is scarcely to be described. It might probably be the case with most nations, that the gods of other countries were held in a sort of secondary reverence, and perhaps in some instances privately worshipped; but of this fact we are certain, that to neglect or disparage the the established worship of the state, was always considered as an offence of the deepest and most heinous nature.

(1.) Athanasius has particularly noticed this in his *Oratio contra Gentes*, tom. i. opp. p. 25.   It has also been pointed out by several modern writers, particularly by Le Clerc in his *Ars Critica*, p. ii. sect. i. cap. xiii. § 11. p. 280 ; and in his *Bibliotheque Choisie*, tom. vii. p. 84.   Also by Dr. Warburton, in his *Divine Legation of Moses*, vol. ii. p. 233, et seq.

VIII. **This diversity of religions did not generate wars.** This diversity of gods, and of religious worship, was never known to generate animosity, or kindle the flames of war between nations, except in the one solitary instance of the Egyptians : and considerable doubts may be entertained whether even in this case a difference of religion alone was the cause of strife.(¹)   Each nation readily conceded to others the right of forming their own opinions, and judging for themselves, in matters of religious concern ; and left them, both in the choice of their deities, and their mode of worshipping them, to be guided by whatever principles they might think proper to adopt.   Although this may appear at first sight to many as a very extraordinary and unaccountable circumstance, yet, when it is examined there will be found nothing in it that should excite either our wonder or surprise.(²)

Those who were accustomed to regard this world in the light of a large commonwealth, divided into several districts, over each of which a certain order of deities presided, and who never extended their views or hopes beyond the enjoyments of this life, certainly could not, with any shadow of justice, assume the liberty of forcing other nations to discard their own proper divinities, and receive in their stead the same objects of adoration with themselves.   The Romans, we know, were jealous in the extreme of introducing any novelties, or making the least change in the public religion; but the citizens were never denied the privilege of individually conforming to any foreign mode of worship, or manifesting, by the most solemn acts of devotion, their veneration for the gods of other countries.(³)

(1.) That the Egyptians were at times engaged amongst themselves in religious wars, *i. e.*, in wars undertaken on account of their gods and their religion, is clear from many passages in ancient authors, the principal of which are brought into one view by Pignorius, in his *Expositio Mensæ Isiacæ*, p. 41, et seq. But if by a religious war be meant that which is undertaken by a nation or people in defence of their religion, or with a view to make another nation or people renounce the religion of their ancestors and adopt theirs, in such case I do not see that those wars of the Egyptians can with any [p. 7] propriety be termed religious ones. The Egyptians engaged in wars with their neighbors, not with a view to make them change their religion, but for the purpose of revenging the injuries that had been done to certain animals which they themselves held sacred. The fact was, that animals, which in some of the provinces of Egypt were reverenced as gods, were in others considered as noxious, and killed whenever they could be found: and hence arose the quarrels and warfare to which we allude.

(2.) See Shaftesbury's *Characteristics*, passim, vol. ii. p. 166. iii. p. 60. 86, 87. 154, &c.

(3.) Vid. Corn. a Bynkershoock, *Dissert. de Cultu peregrinæ Religionis apud Romanos*, in Opuscul. Lug. Bat. 1719, 4to. No. iv. Matth. Ægyptii. *Dissertatio ad Senatus consultum de Bacchanalibus*, tom. vii. Livii Drakenborchiani, p. 197, et seq. Warburton's *Divine Legation of Moses*, vol. i. p. 307, et seq.

IX. **Various kinds of deities.** The principal deities of most nations, consisted of heroes renowned in antiquity, kings, emperors, founders of cities, and other illustrious persons, whose eminent exploits, and the benefits they had conferred on mankind, were treasured up and embalmed in the minds of posterity, by whose gratitude they were crowned with immortal honours, and raised to the rank of gods. An apotheosis had also been bestowed on several of the softer sex, whose virtues or superior talents had improved and thrown a lustre on the age in which they lived. This may easily be perceived by any one who will take the pains to explore the sources of the heathen mythology; and it at once accounts for what must otherwise appear a monstrous incongruity, namely, that of their attributing to those celestial beings the same evil propensities, errors, and vices, that we have daily to deplore as the characteristic frailties of human nature. In no other respects were the gods of the Gentiles supposed to be distinguished beyond mankind, than by the enjoyment of power, and an immortal existence. To the worship of divinities of this description was joined, in many countries, that of some of the noblest and most excellent parts of the visible world; luminaries of heaven in particular, the sun, the moon, and the stars, in whom, since the effects of their influence were constantly to be perceived, a mind or an intelligence was supposed to reside. The superstitious practices of some regions were carried to an almost endless extreme: mountains, rivers, trees, the earth, the sea, the winds, even the diseases of the body, the virtues and the vices, (or rather certain tutelary genii, to whom the guardianship and care of all these things were conceived to belong,) were made the objects of adoration, and had divine honours regularly paid to them. In Egypt this excess of religious culture reached to the worshipping of the most noxious and venomous animals.([1])

(1.) See the learned work of Gerard Jo. Vossius, *De Idololatria*, lib. i, ii, iii.

[p. 8.] X. **Temples and statues of these deities.** Buildings of the most superb and magnificent kind, under the names of temples, fanes, &c. were raised and dedicated by the people of almost every country to their gods, with the expectation that the divinities would condescend to make those sumptuous edifices the places of their immediate residence. They were not all open to the public, but some of them confined to the exercise of private and retired devotion. Internally, those of either description were ornamented with images of the gods, and furnished with altars, and the requisite apparatus for sacrifice.

The statues were supposed to be animated by the deities whom they represented; for though the worshippers of gods like those above described, must, in a great measure, have turned their backs on every dictate of reason, they were yet by no means willing to appear so wholly destitute of common sense as to pay their adoration to a mere idol of metal, wood, or stone; but always maintained that their statues, when properly consecrated, were filled with the presence of those divinities whose forms they bore.(')

(1.) Arnob. *adv. Gentes*, lib. 6. p. 254. edit. Heraldi. Augustin. *de Civitate Dei*, lib. 8. c. 23. p. 161. tom. 7. opp. edit. Benedict. Julian. *Misopogon*, p. 361. opp. edit. Spanheim.

XI. **Sacrifices and other rites.** The religious homage paid to these deities consisted chiefly in the frequent performance of various rites, such as the offering up of victims and sacrifices, with prayers and other ceremonies. The sacrifices and offerings were different, according to the nature and attributes of the gods to whom they were addressed.(') Brute animals were commonly devoted to this purpose; but in some nations of a savage and ferocious character, the horrible practice of sacrificing human victims prevailed. (²) Of the prayers of pagan worshippers, whether we regard the matter or the mode of expression, it is impossible to speak favorably: they were not only destitute in general of every thing allied to the spirit of genuine piety, but were sometimes framed expressly for the purpose of obtaining the countenance of heaven to the most abominable and flagitious undertakings. (³) In fact, the greater part of their religious observances were of an absurd and ridiculous nature, and in many instances strongly tinctured with the most disgraceful barbarism and obscenity. Their festivals and other solemn days were polluted by a licentious indulgence in every species of libidinous excess; and on these occasions they were not prohibited even from making the sacred mansions of their gods the scenes of vile and beastly gratification.(')

(1.) Vid. Jo. Saubertus, *de Sacrificiis veterum*, Lug. Bat. 1699. 8vo. and republished by Crenius.

(2.) See what has been collected on this subject by Columna, in his Commentary on the Fragments of Ennius, p. 29, et. seq. Also Saubertus, *de Sacrificiis veterum*, cap. xxi. p. 455.

(3.) Vid. Matth. Brouerius a Niedeck, *de Adorationibus veterum Populorum*, Traj. 1711, 8vo. Saubertus, *de Sacrificiis*, cap. xii. xiii. p. 343, et seq.

(4.) The impiety and licentiousness which characterised the festivals of heathen nations, are very fully and ably exposed by Philo Judæus, in his treatise *de Cherubim*, p. 155, 156, tom. i. opp. edit. Mangey.

XII. **Their priests.** The care of the temples, together [p. 9.] with the superintendance and direction of all religious ordinances, was committed to a class of men bearing the titles of priests, or flamins. Within the peculiar province of these ministers it came to see that the ancient and accustomed honors were paid to the deities publicly acknowledged, and that a due regard was manifested in every other respect for the religion of the state. These formed their ordinary duties; but superstition ascribed to them functions of a far more exalted nature. It con sidered them rather in the light of intimate and familiar friends of the gods, than in that of officiating servants at their altars; and consequently attributed to them the highest degree of sanctity, influence, and power. With the minds of the people thus prejudiced in their favor, it could be no very difficult thing for an artful and designing set of men, possessed of a competent share of knowledge, to establish and support a system of spiritual dominion of the most absolute and tyrannical kind.

XIII. **Mysteries.** In addition to the public service of the gods, at which every one was permitted to be present, the Egyptians, Persians, Grecians, Indians, and some other nations, had recourse to a species of dark and recondite worship, under the name of mysteries. The practice of certain secret religious rites may indeed be said to have been common to the people of almost all countries except the Romans, who adopted no such usage until the time of Adrian.(') None were admitted to behold or partake in the celebration of these mysteries but those who had approved themselves worthy of such distinction, by their fidelity and perseverance in the practice of a long and severe course of initiatory forms. The votaries were enjoined, under the peril of immediate death, to observe the most profound secrecy as to every thing that passed :(') and this sufficiently accounts for the difficulty that we find in obtaining any information respecting the nature of these recluse practices, and for the discordant and contradictory opinions concerning them that are to be met with in the writings of various authors, ancient as well as modern.(') From what little can be collected on the subject, it should seem that these mysteries were not all of the same nature. In the celebration of some of them, it is pretty plain that many things were done in the highest degree repugnant to virtue, modesty, and every finer feeling. In others, perhaps, the course of proceeding might be of a very different complexion; and it is very probable that in those of a more refined cast, some advances were made in bringing back religion to the test of reason, by inquiring into and exposing the origin and absurdity of the popular superstitions and worship.(') There might, therefore, be some foundation for the promise usually held forth to those who were about to be initiated, that they would be put in possession of the means of rendering this life happy, and also have the expectation opened to them of entering on an improved state of existence hereafter. However this might be, it is certain that the highest veneration was entertained by the people of every country for what were termed the mysteries; and the Christians, perceiving this, were induced to make their religion conform in many respects to this part of the heathen model, hoping that it might thereby the more readily obtain a favorable reception with those whom it was their object and their hope to convert.(*)

(1.) That the Romans practised no sort of mysteries before the time [p. 10.] of our Saviour, is clear from the testimony of Dionysius Halicarnassensis, and others. Aurelius Victor is my authority for considering these secret rites, and particularly the Eleusinian mysteries, to have been introduced at Rome by the emperor Hadrian, whose curiosity was unbounded. *Pace ad orientem composita Romam regreditur. Ibi Græcorum more, seu Pompilii Numæ, cæremonias, leges, Gymnasia, doctoresque curare occœpit ;—atque initia Cereris, Liberæque, quæ Eleusina dicitur Atheniensium modo, Roma percoleret.* Lib. de Cæsarib. cap. xiv. p. 349. edit. Arntzenii. I am aware that the credit of Aurelius Victor has been called in question by several very learned men, but I must confess I know not on what grounds.

(2.) See what has been collected on this subject by Meursius, in his work *de Mysteriis Eleusiniis ;* and by Clarkson, in his *Discours sur les Liturgies,* § 4. p. 36.

(3.) Dr. Warburton has discussed the subject of these mysteries with much ingenuity, though not always with equal felicity, in his celebrated work on *the Divine Legation of Moses,* tom. i. lib. 2. sect. 4. p. 131. s. That great scholar thinks that all the different sorts of mysteries were instituted for the purpose of teaching the doctrine of the immortality of the soul. But this appears to me to be carrying the matter too far. I grant that in some of them, the principles of a rational religion might be inculcated, and the absurdity of the public superstitions exposed; but that this was the case with all, no one can believe who has attended to the nature of the mysteries of Bacchus, the celebration of which, according to Livy, was positively forbidden at Rome. I have myself formerly written on the subject of the mysteries, by way of note to Cudworth's *Intellectual System of the Universe,* tom. i. p. 329. tom. ii. p. 1049 ; and I still retain the same sentiments that I there expressed.

(4.) Vid. Cicero *Disput. Tusculan.* lib. i. cap. 13. tom. 8. opp. ed. minoris Verburgianæ. Lib. i. *de Legibus,* cap. 24. p. 3362. Varro *apud Augustinum de Civitate Dei,* lib. iv. cap. 31. p. 87. tom. 7. opp. Eusebius *Præparat. Evangelica,* lib. ii. cap. 3. p. 61. s.

(5.) They adopted, for instance, in common with the pagan nations, the plan of dividing their sacred offices into two classes : the one public, to which every person was freely admitted ; the other secret or mysterious, from which all the unprofessed were excluded. The initiated were those who had been baptized; the unprofessed, the catechumens. The mode of preparatory examination also bore a strong resemblance, in many respects, to the course of initiatory forms observed by the heathen nations, in regard to their mysteries. In a word, many forms and ceremonies, to pass over other things of the Christian worship, were evidently copied from these secret rites of paganism; and we have only to lament that what was thus done with unquestionably the best intentions, should in some respects have been attended with an evil result.

XIV. **The religion of the Greeks and Romans.** At the time of Christ's birth the religion of Rome had been received, together [p. 11.] with its government and laws, by a great part of the world. The principal tenets of that religion were built on the superstition of Greece ;(¹) but, at the same time there was in some points a material difference between the two. For not to say any thing of the regulations established by Numa and others, relating to the government and support of the state, the people had, in the course of time, adopted much of the old Etruscan mythology, and a place amongst their gods had also been given by them to some of the Egyptian deities.(²)

(1.) Vid. Dionysius Halicarn. *Antiquit. Romanor.* lib. 7. cap. 72. p. 460. tom. i. opp. ed. Hudsoni.

(2.) Vid. Petitus *Comment. in Leges Atticas,* lib. 1. tit. 1. p. 71. s. ed. Batav. Lactantius *Divinar. Institution.* lib. 1. cap. 20.

XV. **The religions of other nations adulterated by the Romans.** But since the conquered nations did not so implicitly conform to the Roman religion as utterly to discard that of their ancestors, a species of mixed religious culture by degrees sprung up in the provinces, partaking in its nature both of the religion of the country, and of that of Rome. It appears to have been the object of the Roman government, at one time, completely to abolish the religious systems of those nations whose sacred rites were of a ferocious and cruel character, or in any shape repugnant to humanity ;(¹) and to introduce their own religion in their stead. The attachment however of those barbarians to the superstitions of their forefathers, entirely defeated the accomplishment of those views, and rendered it impossible to effect any thing beyond a sort of compromise, by which certain of the Roman deities and rites were associated and intermixed with those peculiarly belonging to the conquered countries. Hence it is that we frequently find a deity distinguished by two appellations; the one being its original title, the other that which it had acquired by this kind of denization: and to the same cause we must refer much of that affinity which is often to be perceived between the Roman forms of worship, and those of the nations which they subdued.

(1.) **Vid. Strabo,** *Geograph.* lib. iv. p. 189, 190, where, after descanting on the barbarous and inhuman religious rites of the Gauls, the Germans, and the Celts, he states that every endeavor was used by the Romans to abolish them.

XVI. **The religions of the Indians, Egyptians, Persians, and Celts.** Amongst the most remarkable of the religions which prevailed at that time, may be reckoned those which were cultivated by the Indians, the Persians, the Egyptians, and the Celts. Of these the Indians and Celts are chiefly distinguished, by hav- [p. 12,] ing selected for the objects of their adoration a set of ancient heroes and leaders, whose memory, so far from being rendered illustrious by their virtues, had come down to posterity disgraced and loaded with vice and infamy. Both these nations (or rather classes of men) believed that the souls of men survived the dissolution of their bodies: the former conceiving that all of them without distinction migrated into new terrestrial habitations; whilst the latter on the contrary, considering immortal life as the meed bestowed by heaven on valor alone, supposed that the bodies of the brave, after being purified by fire, again became the receptacles of their souls, and that the heroes thus renewed, were received into the council and society of the gods. The most despotic authority was committed to their priests by the people of either country: their functions were not limited to the administration of divine matters, but extended to the enacting of laws, and the various other departments of civil government.

XVII. **The religion of the Egyptians.** In treating of the religion of the Egyptians, it is necessary to make a distinction; since only a part of it can properly be considered as the general religion of the country, the practice of the rest being confined to particular provinces or districts. The liberty which every city and province enjoyed of adopting what gods it pleased, and of worshipping them under any forms which the inhabitants might think proper to institute, of course gave rise to a great variety

of private systems. In the choice of their public or national
gods, no sort of delicacy was manifested, the chief class of them
being indiscriminately composed of mortals renowned in history
for their virtues, and those distinguished alone by the enormity
of their crimes : such as Osiris, Serapis, Typhon, Isis and others. With the worship of these, was joined that of the constel-
lations, the sun, the moon, the dog-star, animals of almost every
kind, certain sorts of plants, and I know not of what else.
Whether the religion of the state, or that peculiar to any province or city be considered, it will be found equally remote in
its principles from every thing liberal, dignified, or rational;
some parts were ridiculous in the extreme, and the whole in no
small degree contaminated by a despicable baseness and obscurity. Indeed the religion of the Egyptians was so remarkably
distinguished by absurd and disgraceful traits, that it was made
the subject of derision even by those whose own tenets and
practice were by no means formed on the suggestions of a sound
wisdom.(¹) The priests had a sacred code peculiarly their own,
founded on very different principles from those which characterized the popular religion, and which they studiously concealed
from the curiosity of the public, by wrapping it up in characters
the meaning and power of which were only known to themselves. Nothing absolutely certain, it should seem, can be ascertained respecting it; but if we may give credit to what is said
by some ancient authors on the subject, it bore a pretty close
analogy to that system which attributes the production of every
part of the universe to a certain energy or power contained and
operating within itself; putting nature, in fact, in the place of the
Deity.(²)

(1.) See what I have said concerning the religion of the Egyptians in a
note to Cudworth's *Intell. System.* tom. i. p. 415.

(2.) The more occult and abstruse parts of the Egyptian religion have been
investigated with much sagacity and erudition by the learned Paul. Ern. Ja-
blonski in his *Pantheon Ægyptiorum, seu de diis eorum Comment.* 8vo. Francf.
1750.

[p. 13.]   XVIII. **The religion of the Persians.** The Persians
owed their religious institutes chiefly to Zoroaster. The leading
principle of their religion was, that all things were derived from

two common governing causes; the one the author of all good, the other of all evil: the former the source of light, mind, and and spiritual intelligence; the latter that of darkness and matter, with all its grosser incidents. Between these two powerful agents they supposed a constant war to be carried on. Those however who taught upon this system did not explain it all in the same way, or draw from it the same conclusions; hence uniformity was destroyed, and many different sects generated. The opinion of the better instructed seems to have been, that there was one Supreme Deity, to whom they gave the name of MITH-RA, and that under him there were two of inferior degree, the one called OROMASDES, the author of all good, the other ARI-MAN, the cause of all evil. The common people who equally believed in the existence of a Supreme Being, under the title of MITHRA, appear to have considered him as all one with the sun; and it is probable, that with the two inferior deities above-mentioned, they joined others, of whom scarcely any thing can be known at this day.(')

(1.) Dr. Hyde has written a commentary professedly *de veterum Persarum Religione*, 4to. Oxon. 1700; but his work must be read with some caution. Some remarks on the same subject are to be met with in my notes to Cudworth's *Intellectual System*, tom. i. p. 327 and 249, s.

XIX. **These religions suited to the climate, &c. of the countries where they prevailed.** Whoever will attentively examine the nature of the ancient religions, must, I think, readily perceive that nearly all of them were framed by the priests upon principles suited to the climate, the extent, and the civil constitution of the states for which they were respectively designed. Hence, by way of distinction, they may be divided into two classes, the civil, and the military. Under the former may be placed the systems of almost all the eastern nations, the Persians, Indians, Egyptians and others, whose religious institutes were manifestly subservient to the public weal, by promoting the safety and tranquillity of the people, encouraging those arts by which the necessaries of life were multiplied, and securing to the kings and magistrates a due degree of authority and dignity. Within the latter division we would comprehend the religious economy of

all the people of the north ; nations whose every sentiment imbibed from their priests, respecting the gods, and the proper
mode of sacred worship, tended to inspire them with fortitude
[p. 14.] of mind, a contempt of death, a ferocity of disposition,
and every other quality calculated to form a valorous and warlike people. Under governments of a mild and moderate character, the gods were represented as just, placable, and merciful :
in those of the opposite description, the people were made to believe that the deities delighted in severity, were harsh, wrathful,
quickly to be irritated, and with difficulty brought over to the
side of mercy.

     XX. **Virtue and sanctity of morals not promoted by these religions.**
None of these various systems of religion appear to have contributed in the least towards an amendment of the moral principle, a reformation of manners, or to the exciting a love, or even
a respect, for virtue of any sort. The gods and goddesses, who
were held up as objects of adoration to the common people, instead of exhibiting in themselves examples of a refined and supereminent virtue, displayed in illustrious actions, stood forth to
public view the avowed authors of the most flagrant and enormous crimes.(¹) The priests likewise took no sort of interest
whatever in the regulation of the public morals, neither directing the people by their precepts, nor inviting them by exhortation and example, to the pursuit of a wise and honorable course
of life ; but on the contrary indulged themselves in the most unwarrantable licentiousness, maintaining that the whole of religion was comprised in the rites and ceremonies instituted by
their ancestors, and that every sort of sensual gratification was
liberally allowed by the gods to those who regularly ministered
to them in this way.(²) The doctrine of the immortality of the
soul and of a future state of rewards and punishments, had also
been but very partially diffused, and even what had been advanced on the subject was, for the most part, of a very vague
and unsatisfactory nature, and in some respects calculated rather
to corrupt the mind than to produce any good effects. Hence,
at the coming of our Saviour, any notions of this kind found little or no acceptance with those who pretended to any thing beyond a common share of knowledge, and especially the Greeks
and Romans, but were all regarded in the light of old wives

fables, fit only for the amusement of women and children. No particular points of belief respecting the immortality of the soul being established by the public religion, every one was at liberty to avow what opinions he might please on the subject.(³)

(1.) The most learned of the Greeks and Romans admit this : vid. Plato *de Legibus*, lib. i. p. 776, and *de Republica*, lib. ii. p. 430, 431, opp. edit. Ficini. Isocrates *in Orat. in Encomio Busiridis*, p. 452. Seneca *de Vita beata*, cap. xxvi. p. 639, tom. i. opp. Terentius, *Eunuch.* act iii. sc. 5. v. 35. Martialis, lib. xi. epig. 44. From this circumstance, Ovid takes occasion elegantly to caution those females who had a regard for their honor, to avoid the temples of the deities. *Trist.* lib. ii. v. 287, and seq.

> " Quis locus est templis augustior ? Hæc quoque vitet,
> " In culpam si qua est ingeniosa suam.   [p. 15.]
> " Cum steterit Jovis Æde, Jovis succurret in Æde
> " Quàm multas Matres fecerit ille Deus.
> " Proxima adoranti Junonia templa subibit
> " Pellicibus multis hanc doluisse Deam.
> " Pallade conspecta, natum de crimine Virgo
> " Sustulerit quare, quæret Erichtonium.

(2.) See what is said on this subject by Barbeyrac in the preface to his French translation of Puffendorf's work *de Jure Naturæ et Gentium*, last edit. § vi. p. xxii.

(3.) *Polybius Historiar.* lib. vi. cap. liv. p. 693, tom. i. ed. Gronov. According to Sallust, in *Catalin.* cap. li. p. 309, 310, ed. Cortian. Julius Cæsar when delivering himself publicly in the Roman senate, made no scruple of denying that man had any thing to fear or hope for after death: *de pœna possumus equidem dicere id, quod res habet : in luctu atque miseriis mortem ærumnarum requiem, non cruciatum esse ; eam cuncta mortalium mala dissolvere: ultra neque curæ neque gaudio locum esse*. Which speech of Cæsar's, so far from calling down the censure of that great defender and ornament of the stoic philosophy M. Portius Cato, seems rather to have met with his unqualified approbation: For in cap. lii. § 13, p. 332, we find him as it were studiously panegyrising it.—*Bene et composite*, says he, *Cæsar paullo ante in hoc ordine de vita et morte disseruit : falsa, credo, existimans quæ de inferis memorantur ; diverso itinere malos a bonis loca tetra, inculta, fœda, atque formidolosa habere.* Never would these great and leading characters have ventured to speak after this manner in the senate, had it been a part of the public religion to believe in the immortality of the soul: nay, had a belief of this kind even been generally prevalent amongst the people, such sentiments as the above could never have been uttered in public.

XXI. **The lives of men professing these religions, most flagitious.** Under the influence of such circumstances, it is not to be wondered at that the state of society should have become in the highest degree depraved. The lives of men of every class, from the highest to the lowest, were consumed in the practice of the most abominable and flagitious vices: even crimes, the horrible turpitude of which was such that it would be defiling the ear of decency but to name them, were openly perpetrated with the greatest impunity. If evidence be required of this, the reader may at once satisfy himself of the truth of what is here said, by referring to LUCIAN amongst the Greek authors, and to the Roman poets JUVENAL and PERSIUS. In the writings of the former in particular, he will find the most detestable unnatural affections, and other heinous practices, treated of at large, and with the utmost familiarity, as things of ordinary and daily occurrence. Should any one conceive that these or other writers might give the rein too freely to their imagination, and suffer themselves to be carried into extremes by their genius for satire and sharp rebuke, let him turn his attention to those cruel and inhuman exhibitions which are well known to have yielded the highest gratification to the inhabitants of Greece and Italy, (people, who in point of refinement, possessed a superiority over all other nations of the world,) the savage conflicts of the gladiators in the circus: let him cast his eye on that dissoluteness of manners by which the walks of private life were polluted; the horrible prostitution of boys, to which the laws opposed no restraint; the liberty of divorce which belonged to the wife [p. 16.] equally with the husband; the shameful practice of exposing infants, and procuring abortions; the little regard that was shown to the lives of slaves; the multiplicity of stews and brothels, many of which were consecrated even to the gods themselves. Let him reflect on these, and various other criminal excesses, to the most ample indulgence in which the government offered not the least impediment, and then say, if such were the people distinguished beyond all others by the excellence of their laws and the superiority of their attainments in literature and the arts, what must have been the state of those nations who possessed none of these advantages, but were governed entirely by the impulses and dictates of rude and uncultivated nature.(¹)

(1.) A very copious and animated description of the extreme profligacy of manners that characterized the heathen worshippers, is given by Cyprian in the first of his *Epistles,* p. 2. ed. Baluz. Several things likewise on this subject are brought together from ancient monuments by Cornelius Adam, in his *Exercitatio de malis Romanorum ante Prædicationem Evangelii Moribus,* which is the fifth of his *Exercitationes exegeticæ,* Groning. 1712, 4to.

XXII. **The arguments used by the priests in defence of these religions.** It was impossible that the vanity, the madness, the deformity of systems like these, should escape the observation of any who had not renounced both reason and common sense. But to all objections that might be raised, the artful priests were ever furnished with a reply from two sources: first, the miracles and prodigies which they asserted were daily wrought in the temples, and before the statues of the gods and heroes; and, secondly, the oracles, or spirit of divination, by which they pretended that the gods, either by signs, or in words and verses, made known what was about to happen. The deception practised in either case was made the subject of ridicule by many, who saw through the fraud and knavery of the priests; but a regard for their own safety constrained them to observe no little degree of caution in the exercise of this sort of pleasantry. For in all these matters an appearance was constantly maintained, sufficiently specious and imposing to seize on vulgar minds; and the multitude was ever ready, at the call of the priests, to assert the majesty of their gods, and to punish with the utmost severity those who might be charged with having done any thing inimical to the interests of the public religion.

XXIII. **Philosophers.** This state of things rendered it necessary for those who embraced opinions more consonant to reason, and whom it became customary to distinguish by the appellation of philosophers, to temporize in a certain degree; and although they might entertain a just contempt for those notions respecting religion by which the vulgar were influenced, they yet found it expedient to pay the accustomed honours to the gods of the country, and so far to qualify and soften down their doctrines as to render them not obviously repugnant to the ancient established religion. Amongst this class of men there were not wanting some, indeed, who ventured with much point and ingenuity to contend against the popular superstitions and absurd notions respecting the gods; and who, in many respects,

defined the rules of human conduct on principles equally conso-
[p. 17.]   nant to nature and reason; apparently considering every
part of this universe as subject to the governance of an omnipotent, all-bountiful, and pre-excellent deity; and there seems,
therefore, to be no foundation for the opinion which some have
entertained, that all these philosophers were the favourers of impiety, or in fact atheists, denying altogether the existence of a
God.(¹)   It must, however, be acknowledged, that the principles
laid down by many of them went wholly to extinguish every
sense of God and of religion, and completely to do away all distinction between good and evil; and that in the tenets even of
those who espoused the cause of God and of morality, many
things were contained to which no good or rational men could
yield his approbation or assent.(²)   If the very best of these
philosophic systems, therefore, had been substituted in the place
of the ancient popular religions, it may well be questioned
whether it would eventually have been attended with any considerable advantage to mankind.

(1.) There is a remarkable passage in Cicero, which goes near to prove that,
in his time, philosophers of every sect were accounted the adversaries of the
gods and of religion.   It occurs in that part of his treatise *de Inventione*,
where he discusses the nature of probabilities; and lays it down, that all matters of common belief (quæ in opinione posita sunt) are to be regarded as
such.   By way of illustration, he adduces the following examples: "In eo
autem quod in opinione positum est, hujusmodi sunt probabilia: impiis apud
inferos pœnas esse præparatas: *eos, qui philosophiæ dent operam, non arbitrari
deos esse.*"   *De Inventione*, lib. i. cap. 29. tom. i. opp. p. 171. ed. Verburgienæ.
In the time of Cicero, therefore, it was the general opinion that those who
were called philosophers denied the existence of the gods; and hence, according to his judgment, it was not less probable that they did so, than that
there were punishments in reserve for the wicked hereafter.   It is established indeed beyond doubt, by many passages in ancient authors, that the number of
impious and wicked men was very great in that age, and especially amongst
those of the philosophic sects.   Juvenal notices this depravity, Sat. 13. v. 86, 87.

" Sunt in fortunæ qui casibus omnia ponant,
    Et nullo credant mundum rectore moveri,
    Natura volvente vices, et lucis, et anni,
    At que ideo intrepidi quæcumque altaria tangunt."

Philo Judæus also complains in the strongest terms of the great prevalence
of atheism in his time.   Lib. 3. *Allegor. Legis*, p. 93. tom. i. opp.   I do not,
however, think that we ought to give implicit credit to those who involve all
the philosophers of those times in one undistinguishing censure, and insist

that even those were at enmity with religion, in whose writings are to be found the most admirable discussions relative to God, and subjects of a divine nature: and it appears to me that many very learned men of modern times have strained matters too far, in attempting to prove that it was the object of all the ancient sects, either avowedly or in secret, to undermine the fundamental principles of all religion. Can it for a moment be believed that none of [p. 18.] those great and excellent men, whose minds were, as far as we can perceive, uninfluenced by any vicious or illiberal principle, should have been so happy as to possess the faculty of reasoning justly and with perspicuity? Can we conceive that those who expressly acknowledged the existence of a God, and sublimely descanted on the nature of his attributes, were all deceivers and liars, believing one thing, and writing and professing another? Not to notice what has been urged on the subject by authors of more ancient date, that excellent and eminently sagacious writer, Dr. Warburton, has, with a vast deal of ingenuity and abundance of learning, labored to establish this point, in his celebrated work on the *Divine Legation of Moses*, vol. i. p. 332. s. and p. 419. s. He would fain persuade us, that all the philosophers disbelieved and denied the immortality of the soul in private, whatever might be the sentiments they publicly avowed and taught respecting it; and that in reality they gave the place of the Deity to a principle, which they termed the Nature of Things; considering the minds of men to be particles separated from the soul of the universe, and that upon the dissolution of their bodies these particles again sought and were re-united to the source from whence they proceeded. But without objecting that we have no authority for this but the Grecian philosophers, whereas other nations had their peculiar philosophic sects, differing widely in their tenets from those of Greece: laying aside, I say, this objection, we cannot help remarking that this illustrious author has by no means substantiated his accusation by those plain and irrefragable proofs which the importance of the case should seem to demand, but supports it merely by conjectures, coupled with a few examples, and finally by inferences drawn from certain institutes or dogmas of particular philosophers. Now, if accusations are required to be made good only according to these rules; if examples and inferences be deemed sufficient to convict those whose words excite not the least suspicion of any latent criminality,—who, I would ask, shall be accounted innocent? With that mediocrity of talent, and those inferior powers to which alone I can pretend, in comparison with such a man as Warburton, let me only have permission to adopt the same mode of attack against the whole body of Christian divines, as he has availed himself of in regard to the ancient philosophers, and I will undertake to prove that none of them were sincere in what they publicly professed, but that all were devoted to the purpose of slyly instilling into men's minds the poison of impiety.

(2.) By way of specimen, we refer the reader to what is said respecting the absurd tenets of the philosophers of their time, by Justin Martyr, *Dial. cum Tryphon.* p. 4, 5, 6, 7. edit. Jebb.; and by Hermias, in an elegant little work, entitled, *Irrisio Philosophiæ.* If any additional proof were wanting on the subject, enough might easily be collected to form a volume **of** itself.

XXIV. **Two modes of philosophising prevail.** At the time of the Son of God's appearance upon earth, there were two species of philosophy that generally prevailed throughout the civilized world: the one, that of Greece; the other what is usually termed the Oriental. There are many, indeed, who make no distinction between these two kinds of philosophy; but it ap-
[p. 19.] pears to me that, in blending them together, they confound things of a very opposite nature, and betray no trifling want of information respecting matters of antiquity.(') The term philosophy properly belonged to the former; those who were familiar with the Greek language having given to the other the appellation of γνῶσις, or knowledge: to understand the force of which term, it is necessary that we consider the word Θεῦ, or of God, as annexed to it;(²) since the leading tenet of those who professed this species of philosophy was, that by means of their institutes, that knowledge of the Supreme Deity and great First Cause of all things, which it had been the ill fate of mortals to lose, might again be discovered and restored to mankind. The principles of the former, or what was properly called Philosophy, were not confined to Greece, but were embraced by all such of the Romans as aspired to any eminence of wisdom. The followers of the latter were chiefly to be found in Persia, Chaldæa, Syria, Egypt, and the other oriental regions. Many of the Jews had likewise adopted it. Both these sorts of philosophy were split into various sects, but with this distinction, that those which sprang from the oriental system all proceeded on one and the same principle, and of course had many tenets in common, though they might differ as to some particular inferences and opinions; whilst those to which the philosophy of Greece gave rise were divided in opinion even as to the elements or first principles of wisdom, and were consequently widely separated from each other in the whole course of their discipline. St. Paul adverts to each of these systems, (to that of Greece, Col. ii. 8.; to the oriental, 1 Tim. i. 4. iv. 7. vi. 20.) and strenuously exhorts the Christians to beware of blending the doctrines of either with the religion of their divine master (³) To this admo-

nition had those to whom it was directed paid due attention, they would in an eminent degree have consulted the interest of the cause they had espoused. But to the great injury of divine truth, it unfortunately happened that vain and presumptuous men could not be satisfied with that wisdom which leads to eternal life, as it came pure from above; but must needs set about reconciling it, first of all to the principles of the oriental philosophy, and afterwards to many of the dogmas of the Grecian sects.

(1) Every one who has examined this subject thoroughly, must admit that nothing can be better authenticated than the vast and essential difference that existed between the philosophy of the eastern nations and that of the sages of Greece. It is equally well established, that amongst the different doctrines professed by the various oriental sects, that of the ancient Chaldeans and Persians, which regarded matter as the source of all evil, and supposed it to be under the influence and controul of a spiritual agent peculiar to itself, held the chief place, being the most widely disseminated of any, and that on which ingenuity had particularly exercised itself in giving it a variety of modification. It must also, unless I am very much mistaken, be apparent to every unprejudiced inquirer, that in this most ancient philosophy originated all those modes of discipline adopted by the professors of the Gnostic system, and which, though they were in many respects different from each other, had yet, as it should seem, amongst other points of similarity, one common origin and end. It can also be shown, if it should be thought necessary, that the name or [p. 20.] title of " oriental philosophy or doctrine " was known to ancient writers. Amongst other proofs which might be adduced, some extracts from ·Theodotus, one of the Gnostic school, which are subjoined to the Works of Clemens Alexandrinus, are still extant under the following title, which appears to be of very ancient date: Ἐκ τῶν Θεοδότυ καὶ τῆς ἀνατολικῆς καλυμένης διδασκαλίας ἐπιτόμαι. *Excerpta ex Scriptis Theodoti et Doctrina quæ Orientalis appellatur.*

Whether the person who gave this title to the work were himself a Gnostic, or an enemy of the Gnostics, it leaves us in no doubt as to this fact, that the Gnostics mingled none of the principles of the Grecian philosophy with their system of discipline, but framed it entirely after the oriental model. In acting thus, they neither imposed upon others, nor were they deceived themselves.

(2) The word γνῶσις was used by the Greeks to express the knowledge of such things as are not the objects of sense; but are only to be comprehended by the mind or understanding; and since those things which are perceptible to the mind alone are not liable to alteration or change, but continue fixed, and are perennial, the appellation γνῶσις seems to have been

not improperly used to signify that species of knowledge which relates to things of an eternal and immutable nature. Vid. Jac. Thomasii *Origines Historiæ Eccles. et Philosophiæ,* § 25. seq. p. 21. seq. The term appears to have had a similar meaning, when applied to that kind of philosophy which I denominate the oriental ; since it was not conversant with objects of opinion and sense, but occupied itself solely in the contemplation of things of an abstract and unchangeable nature. I conceive, however, that we ought to understand it in a more restricted sense, when we find it applied to that species of philosophy to which the earliest corrupters of Christianity were inclined, and that in this case it was used emphatically to signify the knowledge of the Deity in particular : for it was the boast of teachers of that vain system, that through their means mankind might recover that knowledge of the true God, from which nearly the whole world had long been estranged. The knowledge of the Deity, indeed, since it is infinitely above all other knowledge that can be acquired by man, and is the fountain from whence alone true religion can spring, may certainly in the strongest and most emphatical sense be styled γνῶσις or knowledge. It is in this way that the sacred writers, when speaking of that truth which is our guide to salvation, style it simply ἀλήθεια, truth ; and a faith in Christ, πίστις, faith, without any addition.

(3) The most learned expositors and commentators on the Holy Scriptures, as well ancient as modern, are unanimously of opinion that St. Paul, in the passages to which I have referred, meant to reprove those who, in the then infancy of Christianity, had the presumption to attempt encumbering the beautifully plain and simple doctrines of Jesus Christ with expositions founded on that species of philosophy to which they had given the pompous title of γνῶσις, or knowledge of the Supreme Deity. The remarkable passage, indeed, which I have cited from that inspired writer, in which he warns Timothy to avoid " oppositions of science falsely so called," (1 Tim. vi. 20,) applies so directly to the vain and foolish system styled γνῶσ ς, that even the arguments of those who would willingly give it a different interpretation, instead of invalidating, have rather added strength and confirmation to this construction of it. It is clear from the words of St. Paul, 1st, That there was a particular species of philosophic discipline prevalent amongst the Greeks of his time, to which his friend, would understand him to allude by the appellation γνῶσις. 2dly, That it was not a system cultivated in retirement and privacy, for he speaks of it as a thing openly known, [p. 21.] and familiar to the public. 3dly, That it appeared to him undeserving of such an high and august title ; for he says ; that it is " falsely " (by which we must understand him to mean improperly and without reason) " so called." 4thly, That those who were addicted to this philosophy had been endeavouring to blend its doctrines with those of the Christian religion : for if no one had attempted this, with what propriety could he have admonished Timothy to beware of this sect, and to keep that deposit of divine truth, which had been committed to his trust, pure and uncontaminated by any

admixture with such vain and trifling theories. 5thly, That the professors
of this sort of discipline maintained the existence of certain ἀντιθίσεις or oppositions, which, since they are the only circumstances relating to it that
are noticed by the apostle, may without doubt be considered as having constituted the essential and fundamental principles of the system. What we are
to understand by these oppositions may readily be perceived: for it was an
established tenet with the followers of this doctrine, that light and darkness,
God and matter, the body and the soul, the Supreme Deity, and those
powers by whom they supposed the universe to be governed, were con
stantly at variance and opposed to each other; even man himself, according
to them, was a compound, made up of two adverse and conflicting principles; and the powers of darkness ever occupied in active hostility against
eternal light. Upon the ground of these oppositions they pretended to account for all events and changes whatever, whether natural, moral, or political;
and in fact for every occurrence, good or evil. It is, therefore, with no less
propriety than elegance, that St. Paul intimates his disapprobation of the
whole system, by a strongly marked reprehension of these its distinguishing features.

XXV. **The Greek philosophic sects. The Epicureans.** The more
illustrious sects of the Grecian school, whose doctrines were also
much cultivated by the Romans, may be divided into two
classes: the one comprising those whose tenets struck at the
root of all religion; pretending, indeed, by specious eulogium,
to support and recommend the cause of virtue, but in reality
nourishing the interests of vice, and giving color to almost every
species of criminality; the other being composed of such as acknowledged the existence of a deity, whom it was the duty of
men to worship and obey, and who inculcated an essential and
eternal distinction between good and evil, just and unjust; but
who unfortunately sullied and disgraced what they thus taught
conformably to right reason, by connecting with it various notions, either absurd and trifling in their nature, or taken up
hastily, and with an unwarrantable presumption.(') Under the
first of these classes may be ranked the disciples of Epicurus
and those of the Academy. The Epicureans maintained that the
universe arose out of a fortuitous concurrence of atoms; that
the gods (whose existence they dared not absolutely to deny)
were indifferent as to human affairs, or rather entirely unacquainted with them; that our souls are born and die; that all
things depend on, and are determined by accident; that in every
thing, voluptuous gratification was to be sought after as the
3

chief good ; and even virtue itself only to be pursued, inasmuch
as it might promise to minister at the shrine of pleasure.   The
votaries of a system like this, (and there were but few amongst
the favored children of prosperity, the wealthy, the noble, and
the powerful, who were not captivated by its allurements,)(²)
naturally studied to pass their lives in one continued round of
[p. 22.] luxurious enjoyment : the only restraint they imposed on
themselves arose out of a desire to avoid, at all times, such an
excessive or immoderate devotion to pleasure as might generate
disease, or tend in any other shape to narrow the capacity for
future indulgence.

(1.) The reader will find what we have here briefly stated, respecting the
different sects of philosophers, treated of at large in a very masterly manner
by the learned Brucker, in his *Historia Philosophiæ Critica ;* a work that
will immortalize the erudition of its author, and which no one ought to be
without, who is willing to acquire an accurate knowledge of the success that
attended the labors of those illustrious characters of all ages and nations,
who devoted their talents to the discovery and elucidation of truth.

(2.) The number of those who embraced the Epicurean system was every
where so immensely great, in the age to which we allude, that whole armies
might have been formed of them.   This is sufficiently plain from Cicero
alone, who, in various parts of his works complains of the vast increase of
the Epicurean sect.   Vid. *de Fin. Bonor. et Malorum,* lib. i. cap. vii. p. 2350.
tom. viii. opp. lib. ii. cap. xiv. p. 2388.   *Disput. Tusculan.* lib. v. cap. x. p.
2829, tom. viii. opp.; and many other places to the same purport.

XXVI. **The Academics.** The Academics, although they affected to be influenced by better and wiser principles than those
of the Sceptics, yet entertained maxims of an equally lax and
pernicious tendency with them.   In fact, they subscribed to the
fundamental dogma on which the whole system of sceptic disci
pline was built, namely, that "nothing can be known or perceived with certainty, and therefore that every thing may be
doubted of and questioned."   The only distinction which they
made was this, that whereas the Sceptics insisted that "nothing
should be assented to, but every thing made the subject of dispute ;" the Academics, on the contrary, contended that "we
ought to acquiesce in all things which bear the appearance of
truth, or which may be considered in the light of probabilities."
But since the Academics were ever undetermined as to what
constituted that sort of probability to which they would have a

wise man assent, their doctrine contributed, no less than that of the 'Sceptics, to render every thing vague and unsettled.(') To make it, as they did, a matter of doubt and uncertainty, whether the gods existed or not; whether the soul was perishable or immortal; whether virtue was preferable to vice, or vice to virtue; was certainly nothing less than to undermine the chief and firmest supports of religion and morality. The philosophy of the Academy was at one time so much neglected as to be nearly lost. Cicero revived it, at Rome, not long before the coming of our Saviour;(') and so much weight was attached to his example and authority, that it was soon embraced by all who aspired to the chief honours of the state.(')

(1.) The manner of the Academics cannot be better illustrated than in the words of Cicero, who may be considered as the leader of the sect. [p. 23.] " Ea, quæ vis, explicabo (he is treating of death and the immortality of the soul) ut homunculus unus e multis, *probabilia conjectura sequens.* Ultra enim quo progrediar, *quam ut veri videam similia,* non habeo. Certa dicent ii, qui et percipi ea posse dicunt, et se sapientes esse profitentur." *Tusculan. Disput.* lib. i. cap. ix. p. 2570.

(2.) Multis etiam sensi mirabile videri, eam nobis potissimum probatam esse philosophiam, *quæ lucem eriperet et quasi noctem quamdam rebus offunderet, desertæque disciplinæ et jampridem relictæ* patrocinium nec opinatum a nobis esse susceptum. Cicero *de Natura Deor.* lib. i. cap. iii. p. 2884. This passage of the Roman orator unfolds, without disguise, the nature of the academical philosophy, of which we see he openly avows himself the patron and restorer. He repeats this in cap. v. p. 2886.

(3.) The philosophy of the Academy, inasmuch as it inculcated the uncertainty of every thing, and encouraged a spirit for disputation on all topics, contributed in an eminent degree to sharpen the mental powers, and to strengthen and improve those faculties which give advantage in debate. It cannot, therefore, appear surprising to any one, that at Rome, where every man's power may be said to have been commensurate with his eloquence, the example of Cicero should have stimulated all those who were ambitious of glory and honor, to the cultivation of that philosophy from which he professed himself to have derived so much advantage.

XXVII. **The Peripatetics.** Within the other class of philosophers, that is, of those who manifested a respect for religion, the most distinguished sects were the Peripatetics founded by Aristotle, the Stoics, and the Platonists. The Peripatetics acknowledged the existence of a God; and the obligations of morality; but, at the same time, their tenets were not of a character to inspire a reverence for the one, or a love of the other. The Aristotelian doctrine gave to the deity an influence not much beyond that of the moving principle in a piece of mechanism : considering him, indeed, to be of an highly refined and exalted nature, happy in the contemplation of himself, but entirely unconscious of what was passing here below; confined from all eternity to the celestial world, and instigating the operations of nature rather from necessity than volition or choice. In a god of this description, differing but little from the deity of the Epicureans, there was surely nothing that could reasonably excite either love, respect, or fear. We are unable to ascertain, with any precision, what were the sentiments of the Peripatetic philosophers respecting the immortality of the soul.(')Could the interests of religion or morality, we would ask, be in any shape effectually promoted by teachers like these, who denied the superintendance of a divine Providence, and insinuated, in no very obscure terms, a disbelief of the soul's future existence ?

(1) See what I have said on this subject, in some notes to Cudworth's *Intellect. System*, tom. i. p. 66. 500. and tom. ii. p. 1171. See also a learned [p. 24.] work of the celebrated Jesuit Michael Mourgues, which he entitled, *Plan Theologique du Pythagorisme*, tom. i. let. ii. p. 75, where it is proved that the system of Aristotle excluded the deity from all knowledge of, or interference with, human affairs.

XXVIII. **The Stoics.** The Deity had somewhat more of majesty and influence assigned to him by the Stoics. They did not limit his functions merely to the regulating of the clouds, and the numbering of the stars; but conceived him to animate every part of the universe with his presence, in the nature of a subtle, active, penetrating fire. They regarded his connection with matter, however, as the effect of necessity ; and supposed his will to be subordinate to the immutable decrees of fate : hence it was impossible for him to be considered as the author either of rewards to the virtuous, or of punishment to the wicked. It is well known to the learned world, that this sect denied the immortality of the soul, and thus deprived mankind of the strongest incitement to a wise and virtuous course of life. Upon the whole, the moral discipline of the Stoics, although it might in some respects be founded on unexceptionable principles, the result of sound reasoning, may yet be compared to a body of a fair and imposing external appearance, but which, on a closer examination, is found destitute of those essential parts which alone can give it either energy or excellence.(¹)

(1) The reader will find this illustrated by what I have remarked in my notes to Cudworth's *Intellectual System*, tom. i. p. 517, et seq.

XXIX. **The Platonists.** Of all the philosophers, Plato seems to have made the nearest approach to the principles of true wisdom ; and there are certainly grounds for believing that his system was not wholly unproductive of benefit to the human race. He considered the Deity, to whom he gave the supreme governance of the universe, as a being of the highest wisdom and power, and totally unconnected with any material substance. The souls of men he conceived to proceed from this pre-eminent source ; and, as partaking of its nature, to be incapable of death. He also gave the strongest encouragement to virtue, and equally discountenanced vice, by holding out to mortals the prospect of a future state of rewards and punishments. But even the system of Plato had its defects. For, not to mention his frequent assumption of things without any sort of proof, and the obscure and enigmatical way in which he often expresses himself, he ascribes to that power, whom he extols as the fashioner and maker of the universe, few or none of the grander attributes, such as infinity, immensity, ubiquity, omnipotence, omniscience ; but supposes him to be confined within certain limits, and that the direction of human affairs was committed to a class of inferior spiritual agents, termed dæmons. This notion of ministering dæmons, and also those points of doctrine which relate to the origin and condition of the human soul, greatly disfigure the morality of Plato ; since they manifestly tend to generate superstition, and to confirm men in the practice of worshipping a number of inferior deities. His teaching, [p. 25.] moreover, that the soul, during its continuance in the body, might be considered, as it were, in a state of imprisonment, and that we ought to endeavour, by means of contemplation, to set it free, and restore it to an alliance with the Divine nature, had an ill effect, inasmuch as it prompted men of weak minds to

withdraw every attention from the body and the concerns of
life, and to indulge in the dreams and fancies of a disordered
imagination.(')

(1) The reader will find the objectionable points of the Platonic philosophy
discussed in an eloquent and copious manner by Fra. Baltus, an ingenious
Jesuit, in a work undertaken by him with a view to exonerate the early fathers
from the charge of Platonism, and entitled, *Defense des Peres accusez de Platonisme*, Paris, 1711, 4to. His reprehension, however, is occasionally carried
to an excess ; and he is not always sufficiently attentive to the force and spirit
of the Platonic opinions.

XXX. **The Eclectics.** Since the little of good that presented
itself in the tenets of any of these various sects was sullied and
deformed by an abundant alloy of what was pernicious and
absurd ; and as it was found that no sort of harmony prevailed
amongst philosophers of any description, even though they
might profess one and the same system, but that they were constantly at variance either with themselves or with others; it
occurred to some, who perhaps were more than ordinarily
anxious in their pursuit after truth, that the most ready way of
attaining their object would be to adopt neither of these systems
in the whole, but to select from each of them such of its parts as
were the most consonant with sound and unbiassed reason.
Hence a new sect of philosophers sprang up, who, from the
manner in which their system was formed, acquired the name of
Eclectics. We are certain that it first appeared in Egypt, and
particularly in Alexandria, but the name of its founder is lost
in obscurity ; for though one Potamon of Alexandria is commonly represented as such by ancient writers, it is by no means
clear that this opinion of theirs is correct. However, we have
sufficient authority for stating, (indeed it might be proved even
from Philo Judæus alone,) that this sect flourished at Alexandria at the time of our Saviour's birth.(') Those who originated
this species of philosophy took their leading principles from the
system of Plato; considering almost every thing which he had
advanced respecting the Deity, the soul, the world, and the
dæmons, as indisputable axioms: on which account they were
regarded by many as altogether Platonists. Indeed, this title,
so far from being disclaimed, was rather affected by some of

them, and particularly by those who joined themselves to Ammonius Saccas, another celebrated patron of the Eclectic philosophy. With the doctrines of Plato, however, they very freely intermixed the most approved maxims of the Pythagoreans, the Stoics, the Peripatetics, and the oriental philosophers; [p. 26.] merely taking care to admit none that were in opposition to the tenets of their favourite guide and instructor.([2])

(1) The writings of Philo Judæus are, in every respect, marked by the same species of philosophy that characterizes those of Clemens Alexandrinus, Origen, and other fathers of the Christian church, who were confessedly Eclectics. He chiefly follows Plato, and on this account he is regarded by many in the light of a mere Platonist; but it would be difficult to make this opinion accord with the encomiums which we find him at times bestowing on the Stoics, the Pythagoreans, and other philosophers, and whose maxims and mode of expression he adopts without reserve. We should rather, therefore, consider him as belonging to those who professed themselves to be of no particular sect, but who made it their study to select and appropriate to themselves the most rational parts of every system. Mangey, the learned English editor of Philo's works, did not overlook this, though he suffered so many things else to escape him, but remarks in the preface, p. viii. that his author ought to be classed with the Eclectics.

(2) Justin Martyr mentions, (*Dial. cum Tryphon.* sect. 2. p. 103. opp. edit. Benedict,) amongst other philosophic sects of his time, that of the Theoretics, which he considers as holding a middle place between the Peripatetics and the Pythagoreans. Langus, the translator of Justin, imagines that he applied this denomination either to the Academics or the Sceptics, who assigned no bounds to their doubts and inquiries. This suggestion appears to me to carry some weight with it : but Prudentius Maranus, a Benedictine monk, who some time back published an edition of Justin, maintains a very different opinion, and asserts that by the term Theoretic was meant that species of philosophy which disregards action, and devotes itself entirely to contemplation. I do not think, however, that we can altogether rely on the judgment of this industrious good old man, whose accuracy of conception is not every where alike conspicuous. Justin speaks of the Theoretics as one of the sects that flourished at the time he wrote ; but none of those sects, except the Academics, can be said to have so far embraced the contemplative system as to neglect laying down any rules for the conduct of active life. But is it not possible that the sect which Justin terms the Theoretics might be one and the same with that of the Eclectics? There is certainly nothing in the name that militates against this supposition, since the term Theoretics might naturally enough be used to characterize a class of philosophers who were continually prying, with the most vigilant curiosity, into the maxims and opinions of other sects, and adopted none into their own system but such as had undergone a severe and penetrating scrutiny.

XXXI. **The Oriental Philosophy.** The documents that have hitherto come to light relating to the oriental philosophy are so few, that our knowledge of it is of necessity very limited. Some insight, however, into its nature and principles may be obtained from what has been handed down to us respecting the tenets of several of the first Christian sects, and from a few other scattered relics of it, that may be collected here and there. Its author, who is unknown, perceiving that in almost every thing [p. 27.] which comes under our observation there is a manifest admixture of evil, and that human nature has an obvious leaning to what is criminal and vicious, whilst, at the same time, reason forbids us to regard the Deity in any other light than as the pure and unsullied fountain of good alone, was induced to seek for the origin of this calamitous state of things in a different source.(') But as he could discover nothing besides God, to which this evil influence could be attributed, unless it were the matter of which the world, and the bodies of men, and all other living creatures are formed, he was led to regard this principle as the root and cause of every evil propensity, and every untoward affection. The unavoidable consequence of this opinion was, that matter should be considered as self-existent, and as having exercised an influence entirely independent of the Deity from all eternity. But this proposition imposed on its abettors a task of no little difficulty, namely, that of explaining by what agency or means this originally rude undigested mass of matter came to be so skilfully and aptly arranged in all its parts; how it happens that so many things of a refined and exalted nature are connected with it; and particularly, to account for the wonderful union of ethereal spirits with supine and vitiated fleshly bodies. It was found impossible to solve these points by any arguments drawn from nature or reason; recourse was therefore had to the suggestions of a lively invention, and a fabulous sort of theory was propounded respecting the formation of the world, and that remarkable admixture of good and evil in every thing belonging to it, which so continually obtrudes itself on our notice. The Deity could not, consistently with their views of him, be considered as the author of either; since it must have appeared incredible to those who regarded the Supreme Being as purity and goodness itself, and utterly averse from every thing of an opposite character, that he should have employed himself in giving form and arrangement to a vitiated and distempered mass, or have been anywise instrumental in associating good with evil.

(1.) The ancient fathers of the Christian church, although they could form but a very imperfect judgment of the Gnostic system, since they were unacquainted with its true origin and growth, yet plainly perceived that this species of philosophy was founded on a wish to remove from the Deity every imputation of his being the cause or author of any thing evil. Tertullian says, (*de Præscript. advers. Hæreticos*, cap. vii. p. 119. opp. edit. Venet.) "Eædem materiæ apud hæreticos et philosophos volutantur, iidem retractatus implicantur: unde malum? et quare? et unde homo? et quomodo?" See also Epiphanius, hæres. xxiv. Basilidianor. sect. vi. p. 72. tom. i. opp. ; and beyond all, that fragment of Valentine preserved by Origen, *Dialog. contra Marcionitas*, sect. iv. p. 85. ed. Wettsten. in which he points out with much perspicuity the various steps by which he arrived at that form of religion of which his conscience approved. [p. 28.]

XXXII. **The oriental philosophers divided into sects.** As none more readily disagree among themselves, than those who pretend to resolve the most abstruse and intricate points by the strength of the human intellect alone, it will easily be conceived that those who endeavoured to extricate themselves from the difficulties above noticed, by the assistance of fiction, would of course run into a great diversity of sentiment. Those of the most numerous class seem to have believed in the existence of a being, whom they considered as the prince or power of darkness, upon whom the Prince of light (that is, the Deity himself) made war; and having obtained the victory, made matter the receptacle of the spoil and forces which he had taken from his opponent. Tales like this, of the wars carried on between a good and an evil power, were commonly adopted by all of this sect; but they were far from being unanimous as to the nature of that prince of darkness, or matter, who was thus set in opposition to the Deity. By some, he was considered as of an equal nature with the Author of all good, and of necessity to have existed from all eternity; by others, he was thought to have been generated of matter, which they supposed to be endowed with both animation and fertility; whilst others regarded him as the son of Eternal Light, the offspring of the Deity, who, unable to endure the control of a superior, had rebelled against the author of his existence, **and** erected for himself a separate and distinct estate. The opinion entertained by *another sect* was, that matter was not subject to the dominion of a prince or ruler peculiar to itself, but that it was fashioned and brought into order, and man created, by one of those eternal spirits whom God begat of himself, and who acted not from design, but was stimulated to the undertaking by a sudden accidental impulse. This opinion also, when it came to be discussed and enlarged upon, gave rise to much dissension. Some contended that this architect or fabricator of the world acted with the consent and approbation of the Deity; others denied this. Some supposed that, in the commencement of this undertaking, he was uninfluenced by any vicious principle; but that having accomplished his purpose, he gave himself over to iniquity, and, at the instigation of pride, withdrew men from the knowledge of the Supreme Deity. Others conceived him to have a natural and necessary inclination to what was evil; others imagined that he might be of a middle nature, somewhat between the two; and many esteemed him to be a compound essence, made up of a certain proportion of good and evil. The sentiments of *a third sect* appear to have been formed on an union of those of the two former. According to these, the world, and all things belonging to it, were under the regulation and guidance of three powers, namely, the Supreme Deity, the prince of darkness and of matter, and the creator or maker of the world. I believe I may venture to say, that every one who shall attentively examine the opinions and maxims entertained by some of the Christian sects [p. 29.] of the first century, will readily give his assent to the accuracy of this statement. Of the first class we may account Simon Magus, Manes, and others; the principal leaders of the Gnostics may be ranked under the second; and Marcion, with perhaps some others, may be considered as belonging to the third.

XXXIII. **Certain tenets, however, common to them all respecting the Deity.** Notwithstanding that the various sects of oriental philosophers, who believed matter to be the cause of all evil, were so much divided in opinion as to the particular mode or form under which it ought to be considered as such; there were yet some maxims, or points of doctrine, to which they all subscribed without reserve, and which may be regarded as the principles on which the system in general was founded. In the first place, they were unanimous in maintaining that there had existed from all eternity a divine nature, replete with goodness, intelligence, wisdom, and virtue; a light of the most pure and subtle kind diffused throughout all space, of whom it was impossible for the mind of man to form an adequate conception. Those who were conversant with the Greek language gave to this pre-eminent Being the title of Βυθὸς, in allusion to the vastness of his excellence, which they deemed it beyond the reach of human capacity to comprehend. The space which he inhabits they named πλήρωμα, but occasionally the term αἰὼν was applied to it. This divine nature, they imagined, having existed for ages in solitude and silence, at length, by the operation of his omnipotent will, begat of himself two minds or intelligences of a most excellent and exalted kind, one of either sex. By these, others of a similar nature were produced; and the faculty of propagating their kind being successively communicated to all, a class of divine beings was in time generated, respecting whom no difference of opinion seems to have existed, except in regard to their number; some conceiving it to be more, others less. The nearer any of this celestial family stood in affinity to the one grand parent of all, the closer were they supposed to resemble him in nature and perfection; the farther off they were removed, the less were they accounted to partake of his goodness, wisdom, or any other attribute. Although every one of them had a beginning, yet they were all conceived to be immortal, and not liable to any change; on which account they were termed αἰῶνες, that is, immortal beings placed beyond the reach of temporal vicissitudes or injuries.(¹) It was not, however, imagined that the vast extent of space called πλήρωμα was occupied solely by these spirits of the first order: it was likewise supposed to contain a great number of inferior beings, the offspring of the αἰῶνες, and consequently of divine descent, but who, on account of the many degrees that intervened between them and the first parent, were considered comparatively to possess but a very limited portion of wisdom, knowledge, or power.

(1) Αἰὼν properly signifies indefinite or eternal duration, as opposed to [p. 30.] that which is finite or temporal. It was, however, metonymically used for such natures as are in themselves unchangeable and immortal. That it was com-

monly applied in this sense even by the Greek philosophers, at the time of Christ's birth, is plain from Arrian, who uses it to describe a nature the reverse of ours, superior to frailty, and obnoxious to no vicissitude : Ὀυ γὰρ εἰμὶ Ἀιὼν ἀλλ' ἄνθρωπος, μέρος τῶν πάντων ὡς ὥρα ἡμέρας, ἐνεῆναι με δεῖ ὡς τὴν ὥραν, καὶ παρελθεῖν ὡς ὥραν. Non ego natura sum perennis et immutabilis (it was an error of the translator to render it non ego sum *eternitas*) sed homo, pars hujus universitatis, quemadmodum hora pars est diei. Oportet me non secus ac horam existere et occidere. *Dissert. Epictetearum*, lib. ii. § 5. p. 179. edit. Holstenii. There was, therefore, nothing strange or unusual in the application of the term αἰῶνες, by the Gnostics, to beings of a celestial nature, liable to neither accident nor change. Indeed the term is used even by the ancient fathers of the purer class to denote the angels in general, good as well as bad. The example of Manichæus the Persian, who, according to Augustin, applied the denomination of Ἀιῶνες (which Augustin renders into Latin by the word *sæcula*) to celestial natures of the higher order, seems to prove that the term was adopted in much the same sense by the followers of the oriental philosophy in general, as well by those who were not conversant with the Greek language as those who were. Amongst the commentators on Holy Writ are some of acknowledged erudition and ingenuity, who conceive that αἰὼν has a similar signification in the writings of the New Testament. St. Paul describes the Ephesians, before they were acquainted with the Gospel of Christ, to have walked κατὰ τὸν αἰῶνα τῆ κόσμᾳ τύτᾳ, κατὰ τὸν ἄρχοντα τῆς ἐξυσίας τῆ ἀέρος. In this passage, ἄρχων τῆς ἐξυσίας τῆ ἀέρος, "the prince of those powerful natures which belong to, or have their dwelling in the air," appears to be one and the same with him who is first spoken of as the Ἀιὼν τῆ κόσμᾳ τύτᾳ; and according to this exposition, Ἀιὼν must here unquestionably mean an immutable nature, a spirit or an angel of the highest class. Vid. Beausobre's *Histoire du Manichee*, tom. i. p. 574, 575; as also his *Remarques sur le Nouveau Testament*, tom. ii. p. 7, 8. Jerome and, as it should seem, some others approved of this interpretation. Jo. Alb. Fabricius thinks that the same sense may be given to the term in that passage of the Epistle to the Hebrews, where God is said · by his Son to have made τὸς αἰῶνας· δι ὃ καὶ τὸς αἰῶνας ἐποίησεν. (I. 2.) Quo in loco, says he, per Ἀιῶνας non absurdum sit intelligere angelos. *Codic. Apocryphi Nov. Test.* tom. i. p. 710. Of these interpretations, the first has certainly the appearance of being a just one ; of the latter I cannot say quite so much.

XXXIV. **Opinions of the oriental philosophers respecting matter, the world, the soul, &c.** Beyond that vast expanse refulgent with everlasting light, which was considered as the immediate habitation of the Deity, and those natures which had been generated [p. 31.] from him, these philosophers placed the seat of matter, where, according to them, it had lain from all eternity, a rude, undigested, opaque mass, agitated by turbulent irregular motions of its own provoking, and nurturing, as in a seed-bed, the rudiments of vice, and every species of evil. In this state it was found by a genius or celestial spirit of the higher order, who had been either driven from the abode of the Deity for some offence, or commissioned by him for the purpose, and who reduced it into order, and gave it that arrangement and fashion which the universe now wears. Those who spoke the Greek tongue were accustomed to refer to this creator of the world by the name of Demiurgus. Matter received its inhabitants, both men and other animals, from the same hand that had given to it disposition and symmetry. Its native darkness was also illuminated by this creative spirit with a ray of celestial light, either secretly stolen, or imparted through the bounty of the Deity. He likewise communicated to the bodies he had formed, and which would otherwise have remained destitute of reason, and uninstructed except in what relates to mere animal life, particles of the divine essence, or souls of a kindred nature to the Deity. When all things were thus completed, Demiurgus revolting against the great First Cause of every thing, the all-wise and omnipotent God, assumed to himself the exclusive government of this new state, which he apportioned out into provinces or districts; bestowing the administration and command over them on a number of genii or spirits of inferior degree, who had been his associates and assistants.

XXXV. **Their tenets respecting man.** Man, therefore, whilst he continued here below, was supposed to be compounded of two principles, acting in direct opposition to each other: 1st, a terrestrial and corrupt or vitiated body; 2d, a soul partaking of the nature of the Deity, and derived from the region of purity and light. The soul or etherial part being, through its connection with the body, confined as it were within a prison of matter, was constantly exposed to the danger of becoming involved in ignorance, and acquiring every sort of evil propensity, from the impulse and contagion of the vitiated mass by which it was enveloped. But the Deity, touched with compassion for the hapless state of those captive minds, was ever anxious that the means of escaping from this darkness and bondage into liberty and light should be extended to them, and had accordingly, at various times, sent amongst them teachers endowed with wisdom, and filled with celestial light, who might communicate to them the principles of a true religion, and thus instruct them in the way by which deliverance was to be obtained from their wretched and forlorn state. Demiurgus, however, with his associates, unwilling to resign any part of that dominion, of whose sweets they were now become sensible, or to relinquish the divine honors which they had usurped, set every engine at work to obstruct and counteract these designs of the Deity; and not only tormented and slew the messengers of heaven, but endeavoured, through the means of superstition and sensual attractions, to root [p. 32.] out and extinguish every spark of celestial truth. The minds that listened to the calls of the Deity, and who, having renounced obedience to the usurped authorities of this world, continued stedfast in the worship of the great first Parent, resisting the evil propensities of the corporeal frame, and every incitement to illicit gratification, were supposed, on the dissolution of their bodies, to be directly borne away pure, ærial, and disengaged from every thing gross or material, to the immediate residence of God himself; whilst those who, notwithstanding the admonitions they received, had persisted in paying divine honors to him who was merely the fabricator of the world, and his associates, worshipping them as gods, and suffering themselves to be enslaved by the lusts and vicious impulses to which they were exposed from their alliance with matter, were denied the hope of exaltation after death, and could only expect to migrate into new bodies suited to their base, sluggish, and degraded condition. When the grand work of setting free all these minds or souls, or, at least, the greatest part of them, and restoring them to that celestial country from whence they first proceeded, should be accomplished, God, it was imagined, would dissolve the fabric of this nether world; and having again confined matter, with all its contagious influence, within its original limits, would, throughout all ages to come, live and reign in consummate glory, surrounded by kindred spirits, as he did before the foundation of the world.

XXXVI. **Moral discipline of the oriental philosophers.** The moral discipline deduced from this system of philosophy, by those who embraced it, was by no means of an uniform cast, but differed widely in its complexion, according to their various tempers and inclinations. Such, for instance, as were naturally of a morose, ascetic disposition, maintained that the great object of human concern should be to invigorate the energies of the mind, and to quicken and refine its perceptions, by abstracting it as much as possible from every thing gross or sensual. The body, on the contrary, as the source of every depraved appetite, was, according to them, to be reduced and brought into subjection by hunger, thirst, and every other species of mortification; and neither to be supported by flesh or wine, nor indulged in any of those gratifications to which it is naturally prone; in fact, a constant self-denial was to be rigorously observed in every thing which might contribute either to the convenience or amœnity of this life; so that the material frame being thus by every means weakened and brought low, the celestial spirit might the more readily escape from its contagious influence, and regain its native liberty. Hence it was that the Manichæans, the Marcionites, the Encratites, and others, passed their lives in one continued course of austerity and mortification. On the other hand, those who were constitutionally inclined to voluptuousness and vicious indulgence, found the means of accommodating the same principles to a mode of life that admitted of the free and uncontroled gratification of all our desires. The essence of piety and religion, they said, consisted in a knowledge of the supreme Deity, and the maintaining a mental intercourse and association with him. Whoever had become an adept in these attainments, and had, from the habitual exercise of contemplation, acquired the power of keeping the mind abstracted from every thing corporeal, was no longer to be considered as affected by, or answerable for, the impulses and actions of the body; and consequently could be under no necessity to control its inclinations, or resist its propensities. This accounts for the dissolute and infamous lives led by the Carpocratians, and others, who assumed the liberty of doing whatever they might list; and maintained [p. 33.] that the practice of virtue was not enjoined by the Deity, but imposed on mankind by that power whom they regarded as the prince of this world, the maker of the universe.(')

(1.) Clemens Alexandrinus clearly perceived this discordance of sentiment amongst the oriental sects, and accordingly divides the heretics of his time into two classes; viz. such as deemed every thing lawful for those who maintained a communion with God, and such as believed that man could innocently indulge himself in scarcely any thing. *Stromat.* lib. iii. cap. v. p. 529. The former placed no restraint whatever on their inclinations; the latter made it a point to reduce and afflict their bodies by every species of mortification and self-denial. Slender indeed must be their acquaintance with the writings of antiquity, who would contend that all the followers of the Gnostic absurdities are indiscriminately represented by the Christian fathers of the first century as men of reprobate and dissolute lives. For so far from this being the case, the generality of them acknowledge, that not a few of that numerous class had, by their continence and austerity of demeanor, acquired a reputation for sanctity, and gained to themselves the love and veneration of the multitude. That the greater part, however, of those who affected the title of Gnostics, boldly set all virtue at defiance, and polluted themselves by every species of criminal excess, is manifest not only from the testimony of Christian writers, but also from the accounts given of them by those adversaries of Christianity, Plotinus the Platonic philosopher, and Porphyry. See the treatise of the former, *contra Gnosticos,* cap. xv. p. 213, 214; and of the latter, *de Abstinentia,* lib. i. sect. 42, p. 35, edit. Cantab. But not to enlarge more than is necessary on the subject, there are some striking passages in the writings of the apostles which evidently point to the two opposite systems of morals that were thus drawn from one and the same source. St. Paul (Col. ii. 18, et seq.) mentions, amongst the first corruptors of the Christian religion, those who neglected all care of the body, displaying in themselves a great show of sanctity and wisdom; whilst St. Peter (2 Pet. ii. 1, et seq.) and St. Jude (in Epist.) notice, as belonging to the same class, men who were so impious and depraved as to maintain that the followers of Christ might freely give the rein to their passions, and with impunity obey the dictates of every corrupt inclination.

XXXVII. **Use of this chapter.** The inferences to be drawn from the statement which has thus been given, of the wretched aspect of the whole world at the time of the Son of God's appearance upon earth, must, it is presumed, be sufficiently obvious. To every one who shall peruse it with a mind disposed to be informed, I conceive it will be manifest, that such was the hopeless and forlorn condition into which the human race had fallen at that period, that its recovery could only be effected by a divine instructor and guide, who might overthrow the strong and widely extended dominion of superstition and impiety, and call back unhappy, lost, and wandering man to the paths of wisdom and virtue. But little or no assistance was to be expected from the efforts of man himself against these adversaries; since [p. 34.] we see that even those mortals who were endowed with a superior degree of intellectual power, and who occasionally obtained a glimpse of the true path, were yet unable to proceed in it, but again lost themselves in the mazes of error and uncertainty, and disgraced what little they had acquired of sound wisdom, by an admixture of the most extravagant and absurd opinions. I should also hope, that from this view it will appear of what infinite advantages the Christian religion hath been productive to the world and its inhabitants; I mean not only in a spiritual sense, by opening to us the road that leads to salvation and peace, but also in the many and vast improvements in government and civilization to which its influence gave rise. Take away the influence which the Christian religion has on the lives of men, and you at once extinguish the cause to which alone those unspeakable advantages which we enjoy over the nations of old can be fairly or justly attributed.   [p. 35.]

CHAPTER II.

*Of the civil and religious State of the Jewish Nation in particular,
at the time of Christ's Birth.*

I. The Jewish nation governed by Herod the Great. The condition of the Jews, at the time of the Son of God's advent in the flesh, was not much superior to that of other nations. The reins of their government had been placed in the hands of a Stipendiary of Rome, called Herod, and surnamed the Great, (a title, by the bye, to which he could have no pretensions, except from the magnitude of his vices,) who, instead of cherishing and protecting the people committed to his charge, appears to have made them sensible of his authority merely by oppression and violence. Nature, indeed, had not denied him the talents requisite for a lofty and brilliant course of public life; but such was his suspicious temper, so incredibly ferocious his cruelty, his devotion to luxury, pomp, and magnificence so madly extravagant, and so much beyond his means: in short, so extensive and enormous was the catalogue of his vices that he was become an object of utter detestation to the afflicted people over whom he reigned, and whose subsistance he had exhausted by the most vexatious and immoderate exactions. With a view to soften, in some de-

4

gree, the asperity of the hatred which he had thus drawn on himself, he pretended to adopt the religion of the Jews, and at a vast expence restored their temple, which, through age, had gone much to decay: but the effect of all this was destroyed by his still conforming to the manners and habits of those who worshipped a plurality of gods; and so many things were countenanced in direct opposition to the Jewish religion, that the hypocrisy and insincerity of the tyrant's professions were too conspicuous to admit of a doubt.(')

(1) For an ample illustration of these matters, we refer the reader to the Jewish historian Josephus; and in addition to that author, he may consult Basnage, *Histoire des Juis*, tom. i. part i. p. 27, et seq. Norrisii *Coenotaphia Pisana*. Noldii *Historia Idumœa*, published by Havercamp, at the end of his edition of Josephus, tom. ii. p. 333. 396. Cellarii *Historia Herodum*, which is the eleventh of his *Academical Dissertations*, part i. p. 207. Prideaux's *History of the Jews*. In a word, there has scarcely perhaps been any thing written on the subject of Jewish affairs, from whence he may not derive information.

[p. 36.] II. **Sons and successors of Herod.** On the death of this nefarious despot, the government of Palestine was divided by the emperor Augustus amongst his three surviving sons. Archelaus, the eldest, was appointed governor of Judea, Idumea, and Samaria, under the title of ethnarch, though, by his conduct he made it appear that the title of monarch would have better suited him. Antipas had Galilee and Peræa for his share; whilst Batanea, Trachonitis, Auranitis, with some of the neighbouring territory, were assigned to Philip. The two latter, from their having a fourth part of the province allotted to each, were styled tetrarchs. Archelaus, who inherited all the vices of his parent, with but few or none of his better qualities, completely exhausted the patience of the Jews; and by a series of the most injurious and oppressive acts, drove them, in the tenth year of his reign, to lay their complaints before the emperor Augustus, who, having inquired into the matter, deposed the ethnarch, and banished him to Vienne, in Gaul.

III. **State of the Jews under the Roman Government.** After the removal of Archelaus, the greater part of Palestine which had been under his government was reduced by the Romans into the form of a province, and put under the superintendance of a governor, who was subject to the controul of the president of Syria. This arrangement, it is probable, at first met with the ready concurrence of the Jews; who, on the death of Herod, had petitioned Augustus that the distinct regal form of government might no longer be continued to them, but their country be received under his own immediate protection, and treated as a part of the empire. The change, however, instead of producing an alleviation of misery to this unhappy people, brought with it an intolerable increase of their calamities. To say nothing of the avarice and injustice of the governors, to which there was neither end nor limit, it proved a most disgusting and insufferable grievance to most of them, who considered their nation as God's peculiar people, that they should be obliged to pay tribute to a heathen, and an enemy of the true God, like Cæsar, and live in subjection to the worshipers of false deities. The extortion, likewise, of the publicans, who after the Roman manner were entrusted with the collection of the revenue, and for whose continual and flagrant abuses of authority it was seldom possible to obtain any sort of redress, became a subject of infinite dissatisfaction and complaint. In addition to all this, the constant presence of their governors, surrounded as they were by an host of foreign attendants of all descriptions, and protected by a Roman military guard, quartered with their eagles, and various other ensigns of superstition, in the heart of the holy city, kept the sensibility of the Jews continually on the rack, and excited in their minds a degree of indignation bordering on fury; since they considered their religion to be thereby disgraced and insulted, their holy places defiled, and in fact themselves, with every thing they held sacred, polluted and brought into contempt. To these [p. 37.] causes are to be attributed the frequent tumults, factions, seditions, and murders, by which it is well known that these unfortunate people accelerated their own destruction.

The condition of the Jews who were under Philip and Antipas, the other sons of Herod, was somewhat better; the severe punishment of Archelaus having taught his brothers to beware of irritating the feelings of their subjects by any similarly excessive stretch or abuse of authority.

IV. **Their high priests and sanhedrim.** If any remnant of liberty or happiness could have been possessed by a people thus circumstanced, it was effectually cut off by those who held the second place in the civil government under the Romans and the sons of

Herod, and who also had the supreme direction in every thing pertaining to religion, namely, the chief priests, and the seventy elders, of whom the sanhedrim or national council was composed. The chief priests, according to what is handed down to us of them by Josephus, were the most abandoned of mortals, who had obtained that elevated rank either through the influence of money, or iniquitous pliability; and who shrank from no species of criminality that might serve to support them in the possession of an authority thus infamously purchased. Since all of them perceived that no reliance could be placed on the permanency of their situation, it became an object of their first concern to accumulate, either by fraud or force, such a quantity of wealth as might either enable them to gain the rulers of the state over to their interest, and drive away all competitors, or else yield them, when deprived of their dignity, the means of living at their ease in private. The national council, or sanhedrim, being composed of men who differed in opinion respecting some of the most important points of religion, nothing like a general harmony was to be found amongst its members: on the contrary, having espoused the principles of various sects, they suffered themselves to be led away by all the prejudice and animosity of party; and were commonly more intent on the indulgence of private grudge, than studious of advancing the cause of religion, or promoting the public welfare. A similar depravity prevailed amongst the ordinary priests, and the inferior ministers of religion. The common people, instigated by the shocking examples thus held out to them by those whom they were taught to consider as their guides, rushed headlong into every species of vicious excess; and giving themselves up to sedition and rapine, appeared alike to defy the vengeance both of God and man.([1])

(1.) See Josephus *de Bell. Judaic.* lib. v. cap. xiii. sect. 6. p. 362. edit. Havercamp.

V. **The Jewish worship corrupt.** Two sorts of religion flourished at that time in Palestine; the Jewish and the Samaritan; and what added not a little to the calamities of the Hebrew nation, the followers of each of these regarded those of the other persuasion with the most virulent and implacable hatred; and mutually [p. 38.] gave vent to their rancorous animosity in the direst curses and imprecations. The nature of the Jewish religion may be collected from the books of the Old Testament; but at the time of our Saviour's appearance it had lost much of its original beauty and excellence, and was contaminated by errors of the most flagrant kind, that had crept in from various sources. The public worship of God was indeed still continued in the temple at Jerusalem, with all the ceremonies which Moses had prescribed; and a vast concourse of people never failed to assemble at the stated seasons for celebrating those solemn festivals which he had appointed; nor did the Romans ever interfere to prevent those observances: in domestic life, likewise, the ordinances of the law were for the most part attended to and respected: but it is manifest, from the evidence brought forward by various learned writers, that even in the service of the temple itself, numerous ceremonies and observances, drawn from the religious worship of heathen nations, had been introduced and blended with those of divine institution; and that, in addition to superstitions like these of a public nature, many erroneous principles, probably either brought from Babylon and Chaldea by the ancestors of the people at their return from captivity, or adopted by the thoughtless multitude, in conformity to the example of their neighbours the Greeks, the Syrians, and the Egyptians, were cherished and acted upon in private.(¹)

(1) See Spencer's Treatise *de Ritibus et Institutis Hebræorum a Gentium Usu desumptis, nullibi vero a Deo præceptis aut ordinatis,* which is the fourth in the last Cambridge edition of his grand work, *de Legibus Ritualibus veterum Ebræorum,* tom. ii. p. 1089. See also Joh. Gothofred. Lakemacheri *Observationes Philolog.* lib. i. observ. ii. p. 17, where it is proved that the Jews adopted several of the rites of Bacchus from the Greeks. An account of the various private superstitions which the Jews had derived from foreign nations, and of which the number was not small, may be found in most authors who have treated of the Jewish rites and manners.

VI. **The religion of the Jews.** The opinions and sentiments of the Jews respecting the Supreme Deity and the divine nature, the celestial genii or ministering spirits of God, the evil angels or dæmons, the souls of men, the nature of our duties, and other subjects of a like kind, appear to have been far less extravagant, and formed on more rational grounds than those of any other nation or people. Indeed, it was scarcely possible that they should altogether lose sight of that truth, in the knowledge of which their fathers had been instructed through an immediately divine communication: since it was commonly rendered habitual to them, even at a tender age, to be diligent in hearing, reading, and studying the writings of Moses and the prophets. In every place where any considerable number of Jews resided, a sacred edifice to which, deriving its name from the Greek, they gave the appellation of synagogue, was erected, in which it was [p. 39.] customary for the people regularly to assemble for the purposes of worshipping God in prayer, and hearing the law publicly read and expounded. · In most of the larger towns there were also schools under the management of well-informed masters, in which youth were taught the principles of religion, and also instructed in the liberal arts.(¹)

(1) See Campeg. Vitringa *de Synagoga vetere*, lib. iii. cap. v. p. 667. and lib. i. cap. v. p. 133. cap. vii. p. 156. Besides whom the reader may consult those other authors who have written concerning the synagogues, the schools, and the academies of the Jews, pointed out by Fabricius in his *Bibliographia Antiquaria*, and by Wolfius in his *Bibliotheca Hebraica*.

VII. **Wrong opinions entertained by the Jews respecting God and the angels.** Rational and correct, however, as the Jews appear to have been in those principles and sentiments which they had derived from their sacred code, they had yet gradually incorporated with them so large an admixture of what was false and absurd, as nearly to deprive the truth of all its force and energy. The common opinion entertained by them respecting the nature of God was, unless I am much deceived, closely allied to the oriental doctrine of its not being absolutely simple, but somewhat resembling that of our light. To the prince of darkness, with his associates and agents, they attributed an influence over the world and mankind of the most extensive nature; so predominant, indeed, as scarcely to leave a superior degree of power even with the Deity himself. Of various terrific conceits founded upon this notion, one of the chief was, that all the evils and calamities which befal the human race, were to be considered as originating with this prince of darkness and his ministering spirits, who had their dwelling in the air, and were scattered throughout every part of the universe. With a view, in some degree, to lessen the fear that was very naturally produced by this idea, they were willing to persuade themselves that an art had been divinely communicated to mankind, of frightening and driving away these evil spirits, by the use of various sorts of herbs, by repeating certain verses, or by pronouncing the names of God and of divers holy men; or, in other words, they were led to entertain a belief in the existence of what is termed magic. All these opinions, and others of a kindred nature, were, as it should seem, borrowed by the Jews from the doctrine of the Chaldæans and Persians, amongst whom their ancestors had for a long while sojourned in captivity. Their notions, also, and manner of reasoning respecting the good genii, or ministers of divine providence, were nearly of the same complexion with those of the Babylonians and Chaldæans, as may clearly be perceived by any one who will compare the highly absurd and irrational doctrines maintained by the modern descendants of the Magi, usually styled Guebres, as also by the Arabs, and other oriental nations, concerning the names, functions, state, and classes of angels, with the sentiments anciently entertained by the Jews on these subjects.(¹)

(1) See *Observationes ad Jamblichum de Mysteriis Ægyptior. a* [p.40.] *Thom. Gale*, p. 206 ; also what is said on this subject by Sale, in the preface to his English translation of the *Koran.* Even Josephus himself hints in no very obscure manner, though with some caution, that the intercourse with the Babylonians had proved highly detrimental to the ancient religion of the Jews. See his *Antiquitates Judaic.* lib. iii. cap. vii. sect. 2. p. 140.

VIII. **As also respecting the Messiah, the sum of religion, and other matters.** The greatest part of the Jewish nation were looking with the most eager desire for the appearance of the deliverer, promised by God to their fathers; but their hopes were not directed to such an one as the Scriptures described: they expected not a saviour of souls, but a strenuous warlike leader, whose talents and prowess might recover for them their civil liberty.(') Concerning the reign of this prince here on earth, which it was imagined would last for the term of a thousand years, as also of the profusion of pleasures and luxuries with which it would be attended, of his wars with a terrible adversary, to whom they gave the name of Antichrist,

and finally of his victories and their consequences, **many**
wonderful tales were related; some of which were afterwards
adopted by the Christians. With the exception of merely a
few of the better instructed, the whole nation may be said to
have considered the sum and substance of religion as consisting entirely in an observance of the ceremonies prescribed by
Moses, to which they attached so high a portion of merit, as
to believe that every one who constantly and strictly conformed to them might, with a degree of certainty, look forward to the enjoyment of the blessings of Divine favour, both
in this life and that which is to come. To the calls of humanity and philanthropy the Jews paid not the least attention, except in regard to those who were allied to them by
nature and blood, or were at least so far connected with them
as to belong to the same religious community with themselves. They were even so wholly destitute of every gene-
rous feeling or sentiment towards strangers, as not only to
shun, by every means in their power, whatever might lead to
any thing like an intimacy, or reciprocal interchange of good
offices with them, but also to imagine themselves at liberty to
treat them on all occasions in the most injurious and oppressive manner. It was, therefore, not without reason that they
were taxed by the Greeks and Romans with cherishing an
hatred of the human race.([2])

(1) Basnage, in his *Histoire de Juifs*, tom. v. cap. x. p. 193. treats particularly of the notions which, about the time of our Saviour's coming, were entertained by the Jews respecting the Messiah. Some very learned men of our
own time have considered it as a matter of doubt, whether the Jews in general
looked for a Messiah, or whether the expectation was not cherished by merely
a part of them : and there are those who maintain, that the Pharisees alone are
represented in the writings of the New Testament as looking for a prince or
deliverer; and would hence conclude, that the Sadducees entertained no such
hope. But not to say any worse of this opinion, it appears to me to savour
highly of temerity. I cannot, indeed, pretend to determine what might be the
sentiments of the Essenes, who differed in so many respects from the regular
[p. 41.] Jews, that they can only be considered as half Jews; but I think it is
manifest beyond all doubt, that all the rest of the Hebrews who dwelt in Palestine, and the neighbouring regions, fully expected the coming of a Messiah.
Numberless passages might be cited, which place it out of all controversy that
this consolatory hope was generally cherished in the minds of the people at

large, (see particularly John x. 24, et seq. xii. 34. Matth. xxi. 9.) ; and that not only the Pharisees, but also the Sadducees entertained a similar expectation must, I think, readily be admitted by every one, if it be considered that the sanhedrim, or general council of the nation, together with all the doctors and interpreters of the law, and also the whole of the priesthood, evidently looked for the coming of the Christ. The national council, as appears from the authority of Scripture itself, was composed of Sadducees as well as Pharisees ; and the various orders of priests were made up indiscriminately of those of either sect. If, therefore, it can be ascertained that the whole of the sanhedrim, together with all the priests and doctors, both wished for and expected a Messiah, nothing further can be requisite to prove that the sentiments of the Sadducees were similar to those of the Pharisees on this point. And that such was actually the case, admits not of the least ground for dispute. Herod the Great, alarmed by the coming of the Magi, or wise men from the East, commanded the priests and interpreters of the sacred volume to assemble, and inquired of them concerning the country in which the Messiah would be born. This general assembly of all the learned of the nation, amongst whom were undoubtedly many of the Sadducees, with one accord replied, that, according to the prediction of the holy prophets, the deliverer of the people would be born in Bethlehem. Matth. ii. 4, 5, 6. Not a single individual of them, therefore, appears to have entertained the least doubt of the coming of a Messiah. When John began to execute the divine commission with which he was charged, of baptizing with water, the council at Jerusalem sent messengers to inquire of him whether he were the Messiah or Christ. John i. 20. 25. It is evident, therefore, that this council must have been unanimous in the expectation of a Messiah. Caiaphas the high priest, the president of the Jewish council, required of our Saviour, under the most solemn adjuration, to say whether or not he were the Messiah : and when Jesus answered in the affirmative, that pontiff at once accused him of direct blasphemy, and demanded of the members of the council what punishment ought to be inflicted on him? who all, without exception replied, that a man who could be guilty of such impiety was deserving of death. Matth. xxvi. 63, et seq. The whole council, therefore, we see were of opinion, that for a man to call himself the Son of God, or the Messiah, was an insult to the Divine Majesty, and merited nothing short of capital punishment. But with what propriety, and on what grounds could such a judgment have been with one voice pronounced by this assembly, which comprehended many of the Sadducees, if it was their belief that the notions entertained by the people respecting a Messiah had no solid foundation, but ought to be regarded in the light of a fabulous delusion? Could a man be said to have offered a serious affront to God, by merely endeavouring to give to a popular whim or idle conceit of the vulgar a turn in his own favour? But how, it has been asked by some of the learned, could it be possible for the Sadducees to feel any sort of interest in the coming of a Messiah, when, as is well known, they never extended their views of happiness beyond the present life, and absolutely denied the doctrine of a future state of rewards and punishments? The answer is easy. It was indeed impossible for the Sadducees, consistently with the tenets of their sect, to entertain any expectation of the coming of such a Messiah as God had promised, a spiritual deliverer, a re- deemer of souls; but nothing could be more natural than for men like [p. 42.] them, who maintained that obedience to the law of God would be re- warded in no other way than by an abundance of this world's goods, health of body, riches, and the like, to look with eagerness after such a Messiah as was the object of the ardent hope of the Jewish nation at that period, namely, an illustrious prince, a hero, or vanquisher of the Romans, and a restorer of their lost liberties.

(2) See the authorities collected by Elsner, (*Observation. Sacr. in Nov. Test.* tom. ii. p. 274.) to which, if it were necessary, many others might be added.

IX. **Jewish sects.** Among the various untoward circum- stances which conspired to undermine the welfare of the Jew- ish nation, one of the chief was that, those who possessed a superior degree of learning, and who arrogantly pretended to the most perfect knowledge of divine matters, so far from be- ing united in sentiment, were divided into various sects, widely differing in opinion from each other, not only on sub- jects of smaller moment, but also on those points which con- stitute the very essence of religion itself. Of the Pharisees and the Sadducees, which were the two most distinguished of these sects both in number and respectability, mention is made in the writings of the New Testament. Josephus, Philo, and others speak of a third sect, under the title of the Es- senes;(¹) and it appears from more than one authority, that several others of less note contributed still farther to distract the public mind. St. Matthew, in his history, notices the Herodians; a class of men who, it seems highly probable, had espoused the cause of the descendants of Herod the Great, and contended that they had been unjustly deprived of the greater part of Palestine by the Romans. In Josephus we also find mention made of another sect, bearing the title of the Philosophers; composed of men of the most ferocious cha- racter, and founded by Judas, a Galilean, a strenuous and un- daunted asserter of the liberties of the Jewish nation, who main- tained that the Hebrews ought to render obedience to none but God alone.(²) In fine, I do not think that the accounts given of the Jewish sects or factions by Epiphanius and Hegesippus, as preserved in Eusebius, should be considered as altogether groundless and undeserving of credit.(³)

(1) It is certain that no express mention is made of the Essenes in the writings of the New Testament: several learned persons, however, have imagined, that although the name is not to be found there, yet that the principles and doctrines of this sect are glanced at in various passages. Some, for instance, point to Col. ii. 18, et seq.; others to Matth. vi. 16.; whilst others again fancy that a similar allusion is to be perceived in several other places. It cannot be necessary to enter into a serious refutation of these opinions, since they have no other support than that of mere random conjecture. From this silence of the sacred writings respecting the Essenes, (or, as some perhaps would prefer to have them called, Essees,) the adversaries of religion have taken occasion to insinuate that Christ himself belonged to this sect, and was desirous of propagating its discipline and doctrines in the cities, in opposition to the wishes of the Pharisees and Sadducees. See Prideaux's *Histoire des Juifs*, tom. iv. p. 116. But the opinion is manifestly childish and absurd in itself; and nothing more is required than a comparison of the discipline of the Essenes with that of the Christians, to prove it at once utterly false and void of foundation. Others, influenced by less hostile motives, have suggested as a reason why Christ and his apostles forbore to cast any reprehension on the Essenes, that notwithstanding all their proneness to superstition, they [p. 43.] might probably appear to be actuated by a rectitude of intention, and a sincere desire to worship God aright. Finally, there are some who imagine that the Essenes without hesitation embraced the truth propounded to them by Christ, and became his disciples; and consequently exempted themselves from the censure to which they would otherwise have been exposed. But it appears to me, that no one who will be at the pains attentively to examine the principles and tenets of the Essenes, and to compare them with the history of Christian affairs, can well accede to either of these opinions. At the same time, I conceive, that without going any farther than to the manners and habits of this sect, we may be furnished with a most plain and satisfactory reason why no mention is made of it either by the evangelists or any other of the apostles. Those four historians of the life and actions of Christ, whom we term evangelists, confined their narration to such things alone as were said and done by him in the Jewish cities and towns, and particularly at Jerusalem. In like manner, the epistles written by the apostles were addressed only to Christians who dwelt in cities. But the Essenes, it is well known, avoided all intercourse whatever with cities, and spent their lives in wilds and desert places. It would therefore have been altogether digressive, and out of place, had any notice been taken, in either of the books of the New Testament, of any disputes which either Christ or his disciples might have had with a sect of this description.

(2) Josephus *Antiquit. Judaic.* lib. xviii. cap. ii.

(3) In support of the opinion which I thus profess myself to entertain, that what Epiphanius has recorded concerning the Jewish sects, in the Preface to his book *de Hæresibus*, is probably not wholly fictitious, or unworthy of credit, I will here bring forward a conjecture, which I have never turned in my mind without feeling strongly persuaded of its probability, and that it might with

propriety be submitted to the consideration of the learned. Possibly it may contribute towards dispelling a portion of that obscurity with which ancient history is enveloped. Amongst the various Jewish sects enumerated by Epiphanius, is that hf the Hemerobaptists, a set of people who, according to him, were accustomed to wash their bodies daily, imagining that without this perpetual ablution, it would be impossible for any one to obtain salvation. Now mention is made of this same sect by Hegesippns, a very ancient writer, *apud Euseb. Histor. Eccles.* lib. iv. cap. xxii. p. 143; and Justin Martyr also notices it, *Dialog. cum Tryphon* p. 245. ed. Jebb. merely with this difference, that rescinding the first part of the word, he terms the sect Baptist. In the *Indiculum Hæreseon*, a work which is commonly attributed to Jerome, it is likewise reckoned as one of the Jewish sects. The author of those tracts, which bear the name of *Clementina*, says that one John was the founder of this sect, and that he had under him a company of twelve apostles, besides thirty other select associates. *Homil. secund.* cap. xxiii. p. 633. tom. i. *Patr. Apostol.* The same thing is also said in the *Epitome Gestorum Petri,* which is subjoined to the *Clemintina*, § xxvi. p. 763. If any reliance whatever, therefore, is to be placed in ancient history, the fact seems to be incontrovertibly established by evidence that admits of no suspicion either on the ground of deceit or ignorance, that such a sect as that of the Hemerobaptists did in reality exist amongst the Jews; and we should consequently do wrong in considering every thing recorded by Epiphanius as fabulous, and undeserving of credit. But what appears to me to be by no means an improbable conjecture is, that some of the descendants of these Hemerobaptists have survived even to this day. The learned well know that there exists in Persia and India a very numerous and widely extended class of men, who call themselves Mendai Ijahi or the dis-
[p. 44.] ciples of John; but who, from their appearing to have received a tincture of Christianity, although but in a very slight and imperfect degree, are most commonly styled by Europeans, " the Christians of St. John." The Orientals give them the name of Sabbi or Sabiin. Ignatius a Jesu, a Carmelite, who resided for a long while amongst these people, published an account of them in a particular little work, bearing the following title: *Narratio Originis Rituum et Errorum Chrïstianorum S. Johannis; cui adjungitur Discursus per Modum Dialogi, in quo confutantur* xxxiii. *Errores ejusdem Nationis,* Romæ, 1652, in 8vo. The book is not to be despised, since it contains many things well worthy of attention; but it is deficient in method, and is evidently the production of an untutored genius. Besides what is to be met with in this author, copious accounts have been given of these people by Herbelot, in his *Bibliotheca Orientalis voce Sabi,* p. 726.; and Asseman, in the *Bibliotheca, Oriental. Clement. Vatican;* as also by Thevenot and Tavernier, in the accounts of their travels; and Kæmpher, in his *Amœnitates exotic. fascic.* ii. cap. xi. p. 435, et seq.; and more recently by Fourmont, in the *History of the Academy of Inscriptions, &c. at. Paris;* and others. Bayer also is known to have been engaged in a work expressly on this subject, and which it is probable that he had nearly, if not quite, completed at the time of his death. The origin and nature of this sect have not been as yet satisfactorily determined. We

have sufficient proof before us at this day, that it cannot in any shape be referred to the Christians; for the opinions which those who belong to it entertain respecting Christ, are evidently such only as have been accidentally imbibed from their intercourse with the Chaldean Christians; and they do not pay him any sort of adoration or worship. By most people they are considered as the descendants of the ancient Sabii, of whom frequent mention is made in the Mohammedan law, and in Maimonides. But their manners and tenets by no means accord with those which are ascribed to the Sabii: and in regard to the appellation of Sabii, which is given to them by the Mohammedans, no argument whatever can be drawn from it, since it is well known that this is a generic term, applied by the Arabs to all who are of a different religion from themselves. For my own part, I should rather consider these Christians of St. John as the descendants of the ancient Hemerobaptists, who appear to have flourished in Judea about the time of our Saviour's birth; and I ground my opinion on the following reasons: 1st, These people profess themselves to be Jews, and assert that their forefathers dwelt in Palestine, on the banks of the river Jordan; from whence, according to them, they were driven by the Mohammedans. This is of itself, I think, sufficient to overturn the opinion of those who would confound them with the Sabii. 2dly, They rest their hopes of the remission of sins, and of salvation, on the frequent ablution of the body; an error by which the Hemerobaptists were principally distinguished from other Jews. At this day, indeed, the disciples of John, as they wish to be called, are washed in the river, according to solemn form by the priests, only once in the year; whereas the Hemerobaptists practised a daily ablution of the body; but it is strongly impressed on the minds of all of them, that the oftener this ceremony is performed by any one, the more refined and holy he becomes; and they would, therefore, rejoice if it were possible for them to undergo the like ablution every month, or even every day. It is the avarice of the priest which prevents the frequent repetition of this cere- [p. 45.] mony: money being the only motive by which they can be stimulated to the exercise of the duties of their function. 3dly, The name of the founder of this sect, as that of the Hemerobaptists, was John; from whom they pretend to have received a certain book, which is regarded as sacred, and preserved with the greatest care. It is a common opinion that this John was the same with him who was the forerunner of Christ, and who is styled in Scripture the Baptist; and hence many have been led to conclude, that the people who are styled Sabii are the descendants of John the Baptist's disciples. Ignatus a Jesu. in particular, is of this opinion. See his work above mentioned, cap. ii. p. 13, et seq. But it is plain from the account which, even according to Ignatius himself, these people give of the founder of their sect, that he must have been a person altogether different from the Baptist: for they will not admit that the John, whose memory they hold in such reverence, suffered capital punishment under Herod; but maintain that he died according to the course of nature at a city of Persia, named Sciuster, and was buried near that place. They also relate of him, that he was married, and had four sons. It cannot indeed be denied but that, in some few particulars, the account which they give of this their John corresponds with what is recorded in Holy Writ of John the Baptist; but it appears to me beyond all doubt, that these things, as well as the few facts of which they are in possession respecting Christ, were adopted from the Christians, with whom they sojourned for a while, after their flight from the oppression of the Mohammedans. Perceiving nothing in these things either contradictory or adverse to their tenets, and being, through their extreme ignorance, utterly unqualified for examining into or controverting any points of which they might chance to be informed, they probably without hesitation received and propagated them as a part of their own system. Of the degree of merit that may belong to this conjecture of mine, which I scruple not to say appears to me to have every probability on its side, the public will be better able to judge, when it shall be put in possession of those books which the Christians of St. John hold sacred, and particularly of that one which this sect consider to have been written by their venerated founder. Copies of these books were, a few years since, deposited in the King of France's library; and it may therefore reasonably be expected that, ere long, they will find their way into the hands of the learned. [See another translation of this note, in *Murdock's* Mosheim's Institutes of Eccl. Hist. B. I. cent. I. p. 1. ch. 2. §. p. n. (7,) vol. I. p. 34-36. *Editor.*]

X. **Of the larger sects, their points of concord and disagreement.** The Pharisees, the Sadducees, and the Essnes, the three most distinguished and powerful of the Jewish sects, were cordially united in sentiment as to all those fundamental points which constitute the basis and chief support of the Jewish religion. All of them, for instance, rejected with detestation the idea of a plurality of gods, and would acknowledge the existence of but one almighty power, whom they regarded as the creator of the universe, and believed to be endowed with the most absolute perfection and goodness. They were equally agreed in the opinion, that God had selected the Hebrews from amongst the other nations of the earth as his peculiar people, and had bound them to himself by an unchangeable and everlasting covenant. With the same unanimity they maintained that Moses was the ambas-[p. 46.] sador of heaven, and consequently that the law promulgated by him was of divine original. It was also their general belief, that in the books of the Old Testament were to be found the means of obtaining salvation and happiness; and that whatever principles or duties were therein laid down or inculcated, were to be received with reverence and implicitly conformed to. But an almost irreconcileable difference of opinion, and the most vehement disputes, prevailed amongst them respecting the original source or fountain from whence all religion was to be deduced. In addition to the written law, the Pharisees had recourse to another, which had been received merely through oral tradition. This latter both the Sadducees and the Essenes rejected with contempt, as altogether spurious. The interpretation of the law yielded still further ground for acrimonious contention. The Pharisees maintained that the law, as committed to writing by Moses, and likewise every other part of the sacred volume, had a two-fold sense or meaning; the one plain and obvious to every reader, the other abstruse and mystical. The Sadducees, on the contrary, would admit of nothing beyond a simple interpretation of the words, according to their strict literal sense. The Essenes, or at least the greater part of them, differing from both of these, considered the words of the law to possess no force or power whatever in themselves, but merely to exhibit the shadows or images of celestial objects, of virtues, and of duties. So much dissention and discord respecting the rule of religion, and the sense in which the divine law ought to be understood, could not fail to produce a great diversity in the forms of religious worship, and naturally tended to generate the most opposite and conflicting sentiments on subjects of a divine nature.(')

(1) A collection of what had been written concerning these Jewish sects, by Jos. Scaliger, Drusius, and Serarius, three distinguished authors, who, as it appears, differed in opinion as to many things connected with the subject, was published by Trigland in 2 vols. 4to. 1702, under the following title: *Trium Scriptorum illustrium de Judæorum Sectis Syntagma.* Since that time, Basnage, Prideaux, and numberless other writers, have used their endeavors still farther to elucidate the subject; but the attempt has not, in every case, been attended with equal success.

XI. **Of the Pharisees.** In point of numbers, riches, and power, the Pharisees far surpassed every other Jewish sect; and since they constantly exhibited a great display of religion, in an apparent zeal for the cultivation of piety and brotherly love, and by an affectation of superior sanctity in their opinions, their manners, and even in their dress, the influence which they possessed over the minds of the people was unbounded; insomuch that they may almost be said to have given what direction they pleased to public affairs. It is unquestionable, however, that the religion of the Pharisees was, for the most part, founded in consummate hypocrisy ; and that at the bottom they were generally the slaves of every vicious appetite; proud, arrogant and avaricious; consulting only the gratification of their lusts, even at the moment of their professing themselves to be engaged in the service of their Maker.(¹) These odious features in the character of the Pharisees [p. 47.] caused them to be rebuked by our Saviour with the utmost severity of reprehension ; with more severity, indeed, than he bestowed even on the Sadducees, who, although they had departed widely from the genuine principles of religion, yet did not impose on mankind by a pretended sanctity, or devote themselves with insatiable greediness to the acquisition of honors and riches. The Pharisees considered the soul to be immortal. They also believed in the resurrection of the body, and in a future state of rewards and punishments. They admitted the free agency of man to a certain extent ; but beyond this, they supposed his actions to be controlled by the decrees of fate. These points of doctrine, however, seem not to have been understood or explained by all of this sect in the same way ; neither does it appear that any great pains were taken to define and ascertain them with precision and accuracy, or to support them by reasoning and argument.(²)

(1) Josephus, although himself a Pharisee, yet authorizes this statement. See what he says in his *Antiquitates Judaic.* lib. xvii. cap. iii. ; and also in some other places.

(2) Even Josephus, who must have been intimately acquainted with the tenets of the Pharisees, is very inconsistent with himself in the account which he gives of them, as may easily be perceived by any one who will compare together the different passages relating to them in his works. It would also prove a task of some difficulty to reconcile every thing which he says concerning the opinions of the Pharisees, with what is recorded of them in the writings of the New Testament. Such inconsistency and contradictions can scarcely be accounted for, otherwise than by concluding that a difference of sentiment prevailed amongst the Pharisees on various points; and that their opinions, so far from being fixed and determinate, were in many respects altogether vague and unsettled.

XII. **Of the Sadducees.** The Sadducees fell greatly short of the Pharisees in number as well as influence. This is easily to be accounted for, from the manners and principles of the sect. Their leading tenet was, that all our hopes and fears terminate with the present life ; the soul being involved in one common fate with the body and liable, like it, to perish and be dissipated. Upon this principle, it was very natural for them to maintain, that obedience to the law would be rewarded by God with length of days, and an accession of the good things of this life, such as honors and wealth; whilst the violators of it would, in like manner, find their punishment in the temporary sufferings and afflictions of the present day. But persons impressed with this opinion could not possibly consider any as the favorites of Heaven but the fortunate and the happy; for the poor and the miserable they could entertain no sentiments of compassion: their hopes and their desires must all have centred in a life of leasure, of ease, and voluptuous gratification: and such is exactly the character which Josephus gives us of the Sadducees.(¹) With a [p. 48.] view in some degree, to justify this system, and cast as it were a veil over its deformity, they denied that man had any natural propensity to either good or evil; but insisted that he was left at perfect liberty to choose between the two. A man's happiness and prosperity, therefore, they asserted, depended entirely on himself; and hence if he were poor and miserable, he was not deserving of any commiseration or pity, since his adverse lot was altogether the consequence of his own depravity and misconduct.

(1) According to Josephus, the sect of the Sadducees was of small number, and composed entirely of men distinguished for their opulence and prosperity. *Antiquit. Judaic.* lib. xviii. cap. i. § 4. p. 871. lib. xiii. cap. x. § 6. p. 663. He also represents those belonging to it as entirely devoid of every sentiment of benevolence and charity towards others; whereas the Pharisees, on the contrary, were ever ready to relieve the wants of the poor and the wretched. *De Bell. Judaic.* lib. ii. cap. viii. § 14. p. 166. It likewise appears from his account of them, that they were studious of passing their lives in one uninterrupted course of ease and pleasure; insomuch that it was with difficulty they could be prevailed on to undertake the duties of the magistracy, or any other public function. *Antiquit.* lib. xviii. cap. i. § 4. p. 871. They were also, it should seem, decidedly hostile to the doctrine of fate and necessity; considering all men to enjoy the most ample freedom of action: i. e. the absolute power of doing either good or evil, according to their choice. It would have yielded some gratification to the reader, possibly, had Josephus traced these distinguishing traits in the character of the Sadducees to their proper source; but on this part of the subject he is altogether silent. The deficiency, however, may, I think, be easily supplied; and I will therefore attempt it in a few words. Since the Sadducees believed that the law of Moses was of divine original, they were unavoidably constrained to admit that God promised rewards

to the obedient, and threatened evil-doers with punishment. But as it made a part of their creed, that death puts a final period to the existence of the soul as well as the body, it became with them a necessary point of belief, that the remuneration bestowed by God on the righteous would consist of the good things and enjoyments of the present life; and that its temporal evils, such as poverty, disease, ignominy, and the like, would constitute the punishment of the wicked. Now, it strikes me that every thing which Josephus has handed down to us respecting the Sadducees may readily be accounted for from this one principle: for under the influence of such an opinion, they would necessarily consider the man who abounded in wealth, and other means of worldly enjoyment, as upright and acceptable to God; whilst the miserable, the poor, the destitute, and the diseased, must in like manner have been regarded by them in the light of sinners, hateful in the sight of their Maker. Persons of slender or more moderate means, to say nothing of the afflicted, the indigent, and the naked, could have had no inducement whatever to join themselves to men professing such sentiments; and as the number of these has ever far exceeded that of the rich and the happy, it was impossible for this sect to extend itself so as to become any way numerous. To the same source may likewise be referred that want of humanity, which they discovered towards the necessitous, and those who had to struggle with the ills of adverse fortune: for since it was their belief, that every thing in this life went well with the righteous, and that adversity was the lot only of the wicked, they were naturally led to conclude that the poor and the wretched must, by their crimes and offences, have displeased God, and drawn on themselves the effects of his just indignation; and that to relieve the wants of those who were at enmity with Heaven, or to attempt, by any means, to mitigate or soften down chastisements inflicted by the hand of the Almighty, would be acting in direct opposition to the dictates [p. 49.] both of reason and religion. It is probable, therefore, that in the observance of a harsh and unfeeling carriage towards their unfortunate fellow mortals, they imagined themselves to be actuated by motives of piety and a love towards God. Again, nothing could be more natural for men who conceived that the soul would not survive the body, and that all those who should be found deserving of the favor of Heaven would receive their reward in this world, than to devote themselves to a life of ease and voluptuous gratification: for in vain they might say, would God lavish on his favourites riches and health, or any of the various other means of enjoyment, if he did not intend them to be used for the purpose of rendering the path of life smooth and delightful. According to their view of things, the pleasures and gratifications placed by the bounty of Divine Providence within our reach, ought rather to be considered in the light of rewards which God bestows on the just, by way of remuneration for the difficulties which they may encounter in the study of His law. Unless I am altogether mistaken, our blessed Saviour, in that history of the rich man (whether true or feigned, matters not) which is recorded in St. Luke's Gospel, cap. xvi. v. 19. hath given us a just picture of the manners and way of living of the Sadducees. Dives was a Jew, for he calls Abraham his father; but he was neither a Pharisee nor one of the Essenes, and we may therefore conclude him to have been a Sadducee. Indeed, our Saviour's narrative leaves us in no doubt as to this point; for the request of Dives to Abraham is, that he would send Lazarus to his brethren, for the purpose of converting them to a belief in the soul's immortality, and in the certainty of a future state of rewards and punishments. It is plain, therefore, that during his life-time he had imagined that the soul would perish with the body, and had treated with derision the doctrine maintained by the Pharisees respecting the happiness or misery of a future state; and that the brethren whom he had left behind entertained similar sentiments—sentiments which clearly mark them as the votaries of that impious system to which the Sadducees were devoted. This man is represented as having amassed great wealth. His riches were employed in obtaining for him authority and respect amongst the people: for the eyes of the multitude were studiously drawn towards him, by the splendour and costliness of his apparel; and he fared sumptuously and joyously with his companions every day. Lazarus, a poor wretch, the prey of misery and disease, was suffered to lie languishing at his gate, neglected and scorned, as a being hateful in the sight of Heaven, and undeserving of any commisseration. The writings of Moses and the prophets were not indeed rejected by him; on the contrary, it should seem that he held them in respect. "They have Moses and the prophets," says Abraham. The Holy Scriptures, therefore, it appears, were in the hands of these men; but they would not allow that any thing contained in them would warrant a conclusion that the souls of men would survive the dissolution of their bodies, and be either punished or rewarded in a future state for the deeds done in the flesh. The authority, therefore, of Christ himself may be adduced in support of the greater part of what Josephus has handed down to us repecting the Sadducees. It was impossible for any thing to be more directly repugnant to the manners and opinions which we have just been considering, than the doctrine of the Pharisees, who maintained that there is in mankind a general proneness or inclination to what is evil and vicious, and that consequently great allowances ought to be made for the weakness and corruption of our nature; that many are involved in misery, not so much through their own fault, as in compliance with the all-wise arrangements of Divine Providence, which freely dispenses both good and evil to its creatures, according to its will; whilst the afflictions and sufferings of others are evidently to be attributed to imprudence, to ignorance, to accident, or perhaps to the injustice and tyranny of [p. 50.] wicked men. A man's fortune or circumstances in life, therefore, they contended, could in no wise furnish a just criterion whereby to estimate his uprightness or depravity. On every one of these points, the Sadducees differed from them *toto cœlo;* insisting that man is endowed with the most perfect freedom of will to do either good or evil, without being under the least controul whatever from any impediment either external or internal; and that he is not driven by necessity, or inclined by natural propensity, to either the one side or the other. The happiness of mortals, therefore, being thus made wholly dependent on themselves, if they fail to attain it, it must be entirely through their own fault. At this distance of time, it is impossible to enter more at large into the subject, or to relieve it altogether from the obscurity with which it is enveloped; since we are ignorant of the manner in which the Sadducees might explain and recommend their system, and are equally unacquainted with their mode of reasoning, in answer to the arguments of their opponents.

XIII. **Division of the Essenes.** The Essenes are generally divided by the learned into two classes, the *practical*, and the *theoretical.* This arrangement of the sect is founded upon a supposition that the Therapeutæ, concerning whom Philo Judæus has left us a distinct little treatise, belonged to it. To this opinion I cannot implicitly subscribe, since it has no other support on its side than mere probability; but, at the same time, I do not pretend to say that it may not be a just one. Those whom they call practical Essenes were such as engaged in agriculture, or practised medicine, or any of the other arts, and did not estrange themselves from the society of mankind. The term theoretical they apply to those who, renouncing every sort of bodily occupation, devoted themselves entirely to the exercise of contemplation; and who, to avoid pollution, withdrew themselves from all converse with men of a different persuasion. The practical Essenes were still further divided, according to Josephus, into two branches: the one being characterized by a life of celibacy, dedicated to the instruction and education of the children of others; whilst the other thought it proper to marry, not with a view to sensual gratification, but for the purpose of propagating the human species.(¹) It is possible that these might not be the only opinions and habits, by a difference in regard to which these two classes were distinguished from each other. The monks of Christianity, a description of men that first appeared in Egypt, seem to have taken for their model the manners and scheme of life of the practical Essenes: indeed the account given us by Josephus of the latter corresponds so exactly with the institutions and habits of the early votaries of monachism, that it is impossible for any two things more nearly to resemble each other. Those solitary characters, who came to be distinguished by the appellation of hermits, appear to have copied after the theoreti-[p. 51.] cal Essenes or Therapeutæ.

(1) Josephus *de Bello Judaic.* lib. ii. cap. viii. sect. 13. p. 165, et seq.

XIV. **Of the practical Essenes.** The practical Essenes were distributed in the cities, and throughout the countries of Syria, Palestine, and Egypt. Their bond of association embraced not merely a community of tenets, and a similarity of manners, and particular observances, like that of the Pharisees or the Sadducees; but extended also to a general participation of houses, victuals, and every sort of goods. Their demeanor was sober and chaste; and their mode of life was, in every other respect, made subject to the strictest regulations, and put under the superintendance of governors, whom they appointed over themselves. The whole of their time was devoted to labour, meditation, and prayer: and they were most diligently attentive to the calls of justice and humanity, and every moral duty. Like all other Jews, they believed in the unity of God: but from some of their institutes, it appears that they entertained a reverence for the sun; considering, probably, that grand luminary as a deity of an inferior order, or perhaps regarding him as the visible image of the Supreme Being. The souls of men they imagined to have fallen, by a disastrous fate, from the regions of purity and light into the bodies which they occupy; during their stay in which, they considered them to be confined as it were within the walls of a loathsome dungeon. For this reason, therefore, they would not believe in the resurrection of the body; although it was their opinion that the soul would be rewarded or punished in a life to come, according to its deserts. They also allowed themselves but little bodily nourishment or gratification, fearing lest the immortal spirit might be thereby encumbered and weighed down. It was, moreover, their endeavour, by constant meditation, to withdraw the mind as much as possible from the contagious influence of the corrupt mass by which it was unhappily enveloped. The ceremonies or external forms, enjoined by Moses to be observed in the worship of God, were utterly disregarded by many of the Essenes; it being their opinion that the words of the law were to be understood in a mysterious recondite sense, and not according to their literal meaning. Others of them, indeed, conformed so far as to offer sacrifices; but they did this at home, since they were totally averse from the rites which it was necessary for those to observe who made their offerings in the temple.(') Upon the whole, I should think it no improbable conjecture, that the doctrine and discipline of the Essenes arose out of an endeavour to make the principles of the Jewish religion accord with some tenets which they had imbibed from that system, which we have above spoken of under the title of the oriental philosophy.

(1) Philo, in his book *Quod omnis Probus Liber*, p. 457. tom. ii. opp. edit. Anglic. denies that the Essenes offered up any sacrifices. Josephus, however, in his *Antiquitates Judaic.* lib. xviii. cap. i. § v. p. 871, says, that they did not indeed sacrifice in the temple at Jerusalem ; and for this plain reason, that the Jews would not permit them do so, on account of their refusing to observe the customary national ceremonies; but that, separately, among themselves, they offered up victims to the Supreme Being with more than ordinary solemnity. The learned are divided in opinion as to which of these accounts is most deserving of credit. The generality of them lean to the authority of Philo, and propose, either by an emendation of the words of Josephus, or by giving them a new interpretation, to make him say much the same thing with Philo; on which subject I have already taken occasion to make some remarks, in my notes to Cudworth's *Discourse concerning the true notion of the Lord's Supper.* I must [p. 52.] confess that I see nothing which should prevent us from considering both these accounts as supported, to a certain extent, by the real fact. For, since it appears that the Essenes were so much divided in opinion respecting the marriage state, as that some of them utterly disapproved of entering into it, whilst others freely took to themselves wives; I think it by no means impossible that one part of this sect might be wholly averse from sacrifices of any kind, and consider the law from beginning to end merely in the light of an allegory; whilst the remaining part, thinking that the words of the law ought in some sort to be understood according to their literal sense, might comply with them so far as to offer sacrifices to God, although, in their manner of doing so, they might probably have a regard to some of the principles which they had imbibed from a different source. There are, however, some highly respectable literary characters, to whom it appears altogether incredible that any Jews, who believed in the divine original of the Mosaic law, should have dared to sacrifice in any other place than the temple; and who consequently refuse to place any faith in what Josephus says of the Essenes having done so. But I rather think that I am furnished with the means of making these opponents of the Jewish historian alter their opinion, and of rendering them willing again to restore to him whatever they may have detracted from his credit and authority. The fact is, that I have met with a remarkable passage in Porphyry, the Platonic philosopher, which has never, as far as I can discover, been noticed by any one who has treated of the Essenes, or undertaken to illustrate Josephus: but which clearly vindicates the account of that historian from all suspicion of error, and tends in great measure to remove the obscurity which hangs over his narrative. Porphyry, in his treatise *de Abstinentia a Carnibus Animalium*, lib. ii. § 26. p. 70. assigns a distinguished place to the Essenes,

amongst those whom he commends for abstaining from the flesh of victims.

Καί τοι Σύρων μὲν Ἰουδαίοι διὰ τὴν ἐξ ἀρχῆς θυσίαν, ἔτι καὶ νῦν φησὶν ὁ Θεόφραςος ζαο-
θυτῦντες, εἰ τὸν αὐτὸν τρόπον ἡμᾶς κελεύοιεν θύειν, ἀποςαίημεν ἂν τῆς πράξεως· ὁ γὰς
ἰςιώμενοι τῶν τυθέντων, ὁλοκαυτῦντες δὲ ταῦτα νυκτὸς, καὶ κατ᾿ αὐτῶν πολὺ μέλι καὶ
οἶνον λείζοντες, ἀνήλισκον τὴν θυσίαν θᾶττον, ἵνα τῦ δεινῦ μὴ ὁ πανόπτης γένοιτο θεα-
τής. Καὶ τῦτο δρῶσι, νηςεύοντες τὰς ἀνὰ μέσον τότε ἡμέρας, καὶ κατὰ πάντα τῦτον
τὸν χρόνον, ἅτε φιλόσοφοι τὸ γένος ὄντες, περὶ τῦ θείω μὲν ἀλλήλοις λαλῦσι, τῆς δὲ νυκτὸς τῶν ἀςρῶν ποιῦνται τὴν θεωρίαν, βλέποντες εἰς αὐτὰ καὶ διὰ τῶν εὐχῶν θεοκλυτῦντες.

Proinde Judæi qui Syriam incolunt, propter primum sacrificiorum institutum, eo modo etiamnum animalia, ut ait Theophrastus, sacrificant: quo si nos juberent facere, a ritu immolandi deficeremus. Non enim victimas epulantur, sed eas integras per noctem comburentes, multo melle et vino iis superfuso, sacrificium ocyus consumunt, ne qui omnia videt, facinus hoc intueatur. Hoc autem faciunt, diebus interjectis jejunantes, et per totum tempus, tamquam e philosophorum erant genere, de numine colloquuntur: nocte etiam astra contemplantur, ea intuiti et precibus deum invocantes. It is true, that this passage does not refer to the Essenes by name; and it may therefore, at first sight, appear as if Porphyry and Theophrastus, whom he quotes, were speaking of the Jews at large. But the nature of the account itself thus given of them places it beyond a question, that it was meant merely of some Jewish sect, and indeed of none other than the sect of the Essenes: for not a single particular of what is thus related can be reconciled with the customary practice and usages of the Jews in common; whereas the account corresponds, in every respect, with the institutions and discipline of the Essenes. The Jews of whom it speaks were philosophers; they sacrificed in the night; they did not feast on the things offered; they occupied themselves in contemplating the stars; they revered the [p. 53.] sun; they poured out honey and wine on their sacrifices; they consumed the whole of what was offered with fire; and prepared themselves for the performance of their sacred rights by an abstinence from food. Now nothing could be more foreign than all these things were from the religious observances of the Jews as a nation; whilst, at the same time, they precisely accord with the principles and practices of the Essenes. The fact therefore undoubtedly was, as Josephus represents it, that the Essenes did not bring their sacrifices to the temple, but offered them up at home. It is also easy to perceive the reasons on account of which the Jewish pontiff and priesthood would not permit them to sacrifice in the temple. The gifts, indeed, which they were accustomed to send to the temple, according to Josephus, were not rejected, neither were its doors closed against them personally; but since they would not, in their sacrifices, follow the institutes and usages of their forefathers, but introduced rites of a novel and profane nature, permission to perform them in the temple was an indulgence which it was utterly impossible to grant. 1. It is well known that all Jews (i. e. who were such in reality, and according to the strict sense of the term) were accustomed to feast solemnly on such part of the victims as remained after sacrifice. But this was an abomination in the eyes of the Essenes, who, according to the principles of the oriental philosophy, considered the soul to be held in bondage by the body; and thinking it therefore improper to add more than was necessary to the strength of the latter, supported it merely by a small quantity of meagre food, and abstained altogether from the flesh of animals. 2. The Jews devoted only a part of the victim to the fire; but the Essenes burnt the whole of it with as much expedition as possible. 3. The Essenes poured out upon their burnt offerings an abundance of honey and wine; a practice entirely unknown to the Jews. The honey and wine were no doubt meant as visible signs of certain thoughts or reflections, by which they deemed it proper that the minds of those who were assisting at the sacrifice should be occupied. 4. The Jews offered up their sacrifices in the day-time; but the Essenes during the night. Porphyry gives us to understand that they fixed on the night time for performing these rights, "lest this ungracious act should meet the eyes of him who sees every thing." This usage was exactly conformable to a superstitious notion of the Essenes, of which Josephus has taken notice. He who sees all things, and to whose eyes the Essenes were unwilling that their sacrifices should be exposed, was unquestionably the sun, whom they worshipped as the deity. But neither Porphyry nor Theophrastus has hit upon the true reason why this preference was given to the night time for sacrificing. The author, who assigns the above reason for it, appears to have thought that the Essenes did not consider sacrifice as a thing altogether unlawful in itself, but yet regarded it as an usage by no means pleasing or acceptable to God; and that their offerings in this way were made rather in compliance with the custom of their country, than in obedience to what they deemed to be his will. It being their opinion, therefore, that the offering of sacrifice was an act not grateful in the sight of Heaven, they always performed their sacred rites before the rising of the sun, whom, in some way or other, they considered as holding the place of the Deity; being naturally desirous to avoid doing that which they imagined was not pleasing to the God who sees every thing, so immediately in his presence as it must be during the day-time. But this reason was probably framed from the suggestions of the writer's own imagination, or else drawn from the principles of the more recent Platonic philosophy, since it could have no foundation whatever in a knowledge of the tenets of the Essenes. It appears from Josephus, that the Essenes believed the night to be a more sacred season than the day, and were, therefore, accustomed to perform all those rites and services with which they imagined it behoved them to worship the Deity, before the appearance of the dawn. Throughout the day they conceived themselves at liberty to discourse of the business and concerns of this life; but during the night they permitted themselves to converse only on subjects of a sacred and divine nature. The chief part of the night was spent in contemplation; but before the approach of dawn they recited their prayers and hymns. The day they devoted to labor. The circumstance, therefore, of their sacrificing in the night time, instead of warranting the conclusion which [p. 54.] Porphyry would draw from it, serves rather to prove that they considered the offering up of victims as an usage of the most sacred nature, and as constituting a necessary part of divine worship. The rule which the Essenes thus prescribed to themselves, of reserving the night for the performance of their divine rites, and confining themselves wholly to secular affairs during the day, appears to have excited some astonishment amongst several of the learned, who consider it as in no wise supported by reason. But if a proper opportunity offered itself, I could, without any very great pains, demonstrate that this reverence for the night was founded on the principles of the ancient oriental doctrines, or that system which comes more particularly under the denomination of the Egyptian philosophy. Many of the oriental nations appear, from the earliest times, to have considered the night not only as having a claim to our preference beyond the day on the score of antiquity, but also as being more dignified and sacred. Indeed, they carried their veneration for the night so far, as almost to place it on a footing with the Deity himself. See the particulars which have, with much diligence and care, been collected by the eminently learned Paul Ernest Jablonsky, on the subject of the night, and of the veneration in which it was held by the Greeks, Phœnicians, and Egyptians, in his *Pantheon Ægyptiorum*, lib. i. cap. i. § 7, et seq. p. 10, et seq. It seems indeed extremely probable that the Essenes might consider the night as having some resemblance to that vast unbounded space in which, previously to the existence of the world, of the sun, and of time, the Deity, accompanied only by such natures as were generated of himself, had from all eternity reigned in consummate bliss and glory. 5. It was the custom of the Essenes to continue their sacrifices for several successive nights. The whole season during which these observances lasted, was deemed particularly sacred. They renounced, for the time, their usual occupations, and employed each intervening day in subduing the body by fasting, so that it might not impede the vigor and operations of the mind. The nights were passed in contemplating the stars, which, without doubt, they believed to be animated and filled with a divine spirit. Differing, therefore, so essentially as the Essenes did in all these particulars from the Jewish discipline and law, it can afford matter for surprise to no one that the priests should not have permitted them to offer their sacrifices in the temple at Jerusalem.

XV. **Of the theoretical Essenes, or Therapeutæ.** Notwithstanding that the practical Essenes were very much addicted to superstition, society derived no inconsiderable benefit from their labour, and the strictness of their morals. Those of the theoretical class, however, or the Therapeutæ of Philo, seem to have set scarcely any bounds whatever to their silly extravagance. Although they professed themselves to be Jews, and were desirous to be considered as the disciples of Moses, they were yet, if we except the name, and some few trifling observances, entirely strangers to the Mosaic discipline.(¹) Renouncing every sort of employment, and all worldly goods, they withdrew themselves into solitary places, and there, distributed about in separate cells,

passed the remnant of their days without engaging in any kind
of bodily labour, and neither offering sacrifices, nor observing
any other external form of religious worship. In this state of
seclusion from the world and its concerns, they made it a point
to reduce and keep the body low, by allowing it nothing beyond
the most slender subsistance, and, as far as possible, to draw away
and disengage the soul from it by perpetual contemplation; so
that the immortal spirit might, in defiance of its corporeal imprisonment, be kept constantly aspiring after its native liberty
and light, and be prepared, immediately on the dissolution of the
body, to re-ascend to those celestial regions from whence it originally sprang. Conformably to the practice of the Jews, the
Therapeutæ were accustomed to hold a solemn assembly every
seventh day. On these occasions, after hearing a sermon from
[p. 55.] their præfect, and offering up their prayers, it was usual
for them to feast together,—if men can in any wise be said to
have feasted, whose repast consisted merely of salt and bread and
water. This sort of refection was followed by a sacred dance,
which was continued throughout the whole night until the appearance of the dawn. At first, the men and the women danced
in two separate parties; but at length, their minds, according to
their own account, kindling with a sort of divine ecstacy, the
two companies joined in one, mutually striving, by various shouts
and songs of the most vehement kind, accompanied with the
most extravagant motions and gesticulations of the body, to
manifest the fervid glow of that divine love with which they
were inflamed. To so great an extent of folly may men be led,
in consequence of their entertaining erroneous principles respecting the Deity and the origin of the human soul!

(1) On this subject I agree in opinion with those who consider the Therapeutæ of Philo to have been Jews both by birth and by name, although they
materially differed from the bulk of that people in their sentiments, their institutions, and their manners. For Philo, to whom we are indebted for every
information that we have respecting the Therapeutæ, and who was himself a
Jew, expressly calls them Jews, and the disciples of Moses; and in addition to
this, there are to be perceived in their customs and manners several peculiarities which savour strongly of the Jewish discipline: and this opinion, from the
strength of the arguments by which it may be supported, is, I am convinced,
daily gaining ground. There are, however, even at this day, not a few amongst
the learned who will not yield their assent to it; but I rather suspect that their

scruples and backwardness to be convinced may rather be attributed to prejudice or party attachment, than to any arguments by which the opinion can be opposed. In the first place, several of the dependents on the papal hierarchy, and also some English writers, persist in giving the preference to the ancient opinion of Eusebius, who thought that the Therapeutæ must have been Christians; and would fain avail themselves of this as a proof that the monastic mode of life was originated in Egypt amongst the first institutions of Christianity. Bernard de Montfaucon, a most learned brother of the Benedictine order, having in the notes to his French translation of Philo's treatise, *de Vita contemplativa* published at Paris, 1709, in 8vo. undertaken to support this opinion, it involved him in a controversy with Jo. Bouhier, at that time president of the parliament of Dijon. The latter, a man equalled but by few in point of ingenuity and literary attainments, endeavoured, with great strength of argument, to prove that the Therapeutæ were not Christians; but the monk was not to be driven from his position: perceiving plainly that in yielding to his antagonist on this occasion, he should abandon a point of the utmost importance to himself and his fraternity, in establishing the antiquity of monachism. The contest between these two eminent scholars was carried on amicably; and the correspondence which took place on the occasion was collected into an octavo volume, and published at Paris, in 1712, with this title, *Lettres pour et contre sur la fameuse Question, si les solitaires appellez Therapeutes dont a parle Philon le Juif, etoient Chretiens.* A book of some size, in answer to Montfaucon on this subject, was likewise written by Gisbert Cuper, and of which mention is made in his *Letters*, published by Bayer p. 63, 64. 70. 239. 241. 250. See also Reimari *Vita Fabricii*, [p. 56.] p. 243, et. seq.; but it was never published. Whilst there shall be monks in the world, there will not be wanting men, who, in spite of the most forcible arguments to the contrary, will persist in assigning to the Theraputæ a place amongst the earliest Christians; as is plain from the recent example which we have had in Mich. le Quien, a brother of the Dominican order, who, although a man of considerable ingenuity and learning, has not hesitated to maintain (*Orient. Christian.* tom. ii. p. 332.) that the Therapeutæ were of his fraternity The attempt is awkwardly made, and ill supported; but it is evident that the good man was willing to subject himself to every sort of contempt, rather than renounce the satisfaction which he and his brethren derived from their relationship to these ancient Ascetics. So much the more praise, however, is due to Joseph August. Orsi, a copious and elegant writer, belonging to the same order of monks, but who has had the courage, even in the city of Rome itself, to contend that the Therepeutæ have no claim whatever to be considered as Christians. See the *Ecclesiastical History* written by him in Italian, vol. i. p. 77. Amongst the English, Mangey, the editor of Philo, has prevailed on himself, (though confessedly with reluctance, and under the apprehension of exciting ill will,) to espouse the opposite side of the question to that which is the favorite one of his church. With the assistance of chronological calculation, he clearly demonstrates that, at the time when Philo wrote his account of the Therapeutæ, Christianity had not found its way into Egypt. *Præfat. in Opera Philonis*, p. 111. See also *Opera*, tom. ii. p. 471.

In the next place, there are some distinguished literary characters, though comparatively but few, who will not admit that the Therapeutæ were either Jews or Christians. The learned Jo. Joach. Langius published at Hall, in 1721, two dissertations *de Therapeutis in Ægypto et Essœis*, in which he endeavours to make it appear that these Ascetics were a Gentile philosophic sect, who had interwoven with their system of discipline some few particulars drawn from the religion of the Jews. But the difference between this opinion and that of those who conceive the Therapeutæ to have been Jews, is not so great as the learned author seems to have imagined: for, according to his own account, the discipline of this sect appears to have been taken in part from the Jewish religion, and partly from some species of philosophy; and exactly in this light is the system of the Therapeutæ regarded by all those who contend that they were Jews. These dissertations, therefore, have nothing in them of novelty, unless it be the author's refusal to assent to the general opinion, that the Therapeutæ were Jews. On this point it is not necessary at present to enter into a discussion, although it might be very easily shown that the opinion of this learned writer is destitute of every kind of support; whilst many circumstances offer themselves in favor of those who maintain that the Therapeutæ were Jews, and that, not merely so far as regarded certain institutions and tenets, but really and strictly such by birth and descent. Still further removed from the commonly received opinion is that of Paul. Ernest. Jablonsky, a man eminent for his curious and recondite learning, who, in a treatise written professedly on the subject, has attempted to prove that the Therapeutæ were priests of Egypt, who devoted themselves to the observation of the stars, and those other sciences accounted sacred in that country; in fact, that they were the same with those whom Democritus, as cited by Clement, calls *Arpedonaptæ*. The outlines of his undertaking may be seen in his *Letters to Matur. Veissiere la Croze*, tom. i. p. 178, et seq.; and I trust it will not be long ere the work itself is given to the public. As far as I am capable of forming a judgment of the matter, [p. 57.] the learned author will have to encounter many obstacles of no small consequence, and particularly, amongst other things, that part of Philo's account which represents the Therapeutæ as not confined merely to Egypt, but as having established themselves in various other countries. In truth, he will have a vast deal to teach us, of which we are as yet completely ignorant, before we can be brought to consider the Therapeutæ as having been the priests or ministers of the Egyptian deities.

XVI. **The moral doctrine of these sects.** Neither of these sects, into which the Jewish people were divided, can be considered as having the least contributed towards promoting the interests of virtue and genuine piety. The Pharisees, as was frequently objected to them by our blessed Saviour, paid no regard whatever to inward purity or sanctity of mind, but studied merely to attract the eyes of the multitude towards them, by an ostentatious solemnity of carriage, and the most specious external parade of piety and brotherly love. They were also continually straining and perverting the most grand and important precepts of the divine law; whilst, at the same time, they enforced an unreserved obedience to ordinances which were merely the institutions of men. Matth. xv. 9. xxiii. 13. &c. The Sadducees considered all those as righteous who strictly conformed themselves to the observances prescribed by Moses, and did no injury to the Jewish nation, from whom they had received none. Since their tenets forbade men to look forward to a future state of rewards and punishments, and placed the whole happiness of man in riches and sensual gratification, they naturally tended to generate and encourage an inordinate cupidity of wealth, a brutal insensibility to the calls of compassion, and a variety of other vices equally pernicious and degrading to the human mind. The Essenes laboured under the influence of a vain and depressing superstition; so that, whilst they were scrupulously attentive to the demands of justice and equity in regard to others, they appear to have altogether overlooked the duties which men owe to themselves. The Therapeutæ were a race who resigned themselves wholly to the dictates of the most egregious fanaticism and folly. They would engage in no sort of business or employment on their own account, neither would they be instrumental in forwarding the interests of others. In a word, they seem to have considered themselves as released from every bond by which human society is held together, and at liberty to act in direct opposition to nearly every principle of moral discipline.(')

(1) See what is said by Barbeyrac, in the Preface to his French translation of Puffendorf's *Jus Naturæ et Gentium*, § vii. p. xxv.

XVII. **Lives of the people dissolute and perverse.** Owing to the various causes which we have thus enumerated, the great mass of the Jewish people were, at the time of Christ's birth, sunk in the most profound ignorance as to divine matters; and the nation, for the most part, devoted to a flagitious and dissolute course of life. That such was the miserable state of degradation into which this highly favoured race had fallen, is incontestibly proved by the history of our Saviour's life, and the [p. 58.]

discourses which he condescended to address to them : and it was
in allusion thereto that he compares the teachers of the people to
blind guides, who professed to instruct others in a way with
which they were totally unacquainted themselves; Matt. xv. 14.
John, ix. 39 ; and the multitude to a flock of lost sheep, wandering without a shepherd.   Matt. x. 6, xv. 24.

XVIII. **The oriental philosophy adopted by many of the Jews.** To
all the sources of error and corruption above pointed out, we
have still further to add, that, at the time of Christ's appearance,
many of the Jews had imbibed the principles of the oriental
philosophy respecting the origin of the world, and were much
addicted to the study of a recondite sort of learning derived from
thence, to which they gave the name of *cabbala,* and which they
considered as of great authority; attributing to it, in many respects, a superiority over the plain and simple system of discipline prescribed by Moses.   Abundant proof of this might be
adduced from the writings of the New Testament, as well as from
the early history of Christianity.(') But to pass over other facts
which might be noticed, it is certain that the founders of several
of the Gnostic sects, all of whom, we know, were studious to
make the Christian religion accommodate itself to the principles
of the ancient oriental philosophy, had been originally Jews, and
exhibited in their tenets a strange mixture of the doctrines of
Moses, Christ, and Zoroaster.   This is of itself sufficient to prove
that many of the Jews were, in no small degree, attached to the
opinions of the ancient Persians and Chaldæans.   Such of them
as had adopted these irrational principles would not admit that
the world was created by God, but substituted, in the place of
the Deity, a celestial genius endowed with vast powers; from
whom, also, they maintained that Moses had his commission, and
the Jewish law its origin.   To the coming of the Messiah, or deliverer promised by God to their fathers, they looked forward
with hope ; expecting that he would put an end to the dominion
of the being whom they thus regarded as the maker and ruler
of the world.   Their notions, therefore, so far as they related to
the abolition of the ceremonial law by the coming of Christ,
were certainly more correct than those of the Jews in common.
But their hopes in this respect redounded but little to their credit,
since they were founded on a most grievous error, and were ac-

companied with many strange and unwarrantable conceits, not less repugnant to right reason than to the Jewish religion.

(1) See what has been collected on this subject by Jo. Christ. Wolfius, in his *Biblioth. Ebraic.* vol. ii. lib. vii. cap. i. § ix. p. 206.

XIX. **The Samaritans.** The Samaritans, who perform- [p. 59.] ed their sacred rites on mount Garizim, were involved in the same calamities which befel the Jewish people, and were no less forward than the Jews in adding, to their other afflictions, the numerous evils produced by factions and intestine tumults. They were not, however, divided into so many religious sects; although the instances of Dositheus, Menander, and Simon Magus, plainly prove that there were not wanting amongst them some who were carried away by the lust of novelty, and sullied the religion of their ancestors, by incorporating with it many of the principles of orientalism.(') Many things have been handed down to us by the Jews respecting the public religion of these people, on which, however, we cannot place much reliance, since they were unquestionably dictated by a spirit of invidious malignity. But since Christ himself attributes to the Samaritans a great degree of ignorance respecting God, and things of a divine nature, John, iv. 22, it is not to be doubted that in their tenets the truth was much debased by superstition, and the light in no small danger of being overpowered by obscurity; and that their religion was much more contaminated by error than that of the Jews. In this one thing only can they be said to have shown themselves superior to the Jews, that they did not attempt to gloss over or conceal the many imperfections of their religion, but frankly acknowledged its defects, and looked forward with hope to the time when the Messiah (whose advent they expected in common with the Jewish nation) would communicate to them that larger measure of spiritual instruction, of which they stood so much in need.(²)

(1) The principal authors who have treated of the Samaritans are pointed out by Jo. Gottlob. Carpzovius, in his *Critic. Sacr. Vet. Test.* part ii. cap. iv. p. 585.

(2) John, iv. 25. That the sentiments of the woman who conversed at the well with Christ were the same with those of the Samaritans in general will not admit of a doubt: for from whence could a common person like her have obtained the information she discovers on several points relating to the Messiah, unless from popular traditions current amongst those of her own nation. These sentiments then furnish us with a strong argument in answer to the English

writer Ant. Collins, and others, who contend that the more ancient Hebrews entertained no expectation of a Messiah; but that this hope first sprung up amongst the Jews some short time before the coming of our Saviour. So deep and inveterate was the enmity which subsisted between the Jews and the Samaritans, that it is utterly incredible that a hope of this kind should have been communicated from either of them to the other. It necessarily follows, therefore, that as both of them were, at the time of our Saviour's birth, looking for the appearance of a Messiah from above, they must have derived the expectation from one common source, doubtless the books of Moses and the discipline of their ancestors; and consequently that this hope was entertained long before the Babylonish captivity, and the rise of the Samaritans. I mention only the books of Moses, because it is well known that the Samaritans did not consider any of the other writings of the Old Testament as sacred, or of divine original; and it is, therefore, not at all likely that any information which they might possess, [p. 60.] respecting the Messiah that was to come, should have been drawn from any other source. In the discourse of the Samaritan woman, we likewise discover what were the sentiments of the ancient Hebrews respecting the Messiah. The expectation of the Jews, at the time of our Saviour's coming, was, as we have seen, directed towards a warlike leader, a hero, an emperor, who should recover for the oppressed posterity of Abraham their liberty and rights: but the Samaritans, as appears from the conversation of this woman, looked forward to the Messiah in the light of a spiritual teacher and guide, who should instruct them in a more perfect and acceptable way of serving God than that which they then followed. Now the Samaritans had always kept themselves entirely distinct from the Jews, and would never consent to adopt any point of doctrine or discipline from them; and the consequence was, that the ancient opinion respecting the Messiah had been retained in much greater purity by the former than by the Jews, whose arrogance and impatience, under the calamities to which they were exposed, had brought them by degrees to turn their backs on the opinion entertained by their forefathers on this subject, and to cherish the expectation that in the Messiah promised to them by God they should have to hail an earthly prince and deliverer. Lastly, I think it particularly deserving of attention, that it is clear from what is said by this woman, that the Samaritans did not consider the Mosaic law in the light of a permanent establishment, but expected that it would pass away, and its place be supplied by a more perfect system of discipline, on the coming of the Messiah. For when she hears our Saviour predict the downfall of the Samaritan, as well as the Jewish religion, instead of taking fire at his words, and taxing him, after the Jewish manner, with blasphemy against God and against Moses, (Acts, vi. 13, 14, 15,) she answers with mildness and composure, that she knew the Messiah would come, and was not unapprized that the religion of her ancestors would then undergo a change.

XX. **State of the Jews not resident in Palestine.** So exceedingly great was the fecundity of the Jewish people, that occasionally multitudes of them had been constrained to emigrate from their native country; and at the period of which we are now treating, the descendants of Abraham were to be met with in every part of the known world. In all the provinces of the Roman empire, in particular, they were to be found in great numbers, either serving in the army, or engaged in the pursuits of commerce, or practising some lucrative art. Those of the Jews who thus ventured to establish themselves without the confines of Palestine, were every where successful in obtaining that general sort of encouragement and protection from violence, which was to be derived from various regulations and edicts of the emperors and magistrates in their favour :(') but the peculiarities of their religion and manners caused them to be held in very general contempt, and not unfrequently exposed them to much vexation and annoyance from the jealousy and indignation of a superstitious populace. Many of them, in consequence of their long residence and intercourse amongst foreign nations, fell into the error of endeavouring to make their religion accommodate itself to the principles and institutions of some of the different systems of heathen discipline, of which it would be easy to adduce numerous instances : but, on the other hand, it is clear that the Jews brought many of those with whom they sojourned to [p. 61.] perceive the superiority of the Mosaic religion over the Gentile superstitions, and were highly instrumental in causing them to forsake the worship of a plurality of gods. Upon the whole, the circumstance of the Jews having found their way into almost every region of the habitable globe, may, I think, justly be classed amongst the means made use of by Divine Providence to open a path for the general diffusion of the truths of Christianity. For it is not to be doubted that the knowledge which the Gentiles thus acquired from the Jews, respecting the only true God, the Creator and Governor of the universe, although it might be but partial, and of limited extent, inclined many of them the more readily to lend their attention to the arguments and exhortations which were subsequently used by our Saviour's apostles, for the purpose of exploding the worship of false deities, and recalling men to those principles of religion which have their foundation in reason and in nature.

(1) Vid. Jac. Gronovii *Decreta Romana et Asiatica pro Judæis ad cultum divinum per Asiæ Minoris Urbes secure obeundum*, Lugd. Bat. 1712, in 8vo.

6

THE
ECCLESIASTICAL HISTORY
OF THE
FIRST CENTURY.

I. The birth of Christ. With a view to effect the recovery of the human race from such a deplorable state of wretchedness and disorder, and to instruct mankind in the path that leads to everlasting salvation and peace, the Son of God voluntarily condescended to take upon himself our nature, and to be born of a virgin, a descendant of the royal house of David, in Bethlehem, a city of Palestine. This event, we know, took place under the reign of the emperor Augustus; but as to the identical day, or month, or even year of its occurrence, it is impossible to speak with any degree of precision, since all the historians of the life of our blessed Saviour, with whose writings we are acquainted, are entirely silent as to these particulars: and indeed it should seem that the earliest Christians were not much better informed on the subject than ourselves, since they appear to have been much divided in opinion as to the exact time of this most important nativity.(') Several ingenious and profound scholars have, at different periods, bestowed an abundance of pains on the subject, in the hope of being able to supply this deficiency in the more ancient writers; but none of them have as yet made any discovery that can be said to put the matter out of all doubt.(') But surely it is of little or no consequence that we are uninformed of the particular year and day that ushered in this glorious light to the world: it is sufficient for us to be assured that the Sun of Righteousness hath arisen on our benighted race, that its refulgence hath dispelled the darkness with which the human mind was enveloped, and that nothing intervenes to prevent us from availing ourselves of the splendour and invigorating warmth of its beams.

(1) Vid. Clemens Alexandr. *Stromat.* lib. i. p. 339, 340. Beausobre *Remarques sur le Nouveau Testament,* tom. i. p. 6. If the early Christians had known the precise day of our Saviour's nativity, they would without doubt have distinguished it by a religious commemoration, in the same way as they were accustomed to celebrate the day of his resurrection. But it is well known that the day which is now held sacred as the anniversary of our Saviour's birth, was fixed on in much more recent times than those in which we find the Christians celebrating the descent of the Holy Ghost on the apostles, and the resurrection of Christ from the dead. This circumstance may, I think, be considered as a proof that the friends and companions of our Lord themselves were unacquainted with the day of his birth, or, at least, that they left no memorial behind them concerning it, and that the first Christians, finding the point involved in much obscurity and doubt, would not take upon them to determine any thing about it.

(2) The reader who wishes to obtain a view of most of the opinions that have been entertained respecting the year of Christ's nativity, may consult Jo. Alb. Fabricii *Bibliograph. Antiq.* cap. vii. § ix. p. 187. Some additional arguments and conjectures may be collected from the more recent publications of several [p. 63.] learned men on this subject; but from amongst all these different opinions it is not possible to select one that can be altogether relied on as free from error. [The most elaborate work on this subject is the Chronological Introduction to the History of the Church, by the learned *Samuel Farmer Jarvis,* D. D. Historiographer, &c. New-York. 1845. 8vo. Editor.]

II. **Accounts of his infancy and youth.** The inspired historians of the life and actions of our Saviour have left but little on record respecting his childhood and early youth. Whilst yet an infant, it appears that his parents fled with him into Egypt, in order to shield him from the persecuting violence of Herod the Great. Matt. ii. 13. At twelve years of age we find him in the temple at Jerusalem, disputing with the most learned of the Jewish doctors, who were filled with astonishment at his understanding and knowledge. The remaining part of his life, until he entered on his ministry, he appears to have spent with his parents, exhibiting in himself an exemplary pattern of affectionate filial obedience.(') Farther than this, it should seem the divine wisdom did not think it necessary that we should be informed. But these few particulars not being found sufficient to satisfy human curiosity, some artful unprincipled characters amongst the early Christians had the presumption to avail themselves of the ignorance and inquisitiveness of a credulous multitude in this respect, and, under the pretence of illustrating this obscure part of our Saviour's life, to impose on the public a compilation of ridiculous and nonsensical stories, which they entitled Gospels of the infancy of Christ.([2])

(1) Luke, ii. 51, 52. Several of our best informed scholars do not hesitate to assert with the greatest confidence, that Christ, during his youth, exercised the art of a carpenter, which he had learnt of his parent, and that he assisted Joseph in the different parts of his business. ' Indeed there are some who consider this circumstance as a very honourable feature in our Saviour's character, and who consequently have not been very sparing in their censure on those who do not believe the fact, or at least have ventured to express some doubts on the subject. See Montacute's *Origines Ecclesiasticæ*, tom. i. p. 305, and 384. For my own part, without pretending to dictate to others, I must confess that the matter does not appear to me to have been so clearly ascertained as to be placed beyond all doubt. Those who take the affirmative side of the question rely principally on two arguments: the first drawn from the words of the Jews, Mark, vi. 3. *ὀχ' ὗτός ἐςιν ὁ Τέκτων ὁ υἱὸς Μαρίας*. Is not this *the carpenter*, the son of Mary? The other from a passage in Justin Martyr, in which our Saviour is said to have worked as a carpenter, and made ploughs and yokes. *Dialog. cum Tryphon.* p. 270. I pass over the more recent authorities that are brought forward in support of the fact, as of little moment, since they are all either founded on the above mentioned passage in Justin, or drawn from vulgar report, or the apocryphal gospels. Confining myself, therefore, to the two principal authorities above noticed, I must say that I do not perceive how any argument of much weight is to be drawn from either of them. For as to the remark of the Jews, in which our Saviour is termed the carpenter, I consider it to refer merely to the occupation of [p. 64.] his parent; and that *τέκτων* ought to be understood, in this place, as meaning nothing more than *ὁ τῦ τέκτονος υἱὸς*, the son of the carpenter. In support of this explanation of the term, I may refer to the authority of St. Matthew himself, cap. xiii. 55. and almost every language supplies us with instances which prove that it was a common practice to distinguish a child from others of the same name by giving him a surname derived from the trade or occupation of his parent. The English language furnishes us with examples of this in the surnames of Baker, Tailor, Carpenter, Smith, &c. and what is still more to the point, it is at this day the custom in some of the oriental nations, and particularly amongst the Arabs, to distinguish any learned or illustrious man that may chance to be born of parents who follow any particular trade or art, by giving him the name of such trade or art as a surname, although he may never have followed it himself. Thus, if a man of learning happen to be descended from a dyer or a tailor, they call him the Dyer's son, or the Tailor's son, or frequently. omitting the word son, simply the Dyer, or the Tailor. This fact is so well known to those who are conversant in oriental affairs, that I deem it unnecessary to cite any particular authority for it. I shall not here enter into an inquiry whether the reading of the passage of St. Mark above alluded to, as it stands in our copies, be correct or not. The matter unquestionably admits of some doubt: for it is clear from Mill, that there are many ancient

manuscripts which, instead of τίκτων, have ὁ τῦ τίκτονος; a reading which I certainly shall not take upon me, like him, absolutely to reject, since, as I before observed, it may be supported on the authority of St. Matthew himself. Vid. Millii *Prolegomena in Nov. Test.* § 698. p. 66. It should seem also that Origen understood the words of St. Mark in this sense, since he expressly denies that Christ is called τίκτονα, or a carpenter, in any part of the New Testament. *Contra Celsum*, lib. vi. p. 662. The learned well know that Justin Martyr is not to be considered in every respect as an oracle, but that much of what he relates is wholly undeserving of credit. Possibly what he says, in regard to the point before us, might be taken from one or other of the apocryphal Gospels of the infancy of Christ, which were in circulation amongst the Christians in his time.

(2) Such parts of these Gospels of the Infancy of Christ as had escaped the ravages of time, were collected together, and published by Jo. Albert. Fabricius, in his *Codex Apocryph. Nov. Test.* [And still better by *J. C. Thilo,* Lips. 1832. 8vo. Editor.]

III. **John the præcursor of Christ.** Christ entered on his ministry in the thirtieth year of his age; and, in order that his doctrine might obtain a more ready acceptance with the Jews, a man named John, the son of a Jewish priest, a person whose gravity of deportment and whole tenor of life was such as to excite veneration and respect, was commanded by God to announce to the people the immediate coming of the promised Messiah, and to endeavour to awaken in their senseless groveling minds a proper disposition to receive him. This illustrious character proclaimed himself to be the forerunner or herald of the Messiah, commissioned to call with a loud voice on the inhabitants of the wilderness to amend and make ready their ways for the King that was approaching;(') and having his mind inflamed with a holy zeal, he executed his mission with ardour and fidelity, re-[p. 65.] buking the vices of the nation sharply and without reserve. The form of initiation which he adopted, in regard to all those who promised an amendment of heart and life, was to immerge them in the river, according to the ancient Jewish practice. Matth. iii. 2. Joh. i. 22. Jesus himself, before he entered on his ministry, condescended to comply with this rite, and was solemnly baptized by John in the river Jordan, lest (according to his own words) he should appear to have disregarded any part of the divine law. John finished his earthly course under the reign of Herod the tetrarch. Having had the courage openly to reprove that tyrant for an incestuous connection with his brother's wife, he was in consequence thereof cast into prison, and after some little while beheaded.(²)

(1) If we recur to the manners of the eastern nations, John's comparison of himself to a forerunner, or herald, will be found to possess a peculiar force and beauty. In those countries it has ever been customary, even down to our own times, for monarchs, when they are about to undertake a journey, to send before them, into those regions through which they mean to travel, certain of their servants, who, with a loud voice, admonish the inhabitants to amend the roads, and remove every obstacle that might obstruct or impede the royal progress. By the form of annunciation, therefore, which John made use of, an ardent wish was manifested to exalt the character of the Messiah, by likening his approach to that of the mightiest of monarchs; whilst, at the same time, so far from magnifying the importance of his own services, they are, with the greatest humility, placed on a level with those which were usually executed by inferior servants.

(2) The reader who may wish for more copious information on this subject, is referred to two dissertations of Cellarius *de Johanne Baptista ejusque Carcere ac Supplicio,* which he will find published by Walchius, amongst his *Dissertationes Academicæ,* part i. p. 169; part ii. p. 373.

IV. **The life of Christ.** It cannot be necessary that we should, in this place, enter into a minute detail of the life and actions of Jesus Christ. The writings of the four evangelists are in the hands of every one; and no one who has read them can need to be informed, that for upwards of three years, in the midst of numberless perils and insidious machinations, and in defiance of the most insulting and injurious treatment, he continued with an inflexible constancy to point out to the Jewish people, by a mode of instruction peculiarly adapted to the manners and way of thinking of themselves, and the other nations of the east, the true and only means by which everlasting salvation was to be obtained. It must be equally unnecessary to remark, that he discovered no sort of desire whatever for either riches or worldly honours, but that his life was spent in poverty, and distinguished by such sanctity and innocence, that even his most virulent enemies could find nothing whereof they might accuse him. In regard, likewise, to the divinity of his mission, and the truth of the doctrines which he taught, every one must be apprised that he placed both the one and the other beyond all doubt, not only by referring to various prophecies and oracular passages con-

tained in the writings of the Old Testament, but also by a series of the most stupendous miracles. Of his miracles it may
be observed, that, from beginning to end, they were uniformly
of a salutary and beneficent character, *i. e.* they were, in every
respect, strictly consentaneous to the spirit and tendency of his
ministry, and exhibited no unfaithful types or images of those
spiritual blessings which he was about to communicate to mankind. Had our Saviour come to enforce with rigour the penalties of the law, he might with propriety have established the authenticity of his mission by terrific prodigies and signs; but he
[p. 66.] came as the messenger of divine clemency and pity, and
in no way could the truth or the character of his doctrine have
been more beautifully or emphatically marked than by the wonders of benevolence and love.

V. **Christ seceded from the Jewish church to a certain degree.** In
the line of duty which Christ prescribed for the Jews, he omitted none of those points which were enjoined by the law of Moses; and it is observable, that he joined with the inhabitants of
Palestine in their acts of public worship, and in all other rites
of divine origin. This should seem to have been done, partly
for the purpose of bearing testimony to the divine authority of
the Jewish law and religion, and partly with a view to avoid incurring the hatred and ill offices of the priests and lawyers by
any unnecessary provocation. He made no scruple, however,
openly to predict the downfall, not only of the Jewish state, but
also of the Mosaic worship and religion, and to declare, in the
plainest and most express terms, that under his auspices a new
religious community would be established, founded upon more
perfect principles of worship, and which, extending itself to the
farthermost parts of the earth, would unite the whole human
race in one common bond of fraternal love.(¹) Neither did he
confine himself merely to thus prophesying the rise of a new
and most comprehensive religion, but proceeded at once with his
own hands to lay the foundation of it, by causing his disciples
to baptize with water all those who, either through the preaching of himself or his apostles, had been brought to confess that
he was the Son of God, the Saviour of mankind commissioned
from above; thereby initiating them under a new covenant, the
terms and obligations of which were such as could not fail to

separate them from the rest of the Jewish community. John, iii. 22, 26. iv. 2. Although, therefore, it must be allowed that Christ and his disciples did not formally renounce their connection with the Jewish church, or absolutely withdraw themselves from it; yet it is clear that, in a certain degree, he established a new sect therein, and that in reality he separated both himself and his followers from the rest of the Jews.(²)

(1) Luke xix. John, iv. 21. Matth. x. 32. xvi. 18. John, x. 16.

(2) Several learned men, chiefly amongst the civilians, have had their doubts as to this point, of Christ with his followers having seceded from the Jewish church, and established a new and distinct religious community. But to me the fact appears to admit of no question whatever. Whoever promulgates new principles or precepts—prescribes a new rule of life and conduct—makes use of a certain sacred rite, with a view to distinguish all those [p. 67.] who are willing to conform to those precepts, and who approve of such rule of life, from the rest of the community, and to mark their reception into this sect—holds separate solemn assemblies with these his associates—and, lastly, exhorts them on every occasion to be constant in their adherence to that rule of faith and action which they had thus embraced; such person must, in my opinion, unquestionably be considered as founding a new religious community, and causing his followers, in a certain degree, to forsake that to which they formerly belonged. Now our Saviour did all these things. For, in the first place, he announced himself to all whom he undertook to instruct, as the Messiah promised by God to the ancestors of the Jews; and taught them, that their hopes of eternal salvation ought to be built on his merits alone. Then, those who believed in him were enjoined to love each other as brethren, and informed that the worship required of them by God was not that of sacrifices and external observances, but that of the heart and mind. Next, all who professed themselves ready to espouse these principles, and conform to these precepts, were made to undergo a solemn form of lustration at the hands of his disciples, (John, iv. 2, 3,) and by this regenerating ceremony became invested as it were with the rights of citizenship. And lastly, those who had been thus initiated he associated with himself in the closest ties of intimacy, and caused them publicly to declare the faith and hope which they had in him; convening them frequently together for the purpose of religious worship, and, amongst other things, particularly apprizing them of the approaching downfall of the Jewish state and religion. The fact is likewise supported by other circumstances, but I do not deem it necessary to bring them forward at present. I will, however, take this opportunity of saying a few words respecting the rite of baptism, by which our Saviour ordained that his followers should be received into the kingdom of heaven, or the new covenant. My opinion on this subject entirely corresponds with theirs, who consider this ceremony as having been adopted by the Jews long before the time of our Saviour, and used by them in the initiating of strangers who had embraced their religion. To omit other

arguments of no little weight in favour of this opinion, I think it may be supported on the authority of Scripture itself, and particularly from the account given us in John i. of the embassy sent by the supreme council of the Jews to John the Bapti-t, the forerunner of Christ. For the rite itself, of baptizing with water those who confessed their sins and promised an amendment of life, does not seem to have been regarded by the elders of the Jews in the light of a novelty, or as a practice by any means of an unusual kind. The only point on which they require information of John is, from whence he derived his authority to perform this solemn and sacred ceremony. The thing itself occasioned them no surprise, since daily use had rendered it familiar to them: what attracted their attention was, that a private individual should take upon him to perform it in a way contrary to the established usage of the nation. But unless I am much deceived, an inference of still greater moment may be drawn from this message sent by the Jewish council to John, and which will supply us with the reason why our Saviour adopted this ancient Jewish practice of baptizing proselytes with water: for, as it strikes me, the concluding question put by the messengers evidently implies an expectation in the Jews of that age, that the Messiah for whom they looked would baptize men with water. After John had told them that he was neither the Christ nor Messiah, nor Elias, nor any of the ancient prophets, they finally interrogate him thus: " If thou be not that Christ, nor Elias, nor that prophet, why baptizest thou then?" John, [p. 68.] i. 25. Now if these words be attentively considered, I think it must be allowed that they will unquestionably admit of the following construction: " We, as well as those who sent us, understand that when the Messiah shall come, he will baptize and purify the Jewish race with water; we also expect that Elias, who is to precede him, will use the same ceremony for our initiation : but by what authority is it that you, who acknowledge that you are neither the Messiah nor Elias, assume to yourself the right of doing that which can only properly belong to them to perform—we do not mean the baptizing of strangers, but the descendants of Abraham ?" If this be the fair construction of the messengers' words (and I rather think that but few, if any, will deny it to be so,) we have no farther to look for the reason that in all probability induced our Saviour and his forerunner John to baptize their disciples. An opinion, it appears, prevailed amongst the Jews, that Elias, whose coming was to precede that of the Messiah, and also the Messiah himself, would initiate their disciples by a sacred ablution ; and it was therefore necessary, in order to avoid giving the Jews any pretext for doubt respecting either Christ's authority or functions, that both John and himself should accommodate themselves to this popular persuasion. Of the origin of the opinion itself I know nothing.

VI. **Election of the apostles.** Since it was intended that the religious community thus established by Christ, although confined at first within very narrow limits, should by degrees extend itself to the farthermost parts of the earth, it was requisite that he should select certain persons, who, from their being admitted to a constant and familiar intercourse with him, might acquire that lively degree of faith and zeal, which should enable them, in spite of every obstacle and difficulty, to make their way into the different regions of the world, for the purpose of propagating the religion of their divine Master, and bearing testimony to the exemplary purity of his life, and the stupendous deeds and miracles by which he established the truth of his doctrine. From amongst the great multitude of Jews, therefore, that had joined themselves to him, he chose twelve whom he deemed the most faithful and best fitted for the task; appointing them, in a more especial manner, his ambassadors to the human race, and distinguishing them from the rest of his disciples by the title of apostles.(') The persons thus selected were of mean extraction, poor, illiterate, and utterly unprovided with any of those arts or gifts which are calculated to win the countenance and favour of the world, and to impose on the unwary and credulous part of mankind: and it is intimated in Scripture, (1 Cor. i. 20, 21, et seq.) that such were intentionally chosen, lest the efficacy and fruits of their mission should be attributed to eloquence, to authority, or to any other human and natural cause, and not to the divine power of God. In order, likewise, that the testimony with which they were to be charged might be of the most ample kind, and superior to all exception, he made them his constant and intimate companions through life; retaining them always about his person, except on one occasion when he sent them, for a short space, on a mission to the Jews. Matth. x. 5, 6, 7. Their number being fixed at twelve, has a mani- [p. 69.] fest relation to the Jewish tribes ;(²) and it should seem that Christ intended thereby to intimate to the Jews that he was the Sovereign Lord, the true King, and great High Priest of all the twelve tribes of Israel.

(1) The word apostle, it is well known, signifies a legate, an ambassador, a person entrusted with a particular mission. The propriety, therefore, with which this appellation was bestowed by Christ on those friends whom he thought proper to select for the propagation of his religion throughout the world, is manifest from this its common acceptation. But the reader will, perhaps, discover a peculiar force in this term, and more readily perceive the motives which probably induced our Saviour to apply it to those whom he sent forth, when he is informed that in the age of which we are now treating, this appellation was appropriated to certain public officers of great credit and authority amongst

the Jews, who were the confidential ministers of the high priest, and consulted with by him on occasions of the highest moment. They were also occasionally invested with particular powers, and dispatched on missions of importance, principally to such of their countrymen as resided in foreign parts. The collection of the yearly tribute to the temple, which all Jews were bound to pay, was likewise entrusted to their management, as were also several other affairs of no small consequence. For since all Jews, however widely they might be dispersed throughout the various regions of the world, considered themselves as belonging to one and the same family or commonwealth, of which the high priest residing at Jerusalem was the præfect and head; and as the members of every inferior synagogue, however distant or remote, looked up to Jerusalem as the mother and chief seat of their religion, and referred all abstruse or difficult matters, and any controversies and questions of moment respecting divine subjects, to the decision of the high priest, it was absolutely necessary that this supreme pontiff should always have near him a number of persons of fidelity, learning and authority, of whose services he might avail himself, in communicating his mandates and decrees to those Jews who were settled in distant parts, and in arranging and determining the various points referred to him for decision. My recollection indeed does not enable me to produce any express proofs from ancient authors, that, at the period of which we are speaking, the high priest had any such ministers attached to him under the name of apostles; but I think that I can adduce such presumptive evidence of the fact, as will scarcely leave room for any question on the subject. In the first place, it appears to me that St. Paul himself evidently intimates such to have been the case, in the opening of his epistle to the Galatians, when he terms himself an apostle, not ἀπ' ἀνθρώτων, of men, nor δἰ ἀνθρώτυ by man, but of God himself, and his Son Jesus Christ. Galatians i. 1. For what necessity could there be that this inspired writer should thus accurately define the nature of his commission, and so particularly mark the distinction between himself and an apostle invested with mere human authority, if the Jews, to whom that epistle is principally addressed, had been strangers to that other kind of apostles commissioned by men, namely, apostles sent by the Jewish high priest and magistrates to the different cities of the Roman empire? This interpretation was, long since, given to the words of the apostle by St. Jerome, *Comm. ad Galatas,* tom. ix. opp. p. 124. edit. Francof. *Usque hodie,* says he, *a patriarchis* [p. 70.] *Judæorum apostolos mitti* (constat.) *Ad distinctionem itaque eorum qui mittuntur ab hominibus, et sui qui, sit missus a Christo, tale sumpsit exordium: Paulus apostolus, non ab hominibus, neque per hominem.* These words of St. Jerome, who resided in Palestine, and was every way skilled in Jewish affairs, must, I think, necessarily be allowed to weigh strongly in favour of the above statement respecting the apostles of the high priest. The meaning they convey indisputably is, that in the time of St. Paul, it was the practice of the Jewish high priest to send forth apostles, after the same manner as the Jewish patriarchs were accustomed to do at the time he (St. Jerome) wrote: and there appears to be no reason whatever which should induce us to question the credibility of what is thus said. But let us return to the words of St. Paul, in which, as it appears to me, there is something worthy of remark, which, if my memory does not fail me, has never hitherto attracted the attention of any commentator. St. Paul says, that he is an apostle, not of men, neither by man. He therefore clearly divides human apostles into two classes, *viz.* those who were commissioned merely by one man, and those who were invested with their powers by several. Now what does this mean? Who are these men, and who that single man, who, in St. Paul's time, were accustomed to send amongst the Jews certain persons, whom it was usual to distinguish by the appellation of apostles? I trust that I shall be able in great measure to clear this up. The single man to whom St. Paul alludes could, I conceive, have been none other than the great high priest of the Jews; and the several men who had also their apostles were, as it strikes me, unquestionably the *archontes*, or Jewish magistrates. The learned well know that justice was administered to the Jews who dwelt in the different provinces of the Roman empire, by certain magistrates or vicegerents of the high priest, who were termed after the Greek *archontes*, concerning whom a curious and elegant little work was published by Wesseling, *ad Inscript. Beren.* Traject. ad Rhen. 1738, in 8vo. I take the meaning, therefore, of St. Paul to be, that he neither derived his commission from those inferior magistrates, to whom the Jews who dwelt without the limits of Palestine were subject, nor was he delegated by the chief of their religion, the high priest himself. That these *archontes* had under them certain ministers who were termed apostles, much in the same way as the high priest had, is clear from Eusebius, who says, Ἀπόστολυς δὲ εἰσέτι καὶ νῦν ἔθος ἐστὶν Ἰυδαίοις ὀνομάζειν τὸς τὰ ἐγκύκλια γράμματα παρὰ των αρχον]ων αὐτῶν ἐπικομιζομένυς. Apostolos etiam nunc Judæi eos appellare solent qui *archontum* suorum litteras circumquaque deportare solent. *Comment. in Esaiam*, cap. xviii. in Montfauconii *Collectione nova Patr. Græcor.* tom. ii. p. 424. But I shall leave this conjecture to the consideration of those who may be qualified to judge of it. My present object extends no farther than to show that, in the time of our blessed Saviour, those persons who were delegated by the high priest for any special purpose, or charged with the execution of his commands, were distinguished by the appellation of apostles. It affords an argument of no small consequence in support of the fact as thus stated, that it has been clearly proved by several learned men, and particularly by Gothofred, Petavius, Wesseling, and from various passages in the *Codex Theodosianus*, and other ancient authors, that, after the destruction of Jerusalem, the Jewish patriarchs, who may be said to have, in a certain degree, supplied the place of the high priests, had attached to them certain ministers of great trust and authority under the denomination of apostles. Vid. Jac. Gothofredus *ad Codicem Theodosianum*, tom. vi. p. 251, 252. edit. Ritterian. Dion. Petavius *Animadvers. ad Epiphanium ad Hæres.* xxx. *et de Hierarchia Ecclesiast.* lib. i. cap. vi. p. 16. and lib. ii. cap. ii. [p. 71.] § x. p. 45. *in Dogmatibus Theologicis*, tom. iv. Petr. Wesselingius *de Archontibus Judæor.* p. 91. That these patriarchs should have borrowed the term from the Christians, admits not of a moment's belief; since they regarded every thing pertaining to Christianity with the most inveterate hatred, and revolted with the utmost abhorrence from any thing like a shadow of connection with those who professed it : a circumstance which must have escaped Gothofred, or he never would have concluded that the Jews were unacquainted with the term apostle until after the destruction of Jerusalem. The appellation, therefore, was unquestionably Jewish ; and it appears to me equally indisputable, that the Jewish people were well acquainted with its use and import in the time of our Saviour. These considerations, I think, can leave but little doubt on the mind of any one as to the motives which induced our blessed Lord to denominate, as we are expressly told by St. Luke, vi. 13, that he did, those of his ministers whom he selected for the purpose of making known his precepts to all the nations of the earth, apostles. By the application of this term to those whom he thus delegated, his intention doubtless was to intimate to the Jews that he was invested with all the rights of the supreme head of their religion, and that they ought to look up to him as to the true high priest of the Hebrew nation. It does not appear how many persons of this description the high priest had under him, at the period of which we are speaking ; but I conceive it to be extremely probable that their number corresponded with that of the Jewish tribes. Supposing this to have been the case, it accounts for our Saviour's fixing the number of his apostles at twelve.

(2) To be convinced of this, I think we need only recur to our Saviour's own words, Matth. xix. 28. Luke, xxii. 30. which plainly intimate that the number of his apostles had an express reference to the number of the Jewish tribes.

VII. **And of the seventy disciples.** In addition to these twelve, whom Christ ordained to be the messengers and teachers of his word to the world at large, he selected from his disciples seventy others, whom he sent before him into the different parts of Judæa, whither he meant to come, for the purpose of preparing and disposing the minds of the Jewish people ; so that his own preaching might be the more readily listened to, and attended with the greater effect. Luke, x. 1, &c. Of these seventy mention is only once made by any of the evangelists, and no reliance can be placed on the account which some more recent writers have pretended to give of their names, their journies, and their labours.(') We are not, however, by any means authorized from hence to conclude that they were only once employed by Christ, or that their powers were withdrawn from them after they had fulfilled the object of this their first mission. Their number corresponded with that of the senators who composed the sanhedrim, or chief council of the Jews ; and I therefore consider it as highly probable that Christ, [p. 72.] in the selection of this number, also might intend to impress on the minds of the Jewish people, by an ostensible sign, that the former authority of the high priest and chief council was now abolished, and all power as to divine matters become vested in himself alone.

(1) Some notices or memoirs respecting the seventy disciples, compiled by some of the later Greek writers, were published by Fabricius, at p. 474. of his *Libri de Vita et Morte Mosis, a* Gilb. Gaulmino *illustrati ;* but which Blondell, (*de Episcopis et Presbyteris,* p. 93.) has shown to be utterly undeserving of credit.

VIII. **The fame of Christ extends beyond Judea.** The personal ministry and instruction of our blessed Saviour was confined entirely to the Jews; nor did he suffer his disciples, during his continuance on earth, to go to any of the neighbouring nations. Matth. x. 5, 6. xv. 24. The magnitude, however, of the wonderful things that he performed will not permit us to doubt but that his fame soon diffused itself throughout a great part of the world. Amongst other things which tend to prove this, it is related by writers of no small credit, that Abgarus, the king of Edessa in Syria, being afflicted with a severe disease, besought by letter the assistance of Christ; and that our Saviour not only returned an answer to the king, but also sent him his picture.(') What are considered by some as genuine copies of the letters that passed on this occasion, are still extant. In regard to the fact itself, I see no reason for rejecting it as altogether undeserving of belief; but as to what is said of the picture, I think we may consider it as unquestionably the invention of the Greek writers of a later age: and it appears to me, that the letters carry with them no very obscure marks of forgery and imposition.(')

(1) Eusebius *Histor. Eccles.* lib. i. cap. xiii. p. 31. And Jo. Alb. Fabricius *Codice Apocrypho N. Test.* tom. i. p. 317. Theoph. Sigifr. Bayer enters much at length into the history of Abgarus, in his *Historia Edessena et Osröena,* lib. iii. p. 104, et seq. and p. 358.

(2) The arguments by which the authenticity of this history, and of the letters, which form no inconsiderable part of it, is maintained or denied, are brought together into one view, and contrasted with much judgment by Basnage, in his *Histoire des Juifs,* tom. i. cap, xviii. p. 500. Asseman adopts somewhat of a middle course between the two extremes, considering Abgarus's letter as genuine, but supposing that reputed to be Christ's to have been merely a note or minute of our Saviour's words made by Abgarus's ambassador. *Biblioth Oriental. Clement. Vatican.* tom. i. p. 554. and tom. iii. part.

ii. p. 8. For this opinion he had the authority of Bellarmin. Bayer also is friendly to it, in his *Historia Edessena*, p. 109. On the other hand, the learned [p. 73.] and pious Bouguet would fain persuade us, that both the letters and the history itself were the invention of Eusebius. *Biblioth. Italique.* tom, xiii. p. 121, et seq. I cannot, however, by any means consent to charge a man so devoid of seperstition, and so well affected to the cause of Christianity as Eusebius was, with an imposition of so gross a nature ; and more particularly since I find it impossible to divine any motive or cause which could have incited him to the commission of such an infamous fraud. No man does evil unad- visedly, or without some inducement. Keysler, in the account of his travels, written in German, tom. ii. p. 29. says that amongst other ridiculous monuments of superstition exhibited to the credulous multitude at Rome, is shown the pic- ture which Christ sent to Abgarus on the above-mentioned occasion. But Beau- sobre has demonstrated this part of the story to be void of all semblance of truth, in his *Dissertation des Images de Main divine*, which is to be found in the *Biblioth. Germanique*, tom. xviii. p. 10, et seq.

IX. **Fruits of Christ's ministry.** A considerable number of the Jews, penetrated with astonishment at the many wonderful proofs which Christ gave of his divine authority and power, be- came his disciples; being convinced that he could be none other than the holy one of God, the true Messiah, whose coming was predicted of old by the prophets : and it is clear that many more would have joined themselves to him, had not the priests and lawyers, whose crimes and deceit he exposed without reserve, and rebuked with the utmost severity, exerted all their influence, and made use of various arts and devices to prejudice the minds of a timid and fickle people against him. But it was not long that these enemies of Jesus rested content with giving vent to their animosity merely in this shape. For, finding that it would be impossible for them to retain their credit and authority with the world, and the numerous advantages attendant thereon, in any other way than by the destruction of Christ, they began to lay snares for his life. Our blessed Saviour, perceiving himself to be thus beset, had recourse to the dictates of prudence, and by avoiding, both in his words and actions, as far as was consist- ent with the nature of his function, every thing which might tend still further to inflame the malice of these perfidious men, he for some time succeeded in rendering all their schemes abor- tive. Moreover, when he was at Jerusalem, where there was every reason for him to be most apprehensive of danger, his enmies were withheld from laying hands on him during the day by a fear of the people, who were well inclined towards him; and the place where he passed his nights was not known to any, except his intimate friends and companions.

X. **The death of Christ.** Of these his companions, however, one was at length found, named Judas, who, bartering his salvation for money, agreed, for a reward of no great value, to discover the nightly retreat of his divine Master; who was, in consequence thereof, seized on by a band of soldiers, and hurried away as a criminal to answer charges which involved his life. Betrayed thus infamously into the hands of his enemies, our blessed Saviour was first led before the high priest and chief council of the Jews, by whom, without the least shadow of justice, and merely on testimony of the most vague and contradictory nature, he was pronounced guilty of blasphemy, [p. 74.] and worthy of death. From thence he was taken to the tribunal of Pontius Pilate, the Roman governor, and accused of a crime totally different in its nature from that wherewith he had been first charged, and of which it had been his particular care to avoid incurring even the least suspicion, namely, attempting to excite sedition and conspiracy against Cæsar. Pilate, although he does not appear to have been over scrupulous in the administration of justice, yet discountenanced this accusation, which he at once perceived to be founded in falsehood; and strenuously exerted himself to save a man, for whom, on account of his wisdom and sanctity, it should seem that he felt no little respect. Finding, however, after repeated efforts on the side of mercy, that the multitude, who were stirred up by the chief priests, would not be satisfied with any thing short of the blood of Christ, but persisted to call for it with a tumultuous violence, approaching nearly to a state of insurrection, he was at length induced, though evidently with considerable reluctance, to comply with their demands, and passed on the meek and blameless object of their fury a sentence of death. As our blessed Saviour had taken upon himself our nature with a view to expiate the sins of mankind, and was conscious that the divine councils and decrees had been satisfied by him, and that every purpose for which he took up his abode with man was fulfilled, he used no endeavours to screen himself from this injurious treatment, but

7

voluntarily submitted to undergo the pain and ignominy of a capital punishment, and calmly breathed out his pure and spotless soul upon the cross; praying, even in his agony, for the forgiveness of those who were the merciless and unrelenting authors of his sufferings.(')

(1) It is manifest, from the history of the death of Christ, that he spake most truly when he said, No man taketh my life from me, but I lay it down of myself, John, x. 18.   For how easy would it have been for him, even without a miracle, to have avoided falling into the hands of his enemies?   The insidious designs of the Jewish pontiff and chief priests were well known to him; and it is plain that he was no stranger to the treacherous intentions of his perfidious disciple Judas, since he expressly alludes to them on more than one occasion.   On the other hand, it appears that he had several great and powerful friends, on whom he could have depended for support.   Would he but have quitted Jerusalem, and returned into Galilee, every scheme that had been formed against him must have fallen to the ground.   Indeed, even this was not requisite: for his safety would have been completely secured, had he merely changed the place of his nightly resort, and, lest Judas should have discovered it, dismissed that wicked and deceitful man from his society.   Besides these obvious means, there were others to which he might have had recourse, and which would have proved equally efficient in defeating and bringing to nought the evil councils and designs of the Jewish priests and elders.   But it should seem that he disdained, or at least voluntarily neglected to avail himself of any of those precautions, which a very moderate share of human prudence would have suggested to any man under similar circumstances.   He remained in Jerusalem; he permitted Judas to continue about his person, in the character of an intimate friend; he continued to pass his nights in the usual and accustomed place.   All these circumstances being considered, who is there but must readily perceive that Christ voluntarily subjected himself to the punishment of death, and offered up his life to God as a sacrifice for the sins of mankind?

XI. **His resurrection and ascension into Heaven.** The body of Christ, being taken down from the cross, was laid in a sepulchre which Joseph, one of the Jewish senators, had prepared for him- [p. 75.] self, where it remained until the third day. Early on the morning of that day, our blessed Saviour, according to his own prediction, again resumed the life which he had voluntarily laid down; and by triumphantly rising from the tomb, demonstrated that the divine justice was satisfied, and the path which leads to immortality and life once more rendered easy of access to the human race. During the succeeding forty days, he held frequent converse with his disciples, confirming their faith, and instructing them in the nature of those important functions and duties which he designed them to fulfil. It is observable that, after his return to life, he showed himself to none of his enemies. Amongst other reasons which he might have for this reserve, it is probable that he foresaw that even the appearance of one risen from the dead would produce no salutary impression on men, whose minds were not only blinded by malice, but corrupted by various popular superstitions respecting *manes* and spectres.(¹) At the end of the above-mentioned period, having assembled his disciples, and commanded them to go and preach the gospel unto all nations, he blessed them, and rising sublimely from the earth, was in their presence received up into heaven.

(1) The motives which withheld our Saviour from showing himself to any except his disciples, after his resurrection from the dead, have been sought after with more than ordinary diligence by the learned ; inasmuch as the enemies of Christianity have, for ages, urged this circumstance as a reason for calling in question the truth of his return to life. Now to me it appears that the reasons which influenced Christ on this occasion are readily to be collected from the answer which he puts into the mouth of Abraham, in reply to Dives, who had requested that Lazarus might be sent to his brethren from the dead : " If they hear not Moses and the prophets, neither will they be persuaded though one rose from the dead." Luke, xvi. 30. For, unless I am altogether deceived, we ought to consider this answer as conveying a prophetical intimation in regard to the point before us ; much as if our blessed Saviour had added : " In like manner, there can be no hope whatever that those whom I may have in vain endeavoured to convert by all the force of divine eloquence, and by exhibiting to them so many stupendous proofs of infinite power, during my life, should be brought to believe in me even by my rising from the dead. I shall not, therefore, show myself to my enemies after my resurrection : since I am certain that my doing so would be productive of no good effect." At least, I think it must readily be granted me, that the reason which Abraham gives why no good was to be expected from the mission of Lazarus, applies most aptly and forcibly to the subject before us. Many arguments of considerable weight might be urged in support of the proposition, which I conceive is thus to be deduced from the answer of Abraham ; but I will content myself with bringing forward one only. The Jews had accused our Saviour, during his life, of holding converse with the prince of the devils, and making use of magic. In addition to this, the minds both of the Jews and the Romans were, at that time, possessed with an idea that the *manes* or souls of the dead might be called up from the grave by magical incantation; and that, without this, the spirits of the departed did not unfrequently, either of their own accord, or by command of the prince of darkness, again revisit this earth, and show

themselves to the living under an aërial form. Amongst men who entertained [p. 76.] notions like these, the appearance of our Saviour after his resurrection could have wrought no good effect. Had Christ, after his return to life, appeared openly in the temple, or in other places of public resort, such as the palace of the Roman governor, and the Jewish senate, it is more than probable that his enemies would not only themselves have regarded the circumstance in an unfavourable light, but also persuadsd the multitude, either that the unhappy spirit of Christ had been again raised up by some or other of his disciples who were versed in the arts of magic, or that, being itself filled with indignation, and unable to rest, on account of the violent means by which it had been separated from its earthly abode, it was come back for the purpose of, in some measure, avenging itself by haunting and terrifying mankind.

XII. **Effusion of the Holy Spirit on the apostles.** Those whom Christ had selected as above mentioned to be the witnesses of his life and acts, and the messengers of his gospel to the world, were not, at the time of his ascension, endowed with powers adequate to the discharge of the important functions with which they were invested. Having, therefore, again resumed his station in glory, and sat down at the right hand of the everlasting Father, he, about the fiftieth day from the time of his death, sent down on them from above, according to his promise, the divine power and gifts of the Holy Spirit. Acts, ii. 1. In consequence of this miraculous effusion, their minds became irradiated with celestial light, their faith acquired strength, their knowledge of the will of their divine Master was rendered more perfect, and they were inspired with a zeal and fortitude which armed them against every difficulty that it was necessary to encounter in his service, and enabled them, in the execution of his commands, to triumph even over death itself. One of the most astonishing of the endowments thus bestowed by our Saviour on his apostles, was an instantaneous acquaintance with languages of which they were previously ignorant, so as to qualify them to instruct the different nations of the earth in their own proper tongues.(')

(1) Amôngst the various gifts of the Holy Spirit communicated to the apostles, I do not include the faculty of altering the established laws of nature, or in other words, the working of miracles: for I must confess, I cannot at all comprehend how a faculty like this, which requires infinite power, could be communicated to men. The miracles which the apostles appeared to work were, as I conceive, wrought by Christ himself, on their invocation; and, therefore, when he promised them the power of effecting what men and angels could not accomplish, I imagine nothing more was implied than that he would be

always present to their prayers, and ready to effect, through tne infinite power which he possessed, whatever might in any case appear to be expedient or necessary. Peter commanded the lame man to rise up and walk, and immediately he arose and walked. Acts, iv. 6. But I cannot by any means believe that, on this occasion, an energy or power residing in Peter was transferred into the bodily frame of this poor wretch, so as to produce the restoration of his nerves or muscular action ; or that the apostle could, by a mere act of volition, accomplish this wonderful cure. No ; it is not to Peter, but to our blessed Saviour himself, on whose name Peter called, that this miraculous [p. 77.] restoration of the cripple ought, in my opinion, to be ascribed. In confirmation of this, see the words of Jesus himself, John, xiv. 12, 13.

XIII. **The gospel preached first to the Jews and Samaritans, and then to the rest of the world.** Inspired with the requisite confidence and powers by this communication of succour from above, the apostles entered on their ministry without delay ; endeavouring, first of all, as they had been commanded, to convert the inhabitants of Jerusalem to a faith in Christ, and then directing their efforts to the propagation of his gospel amongst the remainder of the Jewish nation. Luke, xxiv. 47. Acts, i. 8. xiii. 46.) Nor were these their first exertions chilled by any thing like a want of success : for within a very short period, the flock of Christ, which, at the time of his departure, could not be considered otherwise than as small and weak, was augmented and strengthened by the accession of many thousands of Jews. It appears that by one sermon alone of Peter's, three thousand, and that by another, five thousand were added to the Christian community in this its infancy. Acts, ii. 41. iv. 4. A preference having been thus given to the Jews, the apostles, in compliance with the express commands of our Saviour, next extended the blessings of their ministry to the Samaritans. Acts. i. 8. viii. 14. At length, having continued for many years at Jerusalem,(¹) and given a due degree of stability and strength to the several Christian fraternities or churches which had been formed in Palestine, they proceeded to communicate the glorious light of the gospel to the different Gentile nations of the earth ; and in the various regions through which they travelled were successful in establishing the church of Christ to an extent and with a rapidity that are, in every respect, truly astonishing.

(1) That the apostles continued at Jerusalem for many years after the ascension of our Saviour, is manifest from their Acts, which were written by St.

Luke; nor can it be doubted that their stay there was in consequence of the divine command. The reasons on which this divine mandate was founded are, I think, readily to be perceived. In order to establish the Christian common-wealth on a firm and durable basis, and to furnish the churches which were about to be planted in the different nations of the earth with a model after which they might form themselves, it was requisite that the first Christian assemblies should be constituted and instructed with great care, under the imme-diate eye of the apostles themselves. An affair of such magnitude, it will be allowed, must necessarily have required a considerable time for its accomplish-ment. But to this reason was added another of still greater consequence and weight, which imperiously demanded the presence of the apostles at Jerusalem. For being invested, as they were by Christ himself, with the entire guardian-ship and administration of the concerns of his religion, the other disciples who were employed in establishing churches in Judæa, Samaria, and the neighbour-ing territories, were of course subject to their direction, and consequently felt it their duty, in all affairs of difficulty and doubt, to recur to them for advice and instruction. But how could these inferior messengers of divine truth have con-sulted the apostles, or availed themselves of their instruction or commands, if the latter had departed from Jerusalem at an early period, and distributed them-selves about in various parts of the world? The general interests of Chris-tianity, therefore, required that those whom our blessed Saviour had appointed the judges, or, as we ought perhaps rather to say, the arbiters of divine matters, and to whom he had given the power of regulating and determining every thing [p. 78.] relative to the establishing of his religion, should for a certain time re-main together in one place, that so an easy access to them might be had by those who were likely to stand in need of their advice or assistance; and their orders and decrees possess an additional weight and authority, from its being known that they comprised the sentiments, not merely of one or two, but of the whole collective body of those who had been admitted to a more particu lar intimacy with Christ, and were the best instructed in his will. How long the apostles thus continued at Jerusalem, and in what particular year from the time of our Saviour's leaving them they departed on that mission to the Gen-tile nations with which they were charged, is by no means certain. According to the ancient report quoted by Eusebius from Apollonius, a writer of the second century, our Saviour ordered his apostles to remain at Jerusalem for twelve years after his parting from them. Euseb. *Histor. Eccles.* lib. v. cap. xviii. p. 186. and Clemens Alexandr. *ex Prædicatione Petri Stromat.* lib. vi. cap. v. p. 762. Considering the great antiquity of this account, it may perhaps be not altogether undeserving of credit; but, at the same time, we cannot help regarding it with some suspicion, since it is certain that, even in the earliest ages of Christianity, it was no uncommon thing for men to fill up the chasms of genuine history with fictitious conceits, the mere suggestions of their own imagination.

XIV. **The election of a new apostle.** The first concern of the apostles, after our Saviour's ascension into heaven, was to render

their number complete according its first establishment, by electing a man of superior worth and sanctity to supply the place of
Judas, who had perished by a miserable death.   Having, therefore, gathered together the small assembly of Christians which had
been formed in Jerusalem, two men distinguished for their sanctity and faith in Christ were proposed as candidates on this occasion ; the one named Barsabas, the other Matthias.   The whole
assembly then joined in devout prayer to God, that their choice
might not, through human frailty, fall on that man of the two
which was least acceptable in his sight; after which, proceeding
to the election, they either by lot, or rather, as I suspect, by the
suffrages of such Christians as were present, chose Matthias to
fill the office of a twelfth apostle.(')

(1) Acts, i. 15, et seq.   Many things highly worthy of observation present
themselves to notice, in the account which St. Luke gives us of the appointment of Matthias in the room of Judas.   Passing over, however, other things
which might be pointed out, I will, in this place, merely make a few remarks
on the mode and form of the election. All the commentators agree in representing Matthias as having been chosen an apostle by lot, agreeably to the ancient
Jewish practice.   On a more attentive consideration, however, of the words of
the sacred historian, I rather think it would be found that this commonly received interpretation of them is what they by no means authorize.   St. Luke
commences his account by stating, that Peter, in a suitable speech, pointed out
to the people who were assembled the necessity of electing a new apostle.
After this, at verse 23, he adds, that two men equal to the station were set
forth in the midst, in order that one of them might be chosen to [p. 79.]
undertake the office.   As to the persons by whom these men were produced
and recommended, he is quite silent.   His words are simply *καὶ ἔστησαν δύο:*
but I have not the least doubt that we ought, in this place, to consider the
word Ἀπόστολοι as meant to be understood.   For who can possibly believe that
the Christians of the ordinary rank, who were in so many respects inferior to
the apostles, should have assumed to themselves the right of selecting two of
their own order, and recommending them as fit for the apostleship?   I therefore consider it as certain, that the apostles made the selection of these two
persons from amongst the general body of Christians at that time resident in
Jerusalem, and directed the assembly at large to choose one of them for an
apostle.   The narrative concludes with an account of the manner in which this
mandate was complied with ; describing it as follows : *καὶ ἔδωκαν κλήρους αὐτῶν,
καὶ ἔπεσεν ὁ κλῆρος ἐπὶ Ματθίαν,* v. 26.   Now, in this passage all the commentators attribute so much force to the word *κλῆρος,* which properly signifies a lot,
that they unanimously consider the true interpretation of the first branch of the
sentence to be, *et jecerunt sortes eorum,* "and they cast their lots ;" and hence
conclude that Matthias was chosen by lot.   But to me it appears that this inter-

pretation is entirely repugnant to the Greek idiom: for whenever the casting
of lots is spoken of by the Greek writers, we constantly find the verb Βάλλειν
joined with κλῆρος; and therefore, if St. Luke had meant to indicate what these
commentators suppose, he would have written καὶ ἔβαλον κλῆρον, or κλήρους, and
not ἔδωκαν, which latter word was never, at least as far as I know, applied in
this way. It was equally unusual for the Greek writers to add the pronoun
αὐτῶν after κλῆρος, when the latter was used by them in the sense of a lot that
was thrown. They say simply, with Homer, ἔβαλον κλήρους, " they cast lots."
And certainly, what occasion there could be for St. Luke to add this pronoun
in the passage under consideration, if he was speaking of casting lots, I am
quite at a loss to conceive. All the commentators refer it, and, consistently with
their interpretation of the passage, could only refer it to the candidates for the
apostleship, Matthias and Barsabas. But in what sense could those lots be
said to be theirs, which, if the above opinion be just, were thrown in that
assembly? Correctly speaking, can the lots, by which an election is to be
determined, be termed the lots of the candidates or persons to be elected?
Considering the weight of these and other objections, which oppose themselves
to the commonly received interpretation of the above passage, I cannot help
thinking that in these words of St. Luke we ought to understand the term κλῆρος
as having the same signification with ψῆφος, viz. *a suffrage,* or what in common language is termed *a vote;* and that what he meant to say was simply,
this, " and those who were present gave their votes." In this case, it will be
perceived that for αὐτῶν I should substitute αὐτῶν. Considering this to have
been the mode which was adopted for the appointment of a new apostle, it
would, in a very striking degree, correspond with the form which was observed
by the most ancient Christian churches, in electing their teachers and pastors; and which, in my opinion, there is every reason to think was founded on
the manner of proceeding to which the apostles had recourse on this occasion.
When a presbyter or a bishop was to be elected, those who presided over the
church proposed certain candidates for the office, of approved worth and ability. Of these the assembly at large pointed out by their suffrages, and not by
lot, him whom they deemed the most deserving; and whoever had the majority of votes in his favor was considered as elected through divine preference.
Such was the form observed by the primitive churches, and I conceive such to
have been the form to which the apostles had recourse on the above-mentioned
occasion; and that the greater number of those who constituted the then infant
[p. 80.] church of Jerusalem gave their suffrages for Matthias, in preference to
his companion Barsabas. The word κλῆρος, in the latter part of the passage
under consideration, does not mean a lot, but the office or function with which
Matthias was invested; τῆς διακονίας, which must be understood as annexed to
it in order to render the sense complete, being omitted for the sake of brevity.
To perceive at once the force of the term in this place, we need only imagine
St. Luke to have studied conciseness less, and written καὶ ἔπεσεν ὁ κλῆρος (τῆς
διακονίας ταύτης) ἐπὶ Ματθίαν; the sense of which in English is, " and the office
of that ministry (i. e. the apostleship) fell on Matthias." In what I have thus
said, I do not pretend to anything like infallibility, but merely propose a

conjecture, which appears to me to have no small degree of probability on its side, for the consideration of the learned.

XV. **The conversion of St. Paul.** All these apostles were uninformed, illiterate men. Through the gift of the Holy Spirit, indeed, their minds had become fully irradiated with celestial light; but to any other sort of wisdom than that which is from above, they had no pretensions; neither were they at all instructed in any of the different branches of human learning. In the then infancy of the Christian church, however, it was absolutely requisite that, in addition to these, there should be some one appointed who might be able to repress the domineering spirit of the Jewish doctors, by encountering them with their own weapons; and also be qualified, if occasion should require, to enter the field of disputation with the advocates and supporters of the various systems of pagan philosophy. Our blessed Saviour, therefore, revealing himself from heaven in a very wonderful manner to a young man of the name of Saul, but who afterwards changed it for that of Paul, appointed him a thirteenth apostle. Saul, who was a Jew, a native of Tarsus in Cilicia, and belonging to the sect of the Pharisees, had been endowed by nature with great and excellent mental powers, and was eminently skilled in every kind of Jewish learning. He was also conversant with the literature and philosophy of the Greeks. Led away by prejudice and warmth of temper, he was at first the bitter persecuting enemy of Christ and his flock; but as he journeyed on a certain time towards Damascus, with power from the high priest to seize on any Christians whom he might find there, and bring them bound to Jerusalem, he was on a sudden struck to the earth, and so affected by the voice and power of our Saviour, that he became at once a convert to his cause, devoting himself wholly to it, and with the utmost cheerfulness and fortitude, exposing himself to innumerable hardships and dangers on account thereof, throughout the whole course of his future life. Acts, ix. 1, et seq. In how great a degree every interest of Christianity was promoted by the exertions of this illustrious and admirable character, how many churches he founded throughout the greatest part of the Roman empire, how numerous and how formidable the contentions and perils which he encountered and overcame, his own epistles which are still extant, and **the** history of the Acts of the Apostles written by St. Luke, abundantly testify.

XVI. **Of the labours, martyrdom, &c. of the apostles.** In the accounts which have been given by various writers, of the labours, the travels, the miracles, and the deaths of the apostles, there is little that can be altogether depended on, except what is recorded in the books of the New Testament, and a few other [p. 81.] monuments of great antiquity. In this case, as in most others of doubt and uncertainty, a difference of opinion prevails as to what ought to be received, and what rejected. For my own part, I think that we cannot well withhold our credit from such particulars as stand supported by the clear and positive testimony of Origen, Eusebius, Gregory Nanzianzene, Paulinus, Jerome, Socrates, and certain of the more ancient writers who are cited with approbation by Eusebius; but as to any thing that is to be met with merely in the writings of uncertain authors, or those of a later age, I should ever feel inclined to receive it with considerable hesitation and distrust, unless it should happen to be corroborated by documents that admit of no dispute. For when once certain of the Christian writers had been unfortunately tempted to have recourse to fiction, it was not long before the weakness of some and the arrogant presumption of others carried forgery and imposition to an extent, of which it would be difficult to convey to the reader any adequate idea. Amongst various other things that I consider as having been too readily received upon trust respecting the apostles, I cannot help including those accounts which have been handed down to us of their having, for the most part, undergone violent deaths; although I am well aware, that the fact of their having suffered in this way is commonly considered as established beyond dispute.(')

(1) That every one of our Saviour's apostles, except St. John, (who ended his days in the natural way at Ephesus,) underwent capital punishment by command of the civil magistrate, is a report that appears to have been regularly transmitted down from very early ages, and is supported by the testimony of many different writers. The opinion that such was the fact has, moreover, taken such deep root even in the minds of many who would not willingly be thought either credulous or uninformed, that whoever may venture either to

call it in question, or oppose it, must run no inconsiderable risk of being accounted hostile to the fame and reputation of those divine characters. In what I am about to say, it is far from my wish to cast any reflection on those who may have espoused this opinion; but I must, at the same time, claim for myself the liberty of remarking, that the evidence on which they rest their proof of the fact, that the major part of the apostles underwent violent deaths, is by no means so conclusive as they seem to imagine. That Peter, and Paul, and James suffered in this way, is what, on the faith of so many ancient authorities, I am very ready to admit; but there are several considerations which combine to prevent me from believing that their colleagues perished by the same untimely fate. My doubts are founded, in the first place, on the testimony of Heracleon, a very ancient author of the second century, a Valentinian indeed by profession, but most evidently neither an ill-informed nor incautious writer, who, as quoted by Clement of Alexandria, (*Stromat.* lib. iv. cap. ix. p. 595.) expressly denies that Matthew, Philip, Thomas, Levi, and some others, were put to death, in consequence of their having made open profession of their faith in Christ in the face of the civil power. Heracleon is arguing against an opinion which was entertained by certain of the Christians of that age, that the souls of martyrs alone were received up into heaven after death; and contends, that those who had never been called upon to lay down their lives for the cause of Christ, but had merely continued steadfast in faith and holiness of life, would equally, on the dissolution of the body, be admitted to the mansions of the blessed. This opinion he supports by the examples of the above-mentioned apostles, whom, with many others, he concludes to have been exalted to a seat in heaven, although they were never put to the test of making an open profession of their faith in Christ before an earthly tribunal, and sealing it with their blood. Ὀυ γὰρ πάντες οἱ σωζόμενοι ὡμολόγησαν τὴν διὰ τῆς φωνῆς ὡμολογίαν, καὶ ἐξῆλθον. Ἐξ ὧν Ματθαῖος, Φίλιππος, Θωμᾶς, Λευίς, καὶ ἄλλοι πολλοί. *Non enim* [p. 82.] *omnes qui salvi facti sunt, eam* (Christi) *confessionem quæ per vocem* (apud magistratus) *ediderunt, et post eam ex vita excesserunt. Ex quibus est Matthæus, Philippus, Thomas, Levis, et multi alii.* Clement of Alexandria, who makes a quotation from Heracleon, of which this passage forms a part, although he takes occasion in some respects to condemn and reject what he thus brings forward, yet never once intimates the least objection to the above cited words of that author respecting the apostles: a circumstance which plainly indicates that he did not consider them as open to any exception. To this twofold testimony may be added others of no less authority. The apostle Philip is clearly excepted out of the class of martyrs by Polycrates, who states him to have died and been buried at Hierapolis. *Epistola ad Victorem,* apud Eusebium *Histor. Eccles.* lib. v. cap. xxiv. p. 191. Baronius, indeed, *Annal.* tom. i. ad ann. 35. § 141. and many others after him, would have us to understand Polycrates as speaking of that Philip who was one of the seven deacons of the church at Jerusalem, and not of Philip the apostle. But the advocates of this notion stand confuted by Polycrates himself, who says expressly that the Philip of whom he makes mention was one of the twelve apostles. But there is an argument of still greater force and weight to be brought forward on this subject,—an argument, indeed, nearly sufficient of itself to establish the point for which I contend; and that is, that all the writers of the first three centuries, including those most strenuous advocates for the honour and dignity of the martyrs against the Valentinians, Tertullian, Clement of Alexandria, and Origen, reckon no more than three of the apostles as coming within the class of martyrs, namely, Peter, Paul, and James the great. Tertullian says, *Quæ tamen passos apostolos scimus, manifesta doctrina est : hanc intelligo solam acta decurrens.—Quod Petrus cæditur, quod Stephanus opprimitur, quod Jacobus immolatur, quod Paulus distrahitur, ipsorum sanguine scripta sunt. Et si fidem commentarii voluerit hæreticus, instrumenta imperii loquuntur, ut lapides Jerusalem. Vitas Cæsarum legimus : orientem fidem Romæ primus Nero cruentavit. Tunc Petrus ab altero cingitur, quum cruci adstringitur. Tunc Paulus civitatis Romanæ consequitur nativitatem, quum illic martyrum renascitur generositate. Haec ubicumque legero, pati disco : nec mea interest, quos sequar martyrii magistros, sensusne an exitus apostolorum. Scorpiace, cap. xv. p.* 633. edit. Rigaltii. If these words of Tertullian be attentively considered, they will be found to militate strongly against the opinion of those who have been led to believe that all the apostles, except St. John, suffered violent deaths. Tertullian is contending with the Valentinians, who, as we hinted above, denied that there was any necessity of laying down one's life for Christ, and maintained that those of his servants who continued steadfast in faith and holiness of life would obtain salvation equally with the martyrs. To this opinion Tertullian opposes the example of the apostles, who were known to have exposed themselves to sufferings of various kinds in the cause of Christ, and not to have refused encountering even death [p. 83.] itself for his sake. Now if, at that time, even the slightest rumour had prevailed amongst the Christians, that all the apostles of our Lord had sealed their testimony with their blood, this author, who appears to have been never backward in availing himself of vulgar report, would most assuredly have brought it forward on this occasion. On the contrary, however, he with more than ordinary caution contents himself with naming merely three of the apostles as martyrs, viz., Peter, Paul, and James. It is, therefore, fairly to be presumed that he knew of no more; and if he knew of no more, we may rest assured that the Christians of that age were apprized of none besides; for if any one had been able to add to the above list, it must have been Tertullian, who was thoroughly conversant with every part of Christian history, true as well as feigned. Tertullian, indeed, does not attempt to conceal his ignorance of any other of the apostles that could be deemed martyrs. He was a man by no means wanting in penetration or judgment, and was fully aware that the Valentinians, his opponents, might reply, that only a few of the apostles suffered martyrdom,—so few, indeed, that even he himself had not been able to swell the list beyond three. With a view, therefore, to preclude them from parrying the force of his argument in this way, he adds, *Nec mea interest quos sequar martyrii magistros, sensusne an exitus apostolorum :* words which, it must I think, be allowed, make strongly in favour of the point for which I contend. For the meaning intended to be conveyed by them is obviously this : " It can be of no avail for you to object, that a few only of the apostles underwent violent deaths. I do not take upon me to controvert this. It is sufficient for me to have proved that I have the general sense of the apostles on my side, inasmuch as they were both ready and willing to have died for the cause of Christ. But few of them, indeed, were called to so severe a trial of their constancy; but there can be no doubt that it was the meaning and desire of them all to glorify their divine Master by their death. The general sense, then, of these illustrious characters I take as my guide; and, after their example, I desire to die for the sake of Christ, although I am aware that the deaths of the major part of them were different from what they had thus expected and desired."

Influenced by these and other considerations, I am induced to think that the accounts which have been handed down to us, respecting the martyrdom of our Saviour's apostles, were invented subsequently to the age of Constantine the Great. That such accounts should have been invented, may readily be accounted for on two grounds. First, the incredible veneration in which the martyrs were held;—a veneration which had been carried to a great height even in the earlier ages of Christianity, but which increased beyond all measure upon the restoration of tranquillity to the Christian commonwealth by Constantine. For when the martyrs came to be worshipped almost like gods, and to have all those honours paid to them which it was customary for the Greeks and Romans to offer to their demigods and heroes, it might of course be thought necessary to include the apostles within this class, lest they should appear to want that which was considered as the most distinguishing and infallible mark of sanctity and glory. Secondly, the ambiguity attached to the word *martyr* might occasion ignorant men to invent accounts of their tragical deaths. *Martyr*, in the Greek language, signifies any sort of witness: but the term was applied by the Christians in a more eminent sense to that kind of witness, who placed it beyond all doubt that Christ was the centre of all his hopes, by sealing his testimony with his blood. The apostles are denominated μάρτυρες, witnesses, in the former sense, by Christ himself. Acts, i. 8. And the term has evidently no higher import annexed to it, when applied, as it afterwards is, by the apostles to themselves, by way of elucidating the nature of their functions. Acts, ii. 32, &c. It might, however, very easily happen [p 84.] that unlearned persons, not aware of this distinction, might conceive that the word martyr, which they found thus applied to the apostles in the writings of the New Testament, was to be understood in the latter sense; and in consequence thereof, hastily adopt the opinion that they ought to be placed in the same class with those whom it was usual for the Christians to style, in a more eminent sense, martyrs.

XVII. **Churches founded by the Apostles.** Amidst all the uncertainty, however, in which the history of the apostles is involved, it appears to be placed beyond a doubt that they travelled throughout the greatest part of the then known and civilized world, and within a short time, either by themselves, or with the assistance of certain of their disciples who accompanied them in

their travels, and shared their labours, established churches dedicated to Christ in almost all the provinces.(¹) But even here we are
precluded from giving scarcely any thing beyond this general
statement of the fact: the great obscurity which hangs over
nearly every part of the early history of Christianity not only
preventing us from marking with precision the extent of the
apostles' progress, but also rendering it impossible for us, with
any degree of confidence, to name any particular churches as
founded by them, except such as are mentioned in the writings
of the New Testament.(²) Throughout the world there is scarcely,
not to say a nation or people, but even a city of any magnitude
or consequence, in which the religion of Christ may be said to
flourish, that does not ascribe the first planting of its church to
one or other of the apostles themselves, or to some of their immediate and most intimate disciples.   But no reliance whatever
can be placed on traditions of this sort: since it has been pretty
clearly ascertained, that the same spirit of vain glory which
prompted ancient nations to pronounce themselves the offspring
of the soil, or the descendants of the gods, found its way into the
churches of Christ, and induced many of them to suppress the
truth, and claim for themselves a more illustrious origin than in
reality belonged to them.(³)

(1) That the apostles should have made their way to parts of the earth which
at that time were not civilized, nor even known, is what I should think could
scarcely be believed by any one. The weight is vast which those take on their
shoulders, who would fain persuade us that the various accounts which carry
the apostles to America, as well as to Sweden, Denmark, and Lapland, and
even make them penetrate into the interior of Africa, are conformable to truth.

(2) A list of those churches founded by the apostles, of which mention is
made in different parts of the New Testament, is given by Hartmann in his
work *de Rebus gestis Christianorum sub Apostolis,* cap. vii. p. 107 ; as also by
Fabricius, in his *Lux Evangelii toti Orbi exoriens,* cap. v. p. 83, et seq.

(3) Amongst the European nations, there is not one that does not pride
itself on being able to attribute the first foundation of its church either to one
of the apostles, or of the seventy disciples, or to some holy personage bearing
an apostolic commission. The Spaniards boast of having had the light of the
gospel communicated to them by two of the apostles in person, viz. St. Paul
and St. James the Great, as well as by many of the seventy disciples, and of
[p. 85.] those who were the companions of the apostles ; and it would be far
from prudent for any one who wishes to cultivate the good will of these people,
to attempt to undeceive them in this respect. The French, with equal osten-

tation and pertinacity, attribute the conversion of their forefathers to the preaching and labours of Crescent, the disciple and companion of St. Paul, of Dionysius of Athens, the Areopagite, of Lazarus, Mary Magdalene, and I know not of how many others. Throughout Italy, there is scarcely a city which does not pretend to have received the first rudiments of Christianity from either Paul or Peter; and that its first bishop was appointed by one or other of these. Vid. Giannone *Histoire civile du Royaume de Naples*, tom i. p. 74, 75. And it would be hardly possible, indeed I may say it would be altogether impossible, for any one to escape the imputation of heresy, who should venture in any way to indicate his disbelief of this. Vid. Jo. Lami *Deliciæ Eruditorum*, tom. viii. Præf. p. xxxv, xxxvi. and tom. xi. Præfat. The Germans affirm that Maternus, Valerian, and many others were sent to them by the apostles; and that the persons thus commissioned by St. Peter and his colleagues, established some considerable churches in their country. The inhabitants of Britain consider St. Paul, Simeon Zelotes, Aristobulus, and particularly Joseph of Arimathea, as the founders of their church. That the former of these actually extended his travels to that island, and first preached the gospel there, is a fact which has been strongly contended for by many, who chiefly rely on the authority of a passage in the first epistle of Clement of Rome to the Corinthians. The Russians, with the Poles and Prussians, venerate St. Andrew as the parent of their respective churches. All these things, and many others which I shall pass over, were considered as indisputable during those benighted ages, when every species of sound learning, divine as well as human, was overwhelmed and trodden under foot by ignorance and superstition. At present, however, they are regarded in a very different light; and the wisest and best informed scholars give them up for the most part as fictions, invented subsequently to the age of Charlemagne, by illiterate and designing men, who expected that by thus propagating a notion of the great antiquity of their several churches, they should open to themselves a source of profit as well as honour. Vid. Calmet, *Histoire de Lorraine*, tom. i. p. xxvi. Le Beuf, *Dissertations sur l'Histoire de France*, tom. i. p. 192, 193. 198; and others. In one particular, perhaps, as we shall presently take occasion to point out, this opinion may not be strictly correct: but in every other respect it meets with the unreserved assent of all of the present day, who prefer truth to the authority of antiquity; and is expressed with much neatness and force of illustration, by that eminently learned French writer, Jo. Launois, in a dissertation, in which he undertakes the defence of a passage in Sulpitius Severus respecting the first martyrs of Gaul, and which is to be found in the second volume of his works, part i. p. 184. His words are, *Media ætate orta est inter ecclesias super antiquitate originum suarum contentio et certa quædam æmulatio, quæ fecit, ut cum simplicem veritatem ultro oblatam facile proferre poterant, ait Damianus, sategerint, ut mendacia cum labore corfingerent. Etenim dum reconcinnarunt pleraque primorum episcoporum acta, nunc adstipulante nominum similitudine, Trophimum puta Arelatensem, et Paulum Narbonensem, qui sub Decio venerant in Galliam, cum Trophimo et Paulo Sergio, Pauli apostoli sectatoribus confuderunt: nunc eadem vel alia de causa Rufum, e Macedonia Avemo-*

nem, et Lazarum e Cypro Massiliam traduxerunt, nunc alios a secundo vel tertio
[p. 86.] *ecclesiæ sæculo revocarunt ad primum, eosque Petri vel Clementis disci-*
pulo et nobilibus ortos parentibus, quos sæpe nominant, affirmarunt: nunc etiam
alios constituerunt, de quibus per antiquæ traditionis testes, qui ante Caroli Magni
tempus floruerunt, nihil licet quicquam pronuntiare.

To the justness of this statement, so far as it goes, I most readily subscribe; but as to what is further imagined by many of the learned, that it was
not until after the age of Charlemagne that the European churches began to
contend with each other respecting the antiquity of their foundation, and, in
direct violation of the truth, to refer their origin to the apostolic age, I conceive
that it admits of some doubt. To me it appears that those preposterous attempts to carry back the origins of churches even to the times of the apostles,
and to give them a venerable air by trumping up the most idle tales of their
extreme antiquity, are of much older date than the age of Charles the Great:
indeed, I have not a doubt but that this silly sort of emulation had taken possession of the minds of both the Greeks and the Latins, even so far back as
the age of Constantine. That this opinion of mine may not have the appearance of being adopted hastily, or on insufficient grounds, I will support it by
an example drawn from the history of Gregory of Tours, a writer of the sixth
century;—an example which must certainly be allowed to stand in no danger
of suffering by a comparison with the most wonderful of any of these wondrous
tales; indeed, of so marvellous a complexion, as to call for a stretch of credulity to which I rather think but few, if any, of us, are equal. The narrative
occurs in Gregory's book *de Gloria Martyrum,* cap. xii. p. 735. and is as follows: *Tunc temporis a Galliis matrona quædam Hierosolymis abierat, pro devo-*
tione tantum, ut Domini et salvatoris nostri præsentiam mereretur. Audivit
autem quod beatus Johannes decollaretur: cursu illic rapido tendit, datisque mu-
neribus supplicat percussori ut eam sanguinem defluentem colligere permitteret
non arceri: illo autem percutiente, Matrona concham argenteam præparat, trun-
cato:que martyris capite, cruorem devota suscipit: quem diligenter in ampulla po-
situm, patriam detulit et apud Vasatensem urbem, ædificata in ejus honorem eccle-
sia, in sancto altari collocavit. Now I will take upon me to assert, that such a
foolish, such a mad conceit as this, in which the people of Bazadois gloried
long before the age of Charlemagne, never entered into the brain of any monk
subsequently to that period. For these people, we see, were willing to have it
believed that their church existed prior to the death of our Saviour; having,
according to the above statement, been founded not long after the death of
John the Baptist, by a certain devout woman on her return from Palestine,
whither she had been induced to go by the fame of Christ's miracles. But even
this was not enough: they must carry the matter still farther, and pretend that
this pious woman actually built the church at Bazas in Guienne before Christ's
death, dedicated the altar therein with Christian rites, and placed on that altar
the blood of St. John. To such an high and incredible antiquity none other
of the Christian churches ever made pretension, except that of Jerusalem, which
was instituted by Christ himself. The people of Bazadois, however, to my
certain knowledge, even yet cherish this error, considering their honour as in no

small degree involved in the maintenance of it. Such ridiculous extravagance naturally reminds one of the Arcades, who anciently boasted that their race was older than the moon.

XVIII. **The Writings of the Apostles.** But the labours [p. 87.] of the apostles, in the cause of their divine Master, were not restricted merely to journeyings, to watchings, to the cheerful endurance of deprivations and sufferings, to the communication of oral instruction, or to the use of such other means as promised to be instrumental in promoting the edification of those of their own age. The welfare of future generations was likewise the object of their solicitude; and they accordingly made it a part of their concern to commit to writing a code of testimony and instruction, of which the whole human race might avail itself in all ages to come: the Holy Spirit, to whose influence and guidance their minds were in every respect subject, doubtless prompting them to the undertaking. St. Matthew with his own hand wrote a history of the life and actions of Christ, as did also St. John; and St. Peter and St. Paul respectively dictated similar histories to St. Mark and St. Luke.(¹) Certain epistles, also, in which are comprised the leading principles of Christianity, and various precepts or rules of life, were addressed by St. Paul, St. James, St. Peter, St. John, and St. Jude, to the churches which they had established in different parts of the world. At no very great distance of time from the age of the apostles, the Christians, with a view to secure to future ages a divine and perpetual standard of faith and action, collected these writings together into one volume, under the title of The New Testament, or The Canon of the New Testament. Neither the names of those who were chiefly concerned in the making of this collection, nor the exact time of its being undertaken, can be ascertained with any degree of certainty; nor is it at all necessary that we should be precisely informed as to either of these particulars: it is sufficient for us to know that it may be proved by many strong arguments, that the principal parts of the New Testament had been collected together before the death of St. John, or at least not long after that event.(²)

(1) That St. Mark wrote his history of Christ from the dictation of St. Peter, is a fact that stands supported by those great and highly respectable authorities, Papias, apud Eusebium *Histor. Eccles.* lib. iii. cap. xxxix.; Irenæus,

adv. Hæreses, lib. iii. cap. i.; Clemens Alexandrinus, Tertullian, and others. That St. Luke derived the materials of his history from St. Paul, is also asserted by Irenæus, lib. iii. cap. i.; Tertullian, *contra Marcionem*, lib. iv. cap. v.; and others. It is, therefore, not without reason that St. Paul and St. Peter are termed by some the original authors of the gospels of St. Luke and St. Mark.

(2) The insidious attempt made by Toland, in his *Amyntor*, to undermine the divine origin and authority of the canon of the New Testament, gave rise to very warm disputes amongst the learned; and many different opinions were, in consequence thereof, brought forward respecting the authors of that collection, and the time when it was made. For which, see Jo. Ens in his *Bibliotheca sacra, seu Diatriba de Librorum Novi Test. Canone, Amstelod.* 1710, 8vo. Jo. [p. 88.] Mill in his *Prolegomena ad Nov. Testament.* § i. p. 23, et seq. and Jo. Frickius *de Cura veteris Ecclesiæ circa Canonem Nov. Testamenti*, a small work of considerable erudition published at Ulm. To me it appears, that after all that has been brought forward on the subject, the matter remains in great measure undecided. The most general opinion seems to be, that the books of the New Testament were originally collected together by St. John : an opinion for which the testimony of Eusebius (*Histor. Eccles.* lib. iii. cap. xxiv.) is very confidently quoted as an indisputable authority. But it is to be observed, that allowing even the highest degree of weight to the authority of Eusebius, nothing farther can be collected from his words, than that St. John approved of the gospels of St. Matthew, St. Mark, and St. Luke, and added his own to them by way of supplement. Concerning any of the other books of the New Testament, Eusebius is entirely silent.

XIX. **The Apostles' Creed.** To these writings of the apostles it might be proper to add that formulary of faith, which is commonly known by the name of the Apostles' Creed, if any reasonable grounds appeared to warrant that notion respecting its origin, which obtained pretty generally in the Christian world subsequently to the fourth century, and which is entertained by many even at this day, namely, that it was drawn up by the apostles themselves before they departed from Jerusalem on their mission to the Gentiles.(') But to say nothing of the silence of all the most ancient writers as to this point, and equally passing over the fact that this formulary was not uniformly adopted by the Christian churches, which would most undoubtedly have been the case, had they known it to have been dictated by such high authority; omitting, moreover, to lay any stress on the circumstance of its having never been received or accounted as a part of the apostolic writings; it is alone a sufficient refutation of this opinion, that we know for certain that this creed was at first extremely short; and that it was afterwards, by little and little, extended and dilated, according as new errors from time to time sprang up in the Christian community.(²) No one surely will maintain, that we ought to regard that as a genuine formulary of faith prescribed by the apostles, which can be proved to have been amplified in several respects subsequently to their death. [p. 89.]

(1) See what has been with much industry collected on this subject by those highly respectable writers: Jo. Franc. Buddeus, in his *Isagoge ad Theologiam,* lib. ii. cap. ii. § ii. p. 441; and Je. Georg. Walchius, in his *Introductio in Libros symbolicos,* lib. i. cap. ii. p. 87.

(2) That such was the fact has been clearly demonstrated by Sir Peter King, in his *History of the Apostles' Creed, with Critical Observations on its Articles,* London, 1702, 8vo. This work was translated into Latin by Gothofred Olearius, and first printed at Leipsig, 1704, in 8vo.; a second edition was some time afterwards published at Basle.

XX. Causes to which the quick propagation of Christianity must be ascribed. The system of discipline which the apostles, by the authority and command of their divine Master, employed themselves in propagating throughout the world, was not only repugnant to the natural disposition and inclinations of mankind, but also set itself in direct opposition to the manners, the laws, and the opinions of all the different nations of the earth; and as for the persons themselves who were selected to be the propounders of it, they were altogether rude and unskilled in any of those arts by which the human mind is to be rendered docile, and brought to yield assent and obedience. It is impossible, therefore, to account for the astonishingly rapid propagation of the Christian religion amongst so many different nations, part of them of a savage and ferocious character, and part entirely devoted to licentiousness and sloth, otherwise than by receiving with implicit credit the accounts which are given us, by profane as well as sacred writers, of the miraculous gifts by which the apostles were distinguished; namely, that they possessed a faculty of persuasion more than human, that they predicted future events, laid open the secrets of men's hearts, held the operations of nature in control, enacted wonders beyond the reach of any human power, and lastly, were capable of transmitting these supernatural endowments to any on whom they thought proper to confer them, simply by the imposition of their hands on them, accompanied with prayer. Let these things be considered for a

moment as false, and we shall at once find how utterly out of our
power it is to assign any rational cause that could have prevailed
on so large a portion of mankind, within so short a period, to
turn their backs on the allurements of pleasure, to forsake the
religion of their ancestors, and voluntarily to embrace Christianity, at the hazard of life, fortune, honour, and every thing else
that could be dear to them.(')

(1) It is certainly a very ill-advised attempt, and a disgraceful abuse of
talents, for any one to pretend to account for that wonderful revolution in the
sentiments and affairs of mankind, which was thus brought about by a mere
handful of illiterate Jews, from mere natural causes. There are, however,
several who, espousing the principles of Hobbes and others, persist in contend-
.ng that the uncommon degree of benevolence and charity towards the poor
and the miserable, by which the early Christians were distinguished, operated
as a lure in bringing over great multitudes of the necessitous, and others of the
lower class of people, to the profession of Christianity, under the expectation
of having their wants relieved, and being enabled, through the munificence of
others, to pass the remainder of their days in inactivity and ease. But surely
this is a very unwarrantable sporting with reason. For if such were the motives
by which the poor and the indigent were influenced, yet by what incentive—by
what inducement could those be stimulated to become Christians, out of whose
abundance the necessities of the poor and the indigent were supplied? But
can it be necessary to inform those who maintain this opinion, that the idle and
slothful had no place amongst the first Christians; and that St. Paul commands,
" that if any would not work, neither should he eat?" 2 Thess. iii. 6, 7, 8, 9, 10.
Can it be necessary to inform them, that the lazy, the vicious, and the sensual,
were, by order of the apostles, to be expelled from the Christian community?
Can it be necessary to inform them, that every Christian family was charged
with the maintenance of such of its own members as were in need; and that
[p. 90.] those alone were relieved at the public expense, who had no relatives
capable of yielding them assistance? 1 Tim. v. 3. 16, &c. Equally superficial
and futile is the reasoning of those, who would persuade us that great numbers
were induced to embrace Christianity, on account of the infamous lives led by
the heathen priests, and the many extravagant absurdities by which the various
systems of paganism were characterized. Motives of this sort might indeed so
far influence men of sound sense and principle, as to cause them to renounce
the religion of their ancestors : but in no shape whatever could they operate
as inducements for them to embrace a new system, which called upon them to
restrain and mortify their natural propensities : and the profession of which
exposed their lives, their reputation, and every thing else that could be deemed
valuable by them, to the most imminent danger. Others there are who imagine
that the virtues by which the apostles and the earliest converts to Christianity
were so eminently distinguished, such as their continence, their contempt of
this world's goods, their fortitude, their patience, and the like, had that effect
on the generality of mankind, that they were readily prevailed on to adopt

them as their instructors and guides in the road to salvation. Great indeed, I am ready to allow, is the effect which eminent probity and virtue have on the minds of men: nor would I be thought to insinuate that the exemplary lives of the apostles had no weight with those whom they converted to a faith in Christ. But all of us who are acquainted with what we are ourselves, and what human nature is, must be well aware that, although purity of morals and innocence of life may excite the respect and veneration of mankind, they will not often produce imitation under any circumstances,—and hardly ever, if it be manifest that such imitation would be attended with ignominy and danger. We need not be told that virtue itself, and that even of the most exalted kind, is commonly regarded in an unfavourable light, if it require men to renounce the principles and opinions in which they were bred, to abandon their pleasures, and cast off habits to which they have been long attached. And certainly nothing less than this is taught us by the examples of the apostles, who from the purity of their morals, are said to have overcome the world. Indeed, were further proof wanting, the matter is placed beyond all doubt by the example of the Lord and Master of the apostles himself, whose whole life exhibited one uninterrupted course of sanctity and innocence. That the pure and inoffensive lives led by the apostles might so far operate in favour of their cause, as to secure them in some degree from personal violence or injury, is what I can very readily bring myself to believe: but that the strictness of their morals and demeanor, and their contempt of this world's goods, should alone have been sufficient to cause many thousands of men to believe in that Jesus, who was crucified by the Romans at the instigation of the Jews, as the Saviour of the human race;—induce them sedulously to form themselves after the apostolic model;—and finally, inspire them with the resolution to die rather than renounce the principles which they had thus embraced, is what I am certain no one possessed merely of ordinary powers will ever prevail on me to admit. And to pass over many other things, let me only by way of conclusion ask, to what source or to what causes are we to ascribe that astonishing virtue and sanctity in the apostles, by which it is pretended to account for the unanimity and eagerness displayed by such vast multitudes, in laying hold on Christ as the only anchor of salvation?

XXI. **The early Christians for the most part of low condition.** Our opinion in regard to this point is not at all shaken by the arguments of those, who, after the example of Celsus, Julian, Porphyry, and other ancient adversaries of Christianity, call upon us to recollect that the first Christian assemblies [p. 91.] or churches formed by the apostles consisted of men of low degree, of servants, labourers, artificers, and women; in short, that they were wholly composed of uninformed illiterate persons, possessed of neither wealth nor dignity, and who were, of course, easily to be wrought upon and managed by any one even of

very moderate abilities. For, in the first place, what they thus
so confidently press on our attention is not a correct representation of the fact; since we are expressly taught in Scripture,
that amongst those who were converted by the apostles to a
faith in Christ were many persons of wealth, rank, and learning.(') And, in the next place, it is well known to every one
who has had the least experience in human affairs, that men,
even of the lowest class, not only inherit from nature, in common with their superiors, the warmest attachment to life, and
whatever may contribute to their own well-being, but are also
in a far greater degree bigoted to, and consequently much more
jealous over, the customs, opinions, and religious principles
handed down to them from their ancestors, than those of intelligent and cultivated minds, who are possessed of wealth and
authority, and fill the higher stations in life.(²)

(1) The apostles, in their writings, prescribe rules for the conduct of the
rich as well as the poor, for masters as well as for servants; a convincing proof,
surely, that amongst the members of the churches planted by them were to be
found persons of opulence and masters of families. St. Paul and St. Peter
admonish Christian women not to study the adorning of themselves with
pearls, with gold and silver, or with costly array. 1 Tim. ii. 9. 1 Peter, iii. 3.
It is therefore plain, that amongst the early Christians, there must have been
women possessed of wealth adequate to the purchase of bodily ornaments of
great price. St. Paul exhorts the Christians to beware of the philosophy of the
Greeks, and also of that oriental system which was styled γνῶσις. 1 Tim. vi. 20.
Col. ii. 8. Hence it is manifest that amongst the first converts to Christianity
there were men of learning and philosophers, who wished to temper and
improve, as they thought, the doctrine of our blessed Saviour, by incorporating
with it the precepts of their own wisdom. For if the wise and the learned had
unanimously rejected the Christian religion, what occasion could there have
been for this caution? St. Paul's remark, that amongst the members of the
church of Corinth were not to be found many of the noble or the mighty,
(1 Cor. i. 26.) unquestionably carries with it the plainest intimation that persons
of rank or power were not wholly wanting in that assembly. Indeed, lists of
the names of various illustrious persons who embraced Christianity, in this its
weak and infantine state, are given by Blondell, at page 235 of his work *de
Episcopis et Presbyteris*; also by Wetstein, in his Preface to Origen's Dialogue
contra Marcionitas, p. 13.

(2) Ignorance and fear generate and nourish superstition. By how much
the more any one's mind is weak and unenlightened, by so much the stronger
hold will superstitious influence be found to have on it. With a much better
prospect of success, therefore, if superstition stand in your way, may you
undertake to convince ten men than one woman, or a hundred sensible and

well-informed people than ten of such as are ignorant and stupid. Vicious inclination never predominates more strongly than in servants or persons of the lower class: and with far greater ease may you extinguish evil pro- [p. 92.] pensities in six hundred well-born persons of ingenuous mind, than in twenty servants or people of the common order. In my opinion, therefore, if the fact would bear out the adversaries of Christianity in what they thus so confidently urge, that the churches founded by the apostles were made up of men of no account, of low and illiterate characters, servants, women, and the like, it would rather tend to augment than diminish the reputation and glory of those divine teachers.

XXII. **Christ held in great estimation by the Gentiles.** That the apostles, in accomplishing the objects of their mission, derived no inconsiderable assistance from the great fame of their divine Master, which soon spread itself far and wide, and thus preceded them in their journeys, admits of little or no doubt. Authors of no mean credit assure us that, before the departure of the apostles from Jerusalem, the fame of the wonders wrought by Christ in the land of Judea had extended itself throughout a great part of the world, or at least of the Roman empire, and impressed many with the highest estimation of his character. It is even said that some of the Roman emperors themselves entertained an honourable respect for his name, his doctrine, and his acts. Indeed, if Tertullian and some others may be credited, Tiberius, who was in other respects a most execrable tyrant, conceived such an esteem for the character of our Lord, that it was his intention to have assigned him a place amongst the deities publicly worshipped by the Roman people; but that the design fell to the ground, in consequence of its being opposed by the senate. There have not, indeed, been wanting amongst the learned some who consider this as altogether a fabrication; but, on the other hand, men, by no means inferior to these in point of erudition, have brought forward several arguments in its support, which, as it appears to us, are not easily to be answered.(')

(1) Eusebius relates (*Histor. Eccles.* lib. vii. cap. xviii. p. 265.) that many amongst the heathens had procured images of our Saviour, and his apostles, and which were preserved by them in their houses with great care and reverential regard: a striking proof that the Gentiles had been early brought acquainted with the character of Christ, and held it in great respect. The Carpocratians, a celebrated Gnostic sect of the second century, exhibited, according to Irenæus, both statues and pictures of our Saviour, and said that Pilate had caused a likeness to be painted of him. Lib. i. *contra Hæreses*, cap. xxv. p. 105. edit. Massvet. Concerning the favourable disposition manifested by the Roman emperors

towards the Christian religion, there is a notable passage cited by Eusebius, *Histor. Eccles.* lib. iv. cap. xxvi. p. 148. from the apology addressed by Melito of Sardis to Marcus Antoninus, on behalf of the Christians; in which he intimates that the ancestors of the emperor had not only tolerated the Christian religion, in common with other systems, but had also treated it wi.h considerable honour and respect. ῾Ην καὶ οἱ πρόγονοι σοῦ πρὸς ταῖς ἄλλαις θρησκείαις ἐτίμησαν. Quam sectam majores tui una cum cæteris religionibus coluerunt. The same author adds, that Nero and Domitian were the only emperors who had ever suffered them-[p. 93.] selves to be so far influenced by the suggestions of wicked and malevo-lent advisers, as to conceive an ill opinion of the Christian religion, and favour the cause of its adversaries. If Melito be correct in what he thus says, that it was the counsel of evil disposed persons which caused Nero to prosecute the Christians, it should seem that John of Antioch might have some reason for stating, as he does, (*in Excerpt. Valesian.* p. 808, et seq.) that Nero, at his first accession to the purple, was well inclined to the cause of Christ, and favoured the Chris-tians. Tertullian (*in Apologetic.* cap. v. p. 57. ed. Havercamp.) speaks of the intention of Tiberius to have assigned our Saviour a place amongst the deities of Rome, as of a thing publicly and commonly known. The circumstance is repeated after him by Eusebius, Orosius, and others; all of them appearing to rely chiefly on the authority of Tertullian. Vid. Franc. Baldvin. *Commentar. ad Edicta veterum principum Romanorum de Christianis*, p. 22, 23. Alb. Fabric. *Lux Evangelii toti Orbi exoriens*, p. 221. Some of the most learned men, how-ever, of the present day, consider this as altogether incredible; deeming it impossible to reconcile such an intention, either with the disposition of Tiberius, or with the state of the Roman empire at that period. In what way, and to what extent the arguments brought forward by those who take this side of the question have been met and answered by men of no less learning and ingenuity on the opposite side, may be seen in a curious work of Theod. Hasæus, *de Decreto Tiberii quo Christum referre voluit in Numerum Deorum*, Erfurt, 1715, in 4to.; as also in a French Letter of J. Christ. Iseleus, which is pregnant with deep erudition, and printed in the *Biblioth. Germanique*, tom. xxxii. p. 147. and tom. xxxiii. p. 12.

XXIII. **Persecution of the Christians commenced by the Jews.** The very great and daily accelerating progress of Christianity, was, however, contemplated with the utmost jealousy and ap-prehension by the Jewish priests and rulers, who plainly per-ceived that if the people should be prevailed on to embrace this new religion, the law of Moses would no longer retain its dignity, and there would consequently at once be an end of their authority, and of the many emoluments and advantages of which they contrived to make it the source. They, therefore, opposed the doctrine of Christ with all imaginable violence and rancour; and availing themselves of every favourable opportunity to lay hold on his apostles and their disciples, they threw them into prison, were they were threatened and scourged, and had every other species of evil heaped on them without reserve: some of *them being even made to undergo capital punishment. Of the malevolence and injustice which the first teachers of Christianity thus experienced at the hands of the Jews, abundant testimony is left us on record by St. Luke, in the Acts of the Apostles. The most eminent amongst those who suffered death at Jerusalem for the cause of Christ were Stephen, a very devout man, whom the Jews stoned; Acts, vii. 1. St. James, the apostle, the son of Zebedee, whom Herod Agrippa put to the sword; Acts, xii. 1, 2. and St. James the Just, the bishop of the church at Jerusalem, who was slain in a cruel manner, as is shortly noticed by Josephus;(¹) but described more at large by Hegesippus;(²) in whose account, however, there are many things to which no one, who is in the smallest degree conversant with either Christian or Jewish antiquities, can by any means give credit.

(1) *Antiquit. Judaic.* lib. xx. cap. viii. or, according to Havercamp's [p. 94.] division, cap. ix. p. 976.

(2) *Apud.* Euseb. *Histor. Eccles.* lib. ii. cap. xxiii. The exceptions which are, not without reason, taken by the learned to this account of Hegesippus are all brought into one view, and augmented with some additional observations or his own, by Joh. Le Clerc, in his *Historia Eccles. duorum primorum sæculorum,* p. 414, et. seq. Even Joh. Aug. Orsi himself, in his *Ecclesiastical History,* a work of much elegance, written by him in Italian, tom. i. p. 237, et seq. frankly confesses that it is not possible even for the most credulous person to believe every thing related by Hegesippus; and pronounces the account given by Josephus, who represents James as having been stoned to death, as much more deserving of credit. For my own part, I must decline entering into a discussion of the numerous difficulties which give an air of improbability to the narrative of Hegesippus; but since the occasion presents itself, I will just offer a few remarks, which may perhaps be found to throw some light on one passage in it, of which the learned have hitherto professed themselves utterly at a loss to comprehend the meaning. The Jews, according to Hegesippus, proposed this question to James the Just: τίς ἡ θύρα τῆ Ἰησῆ? Quodnam est ostium Jesu? What is the gate or door of Jesus?—To which he is represented as answering, that this gate was the Saviour: καὶ ἔλεγε, τῆτον ἶναι τόν Σωτῆρα. Eusebius *ubi supra.* Now it is truly wonderful to behold how erudition has bewildered itself in attempts to discover the meaning of this question. Hen. Valesius, in his notes on Eusebius, p. 39, says, Ostium, hoc loco est introductio, seu institutio atque initiatio. Ostium igitur Christi nihil est aliud quam fides in Deum Patrem, et in Filium, et in Spiritum Sanctum. In this explanation it should seem as if the learned author fancied that he had given us something very great; whereas, in fact, he

has given us nothing; for his interpretation neither accords with the question of the Jews, nor with the answer of James. Admitting this notion of Valesius to be correct, the Jews must have meant to ask of James, What is faith in the Father, Son, and Holy Spirit? But who, let me ask, can possibly attach any such sense to the words they are stated to have made use of—*Quodnam est ostium Jesu*? What is the Gate of Jesus? And what relation to such a question as the above is to be discovered in the answer of James?—*Ostium hoc est Servator.* The Saviour is the gate. Is the Saviour then a faith in the Father, Son, and Holy Spirit? Indeed it is plain that Valesius himself was by no means satisfied with this explanation; for within a very few words after, we find him at variance with himself, and giving the passage a very different interpretation: *Christi ostium*, says he, *est remissio peccatorum, quæ fit per Baptismum.* This exposition, we see, is of quite a different nature from the one cited above, but yet, not at all more rational or intelligible. The Jews, according to this interpretation, must be understood to have asked of James—*Quænam est remissio peccatorum per baptismum?* What is remission of sins by baptism? To which he answers—*Remissio peccatorum est Servator.* Remission of sins is the Saviour. But I again repeat what I said above. This eminent scholar no doubt meant to throw light on this very obscure passage, and probably pleased himself with the notion that he had done so; but, in fact, he has done nothing of the kind: indeed it may be said, that he has thrown additional obscurity over a place already of itself sufficiently dark. In my opinion, Jo. Le Clerc pursued a much wiser course, by ingenuously confessing his inability to explain this passage as it stands, and intimating a suspicion that it must have been some how or other corrupted. *Quod quid sibi velit*, says he, *non intelligo*, [p. 95.] *neque enim Græcum hoc est, nec Hebraismum ullum similem comminisci possum. Respondet enim Jacobus, punc esse Servatorem, quasi* ϑύϱα *significaret munus aut quidpiam simile. Sed forte locus est corruptus. Histor. Eccles. duorum primor. Sæculor.* p. 416. Le Clerc perceived that this passage in Hegesippus required correction, but he would not undertake the amendment himself. This, however, has been, not long since, attempted by a learned French author, who, in 1747, published at Paris, in 4to. a prospectus *d'une nouvelle Traduction de l'Historien Joseph.* According to this writer, p. 9. the term ϑύϱα, which has been all along considered as Greek, and rendered into Latin by the word ostium or porta, ought in fact to be considered as an Hebraism; and the way in which he proposes to correct the passage in question is by substituting תורה *Torah*, for ϑύϱα, or rather by changing the latter into ϑύϱα. This conjecture is noticed by the learned editors of the *Nova Eruditorum Acta* at Leipsig, in their number for March 1750, p. 142; and they appear to consider it as a peculiarily happy one. *Est tamen* say they, *una inter cæteras conjectura, scita felicis ingenii filia; quam calculos peritorum hominum laturam esse, nulli dubitamus.* The emendation thus offered is, I must own, entitled to every sort of praise on the score of ingenuity; but, at the same time, I cannot go the length of saying that I deem it altogether unobjectionable, and free from doubt; since it appears to me in no shape to accord with the answer of James. Were we to adopt the ingenious correction proposed by this author, the question of the Jews would be this—*Quænam est lex Jesu?* What is the law of Jesus? But what sort of reply to this is conveyed by the answer of James, which, according to the same emendation, must be translated—*Lex Jesu est Servator.* The law of Jesus is the Saviour. What sense or meaning would there be in this? or, in what way can it be regarded as an answer to the question proposed? Is James trifling with the Jews, or does he give them the desired information? Let us leave this conjecture then, and see if it may not be possible to suggest an emenda- tion more consentanous to the object which the Jews evidently had in view. Now I entirely agree in opinion with the above-mentioned learned French author, that, in rendering the Hebrew words made use of by the Jews in the questioning of James, into Greek, a mistake was made by the translator, whoever he might be, whether Hegesippus or another, and that the object of their inquiry was entirely misconceived by him. But it strikes me, that the error is rather to be discovered in the name 'Ιησῦ, than in the term θύρα. The Jews manifestly had it in view to learn from James what he deemed the way or the gate of salvation, or, in other words, the true means of obtaining eternal life. I have, therefore, not the least doubt but that, speaking in their vernacular tongue, they made use of the term יְשׁוּעָה, *Jeschuah,* salvation; and that their question to James consequently was—What is in your opinion the gate of salvation? By what means may we arrive at eternal life? But the Greek translator, either through inattention, or for want of sufficient skill in the Hebrew language, mistaking this term for the proper name of our Saviour Jesus, instead of rendering the question, as he ought to have done, τίς ἡ θύρα τῆς σωτηρίας; What is the gate or door of salvation?—translated it, τίς ἡ θύρα Ιησῦ; What is the gate of Jesus? To the question, when corrected in this way, nothing can be conceived more pertinent or opposite than the reply of James— The gate or door of salvation is our Saviour Jesus Christ: for, in fact, he answers in our Saviour's own words, who, in John, x. 7. says of himself, Ἐγώ εἰμι [p. 96.] ἡ θύρα τῶν προβάτων; I am the door of the sheep. Indeed the event of this examination tends so strongly to corroborate this conjecture of mine, that I rather think it will be considered as having every probability on its side. " On hearing this," (*i. e.* the answer of James,) continues Hegesippus, " some of them were prevailed on to believe in Jesus as the true Christ." Now if the answer of James had that effect on the Jews, as to persuade them to believe that Jesus was the Christ or Messiah,—it follows of necessity that he must have declared Jesus to be the author, or, in figurative language, the gate or the door of salvation.

XXIV. **Enmity of the foreign Jews excited against the Christians.** Moreover, not content with thus accumulating every possible injury on such of the harmless disciples of Christ as were to be found in Palestine, the high priest and rulers of the Jews dis- patched legates or missionaries into all the different provinces, for the purpose of animating their distant brethren with similar sentiments of jealousy and hatred towards the Christians, and

stirring them up to seek for every occasion of annoying and persecuting this inoffensive flock.(¹)   By what is recorded in the
Acts of the Apostles, and other ancient authorities, it appears
that the Jews, throughout every part of the world, discovered
the utmost readiness in obeying this call of their spiritual instructors and governors, and with one consent made it their endeavour, by various calumnies and infamous machinations, to
draw on the Christians the indignation and ill-will of the presidents, the magistrates, and the people at large.   The chief of all
the accusations wherewith the followers of Christ were loaded
by the malice of these their inveterate foes, was that of their
being enemies to the state, and conspirators against the imperial
majesty : in proof whereof, it was alleged that they regarded one
Jesus, a malefactor, who had been put to death by Pilate on very
sufficient grounds, as a monarch sent down to mankind from
above.   To this conduct are to be attributed the many complaints
that we meet with in the writings of the early Christians,
respecting the hatred and cruelty of the Jews, whom they represent as more inimical and malicious in their carriage towards
them than even the pagans themselves.(²)

(1) Frequent mention is made of this by the early Christian writers. See
Justin Martyr *Dial. cum Tryph.* p. 51, 52, 53, 318. edit. Jebb. It is also intimated at p. 109, that the Jews forbad their people even from speaking to the
Christians; and at p. 138. 207, that in their schools and synagogues, the followers of Christ were loaded by these infuriate persecutors with the direst curses
and imprecations: a circumstance of which we find mention also made by St.
Jerome and others. See also Eusebius *Comment. in Esaiam,* cap. xviii. p. 474 ;
in Montfaucon's *Nov. Collect. Patrum Græcor.* tom. ii.

(2) See the passages collected by J. A. Fabricius, in his *Lux Evangelii
toti Orbi exoriens,* cap. vi. § i. p. 121. See also *Epistola Smyrnensis Ecclesiæ
de Martyrio Polycarpi,* § xii, xiii. tom. ii.   *Patr. Apostol.* p. 199, 200.

[p. 97.]   XXV. **Overthrow of Jerusalem and the Jewish nation.**
An effectual check, however, was given to the insatiable rancour
with which the Jews thus persecuted the Christians, about the
seventieth year from our Lord's birth, when Divine Justice delivered up their land, their city, and their temple, to be laid waste and
overthrown, and even their name as a nation to be utterly blotted
out, by the Romans under Vespasian and his son Titus.   This
tremendous scene of carnage, ruin, and devastation, which had

been foretold by our Saviour himself, is very particularly described by the historian Josephus, who was present at the destruction of Jerusalem, and for the most part an eye-witness of all its attendant horrors. The cause which, beyond all others, may be considered as having more immediately contributed to bring down these heavy calamities on the Jewish nation, was the mal-administration of the Roman presidents, to whom the 'government of Palestine had been from time to time committed, and particularly of Gessius Florus, whose oppressive and vexatious conduct was every way calculated to exhaust the patience of this wretched and unfortunate people. Irritated and goaded by insults and severities, to which they saw no prospect of an end, they endeavoured to regain their former liberty ; but their efforts, instead of promoting the object they had in view, served only to accelerate their final ruin, by rendering them at one and the same time a prey to intestine faction and the Roman sword. In the course of a seven years' war there perished of this ill-fated people, according to Josephus, either by fire, the sword, famine, pestilence, or different kinds of punishments, no less a number than one million three hundred and thirty-seven thousand four hundred and ninety. In the fourth year of this memorable contest, the city of Jerusalem was taken, after a six months' siege, and the temple, contrary to the wish of the emperor Titus, consumed by fire. The buildings that escaped the ravages of the flames were afterwards pulled down and levelled with the ground. Throughout the whole history of the human race, we meet with but few, if any, instances of slaughter and devastation at all to be compared with this. In contemplating it, amongst various other things which present themselves to our notice as well deserving of the most serious attention, it is particularly worthy of remark that the Jews themselves, rather than the Romans, must be considered as the authors of that great and tremendous accumulation of evils which signalized this final desolation of the house of Israel.

XXVI. **The ten persecutions of the Christians.** About two years before the breaking out of this war between the Romans and the Jews, the Christians who dwelt at Rome were made subject to very unjust laws, and otherwise experienced the most severe and iniquitous treatment at the hands of the emperor Nero. His example was, in this respect, pretty uniformly copied after by

his successors, during three centuries; although their severity
was not always carried to the same extent: and hence the professors of Christianity had to endure a long series of dire afflictions, or, to use a more familiar term, persecutions, to which an
end was not put until the time of Constantine the Great. We
have been for ages in the habit of considering the number of
these persecutions as decidedly fixed at ten; but the early history
of Christianity does not appear by any means to warrant this.
[p. 98.] If it be meant to speak merely of such persecutions as
were particularly severe, and of general extent throughout the
empire, they certainly did not amount to ten; if, on the contrary,
the lesser ones, or such as may be termed provincial, are designed
to be included, it is equally clear that they exceeded that number.
The persons who first fixed the number at ten, certainly found
nothing on record to authorize their doing so; but were, as it
should seem, led away by a wish to make history in this respect,
accommodate itself to certain passages of Scripture, in which
they imagined it to be foretold that just so many persecutions
would befal the Christians.(')

(1) The notion of the Christians suffering exactly ten persecutions under
the different heathen emperors, is without doubt extremely ancient, and may
be traced back as far as to the fifth century. But notwithstanding this, I will
venture to incur the responsibility of assuring all lovers of truth, that it is
wholly built on popular error, without the least shadow of foundation. The
authors of it are indeed unknown; but thus far is certain, that they did not
derive this opinion from what was to be met with on record, but first of all
imbibed it from a mistaken interpretation of Scripture, and then obtruded it
on the world as a point of history. We have good authority for stating that,
in the fourth century, the number of Christian persecutions had not been exactly ascertained. Lactantius, in his book *de Mortibus Persequutorum*, enumerates only six. Eusebius, in his *Ecclesiastical History*, recounts the sufferings which the Christians had at various periods undergone; but he does not
take upon him to fix the times of persecution at any determinate number. It
may, however, in some measure be collected from what he says, that the
church had experienced nine such seasons of adversity. Sulpitius Severus, in
the fifth century, records the like number: but it appears that, at the time he
wrote, the notion of ten persecutions had begun to be entertained; for, after
enumerating nine that were passed, he gives the Christians to understand that
the tenth, which would be the final one, was not to be expected until the end
of the world. *Exinde*, says he, *tranquillis rebus pace perfruimur : neque ulterius
persequutionem fore credimus, nisi eam, quam sub fine jam sæculi Antichristus
exercebit. Etenim sacris vocibus decem plagis mundum afficiendum pronuntiatum*

est; ita quum jam novem fuerint, quæ superest ultima erit. *Histor. Sacr.* lib. ii. cap. xxxiii. p. 248, 249. ed. Clerici. Now it appears to me scarcely possible to conceive any thing that could more strongly support the position advanced by me in the commencement of this note than this passage does. The Christians of the fifth century, we see by it, had, from their interpretation of some passages of Scripture, (what those passages were Sulpitius does not mention,) been led to entertain a belief that the Christian commonwealth was destined to endure ten principal calamities; but the persecutions recorded in history, they found, did not amount to that number. In order, therefore, to uphold the authority of the sacred volume, they determined that the completion of the predicted number of persecutions was to be looked for in the coming of Antichrist, at the end of the world. But even in that same age, there appear to have been others of the Christians who, although they were equally confident in the persuasion that ten persecutions were predicted in Scripture, yet did not think that the afflictions to be expected from Antichrist were to be included in that number; and therefore endeavoured, by twisting and perverting the history of the Christian church previous to the time of Constantine the Great, to make it exhibit all ten of the calamitous periods which they conceived to be thus foretold in the sacred writings. For this we have the testimony of Augustine, in his work *de Civitate Dei,* lib. xviii. cap. lii. p. 404, 405, tom. [p. 99.] vii. opp. edit. Benedict. where, adverting to this subject, he declares that he can by no means assent to the opinion that only ten persecutions of the Christians are foretold in Scripture : *Proinde ne illud quidem temere puto esse dicendum, sive credendum, quod nonnullis visum est, vel videtur,* (this opinion, therefore, we see, was entertained merely by a few,) *non amplius ecclesiam passuram persecutiones usque ad tempus Antichristi, quam quot jam passa est, id est, decem, ut undecima, eademque novissima, sit ab Antichristo.* In these words Augustine points to the way in which the persecutions were computed, by those who maintained that the church had undergone ten previously to the time of Constantine, and which is similar to the modern mode of computation. With regard to its being correct or erroneous he delivers no opinion, but leaves the question entirely at rest. We are next put by him in possession of the particular part of Scripture on which this notion of the ten persecutions, antecedent to the time of Constantine, was grounded. *Plagas enim Egyptiorum quoniam decem fuerunt, antequam inde exire inciperet populus Dei, putant ad hunc intellectum esse referendas, ut novissima Antichristi persecutio similis videatur undecimæ plagæ, qua Ægyptii, dum hostiliter sequerentur Hebræos, in mari rubro, populo Dei per siccum transiente, perierunt.* We see here, then, the source from whence sprung the notion of the ten persecutions antecedent to the reign of Constantine ; and also the reason why the opinion of Sulpitius was rejected, and the last persecution under Antichrist excluded from that number. Some silly trifling Scriptural commentators of the day had taken it into their heads, that the ten plagues of Egypt were to be regarded as typical of the persecutions that the Christians were to undergo at the hands of the pagans ; and that Pharaoh bore the representation of Antichrist : and hence they were led to consider it as indisputable that ten persecutions of the Chris-

tians must have taken place prior to the reign of Constantine ; and that the
afflictions to be expected from Antichrist ought not to be reckoned as one of
those ten calamitous seasons which it was predicted in Scripture should befal
the church.   It is, however, a circumstance which must, we should presume,
in no small degree excite the reader's astonishment, that these sagacious commentators of Holy Writ should not have perceived that this exposition necessarily implies what it is utterly beyond the reach of belief to credit, namely,
that the Egyptians, and all those on whom the Almighty sent down the ten
dreadful scourges mentioned in Scripture, and particularly Pharaoh, with his
servants and soldiers, who were swallowed up in the Red Sea, were the typical representatives of the innocent and holy Christians, who were persecuted
by the Roman emperors.   For if the ten plagues, with which God afflicted
the Egyptians, are to be considered as typical of the first ten persecutions of
the church of Christ, it necessarily follows that the persons who endured
these plagues must have been the representatives of the early Christians : and
if the miserable overthrow and destruction of Pharaoh and his host is to be
understood as prefigurative of the direful visitation which good men are taught
to expect from Antichrist and his followers, we are equally constrained to
regard the Egyptian king and his army as representatives of the faithful adherents of our Lord, who are to endure the persecuting violence of this arch
[p. 100.] adversary to the cause of Christ.   Indeed, Augustine himself, although
he entertained no doubt but that the words of Scripture had a recondite
meaning attached to them, yet considered this interpretation as futile, and
built on no solid foundation.   *Sed ego,* says he, *illa re gesta in Egypto, istas
persecutiones prophetice significatas esse non arbitror : quamvis ab eis, qui hoc
putant, exquisite et ingeniose illa singula his singulis comparata videantur, non
prophetico spiritu sed conjectura mentis humanæ, quæ aliquando ad verum per-
venit, aliquando fallitur.*   But it should seem that Augustine was not acquainted with all the arguments by which the advocates for the opinion, that
the Christians had undergone ten persecutions, endeavoured to establish this
point, so repugnant to all history.   A principal argument of theirs, (and one
which, to confess the truth, has something specious in it,) was drawn from the
Apocalypse.   St. John sees a harlot sitting on a terrible beast, which had
seven heads and ten horns.   Rev. xvii. 1–10.   There is no question but that
this woman represents Rome ; and St. John expressly tells us, that the ten
horns of the beast signify ten kings.   Rev. xvii. 12.   The same inspired writer
adds, that these ten horns of the beast, or ten kings, should make war with
the Lamb, that is, Christ ; but that he should overcome them. v. 14.   This is
the prophecy which induced the ancient Christians to maintain that ten of the
Roman emperors, prior to Constantine, were at open enmity with the church ;
and to attempt to force on us, in direct opposition to all historic evidence, the
notion that the number of persecutions had been exactly ten.   Their way of
reasoning was this :—Since by the woman whom John saw is to be understood
Rome, and by the ten horns ten kings, there can be no doubt but that these
ten kings must be ten Roman emperors ; and since the wars of these ten kings
with the Lamb, that is, Christ, unquestionably signify their endeavours, by

means of laws and punishments, to extirpate the Christians, and entirely abolish their religion, it is evident that ten Roman emperors would oppress and persecute Christ in the persons of his disciples. But, said they, the successors of Constantine, who at present govern the Roman empire, are Christians: and it is not at all likely that their descendants should renounce the faith: those ten enemies of the Lamb or Christ must, therefore, have lived and made war on him before the reign of Constantine. Not permitting themselves to doubt of the accuracy of this mode of reasoning, it became at once their object so to manage the history of the church, previous to the reign of that emperor, as to make it exhibit the ten regal enemies of our Lord making war upon him, by ten persecutions of his faithful adherents. No one would ever have taken up the notion of the ten persecutions, had it not been for the ten plagues of Egypt recorded by Moses, and the ten horns of the beast mentioned by St. John. There are none who have assumed greater freedom in perverting ancient history than those who, without the requisite talents and information, have taken upon them to expound the sacred Oracles. In confirmation of what I have thus advanced, I will quote merely one passage from Gerhohus *de corrupto Ecclesiæ Statu*, a work published by Steph. Baluzius, in the fifth volume of his *Miscellanea*, p. 77. It is not indeed older than the [p. 101.] twelfth century, but it nevertheless puts us in possession of what was the opinion of prior ages. *Deinde reliqui leones a Nerone usque ad Diocletianum per decem universales persequutiones ita comederunt ac disperserunt gregem Domini, ut illa bestia decem cornibus terribilis Danieli præostensa jam singulis cornibus in singulis persecutionibus debachata, et sanguine sanctorum satiata sit, ultra quam dici possit.* There were some, however, as we learn from the following words of Gerhohus, who were of opinion that by the ten horns of the beast, we ought rather to understand the ten years of the Diocletian persecution: *Et quia ultima persequutione, Diocletiano et Maximiano tyrannizantibus, decem annis vexata est ecclesia, sive in decem universalibus persecutionibus, sive in decem annis ultimæ persecutionis intelligas decem cornua crudelis bestiæ, Romani videlicet imperii, gratanter accipe humiliationem ex tunc illius bestiæ, ita ut foenum quasi bos comedens et præsepe Domini sui agnoscens rore cæli tincta sit, baptizato videlicet Constantino imperatore.*

XXVII. Causes of these persecutions. As the Romans allowed to every citizen the free exercise of his own reason and judgement in regard to matters of a divine nature, and never molested the Jews on account of their religion, it has afforded grounds for surprise to many that they should have discovered a temper so inhuman and implacable in their carriage towards the Christians, a set of men of the most harmless inoffensive character, who never harboured in their minds a wish or thought inimical to the welfare of the state.(') But it is not very difficult to account for this. The Romans, it is true, extended their toleration to every kind of religion, from whence no danger to the public safety was to be apprehended ; but, at the same time, they would not endure that any one should deride or attempt to explode the religion of the state, or that which had the support of the laws: for there existed between the government and religion of the Romans such an intimate connection and dependence on each other, that whoever attacked or endeavoured to undermine the latter, could not of necessity appear to them otherwise than as hostile to the former, and inimical to the dignity of the state. On this account all such of the Jews as lived intermixed amongst the Romans, were particularly cautious in whatever they said or did, to avoid every thing which could be construed into a reflection on the religion or gods of the commonwealth. But the conduct of the Christians was directly the reverse of this: for, laying aside every sort of fear, they strenuously endeavoured to make the Romans renounce their vain and silly superstitions, and were continually urging the citizens to give up and abolish those sacred rites, on the observance of which, as we above remarked, the welfare and dignity of the commonwealth were thought so much to depend. Under these circumstances, it could not well otherwise happen but that the Christians, although they intended no ill whatever to the state, yet should come to be looked upon and treated as enemies of the Roman government.

(1) As every thing which can tend to excite suspicion or doubt in the minds of the ignorant, respecting the divine origin of the Christian religion, is eagerly caught at by those of the present day who undertake to disprove it, it is not to be wondered at that they should endeavour to avail themselves of the anti-[p. 102.] pathy of the Romans to Christianity, in order to throw a shade over its excellence, and discredit its authority. The wisest people, say they, that ever existed upon the face of the earth,—a people in the highest degree distinguished for their humanity, and who were never known in any other instance to molest any mortal whatever on account of his religion, yet pronounced Christianity to be incompatible with the public welfare, and refused it toleration. It will therefore not admit of a doubt, but that there must have been something vicious and highly censurable in the conduct and character of the early Christians, which, if not repressed, threatened eminently to endanger the prosperity and safety of the commonwealth. But as nothing can be more ill-founded than these surmises, they serve only to expose the ignorance of those by whom they are suggested, and to betray their utter want of acquaintance with the ancient Roman history.

XXVIII. **Causes of these persecutions.** It yielded a still further ground for offence, that the Christians did not content themselves with entering the lists against the religion of the Romans only, but also boldly asserted the falsehood and insufficiency of every other religious system in the world; and contended that eternal salvation was to be obtained in no other way than by laying hold on Christ. For the inference which the Romans drew from this was, that the members of this sect were not only immeasurably arrogant and supercilious in their pretensions, but were also filled with hatred towards all those who differed from them in opinion, and were consequently to be regarded as persons likely to sow amongst the people the most inveterate discord, and to occasion disturbances of a very serious nature to the state. For it was of old recognised as a maxim of civil polity, that a sect which not only believes those of every other persuasion to be in the wrong, but also considers every other species of religious culture, except that which its own tenets prescribe, as impious and offensive in the sight of heaven, is ever prone to excite public commotions, and give annoyance to those who do not belong to it. And I have no doubt but that we ought to understand Tacitus as intending to reproach the Christians with cherishing a disposition of this sort, when he represents them as *odii generis humani convictos:* and in like manner, Suetonius, when he attributes to them *maleficam superstitionem.*(¹)

(1) Tacitus, *Annal.* lib. xv. cap. xxxv. Suetonius *in Nerone,* cap. xvi. Some very eminent men have imagined that these historians did not properly distinguish between Jews and Christians, but hastily ascribed to the latter the same *hostile odium adversus omnes alios,* which was not without reason attributed to the former. But it should seem to have escaped those who entertain this opinion, that Tacitus and Suetonius are, in the passages above referred to, evidently speaking of a crime peculiar to the Christians,—a crime of so heinous a nature as to deserve capital punishment. Whatever there might be in the Jews of the *humani generis odium,* it is certain that it did not appear to the Romans in this highly criminal light, or of such a dangerous nature as to be termed *exitiabilis superstitio,* which is the expression made use of by Tacitus in regard to the Christians, since they were freely permitted to take up their abode, and openly to exercise their religion in any part of the empire. It may also be noticed, that Suetonius expressly terms the religion of the Christians *nova superstitio,* a modern superstition; by which he clearly distinguishes them from the Jews, whose religion was well known to be of no recent origin.

XXIX. Causes of these persecutions. Whilst these **[p. 103.]**

considerations had the effect of stirring up the emperors, the senate, the presidents, and the magistrates, to endeavour, as far as in them lay, to arrest the progress of Christianity, by means of the most rigorous laws and punishments; there were others which operated no less powerfully on the people, and particularly on the pagan priesthood, so as to cause them to require of their governors and magistrates, with an importunity approaching even to violence, that the Christians, wherever they could be found, should be put to death: and it not unfrequently happened that, by their clamours and threats, they extorted a compliance with their demands, even from those who would never otherwise have been prevailed on to imbrue their hands in the blood of the just. The Jews were possessed of a splendid temple; the ceremonies attending their religious rites were grand and magnificent; they offered up sacrifices, and had a supreme pontiff, with a numerous priesthood; and their mode of worship was, in several other respects, of a showy and an attractive nature: hence the Jewish religion appeared to the heathens as differing in no very material degree from those of other nations; and the God of the Hebrews was looked upon by them as the provincial deity, who had the immediate and especial care and governance of that particular people. But the Christian mode of worship was accompanied with none of those appendages which constituted the apparent affinity between the Jewish religion and those of other nations: ignorant men, therefore, like the pagan multitude, who imagined that the worship acceptable to the gods consisted in the observance of ceremonies and festivals, and the offering up of victims, at once concluded that the Christians paid no sort of homage to Heaven, and consequently believed neither in a Supreme Being, nor a Providence. When the minds of the people at large had received an impression of this sort, it could scarcely happen but that the most virulent rage for persecution should ensue: for it was inculcated no less strongly by the Roman laws than by those of other states, that men who disbelieved the existence of the gods, ought to be regarded as pests of the human race, the toleration of whom might endanger the state, and be productive of the highest detriment to the best interests of society.

XXX. **Causes of these persecutions.** But this was not all. Attached to the service of that host of deities which the Romans worshipped, both in public and private, there was an immense number of priests, augurs, soothsayers, and ministers of inferior order, who not only derived from it the means of living at their ease, with every luxury at command, but were also, from the sacred nature of the functions with which they were invested, sure to stand high in the estimation of the people, and to possess no inconsiderable degree of influence over them. When all these perceived that it was highly probable, or rather felt it to be morally certain, that if once the Christian religion should become predominant with the public, there would immediately be an end to all the emoluments, honours, and advantages, which they then enjoyed; a regard for their own interests naturally prompted them to endeavour, by every means in their power, to lessen the credit of the Christians, and to render them obnoxious to the people and the magistrates. Associated with these in their efforts to put down Christianity, there was an innumerable multitude of persons of various other descriptions, to whom the public superstitions were a source of no small profit; such as merchants who supplied the worshippers with frankincense and victims, and other requisites for sacrifice, architects, [p. 104.] vintners, gold and silver smiths, carpenters, statuaries, sculptors, players on the flute, harpers, and others; to all of whom the heathen polytheism, with its numerous temples, and long train of priests, and ministers, and ceremonies, and festivals, was a principal source of affluence and prosperity.(')

(1) Acts, xix. 24. An idea of the vast detriment which the interests of these priests and merchants experienced from the rapid spread of Christianity, may be collected from this one passage in Pliny's epistles, lib. x. epist. 97. p. 458. *Satis constat prope jam desolata templa cœpisse celebrari——passimque venire victimas, quarum adhuc rarissimus emptor inveniebatur.*

XXXI. **Calumnies propagated respecting the Christians.** From the enmity of the Jews, and of persons like these, proceeded those horrible calumnies, with which it is well known that the character of the first Christians was very generally aspersed, and which occasioned them to be considered by the magistrates and the people at large as entirely undeserving either of benevolence or pity. Nor is it at all to be wondered at that the slanders to which we allude should, until they were refuted, have been productive of this effect; for the crimes thus falsely imputed to the Christians

were of the foulest and most disgusting complexion. Amongst
other heinous offences whereof they were accused, it was asserted
that even their solemn religious assemblies were polluted by the
commission of the most detestable of crimes: that in the place of
the Deity they worshipped an ass ; that they paid divine honours
to their priests,* in a way in which it would be an unpardonable
violation of decency even to name ; that they were active in promoting sedition, and desirous of bringing about revolutions in the
state.(¹)   And with so much art and address were these malignant falsehoods framed and supported, that they obtained credit
even with those who filled the highest stations in the government.
But what contributed as much as anything to inflame the passions
of the lower orders, and stir them up to acts of revenge, was
the malicious artifice of their priests, in attributing every thing
which could be regarded in the light of a national or general
affliction, to the toleration of the Christian religion : for whether
it were war, or tempest, or pestilence, or any other species of
calamity which befel the public, they equally availed themselves of it,   and assiduously inculcated on the minds of the
people that such was the method in which the gods avenged
themselves of the insults offered them by the Christians.   Instructed thus from what they deemed infallible authority, that
such was the origin and cause of their sufferings, the credulous
multitude thought of nothing but revenge, and demanded of
their magistrates, with the most imperious clamour, the extirpa-
tion of a sect so utterly hateful and pernicious.(²)

(1) The reader who wishes to pursue this topic further, may consult a work,
written by Christ. Kortholt, expressly on the subject of these calumnies, and
entituled, *Paganus Obtrectator, seu de Calumniis Gentilium in Christianos,*
Kilon. 1698, in 4to. ; as also the treatise of Jo. Jac. Huldric, *de Calumniis
Gentilium in Christianos,* Tigur. 1744, in 8vo. : the materials for both of which
were drawn from the Apologies of the early Christians, and other ancient authorities.

(2) See Arnobius *adversus Gentes,* and also the various other writers of the
first ages, who came forward on behalf of the Christians, and defended them
against all these malignant aspersions of their adversaries.

[p. 105.]   XXXII. Martyrs and confessors. Those belonging to
the Christian commonwealth who, during this critical situation

* The original Latin is: *Et pudenda sacerdotum suorum* divinis *honoribus affi-
cere.*—Editor.

of its affairs, fell victims to their piety, and whose constancy in the cause of their divine Master even death itself under a variety of terrific forms had not been able to shake,[1] were thenceforward denominated *martyrs:* an appellation borrowed from the sacred writings, Heb. xi. 39. xii. i. and emphatically applied to these illustrious *witnesses* of the divinity of the Christian religion, in consequence of their having sealed their testimony with their blood. Those who had never been called upon to give this last severe proof of their faith and sincerity, but had nevertheless, at the peril of their lives, and with the hazard of honour, fortune, and every other worldly consideration, made open profession of their belief in Christ in the face of the heathen tribunals, were distinguished by the title of *confessors.* The authority and respect which holy men of either of these descriptions enjoyed amongst their brethren during life, and the veneration in which their memory was afterwards held by the Christians of their own age, were such as almost surpass belief.[2] As time advanced, this reverence for the characters of both martyrs and confessors increased; and being seconded by various opinions respecting these victims of persecution, of an inspiriting nature indeed, but which appear to have been by far too hastily adopted, it had the effect of stimulating others to make equal sacrifices in the cause of Christ, and for his sake to encounter the hazard of a cruel and ignominious death with the utmost readiness and fortitude, and to meet this most severe of human punishments in all its terrors, without the least reluctance or dismay. By degrees, however, it degenerated into a pernicious kind of superstition, and becoming a source of corruptions in the true religion, was eventually productive of no small detriment to the interests of Christianity.

(1) **Respecting** the various kinds of punishment and suffering which the martyrs were made to undergo, the reader may consult a most elegantly printed little work of Ant. Gallonius, the last edition of which is that of Antwerp, 1668, 12mo. A work on the same subject was also published by Casp. Sagittarius at Jena, in 1673, in 4to. But in both of these works there is much that cannot be relied upon; for as to those accounts which have come down to us under the title of *Acta Martyrum,* or " the Acts of the Martyrs," their authority is certainly for the most part of a very questionable nature: indeed, speaking generally, it might be coming nearer to the truth, perhaps, were we to say that they are entitled to no sort of credit whatever.

(2) Both martyrs and confessors were looked upon as being full of the Holy Spirit, and as acting under an immediate divine inspiration. Whatever they said, therefore, was considered as proceeding from the oracles of God; whatever, during their imprisonment, they required or wished to have done, was regarded in the light of a divine command—to disobey which would be the very height of impiety; and whatever they did was accounted as nothing less than the act of God himself, with whose Spirit they were conceived to be filled. Whatever might have been the sins and offences of the martyrs, it was imagined that they were all atoned for and washed away by their own blood, not by that of Christ. (Vid. Clemens Alexandr. *Stromat.* lib. iv. p. 596.) Being thus restored to a state of absolute purity and innocence, it was conceived that they were taken directly up into heaven, and admitted to a share in the divine councils and administration; that they sat as judges with God, enjoying the highest marks of his favour, and possessing influence sufficient to obtain from him whatever they might make the object of their prayers. Annual festivals were appointed in commemoration of their deaths, their characters were made the theme of public eulogies, monuments were charged with transmitting of their names and acts to posterity, and various other distinguished honours were paid to their memories. Those who had acquired the title of confessors were maintained at the public expense, and were on every occasion treated with the utmost reverence. The interests and concerns of the different religious assemblies to which they belonged were, for the most part, consigned to their care and management:—insomuch, indeed, that they might almost be termed the very souls of their respective churches. Whenever the office of bishop or presbyter became vacant, they were called to it as a matter of right, in preference to every one else, although there might be others superior to them in point of talents and abilities. Out of the exceedingly high opinion that was entertained of the sanctity and exalted character of the martyrs, at length sprung up the notion that their reliques possessed a divine virtue, [p. 106.] efficacious in counteracting or remedying any ills to which either our souls or bodies may be exposed. From the same source arose the practice of imploring their assistance and intercession in cases of doubt or adversity, as also that of erecting statues to their memory, and paying to these images divine worship; in fine, to such an height of vicious excess was this veneration for the martyrs carried, that the Christians came at last to manifest their reverence for these champions of the faith by honours nearly similar to those which the heathens of old were accustomed to pay to their demi-gods and heroes.

XXXIII. **Multitude of martyrs.** That the number of those who suffered death in the cause of Christ, during the different persecutions to which the church was exposed for upwards of three centuries, so far from being small, was, on the contrary, very considerable, is a fact that stands supported by the weightiest and most positive evidence. There can, however, at the same time, be no doubt but that many of those whose names are to be found in the immense army of martyrs, which both the Greek and Roman churches laud and worship, might with very great propriety be struck out of the list. To be at once convinced of this, we need only be apprised that the governors and magistrates did not direct their severity promiscuously against the great body of Christians at large, but selected as objects of capital punishment merely such of them as filled the office of bishop or presbyter, or held some other station of rank and consequence in the church, or who had displayed a more than ordinary zeal for the propagation of the Christian faith, or were distinguished for their wealth and dignity.(¹) As for those of a lower order in the church, or of an inferior condition in life, although they might be occasionally imprisoned and called to an account, they were, for the most part, considered by the civil power as beneath notice, and might, without any danger to themselves, be present at the last sad scene of their brethren's sufferings. Whenever, therefore, a Christian of either of the descriptions above noticed was thrown into prison, the deacons and Christians of common rank found nothing to prevent them from visiting him, and otherwise ministering, as far as in them lay, to his assistance and comfort, or finally from accompanying him, after his condemnation, to the place of punishment.(²)

(1) Polycarp. *Martyrium*, § xii. *Acta Fructuosi, in* Ruinarti *Actis Martyrum sinceris*, p. 219. *Cypriani, Epist.* v. xiv. p. 10. 23. edit. Benedict. et plur. al.

(2) Lucian. *in Peregrin.* tom. ii. opp. p. 566. edit. Grævii. Cypriani *Epist.* ii. iv. p. 8, 9. If this statement of the fact be allowed to have its due weight, it must, I think, operate considerably towards placing the celebrated controversy respecting the number of martyrs in a proper light, and thus be highly instrumental in bringing it to a conclusion. That but few, comparatively speaking, suffered death for the cause of Christ, was, as is well known, a favourite position with the famous Hen. Dodwell, a man eminent for his learning and extensive reading, but, as it should seem, headstrong, and apt to run into extremes. The arguments by which he endeavoured to establish it are to be found in the eleventh of his *Dissertationes Cyprianicæ.* This opinion has also been embraced by many other celebrated literary characters, though not on the same grounds. On the other hand, there are several authors who have entered the lists on the opposite side, strenuously and at much length maintaining that the number of the martyrs was very great. Of these, Theod. Ruinart may be considered as taking the lead, in his Preface to the *Acta Martyrum sincera et selecta.* By abating somewhat on either side of the question, we might probably

[p. 107.] arrive pretty near the truth. Were Dodwell's position to be so far modified, as to assert merely that the number of martyrs was considerably less than
is commonly supposed, it must command the ready assent of every one who,
in making up his mind on the subject, has not suffered his judgment to be
misled by popular traditions and idle stories, such as for the most part constitute what are termed the Acts of the Martyrs, but formed his opinion from the
evidence contained in monuments of indisputable credit. On the other hand,
it should seem that the adversaries of Dodwell might be very well able to
substantiate their argument, could they be prevailed on to reduce it simply to
this, that the number of the martyrs was certainly much greater than Dodwell
could ever be brought to allow.

XXXIV. **The Neronian persecution.** Foremost in the rank of
those emperors, on whom the church looks back with horror as
her persecutors, stands Nero, a prince whose conduct towards the
Christians admits of no palliation, but was to the last degree unprincipled and inhuman. The dreadful persecution which took
place by order of this tyrant, commenced at Rome about the
middle of November, in the year of our Lord 64.(¹) As a pretext for his cruelty, Nero did not, according to Tacitus,(²) bring
forward any accusation against the Christians on account of their
religion, but imputed to them the commission of a most heinous
crime against the public. For having himself, by way of sport,
caused some houses to be set on fire, and thus kindled a con-
flagration, by which great part of the city of Rome was destroyed,
he, in order to divert the tide of popular indignation from its
proper channel, denounced the Christians as the authors of this
public calamity, and displayed the utmost eagerness in directing
against them all the vengeance of the state; putting them to
death without mercy, and even making a jest of their torments.
Amongst other horrible cruelties exercised on them by his command, they were wrapped in pitched garments, and, being
fastened to stakes, were lighted up as torches to dispel the darkness of the night; their punishment being thus made to bear
somewhat of an analogy to the crime whereof they were accused.
According to some ancient authorities, both St. Peter and St.
Paul suffered martyrdom under this first persecution ; the former
being crucified invertedly ; the latter beheaded : but this has been
much questioned by subsequent writers, who find a difficulty in
reconciling it with chronology.(³) Of any of the other victims
of Nero's cruelty no memorial is left us whatever ; none even of

their names having escaped the obliterating hand of time : for as to
what is told us by the people of Milan, as well as those of Lucca,
Pisa, Aquileia, Ravenna, and other cities of Italy and Spain, about
their patron saints having been put to death under the Neronian
persecution, it can obtain but little credit with any one of the
least intelligence, since it stands altogether unsupported by any
evidence of weight or authority.   Clement of Alexandria says,
that St. Peter's wife was slain before her husband ;(⁴) but even
this is by no means certain.   This dreadful persecution ceased
but with the death of Nero.   The empire, it is well known, was
not delivered from the tyranny of this monster until the year 68,
when he put an end to his own life : it appears, therefore, that
the Christians must, in this first instance, have been exposed to
every species of insult and outrage, under sanction of the imperial
authority, for a period of no less than four years.

(1) This has been clearly proved by Al. de Vignoles, in two dissertations
de Causa et Initio Persequutionis Neronianæ, which are to be found in Masson's
Histoire critique de la Republique des Lettres, tom. viii. p. 74. 117. and tom. ix.
p. 172. 186.   See also Nicol. Toinard. *ad Lactant. de Mortibus Persequutorum,*
p. 398. ed. Du Fresnoy.

(2) *Annal.* lib. xv. cap. xxxviii.   [p. 108.]

(3) Tillemont. *Histoire des Empereurs,* tom. i. p. 564.   Phil. Baratier, *de
Successione Romanor. Pontificum,* cap. v. p. 60.

(4) *Stromat.* lib. vii. p. 869. ed. Potter.

XXXV. **Limits of the Neronian persecution.** Ancient authors
leave us in much doubt as to the extent of this persecution ; so
that we cannot well say whether Nero made it his object to extirpate the Christians from every part of the empire, or whether his
severity was limited so as for it to fall merely by way of punishment on those who, from their residence at Rome, might be considered as immediately implicated in the crime of setting fire to
the city.   Hence it has arisen that although the learned in
general favour the former opinion, yet we meet with several very
eminent men who propend towards the latter.   Those who will
be at the pains to compare the arguments that are urged on both
sides must at once perceive that there is no possibility of setting
the question so completely at rest, as to leave no room for hesitation or doubt on the subject ; since if the famous Spanish inscription, which there is every reason to consider as a forgery, be

rejected, there is nothing like positive testimony to be brought forward by either party. The weight of probability, however, as well as of argument, is certainly in favour of the more common opinion of the two.(')

(1) According to Lactantius, (*Institut. Divinar.* lib. v. cap. xi. p. 578. ed. Walch.) a collection of all the edicts, published by the different emperors against the Christians, was formerly got together by one Domitius, a celebrated Roman lawyer, and given to the public in a work of his, *de Officio Proconsulis.* If this book were now extant, it would throw considerable light on the general history of the afflictions and calamities to which the early Christians were exposed, and enable us at once to determine this question respecting the extent of the Neronian persecution. But since this work has been for a long time lost beyond the hope of recovery, we have no where now to seek for illustration as to many points, except in conjecture. The first writer that I know of, who took upon him to controvert the commonly received opinion respecting the persecution of the Christians by Nero, was that most eminently learned and ingenious civilian Franc. Balduin, who, in his *Comment. ad Edicta Imperatorum in Christianos,* p. 27, 28. edit. Gundling. maintains that no laws were enacted against the Christians before the time of Trajan ; which, if it could be by any means ascertained for a fact, must at once place it beyond all doubt that Nero's severity was directed merely against the Christians of Rome. Next to him may be reckoned Jo. Launois, who, in the dissertation which he published in defence of a passage in Sulpitius Severus, respecting the first martyrs of Gaul, § i. p. 139, 140. tom. ii. p. i. opp. by way of supporting the opinion there given concerning the first introduction and progress of Christianity in that country, denies that the Neronian persecution extended itself to the provinces. Nearer to our own times, this opinion has been still more ably and at large defended by Hen. Dodwell, in the eleventh of his *Dissertationes Cyprianicœ.* § xiii. p. 59.; and many others, who have since exerted themselves in purging ecclesiastical history of its fables and absurdities, have followed pretty nearly in the same path. Of all the arguments which the writers on this side of the question bring forward, the principal and most cogent one is that which they deduce from the cause which, it is acknowledged [p. 109.] on all hands, gave rise to this persecution. Nero, say they, did not deliver over the Christians to punishment on account of their religion, but in consequence of the crime which he falsely imputed to them of setting fire to the city. But it could never be objected to those of the Christians who lived in distant provinces, and had no connection with Rome, that they had any share in an offence like this; and therefore it is most reasonable to conclude that the vengeance of the public was in no shape directed against them. As to any other reasons that have been adduced in support of this opinion, I feel no hesitation in saying that they are such as have but little weight or certainty in them, and are very easily to be refuted. And even in regard to that argument which I have just noticed as being the principal one that is brought forward on this side of the question, so far is it from appearing to me at all

conclusive, that I rather think those on the opposite side might with equal propriety give a turn to it in their own favour. For it is incredible, they might urge, that the tyrant should permit the brethren and associates of men, who were the reputed authors of so great a calamity at Rome, to continue unmolested, though living at a distance. The public might very naturally feel apprehensive that the Christians in the different provinces were actuated by similar views, and meditated the same attempts as were imputed to those at Rome; and it was, therefore, no more than what the common safety appeared to demand, that the emperor should direct his severity generally against the whole body of those who professed a religion so dangerous and pregnant with destruction. The arguments of those who maintain that the Neronian persecution extended throughout the whole of the empire, possess greater force than those which are adduced on the opposite side; yet they are not so determinate, but that there are some exceptions which may very properly be taken to them. Lactantius, (*de Mortibus Persequutor*, c. 2,) it is urged, says, that it was superstition, or a regard for the religion of his ancestors, which prompted Nero *ad excidendum cæleste templum prosilire*. But to this the advocates for the opposite opinion may well object, that surely, as to this point, more reliance is to be placed on the testimony of Tacitus, who was a more ancient writer than Lactantius, and doubtless by far better acquainted with Roman affairs than he could possibly be. And indeed this superiority in the testimony of Tacitus over that of Lactantius was long since contended for by Alphons. de Vignoles, in an admirable dissertation, which is to be found in Masson's *Histoire critique de la Republique des Lettres*, tom. ix. p. 172. An inscription is next brought forward, which it is pretended was found somewhere in Portugal or Spain, and of which a copy (after Schott and Metellus) is given by Gruter, in his *Inscription. Romanar. Corpus*, tom. 1. p. ccxxxviii. n. 9. Its purport is to extol Nero, in the first place, on account of his freeing the province from robbers; and, in the next place, *ob eandem provinciam his qui novam generi humano superstitionem inculcabant purgatam.* Now if this inscription had come to light through a channel that admitted of no suspicion, it must at once be received as a proof that Nero's persecution of the Christians extended itself to the provinces: for it is clear from a passage in Suetonius, (in *Nerone*, cap. xvi.) that *nova superstitio*, "the new or modern superstition," was the title by which the Romans were accustomed to refer to the Christian religion. But Scaliger and other great men after him have entertained considerable doubts as to the authenticity and authority of this monument, and, in my opinion, not without ample reason: for I may, without danger of contradiction from any, even of the most learned and intelligent of the Spanish writers themselves, state it for a fact that no Spaniard or Portuguese ever had the least glimpse of it. But had any thing like a genuine inscription of this nature ever been discovered, there can be no doubt that it would have been preserved with the utmost care, as a thing of the highest value and importance. I pass over the various other arguments on this side, which any one who may be inclined to examine them will find in the Preface to Ruinart's *Acta Martyrum sincera*, § iii. and will only, by way of conclusion, remark that in my opinion there is nothing which makes more strongly in favour of the general notion respecting [p. 110.] the Neronian persecution, than the disputation of Tertullian with those who endeavoured to disguise their own malice towards the Christians under the cloak of the imperial edicts. For at the time when Tertullian wrote his *Apology*, that is, towards the end of the second century, and before the emperor Severus had enacted any new laws against the Christians, the Roman magistrates were accustomed to reply to any who might come forward on behalf of the Christians, that in this respect nothing was left to their discretion ; for that however desirous they might feel to spare these unfortunate people, it was impossible for them to do so, since the laws were peremptory to the contrary. *Postremo,* says Tertullian, (*in Apologet.* cap. iv. p. 46. edit. Havercamp.) *legum obstruitur auctoritas adversus veritatem, ut aut nihil dicatur retractandum esse post leges, aut ingratis necessitas obsequii præferatur veritati.* This pretence Tertullian attacks with great eloquence, and exposes its weakness and fallacy by various arguments, of which the following is not one of the least forcible.—Those laws to which ye refer, as not permitting you to suffer the Christians to exist, were enacted by princes whose cruelty, impiety and mad fury, ye cannot but regard with detestation, namely, by those monsters of the human race, the emperors Nero and Domitian. Their successors in the government of the empire have all been too deeply impressed with the sentiments of justice and benevolence, to follow their example. Trajan revoked these laws in part, and others have suffered them to fall altogether into neglect. Doth it become you then, I would ask, you to whom we are taught to look up as to men distinguished for wisdom and juridical sagacity, to keep, alive and enforce laws which had for their authors the most unprincipled of mortals? *Quales ergo leges istæ, quas adversus nos soli exequuntur (exequi* is used by Tertullian in the same sense as *ferre* or *sancire*) *impii, injusti, turpes, vani, dementes : quas Trajanus ex parte frustratus est, vetando inquiri Christianos :* (the laws of Nero and Domitian must of course, therefore, have directed that the Christians should be prosecuted:) *quas nullus Hadrianus, quanquam curiositatum omnium explorator, nullus Vespasianus, quanquam Judæorum debellator, nullus Pius, nullus Verus impressit.*—Now if this statement of Tertullian be deserving of credit, and there is certainly no reason whatever to suspect its accuracy, there can be no doubt but that Nero as well as Domitian promulgated edicts against the Christians ; and if such edicts were promulgated, not a question can remain of their having been carried into effect throughout all the provinces. There are some other things which might be pointed out, in addition to what I have thus noticed; but, to confess the truth, it appears to me that nothing of any moment would thereby be added to the evidence already adduced.

XXXVI. **Domitian's persecution.** The persecution of the Christians, which had ceased on the death of Nero, was, towards the end of the. first century, revived by the emperor Domitian, who, taking, as it should seem, the cruelty of the former for his model, began about the year 94 or 95 to afflict the church of Christ afresh. As to the immediate cause of this second persecution, we have no express testimony on record : but if what Eusebius reports be true, (and his statement is, he tells us, grounded not only on ancient tradition, but also on the testimony of Hege-sippus, an author of great antiquity,) namely, that Domitian had ordered every descendant of the House of David to be [p. 111.] put to death; and that in consequence of this, the relations of Christ, who dwelt in Palestine, were called forward, in order that he might know who they were ;—I say, if this may be depended on, we are certainly warranted in concluding that it was the appre-hension of their being implicated in seditious conspiracies against his government that prompted this tyrant to aim at the extirpa-tion of the Christians.(¹) It was during this season of calamity to the church that St. John the apostle was banished to the island of Patmos, after having, as Tertullian and others report, come forth safe and uninjured from the midst of a cauldron of boiling oil, into which his enemies had caused him to be thrown.(²) The principal persons who are said to have suffered at this period, were Flavius Clemens, a consul, and Flavia Domitilla, who was either his niece or his wife. The former is stated to have been put to death, and the latter, to have been commanded to with-draw into the island Pandataria. They were both of them re-lated to the emperor.(³)—It is admitted on all sides that this per-secution was not of any long continuance. Ancient writers, how-ever, are not agreed as to the authority by which it was put an end to: some of them representing Domitian himself as having retracted the orders he gave for persecuting the Christians ; whilst others consider the revocation of them as the act of the senate, upon Domitian's death.(⁴)

(1) Vid. Euseb. *Histor. Eccles.* lib. iii. cap. xix. xx. p. 89. In the account there given, I see nothing whatever that can be deemed difficult of belief. From beginning to end, it has all the appearance of a simple unvarnished narrative. The fact, therefore, seems to have been, that some one, an enemy alike both to the Jews and the Christians, had suggested to the emperor that the Jews looked daily for a king to arise from amongst the posterity of David, who should give law to the whole earth ; that the Christians, in like manner, expected that Christ would soon return, and establish for himself a grand and extensive do-minion ; and that, consequently, both Christians and Jews were to be regarded with a jealous eye, as persons harbouring views dangerous to the state, and

only awaiting their opportunity to break out into open revolt. Insidious whis-
pers of this kind would naturally prompt the tyrant to order, as we are told he
did, that all the posterity of David should be sought after, and put to death;
and that measures should be taken to give an equally effective blow to any designs which might be entertained against him by the Christians. The subject
of the particular year in which this persecution commenced is learnedly discussed by Toinard, in his notes to Lactantius *de Mortibus Persequutorum*, p.
351. edit. Bauldrian.

(2) On this subject the reader may consult what I formerly wrote, in answer
to the venerable Heumann, in the first volume of my *Dissertationes ad Hist.
Ecclesiastic. pertinentes*, p. 497–546. I must confess that the account given by
Tertullian, and after him by Jerome and others, of St. John's being thrown
into a vessel of boiling oil, by command of Domitian, and of his miraculous
deliverance therefrom, appears to me to admit of some doubt. What if, by way
of solving the difficulty, we were to hazard a conjecture that the whole account
might be nothing more than a figure made use of by some one or other, in
order to convey a strong idea of the imminent peril to which St. John had been
exposed, and that Tertullian, instead of taking what was said in a metaphorical
sense, understood it *literally?* To use figures or metaphors of this kind, when
speaking of any one's life or fortune as having been exposed to considerable
danger or hazard, is a practice to which all the people of the east are peculiarly
prone : and we ourselves very commonly say of a man who has been saved
from imminent peril of his life, that he was plucked from the fire or the flames.
In this way some one, in allusion to the very narrow and unexpected escape
[p. 112.] which St. John had experienced, in having the punishment of death,
to which he had been sentenced, commuted for that of banishment, might perhaps say that he had, beyond all hope, got safe out of the burning oil. By a
person strongly disposed, as Tertullian certainly was, to catch at and magnify
every thing which had the appearance of a miracle, an expression of this sort
might very readily be misconceived, and, instead of being taken in a figurative
sense, be understood literally.

(3) Euseb. *Histor. Eccles.* lib. iii. cap. viii. *et in Chronic.*

(4) According to Hegesippus, (*apud Euseb. Histor. Eccles.* lib. iii. cap. xx.)
Domitian, on hearing that there were living in Palestine certain nephews of
that Judas who was called the brother of Christ, descendants of the royal house
of David, commanded them to be brought to Rome, and closely examined them
as to their descent, the extent of their property, and the nature of their expectations in regard to the future reign of Christ. These good and pious men, he
says, without hesitation, acknowledged to the emperor that they had sprung
from the stock of David ; but, at the same time, made it appear to him that their
condition in life was humble, and that they were destitute of every thing like
wealth ; and, finally, they told him that the future kingdom of Christ was not
expected to be of this world, but of heaven, and that it would not commence
until the end of all things here below. Domitian, it is stated, having satisfied
himself as to these points, and considering the men as objects unworthy to
excite apprehension, dismissed them to their homes, and published an edict,

forbidding any further persecution of the Christians in Palestine. In like manner Tertullian reports, (*Apologet.* cap. v. p. 61.) that Domitian, not being altogether deaf to the calls of humanity, at length relented of the violence into which he had suffered himself to be betrayed, and liberated all those whom he had either sent into banishment or imprisoned. Lactantius, on the contrary, in his work *de Mortibus Persequutorum,* cap. iii. states it to have been subsequently to the death of Domitian that peace was once more restored to the church. Xiphilin also, in the *Life of Nerva,* says that it was this prince and not Domitian who called back those that had been sent into banishment for their *heresy.* Orosius and some other writers of inferior authority might, but that I deem it unnecessary, be quoted to the same purport. This difference of testimony will at once be accounted for, if it be permitted us to suppose that Domitian might, some short time before his murder, have published an edict forbidding any further persecution of the Christians; but that his assassination followed too quick on this for the Christians in general to experience any material relaxation of their sufferings until after his death.

XXXVII. **Constitution and order of the church of Jerusalem.** Amidst all this distress and calamity, however, the Christian community had to exult in the most rapid extension of its limits; the labours of the apostles and of their companions and disciples being crowned with such success, that churches dedicated to Christ had by this time been established in nearly all the provinces of the empire. Since all these churches were constituted and formed after the model of that which was first planted at Jerusalem, a review of the constitution and regulations of this one church alone will enable us to form a tolerably accurate conception of the form and discipline of all these primitive Christian assemblies.—The Christians at Jerusalem, then, although they did not [p. 113.] secede from the public worship of the Jews, were yet accustomed to hold additional solemn assemblies of their own, for the purposes of devotion, in which, agreeably to apostolic institution, they joined in offering up general prayers, and in commemorating the death and passion of our Lord by partaking of the holy supper.(¹) It may be considered as not merely probable but certain, that the day of the week on which our Saviour arose from the dead, was expressly set apart for the holding of these solemn assemblies.(²) As to the place of these meetings, it should seem that at the first they were held in such of the private houses of the Christians, as had room adequate to the accommodation of any thing like a considerable number of persons. When the church, however, came to consist of many thousands of people, so that it was utterly impossible for them to assemble with any degree of convenience in one place, it is probable that the members distributed themselves into classes, or, as we should say in modern language, parishes, to each of which was assigned a separate place of meeting, for the purposes of divine worship.(²) The presidency or chief superintendence of the whole church rested with the apostles themselves. Next, under these, were certain men of approved faith and authority, who were distinguished by the Jewish appellation of presbyters or elders. They were no doubt appointed to their office by the apostles, with the consent of the people, and gave their counsel, voice, and assistance in the government of the church at large, or certain parts of it. A considerable portion of the members of this primitive church having to struggle with poverty and distress, their necessities were liberally supplied by the bounty of such of their brethren as were in better circumstances: indeed to such an extent did this spirit of charity prevail amongst the first Christians, that St. Luke represents them as having had all things in common.(⁴) The management and disposal of these contributions of the brethren, towards the relief of the necessitous, were at first entrusted to certain men selected by the apostles from amongst the Hebrews or indigenous Jews; but, it being complained of that these persons were guilty of partiality in the distribution of the alms, the church, by the direction of the apostles, appointed seven others from amongst the Greeks or foreigners, for the purpose of taking care that this branch of the church might for the future experience no similar kind of injury.(⁵) The power of enacting laws, of appointing teachers and ministers, and of determining controversies, was lodged in the people at large; nor did the apostles, although invested with divine authority, either resolve on or sanction any thing whatever without the knowlege and concurrence of the general body of Christians, of which the church was composed.(⁶)

(1) Unless I am altogether deceived, a distinct enumeration of all the different branches of divine worship used in the church of Jerusalem, is given us by St. Luke in Acts, ii. 42. His words are, ἦσαν δὲ προσκαρτεροῦντες, (1.) τῇ διδαχῇ τῶν Ἀποστόλων, (2.) καὶ τῇ κοινωνίᾳ, (3.) καὶ τῇ κλάσει τῦ ἄρτυ, (4.) καὶ ταῖς προσευχαῖς "And they continued steadfast in the apostles' doctrine, and fellowship, and in breaking of bread, and in prayers." Now, with the exception of that only which is termed κοινωνία, i. e. "communion or fellowship," it will, I think, readily be allowed by every one that the account here given refers di-

rectly to the manner in which the brethren at Jerusalem occupied themselves in their religious assemblies. In regard to what is termed communion [p. 114] or fellowship, it is not impossible indeed but that some may hesitate; but it appears to me, that since we find it thus inserted amongst the acts of the church collectively, propriety demands that we should understand it in a sense that may accord with the nature and object of such an assembly. For if the term is to be considered as referring merely to the exercise of a daily private duty, I can see no reason whatever for its being thus introduced to our notice, amongst the different branches of the public worship. We may regard St. Luke, therefore, I conceive, as presenting us, in the above-cited passage, with a sketch of the manner in which the Christians at Jerusalem employed themselves, when they met together for the purpose of joining in the worship of God. In the first place, one or other of the apostles delivered a sermon or doctrinal discourse, for the instruction and edification of the people present. Next followed the communion. The word κοινωνία, "communion," is used in Scripture, as is well known, in an especial sense for liberality towards the poor. See Rom. xv. 26. 2 Cor. viii. 4. ix. 13. Heb. xiii. 16. The apostolic exhortation, therefore, being finished, the brethren who were present, it seems, came forward with gifts or offerings, which they consecrated to God for the relief of the poor and such as were in need. This custom of bringing with them to their solemn assemblies gifts or offerings for the use of the community in general, but more especially the poor, and publicly presenting them previously to the celebration of the Lord's supper, is of the highest antiquity amongst the Christians, and one which uniformly prevailed in all the churches; and that this usage was founded on the practice of the original church at Jerusalem, will not admit of a doubt. The history of Ananias derives no inconsiderable degree of illustration from hence; whilst, on the other hand, the account which we have of that unfortunate man serves to throw light on the nature of the rite itself. The whole relation, as it is given by St. Luke in Acts, v. 1, et seq. tends, in my opinion, plainly to show that Ananias made a tender of his offering to the apostles publicly in the face of the whole assembled church. From what is said in verse 2, we may certainly infer, that when this transaction took place, the whole of the apostles were gathered together. But that the apostles were accustomed thus to meet together in one place, except it were in general assemblies of the church, is what, from its utter improbability, I am persuaded that no one will take upon him to assert. It should seem that a considerable number of other persons were likewise present; for, in verse 5, St. Luke says that great fear came on all who had heard what Peter said. Indeed, from verse 11, it may be collected that the affair took place in the presence of the whole, or at least a great part of the church. It appears that when these things happened, the apostles had near them οἱ νεώτεροι, certain "young men." Now I take it that these were not merely young men of the ordinary class, but ministers of the apostles and the church, through whom the apostolic mandates were communicated, and to whom it belonged, when the church assembled, to make the necessary arrangements, and provide the members of it with every requisite accommodation. For unless we understand these young men to have been of this description, I do not see how it can be accounted for that they alone should at once rise up, and taking up the dead bodies of Ananias and his wife, carry them out and bury them : but if we regard them as inferior ministers in the church, every difficulty is at once removed, and we see plainly the reason why, without waiting for any directions, they came forward of themselves and performed this melancholy duty. And that there must have been public ministers of this sort in the primitive church, no one who is apprized of its nature, and the form of the religious assemblies of the Christians of that age, can possibly entertain a doubt. Certain persons must ever have been necessary to perform such duties, as the keeping of the places of meeting clean and decent, arranging the tables and seats, handing and taking away the sacred volumes, providing the members, when celebrating the feasts of love, with every thing requisite, and clearing the tables at the end of these solemn repasts, with a [p. 115.] variety of other things that might be enumerated. These particulars, I think it must be allowed, tend manifestly to show that the attempt of Ananias to impose on the apostles was made in one of the solemn religious assemblies of the Christians at Jerusalem. It should seem, therefore, that the multitude being gathered together for the purposes of divine worship, and a sermon or instructive discourse having been addressed to them by St. Peter, or some other of the apostles, this wretched man, whose soul appears to have been at once the prey of avarice and ambition, coming forward with the rest, in order to give proof of his *κοινωνία*, "communion or fellowship," advanced to the apostles, and laid at their feet a part of the money for which he had sold a portion of land, accompanying this donative with a declaration that, being touched with compassion for the brethren who were in need, he had disposed of his patrimony to a purchaser, and now begged thus to tender the whole of what it sold for as an offering towards their relief. St. Luke, indeed, who was studious of brevity, records no such speech as having been made by Ananias; but that the man must have come forward with a declaration somewhat to the above purport, is manifest from the terms in which St. Peter's reproof to him is couched. For with what propriety could the apostle have upbraided him with the telling of a lie, unless he had openly professed that what he offered was the full price for which the land had been sold ? Greedy of reputation and honour, Ananias would fain have passed himself on the apostles and the church as a man overflowing with love and charity towards the brethren ; whereas his regard for them had nothing at all extraordinary in it. But although he could have entertained no doubt of the sacred nature of the apostle's character, he was not aware of their possessing the faculty of divination, [Lat. *res arcanas divinandi.*] It is unnecessary for me to state what befel him, in consequence of his audacious duplicity. The corpse being removed, it is probable that one or other of the apostles took occasion, from what had happened, to address the congregation present in the way of admonition. The feast of love and celebration of the Lord's supper doubtless followed. About three hours having elapsed, and the time being nearly arrived for the dismissing of the assembly, the wife of Ananias came in, for the purpose, as I conceive, of partaking in those general prayers with which it was customary for the public service to be concluded. This woman having had the effrontery to re-assert the flagrant untruth which her husband had told, was like him, by an instantaneous visitation, deprived of life. As for the reasons which caused her to absent herself from the early part of the public service, although I am persuaded that it might be possible for me to assign such as would appear by no means unlikely ones, I shall not enter into them in this place, as my doing so would occasion me to digress too widely from the subject which we have at present more immediately under consideration. In these solemn assemblies of the Christians, the κοινωνία, or charitable contribution towards the relief of the necessitous, was followed, according to St. Luke, by the "breaking of bread." The expression "to break bread," when it occurs in the Acts of the Apostles, is for the most part to be understood as signifying the celebration of the Lord's supper, in which bread was broken and distributed: we are not, however, to consider it as exclusively referring to this ordinance of our Saviour, but as also implying that feast of love, of which it was the customary practice of the Christians, even from the very first, always at the same time to partake. That these two things were thus associated together, even in the very earliest infancy of Christianity, is clear from what is said by St. Luke in Acts, ii. 46. For after having there told us that the brethren at Jerusalem continued daily in the breaking of bread at different houses, he immediately adds, that they " did eat their food together with joy and simplicity of heart;" μετελάμβανον τροφῆς ἐν ἀγαλλιάσει καὶ ἀφελότητι τῆς καρδίας. See also Acts, xx. 11. where the breaking of bread, or the celebration of the Lord's supper, is again clearly associated with a feast or repast of the Christians. It appears, therefore, that when, in compliance with our Saviour's injunction, the Christians would break bread together, they also partook of a repast in the nature of a supper. [p. 116.] Their meals of this sort were distinguished by an holy mirth, arising out of the love of Christ and of the brethren; but this hilarity had no connection whatever with anything like sensuality or intemperance. And this is what I understand St. Luke to mean by that simplicity of heart, with which he states the Christians to have eaten their food. For what are we to understand by a heart in a state of simplicity, but a heart altogether devoid of every sensual and depraved appetite? The service terminated with some general prayers, which appear to have been distinctly recited by one or other of the apostles or presbyters, and repeated by the whole congregation after him.

(2) It may, I think, unquestionably be taken for a fact, that the first day of the week, i. e. the day on which our blessed Saviour triumphantly burst the bonds of death, and arose from the grave, was expressly appointed by the apostles themselves, during their continuance at Jerusalem, for the holding of these general solemn assemblies of the Christians for the purposes of public worship. In Acts, xx. 7. we see the Christians of Troas assembling together on the first day after the Jewish Sabbath, in order to celebrate the Lord's supper and the feast of love, and St. Paul adressing them, when thus met, in a discourse of no inconsiderable length. For that by μίαν τῶν σαββάτων, the day on which this meeting is stated to have been held, was meant the day next immediately following the Jewish Sabbath, has been demonstrated by several learned writers

so clearly as to leave no room for dispute. Now who, I would ask, can entertain a doubt but that the Christians of Troas, in dedicating this day to divine worship, were guided by apostolic authority, and the practice of the church at Jerusalem, which it is well known that all the other Christian assemblies took for their model? or, who can believe that the apostle Paul, intimately acquainted as he must have been with the discipline of the church at Jerusalem, would have sanctioned the appointment of any other day for the public worship, than the one on which he knew that the rest of the apostles were accustomed to hold their solemn religious assemblies in that city?

(3) If I may give myself credit for any discernment at all, I am sure I plainly discern this, that the vast multitude of persons converted by the apostles to Christianity at Jerusalem must have been distributed into several companies or classes, and that each company or class had its own proper presbyters and ministers, as also its separate place of meeting for the purposes of religious worship. For let any one, who may find a difficulty in believing this, figure to himself a church composed of eight or ten thousand persons, and then reflect whether such a multitude of people could possibly have assembled together in one place, with any degree of convenience or advantage to themselves;—to say nothing of the very imminent danger to which they would necessarily on such occasions have been exposed, in a city teeming with hostility to the disciples of Christ, and in which any meeting together whatever of the Christians was severely denounced. Could it have been possible, let him ask himself, for them to have joined in the celebration of the Lord's supper, and the feast of love connected with it, with any sort of order or convenience? The more he shall reflect on this, the more apparent must, in my opinion, the impossibility of the thing become to him. Now if it be granted that the church at Jerusalem must of necessity have been classed or divided into several minor assemblies, it follows of course that over each of these assemblies there must have presided certain persons in the character of presbyters, in order to regulate the concerns of the meeting, and see that all things were conducted with propriety and prudence. For a flock without shepherds is sure to wander out of the way, and take the very road which leads to the ruin of its own interests and welfare. These things then being admitted, it appears to me that, divesting the subject of such particulars as may evidently be referred either to the wisdom or the cupidity of much more recent times, the origin of what we term *parishes* may, with every [p. 117.] sort of probability, be deduced from the arrangement and distribution of the primitive and parent church at Jerusalem. I do not know whether I may go so far as to say that I have the authority of St. Luke expressly on my side, when he says, in Acts, ii. 46. and v. 42. that the Christians at Jerusalem assembled together, κατ᾽ οἶκον, to break bread. The commentators in general conceive these words to indicate, that the Christians did not hold their meetings always in the same place, but sometimes in this house, sometimes in that, with a view to avoid, as far as possible, disturbance by the Jews. But for my own part, I cannot see any thing whatever that should prevent us from giving to the expression κατ᾽ οἶκον, the meaning of *in diversis domibus*, " in different houses;" and understanding the apostle in the same sense as if he had expressed himself

here as he has done in Acts, viii. 3. xx. 20. and written κατὰ τὰς οἴκας, which is the same as ἐν τοῖς ᾽οἴκοις. Indeed this latter sense is by far more suitable to the words than the former one, since it is certain that the singular number is most frequently put for the plural. In the ancient Vulgate, we find the expression taken in this sense; the translator not altogether unaptly rendering the Greek words κατ᾽ οἴκον by *circa domos.* Nor did it escape our countryman, the blessed Luther, that this was the way in which they ought to be understood; and he well translates them, " .Sin und ßer in den .Säufern." And it appears to me, that St. Luke is to be considered as speaking in allusion to these houses in which the brethren at Jerusalem were accustomed to assemble, when he states St. Paul, before his conversion, to have entered κατὰ τὰς οἴκας, "into the houses," and dragged away the Christians captive from thence. Acts, viii. 3. For I can by no means persuade myself, that Paul and his attendants burst into private houses of the citizens of Jerusalem, and dragged away from thence any men and women whom he might suspect of being Christians. Is it to be believed that in Jerusalem, a city at that time under the dominion of the Romans, any man would have been permitted to violate at pleasure the rights of peaceable citizens, who had never been convicted of apostacy from the religion of their ancestors? I conceive, therefore, that the houses, into which Paul thus entered were those in which the Christians were wont to hold their meetings, during the night season, for the purposes of divine worship; and that taking the opportunity, with the assistance of the servants of the high priest, to break in upon the brethren at the time of their being thus assembled, he laid hold of as many of them as were not able to make their escape, and put them in bonds, as offenders taken in the very act itself.

The sentiments which I have thus been led to entertain respecting the partition or distribution of the church at Jerusalem, occasion me to regard what St. Luke says, in Acts, xv. of the assembly, or, to use a more familiar term, the council of that church, convened in order to decide on the controversy that had arisen at Antioch, in a light somewhat different from that in which it is commonly viewed. If merely the words of the divine historian are to be taken into the account, we must indeed unavoidably conclude, as every commentator whom I had the opportunity hitherto of consulting has done, namely, that the whole multitude of Christians who dwelt at Jerusalem, met together and discussed the question proposed by the deputies of the church at Antioch. But if we bring this conclusion to the test of reason, the thing appears at once to be utterly incredible. For what house could there possibly have been in Jerusalem capable of containing such an immense number of persons? or, how could such a multitude have assembled together in one place, in a city swarming with enemies and informers, but under the greatest degree of dread, and at the utmost peril of their lives and every thing they might possess? I can, therefore, scarcely permit myself to doubt that this assembly or council consisted merely of the apostles and presbyters, and a certain number of select persons, to [p. 118.] whom the church had delegated its power and authority; and that by ᾽ὅλην τὴν ἐκκλησίαν, "the whole church," which St. Luke states, at verse 22, to have assented to the proposal of St. James, we ought to understand merely a certain part of it, which had been invested with the power and authority of determining the proposed question.

(4) There is an ancient opinion, (it is not, however, older than the fourth century,) that the same community of goods existed amongst the members of the church at Jerusalem, as did of old amongst the Essenes, and does at present amongst the monks. But the notion is utterly destitute of any thing like a solid foundation, and has no other support than merely the words of St. Luke, who, in Acts, ii. 44. iv. 32. says that the Christians had all things in common:—words which, however they may at first strike the ear, can certainly never of themselves justify any such conclusion; since an abundance of examples might be brought from ancient authors to prove that we may with the greatest propriety annex to them a very different sense, and consider them as implying a communion merely of the *use*, not of *possession*. Indeed, that such is the acceptation in which they ought to be taken, is manifest from the address of St. Peter to Ananias, (Acts, v. 4.) without recurring to other authority. The reader who may wish to pursue this subject further will find it more amply discussed in a particular treatise of mine, *de vera Natura Communionis Bonorum in Ecclesia Hierosolymitana*, which stands the first in the second volume of my *Dissertationes ad Historiam Ecclesiastic. pertinentes.*

(5) Respecting these seven men, to whom the care of the poor was committed by the church of Jerusalem, I cannot say that my sentiments altogether correspond with those which it should seem are entertained by the generality of people. From the very first rise of the church at Jerusalem, there were without question certain persons whose office it was to take care of the poor : it is not possible that the church could have been without them. Had the apostles taken upon themselves the management and distribution of the alms, there can be no doubt but that they would have dispensed them religiously, and without the least partiality ; nor would there have been any grounds afforded for those complaints of the foreign Jews against the natives, which gave rise to the appointment of the seven men. For who can possibly suppose that the apostles could have been either so inattentive or so regardless of their duty, as to give to the widows of Jews a preference to those of Greeks ? In Acts, vi. 1. the Greeks or foreign Jews are not represented as murmuring against the Apostles, on account of the improper distribution of the alms, but against the Hebrews or native Jews generally. It appears, therefore, (and it is a circumstance particularly necessary to be attended to,) that before those seven men were elected, there were certain persons at Jerusalem, appointed either, as is most likely, by the apostles alone, or otherwise by the suffrages of the people in general, to make distribution of the alms offered by the affluent for the relief of the necessitous : in short, there were deacons in point of fact, before there were any such by name. These ministers, however, having been selected from amongst the indigenous Jews, who in number far exceeded the foreign ones, it was found that they were not strictly impartial, but were apt to lean a little more than was right in favour of their fellow citizens, and those of their own country, and discovered a greater readiness in relieving the widows of native Jews than the others. The foreign Jews,

whom St. Luke terms Greeks, being much dissatisfied at this, and murmuring greatly against the Hebrews on account thereof, the apostles convoked the members of the church, and commanded them to nominate seven men of approved faith and integrity, to whom the management of the concerns of the poor might without apprehension be committed. The people com- [p. 119.] plied with these directions, and chose by their suffrages the appointed number of men; six of them being Jews by birth, and one a proselyte, of the name of Nicolaus. They then brought them to the apostles, who consecrated them by prayer and the laying on them their hands. These seven deacons, as we commonly call them, were all of them chosen from amongst the foreign Jews. This I think is sufficiently evident, from the circumstance of their names being all of them Greek ones: for the Jews of Palestine were not accustomed to adopt names for their children from the Greek, but from the Hebrew or Syriac languages. These circumstances considered, I cannot by any means bring myself to believe that these seven men were entrusted with the care of the whole of the poor at Jerusalem. For can any one suppose that the Hebrews would have consented that the relief of their own widows and poor should be thus committed to the discretion of the Jews of the foreign class? The native Jews would, in this case, have been liable to experience the same injustice from the foreign brethren, as the latter had to complain of, whilst the alms were at the disposal of the Hebrews; and instead, therefore, of at once striking at the root of the evil which they proposed to cure, the apostles would, by such an arrangement, have merely applied to it a very uncertain kind of remedy. Besides, the indigenous Jews made no complaints against those who had hitherto managed the concerns of the poor; and consequently there could be no necessity for their dismissal from office. It appears to me, therefore, clear beyond a doubt that those seven men were not invested with the care of the poor in general, but were appointed merely as curators of the widows and poor of the foreigners or Greeks; and that the others continued under the guardianship of those who, prior to the appointment of the seven, were entrusted with the superintendence and discretionary relief of the whole. Camp. Vitringa saw the matter evidently in this light, as is plain from his work *de Synagoga vetere*, lib. iii. part ii. cap. v. p. 928. In regard to what is urged in opposition to him by B. Just. Hen. B hmer, *Diss.* vii. *Juris Eccles. antiqui,* § xxii. p. 378. it is of very little weight indeed. In fine, I do not see how it is possible for any one to be of a different opinion from that which I thus state myself to have formed on this subject, unless he maintain either that there were no persons whose office it was to take care of the poor in the church at Jerusalem, prior to the appointment of these seven men,—or that, upon the election of the latter, the primitive curators or guardians of the poor were dismissed as persons unworthy of being any longer continued in the trust. But of these two positions, the one is utterly destitute of every sort of probability, and the other implies a disregard of the dictates of equity and fraternal love. As to the reason which caused the number of these men to be fixed at seven, I conceive that it is to be found in the state of the church at Jerusalem, at the time of their appointment. The Christians in that city, it strikes me, were most likely divided into seven classes; the members of each of these divisions having a separate place of assembly. It was therefore deemed expedient, I take it, that seven curators should be appointed, in order that every division might be furnished with an officer or superintendent of its own, whose immediate duty it should be to take care that the widows and the poor of the foreigners should come in for an equitable share of the alms and benefactions, and to see that due relief was administered according to the necessities of the different individuals. It appears to me impossible for any one to assign any more probable reason for the adoption of this number, unless perhaps he should pretend to find some sacred or mystical qualities in it; but the futility of any conjecture of this sort would be manifest on the slightest scrutiny. I cannot, therefore, help considering it as a mark of great superstitious weakness in some of the ancient churches, that they should have given their sanction to such a notion as that there should, in no case, be more or less than seven deacons appointed, lest the apostolic rule in this respect, [p. 120] (a rule which cannot be shown to exist any where but in fancy,) should be broken through or infringed: and I think that those had much more reason on their side who confined themselves to no particular number, but appointed as many deacons as the state and condition of the church appeared to require. But it is not impossible that the authority of St. Luke may be brought forward against me on this occasion, and I shall perhaps be told that he represents the whole church of Jerusalem as having been convened by the apostles, and the whole church as joining in the election of the seven men, (Acts, vi. 2. 5.); and that from hence it should seem reasonable to conclude that the tutelary powers with which these men were invested related not merely to a particular branch of the people, but to the multitude at large: for if the Greeks were alone to be benefited by their labours, the Greeks alone would have been the proper persons to make the appointment. But I cannot say that I perceive much force in this objection.—For not to notice that in many parts of Scripture the whole of a thing is mentioned, when only a part thereof is meant to be understood, it is evident that equity, no less than the critical situation of the church in those times, most urgently demanded that the Hebrews should not be excluded from being present at, and taking a part in, the whole of this transaction. For the Hebrews contributed in no less a degree than the Greeks towards the support of the fund, from whence the relief for the poor was drawn; and a separation pregnant with the greatest danger at that period might well have been apprehended, had the Greeks been ordered to treat of their concerns separately, and a set of public ministers been appointed, without the Hebrews being called to take a share in their election. That St. Luke does not absolutely give us this statement of the matter is a circumstance of no consequence whatever; since we know that the sacred penman contented himself with shortly touching on the leading points of the early history of the church, and left to his readers a very ample scope for filling up and perfecting, by means of meditation and conjecture, what they might thus receive from him under the form of a sketch or merely in outline.

Entertaining then these sentiments on the subject, I cannot but feel myself compelled to withhold my assent from many things which, in later times, have been contended for by several persons of no small weight and erudition, respecting these deacons of the church at Jerusalem. For the most part they maintain, that it was not a function of the ordinary kind with which these seven men were invested, but one of an extraordinary nature; that their office was not one which was common to the church in general, but exclusively appropriate to the church at Jerusalem; and that the deacons, therefore, of whom St. Paul in his epistles makes mention, must have been of a different order from those of Jerusalem. In support of this opinion they adduce the following reasons: 1st, It is urged that the appointment of the seven men at Jerusalem was rendered necessary by the communion of goods which prevailed in the church of that city; but that this kind of communion being unknown in the other Christian churches, there could be no occasion for their appointing any officers of a similar kind. But this reason, inasmuch as it is founded entirely on the ancient erroneous notion respecting the nature of the communion of goods in the church at Jerusalem, which may now, I think, be considered as wholly exploded, falls at once of itself to the ground. There was unquestionably the same community of goods in all the other early churches as in that of Jerusalem; and I have no hesitation in saying that whoever may have entertained the notion, that the individual possession or ownership of things was given up and renounced by the members of the church of that city, has suffered himself to be grossly imposed upon by monkish artifice. It is moreover most clearly manifest from St. Luke's account of the affair, that it was not a communion of goods which occasioned the appointment of these seven men, but the desire of preventing for the future any partiality in the administration of relief to the necessitous. Had no [p. 121.] such tendency to partiality found its way into the church at Jerusalem, a community of goods, even supposing it to have been adopted there, might have been very well regulated and administered without the superintendence of any such officers as these seven men. 2dly, They say that the deacons of whom St. Paul makes mention in his epistles, and still more particularly those who in after ages discharged the functions of deacons in the church, had not the care of the poor committed to them, but were occupied in duties of another nature; and that, therefore, they must have been of an order altogether different from the seven men in the church of Jerusalem. But the insufficiency of this reason also may, I think, be made appear without much difficulty. For if it were true, as these learned persons assert it to be, that neither the deacons alluded to by St. Paul, nor those of after ages, were entrusted with the care of the poor, it still would not amount to a proof that these deacons did not derive their origin from the appointment of the seven men in the church of Jerusalem. An abundance of instances might easily be brought forward, to prove that the titles of offices are frequently retained without the least alteration, although the duties attached to those offices may, from various causes, have gradually undergone a change. But in my opinion the fact was not such in reality, as it is thus assumed to have been: for although it is true that the deacons of after times had other duties assigned them to fulfil, yet in none of the churches were they altogether removed from the management and superintendence of the relief of the poor. As the riches of the church increased, the bishops contrived by degrees to draw into their own hands the more honourable and lucrative part of the charge; but as to such branches of it as had any thing of trouble or inconvenience connected with them, they willingly left them under the superintendence and management of the deacons. Amongst the Latins, the churches from whence the poor, the strangers, the widows, the old people, and the orphans, had the alms dealt out to them, and adjoining to which were houses or apartments in which the poor were maintained, were always of old denominated *diaconiæ*, (indeed the term is not even yet become obsolete,) and the persons who had the care of such churches and houses were always taken from the order of deacons. Vid. Lud. Anton. Muratori *Antiquitates Italicæ medii Ævi*, tom. iii. p. 571, et seq. Du Cange *in Glossar. Latin. med. Ævi voc. Diaconia, Diaconites, Diaconus*. At Rome, even down to our own times, we see the cardinal deacons, as they are called, have the care of churches of this kind, from the revenues of which the poor are furnished with subsistence, and to which there are attached certain houses for refection, and what are termed Hospitals. Add to this, that all the ancient churches were unanimous in referring back the origin of their deacons to the church of Jerusalem; and on this account the greater part of them, as is well known, would never consent that the number of them should be more than seven. But why should I multiply words? There must have been, as I have already shown, certain persons who acted as curators or guardians of the poor at Jerusalem, prior to the appointment of those seven men to that office; nor could any church in that early age, when it was most religiously provided that no brother or sister should want, in fact be without such. The thing speaks for itself; and with such an obstacle in his way, I conceive that scarcely any one will find it an easy matter to persuade himself that the function with which those seven men were invested was of an extraordinary nature, or that it ought to be regarded as having been by any means exclusively appropriate to the situation and circumstances of the church of Jerusalem. In saying this, however, I would be understood as disposed most readily to admit, that this office was not of divine origin, or instituted by our [p. 122.] Saviour himself: for St. Paul, in enumerating the offices that were of divine institution in the Christian church, 1 Cor. xii. 28. Ephes. iv. 11. makes no mention whatever of deacons, although in other places he points out what manner of persons it was fitting that they should be : a circumstance that I could wish to press on the attention of those who contend that Christ himself instituted the three orders of bishops, priests, and deacons; and that, therefore, such churches as have no deacons are to be regarded as defective in their constitution.

Just. Hen. Böhmer, an eminent and deservedly illustrious lawyer of our own times, has started a conjecture that the seven men above alluded to were presbyters of the church of Jerusalem. This notion he appears to have espoused, with a view to its yielding him assistance in proving that our modern spiritual teachers possess nothing in common with the presbyters of the primitive church, and that no distinctions were ever introduced by Christ and his apostles amongst either the teachers or the people. *Dissert. Juris Eccles. antiqui,* diss. vii. § xx. p. 373, et seq. Long before this, Bilson, bishop of Winchester, had endeavoured to establish a point, which, could it be ascertained for a fact, would strongly support the opinion of Bœhmer, namely, that under the denomination of presbyters, in the books of the New Testament, deacons are also included. See his work *on the perpetual Government of Christ's Church,* cap. x. p. 179, 180. London, 1611, in 4to. But amongst all the different passages which he cites in order to prove this, there is not a single one that can be said to yield him even a moderate degree of support. Dr. Gilbert Burnet, another English bishop, and one who has obtained for himself a most distinguished rank amongst the writers of our own age, appears disposed to place the seven men in question on a level nearly with the apostles themselves. The deacons of whom St. Paul makes mention, and for whom his instructions were designed, this prelate will not allow to have been either inferior ministers of the church, or curators of the poor, but contends that they were presbyters. See his *History of the Rights of Princes in the disposing of Ecclesiastical Benefices,* Pref. p. xiv. et seq. The reader will perceive that in this opinion also there is something nearly allied to that of Bœhmer. But it is evident that all these learned writers, as well as others, who reject the ancient notion respecting the seven men appointed by the church of Jerusalem, and endeavour to impose on us a new one of their own in its stead, do so merely with a view to the support of other opinions, which it is their object to establish. Thus Bœhmer, by converting the deacons of old into presbyters, would prove that our modern spiritual teachers bear no resemblance whatever to the presbyters of the primitive church. Bilson, a defender of episcopacy, found himself opposed by what St. Paul says in 1 Tim. v. 17.; and from which passage it has been usual to infer that it did not belong to all the presbyters of the primitive church to teach, but that some were appointed to see to its well ordering and government; and in conformity to this, we see the presbyterians, as they were called, in addition to their teaching presbyters, appoint others whom they term ruling or governing presbyters. But the episcopalians will not admit of any such presbyters as those of the latter kind; and therefore, by way of obviating the force of the passage above referred to, Bilson maintains, though without the least foundation, that by the term presbyters we ought in this place to understand St. Paul as meaning not only presbyters but deacons, and that those presbyters amongst the ancient Christians who did not preach, were none other but deacons. With a view to give some degree of colour and authority to this hasty and ill-founded opinion, he contends [p. 123.] that the term presbyter was commonly applied of old both to presbyters or teachers and to deacons. The object of Burnet was to drive the presbyterians from another ground, on which they were wont to assail episcopacy. The presbyterians, it is well known, assert that in the books of the New Testament mention is made of no more than two classes of the sacred order; *viz.* those of presbyters and deacons; and hence they maintain, that in the apostolic church the degree of bishops, according to the modern sense of the term, was altogether

unknown.   Burnet, by way of rendering their plan of attack on this ground in-
effectual, would willingly persuade us that by the term presbyters, in the writings
of the New Testament, are meant bishops in the modern sense of the word ;
and that the persons whom we therein find styled deacons, were of the same
degree as those to whom in after-times the title of presbyters was given.   From
these examples it is plain that to such an extent may the spirit of party, and a
desire to vindicate a favorite hypothesis prevail, that even the wisest men shall
not be proof against their deception, but become the advocates of opinions
that have no authority or probability whatever to support them.   What Bilson
has advanced, I regard as utterly unworthy of any thing like a serious refutation ; for I will take upon me to affirm that, unless it be by the assistance of
perversion and wrong interpretation, there is not a single passage in the New
Testament to be produced in his favour.   Burnet, which is much to be wondered at in a man of his penetration and sagacity, did not perceive that the
opinion which he wished to inculcate, with a view to support episcopacy, was
in fact calculated to make directly against it.   For let us suppose for a moment, that in those passages, where the term presbyter occurs, we ought to
understand it in the sense of bishop according to modern acceptation, and that
where deacons are spoken of, we should consider presbyters as meant, and the
conclusion unavoidably must be, that the first churches had each of them several such bishops : a conclusion which, if supported by just premises, would of
necessity derogate most materially from the dignity and authority of the episcopal character.   In Acts, xx. 17. we find St. Paul calling to him the presbyters
or elders of the church of Ephesus.   According to bishop Burnet, then, the
church of Ephesus had not merely one, but several bishops.   St. James ad-
monishes the sick to call   for   τὰς πρεσβυτέρας τῆς ἐκκλησίας,   "the presbyters or
elders of the church."   Trusting to the same authority, therefore, we must
conclude that each individual church had a number of bishops belonging to it.
St. Paul directs Titus, whom he had left in Crete, to ordain presbyters or elders
in every city.   Tit. i. 5.   Conformably then to the exposition of the above
mentioned learned prelate, we must understand this as meaning that a variety
of bishops were to be appointed in every city.   But will any bishop, let me
ask, endure to hear of this?   I intentionally pass over some other arguments
which would prove this notion to be altogether groundless, since I should consider it a waste of time to combat, at greater length, a proposition, in which I
cannot perceive even a shadow of probability.   If the opinion of Bœhmer be
adopted, *viz.* that the seven men appointed by the church of Jerusalem were
presbyters, it must necessarily be admitted that the presbyters ordained by the
apostles themselves, or by their direction, in the various other churches, were
altogether of a different order from those of Jerusalem : for it is clear beyond
a question, from what is said in St. Paul's epistles concerning presbyters, that
those there spoken of had nothing to do with the relief of the poor, or the
distribution of the alms, but were solely occupied in instructing the brethren
and governing the church.   To refer but to one passage out of many, for they
are all in substance the same, consult the picture of a presbyter or bishop, as it
is given in 1 Tim. iii. 1.   But that the functions of the presbyters of the church

of Jerusalem should have differed in so material a point as this from those of the presbyters of any other church, (the church of Ephesus for example, whose presbyters are directed by St. Paul, Acts, xx. 28. to occupy themselves in feeding the church of God, and warding off from it all noxious errors,) is so incredible and contradictory to every kind of probability, that I cannot believe it possible for any one possessed of even a common degree of erudition [p. 124.] to be so far imposed on as to receive it for the fact. Indeed, when I consider the arguments by which this illustrious jurist has endeavoured to establish his opinion, I cannot help suspecting that they could never have wrought in a mind of such intelligence as his, that conviction which he would willingly have had them produce in the minds of other people. The arguments to which I allude are two. The first of them is drawn from the silence of St. Luke. This inspired writer, it is urged, makes no mention whatever of any election of presbyters in the church of Jerusalem ; and therefore we must regard these seven men as having been the presbyters of that church. But surely it cannot be possible that any one should be so ignorant as not to know, that there are several things of no small moment passed over by St. Luke without the least notice : and with regard to his silence respecting the election of presbyters in the church of Jerusalem, I account for it by supposing that their first appointment was coëval with the establishment of the church itself. And in this place, I must beg once more to direct the reader's attention towards those νεώτεροι or νεανίσκοι, "young men," who carried forth the dead body of Ananias, Acts, vi. 6. 10. and whom I have above shown to have been public ministers of the church. For unless I am much deceived, the title thus given to them is of itself a proof that there were others at that time belonging to the church who were termed πρεσβύτεροι, "elders ;" and if I am right in this, it is manifested that, besides the apostles, there were presbyters in the church of Jerusalem some time before the appointment of the seven men took place. And that such must have been the fact will appear still more certain, if we consider how utterly incredible it is that a church so vastly numerous as that of Jerusalem was, and divided as it must have been of necessity into various minor assemblies, to each of which a separate place of meeting was assigned, could by any means have dispensed with the want of a set of men of this description. As for those that are termed " the young men," I have little or no doubt but that they were the deacons, to whom the care of the poor was committed by the apostles before the election of the seven men ; other duties, however, being then, in like manner as in after-times, annexed to their office. Let us now examine what force there may be in the second argument adduced by this eminent civilian, and to which he attributes a considerable degree of weight. It is clearly manifest, says he, from Acts, xi. 29, 30. that the presbyters or elders of the church of Jerusalem had the management of the concerns of the poor ; and therefore these presbyters could have been none others than those seven men, to whom the care of the poor was committed. On this argument he expatiates at great length, for the purpose principally of showing that, in addition to their other duties, it also belonged to the presbyters of the church, in the second, third, and fourth centuries, to take care that the necessities of the poor were relieved. But as no one ever entertained a doubt of this, I shall merely inquire whether what is said in Acts, xi. 29, 30. will justify the inference which this very learned writer would draw from it. The Christians of Antioch, we are there told, being given to understand that many of the brethren belonging to the church of Jerusalem were in want, determined to send relief unto them by the hands of Paul and Barnabas. These contributions are stated to have been sent to the presbyters or elders; and hence this learned author concludes that the presbyters were those seven men who had been elected curators or guardians of the poor. But in this conclusion of his there are confounded together two things altogether distinct, *viz.* the custody or care of the charitable fund in the aggregate, and the daily distribution of what might be necessary for the relief of the different individuals in distress. That the seven men were never entrusted with [p. 125.] the first of these, must be evident to any one who will attentively read the history of their appointment. It was the latter, or the daily distribution of relief to the necessitous, which was committed to their management. The Christians of Antioch, therefore, judged rightly in sending their contributions, not to the deacons, but to the presbyters or elders. The only inference, then, that can properly be drawn from this passage is, that in consequence of the disturbance which had arisen in the church of Jerusalem, respecting the improper distinction that was made in administering relief to the poor, the apostles, by way of preventing, for the future, even a shadow of suspicion from lighting on themselves, came to the resolution of having nothing more to do with the custody of the poor's fund, but transferred the keeping thereof to the presbyters or elders. Before these dissensions took place, it was the practice to lay whatever might be designed for the relief of the poor, at the apostles' feet, during one or other of the solemn assemblies of the brethren. At that time, therefore, the poor's fund was at the disposal of the apostles; and certain persons of the Hebrew nation were entrusted by them with the distribution of relief to those who were in want, according to their necessities. The integrity of these inferior ministers, however, having been called in question, the apostles recommended that the foreigners should elect certain curators or guardians for the poor of their own class; and declining to have any thing further to do with the pecuniary concerns of the church, directed that the custody of the contributions for the relief of the necessitous should thenceforward be committed to the presbyters.

(6) There can be no doubt but that the apostles might have filled up a vacancy in their own number, without any reference to the multitude: yet wo find them convoking the general body of Christians to take a share in this matter. When the seven men were to be appointed, the whole affair was, we see, submitted by the apostles to the judgment of the church at large. When a question arose at Antioch respecting the authority of the law of Moses, (Acts, xv.) the apostles, inasmuch as they were constituted by Christ himself expounders of the divine will, might with the greatest reason have taken the cognizance and determination thereof to themselves; yet we find them here again convoking and taking counsel with the whole church. I conceive it to be unnecessary, or otherwise it would be easy to point out

several passages in St. Paul's epistles, which lead to the same inference with the above.

XXXVIII. **Presbyters of the primitive church.** When a number of Christians, therefore, were collected together sufficient to form a church, certain men of gravity and approved faith were without delay appointed, either by the apostles themselves, or their companions, with the assent of the multitude, to preside over it, under the title of presbyters or bishops. By the former of these titles was implied the prudence of old age, rather than age itself, in those who bore it; the latter had an allusion to the nature of the function wherewith they were charged.(') Of these presbyters it is a commonly received opinion, (founded on the words of St. Paul, 1 Tim. v. 17.) that a part only took upon them to instruct the people, and deliver exhortations to them in their solemn assemblies, after the manner of the apostles; and that such of them as had not either received from nature, or acquired by means of art, the qualifications requisite for this, applied themselves to promote the prosperity and general interests of the church in some other way.(²) But since St. Paul requires in express terms that a presbyter or bishop should possess the faculty of teaching, it is scarcely possible, or rather impossible, to entertain a doubt, but that this distinction between teaching and ruling presbyters was after a short time laid aside, and none subse- [p. 126.] quently elected to that office but such as were qualified to admonish and instruct the brethren. The number of these elders was not the same in every place, but accommodated to the circumstances and extent of the church. The endowments which it was requisite that a presbyter should possess, and the virtues which ought to adorn his character, are particularly pointed out by St. Paul in 1 Tim. iii. 1. and Tit. i. 5.; and it cannot be questioned that his injunctions on this subject were strictly adhered to, in those early golden days of the church, when every thing belonging to it was characterized by an ingenuous and beautiful simplicity. It must, however, I conceive, be so obvious to every one as scarcely to need pointing out, that in the requisite qualifications thus specified by the apostle, there are several things which apply exclusively to those times, when Christianity had scarcely established a footing for itself in the world, and the state of manners was far different from what it is at the present day.

11

(1) That the terms *bishops* and *presbyters* are applied promiscuously, as synonymous in the books of the New Testament, is most clearly manifest from Acts, xx. 17. 28. Philipp. i. 1. Tit. i. 5. 7. With regard to the term *presbyter*, the reader will find its force and use well illustrated by Camp. Vitringa, in his work *de Synagog. retere*, lib. iii. part i. cap. i. p. 609; and also by that eminently learned theologist and ornament of his country, Jo. Bened. Carpzovius, in his *Exercitationes in Epist. ad Hebr. ex Philon.* p. 499.

(2) Acceding, as I readily do, to the commonly received interpretation of St. Paul's words, 1 Tim. v. 17. and feeling not at all inclined to controvert the opinion of those who, chiefly on the strength of this passage, maintain that in the infancy of Christianity it was not the province of every presbyter to teach; I yet must own, that without some further support than what is afforded to it by these words of the apostle, the distinction between teaching and ruling presbyters does not appear to me to be in every respect so well established as to be placed beyond the reach of doubt. In no part whatever, I believe, of the New Testament, is the verb κοπιάω made use of, either absolutely or conjoined with the words ἐν κυρίῳ or ἐν λόγῳ, to express the ordinary labour of teaching and instructing the people. But I observe that St. Paul, in various places, applies this verb, and also the noun κόπος, sometimes separately, and at other times connected with certain other words, in an especial sense to that kind of labour which he and other holy persons encountered in propagating the light of the gospel, and bringing over the Jews and heathens to a faith in Christ. In Rom. xvi. 12. (to pass over what is said in verse 6. of one Mary) the apostle describes Tryphæna and Tryphosa as labouring in the Lord; and Persis, another woman, as having laboured much in the Lord, or, which is the same thing, for the sake of, or in the cause of the Lord. Now what interpretation can be given to this, unless it be that these women had assiduously employed themselves in adding to the Lord's flock, and in initiating persons of their own sex in the principles of Christianity? The word appears to me to have the same sense in 1 Cor. iv. 12. where St. Paul says of himself, καὶ κοπιῶμεν, ἐργαζόμενοι ταῖς ἰδίαις χερσί, "and we labour, working with our own hands." By labouring, I here understand him to have meant labouring in the Lord, or for Christ; and the sense of the passage appears to me to be,—" although we labour for Christ, and devote our life to the spreading the light of his gospel [p. 127.] amongst mankind, we yet derive therefrom no worldly gain, but procure whatever may be necessary to our subsistence by the diligence of our hands." And when in the same epistle, 1 Cor. xv. 10. he declares himself to have laboured more abundantly than all the rest of the apostles, περισσότερον αὐτῶν πάντων ἐκοπίασα; his meaning unquestionably is, that he had made more converts to Christianity than they. It would be easy to adduce other passages, in which by labouring, whether it occur absolutely or in connection with some explanatory addition, is evidently meant not the ordinary instruction of the Christians, but the propagating of the gospel amongst those who were as yet ignorant of the true religion; but I conceive that the citations which I have already made will be deemed sufficient. We see, therefore, that it might not without some show of reason and authority be contended that by

τρειςβυτέρυς κοπιῶντας ἐν λόγῳ καὶ διδασκαλίᾳ, "the elders who labour in the word and doctrine," are to be understood such of the presbyters as were intent on enlarging the church, and occupied themselves in converting the Jews and heathens from their errors, and bringing them into the fold of their divine Master,—and not those whose exertions were limited to the instructing and admonishing of the members of the church, when assembled for the purpose of divine worship. No one can doubt but that amongst the elders to whom the care of the churches was committed, there must have been many whose holy zeal carried them beyond the limits of that particular assembly over which they presided, and urged them to use every endeavour for the propagation of the gospel amongst their benighted neighbours; and nothing could be more natural than for such to be pointed out as more especially deserving of an higher reward, and worthy to be held in greater esteem than the rest. This interpretation appears to me to receive no inconsiderable confirmation, when I compare the passage in question with another of a similar nature in St. Paul's epistle to the Thessalonians: Ἐρωτῶμεν δὲ ὑμᾶς ἀδελφοὶ εἰδέναι τὸς κοπιῶντας ἐν ὑμῖν, καὶ προϊσαμένυς ὑμῶν ἐν κυρίῳ, καὶ νȣθετȣντας ὑμᾶς, "and we beseech you, brethren, to know them which labour among you, and are over you in the Lord, and admonish you." 1 Thess. v. 12. Now nothing, I think, can be more manifest than that the apostle, in this place, alludes to the maintaining and honouring of the presbyters or elders. I have not the least idea of any one's denying it. Apparently he distinguishes them into three classes, viz. 1. κοπιῶντας, those who laboured; 2. προϊσαμένȣς, those who ruled or presided; and, 3. νȣθετȣντας, those who taught or admonished. But it is not so much to this point that I would wish to direct the reader's attention, as to the circumstance that τὸν κόπον, "the labour" of the ministers of the church is here clearly spoken of by the apostle as a thing distinct from νȣθεσία, "admonition or exhortation:" from whence it may naturally be inferred that the presbyters who are said by him to labour were different from those who instructed the members of the church, when assembled, in the nature of their faith and duties, or, in other words, "admonished them." The verb κοπιάω is here put absolutely; but there can be no doubt but that we ought to understand the words ἐν λόγῳ καὶ διδασκαλίᾳ, as in 1 Tim. v. 17, or ἐν κυρίῳ, as in Rom. xvi. 12. as annexed to it. Indeed, it does not appear to be altogether necessary that we should call in any further aid than is afforded by the passage itself, for determining the force of the word in this place: for probably the generality of people will be disposed to consider the words ἐν Κυρίῳ as common to all the three members of the sentence, and as having, notwithstanding their immediate connection with προϊσαμένȣς, a reference likewise to the terms κοπιῶντας and νȣθετȣντας. In my opinion, therefore, the apostle, in the passage before us, is to be understood as addressing the Thessalonians thus: "I earnestly entreat you to take care that your presbyters be liberally supplied with every necessary; first of all, those who labour among you with all their might [p. 128.] to propagate the faith of Christ, and augment his flock;—and, in the next place, those who govern the church, and admonish and instruct you by their voice and example."

XXXIX. **Election of the presbyters, their stipends, &c.** That the presbyters of the primitive church of Jerusalem were elected by the suffrages of the people connot, I think, well be doubted of by any one who shall have duly considered the prudence and moderation discovered by the apostles, in filling up the vacancy in their own number, and in appointing curators or guardians for the poor. This power of appointing their elders, continued to be exercised by the members of the church at large, as long as primitive manners were retained entire, and those who ruled over the churches did not conceive themselves at liberty to introduce any deviation from the apostolic model.(¹) The form of proceeding in this matter was unquestionably the same in the first age as we find it to have been in the second and third centuries. When at any time the state of the church required that a new presbyter should be appointed, the collective body of elders recommended to the assembly of the people one or more persons, (in general selected from amongst the deacons,) as fit to fill that office. To this recommendation the people were constrained to pay no further respect than it might appear to them to deserve.(²) Indeed it is placed beyond a doubt, that the multitude, so far from always adopting the candidates proposed by the presbyters, were accustomed not unfrequently to assert the right of judging wholly for themselves, and to require that this or that particular person, whom they held in higher esteem than the rest, should be advanced to the office of an elder. When the voice of the multitude, in the election of any one to the sacred ministry, was unanimous, it was considered in the light of a divine call. In compliance with the express commands of our Lord himself and his apostles, these teachers and ministers of the church were, from the first, maintained and supplied with every necessary by the people for whose edification they laboured; 1 Cor. ix. 13, 14. 1 Tim. v. 17. Gal. vi. 6. 1 Thess. v. 12, 13 ; a certain portion of the voluntary offerings, or oblations as they were termed, being allotted to their use. It will easily be conceived that whilst the churches were but small, and composed chiefly of persons of the lower or middling classes, the provision thus made for the support of the presbyters and deacons could not be very considerable.

(1) What St. Paul says, Tit. i. 5. of his having left Titus in Crete, for the purpose of ordaining presbyters in the churches there, militates in no respect

against the above statement. In executing the commission with which he was entrusted, Titus might, and doubtless did, consult the wishes of the people, and not appoint any to the office of presbyter but such as he found were approved of by them.

(2) It is plain from hence, that what we term the right of presentation, (except in as far as it is at present compulsory,) has nothing in it repugnant to the practice of the church in the earliest times. Our Saviour's [p. 129.] apostles, we see, exercised a right of this kind, when it became necessary to fill up the vacancy in their own number, occasioned by the fall of Judas; and in after-ages, until the right of patronage, as it is called, found its way into the church, a similar right of presentation was uniformly recognized as belonging to the bishops and collective bodies of presbyters. Nor will any one, it is presumed, take exception to this, who shall reflect that, the generality of the individuals constituting the church of Christ are of necessity incapable of estimating the extent of a man's endowments, or of judging how far one may excel another in the qualifications requisite for teaching, and are apt rather to follow the bent of their own wayward humours and prejudices than to listen to the voice of reason and prudence; and how expedient and requisite, therefore, it is, that when a bishop or presbyter is about to be elected, certain persons of discretion and experience should be commissioned to point out to the multitude one or more fit objects for their choice. I pass over the extreme difficulty which is for the most part experienced, even in small assemblies, in conducting an election with any degree of harmony or order, where there are a number of rival candidates for a vacant place, unless there be some one appointed to officiate as superintendent or moderator. For the multitude, if left entirely to itself on such an occasion, is sure to have its proceedings distracted by a conflict of discordant interests and opinions. It must be observed, however, that prior to the age of Constantine the Great, notwithstanding this right of presentation, the most perfect freedom of choice still resided with the people; the multitude being at liberty to reject the persons thus recommended to them, without assigning any reason for their so doing, and either to fix on others for themselves, or else demand that fresh candidates should be proposed to them by the bishop or presbyters. In this respect the right of presentation, as it is now exercised, differs very materially from that which was recognised in the primitive church.

XL. The prophets.

By far the greater part of those who embraced the Christian religion in this its infancy being of mean extraction, and wholly illiterate, it could not otherwise happen but that a great scarcity should be experienced in the churches of persons possessing the qualifications requisite for initiating the ignorant, and communicating instruction to them with a due degree of readiness and skill. It pleased God, therefore, to raise up in every direction certain individuals, and by irradiating their minds with a more than ordinary measure of his holy Spirit, to render them fit instruments for making known his words to the people, and imparting instructions to them, in their public assemblies, on matters relating to religion. These are they who, in the writings of the New Testament, are styled prophets.(') Whoever professed himself to be under the influence of a divine inspiration, and claimed attention as an extraordinary interpreter of the will of God, had permission granted him to speak in public: for, without hearing him, it was impossible for any one to say whether his pretensions to inspiration were or were not well founded. When once he had spoken, however, all uncertainty with regard to his commission was at an end; for there were in the churches persons instructed of God, who could discern by infallible signs between a true prophet and one who falsely pretended to that character. The apostles also had left on record certain marks, by which one specially commisioned from above might clearly be distinguished from an impostor. 1 Cor. xii. [p. 130.] 2, 3. xiv. 29. 1 John, iv. 1. This order of prophets ceased in the church, when the reasons which gave birth to it no longer existed. For when the affairs of the church took a prosperous turn, and regular schools or seminaries were instituted, in which those who were designed for the sacred ministry received an education suitable to the office, it consequently became unnecessary that God should any longer continue to instruct the people by the mouths of these extraordinary ministers or prophets.(²)

(1) It appears to me that the function of these prophets, as they are styled, is too much narrowed by those who would have us believe that they were merely interpreters of the sacred writings, and more especially of the prophecies delivered under the old covenant. It was a common thing I grant, for these prophets to adduce proofs of the truth and divine original of the Christian religion from the inspired writers of the Old Testament. I am ready also to grant that not unfrequently particular passages in the Old Testament, the genuine sense of which had either escaped the Jewish doctors, or been obscured by them, were, through the sagacity of these prophets, illustrated and placed in a proper point of view. But notwithstanding this, I am persuaded that whoever shall with calmness and deliberation examine and compare with each other the different passages in the New Testament, in which mention is made of these prophets, cannot fail to perceive that they did not confine themselves merely to the interpretation of the Scriptures. On this subject I have already given my sentiments to the public at some length, in a particular tract *de illis, qui Prophetæ vocantur in novo Fœdere*, which

is to be found in the second volume of my *Dissertationes ad Historiam Ec-clesiastic. pertinentes.* We have no positive testimony that there were prophets in all the early churches; but it appears extremely probable that such was the case, since St. Paul, in enumerating the ministers of the church appointed by God himself, assigns the second place to the prophets. 1 Cor. xii. 28. Ephes. iv. 11.

(2) There can be no doubt but that, from almost the very first rise of Christianity, it was the practice for certain of the youth, in whom such a strength of genius and capacity manifested itself as to afford a hope of their becoming profitable servants in the cause of religion, to be set apart for the sacred ministry, and for the presbyters and bishops to supply them with the requisite preparatory instruction, and form them by their precepts and advice for that solemn office. On this subject St. Paul, in the latter of his epistles to Timothy, ii. 2. expresses himself in the following terms: καὶ ἃ ἤκουσας παρ' ἐμοῦ διὰ πολλῶν μαρτύρων, ταῦτα παράθου πιστοῖς ἀνθρώποις, οἵτινες ἱκανοὶ ἔσονται καὶ ἑτέρους διδάξαι; "and the things that thou hast heard of me among many wit-nesses, the same commit thou to faithful men, who shall be able to teach others also." The apostle here, we see, directs Timothy, in the first place to select from amongst the members of the church a certain number of men, who might appear to him to possess the talents requisite for conveying instruction to others, and who were persons of· tried and approved faith. For it will not admit of a doubt that by the πιστοὶ ἄνθρωποι, "faithful men," here alluded to, we ought to understand not merely believers, or those holding the faith, but persons of approved and established faith, to whom things of the highest moment might be entrusted without danger or apprehension. Secondly, to the persons thus selected he was to communicate and expound that discipline, in which he himself had been instructed by St. Paul before many witnesses. Now it is evident that St. Paul could not by this mean that they were to be taught the mere elements or rudiments of the Christian religion; for with these every one professing Christianity was of course brought acquainted; and doubtless, therefore, those whom the apostle in this place directs Timothy to instruct, must have known and been thoroughly versed in them [p. 131.] long before. The discipline, then, which Timothy had received from St. Paul, and which he was thus to become the instrument of communicating to others, was without question that more full and perfect knowledge of divine truth as revealed in the gospel of Christ, which it was fitting that every one who was advanced to the office of a master or teacher amongst the brethren should possess, together with a due degree of instruction as to the most skilful and ready method of imparting to the multitude a proper rule of faith, and correct principles of moral action. But what is this, I would ask, but to direct Timothy to institute a school or seminary for the education of future pres-byters and teachers for the church, and to cause a certain number of persons of talents and virtue to be trained up therein, under a course of discipline similar to that which he himself had received at the hands of St. Paul? It may moreover, be inferred from these words, that the apostle had personally discharged the same office which he thus imposes on Timothy, and applied

himself to the properly educating of future teachers and ministers for the church : for it appears by them that he had not been the tutor of Timothy only, but that his instructions to this his favorite disciple had been imparted διὰ πολλῶν μαρτύρων, " before many witnesses;" διὰ having, in this place, unquestionably the force of the preposition ἐνώπιον. To determine, indeed, whom we ought to understand by the persons thus termed " witnesses," has occasioned no little stir amongst the commentators. According to some we should connect them with the following word παράθν, and consider St. Paul as saying, διὰ πολλῶν μαρτύρων παράθν, " transmit by many witnesses." Others would have us understand by these witnesses, the presbyters who ordained Timothy to the sacred ministry by the laying on of hands, 1 Tim. iv. 14.; and conceive that, immediately previous to such ordination, St. Paul had, in the presence and hearing of these presbyters, recapitulated and again inculcated on the mind of his adopted son in the faith the chief or leading articles of the Christian religion: whilst others, again, imagine that the persons here alluded to, were witnesses of the life, actions, and miracles of our Lord. But of these and some other conjectures on the subject, which it is needless to enumerate, there is not one but what is encumbered with considerable difficulties. A much more natural way of resolving the point, as it appears to me, is by supposing that St. Paul had under him, in a sort of seminary or school which he had instituted for the purpose of properly educating presbyters and teachers, several other disciples and pupils besides Timothy; and that the witnesses here spoken of, before whom Timothy had been instructed, were his fellow-students, persons destined like him for the ministry, and partakers together with him of the benefits that were to be derived from the apostle's tuition. It is highly credible, I may say indeed it is more than credible, that not St. Paul alone, but also all the other apostles of our Lord applied themselves to the properly instructing of certain select persons, so as to render them fit to be entrusted with the care and government of the churches ; and, consequently, that the first Christian teachers were brought up and formed in schools or seminaries immediately under their eye. Besides other references which might be given, it appears from Irenæus *adrers. Hæreses*, lib. ii. cap. xxii. p. 148. ed. Massuet. that St. John employed himself at Ephesus, where he spent the latter part of his life, in qualifying youth for the sacred ministry. And the same author, as quoted by Eusebius, *Histor. Eccles.* lib. v. cap. xx. p, 188. represents Polycarp, the celebrated bishop of Smyrna, as having laboured in [y. 132.] the same way. That the example of these illustrious characters was in this respect followed by the bishops in general, will scarcely admit of a doubt. To this origin, in my opinion, are to be referred those seminaries termed " episcopal schools," which we find attached to the principal churches, and in which youth designed for the ministry went through a proper course of preparatory instruction and discipline under the bishop himself, or some presbyter of his appointment.

XLI. **The origin of bishops.** Whilst the Christian assemblies or churches were but small, two, three, or four presbyters were found amply sufficient to labour for the welfare, and regulate the concerns of each : and over a few men like these, inflamed as they were with the sincerest piety towards God, and receiving but very moderate stipends, it was not required that any one should be appointed to preside in the capacity of a ruler or superintendant. But as the congregations of Christians became every day larger and larger, a proportionate gradual increase in the number of the presbyters and ministers of necessity took place; and as the rights and power of all were the same, it was soon found impossible, under the circumstances of that age, when every church was left to the care of itself, for any thing like a general harmony to be maintained amongst them, or for the various necessities of the multitude to be regularly and satisfactorily provided for, without some one to preside and exert a controuling influence. Such being the case, the churches adopted the practice of selecting, and placing at the head of the council of presbyters, some one man of eminent wisdom and prudence, whose peculiar duty it should be to allot to his colleagues their several tasks, and by his advice, and every other mode of assistance, to prevent as far as in him lay the interests of the assembly, over which he was thus appointed to preside, from experiencing any kind of detriment or injury.(1) The person thus advanced to the presidency, was at first distinguished by the title of " the angel" of his church ; but in after-times it became customary to style him, in allusion to those duties which constituted the chief branch of his function, " the bishop."(2) In what particular church, or at what precise period, this arrangement was first introduced, remains nowhere on record. It appears to me, however that there are the strongest reasons for believing that the church of Jerusalem, which in point of numbers exceeded every other, took the lead in this respect; and that her example was gradually copied after by the rest in succession, according as their increase in size, or their situation in other respects, might suggest the propriety of their doing so.(3)

(1) This statement respecting the origin of the order of bishops must, I am persuaded, obtain the assent of every one who knows what human nature is, and shall reflect on the situation of things in that early age, and also on the jealousies, dissensions, and various other embarrassing evils, that are incident to collective bodies of individuals who are all on a footing of equality. That the first churches had no bishops, may, I think, very clearly be proved

from the writings of the New Testament.—I do not mean from the circumstance to which so much weight is by many attributed, viz. that it is not unusual to find therein the term bishop applied to presbyters in general: for
those who take the opposite side of the question will say in reply, that persons
invested with the prelacy were at first distinguished by another name; but
that, after some time, the term bishop ceased to be applied to presbyters of
the common order, and was appropriated exclusively to the chief or presiding
presbyters. But the evidence which, as I have stated above, I deem conclusive
[p. 133.] as to this point is this,—that neither in the Acts of the Apostles, nor
in St. Paul's epistles, although in both express mention is frequently made of
presbyters and deacons, do we find the least notice taken of any church having
been subject to the authority or rule of a single man. It appears to me, however, equally certain that the churches did not long continue under the care
and management of councils of presbyters, amongst whom there was no distinction of rank; but that in the more considerable ones at least, if not in the
others, it came, even during the life-time of the apostles, and with their approbation, to be the practice for some one man more eminent than the rest, to be
invested with the presidency or chief direction. And in support of this opinion
we are supplied with an argument of such strength in those "angels," to whom
St. John addressed the epistles, which, by the command of our Saviour himself, he sent to the seven churches of Asia, Rev. ii. iii. as the presbyterians, as
they are termed, let them labour and strive what they may, will never be able
to overcome. It must be evident to every one, even on a cursory perusal of
the epistles to which we refer, that those who are therein termed "angels"
were persons possessing such a degree of authority in their respective
churches, as enabled them to mark with merited disgrace whatever might
appear to be deserving of reprehension, and also to give due countenance and
encouragement to every thing that was virtuous and commendable. But even
supposing that we were to wave the advantage that is to be derived from this
argument in establishing the antiquity of the episcopal character, it appears
to me that the bare consideration alone of the state of the church in its
infancy, must be sufficient to convince any rational unprejudiced person, that
the order of bishops could not have originated at a period considerably more
recent than that which gave birth to Christianity itself. For it is impossible
for any one who is acquainted with what human nature is, and knows how
things were circumstanced in the first ages, to believe that a proper harmony
could be maintained amongst the presbyters, or that the assemblies of the
church could be convened and regulated, or any factions or disturbances that
might arise amongst the people be repressed and composed, or that many
other things which might be enumerated could be accomplished with any
degree of promptitude, regularity, and ease, without some one being appointed
to act in the capacity of moderator or president. If I figure to myself an
assembly composed of merely a moderate number of people,—say, for instance, a hundred,—and suppose such assembly to be placed under the care
of one or two excellent persons, possessing hearts filled with love towards
God and man, and entirely devoid of ambition and cupidity of wealth, I can

very well conceive that, owing to the paucity and sincere piety of the assembly itself, as well as of those entrusted with the care and management of its concerns, it might be possible for its affairs to be conducted with the greatest regularity, and for its proceedings not to be disgraced by any thing like confusion or party spirit. But when I enlarge upon this idea, and present to my mind's eye a multitude consisting of perhaps four or five hundred persons, (a multitude, too, not receiving laws from a superior, but legislating entirely for itself, and classed or distributed under perhaps ten different presbyters or teachers all on a footing of the most perfect equality,) the case becomes entirely altered, and I should deem it no less essential for such a multitude to have some individual leader or guide assigned to it, than for a legion of soldiers to have its proper commander or tribune.

(2) The title of "angel" is applied by our Lord himself to the presidents of the seven churches of Asia, Rev. ii. iii.; and hence it may fairly be inferred that persons of that description were usually styled so in the first century: for it is not to be imagined that our Saviour addressed those chiefs of their churches by a new and unaccustomed title. As to what has been urged by several learned persons, respecting the peculiar significance and force of this appellation, it appears to me for the most part as rather speculative and curious than well founded and important. For since the term ἄγγελος signifies in general a legate, or person accredited either of God or man, and those presidents of the churches were regarded as being, in an especial degree commissioned of God, it, in my opinion, requires no very great depth of research to account for their being styled angels, at a time when, in conformity to the practice of the apostles themselves, it was customary for the title of bishop to be applied to presbyters in general, and consequently some other appellation was [p. 134.] found necessary, in order to distinguish the chief presbyters from those of the ordinary rank. A more just or appropriate title than this could scarcely have been fixed on. As the term, however, could not be deemed altogether free from ambiguity, and might perhaps be found to give occasion for some aspiring individuals to over-rate their own consequence, and fancy themselves nearly on a level with those who are in the strict sense of the word styled angels, (for even the merest trifles are sufficient to supply men with arguments for vanity and pride,) it was probably thought better to exchange this title for one more definitive and humble, and to substitute for it that very one which had previously been common to the presbyters at large; so that these presidents might thereby be constantly reminded that they were merely placed at the head of a family of brethren, and that their function differed not in its nature from that wherewith all the elders were at the first invested. It appears to me, therefore, that in the appellation ἄγγελος τῆς ἐκκλησίας, the word Θεὸς is to be supplied; and that the title ought to be understood as running thus, Ἄγγελος τῦ Θεῦ τῆς Ἐκκλησίας, *i. e.* a person especially commissioned of God, or one who occupies the station of a divine legate in the church.

(3) As the early churches are well known to have taken all their institutions and regulations from the model exhibited to them by the church of Jerusalem, it appears to me that scarcely a doubt can be entertained of their having been

also indebted to this last-mentioned venerable assembly for the example of appointing some one man to preside over the presbyters and general interests of each individual church, and that the first instance of any one's being invested with the episcopal office occured in that city.   This much at least is certain, that no church whatever can be proved to have had a bishop prior to that of Jerusalem ; and that none of the ancient accounts and notices of bishops, which are to be met with in Eusebius and other authors, do ascend so high as those of Jerusalem.   All ancient authorities, from the second century downwards, concur in representing James the Younger, the brother of our Lord after the flesh, as the first bishop of the church of Jerusalem, having been so created by the apostles themselves. Vid. *Acta sanctor. Mens. Maii,* tom. i. p. 23.   Tillemont, *Mémoires pour servir a l'Histoire de l'Eglise,* tom. i. p. 1008, et seq.   Now if this were as truly as it is uniformly reported, it would at once determine the point which we have under consideration, since it must close the door against all doubt as to the quarter in which episcopacy originated.   But I rather suspect that these ancient writers might incautiously be led to form their judgment of the state of things in the first century from the maxims and practice of their own times, and finding that, after the departure of the other apostles on their respective missions, the chief regulation and superintendence of the church at Jerusalem rested with James, they without further reason concluded that he must have been appointed the bishop of that church.   It appears indeed, from the writings of the New Testament, that, after the departure of the other apostles on their travels, the chief authority in the church of Jerusalem was possessed by James.   For St. Paul, when he came to that city for the last time, immediately repaired to this apostle ; and James appears to have thereupon convened an assembly of the presbyters at his house, where Paul laid before them an account of the extent and success of his labors in the cause of his divine Master.   Acts, xxi. 19, 20.   No one reading this can, I should think, entertain a doubt of James's having been, at that time, invested with the chief superintendence and government of the church of Jerusalem ; and that not only the assemblies of the presbyters, but also those general ones of the whole church, in which, as is clear from verse 22, was lodged the supreme power as to all matters of a sacred nature, were convened by his appointment.   But it is to be observed that this authority was no more than must have devolved on James of course, in his apostolic character, in consequence of all the other [p. 135.] apostles having quitted Jerusalem ; and that therefore this testimony of St. Luke is by no means to be considered as conclusive evidence of his having been appointed to the office of bishop.   Were we to admit of such kind of reasoning as this,—the government of the church of Jerusalem was vested in James, therefore he was its bishop,—I do not see on what grounds we could refuse our assent, should it be asserted that all the twelve apostles were bishops of that church, for it was at one time equally under their government.   But not to enlarge unnecessarily.—The function of an apostle differed widely from that of a bishop ; and I therefore do not think that James, who was an apostle, was ever appointed to or discharged the episcopal office at Jerusalem.   The government of the church in that city, it rather appears to me, was placed in the hands of its presbyters, but so as that nothing of moment could be done without the advice and authority of James; the same sort of respectful deference being paid to his will as had formerly been manifested for that of the apostles at large. But although we deem those ancient writers to have committed an error, in pronouncing James to have been the first bishop of Jerusalem, it may without much difficulty be demonstrated that the church of that city had a bishop sooner than any of the rest, and consequently that the episcopal dignity must have taken its rise there. The church of Jerusalem, at the time of that city's being taken and finally laid waste by the emperor Hadrian, towards the middle of the second century, (about the year of our Lord 137 or 138,) had had fourteen bishops, without our reckoning James as one of them. A list of their names is given us by Eusebius, (*Hist. Eccles.* lib. iv. cap. v. p. 117.) who derived his information in this respect, not from any vague report or tradition, but from certain ancient written documents which had come under his own immediate inspection: ἐξ ἐγγράφων. At that period, according to the same historian, the church of Rome had had no more than seven bishops, and that of Alexandria only five. He likewise represents (*Hist. Eccles.* lib. iv. cap. xx. p. 141.) the church of Antioch as having, even so late as in the reign of the emperor Marcus Antoninus, been under the government of merely its sixth bishop. The number, then, of bishops who had filled the see of Jerusalem having, in the time of Hadrian, reached to more than double that of the prelates of any other of the more considerable churches, it appears to me that we are amply justified in concluding that the church of that city placed itself under a bishop long before either of the rest, and that the other churches were successively induced to follow her example. Eusebius indeed says, that he had not been able to ascertain exactly how many years each of these bishops had held the see; but that, according to common report, they all presided but for a short time. But this in no respect militates against the above conclusion. If we assign, as surely we may at the least, to each of these bishops three years, we shall find it give us somewhat above forty years as the term of their government altogether. Should we, however, be of opinion that the church of Jerusalem (which, from its amplitude, and the great number of its presbyters must have felt in a very eminent and pressing degree the necessity of having a chief ruler or president) was, as is most probable, induced, immediately on the martyrdom of James the Just, to place itself under the superintendence and care of a bishop, we may, in such case, allow a much longer period to the government of the fourteen prelates mentioned by Eusebius: for it has been resolved by the learned, apparently on very sufficient grounds, that James was put to death in the year of our Lord 62, which was more than seventy years prior to the final overthrow of Jerusalem by Hadrian. But in whatever way our calculations as [p. 136.] to this point may be made, it will be equally placed beyond dispute that the church of Jerusalem had over it a bishop long enough before the close of the first century after Christ; and this being established, it will scarcely, I had almost said it cannot, be denied that the episcopal dignity must have **originated** in and passed to the other churches from that of Jerusalem.

XLII. **Rights, &c. of the first bishops.** That these bishops were, on their creation, invested with certain peculiar rights, and a degree of power which placed them much above the presbyters, will not be disputed by any unprejudiced or impartial person: but we are not possessed of sufficient information on the subject, to enable us to state with exact precision the extent to which those rights and that power reached during the first century. It is certain, however, that it would be forming a very erroneous judgment, were we to estimate the power, the revenue, the privileges, and rights of the first bishops, from the rank, affluence, and authority attached to the episcopal character in the present day. A primitive bishop was, as it should seem, none other than the chief or principal minister of an individual church, which, at the period of which we are speaking, was seldom so numerous but that it could be assembled under one roof. He taught the people, administered what are termed the sacraments, and supplied the ailing and the indigent with comfort and relief. With regard to the performance of such duties as it was impossible for him to fulfil or attend to in person, he availed himself of the assistance of the presbyters. Associating, likewise, these presbyters with him in council, he inquired into and determined any disputes or differences that might subsist amongst the members of his flock, and also looked round and consulted with them as to any measures which the welfare and prosperity of the church appeared to require. Whatever arrangements might be deemed eligible, were proposed by him to the people for their adoption, in a general assembly. In fine, a primitive bishop could neither determine nor enact anything of himself, but was bound to conform to and carry into effect whatever might be resolved on by the presbyters and the people.(') The episcopal dignity would not be much coveted, I rather think, on such terms, by many of those, who, under the present state of things, interest themselves very warmly on behalf of bishops and their authority. Of the emoluments attached to this office, which, it may be observed, was one of no small labour and peril, I deem it unnecessary for me to say anything: for that they must have been extremely small, cannot but be obvious to every one who shall consider that no church had, in those days, any other revenue than what arose from the voluntary offerings, or oblations as they were termed, of the people, by far the greater part of whom were persons of very moderate or slender means; and that out of these offerings, in addition to the bishop, provision was to be made for the presbyters, the deacons, and the indigent brethren.

(1) All that we have thus stated is clearly to be proved from documents of the first ages. Of this the reader may satisfy himself, by consulting, amongst other works, Bingham's *Origines Ecclesiasticæ*, and Beveridge's *Codex Canonum primitivæ Ecclesiæ*.

XLIII. **Rural bishops and dioceses.** It was not long, [p. 137.] however, before circumstances became so changed, as to produce a considerable extension and enlargement of the limits, within which the episcopal government and authority had been at first confined. For the bishops who presided in the cities, were accustomed to send out into the neighbouring towns and country adjacent certain of their presbyters, for the purpose of making converts, and establishing churches therein; and it being of course deemed but fair and proper that the rural or village congregations, which were drawn together in this way, should continue under the guardianship and authority of the prelate by whose counsel and exertion they had been first brought to a knowledge of Christ and his word, the episcopal sees gradually expanded into ecclesiastical provinces of varied extent, some greater, some less, to which the Greeks in after times gave the denomination of dioceses. Those to whom the instruction and management of these surrounding country churches were committed by the diocesan were termed chorepiscopi, *i. e.* τῆς χώρας ἐπισκοποὶ, "rural bishops." Persons of this description are doubtless to be considered as having held a middle rank between the bishops and the presbyters: for to place them on a level with the former is impossible, since thay were subject to the diocesan; but at the same time, it is manifest that they were superior in rank to presbyters, inasmuch as they were not accustomed to look up to the bishop for orders or direction, but were invested with constant authority to teach, and in other respects to exercise the episcopal functions.(1)

(1) The reader will find this subject very copiously treated of in the following (amongst other) works: Morin. *de sacris Eccles. Ordinationibus*, part i, exerc. iv. p. 10, et seq.; Blondell. *de Episcopis et Presbyteris*, § iii, p. 93. 120, et

seq ; Bevereg. *in Pandect. Canonum ad Canon.* xiii. *Concilii Ancyrani,* tom. ii.
p. 176 ; Ziegler. *de Episcopis,* lib. i. cap. xiii. p. 105, et seq. ; Pet. de Marca *de
Concordia Sacerdotii et Imperii,* lib. ii. cap. xiii. part xiv. p. 159, et seq. ;
Boehmer. *Adnotat. ad illum,* p. 62, 63 ; Thomassin. *Disciplina Eccles. vet. et nov.*
part i. lib. ii. cap. i. p. 215 : the learned authors of which are divided in opinion
as to whether the " chorepiscopi" belonged to the episcopal order, or to that
of presbyters. But it appears to me, that whoever shall attentively consider
what has been handed down to us respecting these " rural bishops," must
readily perceive that they cannot with propriety be ranked under either of
those orders. In fact, I conceive that the question would never have been
agitated amongst men of erudition, had it not been for a preconceived notion,
too hastily taken up by them, that all the ministers of the primitive church
were to be classed under one or other of the three orders of bishops, presbyters, or deacons.

XLIV. **Deacons and deaconesses.** In addition to these its governors and teachers, the church had ever belonging to it, even
from its very first rise, a class of ministers, composed of persons of
[p. 138.] either sex, and who were termed deacons and deaconesses.
Their office was to distribute the alms to the necessitous ; to carry
the orders or messages of the elders, wherever necessary ; and to
perform various other duties, some of which related merely to
the solemn assemblies that were held at stated intervals, whilst
others were of a general nature. That the greatest caution and
prudence were, in the first ages, deemed proper to be observed in
the choice of these ministers, appears plainly from St. Paul's directions on the subject. 1 Tim. iii. 8. et. seq. From what is
afterwards said by the apostle, at verse 13. of the same chapter,
learned men have been led to conclude, and apparently with
much reason, that those who had given unequivocal proof of their
faith and probity in the capacity of deacons, were, after a while,
elected into the order of presbyters. The deaconesses were widows
of irreproachable character and mature age. In the oriental
countries, where, as is well known, men are not permitted to have
access to the women, the assistance of females like these must
have been found of essential importance : for, through their
ministry, the principles of the Christian religion could be diffused
amongst the softer sex, and various things be accomplished in
relation to the Christian sisterhood, which, in a region teeming
with suspicion and jealousy, could in no wise have been consigned
to or undertaken by men.(')

(1) The origin of the order of deacons is, in my opinion, unquestionably to be referred back to the primitive church of Jerusalem; but the reader will have perceived, from what I have above remarked on the subject, that I do not agree with the majority of writers in considering it as having taken its rise in the appointment of the seven Greeks spoken of in the Acts of the Apostles.* For that there must have been ministers who discharged the functions of deacons in the assembly of the Christians of that city, prior to such appointment, will not with me admit of a doubt: since, not again to bring forward other reasons, it is evident that the business of the church could by no means have been properly conducted, without the assistance of persons acting in that capacity. The more attention, likewise, that I bestow on those "young men," who appear to have been in waiting on the apostles, and committed the bodies of Ananias and his wife to the earth, the more am I convinced that they were in fact none other than deacons. The seven men subsequently appointed I conceive to have been public ministers, differing in no respect from those whom, for the sake of distinction, we will term original deacons, except only that their sphere of duty was limited to that part of the church which was composed of foreigners. Now if this opinion be correct, as it really appears to me to be, there is at once an end of the notion entertained by some, that the deacons of after-ages differed from those of the primitive times; for that it was the office of the original or primitive ones to take care of the poor, but that those of after-times had duties of a very different nature assigned to them by the bishops. To me it seems clear that no such alteration took place in the functions of the deacons, but that, from the first, it was their duty to render themselves serviceable in all things which might be required of them by the situation and circumstances of the church at that time. Whether or not there were any such characters as those of deaconesses known in the church of Jerusalem, is what I have not the means of ascertaining with any degree of certainty. I think, however, it may very well admit of a conjecture, that those widows who were neglected by the Hebrew deacons, (Acts, vi. 1.) might be women acting in the capacity of deaconesses amongst the Greeks. That the handmaids of the churches were in that age termed "widows," in an absolute sense, is manifest beyond a doubt, and may in particular be proved from the words of St. Paul himself, 1 Tim. v. 9, 10. As far as my penetration is able to reach, I can perceive nothing that can be considered as at all opposing itself to this conjecture; but, on the contrary, several things present them- [p. 139.] selves to notice tending rather to support it. Of the arguments which may be adduced in its favour, I think it is not one of trifling force that the Hebrews, against whom the complaint is made, are not accused of having neglected any of the foreign poor besides the widows. Most assuredly the Greek Jews who dwelt at Jerusalem must have had other persons amongst them who required relief as well as their widows! Then how came it to pass that their widows alone should have had cause given them by the Hebrew deacons to murmur and complain of neglect? Now if by the term widows we here understand

* Vid. supr. sec. xxxvii. note [5] p. 152.

deaconnesses, it will be possible to assign no very unsatisfactory reason for this. The number of the Greek converts was undoubtedly not so great as that of the Hebrew ones: the duties, therefore, which the "widows" of those Greeks or foreigners had to discharge must have been executed with less labour and inconvenience than fell to the lot of the indigenous matrons, in the performance of their functions. Perceiving, then, that the trouble encountered by the foreign class of widows was disproportionate to that which necessarily attached itself to the services of the others, and being also perhaps somewhat influenced by a partiality towards those of their own nation, the Hebrew ministers, who were entrusted with the distribution of the alms, might probably conceive that there could be no impropriety in their granting relief on a more liberal scale to the widows of the indigenous Jews than to those of the foreign class. But leaving it to others to determine on the validity of this conjecture, I pass on to the notice of a few things which have suggested themselves to me, on a reconsideration of the history of the controversy above alluded to between the Jews and the Greeks, as given us by St. Luke. In the opening of his narrative, the sacred historian tells us that "there had arisen a murmuring of the Grecians against the Hebrews." Being particularly studious of brevity, however, he omits adding some things which yet are necessary to be understood by his readers, in order to their forming a proper judgment of the affair. In the first place, then, although no such thing is expressed, yet it is evident from the context that we must consider the Greeks as having come to the apostles, and complained to them of the ill conduct of the Hebrews. It could not, however, surely have been against all the Christian converts of the Hebrew race, at that time dwelling in Jerusalem, that complaint was then preferred. For no one that is in his senses can believe that the whole body of Hebrews should have deliberately concurred in a wish to wrong the widows of the foreigners, or have agreed together that less relief should be afforded to them than to the others. The complaint there can be no doubt related merely to those indigenous Jews, to whom the relief and care of the poor had been committed by the apostles. We must also conclude that the Greeks, who were the bearers of this accusation, preferred at the same time, on behalf of their church, a request that the apostles would take upon themselves the future distribution of the alms, and the administration of whatever else might relate to the poor. . For unless we conceive this to have been the case, it is impossible to account for the speech which is stated to have been made by the apostles to the multitude when assembled. Had no such direct application been made to them to take upon themselves the office, what room could there have been for their so formally declining it? Taking it, however, for the fact, that such request was made, as we are certainly well warranted in doing by the words of the apostles themselves, what follows will be found to correspond in a very striking degree with every thing precedent, and the whole affair is at once rendered clear and intelligible. The address delivered by the apostles, on this occasion, to the general assembly of the church, we may suppose to have ran somewhat in this way:—"Brethren, we are given to understand by the Greeks, that their widows have not experienced, in point of charitable assistance that degree of justice which they had a right to expect at the hands of the ministers of the church: and they have, in consequence thereof, expressed a wish that we ourselves would undertake to see that things of this kind should be properly managed for the future. To this, however, we cannot by any means consent: for were we to comply with the request thus made to us, and take upon ourselves the business of administering relief to the poor, we should inevitably be obliged to neglect the most important part of our function, which consists in unfolding the truths of divine revelation, and extending the bounds of the Christian community, or at least should not be able to devote [p. 140.] ourselves to it with that degree of attention and assiduity which the will of God requires. The remedy, therefore, which we will, with your consent, apply to the evil complained of, shall be this.—Choose ye from amongst yourselves seven men, on whose faith and integrity ye can rely, to superintend this business, and recommend them to us. From those whom ye may thus point out, as persons worthy to be entrusted with the guardianship and care of the poor, you will not find us in any wise disposed to withhold our confidence." For further information with regard to the deacons and deaconesses of the primitive church, the reader is referred to what has been written by Caspar Ziegler on the subject; as also to Basnage's *Annal. Politico-Eccles. ad Ann.* xxxv. tom. i. p. 450.; and Bingham's *Origines Ecclesiast.* lib. ii. cap. xx. p. 296, et seq.

XLV. **Constitution and order of the primitive churches. The People.** From these particulars we may collect a general idea of what was the form and constitution of those primitive Christian associations, which in the language of Scripture are termed *churches.* Every church was composed of three constituent parts: 1st, Teachers who were also invested with the government of the community, according to the laws; 2dly, Ministers of each sex; and 3dly, The multitude of people.(¹) Of these parts, the chief in point of authority was the people: for to them belonged the appointment of the bishop and presbyters, as well as of the inferior ministers;—with them resided the power of enacting laws, as also of adopting or rejecting whatever might be proposed in the general assemblies, and of expelling and again receiving into communion any depraved or unworthy members. In short, nothing whatever of any moment could be determined on, or carried into effect, without their knowledge and concurrence. All these rights came to be recognised as appertaining to, and residing in the people, in consequence of its being entirely by them that the necessary means were supplied for maintaining the teachers and ministers, relieving the wants of the indigent, promoting the general interests and welfare of the community, and averting from

it occasionally impending ill.   The contributions thus furnished
consisted of all kinds of offerings, or *oblations* as they were commonly termed, which every one according to his ability, and of
his own free will, without any sort of demand or admonition,
brought with him to the assembly, and threw into the common
stock.   After some little while, it was judged expedient to divide
the multitude into two orders or classes, *viz.* that of the *faithful*,
and that of the *catechumens.*(²)   Of these, the former were such
as had been solemnly admitted members of the church by the
sacrament of baptism, and publicly pledged themselves to God
and the brethren that they would strictly conform themselves
to the laws of the community, and who, in consequence thereof,
possessed the right of voting in the public assemblies, and of
being present at, and taking a share in, every part of divine worship.   The latter were those converts who, not having gone
through the course of preparatory discipline and probation prescribed by the rules of the church, remained as yet unbaptized,
and whose title to the rights of Christian fellowship was conse-
[p. 141.] quently deemed incomplete.   These were not permitted
to be present at the solemn assemblies of the church, or to join
in the public worship ; neither were they suffered to participate
of the Lord's supper.   All the members of the Christian community considered themselves as being on a footing of the most
perfect quality.   Amongst a variety of other proofs which they
gave of this, it was particularly manifested by their reciprocally
making use of the terms " brethren," and " sisters," in accosting
each other.(³)   On the ground of this sort of spiritual relationship,
the utmost care was taken that none should be suffered to languish
in poverty or distress ; since, whilst the means of assistance were
not wanting, it would have been contrary to the laws of fraternal
love to have permitted any brother or sister to remain without
the necessaries of life.(⁴)   That even in this early age, there was
in the church a mixture of the bad with the good, is what no one
can doubt :—it is impossible, however, that any one belonging
to the Christian community could have openly persisted in a
wicked, flagitious course of conduct ; since it was particularly enjoined both by Christ and his apostles, that if repeated admonition and reproof should fail to produce repentance and amendment of life in any who might pollute themselves by a depraved

demeanor, or by flagrantly violating the laws of morality and religion, they should be excommunicated, or in other words, be expelled from every kind of intercourse and association with the faithful.(⁵)

(1) Of all that I here state, the greater part is, with a very moderate degree of trouble, to be proved from Scripture itself. Indeed the authenticity of it has been already so proved. I shall, therefore, content myself with merely adding a few observations, illustrative of such things as may appear to require some elucidation.

In the *first* place, then, it may be proper for me to remark, that in enumerating the constituent parts of a church, I have intentionally avoided making use of the terms *clergy* and *laity* :—not that I can perceive any thing objectionable in these terms, when properly explained ; but lest, by my having recourse to them, I should afford occasion to some to doubt of my impartiality. I cannot, however, avoid taking this opportunity of professing myself to be utterly unapprised of any good that has resulted from the violent and long continued disputes which have been carried on, respecting the antiquity and origin of these appellations. For my own part, I agree in opinion with those who conceive them to have come very early into use,—in fact, to have been nearly coëval with the first rise of Christianity ; but, at the same time, of any thing that is to be gained by establishing this opinion, I am altogether ignorant. In like manner am I an entire stranger to any advantage that is to be expected from the carrying of their point, by those who undertake to prove that these terms were not known in the church prior to the third century. Facts and ordinances constitute the proper objects of our attention when inquiring into the state of the primitive church, not particular appellations or terms, which, whether they be of ancient or of modern origin, can in no shape alter the nature of things. In order to acquire a proper knowledge of the latter, we must pursue a course of study far different from that of words.

(2) At the first, there was no distinction recognised in the church between the *faithful* and the *candidates for baptism*, or catechumens ; nor do I think that any vestige of such a division of the people is to be found throughout the whole of the New Testament,—any, at least, that can be deemed clear and indisputable. Whoever, through the powerful operation of divine truth, had been brought to profess a belief in Christ as the Saviour of the human race, although they might in other respects be uninformed, and various errors might still remain to be rooted out of their minds, were yet baptized, and admitted into the fellowship of Christ's kingdom. The growth and increase of the church would have been beyond measure retarded. had no one in those early times been received into the Christian community but such as had gone through a long course of probation, and had acquired an accurate knowledge of the religion they were about to embrace. When Christianity, however, had obtained for itself somewhat of a more stable footing, so that in many [p. 142.] places very large congregations of its professors were established, it was deemed expedient that none should be received into the church but such as

had made themselves thoroughly acquainted with the Christian discipline, and had given convincing proofs of their possessing a sincere and upright mind. This regulation being once introduced, it unavoidably gave rise to the distinction between the *faithful* and the *catechumens*, or between those who were *fully* and such as were merely *partially* admitted into the Christian fellowship. Many have written on the subject of the catechumens, and particularly Tob. Pfanner, in whose book, however, I have to regret the same deficiency that occurs in almost every other work on Christian antiquities, namely, that although the things themselves be perspicuously discussed, and satisfactorily established by a reference to ancient authorities, yet the causes to which the laws and institutions of the primitive church owed their rise are either wholly passed over, or but slightly hinted at. This defect, however, is not of so serious a nature but that it may, without much difficulty, be supplied by any one of common learning and capacity.

(3) Respecting the terms "brethren" and "sisters," thus made use of to denote the perfect equality that was understood to exist amongst all the members of the Christian community, there was a book published at Goslar, 1703, in 8vo. by Gothofred Arnold, under the title of *Historia Cognationis spiritualis veterum Christianorum*. Like all the other works, however, of that author, who, although a well-intentioned man, and one by no means destitute of learning, was yet possessed of but a very moderate share of sagacity or judgment, it exhibits an undigested farrago of facts and opinions, by which the mind of the reader is embarrassed and distracted, instead of being gratified and enlightened.

(4) What St. Luke has left us on record in Acts, iv. 34. respecting the primitive church at Jerusalem, namely, that none of its members lacked or were in want, may, in the strictest sense, be applied to all the other early churches. Since the Christians considered themselves to be all on an equal footing, and all united in one common bond of fraternal love, they of course deemed it incumbent on them to take care that none of their number should be destitute of the necessaries of life ; but that, if any were in want of these, their necessities should be supplied out of the abundance of the others. Amongst those of the present day, however, who pique themselves on the faculty of seeing farther into things than other people, there are not a few who take exception to this liberality of the primitive Christians towards their poor, on the score of imprudence, —alleging that it tended to the encouragement of idleness and sloth. They are also fond of adding, that the compassion and regard thus shown for the indigent and necessitous, must be considered as the cause which, beyond all others, contributed to the rapid propagation of the Christian religion : for that, under the expectation of being supported in ease and comfort by the liberality of others, without any care or pains of their own, vast crowds of idle, worthless, lazy people were led to embrace with eagerness the Christian fellowship. But that any thing like this should be urged by men, who would fain be thought no strangers to the apostles' writings, is truly amazing. Had those writings ever been perused by them with attention, nothing but the most wilful and inveterate blindness could have prevented them from perceiving that the liberality

of the Christians towards their poor was regulated by the most discreet provisions, so as to render it nearly impossible that the munificence of the church could be either abused or misapplied. In the first place, it is expressly enjoined by St. Paul, that none should be included in the number of the poor who would not endeavour, as far as they were able, to support themselves by honest labour. Indeed, they were not only to be refused relief, but were to be absolutely expelled from the church. All, likewise, that did not conduct themselves as became the disciples of Christ, were to be withdrawn from, and to be denied the benefits of Christian charity. 2 Thess. iii. 6–12. In the next place, we find it laid down in clear and express terms, as the duty of every Christian [p. 143.] family to provide, as far as they were able, for those of their own kindred, and not suffer them to become a burden to the church. 1 Tim. v. 3. 16. By another apostolic admonition, particular care is enjoined to be taken that evil-disposed persons might not be furnished, through the bounty of the church, with the means for vicious gratification. And lastly, in addition to all this, it is still further directed that the number of those to whom public relief was granted, should not be suffered to increase beyond measure, or so as to press too hard on the means of those by whom such relief was supplied. It was not, therefore, every one who might happen to be destitute, or in need, that was regarded by the primitive church in the light of a pauper, meriting charitable assistance. To entitle a man to public relief amongst the first Christians, it was necessary that he should appear to be duly impressed with a proper sense of his duty towards God and mankind ; and that he should not either be capable of procuring a subsistence for himself by any exertions of his own, or have any relatives or connections to whom he might with any degree of justice or propriety be referred for assistance adequate to his wants.

(5) It appears to me that if the voice of reason and common sense be attended to, not a question can for a moment exist as to the justice and propriety of expelling from any community all such of its members as may forfeit the pledge publicly given by them on their being admitted into such community, and contemptuously persist in an open violation of its laws. The dictates of reason, indeed, as to this point, are, in my opinion, so unequivocally clear and imperative, that I am altogether filled with astonishment when I reflect on the number of eminently learned men,—men, too, particularly versed in the principle and nature of laws, divine as well as human, who have not scrupled peremptorily to maintain that the practice of excommunicating evil-doers, or expelling them from the church, has no other support or foundation than the ancient Jewish law, or the mere arbitrary will of the first Christians. But the influence which opinions, that we have been once led to entertain and approve of, have on our future judgment is incredible. Whatever may appear to oppose itself to them is not for a moment to be listened to, however well it may be supported by either argument or evidence. To enter into any serious discussion of the matter, however, in this place would be useless, since there is not the least ground to hope for a revival of this pious and salutary custom in times like the present.

XLVI. **Teachers and ministers.** Both the teachers and the ministers of the church, when their appointment had received the approbation of the people, were consecrated by the presbyters to their office by prayer and the imposition of hands ;—a practice which the Christians adopted from the Jews, probably on account of its very high antiquity, and the great appearance of piety which it carried with it. The duties of the presbyters consisted in instructing and exhorting the multitude, both publicly and in private. It belonged to them also to endeavour, by argument and persuasion, to convince and bring over the adversaries and enemies of the faith. Tit. i. 9. 2 Tim. ii. 24. The converts were baptized by them. They also presided at the feasts of love, and celebration of the Lord's supper. In short, they were invested with the superintendance and management of everything which might be essentially connected with the welfare and prosperity, either of the church in its collective capacity, or of its several members individually. When it came to be the practice for a chief or presiding presbyter to be appointed, under the title of " bishop," the province of teaching, and also the direction and management of every thing of a sacred nature, was transferred to him. As it was not, however, to be expected that one man could be equal to the personal discharge of duties so various and extensive, he had the power of committing to either of the elders the fulfilment of such of them as that elder might appear to him to be particularly well qualified to execute. When anything of more than or-[p. 144.] dinary moment occurred, the bishop called together the presbyters, and consulted with them as to what was necessary or proper to be done. Having thus taken council with the elders, he next convened a general meeting of the people, to whose determination every thing of importance was always finally referred, and submitted to them, for their approval or rejection, the measures which appeared to him and the presbyters as either requisite or eligible to be pursued. Acts, xxi. 18. 22. The bishop was commonly chosen from amongst the presbyters, and the presbyters for the most part, taken from the class of deacons. The people, however, were not bound to abide by this rule ; and it was occasionally departed from, when the probity, the faith, and the general merits of any individual amongst the multitude pointed him out as a person deserving of preference. That the income or stipend of the several teachers and ministers of the church could have been but small, whilst, at the same time, the trouble and perils which they necessarily had to encounter in the discharge of their functions were manifold and great, is so apparent as not to admit of a doubt. But in those primitive times of which we are now treating, a Christian pastor's station in the scale of dignity and honour was, for the most 'part, estimated by the magnitude of the benefits derived from his labours, and not by the extent of his revenue, or of any other kind of pecuniary remuneration, that might be attached to his office.

XLVII. **Order of proceeding, when assembled.** The particular form or manner of proceeding in those solemn assemblies, which were held at stated intervals for the purpose of divine worship, does not appear at the first to have been every where precisely similar.([1]) It was frequently required that much should be conceded to place, to time, and to various other circumstances. From what is left us on record, however, in the books of the New Testament, and some other very ancient documents, it appears that the course observed in most of the churches was as follows. After certain introductory prayers, (with the offering up of which there can be no doubt but that the service commenced,) a select portion of Scripture was read by one or other of the deacons. The lesson being ended, some presbyter, or, after the appointment of bishops, the bishop, addressed himself to the people in a grave and pious discourse; not, as it should seem, composed according to the rules of art, but recommending itself to attention and respect through the unaffected piety and fervent zeal of the preacher. In this discourse, the multitude were exhorted to frame their lives agreeably to the word which they had heard read, and to embrace every occasion of proving themselves worthy disciples of that Divine Master, whose followers they professed themselves to be.([2]) Some general prayers (the extemporaneous effusions, as it should seem, of a mind glowing with divine love) were then offered up aloud by the officiating minister, and repeated after him by the people. If there were any present who declared themselves to be commissioned of God to make known his will to the people, I mean persons professing themselves to be prophets, they were now at liberty to address the congregation. After having heard what they had to say, it was referred to the acknowledged prophets, to determine whether they spake under the influence of a mere natural impulse, or were prompted in what they delivered by a divine inspiration. To this first solemn act of public worship succeeded a second, which commenced with the offering of certain voluntary gifts, or oblations, which all those who were possessed of sufficient ability, were accustomed to bring with them, and present to the elders. From what was thus offered, the presiding minister selected so much as might appear to him to be necessary for the [p. 145.] celebration of the Lord's supper, and consecrated it to that purpose in a set form of words; the people expressing their approval of his prayers, by pronouncing aloud the word "amen" at the conclusion of them. After partaking of the Lord's supper, the assembly sat down to a sober and sacred repast, denominated the feast of love. In this, however, the same order was not observed in all the churches. At the breaking up of the assembly the brethren and sisters exchanged with each other what, from its being meant as a token of mutual good will, was termed the kiss of peace. How truly admirable the simplicity by which the rites of our holy religion was characterized in these its infant days !(²)

(1) Next to the writings of the New Testament, the most ancient authority that we have respecting the forms and method observed by the Christians of the first century, in their assemblies for the purpose of divine worship, is Pliny the Younger, a Roman of considerable eminence, who held the office of propraetor of Bithynia under the emperor Trajan. The particulars relating to this subject, which are contained in that well-known letter of his to his imperial master, (the xcviith of the xth book,) on which so much attention has been bestowed in the way of illustration by the learned, were collected, as he himself expressly intimates, from the mouths of a number of persons who, intimidated by the fear of death, had renounced Christianity, and returned back to the worship of the Roman deities. The generality of people would, in all probability, have given implicit credit to so many persons, when thus found to agree in one and the same account: but to the mind of Pliny, a man, as it should seem, beyond measure cautious and circumspect, this united testimony did not appear altogether conclusive. Informed, as he was, of the various reports that were in constant circulation amongst the priests and populace, respecting the infamous clandestine practices and vile repasts of the Christians, and finding no correspondence whatever between those reports and the testimony of the above-mentioned repudiators of Christianity, (for they were all of them unanimous in asserting that, in the assemblies of the Christians, nothing was ever done in which it might be deemed at all disgrace-

fu⁻ for a virtuous man and good citizen to join,) he seems to have been apprehensive of being made the dupe of dissemblers, and to have entertained some doubt as to whether he ought to give the preference in point of credit to general report, or to the evidence of these particular witnesses. With a view, therefore, to arrive at greater certainty as to this point, he subjected two deaconesses of the Christians who fell into his hands, and who appear to have been of the rank of servants, to the torture, expecting thereby to obtain a full disclosure of the truth. Of the information that was extorted from them he speaks merely in general terms. *Quo magis*, says he, *necessarium credidi,* (it is apparent, therefore, that he entertained some suspicion as to the accuracy of the testimony of those renunciators of Christianity whom he had before examined,) *ex duabus ancillis, quæ ministræ dicebantur, quid esset veri et per tormenta quærere. Sed nihil aliud inveni quam superstitionem pravam et immodicam.* From these words of the proconsul, we may collect that he succeeded in obtaining from these women some additional testimony; but it is, at the same time, clear that he had been able to extort from them nothing whatever that tended, in any respect, to contradict or invalidate the account given by those whom he had before examined. The expression *superstitio prava et immodica,* although it conveys somewhat of a degrading and injurious imputation, and was evidently intended by Pliny so to do, has yet nothing in it which can be said in any wise to sully or derogate from the pure and sacred character of Christianity. The term "superstition" is applied by him [p. 146.] to it, in consequence of its being a religion which differed in its principles and nature from that of the Romans, and which discountenancing the worship of their ancient deities, would substitute for it that of Jesus Christ. The epithet *pravus* was, we know, used to denote in any thing the opposite quality to *rectus:*—the latter, therefore, implying a consonancy with that which is fit, proper, and agreeable to rule; the former must, of course, be understood as indicating a want of such consonancy. By terming Christianity then *prava superstitio,* nothing more appears to have been meant than that it was a religion of an opposite character to the approved and established Roman mode of worship. The Romans, for instance, were accustomed to offer up victims to their gods, and to dedicate to them temples, altars, statues, and images. Their invocations and prayers to them were also accompanied with a long and varied train of ceremonies. But the Christian mode of worship was, on the contrary, in every respect characterised by the utmost plainness and simplicity. To Pliny, therefore, the latter, inasmuch as it opposed itself to what had received the sanction of long established and general usage, had the appearance of being (*prava*) founded in perversion and error. He likewise applies to it the epithet *immodica,* meaning thereby, as it should seem, that it was a religion of extravagance,—a religion not limited either by the bounds which the wisdom of antiquity had prescribed, or by those which were to be deduced from the dictates of philosophy. *Immodicus* was, we are certain, a term used by the Romans to characterise any thing by which a person was led into extravagance, or carried away beyond the bounds or rule assigned by reason, or the laws of the state. Now Pliny could have known no other bounds or rule for religion than the two above mentioned, namely, the rule prescribed by reason or philosophy, and that laid down by the Roman laws: and it appears to me, therefore, that by denominating the Christian discipline *immodica*, it was unquestionably the intention of this illustrious writer to intimate that it imposed greater and more difficult duties on mankind than were prescribed either by philosophy or by the ancient religion of the Roman people. With regard to the love of mankind, for instance, the principles recognized by the Roman people at large, and even by the most excellent of their philosophers, were that we ought to love and cherish our friends, and that no wrong or injury should be done to any one except our enemies: the latter, however, might, according to them, be without impropriety hated, and in every possible way vexed and persecuted. But the divine author of Christianity enjoins that our love of each other should be limited by no such bounds, but extend itself even to our enemies and greatest foes. By a Roman, then, the principles of Christianity might, in this respect, very naturally be considered as (*immodica*) exceeding the bounds of propriety. I have been induced thus to bestow some little pains in the illustration of these words, from my observing that the various learned commentators on Pliny have passed them over with but a slight notice. On the whole, it appears to me, that at the moment when this illustrious writer intended nothing less than to pay any sort of compliment to Christianity, he in fact pronounced its eulogium ; and that, by the very terms which he applied to it in the way of reproof, he in reality establishes its claim to the character of superior wisdom and excellence.

Let us now turn our attention towards, and briefly examine those particulars, respecting the forms of divine worship observed by the first Christians, which Pliny states himself to have obtained from the many witnesses which he had examined, of whom some had renounced Christianity, others not. Great as is the number of commentators, who have gone before us in this path, we may yet, I rather think, be able to pick up something in the way of gleaning. In the first place, I will lay before the reader the words of Pliny himself, from the Gesnerian edition of his works, the most correct of any that have as yet been given to the public. *Adfirmabant autem, hanc fuisse summam vel culpæ suæ vel erroris, quod essent soliti stato die ante lucem convenire : carmenque Christo, quasi deo, dicere secum invicem : se que sacramento non in scelus aliquod obstringere sed ne furta, ne latrocinia, ne adulteria committerent, ne fidem fallerent, ne depositum appellati abnegarent : quibis peractis, morem sibi discedendi fuisse, rursusque* [p. 147.] *coeundi ad capiendum cibum, promiscuum tamen et innocuum.* " They affirmed the whole of their guilt, or their error, was, that they met on a certain stated day before it was light, and addressed themselves in a form of prayer to Christ, as to some god, binding themselves by a solemn oath, not for the purposes of any wicked design, but never to commit any fraud, theft, or adultery, never to falsify their word, nor deny a trust when they should be called upon to deliver it up: after which, it was their custom to separate, and then reassemble to eat in common a harmless meal." (Melmoth.) Now it must immediately, I think, be remarked by every one who shall peruse this passage with attention, that the sketch which it exhibits of the forms observed by the Christians in their solemn assemblies is throughout but an imperfect one, and that in many respects it is wholly deficient. Not a word, for instance, is said of the exhortation or sermon usually delivered by one of the presbyters or the bishop, or of the reading a portion of the Scriptures; nor is there any notice taken of the celebration of the Lord's supper, or of the oblations which it was customary for the communicants to offer. In making his report to Trajan, Pliny probably saw no necessity for setting down all that he had learnt from the witnesses, but deemed it sufficient to lay before the emperor merely such particulars as would give him an insight into the nature of the Christian discipline, and satisfy him that those who had embraced it were far from being of a character either so detestable or dangerous as that which was attributed to them by vulgar report. For Pliny's epistle, from beginning to end, is unquestionably to be regarded in the light of an apology for the Christians; the object of it evidently being to refute those calumnies under which they laboured, and to incline the emperor to treat with lenity and compassion a set of men, who, although they had espoused a different religion from that of the Romans, yet appeared to him to cherish no principles either of a vicious or dangerous tendency. In addition to this, it must necessarily be observed, (and it will presently be rendered more strikingly manifest,) that the information thus communicated by Pliny to the emperor is conveyed rather in terms and phrases of his own, than in those which it is at all likely that the Christians whom he had examined made use of; and that, in a certain degree, his description of the Christian sacred rites obviously, and as it were by way of illustration, accommodates itself to the Roman way of thinking on the subject. This, I have no doubt, was the result of design; his object in it being, as I conceive, to render the matter more intelligible and easy of apprehension than it would otherwise have been to Trajan, who was an utter stranger to the maxims and institutions of the Christians, and wholly unacquainted with their affairs. Had Pliny, in his account of the Christian principles and customs, made use of Christian terms and phrases, the emperor would in all probability have found no small difficulty in ascertaining the meaning of many of them, and might possibly have understood some parts of the letter in a sense very different from that which it was the object and intention of the writer to convey. But to come to particulars.— The account commences by stating in general terms, that the solemn assemblies of the Christians were held on a certain fixed day. This fixed day, as may be proved from the epistle itself (and in another place I have so proved it,) was the same with that which we at present consider as sacred, namely, the first day of the week, the day on which our blessed Saviour arose from the dead. B. Just. Hen. Bœhmer would indeed have us to understand this day to have been the same with the Jewish Sabbath; but notwithstanding all that he has urged in his dissertation *de Stato Christianorum Die*, (which stands first in that series of tracts, in which he undertakes to illustrate the sacred rites, &c. of the Christians from Pliny,) I rather think that he has not succeeded in making any converts to his opinion amongst those who have read what Pliny says with attention, and taken the pains to make themselves acquainted with ancient manners. On this stated day, the Christians of Bithynia, it appears were accustomed to hold two distinct meetings; the one before sun-rise, for the worship of God, and furtherance of piety; the other in the course of the day, most probably about the time of noon, for the purpose of partaking together of a common meal or repast. With the Christians of other countries it was not the custom thus to divide their sacred offices; but they went through the whole of whatever might be enjoined with regard to public worship at one and the same meeting. It is by no means difficult, however, to assign a very sufficient reason for this deviation of the Bithynian Christians from the general practice. Exposed, as they were on all sides, to the treachery of malignant foes, it would have been impossible for them to have met and gone through their forms of public worship during the day. There assembly for this purpose, therefore, was held before sun-rise. To have joined in a meal, however, at this early hour would not have been seasonable or convenient; and the feast of love was, threfore, deferred until that time [p. 148.] of the day, which in those regions was customarily allotted to bodily refection. The public worship, for the performance of which the first of these meetings was held, commenced with the offering up of prayers, in which they gave praise to Christ, and extolled the blessings to mankind of which he was the author. These prayers Pliny states them to have recited *secum invicem*. Now by the former of these words, I conceive him to have meant, that the prayers thus offered up were general ones, in which every person present joined. With regard to the term *invicem*, learned men have imagined that we ought to understand it as indicating the manner in which these prayers were recited; and that it has, in this place, a similar import with *alternatim;* implying, as they would have it, that in the assemblies of which we are speaking, the Christians divided themselves into two choirs, and that the praises of Christ were alternately celebrated by each. For my own part, I should not by any means wish to be understood as pronouncing this opinion to be erroneous; but, at the same time, I cannot help observing that it appears to me not at all improbable that Pliny might have recourse to the term *invicem*, by way of briefly expressing what the Christians had told him, of its being usual for one of their presbyters, or their bishop, first to recite the form of prayer, and then for the people to repeat it after him, and add the word "amen" at the conclusion. Were the term to be considered as having this reference, we should unquestionably find less difficulty in making it accord with what we know of the forms and usages of the early ages. As to the force or precise meaning of the words *quasi deo*, I must confess that I really do not feel myself at all competent to speak with decision. For it appears to me to be altogether uncertain whether Pliny, in this place, makes use of words of his own, or adopts those of the Christians whom he had examined. If the expression is to be considered as Pliny's own, it certainly cannot be adduced as a proof that those Christians entertained a similar opinion with ourselves as to the divinity of Christ; for *deus*, as is well observed by that excellent scholar and sagacious commentator, Jo. Matth. Gesner, in his remarks on this passage, was a term in the use of which the Romans allowed themselves considerable latitude; and so far from considering it as exclusively appropriate to the divine nature, were in the habit of not unfrequently applying it to spiritual beings of a very inferior order. On the other hand, could it be ascertained that *quasi deo* were the words of the Christians whom Pliny examined, there must at once be an end to all doubt as to the fact of those Christians having worshipped our blessed Saviour as the Supreme Deity.—With regard to the word *carmen*, it admits of some question whether we ought to understand by it that these prayers of the Christians were composed according to the rules of metre, and consequently sung; or whether the term is to be considered as implying in this place, what we frequently find it applied to elsewhere, merely a set form of words in prose. Some of the highest authorities, including the celebrated Gesner, lean in favour of the latter construction ; and influenced chiefly by the weight of such judgment, I was led to give preference to this opinion in my *Histor. Christian. Institutiones majores*, sæc. i. The former construction of the word has, however, found an able advocate in a learned writer, whose masterly discussion of the subject, under the assumed title of *Hymnophilus*, is to be found in the fifth volume of the *Miscellanea Lipsiens. nov.* of the learned Menckenius. After having compared together the different arguments brought forward on either side, I must confess it now appears to me scarcely possible to say which way the scale preponderates. Those eminent scholars, to whose opinion I formerly subscribed, bring forward, in support of their construction of the word, the authority of a great number of ancient Latin writers, and beyond all, that of Pliny himself, in whose writings they observe, the word *carmen* is several times put for prayers in prose. The verb *dicere*, too, they bid us remark, which Pliny in this place joins with *carmen*, will not admit of the supposition that compositions in verse were here alluded to ; for that had real verses been meant, they would have been stated (*cani*) to be sung, not (*dici*) said. But of these arguments, neither the one or the other can be deemed conclusive. For as to the first, it can by no means be allowed [p. 149.] to follow, that because the word *carmen* is frequently put by Pliny and others for a composition in prose, it may not have a different signification in the passage in question; and particularly if it be considered that in the one case it is used in an extraordinary sense, but in the other merely in an ordinary one. And with regard to the argument deduced from the word *dicere*, a variety of passages might be quoted, which would show that this verb was occasionally put for *cantare*, and associated with *carmen* in its strict sense. In the *Carmen sæculare* of Horace, for instance, ver. 6, 7, 8, we find,

> " *Quo Sybillini monuere versus*
> *Virgines lectas, puerosque castos,*
> *Diis, quibus septem placuere colles,*
>   Dicere carmen.*"

Indisputably alluding to the singing of a hymn, or composition in verse. Virgil too, when speaking of the hymn which the husbandmen were accustomed to sing to Ceres, before putting the sickle to the corn, *Georg.* lib. i. ver. 348, et seq. says,

> ————————————————" *Neque ante*
> *Falcem maturis quisquam supponat aristis,*
> *Quam Cereri, torta redimitus tempora quercu,*
> *Det motus incompositos, et* carmina dicat.*"

And again, when describing a part of the inhabitants of the Elysian Fields as occupied in song and dance, *Æneid.* lib. vi. ver. 644.

> " *Pars pedibus plaudunt choreas, et* carmina dicunt."

The very learned writer, to whom I have above alluded as taking with others the opposite side of the question, rests his argument principally upon the word *carmen*,—reminding us that it strictly and properly signifies a song, and contending that the strict and proper signification of a word is not to be departed from, unless through evident necessity. Now all this is certainly very well observed. But the advocates for the former opinion may reply, that this learned writer himself is one of the first to break through the rule which he thus prescribes to others, of adhering to the strict and proper signification of words, by insisting that we ought to understand Pliny as using *dicere* in the sense of *cantare:* for that this is literally rejecting the plain and commonly accepted meaning of the former verb, and annexing to it a remote and unusual signification, without any apparent necessity for so doing. In support of this construction, indeed, he adduces the authority of Eusebius and Tertullian: the latter (in *Apologetic.* cap. ii.) making use of the term *canere*, as expressive of Pliny's meaning; and the former (in his *Ecclesiastical Hist.* lib. iii. cap. 33.) rendering the words *carmen dicere* into Greek by the verb ὑμνεῖν. Now this is certainly a circumstance not unworthy of remark; but, at the same time, it cannot be considered as altogether so conclusive as to place the matter beyond doubt: for were the question to be agitated, it is very possible that much difference of opinion might be found to prevail with regard to the merits of Tertullian and Eusebius as translators of Pliny. As to any thing else connected with this point, I purposely pass it over.

These prayers, then, whether in verse or in prose, having been offered up, the Christians, according to Pliny, *sacramento se obstringebant, &c.* " bound themselves by an oath not to commit theft, robbery, or any other crime forbidden by law. But in this instance, it is plainly to be perceived that we have not the words of the Christians themselves given to us. The terms here used must be considered as belonging entirely to Pliny, who endeavoured, by clothing the information he had taken down from the mouths of the Christians in a Roman dress, to render it easier of comprehension to the emperor, and thus the more readily to satisfy him of the innocent and harmless character of the religion which these people professed. With regard to what he here first says, of its having been the practice of the Christians in their assemblies, *sacramento se obstringere*, "to bind themselves by an oath," that is, *to swear*, [p. 150.] that they would lead a chaste life, &c. it is altogether a misrepresentation of the fact . and I know not how to account for it, that learned men, who do not appear to have been ignorant of the utter dislike which the early Christians had to oaths of any sort, should for a moment have brought themselves to believe that such was the case. For is it at all credible that men so exceedingly reserved and scrupulous in swearing, be the occasion what it might, should have regularly bound themselves by an oath, whenever they assembled together for the purposes of divine worship? This difficulty has not indeed escaped the observation of some men of erudition, and they have endeavoured to obviate it by suggesting that when the Christians, in the course of their examination, made mention of their *sacraments*, Pliny might not be aware of their meaning, but conceive that the term was used by them in its literal Roman sense; whereas what they alluded to were certain rises of their own, to which they had given the denomination of sacraments, namely, baptism and the supper of the Lord. The conjecture is certainly ingenious, but beyond this we can allow it to possess no merit whatever. For not to mention other things by which it might be shown to be utterly destitute of foundation, its fallacy is rendered sufficiently apparent by Pliny himself, who expressly states that sacrament of which he speaks, to have been comprehended in the first part of the Christian worship; whereas the celebration of what were termed sacraments by the Christians, did not belong to that portion of their divine service. The Lord's supper, in particular, is known to have always formed a branch of that latter or concluding part of their public worship, to which we shall presently advert. To me it appears most likely, that the Christians simply represented themselves as making a solemn promise to the Almighty, whenever they assembled together, that they would strive to lead a life of purity and innocence; and that Pliny, perceiving little or no difference between a promise of this sort and an oath, by way of making a stronger impression on Trajan's mind, preferred expressing himself after the Roman manner, and stated them *sacramento se obstringere*. It yields a further argument against our believing that the Christians were accustomed in their assemblies to take an oath to the above effect, that not the least vestige whatever of any such periodical repetition of the articles of their profession is to be met with in any of the monuments of antiquity; nor was it at all necessary. The practice was, for those who embraced Christianity, once, namely, at the time of their initiation, to pledge themselves solemnly to God that they would lead a life conformable to the religion they had espoused. After having done this, they do not appear to have been continually called upon for a repetition of their engagement, but were merely admonished publicly by the presbyters to beware of departing from, or forfeiting the solemn promise thus made. Finally, what Pliny thus reports to the emperor concerning the Christians, *viz.* that they solemnly pledged themselves to abstain from the commission of any acts that were forbidden as criminal by the Roman laws, such as theft, robbery, adultery, violation of compacts, refusal to restore any thing given merely in pledge, and the like, can never be considered as having constituted any very striking feature in that most pure and holy system of moral discipline, which the professors of Christianity made it their object to cherish and inculcate. Restrictions of this sort might doubtless occupy a subordinate place in the Christian code; but its injunctions mainly respected duties of a higher and more important nature:—that we were, for instance, to cherish the most unbounded reverence for God and his will; that our love should be extended universally to all mankind; that we should ever be ready to do good, even to our enemies; and should earnestly strive to subdue, and as it were extinguish, within ourselves, every sort of unlawful appetite. There can be little or no doubt that the Christians whom Pliny examined pointed out these things to him, but that he deemed it unnecessary to notice them; conceiving that every purpose he had in view would be sufficiently answered, by his representing to Trajan that no incongruity subsisted between the Christian discipline and the Roman laws, but that whatever was interdicted as criminal by the one was as strictly prohibited by the other. To me it appears most likely, that the account given by the Christians on this occasion was to the following purport:— That after offering up their prayers to Christ, it was customary for one or [p. 151.] other of their ministers to read a portion of those Scriptures which they held sacred. That a solemn oration or sermon was then delivered by a presbyter, or the bishop, in which those present were exhorted to make what they had heard, the rule of their faith and conduct; abstaining, as far as in them lay, from the commission of evil of any kind; and that it was usual for all of them to promise, silently within themselves, that they would do so. If any refused to conform themselves to the word, agreeably to this admonition, and preferred continuing in the practice of iniquity, they were excluded from all communication with the assembly. And this is the sense which Tertullian, who perceived how widely Pliny's account, if taken literally, would differ in this respect from the practice of the first Christians, annexes to the passage in question. *Allegat,* says he, alluding to this letter of Pliny's, *nihil aliud se de sacris eorum comperisse, quam cœtus ante lucanos ad canendum Christo ut deo, et ad confœderandam disciplinam, homicidium, adulterium, fraudem, perfidiam, et cætera scelera prohibentes.* (*Apologetic.* cap. ii.) The reader will perceive that this exactly corresponds with what I have above remarked. Nothing is here said of the taking of any oath; nothing of any reiteration of the baptismal vow · on the contrary, the crimes which Pliny states the Christians to have abjured, are here represented as being merely prohibited, meaning doubtless forbidden by the mouth of the preacher.

At their second meeting, it was the practice of the Christians to celebrate the feast of love, and the Lord's supper; of which two rites Pliny speaks in the following terms: *Rursusque coeundi ad capiendum cibum, promiscuum tamen et innoxium.* *Promiscuus cibus,* it appears to me, is here put to denote food of the opposite quality to that which is exquisite and delicate. By this expression, therefore, it should seem, that Pliny meant to do away that suspicion of indulging in luxury and voluptuous excess, which the enemies of the Christians had excited against them; and to satisfy the emperor that in their repasts they made use of nothing costly or delicate, but merely the plain and ordinary articles of food. The epithet *innoxius* was unquestionably intended by him to operate in direct refutation of a calumny respecting the Christians, which had been very generally propagated throughout the confines of the Roman empire, and had served to kindle amongst the lower orders of the people a wonderful degree of animosity towards them, namely, that of their occasionally joining in a sort of Thyestean banquet,—a charge of which we find frequent notice taken in the different apologies of the early Christians.

(2) There are several, not to speak merely of men of ordinary learning, but also of the better informed, who maintain that any individual amongst the Chris-

tians was, in this first age, at liberty to assume the office of a teacher in their solemn assemblies, and might there openly deliver his sentiments on divine subjects, for the benefit of the fraternity at large. A very unwarrantable use, however, has been made of this opinion by some of the present day, who aim at bringing about a new order of things in the Christian commonwealth, and would fain abrogate all rule; and jumbling every thing together, do away all sort of distinction between teachers and learners. For my own part, could I perceive, that such an opinion was in any respect well founded, I would at once, without the least hesitation, acknowledge it. In fact I could, in the present instance, have no temptation whatever to disguise the truth; since, having never filled the office of a public teacher in the church, my interest is not at all involved in the question: and besides I well know, that should such or such appear to have been the customary or established practice of the first ages, it by no means follows that it ought not to have been deviated from in succeeding generations. But I most solemnly declare, that amongst the various arguments and proofs which are adduced in support of the above opinion, even by those of the learned who have espoused it, I have not been able to find any thing whatever that can, in my opinion, be considered as satisfactory, — I will not say by a man of acuteness and penetration, but by any one of common sense and understanding. So far as this, indeed, undoubtedly appears clear, that any one, whether he were a presbyter, or a bishop, or merely a person of the ordinary class, might use his endeavours to propagate the Christian Religion, [p. 152.] and exert himself to the best of his abilities in making known the blessings of celestial truth to those who lay chained in darkness and superstition. But does this, let me ask, at all support the idea that the office of teaching in the public assemblies of the Christians might be assumed by any of the brethren *ad libitum!* It is also unquestionable that the primitive Christians, in conformity to the direction of the apostles, were accustomed to admonish, exhort, and reprove each other. But there can be no doubt that this was done privately, and not openly in the face of the whole congregation, when assembled for the purposes of public worship. Finally, no one denies that the prophets, or those who asserted themselves to be under the influence of divine inspiration, had liberty to speak in the solemn assemblies of the church. But it appears to me truly astonishing that any one should bring forward this as an argument in favour of the opinion, that the office of teaching in public might of right be assumed by any of the brethren indiscriminately. If I am capable of forming any judgement at all on the subject, I am sure that what we know of these prophets, so far from yielding any argument in favour of such an opinion, makes directly the contrary way. It appears to me in fact altogether incontrovertible, that the prophets only had liberty to preach, and consequently that the liberty of preaching could not have belonged of common right to all the brethren: and that so far from its having been the practice for every one to address the brethren in their public assemblies, who might feel inclined so to do, this privilege was confined merely to those who had given satisfactory proof of their being divinely commissioned to instruct the church.

(3) The reader will find these particulars more fully discussed and illustrated

in Bingham's *Origines Ecclesiasticæ*, Cave's *Primitive Christianity*, Goth. Arnold's work *de Vita et Moribus primorum Christianorum*, and the writings of various other authors. It may not, however, be improper to apprise him that considerable caution ought to be observed in reading books of this sort; since, to pass over other things, the authors of them have not been on all occasions sufficiently particular in the choice of their authorities, neither have they made a proper distinction with regard to times, or between such things as are certain and indisputable and such as are merely probable.

XLVIII. **All the primitive churches independent.** Although all the churches were, in this first age of Christianity, united together in one common bond of faith and love, and were in every respect ready to promote the interests and welfare of each other by a reciprocal interchange of good offices; yet with regard to government and internal economy, every individual church considered itself as an independent community, none of them ever looking in these respects beyond the circle of its own members for assistance, or recognizing any sort of external influence or authority. Neither in the New Testament, nor in any ancient document whatever, do we find any thing recorded, from whence it might be inferred that any of the minor churches were at all dependent on, or looked up for direction to, those of greater magnitude or consequence: on the contrary, several things occur therein, which put it out of all doubt that every one of them enjoyed the same rights, and was considered as being on a footing of the most perfect equality with the rest.(') Indeed it cannot,—I will not say be proved, but even be made to appear probable, from any testimony divine or human, that in this age it was the practice for several churches to enter into, and maintain amongst themselves that sort of association, which afterwards came to subsist amongst the churches of almost every province:—I allude to [p. 153.] their assembling by their bishops, at stated periods, for the purpose of enacting general laws, and determining any questions or controversies that might arise respecting divine matters.(²) It is not until the second century that any traces of that sort of association, from whence councils took their origin, are to be perceived: when we find them occurring here and there, some of them tolerably clear and distinct, others again but slight and faint: which seems plainly to prove that the practice arose subsequently to the times of the apostles, and that all that is urged concerning the councils of the first century, and the divine authority of councils, is sustained merely by the most uncertain kind of support, namely, the practice and opinion of more recent times.(²)

(1) It appears indeed from the Acts of the Apostles, that the dignity and authority of the church of Jerusalem was forawhile very great. In cap. xv. we find the Christians of Antioch referring their disputes concerning the necessity of observing the law of Moses, to the judgment of this church; and it seems extremely probable that other churches might act in a similar way. St. Paul too, although acting under an immediately divine commission, yet made it a point to commend himself and his doctrine to the favour and approval of the apostles and the church of Jerusalem. Gal. i. 18. ii. 7, 8, 9. But the authority thus recognised in this particular church, did not arise so much out of any thing like a superiority over the other churches, (for it never laid claim to any such pre-eminency,) as from the circumstance of its being under the immediate care and government of our Lord's apostles, who were expressly constituted by Christ himself supreme directors and judges of all matters connected with religion. Properly speaking, it was not to the church of Jerusalem, but to the apostles who presided over it, that the other churches had recourse for direction. To confess the truth, however, it is not improbable that in dubious matters, even in the absence of the apostles, application might oftener be made to this church than to any other for advice. For in the church of Jerusalem there must have been a far greater number of inspired persons than was to be met with in any of the other churches; since the Holy Spirit, at the time of its miraculous effusion, recorded in Acts, ii. did not descend merely on the apostles, but was poured out generally on all the disciples of Christ in that city. The churches of Asia, I have not the least doubt, recognized a similar authority in that of Ephesus, during the time that St. John presided over it. Indeed it appears to me not at all unlikely, that the honour of being occasionally looked up to by neighbouring churches for an example, both as to faith and practice, might be a distinction enjoyed by all such of the churches, as had had the good fortune to be under the immediate tuition and care of any of the apostles. Should any one require it, I will concede even more than this; for I am sure it is my wish most readily to grant whatever can reasonably be expected of me. I will admit then, that it was for some time customary for all the apostolical churches, that is, those which had been founded and instructed by the apostles themselves, to be consulted respecting any new opinions that might be suggested, or any controversies that might arise respecting religion. Of this custom abundant testimony is to be collected from the writers of the second century. The spiritual instructors of that age appear to have thought, and in my opinion not without reason, as things were then situated, that with regard to matters of faith and doctrine, it was not likely that any should be better informed than those [p. 154.] who had been under the immediate tuition of the apostles themselves. In the case too, of any one's taking upon him to disseminate new opinions, and endeavouring to shelter himself under apostolic authority, no more effectual way of

repressing his presumption could present itself than that of referring to the testimony of the churches which the apostles themselves had founded. See, for instance, Tertullian *de Præscript. advers. Hæreticos.* It is a most egregious mistake, however, for any one to imagine that we have in this any thing like a proof of an inequality having subsisted amongst the early churches, or of a judicial power having been possessed by such of them as were apostolical. For to pass over other things which might be urged, it was not to the churches, but to the apostles, the founders of those churches, whose counsel and discipline were supposed still to prevail in those assemblies, that this judicial power was attributed; and by degrees, as the decisions and authority of councils came to have more weight and influence, this ancient practice of recurring to the testimony of the apostolical churches fell into disuse. In fact, the thing was as much a matter of choice then, as at present it is with any one whether or not he will refer any doubts, with which he may be perplexed, to be resolved by a college of divines in an university. Certain I am that no proof whatever can be brought to show that this sort of reference to the apostolical churches was at all compulsory, or that their determinations were considered of such authority as for it to be deemed impious in any one to decline complying with them. A great reverence was undoubtedly, during the first ages, entertained for such of the churches as had been long under the immediate instruction of any of the apostles; but if any one thing be certain, I am persuaded this is,—that these churches never possessed the power of governing or controuling the rest according to their will.

(2) In St. Paul's epistles there are several passages, which plainly prove that the first churches were held together by no bond, save only that of faith and mutual love : and that each was governed and regulated by its own laws and institutions. Those seven epistles addressed to the Asiatic churches, with which the Revelations open, exhibit likewise indisputable testimony to the same effect. In the first place, nothing whatever is to be found in these epistles to warrant even a conjecture that these seven churches were united together by any sort of consociation, or that they were accustomed to assemble one with the other in the way of council : on the contrary, the circumstance of our Saviour's not directing what he had to say to them collectively, but, whether it be in the way of commendation, of reprehension, or of admonition, addressing himself to each one separately, tends unquestionably to prove that they had nothing in common, save that of their being of one and the same religious profession. Had it been usual for the bishops of these churches to assemble and consult together at stated periods, or when any thing new or extraordinary might occur, as was the practice in the second century, it is not at all probable that the circumstance would have been passed over by our Saviour without the smallest notice ; but that on the contrary, he would have recommended to the pastors thus associated the cultivation of prudence and harmony, and would have attributed to them chiefly whatever presented itself either as exceptionable or praise-worthy in the state of these churches. Again, another argument of still greater cogency is to be drawn from these epistles :—for it appears by them that there was a considerable diversity in the tenets and regulations of these seven

churches. The Nicolaitans, for instance, whoever they might then be, were wholly excluded from the church of Ephesus, Rev. ii. 6.; whereas in [p. 155.] that of Pergamos they had free toleration, Rev. ii. 15. The members of the church of Thyatira suffered those to continue of their number who ate with the worshippers of false deities in their temples, and were addicted to fornication; things which were for the most part held in utter abomination by the rest. Now if the heads of churches, thus situated in one and the same province, had been accustomed occasionally to meet for the purpose of consulting together, and deliberating on the best means of promoting the common welfare of the assemblies over which they presided, in what way are we to account for the existence of this diversity of sentiments and moral discipline amongst them? Had it at that time been the practice to hold councils, the case of the Nicolaitans would without doubt have been discussed therein; and either their tenets would have been sanctioned by the general voice, or the sect would have been excluded from the churches altogether.

(3) It is very common for that assembly of the church of Jerusalem, of which we read in Acts, xv. to be termed the *first council ;* and if people choose still to persist in giving it this denomination, I shall certainly not trouble myself so far as to fall out with them about it. I would wish them, however, to understand that this is applying the word *council,* in a way altogether inconsistent with its true import. The congregation that is stated to have met on this occasion was nothing more than an assembly of the members of one individual church, consisting of the apostles, the elders, and the people. Now if the term council could properly be applied to such an assembly as this, it would follow as a necessary consequence that more councils were held in the first century than in any subsequent one; whereas even the warmest advocates for their early origin are ready to admit, that in this age they were not by any means frequent. In fact, it was a common practice in all the churches, at this period, for the members to hold meetings after the manner of that above alluded to as having been convened at Jerusalem, for the purpose of consulting together, and deliberating on matters relating to religion and divine worship: and therefore, if such a meeting is to be termed a council, it may even be said that there were more councils held in the first century than in all the subsequent ones down to our own time put together. A council, properly speaking, means an assembly of several associated churches, or a congregation of delegates representing a number of churches so united, in which the common welfare of the whole is made the subject-matter of consultation ; and such things are resolved on and enacted as may appear to the members constituting such an assembly, or to the major part of them, eligible, and fraught with a promise of conducing to the general good. Now, that such an assembly as this was even once held in the first century, is what I am sure no one, let him take what pains he may, will ever be able to find in the history of that age. As the cause of Christianity, however, advanced, and its concerns became more extensive, so that the churches composing an ecclesiastical province, assumed, as it were, the form of a republic made up of various minor districts, it became necessary, in order to preserve tranquillity and a mutual good understanding amongst them, that several parti-

culars should be occasionally discussed in a general meeting, composed of legates or deputies from each.

XLIX. But few persons of erudition amongst the primitive Christians. The apostolic fathers. In the age of which we are now treating, it was not deemed so essentially requisite in a teacher that he should be distinguished for profound or extensive knowledge, either human or divine, as that he should be a man of virtue and probity, and, in addition to a due measure of gravity, be possessed of a certain degree of facility in imparting instruction to the ignorant. Had the apostles indeed thought otherwise, and directed that none but men of letters and erudition should have been elected to the office of presbyters, it would not have been possible for the churches to have complied with such a man- [p. 156.] date; since, at that time, the number of the wise and learned who had embraced the faith of Christ was but small, and as it were of no account. The Christian writers of the first century consequently were not many; and from the labours of the few whose works have reached us, whether we consult such as have been handed down whole and entire, or such as carry with them the marks of interpolation and corruption, it is uniformly evident that, in unfolding the sacred truths of Christianity to the world, the assistance of genius, of art, or of human means of any other kind, was but little, if it all, courted. For if the mind of a reader is not to be charmed or wrought upon by sanctity of sentiment, simplicity of diction, or the effusions of a genuine unaffected piety, it will be in vain for him to seek for either gratification or improvement in the perusal of the writings to which we allude. All these authors, although by no means on a level in point of dignity and judgment, are yet usually classed together under the general title of " the Apostolic Fathers ;" alluding as it should seem, to their having conversed with the apostles themselves, or with some of their immediate associates, and their works have, in consequence, been most commonly edited together. On this account, it may be the better way perhaps for us to collect here into one view whatever we may judge necessary to be known respecting them, than to postpone any part of it to a subsequent period ; although Ignatius, Polycarp, and Hermas, rather belong to the second century, as that was the age in which they wrote and died.(')

(1) Whatever writings could in any way be ascribed to the apostolic fathers, whether good, bad, or indifferent, were all of them collected together by Jo. Bapt. Cotelerius, a French divine, and published by him in two volumes, illustrated with long and learned notes. This work was afterwards twice re-printed at Amsterdam, with various additions by Jo. Le Clerc. The better part of these fathers has also been given to the public, but without comment, by Tho. Ittigius, in his *Bibliotheca Patrum Apostolicorum.* They have been translated into English by Wake, archbishop of Canterbury; into German, by Gothofred Arnold; and the better part of them into French, by Abr. Ruchat.

L. **The genuine writings of Clement of Rome.** At the head of these writers stands that Clement who, from his having been bishop of Rome, is usually, by way of distinction styled the Roman ; a man of unquestionably the highest authority, since we find other authors, with a view to obtain for their opinions and writings a favourable reception with the public, prefixing to them his name. The common accounts that we have of his life, the incidents by which it was chequered, and the manner of his death, are for the most part undeserving of credit, at least they are by no means well authenticated.(') There are extant two epistles of his in Greek addressed to the church of Corinth, at a time when it was distracted by intestine faction. Of these the first is generally, and I think not without reason, considered as indisputably genuine in the main ; although a very ill applied industry appears to have been subsequently exercised upon it by some one or other, probably, however, without any evil design, in the way of interpolation.(²) The authenticity of the latter one has [p. 157.] been regarded, even from a very remote period, as somewhat questionable, though it is not easy to say on what grounds, since there seems to be nothing whatever in it that is manifestly irreconcileable with what we know of the genius and character of Clement.(³)

(1) Vid. Jo. Ernest Grabe *Spicileg. Patrum Sæc.* i. p. 264 ; Tillemont *Memoires pour servir a l'Histoire de l'Eglise*, tom. ii. part i. p. 269; Phil. Rondinin. lib. ii. *de S. Clemente Papa et Martyre, ejusque Basilica in Urbe Roma*, 1706, 4to. Some time back, when a Sepulchre, bearing the name of Clement, was unexpectedly laid open at Rome, a good deal of discussion took place amongst the learned of Italy respecting Clemens Romanus. With regard to these investigations, however, the wisest and best-informed writers do not scruple to avow that the history of this venerable man is involved in great obscurity ; and that several things, which have been hastily considered as re-

lating to him, belong properly to Flavius Clemens the consul, who was put to death by Domitian. See the Dissertations of the Jesuit Zacharias, and of Vitry, which were published by Angelus Calogera, in his *Opusc. Scientific.* tom. xxxiii. p. 300. 350, et seq.

(2) This interpolation was first detected by Hieron. Bignonius, who communicated what he had thus remarked in a letter to Grotius. See Cotelerii *Patres Apostolici*, tom. i. p. 133, 134. The discovery was further prosecuted, not however without caution, by Ed. Bernhard, in some annotations of his on Clement, which were published by Le Clerc, in the last edition of his *Patres Apostolici.* The learned Hen. Wotton, it is true, in his notes on this epistle, leaves no means untried to do away this imputation, and to persuade us that the letter in question has been handed down pure and unvitiated by any sort of corruption whatever. But the labours of this eminent scholar, so far from establishing his point, may be said to have been completely thrown away; since it is as clear as the light itself, that there are several passages in this epistle altogether irrelevant to the writer's purpose, and which hold no sort of connection or correspondence with what precedes or follows them: indeed some of them are manifestly taken from Clement of Alexandria. For my own part, I should think that it might be very possible for an attentive and skilful person to remove from this venerable author's robe, (if I may be allowed to apply the term robe to an epistle that has no pretensions to either learning or eloquence,) these patches with which it is at present disfigured; and it appears to me to be a kind of task which it might prove well worth the while for any judicious scholar to undertake.

(3) A list of the different editions of these epistles that have been published, is given by Jo. Albert. Fabricius, in his *Biblioth. Græc.* lib. iv. cap. v. p. 175, et seq. It does not, however, include the most accurate one of all, *viz.* that printed at Cambridge in 1718, in 8vo. by Hen. Wotton, and enriched with various notes and dissertations of his own, and of several other learned men.

[p. 158.]   LI. Supposititious writings of Clement. In addition to these epistles, there have been attributed to Clement the following works: 1. Eight books of *Apostolical Constitutions*, a work of undoubted antiquity, but, at the same time, of uncertain date; the production of an author beyond all measure, austere, and who, as it should seem, entertained a thorough contempt for intellectual culture of any kind. The most probable origin that we can assign to this work is, that some ascetic writer having drawn up a form of church government and discipline, upon what he conceived to be apostolic maxims, he, in order to gain for it more attention and respect, attributed it at once to the apostles themselves, pretending it to have been received direct from them by their disciple Clement.(') 2. A set of *Apostolical Canons*, or Ecclesiastical Laws, eighty-five in number, which the person who framed them wished to be considered as having been enacted by the apostles, and transmitted by them to Clement. It should seem to be not at all unlikely that these Canons and the above-mentioned Constitutions might originate with one and the same author. Be that as it may, the matter of this work is unquestionably ancient; since the manners and discipline of which it exhibits a view are those which prevailed amongst the Christians of the second and third centuries, especially those resident in Greece and the oriental regions.([2]) With respect to its form, however the work is commonly looked upon as belonging to a more recent age. 3. *The Recognitions of Clement*, in ten books. This is a narrative entirely fictitious, but at the same time of an agreeable interesting nature, and of considerable use in bringing us acquainted with the tenets of the Gnostics, and enabling us rightly to comprehend the state of Christian affairs in the age to which it refers. The work professes to be an account of the travels of St. Peter, and his disputes with Simon Magus, the leader of the Gnostics, written by Clement; in reality however it appears to have come from the pen of an Alexandrian Jew, who had but partially embraced Christianity, and still cherished errors of the grossest kind. Considerable hostility is nevertheless manifested by him towards the tenets of the Gnostics, and in some respects he proves himself to be neither a weak nor an unskilful adversary. For some time these Recognitions were known to the public merely through the medium of a Latin translation by Rufinus: we may consider the Greek text as having been first published by Cotelerius in his Patres Apostolici. For although the Clementina, as printed by Cotelerius, differ in many respects from the Recognitions, yet in both the argument of each respective book is the same, in both the same order of narration is observed, and a similar correspondence between them prevails in the winding up and conclusion of the narrative: in fact it should seem that one and the same book was anciently edited twice, or perhaps oftener, under a somewhat different form.([3])

(1) The various opinions entertained by the learned, respecting the Apostolical Constitutions and Canons, have been collected into one view by Tho. Ittigius, in a dissertation *de Patribus Apostolicis*, prefixed to his *Bibliotheca Patrum Apostolicorum;* as also by Jo. Franc. Buddeus, in his *Isagog. in The-*

ologiam, part ii. cap. v. p. 742, et seq. There are likewise two learned disser-
[p. 159.] tations on the same subject, annexed by Jo. Phil. Baratiere, to his
work *de Successione Romanor. Episcoporum primorum,* p. 229, and 260 ; the
object of one of which is to prove that these Constitutions are not, as many
pretend, interpolated ; whilst that of the other is to make it appear that they
were compiled about the beginning of the second century. As to the first of
these points, the generality of people will, I rather think, feel disposed to agree
with him ; but with regard to the latter, I conceive that his arguments will
not be deemed conclusive by many.

(2) This has been proved, I think, beyond all controversy by that most
able investigator of Christian antiquities, Bishop Beveridge, as well in his annotations on these canons, as in a separate work on this subject, published by
him (Lond. 1678, in 4to.) under the title of *Codex Canonum Ecclesiæ primi-
tiræ vindicatus et illustratus.*

(3) Concerning this work (which those who may be induced to consult it,
will find to throw considerable light on several ancient matters and opinions,
and to yield more assistance towards comprehending the mysteries in the discipline of Simon Magnus and others of the Gnostics, than all the other early
writers put together) I have spoken more at large in my dissertation *de turbata per recentiores Platonicos Ecclesia,* § XXXIV. See my *Syntagma Dissert.
ad Hist. Eccl. pertin.* vol. i. I do not however consider myself as having,
either here or even there, pointed out every ground on which it has a claim to
our attention.

LII. **Ignatius and his Epistles.** Next after Clement in point of
time comes Ignatius, to whom St. Peter himself is said to have
committed the care and superintendance of the church of Antioch,
and who, by command of the emperor Trajan, was delivered over
as a prey to wild beasts in the theatre at Rome.(¹) There are extant several Epistles with the name of Ignatius prefixed to them ;
but a question having been made as to their authenticity, a deal
of learned and elaborate discussion has taken place on the subject
amongst men of erudition, and the point has been contested by
them with considerable vehemence; some asserting them to be
spurious, others insisting on it that they are genuine.(²) The
most prevailing opinion appears to be that the seven which are
reputed to have been written by him in the course of his journey
to Rome, namely those respectively addressed to the Smyrneans,
to Polycarp, to the Ephesians, to the Magnesians, to the Phila-
delphians, and to the Trallians, as they stand in the edition of
them published in the seventeenth century, from a manuscript
in the Medicean library at Florence are unquestionably genuine;

though there are not wanting those who, on account of its dissimilitude of style, consider the authenticity of the Epistle to Polycarp as less to be depended on than that of the other six. As for the rest of these Epistles, of which no mention whatever is made by any of the early Christian writers, they are commonly rejected as altogether spurious. The distinction thus generally recognized in favour of the above-mentioned particular letters is grounded on reasons of no little force and weight, but at the same time they are not of such a conclusive nature as to silence all objection : on the contrary, a regard for truth requires it to be acknowledged, that so considerable a degree of obscurity hangs over the question respecting the authenticity of not only a part, but the whole of the Epistles ascribed to Ignatius, as to render it altogether a case of much intricacy and doubt.(²)

(1) For a copious account of Ignatius we refer the reader to Tillemont's *Memoires pour servir a l'Histoire de l'Eglise*, tom. ii. p. ii. p. 42. 80. Several others also have employed their pens on this subject, as may be seen [p. 160.] in the *Biblioth. Græc.* of Fabricius, lib. v. cap. i. p. 38, where likewise the different editions of the Epistles of Ignatius are enumerated, and a view is taken of the disputes amongst the learned to which they have given rise.

(2) But few probably would ever have interested themselves much in this question concerning the genuineness of the Epistles of Ignatius, had they not been found to favour the cause of those who contend for the divine origin and great antiquity of episcopal government. But the Presbyterians as they are termed, and those amongst us who are for doing away every thing of which the teachers of the church might avail themselves, in order to maintain a distinction between themselves and the people, perceiving this, have attacked these letters with all the warmth of party spirit, and occasionally suffered themselves to be betrayed into so much violence on the subject, as rather to lessen their own credit than that of the Epistles in the eyes of a judicious reader. The Episcopalians have also, not unfrequently, run into the same fault ; and in their eagerness to prove a want of penetration and judgment in their adversaries, have shown a deficiency of candour and liberality in themselves. For my own part, I cannot perceive that it would be of any great consequence to either party to obtain the victory in this case ; since it by no means appears to me that the cause of episcopacy is so far dependent on these Epistles for support, as that it must stand or fall accordingly as they may be adjudged to be either genuine or spurious. But the conduct of even our greatest scholars may, in some instances, be said to resemble that of advocates in courts of law, who frequently contend with more asperity and earnestness for minor or collateral points, than for the principal matter in dispute.

(3) That the six or seven letters above pointed out have in them somewhat of a genuine cast is, I think, unquestionable, and rendered particularly

manifest by (amongst others) Bishop Pearson in his *Vindiciæ Ignatianæ*, a work of great excellence, and replete with profound learning. As to the quantity however of what may thus be considered as authentic, I must confess myself unable to determine. There are extant, as is well known, two editions of the Epistles ascribed to Ignatius; the one an ancient one, and the more comprehensive of the two; the other, that which was published in the 17th century, first of all by Isaac Vossius, and afterwards by Sir Thomas Smith, from the Medicean manuscript, and in which are not to be found several things that are contained in the former. Of these editions the latter has, in general, the preference given to it by those of the present day who wish to uphold the authority of Ignatius, inasmuch as it accords better with the tenets and opinions now generally prevalent in the Christian church than the other, in which some passages and expressions occur which cannot well be defended or reconciled with what are commonly deemed orthodox sentiments respecting God and the Saviour of mankind. This is not however considered as by any means a satisfactory reason for rejecting the other edition by some, who with truth remark, that prior to the existence of controversies in the church, its members appear to have allowed themselves considerable latitude both in thinking and speaking, and that consequently the rules of expression to which we of the present day find it necessary to confine ourselves, must not be too strictly applied as a standard whereby to judge of anything that may occur in the writings of the early Christians. There are therefore not wanting those who consider the more ancient and fuller edition as the best; amongst whom we may mention Jo. Morin (*de sacr. Ordinat.* p. iii. exerc. iii. cap. iii.) and W. Whiston: the latter of whom, in a work printed at London, 1710, in 8vo. endeavours to prove that Athanasius contrived to get every thing which seemed to militate against the Nicene dogma concerning the existence of three persons in one God, to be expunged from the Epistles of Ignatius, lest the tenets of himself and his associates might appear not to be in unison with the sentiments of so respectable a writer. As for what Whiston would thus insinuate respecting Athanasius, it is unquestionably to be regarded as nothing more than one of those dreams of [p. 161.] fancy by which men are sometimes led astray, when they pay more attention to the suggestions of their own imagination than to the dictates of right reason; but it must at the same time be acknowledged that the opinion entertained by him, in common with other learned men, that a preference ought to be given to the more ancient and fuller edition of the Ignatian Epistles, although it may be questioned and opposed, can yet by no means be wholly set aside, or proved to have no foundation in truth. Le Clerc has attacked this opinion with no little force, in an express dissertation annexed to the last edition of the *Patres Apostolici*, tom. ii. p. 501, et seq.; as has also Wotton in the preface to his edition of the Epistles of Clement, p. clxxxv. et seq.; but should any one be inclined to enter the lists in defence of the opposite side of the question, he will not have far to seek for a reply. To me it appears not at all impossible that the longer epistles should have been curtailed or epitomized by some one or other; and it might, in my opinion, therefore be urged with some show of reason, that the shorter epistles published by Vossius are merely an abridgment of the longer ones, made by some unknown person, who was probably apprehensive lest any loose and incautious expressions of Ignatius might prove of detriment to the orthodox belief respecting the divine Trinity. But to whichsoever edition we may give the preference, we shall never, under the present circumstances, let us endeavour what we may, be able to exonerate these letters from all suspicion of corruption and interpolation. Upon the whole, it appears to me, that this great controversy respecting the Epistles of Ignatius, although it has occupied the attention and talents of so many eminent men, remains as yet undecided, nor do I think that it can ever be satisfactorily determined, unless further light should be acquired by a discovery of some more ancient copies, or of some more explicit early authorities than those we are already in possession of on the subject. The letters themselves, come from what pen they may, are indisputably of very ancient date ; and that they are not altogether a forgery is in the highest degree credible : but to ascertain with precision the exact extent to which they may be considered as genuine, appears to me to be beyond the reach of all human penetration.

LIII. **Polycarp and Barnabas.** The Epistle to the Philippians which is attributed to Polycarp, bishop of Smyrna, who had been one of St. John's disciples, and who, about the middle of the second century, suffered martyrdom at a very advanced age, has merely a questionable claim to credit; in consequence of which it is regarded by some as spurious, though others consider it to be genuine.(') The Epistle that has come down to us with the name of Barnabas affixed to it, and which consists of two parts, the one comprising proofs of the divinity of the Christian religion derived from the books of the Old Testament, the other, a collection of moral precepts, is unquestionably a composition of great antiquity, but we are left in uncertainty as to its author. For as to what is suggested by some, of its having been written by that Barnabas who was the friend and companion of St. Paul, the futility of such a notion is easily to be made apparent from the letter itself; several of the opinions and interpretations of Scripture which it contains, having in them so little of either truth, dignity, or force, as to render it impossible that they could ever have proceeded from the pen of a man divinely instructed.(')

(1) A list of authors who have written particularly respecting Poly- [p. 162.] carp, is given by Jo. Alb. Fabricius in his *Bibliotheca Græca*, lib. v. cap. i. p. 47 et seq. The most distinguished of these is Tillemont, whose diligence has never been surpassed by either of the others. See his *Memoires pour servir a l'Histoire de l'Eglise*, tom. ii. p. ii. p. 287, et seq. The year and month of this father's death have been made the subject of particular discussion by (amongst others) Bara-

tier, in his work *de Successione Romanorum Pontificum*, and the Abbé Longerue, in a dissertation *de Anno Macedonum*, which is to be found in J. D. Winckler's *Sylloge Anecdotorum* p. 18. 25. But since the grounds and arguments relied on in this discussion, are chiefly drawn from the Greek Epistle of the church of Smyrna respecting the death of Polycarp, first published by Bishop Usher, it appears to me that very great doubt and uncertainty must continue still to hang over the point. For whoever will attentively consider that Epistle, and compare it with what is given us from it by Eusebius in his *Ecclesiastical History*, lib. iv. cap. xv. cannot fail to perceive that it has been corrupted and interpolated by some weak and superstitious person, who, in his endeavours, to multiply miracles, descends even to trifling, and occasionally falls into the absurdity of disagreeing with himself.

(2) With regard to Barnabas and his Epistle, the reader may consult, amongst other works, Fabricii *Biblioth. Græc.* lib. iv. cap. v. § xiv. p. 173, and lib. v. cap. i. § iv. p. 3. Thom. Ittigii *Select. Histor. Eccles. Capit.* sæc. i. c. i. § xiv. p. 20.—Basnage, in his *Histoire des Juifs*, tom. iii. cap. xxvi. p. 558, has pointed out and corrected some of the more flagrant errors of this writer, but not all. For he has adopted many, and that too in things with regard to which it would have been easy for him to have obtained more accurate information. With respect to the real origin of this letter, I do not, for my own part, see any just grounds for believing it to have been written by some artful man, who, the more readily to gain readers and proselytes, introduced it to the world as an Epistle of Barnabas the companion of St. Paul. In fact I can perceive nothing whatever that should lead one even to suspect a thing of the kind : and the opinion therefore to which I incline is, that some Jew of the name of Barnabas, a man, as it should seem, not wanting in piety, but of a weak and superstitious character, being actuated by a wish to forward, to the utmost of his ability, amongst his brethren, the cause of that most holy religion to which he had himself become a convert, drew up and sent out into the world this Epistle; but that the early Christians, led away by a name for which they entertained the highest reverence, attributed it at once to that Barnabas who was the friend and companion of St. Paul.

LIV. **Hermas.** The list of apostolical fathers closes with Hermas, a writer of the second century, who, according to early authorities, was brother to Pius, bishop of Rome.(') His book, which is now known to the world merely through the medium of a Latin translation, was originally written in Greek, and is entitled " *The Shepherd*," the principal character introduced in it being that of an angel who had assumed the form and garb of a shepherd, and who, under this disguise becomes the instrument of conveying to Hermas instruction and admonition from above. [p. 163.] The object of this author evidently was, to impress the world with the belief that his book was not the offspring of any human understanding or talents, but that whatever it contained had been derived either from God himself or from the above-mentioned angelic shepherd. But there is such an admixture of folly and superstition with piety, such a ridiculous association of the most egregious nonsense with things momentous and useful, not only in the celestial visions which constitute the substance of his first book, but also in the precepts and parables which are put into the mouth of the angel in the two others, as to render it a matter of astonishment that men of learning should ever have thought of giving Hermas a place amongst the inspired writers. To me it appears clear that he must have been either a wild disordered fanatic, or else, as is more likely, a man who, by way of more readily drawing the attention of his brethren to certain maxims and precepts which he deemed just and salutary, conceived himself to be warranted in pretending to have derived them from conversations with God and the angels.([2])

(1) Amongst the learned there have not been wanting some, [among the Britans and the adherents to the Roman Pontif,] who, from a wish, to exalt the character and authority of Hermas, the author of " The Shepherd, " the writer to whom we here allude, have strained every nerve to persuade us that he was a different person from that Hermas whom ancient authors speak of as having been brother to Pius, bishop of Rome. What they maintain is, that the author of " The Shepherd, " was either that Hermas spoken of by St. Paul in Rom. xvi. 14. ; or if this should not appear to be probable, still that he was a very ancient writer , who lived in the time of Clement of Rome, and before the destruction of Jerusalem ; a position which must at once fall to the ground, were it to be admitted that " The Shepherd " was written by the brother of Pius, bishop of Rome, since the Romish see was filled by no one of that name until the second century. No one has displayed greater learning in defence of this point, or entered into it more fully, than Just. Fontaninus : vid. *Histor. Literar. Aquiliens.* lib. ii. cap. i. p. 63, et seq. But notwithstanding all that has been urged by him and others, it is most clearly manifest that the early writers who make mention of Hermas, the brother of Pius, understood him to be one and the same with that Hermas who was the author of "The Shepherd. " To me it appears impossible for any one to doubt this who will attentively consider the following passage in the verses against Marcion, to be found amongst Tertullian's works, lib. iii. cap. ix. p. 366, edit. Venet. ; and which, if wrongly attributed to Tertullian, were yet certainly written by some very ancient author—

> " *Jamque loco nono cathedram suscepit Hyginus,*
> *Post hunc deinde Pius, Hermas cui germine frater*
> *Angelicus Pastor, quia tradita verba loquutus.* "

Now the opinion of learned men with regard to this passage has been, **that**

14

Hermas is here styled an *angelic pastor*, that is a teacher rivalling the angels, and possessed of angelic excellence. But that this is a mistake is evident from the context,—*quia tradita verba loquutus.* For supposing the above opinion to be just, we have here the reason assigned for the writer's applying to Hermas the title of *Angelic Pastor:* but who, let me ask, can possibly see in these words even the shadow of a reason to justify the appellation? Could the circumstance [p. 164.] of his having spoken *tradita verba*, or "words transmitted from above," give Hermas a claim to the title of *Angelic Pastor?* If it did, the title is certainly not due to him alone, but belongs also to every sound Christian preacher; for all such men teach and speak words which came from God himself, and were commanded by him to be put in writing. The more natural conclusion then is, that it is not to Hermas that the magnificient title of Angelic Pastor has relation in this passage, but to some other person; nor does there appear to me to be the least difficulty whatever in immediately pointing that other person out. Not a question, as it strikes me, can exist but that the appellation refers to the work called "The Shepherd," which was written by Hermas, and in the second and third book of which an angelic pastor or shepherd is introduced as communicating to the author what is there recorded; and what Tertullian meant to intimate in my opinion, undoubtedly was, that the Hermas of whom he spake was the same with him to whom an angel, under the form and garb of a shepherd, had communicated and explained certain mandates from above. If the common reading indeed of this passage be retained, I am ready to allow that the sense which I would thus annex to it may appear to be not altogether obvious or plain: but it will not admit of a doubt that this reading is corrupt. Even those who may be against me as to the above interpretation of the passage, must yet allow this to be the fact: for as the words stand at present, it is impossible to annex to them any sense whatever. The correction, I should propose, would be, to transfer the comma which follows the word *pastor*, back to the word *frater* at the close of the preceding line, and to exchange the particle *quia* in the third line for the pronoun *cui:*

> ———————————— *" Hermas cui germine frater,*
> *Angelicus Pastor cui tradita verba loquutus. "*

Corrected in this way the passage at once loses its obscurity, and becomes in every respect clear and intelligible. " Pius, " says Tertullian, "has a natural brother called Hermas: I mean the person of that name who enjoyed the rare felicity of receiving from the mouth of an angelic pastor, or angel who assumed the form and guise of a shepherd, words transmitted from the Deity himself." That I should point to a variety of passages in the writings of other ancient authors, which explicitly corroborate the testimony of Tertullian in this respect, by attributing " The Shepherd " to that Hermas who was the brother of Pius, is, I conceive, not by any means necessary. For there was fortunately brought to light, some few years since, a work of unquestionable authority, the production of an author cotemporary with Hermas, and containing a passage which places it beyond all dispute that the book which we have extant under the title of " the Shepherd " was written in the second century, by the brother of Pius, bishop of

Rome. It is a fragment (the exordium being wanting) of a small work concerning the canon of the holy Scriptures, and was published by L. Ant. Muratori, in his *Antiquitates. Ital. Med. Ævi*, tom. iii. diss. xliii. p. 853, et seq. The
author of it is unknown. Muratori attributes it to Caius, a presbyter of the
church of Rome, who lived in the latter part of the second century; but the
point is by no means placed beyond doubt. Of this however we are certain,
from the evidence of the book itself, that the author, whoever he might be, compiled it in the second century, and during the time when Hermas was alive. In
this very valuable fragment we meet with the following testimony respecting
Hermas, the author of "the Shepherd:" "*Pastorem vero nuperrime temporibus
nostris in urbe Roma Herma conscripsit, sedente cathedra urbis Romæ* [p. 165.]
Ecclesiæ Pio *episcopo* fratre ejus.—Nothing surely can be more explicit than
this; and there is consequently no room left for further dispute amongst the
learned respecting either the age, the kindred, or the condition of Hermas. To
this passage succeeds another no less worthy of remark, since it brings us acquainted with the degree of estimation in which Hermas was held as a writer
by the Latin church. The construction of the paragraph is indeed not the most
elegant imaginable, but it nevertheless leaves us in no doubt as to the fact
that the writings of Hermas were not included within the canon of sacred Scriptures: *Et idco legi eum quidem oportet, se publicare vero in ecclesia populo, neque
inter prophetas completum numero, neque inter apostolos in finem temporum potest.*
"The Shepherd," says this writer, "may properly enough be perused by pious
persons in private, but it is not a work fit to be read publicly in assemblies of
the church, or deserving of being classed with the writings of either the prophets or the apostles."—The just discrimination exhibited in this passage reflects no little honour on the Latin churches, inasmuch as it proves them to have
been more discreet and cautious in their judgment than the Greeks were, who
for the most part regarded Hermas as an author not inferior to the prophets and
apostles. Hermas himself, as I shall presently take occasion to show, was unquestionably desirous of having a place assigned him amongst the sacred writers:
but the teachers of the Latin, and especially the Roman churches, notwithstanding they were told that his book contained the discourses of an angel and the
church, and that the precepts therein delivered were the very words of God himself, notwithstanding also that they knew the author was brother to Pius the
Roman pontiff, as we should now call him, yet would they not suffer themselves
to be imposed upon, but candidly and boldly affirmed, that neither the visions
of Hermas nor the discourses of his angelic instructor, were entitled to any
credit. Out of respect, as I conceive, to the brother of a man of considerable
authority, and a Roman bishop, they did not go the length of prohibiting the
use of the book altogether, but permitted it to be perused with a view to pious
edification in private; they however would not consent to its being read in
public to the people. It must indeed be acknowledged that the Latin, and especially the Roman Christians, manifested from the first a greater degree of
circumspection and prudence in drawing the line between such writings as were
really and truly the fruit of divine inspiration and such as falsely pretended to
that character, than those of Greece and the oriental regions, whose precipitancy

was such, that, had their judgment been made the criterion, the canon of the New Testament would have come down to us by far more bulky in size than it is at present, and disgraced by writings which are now by common consent regarded as apocryphal. Whilst we are on the subject, I will add a word or two respecting the reason which some of the learned assign as chiefly inducing them to consider the author of the work now extant under the title of "the Shepherd" and Hermas, who was brother to Pius, as having been two different persons. In the *Liber pontificalis* and some other ancient writings, there is a passage cited respecting the celebration of Easter, from a book called "the Shepherd," written by Hermas, the brother of Pius, but which is no where to be found in the work that has reached us under that title. See Jo. Alb. Fabricii *Codex Apocryphus Novi. Testam.* tom. iii. p. 761. Hence they infer that the Shepherd written by Hermas, the brother of Pius, was a different book from the Shepherd that we are in possession of. But this way of reasoning, although it might be fair enough if the work were extant in the original Greek, and we certain that it had come down to us entire, will yet by no means hold good [p. 166.] under the existing circumstances, since the work is known to us merely through a Latin translation, and it is far from being impossible that this translation, should be incomplete. To me it appears not at all unlikely that those of the Greek and oriental Christians, who were styled *Quartadecimans*, might expunge from " the Shepherd " the passage above alluded to respecting the time of keeping Easter, inasmuch as it militated against the opinion which they themselves entertained on the subject.

(2) Several things, which I cannot well enter into in this place, conspire to impress me with the opinion that Hermas could never have been so far the dupe of an over-heated imagination, as to fancy that he saw and heard things which in reality had no existence, but that he knowingly and wilfully was guilty of a cheat, and invented those divine conversations and visions which he asserts himself to have enjoyed, with a view to obtain a more ready reception for certain precepts and admonitions which he conceived would prove salutary to the Roman church. At the time when he wrote, it was an established maxim with many of the Christians, that it was pardonable in an advocate for religion to avail himself of fraud and deception, if it were likely that they might conduce towards the attainment of any considerable good. Of the host of silly books and stories to which this erroneous notion gave rise from the second to the fifteenth century, no one who is acquainted with Christian History can be ignorant. The teachers of the Roman church themselves appear to me to have considered Hermas as having written his work upon this principle, and not to have altogether disapproved of it. For as we have seen above, they permitted his book to be circulated and perused, with a view to pious edification in private, but would not allow it to be read publicly in the assemblies of the church. From their refusal of the latter it may fairly be inferred, that they did not regard the visions of Hermas, or the precepts and advice of the angel with whom he pretended to have conversed, in the light of divine communications : but their acquiescing in the former, very plainly shows, that the kind of fiction to which this author had recourse, appeared to them to be such as was warrantable, and that

they did not think it unjustifiable to practice imposition on the multitude in the way of instruction, or to invent pious stories for the sake of more readily commanding their attention. Had they believed Hermas to have written under the influence of divine inspiration, they would not have dared to deny his work a place amongst the sacred writings, and pronounce it unfit to be read in public: but on the other hand, had they felt indignant at the cheat practised by him, or disapproved of the guile to which he had recourse, they unquestionably would never have recommended the perusal of his work to Christians in private, as useful and likely to confirm their piety. That Hermas himself, however, was desirous of having a place assigned him amongst the inspired writers, and to have his work read in the public assemblies of the Christians as the writings of the prophets and apostles were, is plain from what occurs at the end of the second vision in his first book, (edit. Fabrician. p. 791.) The church, which he represents as having appeared to him under the form of an aged matron, is there made to inquire, *Si jam libellum dedisset senioribus?*—"If he had yet given his book to the elders?" meaning the presbyters of the Roman church. His reply is in the negative, *adhuc non.* Hearing this, the church thus continues: *Bene fecisti: habeo enim quædam verba edicere tibi. Cum autem consummavero omnia verba, aperte scientur ab electis.* Admirably well observed indeed! The meaning of these words as is unquestionably proved by what subsequently occurs, is nothing less than this: "After I shall have finished what I have in charge to communicate to thee from above, the book must be sent to all the Christian churches, and be read publicly therein, that no one may be ignorant of the divine will." We shall add what follows, as it most clearly evinces not only the deceit of the man, but also that he had the arrogance [p. 167.] to aspire at being associated with the sacred writers. *Scribes ergo duos libellos, et mittes unum Clementi, et unum Graptæ. Mittet autem Clemens in exteras civitates: illi enim permissum est. Grapte autem commonebit viduas et orphanos. Tu autem leges in hac civitate cum senioribus qui præsunt ecclesiæ.* The Clement here spoken of must without doubt have been a man of the highest authority, since the power is attributed to him of sending round, and recommending to the foreign churches, such writings as might appear to be the fruit of inspiration; and he could consequently be none other than that Clement whom, by way of distinction, we usually style "the Roman:" for such preeminence and authority was never possessed by any one else of that name amongst the early Christians. The commentators on Hermas therefore are, in my opinion, right in considering him as the person here meant. Clement it is pretended was, at the time when Hermas wrote, absent from the Roman church over which he presided. For it was well known, that although that church was the principal and more immediate object of his care, yet that he frequently made excursions to the neighbouring cities, with a view to extend and strengthen the interests of the Christian community, the duties appertaining to his office in the church of Rome being, during his absence, committed to the elders. The book then was to be sent to him at some no very distant city where he was staying, and he was to circulate it amongst all the other churches of Italy, by whom he was looked up to as a father, and give directions for its being read in their public assemblies. The object of this author therefore, who in fact wrote long after the death of Clement, namely under the pontificate of Pius, about the middle of the second century, evidently was to render the inspiration of his work less questionable, by making it appear as if it had been written at an earlier period, and during the life-time of Clement. This circumstance must of itself surely be enough to convince every one that the man acted on the principle of deception, and had it in view to take advantage of the simplicity of his Christian countrymen. In the Roman church, to which he himself belonged, a copy of the book was to be handed to the elders, to whom the regulation of all sacred matters was committed during the absence of Clement, in order that they might direct it to be read publicly to the people in their solemn assemblies. But even this was not deemed sufficient. Recollecting that the widows oppressed with age and infirmities, and the children as yet unbaptized, would not be present at those assemblies, he took care to provide for another copy being sent to Grapta, a woman who officiated as a deaconess, for the purpose of being read to the widows and orphans. As we have touched on the subject, it may not be amiss just to remark by the way, that some little light appears to be thrown by this passage on the duties appertaining to the office of the deaconesses, inasmuch as it seems plainly to show that they were entrusted with the instruction and ordering of the feeble women and children. Upon the whole, it is manifest that Hermas wished to make the Christians of Rome believe that his book had been considered as of the number of inspired writings, and been read in public during the time of their highly venerated and holy pastor Clement, and that consequently they themselves might, without hesitation, bestow upon it a similar honour. But to be brief. The Pastor of Hermas is a fictitious work, of much the same kind with what are termed the Clementina and the Recognitions of Clement. In its plan however it is somewhat inferior to these, as instead of mortal characters conversing, we have the Deity himself, and his ministers or angels introduced on the scene.

[p. 168.] **LV. Origin of dissensions and errors in the Primitive Church.** That disputes and dissensions should not have been altogether unknown in the first Christian churches, or that errors of no small moment should have been engendered by some of them, can occasion no very great surprise to any one who shall reflect on the nature of their constitution, and the situation of things in the age of which we are treating. For the Christian fraternity was at that period composed in part of Jews and partly of Gentile worshippers, *i. e.,* of people altogether differing from each other both in their opinions and manners; and of whom the former could by no means be induced to renounce their attachment to the law of Moses whilst Jerusalem was in existence, nor could the latter, without the greatest difficulty, prevail on themselves to endure with any becoming degree of moderation the superstition and imbecility of the Jews. Associated with these were also others of a middle class, who had either unconditionally embraced the maxims of the oriental philosophy respecting the nature of matter, the origin of this world, the conjunction of ethereal spirits with terrestrial bodies, and their expected future deliverance, or had else espoused them under certain modifications deduced from the principles of the Jewish religion. And from any of these no other conditions had been exacted previously to their being received into the Christian community by baptism, than that they should solemnly profess a belief in Christ as the Lord and Saviour of the human race, and declare themselves to be desirous of leading an innocent and holy life for the future, agreeably to his commands. Nothing like a regular course of preparatory institution had been gone through, no formal examination as to principles or opinions had taken place, no pains had been used even to root out from the minds of the converts any erroneous notions which they might have conceived or imbibed. In fact, a naked faith was all that in this infancy of the Christian church was required of any who were desirous of being admitted within its pale. A fuller and more perfect insight into its doctrines was left to be acquired in the course of time. That amongst men of this description then, allied closely indeed in point of moral worth and sanctity of demeanor, but at the same time differing widely from each other as to various matters of opinion, there should have occasionally arisen some disputes and controversies, was a circumstance so much within the ordinary course of things, as surely to yield no ground whatever for surprise.

LVI. **The first controversy, respecting the necessity of observing the law of Moses.** The first controversy by which the peace of the church appears to have been disturbed, was that which was kindled in the church of Antioch by certain Jews, who, conceiving that the ceremonial law promulgated by Moses was designed to be of perpetual duration, and that the observance of it was consequently necessary to salvation, contended that its ordinances ought to be complied with even by those of the Gentiles who had been converted to Christianity : Acts, xv. 1. et seq. Being unable to come to any agreement as to this point amongst themselves, the Christians of Antioch deputed Paul and Barnabas to consult with the apostles on the subject. The latter, having submitted the matter to the consideration of the church of Jerusalem, the controversy was at length, with the general consent, put an end to by them in the following way, namely, that such of the Christian converts as were of the Jewish nation should be at liberty to conform themselves to the Mosaic ritual, but that those of every other description should not be considered as [p. 169.] under any obligation whatever to comply with the ceremonies of the Jewish law. Lest the minds of the Jewish converts, however, should be too far alienated from the Gentile brethren, it was required of the latter to abstain from those things which were regarded as polluting and abominable by the Jews, namely, from partaking of those feasts which it was usual for pagan worshippers to prepare from the victims offered to their false gods, and from joining in the obscene libidinous indulgences with which the celebration of these feasts was in general accompanied, as likewise from blood and the flesh of animals strangled.(¹)

(1) It is common for us to term the assembly in which this controversy was settled, the first Christian council, and to consider it as the original or prototype of all the councils of after ages. Nay there are many who will go even farther, and maintain that the divine right of councils is to be proved from this assembly. " The apostles," say they, " by calling together the church of Jerusalem on this occasion, had it in view to point out to posterity, that controversies respecting religion were to be submitted to the cognizance and decision of councils." But the truth of the matter is, that we have learnt to think and speak thus from the friends to the papacy, who, after searching the Scriptures in vain for something that might establish the divine authority of councils, were at length constrained to lay hold on this convocation of the church of Jerusalem by the apostles, as on a sheet anchor or last hope. For my own part, I see no particular objection to any one's giving the denomination of a council to this assembly if he think fit; since it was anciently usual for any lawful assembly to be termed a council; and it can be shown by many examples, that a meeting of merely the teachers of a single individual church was frequently so styled. Vid. J. Gothofred *ad Codicem Theodosianum*, tom. vi. p. 28. ed. Ritterian. But as to those meetings of the heads of the church which have been, from time to time, held subsequently to the second century, and which are properly termed councils, the assembly at Jerusalem, to which we allude, bears no resemblance whatever to them, and it is consequently idle for any one to think of deducing the origin of such conventions from that source. This want of resemblance is admitted by the acute and ingenious father Paul Sarpi, himself a Romanist, in his *History of the Council of Trent*, see lib. ii. p. 240. of the French translation

of it by Courayer; but it at the same time appeared to him that he had hit upon a circumstance which would bear him out in maintaining, that the assembly at Jerusalem might still, in the strict sense of the term, be styled a council; and this was, that not only the apostles, the elders, and the brethren of Jerusalem, but also Paul and Barnabas, the deputies from the church of Antioch, are stated to have spoken therein. The title of "the first Council," he therefore thought might very justly be continued to this meeting. But surely it is scarcely possible for any reasoning to be weaker than this. Did it indeed appear that the deputies from Antioch had voted, or sat as judges in this assembly, in the same way as the elders of Jerusalem did, the argument might not be altogether destitute of force: but instead of this being the case, it is evident that they pretended to nothing beyond the character of deputies, and left the determination of the point wholly to the apostles and the other members of the church of Jerusalem. Speak they undoubtedly did, and it was necessary that [p. 170.] they should speak; but it was not in the way of offering any opinion of their own as to the matter in question that they did so. In addition to this it is to be remarked, that the point in dispute was not resolved in this assembly by the number of votes, as was the custom in councils, but was determined solely by the judgment of the apostles. Had the suffrages been taken, it was possible that of the two opinions the wrong one might have prevailed: for a greater part of the Christians of Jerusalem were strongly attached to the Mosaic law, and contended warmly for its authority in this very assembly. But, by the speeches of Peter and James, an end was put to all dissensions, and a mode of determination suggested to which the multitude deemed it incumbent on them to make no opposition. We have not therefore, here any thing in the least resembling a council: for the decision, it is plain, was not that of the church of Jerusalem, but of the apostles, by the interposition of whose opinion an end was at once put to the doubts and disputes of the church. Viewing the matter in this light, I find myself unable altogether to fall in with the opinion expressed on the subject by Just. Hen. Bœhmer, in his *Dissert. Juris Eccles. Antiqui,* diss. iii. § lxxi. p. 218, and elsewhere, who would consider the decision of this assembly in the light of an award, as the lawyers term it, conceiving the church of Antioch *per modum compromissi caussam controversam decisioni apostolorum et matricis ecclesiæ submisisse.* It should seem not improbable that the original author of this opinion might be father Paul Sarpi himself, as we meet with it in his *History of the Council of Trent,* lib. ii. p. 240, though expressed there but shortly, and with some reserve. But to me it appears that, in the first place, there is no foundation for what he sets out with assuming, namely, that the Christians of Antioch referred the determination of their controversy, not to the apostles only, but also to the whole church of Jerusalem. For it is most clearly manifest, from the statement of St. Luke, Acts, xv. 2, that the persons referred to as judges on this occasion were solely the apostles and the elders, the latter of whom were well known to be of the number of those who enjoyed divine illumination in common with the apostles, and not the whole congregation of Christians resident at Jerusalem. The apostles and presbyters, it is true, when they were about to investigate and determine the question by which the church of Antioch was divided, convoked an assembly of the people; but their doing so was a matter of discretion, not of necessity : for had they chosen it, they might, from the power that was given them of God, have proceeded of themselves to decide the point in dispute, in the absence of the people, and without in the least consulting them : of the exercise of which power by them we have a striking instance afforded us, in their checking the disposition which the people discovered to run into parties, and pointing out in what way the affair should be determined. In the next place, and which is to me an objection of still greater force, the apostles must, if this opinion be adopted, be considered merely in the light of referees or arbitrators, elected at the will of the contending parties, for the purpose of settling their dispute : whereas they had been constituted judges of all controversies like this, respecting religion, by divine appointment; and it was, therefore, not left to the option of the Christians of Antioch, whether they would refer the determination of their dispute to them or not. In a case like theirs, they were enjoined by nothing less than divine authority to have recourse to the tribunal of the apostles. Lastly, the very words themselves in which the decree, in this case, is conceived, forbid us to view it in the light of an award or judgment of arbitrators indifferently appointed by the parties. For it is not in terms of their own that the apostles make this decree, but what they ordain is expressly stated to be so done by the command and authority of the Holy Spirit. Ἔδοξε [p. 171.] τῷ ἁγίῳ πνεύματι καὶ ἡμῖν. "*It seemed good to the Holy Ghost and to us.*" In which passage the words τῷ ἁγίῳ πνεύματι, "*to the Holy Ghost,*" must be referred to the apostles, through whom the Holy Spirit, by whom they were influenced, spake, commanded, and adjudged. The meaning is—"It seemed good to the apostles, in whom the power of the Holy Spirit is resident, and whom the same spirit animates." A similar mode of expression is made use of by St. Peter, in that terrible denunciation wherewith he overwhelms Ananias, for having attempted to practise deceit on the apostles: Acts, v. 3, 4. *Why hath Satan filled thine heart to lie to the Holy Ghost?* (that is, to us in whom the Holy Spirit is resident. *Thou hast not lied unto* (mere) *men, but unto God* (who dwelleth in us). The words καὶ ἡμῖν, "*and to us,*" which follow, do not refer to the apostles, but to the elders and brethren of the church of Jerusalem, who are joined with the apostles in the beginning of the letter. For the denomination of "the Holy Ghost was not of course considered as embracing these, since they enjoyed merely an ordinary illumination of the blessed Spirit. The above remarks are submitted to the consideration of the reader, in consequence of my observing that the force of these words has hitherto escaped the attention of commentators.

LVII. **Controversy respecting the law of Moses.** Constantly bearing in mind the decree which he had thus received from the mouths of the apostles themselves at Jerusalem, we find St. Paul not only making it his endeavour, both in the churches of which he was the immediate founder, and likewise in those to which he

addressed epistles, to repress with every possible energy the attempts of the Jewish converts to impose on the necks of their
Gentile brethren the yoke of the Mosaic covenant, but also
labouring by degrees to extinguish in the minds of the Jews
themselves that blind and immoderate partiality which they
entertained for this law of their forefathers. From his epistles,
however, it appears that, in his attempts to accomplish these objects, he was ever most violently, and not unfrequently successfully, opposed by the Jews ; the mistaken zeal and intemperate
warmth of some of whom led them into such extremes, that they
hesitated not at making use of every means to excite a general
feeling of ill-will towards St. Paul, and to detract from the high
character of this great apostle of the Gentiles, who could justly
boast of having, in the most marked and emphatical manner,
been called to the ministration of the word by the voice of our
Lord himself. On the other hand, it was not without considerable difficulty that the Gentile converts could be brought to endure with patience that the Jews should thus obstinately persist
in refusing to recede from the customs and institutions of their
forefathers, and that they themselves should yield obedience to
the decree of Jerusalem, which forbad them to partake of meats
offered to idols, or to be present at the feasts of heathen worshippers. As for any disputes of inferior moment, of which description there are some particularly adverted to, and others incidentally noticed, by St. Paul in his Epistles, I purposely pass them
over in silence, as possessing no claim to our attention.

[p. 172.] LVIII. **Schism generated by this controversy respecting
the Mosaic law.** Invincible nearly as the attachment of the Jewish converts to the law of ceremonies appeared for a long while
to be, the destruction of their national city and temple by
the Romans caused it sensibly to fall into the wane amongst
such of them as had taken up their abode without the confines
of Palestine.(') By the immediate inhabitants of that region,
however, who appear to have been buoyed up with the hope that
it would not be long before they should obtain permission of the
Romans to rebuild both their temple and the city, a belief continued still to be retained that the authority of the law of Moses
was ever to be regarded by the descendants of Abraham as alto-

gether sacred and inviolable. To the delusive expectations of
these latter, an end was not put until Jerusalem had experienced
its second and final overthrow, under the reign of the emperor
Hadrian; when, every hope respecting the restoration of their
city having vanished, a part of the Jewish brethren were prevailed on to renounce the institutions of Moses, and to embrace
the freedom that was held out to them in the Gospel of Christ;
others of them, however, gave the preference to continuing under the bondage of their ancient system of discipline, and in consequence thereof withdrew themselves from the assemblies and
society of the rest. Those who thus inflexibly persisted in encumbering the profession of Christianity with the observances
of the Mosaic ritual, had the denomination of *Nazarenes* and
Ebionites given to them by the other Christians, or otherwise assumed these titles of their own choice by way of distinction.(²)

(1) Eusebius has left it on record, (*Histor. Eccles.* lib. iii. cap. xxxv. p.
106.) that, on the overthrow of Jerusalem and burning of the temple, a vast
number of the Jews (μυρίων ἐκ περιτομῆς) were induced to embrace Christianity. Hence it is manifest how greatly the calamities to which they were
exposed, contributed towards lessening the attachment of the Jewish people
to the law of their forefathers.

(2) Of this schism or secession we shall treat more particularly when we
come to the reign of Hadrian, in our history of the second century. The Ebionites and Nazarenes have, I well know, always hitherto been classed with the
sects of the first age, but to me this appears irreconcilable with reason. For
it can be indisputably proved, that those of the Christians who persisted in
adhering to the observance of the law of Moses, did not separate themselves
from the rest of the brethren, until Jerusalem, which had just begun to rise
again from its ashes, was secondly, and finally, laid waste by the Romans, in
the time of the emperor Hadrian; and that it was upon their so separating
themselves, and not before, that they came to be distinguished by the titles of
Ebionites, and Nazarenes, and were numbered amongst the corrupters of
Christianity. Previously to their acting thus, they were regarded by no one
in any other light than as true Christians. During the first century, they certainly had not by any means forfeited their claim to the title of brethren, although they had given proofs of weakness and a want of further light. Heretics, it is true, they became, but this was at a subsequent period, when they
refused any longer to hold fellowship with those who had discernment enough
to perceive, that Christ had relieved the necks of even the Jews themselves
from the yoke and burden of the law.

LIX. **Controversy respecting the means of obtaining justification
and salvation.** Nearly allied to these disagreements and conten-

tions, respecting the necessity for observing the Mosaic law of ceremonies, although of infinitely greater moment, was [p. 173.] a dispute stirred up by the Jewish doctors at Rome, and in others of the Christian churches, concerning the means whereby we are to arrive at justification and salvation. For whereas the doctrine taught by the apostles was, that our every hope of obtaining pardon and salvation ought to centre in Christ and his merits, these Jewish teachers, on the contrary, made it their business to extol the efficacy and saving power of works agreeable to the law, and to inculcate on men's minds, that such as had led a life of righteousness and holiness, might justly expect to receive eternal happiness from God as their due. To this doctrine, inasmuch as it went materially to lessen the dignity and importance of our blessed Saviour's character, and was founded on a false estimate of the strength of human nature, as well as repugnant to the voice and authority of the moral law itself, St. Paul opposed the most unremitting and particular resistance.(')

(1) It is clear, from St. Paul's Epistle to the Romans, that there were, besides this, other controversies in agitation at that period : but as the apostle, aware that he was addressing himself to persons to whom the subjects in dispute were familiar, omits the mention of several important particulars, doubtless well known to the Romans, but in regard to which we of the present day are, as it were, wholly in the dark, it is scarcely possible for any one, at this distance of time, to form any thing like a clear and precise notion of what these questions involved. The reader will find every thing that can, with any degree of certainty or apparent probability, be said on the subject, collected together and arranged by the following authors: Herm. Witsius, *Miscell. Sacr.* tom. ii. exerc. xx, xxi, xxii. p. 665, et seq.; Camp. Vitringa, *Observation. Sacr.* lib. iv. cap. ix, x, xi. p. 952; Jo. Franc. Buddeus, *Lib. de Ecclesia Apostolic.* cap. iii. p. 111, et seq. In these works there are indeed not a few things advanced which are founded merely in conjecture, and might, without taking any very great pains, be proved futile, and wholly destitute of substantial support ; but, since we have it not in our power to substitute any thing more certain in their stead, it may be as well, perhaps, to leave them untouched, as to displace them for the purpose of bringing forward merely a fresh set of conjectures.

LX. **Heretics commemorated by the apostles.** With these supporters of the law of Moses, these mistaken advocates for the strength of human nature, by whose contentious spirit the church of Christ was prevented from enjoying a perfect tranquillity even in this its golden age, we find ancient as well as modern writers very commonly joining the following persons, of whose apostacy or errors St. Paul and St. John make mention in their epistles, namely, *Hymenæus, Alexander, Philetus, Hermogenes, Phygellus, Demas,* and *Diotrephes.* For they conceive all these to have been the founders of sects, or at least to have been the authors of various pernicious errors, through the introduction of which into some of the churches, Christianity experienced a partial adulte-ration.(¹) But it appears to me, that if what the sacred writers have left us on record respecting these men be maturely weigh-[p. 174] ed, the inclination of opinion must be that, with the exception of *Alexander, Hymenæus,* and *Philetus,* it is rather of a dereliction of Christian duty and charity that they are accused, than of perverting Divine truth, or entertaining any heretical opinions.(²)

(1) See Vitringa and Buddeus *loc. supr. indicat.* also Tho. Ittigius *de Hæresiarchis Ævi Apostolici et Apostolico proximi,* sect. i. cap. viii. p. 84, et seq.

(2) In 2 Tim. i. 15. we find St. Paul complaining that he had been deserted by all who had accompanied him from proconsular Asia, of which *Ephesus* was the chief city, to Rome. Of those he, for some particular reasons no doubt, though we are unacquainted with them, points out *Hermogenes* and *Phygellus* by name. The probability is, that these men, upon finding St. Paul cast into prison, considered his fate as pretty well decided, and despairing ever to see him regain his liberty, and continue the travels he had meditated, they left Rome, and returned into their own country. That their conduct in this respect was highly blameable, is what every one must admit: for to desert a brother, and, much more, one of God's apostles, whose life is in jeopardy, and to whose protection and comfort one might contribute by continuing with him, is certainly to evince both a levity of mind and also a forgetfulness of Christian obligation: but the inconstancy of these men has surely nothing in it that can authorise us to conclude, that, in returning home, they had it at all in view to become opponents of the principles which had been taught them by St. Paul, or meditated the introduction of any innovations into the Christian church. Of the number of these inconstant brethren there was also one *Demas,* whom St. Paul, in cap. iv. v. 10. of the same epistle, represents as having left him, and gone to Thessalonica, being captivated with the love of this world. In reprobating the conduct of this man, both ancient writers and modern ones seem to have set no bounds whatever to their indignation: those who except him out of the class of heretics, do it merely for the purpose of attaching to him a worse denomination, namely, that of an absolute apostate from Christianity. But for my own part, I see nothing in the words of St. Paul which can warrant us in drawing a conclusion so severe against him. The apostle does not accuse Demas of having forsaken Christ, but of having deserted him, Paul: which latter it was certainly very possible for him to do, and yet to remain

steadfast in the faith of Christ. Nor does the reason which the apostle assigns for this man's having forsaken him, by any means imply a defection from Christ. For in Scripture those are said to love the world who prefer the enjoyment of the luxuries, the comforts, and the security of this life to the duties which Christianity enjoins us to fulfil. It appears to me, therefore, that the misconduct wherewith St. Paul is to be understood as reproaching Demas, amounted to no more than this, that he had consulted his ease and convenience rather than his duty, and preferred retiring to a life of safety and quietness at Thessalonica, to continuing any longer a partaker of the ignominy, dangers, and toils, which the companions and friends of St. Paul had continually to encounter at Rome: that the man had very much misconducted himself is unquestionable, but there are certainly no just grounds for believing him to have incurred that high degree of criminality which we so generally find attributed to him. *Crescens* and *Titus*, who are mentioned by St. Paul in the same verse with Demas, are stated to have gone into Galatia and Dalmatia, so that they had in like manner quitted their captive master : but their departure from him was for the best of purposes, namely, to propagate the religion of Christ in those provinces ; and they went with his consent and appro- [p. 175] bation : whereas the object of Demas in quitting Rome was altogether dishonourable, and unworthy of a disciple of Christ, for he withdrew from thence that he might shelter himself from danger, and spend his days in tranquillity and ease.—*Diotrephes* is censured by St. John, in his third epistle, on a twofold account. First, that he had arrogated to himself a pre-eminence in the church to which he belonged, and which had probably been committed to his superintendence : and secondly, that he had conducted himself in a harsh and unfeeling manner towards certain of the brethren, who had deserved well of Christianity, and consequently had a claim to far different treatment at his hands. The circumstances of the case appear to have been these. Certain members of the church to which Diotrephes belonged had gone forth for the purpose of propagating the Christian religion amongst the neighbouring nations. Upon their return, they brought with them some strangers or foreigners whom they had initiated in the principles of Christianity, and also a letter from St. John, commending the faith and zeal which they displayed in the cause of Christ, and desiring that they and their companions might be hospitably lodged and entertained during their stay, as was the custom amongst the early Christians, and that on their again going forth they might be supplied, through the public liberality, with every thing which might tend to encourage and forward them in undertaking a fresh mission amongst the Gentiles. But Diotrephes, it seems, spurned at the recommendation of St. John, and not only forbad these good and useful men from being maintained out of the public fund, or at the expense of the church, but also went to the length of excommunicating those who had been induced to yield them some occasional private assistance.

It will scarcely then, I had almost said it cannot, be denied me to infer from the above that Diotrephes must have been the Bishop of this church. For how could it have been possible for a private individual to have excommunicated any

of the brethren with whom he might be at enmity? or by what means could such
an one have brought it about, that a letter from one of Christ's apostles should
be treated with neglect and contempt?   Some particular reason or other there
unquestionably was, that induced this haughty character to conduct himself in
the manner above stated; and it must, no doubt, have been such a reason as had
all the appearance of being a just and an honourable one.   Learned men have
imagined that this reason is to be discovered in the quality or condition of the
persons whom he excommunicated. Diotrephes they suppose to have been originally a Gentile, and those whom he refused to receive Jews: and hence they conclude that the contempt entertained by the former for the latter had gained so
complete an ascendency over his mind that he could not forego the opportunity
of manifesting it, even at the expense of violating the most sacred law of charity. This conjecture may, perhaps, at first sight, be thought to carry with it somewhat of a specious air; but if put to the test, there will be found in it nothing
that can possibly have any weight with a considerate person at all conversant in
Christian history.   For, not to rest on the circumstance of its being unsupported by any sort of authority, except what is supplied by the name Diotrephes,
which is certainly a Greek one, but of itself can surely never be considered as
yielding an argument of the least cogency or force; and equally passing over the
fact of their being no sort of memorial extant which can warrant us in believing
that the Gentile Christians ever permitted themselves to be so far carried away
by their hatred and contempt of the Jews, as to refuse to consider them as brethren, and withhold from them even the common fruits of charity ; it is plain, from
the fifth verse of St. John's Epistle, that those whom Diotrephes treated with
such harshness were members of that church over which, it should seem, that he
presided.   The apostle, indeed, speaks of the Christians to whom he alludes as
consisting of two classes,—ἀδελφὸς, or brethren, and ξενὸς, foreigners or stran-
[p 176.] gers.   But, since he is treating of Christians sojourning in one and the
same church, and makes use of the term "brethren" in opposition to that of
"strangers," there can be no doubt but that by the former he meant those who
had been regularly admitted into fellowship with the church, and by the latter
such as had not been so admitted.   There are some, I am well aware, who think
St. John is to be understood as meaning by "brethren," Jews—and by "strangers," Greeks; but it cannot be shown either that the term "brethren" was ever
used by the apostle in this restricted sense, or that it was customary for the
Greek converts to be styled ξενοι, or strangers.   What we set out, therefore, with
observing, seems scarcely to admit of any question, namely, that certain members of the church which was under the care of Diotrephes had gone forth with
a view of propagating Christianity amongst the people of the neighbouring district, and on their return brought with them some of their disciples, and also an
epistle addressed by St. John to the church to which they belonged.   And now,
to give my own opinion as to the reason of their being so ungraciously received
by Diotrephes, I think the cause of all his ill-will towards them is plainly pointed at by St. John himself.   To every one perusing his Epistle it must be obvious, that the apostle introduces at ver. 7. somewhat of an apology to Gaius, to
whom he writes for the journey which these good men undertook in the cause

of Christ. First, he says, that their motive was good, that they went forth with the best mind and intention, being desirous only of contributing to the honor of God. Then he adduces it as further commendable in them, that, although they might reasonably have expected to be furnished with the necessaries of life by the people among whom they sojourned, they yet preferred maintaining themselves by the labour of their hands, and refused every sort of recompence, gratuity, or reward. Now it is clear, that what these men had done, could require no such defence or justification in the eyes of Gaius, for it appears that he had already befriended their cause, and we may therefore, I think, fairly infer, that what is thus said by the apostle was meant as an answer to the pretext by which Diotrephes pretended to justify his very harsh and unchristian-like conduct. St. John, it is observable, seems tacitly to admit that there was something irregular in the journey undertaken by these men, for the purpose of converting their heathen neighbours, and occupies himself in showing, that if the end of their going forth, and the manner in which they conducted themselves were attended to, this irregularity of theirs must appear to be but of small moment. To be brief then, it strikes me that the truth of the matter was this, that these good men had grievously offended Diotrephes, by having taken upon them this mission to the Heathen without his consent or knowledge, and gone forth rather in compliance with the dictates of their own consciences than under any direction or authority from him. On their return, therefore, it was in vain that they looked up to this haughty character for countenance or support: not even the recommendatory letter which they had procured from St. John, could have the effect of appeasing his wrath, or dissuade him from giving full vent to his indignation. Now, in early times, it undoubtedly was the custom for such of the members of any church as might be desirous of imitating the example of the apostles, and propagating the Gospel amongst the Heathen, to apply to the bishop for his licence, and to enter on their travels under his sanction. Ignatius, in almost all his epistles, inculcates this maxim—Μηδεὶς χωρὶς τῶ ἐπισκόπῳ τὶ πρασσίτω τῶν δυηκόντων εἰς τὴν ἐκκλησίαν. *Sine episcopo nemo faciat eorum aliquid quæ ad acclesiam spectant :* vid. *Epist. ad Smyrnæos,* § viii. *ad Trallianos, ad Philadelph. ad Polycarpum ;* and it would be easy to produce innumerable passages from writers before the reign of Constantine, all tending to show, that in the first ages of Christianity it was unlawful for any thing appertaining to religion to be either done or undertaken without the knowledge and consent of the bishop. The crime of Diotrephes, therefore, was not that of having assailed any of the received principles of the Christian religion, but of having discovered an unwarrantable degree of asperity and rigour in the maintenance of his own [p. 177.] importance and dignity. For he, in the first place, manifested a latent pride of heart, in withholding from a set of pious and innocent men, who, in point of fact, were entitled to every sort of encouragement, the good offices and hospitality of the church, merely because they had not paid the proper attention to his authority and rights: and in the next place, he betrayed a still more inexcusable spirit of arrogance, in spurning at the authority and recommendation of one of Christ's apostles, to whose judgment and authority it became all bishops and churches to pay the utmost deference. This evidently is the offence which St.

15

John censures in these words:—ὁ φιλοπρωτευών αὐτῶν ἐκ ἐπιδέχεται ἡμᾶς. "He who loveth to have the pre-eminence among them receiveth us not." The apostle does not, as is commonly imagined, reprehend him for aspiring to the presidency of the church to which he belonged: for, as I before observed, he must, at the time of his offending, have been at the head of that church: but what he means to censure (as the words themselves indicate beyond all controversy) is that which he considers, as a mark of an inordinately ambitious mind—a mind carried away by the lust of power, namely, that he had dared to assume to himself an authority superior even to that of an apostle. The plain sense of the words is this—"But their Diotrephes, who affects to be greater than any of the apostles, sets at nought my intreaties and authority."

If the men, then, of whom I have been speaking, be taken from the class of the heretics of the first century, there will remain merely Hymenæus, Philetus, and Alexander. Hymenæus, the first of these, is in 1 Tim. i. 20. associated by St. Paul with Alexander: in 2 Tim. ii. 17. however, we find the apostle speaking of him in conjunction with Philetus. That one and the same man is referred to in both these places has never, as far as I know, been yet called in question by any one. But upon attentively considering and comparing together the two above cited passages, I must confess that there appears to me very great reason to doubt whether the Hymenæus mentioned in the first Epistle to Timothy be the same with, or a different man from him, who is spoken of in the last Epistle. Indeed I think that I might almost, with some confidence, take upon me to assert that they were two distinct characters, having nothing in common but the name. In the first place, it is worthy of remark, although it certainly does not go the length of wholly deciding the point, that the companion in error, whom we find associated with Hymenæus in the former passage, is not the same person with whom his name is joined in the latter one. Secondly, it makes still more strongly in favour of my opinion, that the Hymenæus mentioned in the first Epistle, was, together with his associate, delivered over by St. Paul to the evil one, to be tormented until he should desist from blaspheming Christianity, 1 Tim. i. 20. a circumstance, surely, by no means easy to be reconciled with what is recorded of the Hymenæus spoken of in the second Epistle, who is not represented as being under any kind of restraint, but as going about perverting as many of the Christians as he could, and disseminating his errors with no small degree of success. How, let me ask, could it have been possible for a man to do this, whom the apostle had subjected to the power of the Prince of Darkness, for the purpose of bridling his blasphemous tongue? Finally, there appears to have been as much difference between the one and the other Hymenæus, as there is between an open enemy of Christianity and an artful insidious corrupter of it. The words of St. Paul place it beyond all doubt that the Hymenæus first spoken of by him was, [p. 178.] in every respect, a detestable character. His exhortation to Timothy is, that he should unite πίσιν *faith,* i. e. a belief of the religion of Christ, with ἀγαθῇ συνειδήσει, *a good conscience.* Holiness of life, or piety, is what is meant; the fruit of which is *a good conscience,* or a mind conscious to itself of no evil, and therefore peaceful and happy. The importance and necessity of attending to this admonition he exemplifies by the case of Hymenæus and Alexander, both of whom had discarded τὴν ἀγαθὴν συνείδησιν, *a good conscience, i. e.* had plunged into an evil course of life, and turned their backs on the divine law: this corruption of their morals being once wrought, their progress in iniquity became accelerated, and these wretched men, at length, made perfect shipwreck, as it were, of faith, arriving by degrees at such a pitch of callous depravity, as not only to think ill of Christianity, but also publicly to blaspheme its doctrines. To "make shipwreck concerning faith," is, I think, manifestly to be understood as the same with apostatizing from the Christian faith or religion. These two men, therefore, having given themselves up to a life of wickedness and impiety, were at length led on to renounce Christianity altogether. But the Hymenæus spoken of in the latter epistle, although he was involved in very great culpability, was yet not such a monster as this. He had not apostatized from Christianity, but merely given a corrupt interpretation to a part of its doctrines, namely, that which respects the future resurrection of the body. The probability is, that inclining, in this respect, rather to the principles of those philosophers who maintained that the body is, as it were, the prison of the rational soul, and matter the source of all evil, than to the doctrine taught by the apostles, he asserted that what Christ had delivered respecting the resurrection of the body, was not to be understood in a literal sense, but that what he meant to promise was a new life to the souls of men, not to their bodies. The apostle does not attribute to this man and his associate many errors. His course of life does not appear to have been flagitious, nor, like the other Hymenæus, had he, from a habit of sinning, taken occasion to deprave religion. Moreover, we do not find it imputed to him that he had been instrumental in causing others to lead a life of wickedness and impiety; although, as the apostle pretty plainly intimates, there was a tendency in his error to injure the cause of piety, and countenance an indulgence of our appetites. On these accounts St. Paul is led to speak of him with some degree of moderation, whereas his reproof of the other Hymenæus is couched in terms of the greatest severity and vehemence. In fact, he appears rather to lament his fall than to chide it. With regard to the Alexander of whom St. Paul makes mention in his first Epistle to Timothy, my opinion is precisely the same with that which I have above expressed respecting the Hymenæus there spoken of in conjunction with him, namely, that he was a different man from the one referred to under the same name by the apostle, in his second Epistle, and from whom he states himself to have received great injury at Rome. 2 Tim. iv. 14. And it appears to me that St. Paul had it in view to mark the distinction between them, when he added to the name of the latter the denomination of the craft which he exercised, calling him Ἀλέξανδρος ὁ χαλκεὺς, "Alexander the coppersmith." The meaning of this addition, it strikes me, was to distinguish the man of whom he spake from others of the same name who were known to Timothy, and particularly from him whom the apostle had, in his former Epistle, accused of perfidy to the cause of Christ. The Alexander first spoken of, it is also to be remarked, had, in order to prevent Christianity from suffering further from his blasphemy, been delivered over by St. Paul into the power of the evil one; and [p. 179.] how then, it may be asked, could he have insulted St. Paul at Rome, and thrown impediments in the way of his doctrine?

LX. **Gnostic heretics.** But by none of its adversaries or corrupters was Christianity, from almost its first rise, more seriously injured; by none was the church more grievously lacerated, and rendered less attractive to the people, than by those who were for making the religion of Christ accommodate itself to the principles of the oriental philosophy respecting the Deity, the origin of the world, the nature of matter, and the human soul. We allude to those who, from their pretending that they were able to communicate to mankind, at present held in bondage by the Architect of the World, a correct knowledge (γνωσις) of the true and ever-living God, were commonly styled Gnostics. This calamity was foreseen by St. Paul, and is predicted by him in 1 Tim. iv. 1.(') We find him also, in various parts of his Epistles, exhorting the followers of Christ to maintain the discipline of their blessed Master whole and uncontaminated by any of the fables or inventions of the philosophers of this sect. 1 Tim. vi. 20.; 1 Tim. i. 3, 4.; Tit. iii. 9.; Col. ii. 8. But an insane curiosity, and that itch for penetrating into abstruce or hidden things, by which the human mind is so liable to be tormented, caused many to turn their backs on the advice and admonition of the apostle and his associates, and no sooner did some of the Gnostics gain a footing in the recently established Christian churches, than the principles that they maintained respecting the first origin of all things, and the causes for which Christ came into this world, and to which their great austerity of demeanour, and rigid abstinence from even the lawful gratifications of sense, communicated an imposing gloss, were by numbers received with open ears, and suffered to take entire possession of their minds. To no purpose was it that the apostles and their disciples pointed out the emptiness of all these things, and how very incongruous they were with the genuine Christian discipline, although they might carry with them a specious show of somewhat like recondite wisdom.(') Intoxicated with a fondness for these opinions, not a few of the Christians were induced to secede from all association with the advocates for the sound doctrine, and to form themselves into various sects, which, as time advanced, became daily more extensive and numerous, and were for several ages productive of very serious inconveniences and evils to the Christian commonwealth.(')

(1)Although some difference of opinion may subsist with regard to this prediction of St. Paul, I am yet persuaded that every one who has made himself acquainted with what the Gnostic discipline was, will readily admit that that system is more particularly pointed at in the passage referred to in the text, notwithstanding that no necessity may appear to exist for considering [p. 180.] it as exclusively applicable thereto. Numerous are the passages in the other Epistles of the New Testament, as well as in those written by St. Paul, which strike at this system, and call loudly on the Christian churches to beware of it; in fact more numerous, perhaps, than the generality of commentators appear to have imagined. I cannot say that I agree in every thing with Hammond, who, in his *Annotations on the New Testament*, translated into Latin by Le Clerc, and also in his book *de Episcopatus Juribus Dissert. prim. de Antichristo*, cap. iii. p. 11, et seq. takes upon him to apply several passages in the New Testament to the Gnostics, on no other ground, as it should seem, than that of a very slight accordance in terms. There are, however, many observations of his from which it would be inconsistent with candour to withold our assent.

(2) The emptiness and folly of this system of discipline, is most aptly pourtrayed and exposed by St. Paul in 1 Tim. i. 4.; Tit. iii. 9.; 2 Tim. ii. 16.

(3) Learned men are not agreed as to the time when the first sects of the Gnostics were founded. Many of them place implicit faith in the authority of Clement of Alexandria, who says it was after the death of the apostles, in the reign of the emperor Hadrian, that these sects were established, and the integrity of the church was destroyed. *Stromat.* lib. vii. cap. xvii. p. 898, 899. With this testimony they conceive also that of Hegesippus to coincide, who, in a passage preserved by Eusebius, (*Histor. Eccles.* lib. iii. cap. xxxii. p. 104, and lib. iv. cap. xxii. p. 142.) reports the church to have remained a pure virgin until the time of Trajan, but that after the death of the apostles the leaders of divers sects began openly to make their appearance. Others, however, are of opinion that some congregations were formed by certain of the Gnostic tribe, in opposition to the churches of apostolic foundation, even so early as the first century, and during the lifetime of the apostles themselves. And this opinion seems to be favoured by what St. John says, 1 John, ii. 18, et seq. of many Antichrists having gone forth from the church, as well as by what has reached us respecting Cerinthus, and the Nicolaitans, who were heretics of the first century, and tainted with the Gnostic opinions. Conflicting as these sentiments are, it appears to me not at all impossible to reconcile them, without requiring a sacrifice of the point of honour to be made by either party. That dissensions, arising out of the attempt to blend the principles of Gnosticism with Christianity, had been generated in the churches previously to the second century and the reign of the emperor Hadrian, and that some of those who were devoted to those principles, having drawn to them a number of partisans, had proceeded to the length of holding separate assemblies with their disciples is most manifest, not only from the apostolic epistles, but also from other ancient monuments. Nor is this at all opposed by the words of Clement or Hegesippus. For it should seem that what these writers say may, in fact, be

considered as amounting merely to this, that in the reigns cf Trajan and Hadrian, the patrons of heresy came forward with greater boldness than before, and laying aside the caution and reserve with which they had hitherto maintained their doctrines, made open profession of their dissent from the rest of the Christians, endeavouring likewise, by every means in their power, both to augment the number of their partisans and also to place their different sects or fraternities on a firm and stable basis: though, with regard to what is said by Hegesippus, it may perhaps admit of a question, whether it is to be considered as relating merely to the church of Jerusalem, as some of the learned imagine, or, as others conceive, to the church at large. In short, the fact appears to have been, that during the first century the sects formed by those who were for interpreting the doctrines of Christianity according to the principles of the ancient philosophy of the Magi, were neither large, nor held in much account, their internal organization being at that time but very imperfect; but, that [p. 181.] about the commencement of the second century, they burst through the obscurity by which they had been enveloped, and assumed for themselves a regular determinate form, under certain acknowledged leaders, and subject to a system of laws and regulations peculiarly their own. .

LXI. **Nature of the Gnostic discipline.** It is, however, by no means difficult to point out the way in which these people contrived to make the religion of Christ appear to be altogether in unison with their favorite system of discipline. All the philosophers of the East, whose tenets, as we have seen, were, that the Deity had nothing at all to do with matter, the nature and qualities of which they considered to be malignant and poisonous—that the body was held in subjection by a being entirely distinct from him to whom the dominion over the rational soul belonged—that the world and all terrestrial bodies were not the work of the Supreme Being, the author of all good, but were formed out of matter by a nature either evil in its origin, or that had fallen into a state of depravity—and, lastly, that the knowledge of the true Deity had become extinct, and that the whole race of mankind, instead of worshipping the Father of Light and Life, and source of every thing good, universally paid their homage to the Founder and Prince of this nether world, or to his substitutes and agents: I say all these looked forward with earnest expectation for the arrival of an extraordinary and eminently powerful Messenger of the Most High, who, they imagined, would deliver the captive souls of men from the bondage of the flesh, and rescue them from the dominion of those Genii by whom they supposed the world and all matter to be governed, at the same time communicating to them a correct knowledge of their everlasting Parent, so as to enable them, upon the dissolution of the body, once more to regain their long lost liberty and happiness. An expectation of this kind even continues to be cherished by their descendants of the present day. Some of these philosophers then, being struck with astonishment at the magnitude and splendour of the miracles wrought by Christ and his apostles, and perceiving that it was the object of our Lord's ministry both to abrogate the Jewish law, a law which they conceived to have been promulgated by the Architect or Founder of the World himself, or by the chief of his agents, and also to overthrow those gods of the nations whom they regarded as Genii placed over mankind by the same evil spirit; hearing him, morever, invite the whole world to join in the worship of the one omnipotent and only true God, and profess that he came down from Heaven for the purpose of redeeming the souls of men, and restoring them to liberty, were induced to believe that he was that very messenger for whom they looked, the person ordained by the everlasting Father to destroy the dominion of the founder of this world as well as of the Genii who presided over it, to separate light from darkness, and to deliver the souls of men from that bondage to which they were subjected in consequence of their connection with material bodies.

LXII. **Nature of the Gnostic discipline.** The principles [p. 182.] and nature of this system of discipline, however, were such as to render it impossible for its votaries to yield their assent to many things which were delivered by Christ and his apostles, or to interpret them according to their obvious and commonly accepted sense. To have done so would have been acting in direct opposition to certain leading maxims, which were considered by persons of their persuasion as indisputable truths.(') To various articles, therefore, propounded in the Christian code as essential points of belief, they utterly refused their assent: such, for instance, as that which attributes the creation of the world to the Supremé Being, and those respecting the divine origin of the Mosaic law, the authority of the Old Testament, the character of human nature, and the like: for it would have amounted to nothing short of an absolute surrender of the leading maxims of the system to which they were devoted, had they not persisted in maintaining that the Creator of this world was a being of a nature vastly inferior to the Supreme Deity, the Father of our Lord, and that the law of Moses was not dictated by the Almighty, but by this same inferior being, by whom also the bodies of men were formed and united to souls of ethereal mould, and under whose influence the various penmen of the Old Testament composed whatever they have left us on record. In addition to the articles of Christian belief, which they felt themselves constrained thus peremptorily to reject, there were others which they found it necessary to explain after their own manner, in order to render them compatible with the principles of the oriental discipline. Respecting Christ and his functions in particular, it was requisite for them, in support of their tenets, to maintain that he was to be considered as inferior to the Supreme Being, and as never having in reality assumed a material body. Their adoption of the former of these positions was an inevitable consequence of their believing, as they universally did, that the Deity had existed from all eternity in a state of absolute quiescence, but that at length, after ages spent in silence and repose, he begat of himself certain natures or beings after his own likeness, of whom Christ was one : to the maintenance of the latter they were constrained by that leading maxim of the oriental system, that all matter was intrinsically evil and corrupt. Consistently with these sentiments, they moreover found themselves called upon to deny that Christ, in reality, either underwent what he is reported to have suffered, or died, and returned again to life, as is recorded of him. In their exposition of this doctrine, however, they did not all of them follow precisely the same plan. Again, in regard to the purposes for which Christ came into the world, the principles of their system rendered it necessary for them to assert, that it was not with a view to expiate the sins of mankind, or to appease the wrath of an offended Deity, that he relinquished for a while his abode in the Heavens, but merely in order to communicate to the human race the long lost knowledge of the Supreme Being ; and that, having put an end to the usurped dominion of the arrogant founder of this world, he might point out to the souls of men (those spirits of ethereal origin unhappily confined in earthly prisons) the means of recovering for themselves their native liberty and happiness. Finally, to pass over

some other points which might be noticed, these votaries of
orientalism were compelled, in support of their favourite maxim
respecting the malignant nature of matter, to discoun- [p. 183.]
tenance every idea of a future resurrection of men's bodies from
the dead, and to maintain that what is said in Scripture on the
subject is altogether figurative and metonymical. In their manners and habits the Gnostics were for the most part melancholy
and austere. Indeed, allowing the principles and notions which
they cherished respecting matter and the origin of our earthly
forms to be just and correct, it cannot but follow, that to obey
the instincts of nature, or to indulge in any sort of bodily gratification, must be contrary to reason, and even criminal. Strange,
however, as it may appear to those who are not aware of the
discordant conclusions which different men will sometimes deduce from the same premises, it is most certain that some of this
sect conceived themselves to be warranted by these self-same
principles in plunging, with the most barefaced effrontery, into
every species of libidinous and vicious excess.(²)

(1) The early Christian fathers, who were acquainted with none other besides the Grecian system of philosophy, perceiving that some of the dogmas of
the Gnostics coincided with the principles of the Platonists, were induced to
conclude that the discipline of the former had been altogether generated by a
conjunction of the platonic philosophy with Christianity: to this opinion great
numbers of the learned of modern days have likewise subscribed, so many indeed, that they are scarcely to be enumerated. After having, however, examined
the subject with every possible degree of impartiality and attention, I am most
thoroughly convinced that the founders of the Gnostic schools cannot, with the
least propriety, be reckoned amongst the followers of Plato. With regard to
certain particulars taken separately, I am very ready to admit that there is no great
want of resemblance between the Platonic philosophy and the doctrine of the
Gnostics; but only let the two systems be compared together, as they ought to
be, *in toto*, and the great dissimilarity that exists between them becomes at once
conspicuous. That long series of *æons*, for instance, of either sex, through which
the Gnostics uniformally deduce the connexion of the Deity with matter, is a
thing altogether unknown to the system of Plato: whilst, on the other hand, the
Platonic doctrine respecting the nature of the Deity and the origin of this world,
as exhibited by the Athenian sage in his *Timæus*, is in no respect whatever to
be reconciled with the tenets of the Gnostics. The Deity is represented by Plato
as eternally active and energetic, by the Gnostics as altogether passive and quiescent. According to the former, this world is eternal, and a work of beauty not
at all unworthy of the Almighty hand that framed it: by the latter, it is regarded as an ill-formed mass, the destruction of which is an object of desire and me-

ditation with the Deity. In the opinion of the Platonists, this world and its inhabitants are governed either immediately by the Deity himself, or through the ministration of dæmons commissioned by him : but according to the Gnostic scheme, an absolute and entire dominion over the human race, and the globe we inhabit, is exercised by the founder of the material world, a being of unbounded pride and ambition, who makes use of every means in his power to prevent mankind from attaining to any knowledge of the true God. In addition to what are here enumerated, many other points of difference between the two systems will readily be perceived by any one who will divest his mind of all bias or prejudice, and be at the pains of perusing the little book written by Plotinus the Platonist, in opposition to the Gnostics. Porphyry moreover, the disciple of Plotinus, says, in the *Life of his Master*, cap. xvi. p. 118. expressly, that the Gnostics considered Plato as a minute philosopher, who had never ascended in mind and thought to the first principles of all things. But not to multiply (p. 184.) words : it is allowed by all that the discipline of Manes was the genuine offspring of the ancient philosophy of the East, or that of the Persians and Chaldæans: but this discipline, if we except the conclusions of some of its dogmas, corresponds so exactly in all respects with that of the Gnostics, that it is scarcely possible for any two systems to appear more familiar to each other : that they were both, therefore, drawn from one and the same source, surely, cannot admit of a doubt.

(2) Amongst the learned, and more particularly amongst those of our own times, there have not been wanting several who have stood forward, with considerable ingenuity and eloquence, as the advocates and defenders of the Gnostics. The professed object of some of these has been merely to extenuate, as far as possible, the errors of this sect, and in the way of explanation to offer every kind of apology for them of which the nature of the case will admit. Others of them, however, have endeavoured to clear those corrupters of Christianity from every sort of reproach, insisting on it that the ancient authors, from whom we derive our knowledge of their principles and tenets, are to be regarded either as malignant and invidious accusers, or else as ill-informed and incompetent judges. But, notwithstanding all the respect that may be due to authority so commanding, we cannot help saying, that to us these eminent writers appear to have, in this instance, laboured to as little purpose as they would have done in attempting to wash a blackamoor white, and thrown away their time and talents on behalf of a cause which is altogether desperate, and admits of no defence. If there be any truth at all in history, not a doubt can exist but that the religion professed by this sect was of a nature diametrically opposite to that which is propounded to mankind in the writings of the New Testament. If taken up separately indeed, and exhibited apart by themselves, it may be very possible for ingenuity to give to certain particulars of the Gnostic system an air of soundness and truth : but only let the parts thus selected be referred to their proper stations in the general scheme, and the fallacy will at once become apparent. That the ancient Christian writers were actuated by malice in framing their reports of the Gnostics, and incurred the guilt of slandering a worthy set of men, for the purpose of securing to themselves an absolute sway, is what no good person, who

is acquainted with the situation of things in those early times, will easily be induced to believe, and what, I am sure, this one consideration alone is enough to prevent any one in his senses from crediting, namely, that a variety of writers, separated widely from each other in point of time, place, manners, studies, and attachments, have handed down to us precisely one and the same account of the Gnostic principles and opinions. By every unprejudiced and impartial person, this concurrence of testimony will, I am persuaded, be allowed so completely to do away all suspicion of slander and misrepresentation, as to render any further evidence to this effect altogether superfluous. Were it at all necessary, other circumstances, not less cogent and conclusive, might easily be brought forward. With regard to those who would have us believe that the principles and maxims of the Gnostics were in reality sound and correct, but that these philosophers, having made use of new and unaccustomed terms and phrases in propounding their opinions to the world, their meaning was hastily misconceived by their adversaries, I must confess that I do not see how this suggestion of theirs much helps the matter. Were we to admit this representation of the case to be just, the only effect it could have on our minds, would be to make us no longer regard the Gnostics in the light of persons led away by error, and too great a fondness for certain opinions of their own, but as men acting under the influence of folly and impiety. For, unquestionably, men who could prevail on themselves to cloak up and disguise sentiments, which they knew to be sound and just, in pompous obscurities, and a high sounding theatrical kind of phraseology, must either have had it in view to impose on the world, and in this silly way to acquire for themselves the reputation of superior wisdom, or otherwise have been complete drivellers, and entirely deprived of their wits. And as for those whom this sort of senseless and bombastic language, which the perspicuity and simplicity of Holy Writ most strongly, although tacitly, condemns, could so far charm as to make them anxious to convert their brethren to a sense of its excellence and beauty, and who, rather than renounce this silly and obscure kind of jargon, would stir up dissensions in the church, and split it into sects, they cannot be regarded in any other light than that of wicked and presumptuous men, the enemies of love, peace and harmony, or, in a word, than as the pests and canker-worms of the Christian community. But, even granting that [p. 185.] the meaning of these men might in some respects be misunderstood, it is yet very easily to be proved that the ancient Christian writers are, for the most part, strictly correct in their representation of the Gnostic principles and opinions, and that the members of this sect gave themselves so entirely up to the suggestions of a disordered imagination, as altogether to set common sense and reason at defiance.

LXIII. **Arguments urged by the Gnostics in defence of their system.** That the principles and opinions which we have been considering, as well as others of their tenets and maxims, were repugnant not only to the doctrine openly delivered by Christ himself, but also to the tenor of those writings which are considered by the whole body of Christians as the rule and standard of their religion, is what the generality of the Gnostics did not attempt to deny. In truth, the fact was too glaring to admit of a question. They, however, took care not to be unprepared with arguments, whereby to defend and support the system of discipline to which they were devoted. By the leaders of some of their sects it was contended, that the religion propounded by Christ was of two sorts; the one of easy comprehension, and suited to the capacity of the vulgar; the other sublime, and to be understood only by persons of refined intellect. The former they represented as being contained in the books of the New Testament, the latter as having been unfolded by Christ to his apostles alone, in private. For their own knowledge of the latter they professed themselves to be indebted to certain disciples of the apostles Peter, Paul, and Matthias.(¹) Others pretended that their leading tenets and maxims were drawn from the oracles and visions of Zoroaster and other divinely instructed sages of the East, as likewise from certain secret writings of Abraham, Seth, Noah, and other holy men of the Jewish nation, who flourished long before the time of Christ; a pretence which, in the age of which we are speaking, was certainly not wholly destitute of colour, since there were various fictitious writings in the hands of many at that time, which a set of villainous and artful men had palmed on the world as the productions of those great and sacred characters.(²) Some took upon them to exclude from the sacred code all such writings of the New Testament as appeared to militate with any degree of force 'against their principles, and to substitute in their places other gospels and epistles of their own forging, but which they pretended to have been written by certain of our Lord's apostles, such as Peter, Thomas, and Matthias.(³) Others, again, maintained, that the ordinary copies of the New Testament were corrupted, and in proof of this produced what they pretended to be correct ones, and in which, either through their own artifice, or want of care in the transcribers, a difference of reading presented itself in those passages which were adverse to the Gnostic tenets. Lastly, there were many of them who insisted on it, that, in the words of Scripture there was enveloped a recondite meaning; (an opinion, indeed, at that time commonly entertained even by persons of strictly orthodox sentiments;) and, upon this principle, were [p. 186.] continually labouring in the most silly and puerile way, by the squeezing and torturing of words, to wring from them that assistance and support, which, without resorting to such means, they could in no wise be made to yield.

(1) Vid. Irenæus *adv. Hæreses.* lib. i. cap. xxv. § v. p. 104. & lib. iii. cap. v. p. 179. ex-division. Renat. Massuet., Clemens Alex. *Stromat.* lib. vii. cap. xvii. p. 898. 900.

(2) Vid. Porphyr. *in Vit. Plotini,* cap. xvi. p. 118. edit. Fabric. Clemens Alex. *Stromat.* lib. i. cap. xv. p. 357. lib. vi. cap. vi. p. 767. Eusebius *Histor. Eccles.* lib. iv. cap. vii. p. 120. Epiphanius *Hæres.* xxvi. § viii. p. 59. 84. *Hæres.* xxxix. § v. p. 286, &c. *Constitutiones Apostolicæ,* lib. vi. cap. xvi, p. 348. et seq. tom. i. *Patr. Apostolic.* and various other authorities.

(3) Jo. Alb. Fabricius will be found to illustrate this the best of any one, in his *Cod. Pseudepigraph. Nov. Test.* The reader may also consult Beausobre *Histoire du Manichée,* tom. i. p. 344, et seq.

LXIV. **The Gnostic Factions.** Great was, indeed, the detriment which the interests of Christianity experienced from this presumptuous sect, which arrogated to itself a correct and perfect knowledge of the Deity: but in a much heavier degree would the malign influence of its doctrines have been felt, had they been urged with a due measure of uniformity and consistence. Fortunately, however, it happened, that from its very first rise, this faction was split into various parties, the leaders and directors of which were as much at variance among themselves as with the Christians, whose tenets they stigmatized as highly derogatory to the character of the Deity, inasmuch as they attributed to him the creation of the world. For, although all of them took for their ground-work the same principles, yet when they came to enter into particulars, and proceeded to bring the different points of their doctrine to the test of a closer examination, for the purpose of ascertaining their due force, and reconciling them with each other, as well as of adapting them to the principles of the Christian religion, the difference of opinion that sprung up amongst these pretenders to superior knowledge was truly astonishing. All of them, for instance, were unanimous in regarding the Supreme Deity as a being altogether different from the creator and governor of this world: but as to the precise nature of this last mentioned being, and also the degree of his inferiority to the Father of our Lord, considerable controversy prevailed. Again, all of them were agreed in considering matter as intrinsically evil and corrupt, and as the womb and nurse of all those vicious desires and propensities wherewith mankind are continually tormented; but whether such had been its pernicious nature or quality from all eternity, or whether it had accidentally become thus depraved; whether it was animate or inanimate, and whether it were possessed of a generative faculty, and could of itself produce living beings or not, was made the subject of very violent contention. That Christ was the Son of the Supreme Deity, and was sent into the world for the purpose [p. 187.] of liberating the souls of men from the wretched bondage in which they were held by the body, was what all of them professed to believe : by some, however, his character was estimated higher than by others; and with regard to the body which he assumed, it was asserted by some to have been merely a visionary form; whilst others maintained it to have been a frame of an ethereal and celestial nature. A similar disagreement of opinion prevailed amongst them respecting a variety of other things. Nor have we far to seek for the cause which gave rise to these manifold dissensions. For, in the first place, the oriental philosophy, to which the Gnostics were addicted, having no foundation whatever in the principles of sound reason, but being grounded merely on various refined conceits, the offspring of human ingenuity, had for a long while been split into a great number of parties and sects.(') In the next place, a considerable portion of the Gnostics had, previously to their embracing Christianity, assigned no limits whatever to their philosophical speculations; whereas others of them, who were of Jewish extraction, had, in a certain degree, restricted and modified the system of discipline to which they were attached, by incorporating with it various particulars of the law and institutions of Moses. By some again, the principles of Gnosticism had been united with certain maxims derived from a rude and superstitious kind of astronomical knowledge, by the cultivation of which different nations of the East, and particularly the Egyptians, had much corrupted their minds; whilst by others this study of the heavenly bodies was either altogether neglected, or attended to only to be treated with contempt. Finally, in addition to the above-mentioned sources of disagreement, it may be remarked, that the attempt to blend philosophy, under any certain or particular form, with religion, no matter whether true or false, has never failed very quickly to produce much difference of opinion amongst those who have made it, and to supply them with a variety of grounds for disunion, contention, and dispute.

(1) The learned Thomas Hyde, a man eminently skilled in oriental matters and opinions, expresses himself as follows in his *Historia Religionis veterum Persarum,* cap. i. p. 26. " *Cum itaque in hac religione* (i. e. the religion of the magi, which assigned to matter a peculiar governor or ruler, and denied that this world had been created by the Supreme Deity, the author of all good) *fuerint sectæ pluresquam* 70, (*uti etiam sunt in Christianitate*) *non est expectandum, ut omnia, quæ de eorum religione forte dicta fuerint, pertineant ad magos orthodoxos, sed aliqua etiam ad hæreticos.—Magorum secta orthodoxa ea est, quæ de duobus principiis credit unum fuisse æternum, alterum vero creatum. Hæretici autem fuere tam alii qui in processu hujus operis enumerantur, quam magi dualistæ, statuentes, hæc duo principia fuisse æterna, et alii in aliis rebus minus orthodoxe sentientes."* With regard to the position here laid down, that that particular sect of the magi which believed that the Prince or Governor of Darkness and Matter derived his existence from the Supreme Deity, was the predominent and principal one, it should seem to be not altogether established beyond the reach of doubt, but in every, other part of his statement respecting the dissensions of these philosophers, this illustrious scholar is indisputably most correct.

LXV. **Simon Magus.** At the head of the heretics of this age, and particularly of the Gnostics, we find the ancient fathers of the church unanimous in placing a *Simon Magus,* whom [p. 188.] they assert to have been one and the same with him whose depravity and perfidy was so severely reprobated by St. Peter at Samaria: Acts, viii. 9, 10.(') Being in possession of no testimony or other means whereby to controvert their authority with regard to the identity of Simon Magus, and that Simon who was accounted the parent or chief leader of the Gnostics, it appears to me that we have no alternative but to acquiesce in it; although there are not wanting several very eminently learned men who cannot prevail on themselves to concede even thus much.(²) But as to the remainder of what they thus state respecting this Simon, I must confess that it seems to me to be entitled to no sort of credit whatever. For from everything which even they themselves have handed down to us concerning the man, it is manifest beyond dispute that he cannot with the least propriety, be included in the class of heretics or corrupters of the

Christian religion, but is to be reckoned amongst the most hostile of its adversaries, inasmuch as he hesitated not to revile and calumniate the character of our blessed Saviour, and made use of every means within his power to impede the progress of Christianity : pretending at the same time that he himself, and a female associate of his, of the name of Helen, were persons really commissioned from above for the purpose of enabling the souls of men once more to regain their native liberty and light.(')

From this one circumstance alone, supposing that we were to lay out of the case various other corroborative proofs, it is plainly to be perceived that there must have been some mistake with regard to the Gnostic Christians being considered as the disciples of Simon, and his being accounted the parent or inventor of the Gnostic philosophy. The principles and maxims of this species of philosophy had become familiar to the people of the East long before the time of Simon's applying himself to the study and culture of it in Egypt ; and as to his having been the chief leader of the Gnostics, it is certain that not one of their sect held him in the least reverence.(') The probability is, that the early fathers, perceiving the similarity that subsisted between Simon's tenets and those of the Gnostics, and being, notwithstanding their proficiency in Greek literature, but mere novices in Oriental learning, and consequently not aware of any one's having philosophized after this manner previously to him, were induced to believe that the whole tribe of Gnostics had proceeded from his school.

(1) It ought not perhaps to be passed over unnoticed, that not a few writers, ancient as well as modern, have assigned the chief place amongst the heretics of the first century to *Dositheus*, or as he is termed by the Chaldeans, Dosthai. That a man of this name existed about the time of our Saviour, and that he endeavoured to bring about a change in the religion of his countrymen the Samaritans, and became the founder of a sect which continued to exist in Egypt even down to the sixth century, is unquestionably certain. Vid. Origen, lib. vi. *contra* Cels. p. 282. Eulogius apud Photium *Biblioth* Cod. ccxxx. p. 883. et seq. But the fact is, that instead of being included in the class of heretics, he ought rather to have a place assigned him amongst lunatics and madmen, or amongst those who, from a deranged state of intellect have been induced to obtrude themselves on the attention of the world as persons especially commissioned of God. For from the memorials that are extant respecting him, although they are neither very numerous nor explicit, it is clearly to be perceived that the man had been induced, not, as it should seem, so much through arrogance as from downright folly and inanity, to attempt passing himself on the

Samaritans as the Messiah. Vid. Origen, *adv. Celsum*, lib. i. p. 44. lib. [p. 189.] vi. p. 282. *Comm. in Johannem*, tom. ii. opp. p. 219. Eulogius apud Photium *Biblioth.* p. 883. The impious scheme which he had formed having been communicated to the Samaritan high priest, orders were issued for his apprehension with a view to punishment. By a precipitate flight, however, he escaped being taken; and seeking refuge in a remote cave, either voluntarily starved himself to death, or perished for want of being supplied with the necessaries of life. Vid. Epiphanius *Hæres.* xiii. p. 30. tom. i. opp. *Chronicon Samaritanum* apud Abr. Echellensem *Adnotat. ad Hebed-Jesu Catalog. Libror. Chaldaicor.* p. 162.

(2) Camp. Vitringa in the first place, and after him the venerable Christ. Aug. Heumann, and Isaac Beausobre, contend that there were two Simons Magi, and that the ancient fathers, through mistake, attributed the errors and faults of a certain Gnostic philosopher of the name of Simon, to that Simon of whom mention is made in the Acts of the Apostles as having imposed on the credulity of the Samaritans. Considerable difficulty however presents itself in the way of our assenting to this conjecture, since there is no testimony or argument of any force to be brought in support of it, nor is there any thing that opposes itself to probability in the commonly received opinion. Isaac Beausobre has indeed in his *Dissertation de Adamitis*, p. 2. subjoined to L'Enfant's History of the Hussite War, § 1. p. 350. et seq. come forward with no less than eight different arguments in proof of their having been more than one Simon Magus; but of the force of either or all of these arguments I will leave those to judge who will be at the pains of perusing with attention a dissertation published by me some time since on behalf of the opposite side of the question, or *de uno Simone Mago*.

(3) Unanimous as the Christian writers of the first three centuries, who make mention of Simon Magus, are in placing him at the head of the heretics of the first age, it is yet manifest, from every thing which they relate of him, that he could not have belonged to that class, but was an open and determined enemy of the Christian religion in all its branches. Origen (lib. v. *advers. Celsum*, p. 272.) expressly excludes the Simonians from the number of the Christian sects, and states that Jesus was not the object of their veneration, but Simon. And with this accords the testimony of all the rest; some of them indeed not making use of terms equally clear and explicit, but at the same time attributing to Simon principles and opinions which can leave no doubt on our minds as to the fact, inasmuch as they could never have been entertained by any man who had not set Christ far beneath him, and arrogated to himself all the dignity and consequence attached to the character of a divine legate; and hence it came to pass that the Simonians, as is recorded by Origen and Justin Martyr (*Apolog. pro Christianis secunda*, p. 70.) as well as others, experienced no sort of disturbance or molestation at a time when the Christians were constantly exposed to perils of the most formidable kind : for it was publicly known to every one, that so far from being the followers of Christ, they were the enemies of his doctrine. About twenty years since when, if I mistake not, I first suggested this opinion, there were some to whom it appeared almost as sacrilege to call in question the many high and sacred authorities by whom Simon was pronounced to be the

parent of heresy, and to bring into dispute a matter which had received the sanction of so many ages. The opinion however has, on the strength of its own
evidence, in the course of time obtained for itself many patrons, and was not
long since, adopted by the learned Jo. Augustin. Orsi, in the *Ecclesiastical His-*
[p. 190.] *tory* written by him in Italian under the particular patronage of the
pope, tom. i. p. 348.

(4) The most positive testimony as to this is supplied by Irenæus himself,
whom we cannot suspect of having misrepresented the fact, since he is otherwise loud in his condemnation of the Gnostics, on the very ground of their being the followers of Simon. None of the Gnostic sects, he observes, (lib. i. *adv.*
Hæreses, cap. xxvii. § 4. p. 106.) were willing *nomen magistri sui* (Simonis) *con-*
fiteri, but on the contrary, all of them were accustomed *Christi Jesu nomen tan-*
quam irritamentum proferre. Their repudiation of Simon, he adds, was altogether an artifice, by which they hoped to impose the more readily on the simple
and the ignorant, and to free their character from every sort of stain. But in this
he certainly does them wrong.

LXVI **The history of Simon.** The history of Simon is briefly
this. He was by birth a Samaritan, but having gone down into
Egypt, he was induced to continue there for some time, and apply himself to the study of the various arts which were cultivated by those who termed themselves *magi*, and the scourges
of evil dæmons. Upon returning into his own country, he contented himself for awhile with practising on the credulity of the
multitude by means of the powers of deception which he had
thus acquired. But having been a witness of the real miracles
wrought by Philip the deacon, at Samaria, in confirmation of the
truth of the doctrine which he preached, he professed himself
a convert to Christianity, cherishing, as it should seem, a hope
that by so doing he should ultimately, either through obsequi-
ousness or bribery, find a way to obtain for himself the faculty
of working similar wonders, and hence have divine honours paid
him by the people. An impious attempt which he made to
realize these expectations having met with its merited chastise-
ment from St. Peter in that severe and memorable reproof which
stands recorded in Acts, viii. 9, 10. he betook himself again to
his former evil courses, and associating with him a woman of the
name of Helen, spent the remainder of his days in wandering
about through various provinces, endeavouring, wherever he
came, by means of the different tricks and artifices of which
he had made himself master, to impose on weak and ignorant
minds, and make them believe that the two chief faculties of the

Supreme Deity, the one being in its nature masculine, the other feminine, were actually resident in the bodies of himself and his female companion, having been sent down from above for the purpose of controuling the power of those enemies and tormentors of the human race, the creator of this nether world and his subordinate agents ; and of stirring up the minds of men, in spite of their unhappy alliance with vile matter, to the acknowledgment and worship of the only true God. This certainly is all that can with truth, or with any great semblance of truth, be said of this extraordinary character; at least a considerable degree of suspicion attaches itself to whatever else is reported of him.(') In what place, and under what circumstances, his mortal career terminated is altogether uncertain : for as to what several ancient authors report of his having, in consequence of the prayers of St. Peter, fallen headlong from a vast height in an attempt to fly which he made at Rome in the reign of the emperor Nero, and received thereby such wounds as shortly afterwards occasioned his death, it is a tale to which no credit is at present given, except by such as are the dupes of superstition, or ready to swallow down every thing that has the support of antiquity on its side. Nor is any belief now placed by the [p. 191.] generality of people, in what Justin Martyr says of the Romans having honored Simon with an apotheosis, and erected a statue to his memory ; although it appears to be pretty certain, that the sect which he founded continued to exist in the third, and even down to the fourth century, and persisted to the last in paying a sort of honorary worship both to him and his concubine.(²)

(1) Those who may be desirous of possessing themselves of every thing that has been handed down to us respecting Simon, may consult the 2d vol. of Tillemont, and those other authors who are recommended by Sagittarius in his *Introductio ad Historiam Ecclesiasticam.* We should wish the reader to understand this reference as equally applicable to the various other sects of which notice may be taken in the course of this work, as we shall studiously make it our endeavour to avoid, as far as possible, adding to its bulk by any unnecessary repetition of references to books or authorities.

(2) The much agitated questions respecting the manner of Simon's death, and the statue said to have been erected to his memory at Rome, are in some measure grown obsolete, but cannot by any means as yet be said to have been set completely at rest; inasmuch as there are still to be found many who, on such occasions, are always vastly alarmed lest the authority and credit of anti-

quity should experience any diminution: others again, who imagine that the
greater credit is due to a thing in proportion as it is more wonderful and out of
the common course: and finally, others whom superstition so blinds as to render them altogether incapable of discerning the truth. (I.) With regard to what
is related by Arnobius, a writer of the third century, and after him by various
ancient authors, of Simon's flying in the air by the assistance of the evil spirit,
and of his being precipitated to the ground, in consequence of the prayers of
St. Peter, it is in the highest degree incredible and absurd. Simon was a slight-
of-hand man, a mere juggler, not such a character as the Prince of Darkness
would have selected to affright and mislead mankind. Besides, who is there so
ignorant as not to know how little faith is to be placed in what ancient authors
relate of magicians, and prodigies wrought by the assistance of the devil? Moreover, the most respectable of the early Christian writers, and beyond all Eusebius, the parent, as we may call him, of ecclesiastical history, say not a syl-
lable respecting this event, which, if it had in reality occurred, must surely
have been deemed worthy of being perpetuated throughout all ages: it is plain
therefore, that they either were entirely unacquainted with it, or else accounted
it nothing better than a mere idle story of the vulgar. In whichever way their
silence be interpreted, it is equally conclusive against the things ever having
happened. It appears to me however extremely probable, that the tale might
not be altogether of fabulous invention, but originate in a mistake, and be
founded on an event which actually did occur at Rome during the reign of the
emperor Nero. From the testimony of Suetonius, Juvenal, and Dio Chrysos-
tom, it seems to be placed beyond a doubt, that some poor wretch who had pretended to possess the art of flying, and been presumptuous enough to solicit an
opportunity of exhibiting a specimen of his ability in the theatre of Rome, did
actually commit himself to the air, and being immediately precipitated to the
ground, was literally dashed to pieces; the emperor himself, in whose presence
the feat was essayed, being sprinkled with some of his blood. Sueton. *in Nerone,* cap. xii. p. 23. Now it is certainly not at all unlikely that the name of this
unfortunate rival of Icarus might be Simon, and that the Christians, upon hearing that a magician (for so the common people at that time, termed every one
who practised any unusual or extraordinary arts) of this name had come to
such a disastrous end, might at once conclude that it was that very Simon the
[p. 192.] magician whose depravity and wickedness had long been in every
one's month; and since they were accustomed to attribute every thing by which
either the community or the church was materially benefited, to the effect of
prayer, might be led to think that God had wrought destruction on this determined enemy of the true religion at the instance of St. Peter, who was perhaps
at that time sojourning at Rome. Piety having at once given rise to the idea, it
is easily to be conceived that ingenuity would not be long in supplying all the
little minutiæ of circumstances. (II.) With regard to the statue which Justin
Martyr, and after him Tertullian and others, report to have been erected by the
Romans to the memory of Simon Magus, a discovery which was made in the
Tiberine island at Rome, about the year 1574, of a marble base or pedestal inscribed to Semo Sancus, the ancient Deus Fidius, has induced many of the

learned to think that the above-mentioned fathers, in consequence of their possessing merely a superficial knowledge of the Roman superstitions and ancient popular deities, were led into a mistake, and that what they conceived to be a monument raised in honour of Simon, was in fact a statue dedicated to this ancient deity of a somewhat similar name: an error into which they might the more easily fall, if, as was by no means unusual, the sculptor had in the inscription, put Simoni for Semoni. Several instances of such commutations of the letters E and I are given from different authors by the learned Jo. Casp. Hagenbuchius in his *Epistolæ Epigraphicæ*, p. 70. vid. Anton. van Dale's Dissertation *de statua Simonis*, annexed to his work *de Oraculis*, p. 579. Salom. Deylingius *Observat. Sacr. Lib.* 1. *Observ.* xxxvi. p. 140. Beausobre *Histoire de Manichée*, tom. i. p. 203. 395. Longerue in *Sylloge Anecdotorum* Ven. Jo. Dict. Winckleri, p. 211. as well as innumerable other authorities. So strongly supported indeed is this conjecture by different circumstances, that apparently it would be doing it no more than justice were we to give it a higher denomination. Yet such an amazing weight and influence have the names of Justin and Tertullian with some men, men too, by no means deficient either in point of sagacity or liberal information, that they will rather, on the faith and authority of these fathers, give credit to that which carries with it every stamp and indication of error, than adopt the judgment of some of our greatest literary characters, who not only show it to be in the highest degree probable that these fathers laboured under a misconception or mistake, but also point out a way in which every unprejudiced person must allow it to be very possible that such a misconception or mistake might have originated. See in addition to Tillemont *Memor.* tom. ii. p. i. p. 340. Styan Thirlby *ad Justin. Martyr.* p. 40. Prudent. Maranus the late editor of Justin, *Præfat. ad Justinum*, p. iii. c. vi. p. lxxxv. Jos. August. Orsi in his *Ecclesiastical History*, written in Italian, tom. ii. p. 119. as also what is contended for respecting this statue by a learned writer in the *Museum Halveticum*, tom. ii. p. 617. The chief of all the arguments that have been brought forward in favour of this statue is, that it is not to be believed that men like Justin Martyr and Tertullian, to whom the Roman language and religion were familiar, could have been so far deceived as to mistake the deity Semo Sancus for Simon Magus. But, for my own part, when I recollect how many other errors these fathers have inadvertently admitted into their works, I must confess that I see no difficulty at all in giving them full credit for such a blunder as this: whilst on the other hand, every thing whatever seems to oppose itself to my believing that the Romans could for a moment have so far discarded every sense of propriety, as to assign to a Jew or Samaritan of infamous reputation, to a man in fact no better than a juggler or a mountebank, a place amongst their gods, and to honour his memory with a statue. Concerning Helen, the associate of this [p. 193.] despicable mortal, I shall enter into no discussion or inquiry. The labours of the learned with regard to her history, have hitherto only tended to involve nearly the whole of it in difficulties and obscurity. Of the fact of her having existed, however, there can be no doubt, unless all that has come down to us respecting Simon be untrue; for Irenæus, Eusebius, and Augustin, all agree in stating that her image was preserved, and had a sort of worship paid to it by the Simonians, and according to Origen, *contr. Cels.* lib. v. p. 272. the respect which they thus manifested for the memory of this woman caused them to be occasionally styled Helenians.

LXVII. **Tenets of Simon.** The principles on which the discipline of Simon was founded, appear to have been much the same with those which were recognized by all the different sects of the Gnostics. The Supreme Deity, for instance, to whom he attributed every possible degree of excellence, had, according to his tenets, existed from all eternity, and at a certain period begotten of himself a number of æons, or natures after his own likeness. Again, matter, which he regarded as being radically corrupt, was represented by him as having in like manner existed eternally, and being possessed of a generative faculty, to have become the parent and the author of all evil, as well as of various other viciously disposed natures. The creation of this world he considered as having been brought about by a female æon, with the assistance of certain powerful genii, without the concurrence or sanction of the Supreme Deity. By this creator of the world, he maintained, who was herself of a divine nature and origin, were generated an incredible number of living souls, whom she united with bodies composed of matter, and consequently corrupt. Man, therefore, according to him, was compounded of two parts, the one celestial, the other terrene ; the one divine, the other depraved. The human race he represented as held in bondage by the founders or creators of this world, and as living in utter ignorance of the Supreme Deity, who contemplating with sorrow the disastrous situation and miserable servitude into which such a number of æthereal spirits were thus unhappily plunged, was in the highest degree solicitous that they should be stimulated to pursue that path which, upon their release from the body, would conduct them to his immediate residence, the seat of everlasting joy and happiness, to which this pretended philosopher, in common with the rest of the Gnostics, gave the appellation of *pleroma.* The course pointed out by him to be observed by the souls who were desirous of attaining to this blissful state, was to cast off all obedience to the founders of this world, by whom he professed himself to mean those beings who were commonly worshipped as deities by the multitude, and to endeavour by means of meditation and mental exertion, to elevate themselves, and approach as nearly as possible to the supreme source of all good. Souls not inflamed with such a wish, were, upon the dissolution of their present earthly prisons, to pass into new bodies until they should arrive at a knowledge of their great and everlasting parent. The laws to which the nations of the earth paid obedience, not excepting even the peculiar code of the Jews, were, he maintained, all fabricated by the founders of this world for the purpose of perpetuating the bondage of captive souls, and that they might therefore be disregarded with impunity by all such minds as had acquired illumination from the fountain of all wisdom. When the projected deliverance of the [p. 194.] souls of all mankind from the captivity of matter had been finally accomplished, and they had again joined their first great parent in the regions above, the whole fabric of this nether world and all its dependencies, which he pronounced to be a rude and imperfect work, would, according to his tenets, experience an overwhelming and utter destruction at the hands of the Deity. The discipline of Simon, however, differed most essentially from that of the Gnostic Christians in its principal feature, since, instead of joining with them in paying homage to the Saviour of mankind, his aim evidently was to wrest from Christ the glory of man's recovery, and make it the inheritance of himself and his concubine. For he pretended that the greatest and most powerful æon, of the masculine sex, was actually resident within himself, and that the mother of all souls had in like manner taken up her abode in the corporeal frame of his companion Helen ; and asserted that he was in an especial manner commissioned by the Most High for the three-fold purpose of communicating to captive souls the knowledge requisite for their deliverance, of overthrowing the dominion of the founder of this world, and of delivering Helen from the subjection in which she had long been held by the subordinate agents or associates of this author of all evil.(')

(1) In the accounts given us by ancient writers of the religion and discipline of Simon, the student finds himself occasionally embarrassed by a want of coherence and perspicuity. By no one has the subject been handled with greater clearness and precision than by the uncertain author of *The Recognitions of Clement* and *The Clementina*, who under the form of a disputation between St.

Peter and Simon, throws considerable light on several things but very imperfectly and confusedly treated of by other writers. Nor do I see any just reason
that should prevent us from yielding him every sort of credit as an expounder
of the tenets of Simon, since he lived in an age when the sect of the Simonians
was still in existence, and has certainly recorded nothing that is in any material
degree repugnant to the accounts given by other authors. As for intentional
misrepresentation or falsehood, it is difficult to conceive any inducement that he
could have had to be guilty of it.

LXVIII. **Menander.** The second station in the class of heretics derived from the Gnostics, is in general assigned by ancient
writers to Menander, another Samaritan, whom they represent
as having been initiated in the school of Simon. But little credit, however, can be given to this, after comparing together the
accounts which Irenæus, Justin, Tertullian, and a few others,
have handed down to us respecting this man. For from what
they say, it is plain that his object was to supplant both Christ
and Simon, and to pass himself on the world as the Saviour of
mankind, or an æon sent down from above for the purpose of
effecting the salvation and deliverance of the souls of the human
race, by communicating to them a knowledge of the true God; a
circumstance which places it beyond all doubt, that he came
neither within the description of a heretic, nor that of a Simo-
nian. The opinion of the early writers above alluded to, respecting him, was in all probability, grounded on their perceiving that
his tenets and doctrine respecting the Deity, the nature of matter, the origin of this world, and the souls and bodies of its inha-
[p. 195.] bitants, were nearly similar to those which were entertained and taught by Simon and the Gnostic Christians. From
what has reached us respecting Menander, I should conceive his
character to have been rather that of a weak enthusiast than of
an artful impostor. The sect which he founded existed but for
a short period, and appears to have been always confined within
very narrow limits.(')

(1) On this subject the reader may consult Irenæus, lib. i. cap. xxiii. p. 100.
Epiphanius *Hæres.* xxii. p. 61. Justin Mart. *Apolog.* ii. p. 69. Theodoret, *Hæret.
Fabular.* lib. i. cap. ii. p. 193. tom. iv. opp. Tertullian *de Anima*, cap. l. p. 187.
de Resurrect. cap. v. p. 205. Recourse may also be had to Ittigius, Tillemont,
Nat. Alexander, S. Basnage, in *Annal.* and other recent authors who have di-
rected their attention to the elucidation of the early Christian History.

LXIX. **The Nicolaitans.** Since Simon and Menander cannot properly be said to come within the descriptions of heretics, it follows of course that at the head of those Christians who were tainted with the Gnostic heresies we must place the Nicolaitans, provided that the Nicolaitans who are rebuked by our blessed Lord in Rev. ii. 6. 14, 15, be the same with those who under that denomination are reckoned by the writers of the second century amongst the sects of the Gnostics.(¹) The generality of ancient writers consider Nicolaus, one of the seven men elected by the church of Jerusalem, as having been either directly or indirectly the author of this sect. It should seem, however, as if their opinion as to this was founded rather on uncertain report and conjecture than on any testimony that can be relied on.(²) Our blessed Saviour states the Nicolaitans to have incurred his displeasure in consequence of the laxity of their morals, and their continuing to partake of meats offered to idols, and to indulge in fornication, contrary to the Apostle's injunction, Acts, xv. 29, but he does not charge them with entertaining any heretical principles or opinions. By the writers of the subsequent ages, however, they are represented as having adopted the Gnostic maxims respecting the existence of two principles, the one of light, the other of darkness, the origin of the visible world, the ministry of æons, and the like. Over every thing relating to this sect there hangs a degree of obscurity which we believe it will ever be found beyond the power of human ingenuity to dispel.(³)

(1) The opinions of such of the learned as either deny that such a sect as that of the Nicolaitans ever existed, or maintain that it took its name, not from any particular person who might be the founder of it, but from the accordance of its principles with the impiety of Balaam, have been made the subject of particular investigation by me in a dissertation, which is to be found at [p. 196.] p. 395. of vol. i. of my *Syntagma Dissertationum ad Historiam Eccles. pertinent.*

(2) Cassianus, *Collation.* xviii. cap. xvi. p. 529. edit. Francf. 1722. fol. says, *Nam licet hunc Nicolaum quidam asserant non illum fuisse qui ad opus ministerii ab Apostolis est electus, nihilo tamen minus eum de illo discipulorum fuisse numero negare non possunt.*

(3) Irenæus *adv. Heres* lib. iii. cap. xi. p. 188. Tertullian *de Præscript. Hæret.* cap. xlvii. p. 128. Clemens Alex. *Stromat.* lib. iii. cap. iv. p. 524. Augustin *de Heres.* cap. v. p. 60. To these I omit adding Epiphanius, because he confesses that what he says of the *Nicolaitans* belongs equally to all the different sects of the Gnostics. Upon a comparison of the grounds on which our blessed Saviour's rebuke of the Nicolaitans is founded, with the errors which are attri-

buted to them by the writers of after-times, I must confess that I cannot help entertaining very considerable doubts whether the Nicolaitans mentioned in the Revelations were the same with the Nicolaitans of Clement and others, or a different sect. Had the Nicolaitans with whom our Saviour was so much displeased been devoted to the Gnostic discipline and opinions, they would not, in my humble judgment, have been reproved by him merely on account of their reprehensible course of life, but their erroneous principles would likewise have been made the subject of animadversion, and his followers would have been cautioned against imbibing any of their extravagant and pernicious tenets. For surely these principles were pregnant with no less, or rather a greater degree of danger, to the minds of the simple and artless Christians, than was to be apprehended from the offensive improprieties and vices in which the Nicolaitans indulged, in direct opposition to the apostolic precepts. And is it to be believed, that our blessed Saviour, when enjoining his followers to avoid associating with the Nicolaitans, on account of their incontinence, would not have touched on, or in the slightest degree alluded to the origin or fount from whence this laxity of morals had proceeded? The probability, as it appears to me, is, that in the second century amongst the numerous leaders of the different Gnostic sects which were at that time springing up in almost every direction, there might be one of the name of *Nicolaus*, who might give to his followers the denomination of *Nicolaitans*, and that the title, thus acquired by this sect, having reached the ears of the early Christian fathers, who as we well know, were very apt occasionally to fall into mistakes as to matters of this kind, they were hastily led to consider these sectaries as being one and the same with the Nicolaitans mentioned by St. John in the Epistles to the seven Asiatic churches: and since they knew of no man of the name of Nicolaus who had attained to any degree of reputation or consequence in the Christian community, except him who is mentioned in Scripture as having been elected one of the seven ministers of the church of Jerusalem, they at once concluded that this sect must have owed its origin to him. My desire is to be understood as throwing out these suggestions rather in the way of conjecture, than as pretending to speak with any degree of peremptoriness as to this point. I will not however scruple to say, that I think I have at least a strong probability in my favour.

LXX. Cerinthus. In the same age with St. John and the Nicolaitans, flourished, as is commonly thought, the Jew Cerinthus, though there are not wanting some who consider him as having lived in the second century, and long posterior to the time of [p. 197.] John.(') Having devoted himself for some time to the study of letters and philosophy at Alexandria in Egypt, he at length engaged in one of the most difficult undertakings imaginable, namely, that of harmonizing the principles of the Gnostic discipline and those of Christianity, with the peculiar maxims and opinions of the Jews. From the principles of the Gnostic philosophy he adopted those which respect the pleroma, the æons, the origin of this world, and the great length of time through which the human race had remained in utter ignorance of the supreme Deity, together with all such maxims and tenets as were intimately connected with these. As he could not however, with consistency, admit into his system any thing absolutely repugnant to the Jewish religion, it became necessary for him in part to qualify what he thus adopted, and he accordingly relinquished the position that matter was intrinsecally evil and corrupt, inasmuch as it set itself in opposition to the belief entertained by the generality of the Jews respecting the future resurrection of men's bodies. The character likewise of the founder of this world, whom he considered as the legislator and governor of the Jewish people, was much softened down by him. The depravity, pride, and cruelty attributed to this Being by the Gnostics were all thrown into the shade, and he was represented as one of the most powerful genii, although unfortunately estranged from the true God. In the creation of this world he was not supposed to have acted without the knowledge and permission of the Deity, or to have been influenced by any improper motive. By way of reconciling this strange jumble of opinions with Christianity, Cerinthus maintained, that the supreme Deity, being displeased with the uncontrouled dominion usurped by the founder of this world and his subordinate agents over the human race, which had by degrees degenerated into the most irrational tyranny, resolved at length to put an end to it, and with this view to send down amongst mankind a celestial legate, or messenger, who should remove from their minds that cloud of superstition and ignorance with which they were oppressed, and by communicating to them a knowledge of their first great Parent, instruct them in the way of regaining their native liberty and happiness. Amongst the sons of men no corporeal receptacle was deemed by the Almighty wisdom to offer so fit an abode for an heavenly guest of this kind as the body of Jesus, the legitimate child of Joseph and Mary, a person eminently gifted with talents and understanding. Upon him therefore it was ordered, that one of the ever-blessed æons, whose name was Christ, should descend in the shape of a dove at the time of his baptism by John. Jesus then having the æon Christ thus united with him, commenced, ac-

cording to Cerinthus, a vigorous attack on the power and dominion of the founder of this world and his associates, endeavouring to convince the Jews that the one only supreme God was
alone deserving of their worship, and confirming the truth of his
doctrine and precepts by various miracles and signs. The result,
however, of these his labours in the cause of the Deity was unfavourable: for the Jewish elders, at the instigation of that Being
whose empire was thus seriously invaded, and whose energies
were of course exerted to the utmost for the preservation of his
usurped authority, laid violent hands on Jesus and put him to
death on the cross. In the ignominy and horrors of this punishment nothing was supposed to have been involved beyond the
bare corporeal frame of the man Jesus, the Nazarene: for immediately on the seizure of his person by the Jews, the divine principle, or Christ, by which it had been animated, took its depar-
[p. 198.] ture from the earth and returned to the blissful regions of
the pleroma, from whence it had originally proceeded. The way
chalked out by Cerinthus for obtaining salvation partook in like
manner of the Gnostic, Jewish, and Christian schemes. According to him it was incumbent on all who were desirous of arriving
at future happiness to relinquish every sort of homage which they
might have been accustomed to pay to the founder of this world
(who previously to the time of Christ had been the leader of the
Jewish people) and his associates, or to any of the various Gentile deities, and to make the Supreme Deity, and father of Christ,
together with Christ himself, the only objects of their reverential
worship. Such parts of the law of Moses as Jesus by his example
had sanctioned, he pronounced fit to be still observed, the rest to
be disregarded. Finally, he declared it to be necessary that in
all their actions they should strictly conform themselves to the
law of Christ. To those who should continue stedfast in their
obedience to these precepts he held out the promise of a future
resurrection from the dead—enjoyments of the most exquisite
nature during Christ's reign here upon earth—and subsequently,
a life of immortality and endless joy in the blissful regions above.
For, adhering to the Jewish way of thinking in this respect,
Cerinthus held, that upon the resurrection of our bodies
Christ would be again united with the man Jesus, and having founded a new city on the site of the ancient Jerusalem,

would reign there in triumphant splendor for the space of a thousand years.(²)

(1) See Sam. Basnage *Annal. Politico-Ecclesiast.* tom. ii. p. 6. Petr. Faydit *Ecclaircissemens sur l'Histoire Ecclesiastique des deux premieres Siecles,* cap. v. p. 64. Fred. Adolph. Lampius, *Comm. in Evangel. Johannis Prolegom.* lib. ii. chap. iii. §xvii. p. 182. all of whom are of opinion that Cerinthus lived about the time of Hadrian or Antoninus Pius. The arguments on which their opinion is grounded have been replied to by Jo. Franc. Buddeus in his work *de Eccles. Apostolic.* cap. v. p. 412. The principal argument relied on by those of the learned who dissent from the common opinion is, that the early fathers, for the most part, place Cerinthus after Carpocrates in the catalogue of heretics, which latter, without dispute, lived and taught in the second century; a circumstance which doubtless would carry with it considerable weight, did it appear that the early Christian writers had paid due attention to the regular order of time in their enumeration of heretics: but instead of this, we know the fact to be that the names of heretics are set down by Irenæus, Tertullian, Clement, and others, at random, without any regard being had to the times in which they lived.

It is asserted by Irenæus, Jerome, and others, that St. John wrote his gospel, and particularly the commencement of it, with an express view to the confutation of the erroneous tenets of Cerinthus respecting Christ. See Tillemont's *Memoires,* tom. i. p. iii. p. 936. This is denied by some more recent writers, but on grounds not altogether satisfactory. See a small work of Geo. L. Oeder, *de Scopo Evangelii Johannis,* published at Leipsig in 1732, in 8vo.

(2) In the view which I have here given of the Cerinthian discipline, I am borne out by the express testimony of ancient writers. My account, [p. 199.] however, amounts to nothing more than an imperfect sketch. For from no ancient author could I obtain that full degree of information respecting the Cerinthian system of religion which alone could enable me to exhibit a complete and satisfactory view of it; a thing which it would gratify me highly to have done, since in point of reason and ingenuity the author of it appears to have possessed a superiority over the rest of the Gnostics. It cannot indeed be denied, that by the generality of those writers who speak of him he is represented as devoid of understanding, libidinous, depraved, a man who held out, as an allurement to his followers, the promise of a free indulgence in obscene gratifications during the future reign of Christ upon earth. But really, as far as I am capable of forming a judgment on the matter, the blemishes and defects of his character appear to have been very unreasonably magnified by his accusers. In his opinions I perceive, it is true, the marks of a mind not sufficiently purified, and disposed not unfrequently, to deviate from the path of sound reason: but nothing whatever bespeaking a propensity to vicious or libidinous indulgences: nothing indicating a love for or pursuit of illicit pleasures: there are even some things in them which make in his favour, and prove him to have been destitute neither of sense nor of spirit. How, let me ask, could it be possible that the kingdom which it was asserted Christ would hereafter establish at Jerusalem,

should have been held forth in promise as a sink of immorality, vice, and concupiscence, by one who entertained the highest reverence for the wisdom, justice, and virtue of Jesus of Nazareth, and maintained that it was his superior sanctity and knowledge which induced the Deity to select his corporeal frame as a fit terrestrial residence for his offspring Christ, the chief of the celestial æons? How could this have been done by one who was constantly propounding Jesus as a model of virtue and wisdom to mankind? By one again who inculcated the necessity of strictly observing that part of the law of Moses to which Jesus himself had conformed? Is it to be believed, that Cerinthus could have excited or countenanced in his followers an expectation that in the looked for kingdom of 1000 years, during which, according to him, Christ, the immediate offspring of the Supreme Deity, united to the person of Jesus, the most intelligent and sacred of human beings, was to reign here on earth, every moral tie would be dissolved, and mankind be left at liberty to gratify their inordinate desires without restraint? Or in other words, that the greatest and best of potentates, the immediate offspring of the Deity, would become the instrument of promoting amongst a set of subjects newly recalled to life, the perpetration of all those crimes and flagitious enormities of which he had in times past expressed his utter detestation? To my mind this appears so remote from all probability, that I know not how to account for so many learned men's having insisted on it that Cerinthus held forth to his followers the prospect of their being permitted to riot without restraint in one continued scene of the grossest sensuality during the expected future reign of Christ here upon earth. I am at no loss however, in assigning this accusation to its proper source. Not a doubt can exist but that it originated with Caius, the presbyter and Dionysius Alexandrinus, two writers of the third century, as appears from Eusebius *Histor. Eccles.* lib. iii. cap. xxviii. p. 100. To prior ages it was utterly unknown. But at the time when the above-mentioned authors wrote, the dispute with the Chiliasts, or those who maintained that Christ would hereafter reign upon earth for the space of a thousand years, was carrying on with considerable warmth, and the object of these writers evidently was to repress this doctrine. With a view therefore the more readily to accomplish their end, they made it appear that the original author or parent of Chiliasm amongst the Christians was Cerinthus, a pernicious character, and one who had long since been condemned. And this, perhaps, might be allowable enough : but not content with this, they, by way of still more effectually preventing the Christians from every imitation of Cerinthus, deemed it expedient to augment the popular antipathy against him, and to persuade the multitude that he was a distinguished patron of vice and iniquity; and that it was [p. 200.] impossible for any one who was not inimical to the cause of piety and virtue, to approve of or countenance his doctrine respecting the future reign of Christ upon earth. Should it be objected to me, as it probably may, that this case of mine rests merely on supposition, and is grounded on no positive evidence, I confess it. But when it is considered that prior to these adversaries of Chiliasm, no one had ever attributed to Cerinthus so gross an error; when it is remembered that this very error with which he is charged is by no means to be reconciled with the other parts of his doctrine; in fine, when we reflect how utterly incredible it is that any man, not altogether bereft of his senses, should make an unrestricted license to riot in obscenity and filth the characteristic feature of a kingdom over which Jesus Christ was triumphantly to reign ; I rather think that but few things will appear to have a greater weight of probability on their side than the conjecture which I have thus hazarded.

Having relieved Cerinthus from the weight of this reproach, I will now advert to some particulars connected with the history of his system of discipline, in regard to which it were to be desired that further light could be obtained. (I.) It may be recollected that I have said Cerinthus differed in opinion from the rest of the Gnostics respecting the nature of matter. Now for this I cannot vouch any ancient authorities, but it struck me as very fairly deducible from certain of his tenets. For since he believed Jesus to have been a real man, born according to that law by which all other mortals are produced and yet considered CHRIST, who was of a divine nature, as having been united in the most intimate connection with him; and since it was likewise a part of his creed that men's bodies would hereafter be restored to life from the dead, it surely must be impossible that he could have regarded matter as the fountain and seat of all evil. In this respect I should have supposed him to have been of the same opinion with those philosophers of the East who considered matter as having been originally produced by the Deity, and who consequently could not regard it as absolutely and intrinsecally corrupt. What it was that Cerinthus looked upon as the cause of evil is not mentioned by any ancient author, nor is it to be collected from any maxims or tenets of his that have been handed down to us on record. (II.) A considerable degree of obscurity likewise hangs over the opinion entertained by him respecting the founder of this world. His notions of this Being appear to have been that he was of an order vastly inferior to the Supreme Deity, but altogether devoid of malice and arrogance ; and that although he had lost all knowledge of God, the governor of all things, yet that his work was undertaken and completed with the knowledge, consent, and assistance of the Most High. Since it was not his wish to abrogate the whole of the Jewish law, although he considered it as having been framed by the founder of this world, but meant that a part of it should remain in force, it is plain that he must have attributed to this Being a portion of diving wisdom and illumination. It strikes me, therefore, that Cerinthus must have conceived that the Supreme Deity, by means of one of those celestial natures whom the Gnostics term æons, excited the Being who afterwards became the founder of the world, and who at that time perhaps presided over one or other of the heavenly orbs, to undertake the reducing into order and form the rude and undigested mass of matter which had through infinite ages been emanating from the bosom of Omnipotence, as also to replenish it with inhabitants, and give to those inhabitants a set of laws. That the Deity moreover was not at first displeased with the dominion which this Being and his associates in labour assumed over the human race : but that in process of time, upon observing that the founder of the world, who had reserved to himself the government of the Jewish people, and in a much greater degree those of his associates to whom the other nations of the earth had been rendered subject, had departed widely from the principles of sound wisdom, he determined by the mission of Jesus Christ to put an end to their tyranny. As no means present themselves for our obtaining a further insight into the opinions of Cerinthus as to these points, we are constrained· to leave the subject as we found it, enveloped in obscurity. (III.) One of the accusations brought against Cerinthus by ancient writers, is that of his having entertained too great a partiality for the law of Moses: an accusation which I must confess I think to [p. 201.] be by no means an ill-founded one.   For it would be easy to point out several parts of his discipline which prove, to demonstration, that an attachment to the Jewish rites and opinions had gained a strong and predominating influence over his mind.   And they are therefore in an error, who, with Basnage and Faydit deny him to have been of the Jewish religion, as well as those who, with Massuet (*Diss. in Irenœnum*, i. art. vi. p. lxv.) assert that what is said by ancient authors of his having had it in view to reconcile the Jewish religion with Christianity is not deserving of credit.   What is commonly reported, however, of his having wished to impose on the necks of the Christians an observance of the whole law, is equally remote from the truth.   The nature of his system of discipline did not admit of this; for in many respects it went to show that the author of the law of Moses, *i. e.* the founder of this world, had erred : and since it was inculcated by Cerinthus that no sort of homage should for the future be paid to this Being, but that the Supreme Author of every thing and the Father of Christ should alone be worshipped by the Jews as well as all other nations, it must of necessity have been a part of his scheme, that all those rites which were so peculiarly appropriate to the God of the Jews as not to admit of their being transferred into the service of another and a superior Deity, should be abolished.   Moreover, both Epiphanius and Philaster, the latter in his book *de Hœresibus*, cap. xxxvi. p. 78. the former, *Hœres.* xxviii. § 2. p. iii. expressly say, that it was *a part* only of the law of Moses which appeared to Cerinthus worthy of being retained, and to which he thought the Christians might with propriety conform.   It is observable, however, that Dionysius Petavius, the Latin translator of Epiphanius, has skipped over the words ἀπὸ μέρος in the original, and it seems not at all unlikely that this negligence of his may have given occasion to many to think that Cerinthus wished to encumber Christianity with an observance of the whole of the law of Moses.   And here, should any one be desirous of knowing what part of the old law it was that Cerinthus thought to be of perpetual obligation, and what part he considered as having been abrogated by Christ, our reply must be, that it is a question involved in great obscurity, and consequently, one not easily to be resolved. The most probable conjecture appears to be, that he took the example of Christ for a standard or rule, deeming it proper that all those things to which Christ, during his union with the man Jesus, had conformed, should be observed and complied with by those who profess themselves to be his followers.   An opinion which indeed Epiphanius seems greatly to countenance, when in *l. c.* § v. p. 113, he says, that the Cerinthians, after the example of Christ, supported the authority of the law of Moses.   (IV.) At the first sight it seems somewhat wonderful that a man who conceived it proper to reject a part of the Mosaic law, should yet deem it fit to retain the Jewish persuasion respecting the future millenary reign of the Messiah here upon earth, an idle notion which had its rise long after the promulgation of the law. But upon a more attentive review of the discipline of Cerinthus, I think I can perceive the reasons which induced him to promote rather than repress the expectation of an empire of this kind. The holy, wise, and innocent man Jesus, in whose corporeal frame Christ had taken up his residence during his abode here on earth, had, according to the Cerinthian scheme, experienced great injury at the hands of this his celestial guest. For when the Jews, in consequence of his having attacked their lawgiver and Deity, proceeded to lay violent hands on Jesus, Christ, by whose instigation and command he had done so, instead of supporting him against them, at once took his departure and left this unhappy mortal, unbefriended and defenceless, to sink under the torments and the fury of his enraged enemies. Now a desertion of this kind could not fail to carry with it an air of much injustice and ingratitude. For what can be conceived more unprincipled than in a time of the greatest peril to desert a good and eminent character, through whom [p. 202.] one may have taught and acted, and leave him to be tormented and put to death by his enemies? By way therefore of relieving the character of the Deity and his son Christ from this blemish, Cerinthus deemed it expedient to promote amongst his followers a belief that Christ would one day or other even here upon earth, make ample recompense to his former mortal associate, both in honours and rewards, for all the injuries and sufferings to which he had been subjected on his account. For that at a fixed time he would again descend from above, and renewing the union which had formerly subsisted between him and Jesus, make him his partner in a triumphant reign of one thousand years' duration. Contrasted with this magnificent and lasting recompense, the calamities endured by Jesus on account of Christ become light and insignificant. (V.) It is sufficiently clear that the Cerinthian sect flourished chiefly in that part of Asia which was anciently termed Proconsular Asia, or Lydia, and of which the principal city was Ephesus, where St. John spent the latter part of his days. But as to the extent of this sect, or the time when it became extinct, we have no certain information. Its existence should seem not to have been protracted beyond the second century. Isaac Beausobre, indeed, in his *Dissert. sur les Nazareens*, which is to be found in the supplement to his *Historia Hussitica*, p. 144, has attempted, from some words of the emperor Julian, apud Cyrillum, lib. vi. *contra Julian*, p. 333, to prove that the Cerinthians were not extinct even in the fourth century. But the fact is, that he did not sufficiently attend to what is said by Julian. What the emperor remarks is this, that there were certain of the Christians who thought that "the Word" of which St. John speaks, was distinct from Jesus Christ. These Christians Beausobre conceives to have been Cerinthians, but he is mistaken. For Cerinthus did not differ from the rest of the Christians in making a distinction between "the Word," or the divine nature, and the man Jesus Christ. All Christians do this; at least all who assent to the decrees of the Council of Nice. St. John himself clearly does so when he says that the Word was made flesh. John, i. 14. What distinguished Cerinthus from other Christians was

17

his denying that the Word coalesced in one person with Jesus, and contending that the latter was thirty years of age when Christ descended on him, as also that upon the seizure of Jesus by the Jews, Christ withdrew from his person, and returned to the place from whence he had come. His opinion of Christ in this respect bears somewhat of a resemblance to that which is commonly attributed to Nestorius, dividing Christ Jesus into two distinct persons. His tenets, however, were by far worse than what the Nestorian maxims countenance, and we therefore cannot agree with **Faydit, Lampius,** and other learned men, who consider Cerinthus as having, in point of fact, been a Nestorian before the time of Nestorius.

END OF THE FIRST CENTURY.

THE

ECCLESIASTICAL HISTORY

OF THE

SECOND CENTURY.

I. **Propagation of the Christian religion.** The Christian religion, which in the course of the former age had made its way throughout a considerable portion of the world, and pervaded nearly the whole of the Roman empire, was, in the century on which we are now about to enter, by the zeal and incredible exertions of its teachers, still more widely diffused, and propagated even amongst those nations, which on account of their ferocity and the loathsomeness of their manners were justly regarded with horror by the rest. Being destitute of any documents on the subject that can properly be relied on, it is impossible for us, with any degree of exactness, to specify either the time, circumstances, or immediate authors, of this further diffusion of the blessings of the gospel, or particularly to distinguish the provinces which had hitherto remained uncheered by, and now first received the light of celestial truth from those to which it had been communicated in the former century. We must rest satisfied therefore with being able to ascertain, in a general way, from the unexceptionable testimony of writers of these and the following times, that the limits of the church of Christ were, in this age, extended most widely; in so much, indeed, as to make them correspond very nearly with the confines of the then known habitable world.(')

(1) Some very striking passages respecting the amplitude and extent of the Christian community, are to be met with in the works of those most excellent writers of the second century, Justin Martyr, Irenæus, and Tertullian, writers, of whom it is not too much to say, that they are, in general, most deserving of unlimited credit. ὃ δὲ ἵν says Justin, (*Dialog. cum Tryphone*, p. 341. edit. Jebbian.) γὰρ ὅλως ἐςὶ τὸ γένος ἀνθρώπων, εἴτε βαρβάρων, εἴτε Ἑλλήνων, εἴτε ἁπλῶς ὡτινίων ὀνόματι πρόσαγορευομένων, ἢ ἀμαζοβίων, ἢ ἀδίκων καλυμένων, ἢ ἐν σκηναῖς κτηνοτρόφων οἰκούντων, ἐν οἷς μὴ διὰ τῦ ὀνόματος τῦ ςαυρωθέντος Ἰησῦ,

εὐχαὶ καὶ εὐχαριϛίαι τῶ πατρὶ καὶ ποιητῆ τῶν ὅλων γίνονται. *Ne unum quidem est genus mortalium, sive barbarorum, sive Græcorum, seu etiam aliorum omnium, quocumque appellentur nomine, vel in plaustris degentium, vel domo carentium, vel in tentoriis viventium, et pecoribus vitam tolerantium, inter quos per nomen crucifixi Jesu supplicationes, et gratiarum actiones patri et fabricatori omnium non fiant.*——Subsequently, at p. 351. he again expresses himself much to the same purport, though in fewer words. Now admitting, what indeed is too obvi-[p. 204.] ous to be denied, that there is in this somewhat of exaggeration, since long after the age of Justin there were many nations of the earth which had not been brought to a knowledge of Christ, still there could have been no room for this very exaggeration, had not the Christian religion been at that time most extensively diffused throughout the world. Irenæus, disputing with the Valentinians, (lib. i. *adv. Hæres.* cap. x. p. 48. edit. Massuet.) opposes to them the entire Christian church, which he represents as *extended throughout the whole world, even to the uttermost bounds of the earth.* From this immense multitude of Christians in the general, he then selects certain particular churches widely separated from each other in point of situation, and sets them in opposition to his adversaries. Καὶ ὅτε αἱ ἐν Γερμανίαις ἱδρυμέναι ἐκκλησίαι ἄλλως πεπιϛεύκασιν, ἢ ἄλλως παραδιδόασιν, ὅτε ἐν ταῖς Ἰβερίαις, ὅτε ἐν Κελτοῖς, ὅτε κατὰ τὰς ἀνατολὰς, ὅτε ἐν Αἰγύπτω, ὅτε ἐν Λιβύη, ὅτε αἱ κατὰ μέσα τῦ κόσμυ ἱδρυμέναι. *Ac neque hæ quæ in Germaniis sitæ sunt Ecclesiæ aliter credunt, aut aliter tradunt, nec quæ in Hiberiis, aut Celtis, neque hæ quæ in oriente, neque hæ quæ in Ægypto, neque hæ quæ in Libya, neque hæ quæ in medio mundi constitutæ.* In support of the doctrine then for which he is contending, we see Irenæus here calls to witness churches from all the three grand divisions of the world which were at that time known. From Europe, the Germanic, the Iberian or Spanish and the Celtic or Gaulish. He himself lived amongst the Celts, and was a near neighbour to the Germans and Iberians ; and must consequently have been most intimately acquainted with the situation of Christian affairs in those parts. From Asia he adduces the churches of the East, by which I conceive him to mean those which had been planted at the eastern extremity of Asia. Finally, from Africa he calls to his support, the churches of Egypt and Libya. To what churches he alludes when he speaks of those "situated in the centre of the world," it is not very easy to say. The commentators on Irenæus would have us to understand him as having in view the churches of Palestine, since it appears that anciently Palestine was, by some, considered as situated in the centre of the world. How far this may be just I am unable to say. Possibly the word κόσμος, or *world*, might be put by Irenæus, as it is by others of the ancient writers, for the Roman empire. Annexing this sense to the word, the centre of the world would be Italy, which was as it were the heart of the Roman empire. Another interpretation has been offered to the world by Gabriel Liron, a learned monk, of the order of the Benedictines, (*Singularités Historiques et Litteraires*, tom. iv. p. 197.) who supposes that by the centre of the world was meant Asia Minor, Greece, Thrace, Illyricum, Pannonia, Italy and the Isles; in short all those parts which were surrounded by the countries which he had before enumerated. Tertullian gives a more copious list than Irenæus, of the nations that had embraced Christianity, although perhaps less to be depended on. *In quem enim alium*, says he, (in lib. *adv. Judæos*, c. vii. p. 212. edit. Rigalt.) *universæ gentes crediderunt, nisi in Christum qui jam venit ? Cui enim et,* (there seems to be some deficiency or corruption of the text in this place,) *aliæ gentes crediderunt: Parthi, Medi, Ela-mitæ, et qui inhabitant Mesopotamiam, Armeniam, Phrygiam, Cappadociam, et incolentes Pontum, et Asiam, et Pamphyliam: immorantes Ægyptum, et regionem Africæ quæ est trans Cyrenem inhabitantes ! Romani et incolæ ; tunc et in Hieru-salem Judæi et cæteræ gentes: ut jam Getulorum varietates, et Mauro-* [p. 205.] *rum multi fines: Hispaniarum omnes termini, et Galliarum diversæ nationes, et Britannorum inaccessa Romanis loca, Christo vero subdita, et Sarmatarum, et Da-corum, et Germanorum, et Scytharum, et abditarum multarum gentium et provincia-rum et insularum multarum nobis ignotarum, et quæ enumerare minus possumus : in quibus omnibus locis Christi nomen, qui jam venit, regnat.* Considering this passage as perfectly explicit, and every way worthy of credit, various of the learned have not hesitated on the faith of it, to pronounce that the Christian re-ligion had, at this time obtained for itself a footing in all the different nations here enumerated. For my own part were I to follow them in this, it would not be without a strong apprehension that I might plunge myself into difficulties not easily to be surmounted. In fact, it appears to me, that Tertullian puts on here a little of the rhetorician, as he does in many other parts of his writings, and relates some things which it would strangely puzzle me, or any one else to demonstrate. In the first place, it is to be remarked, that the middle part of the above passage is taken from the Acts of the Apostles, and that, with the excep-tion of the Armenians, it exhibits a catalogue of precisely the same nations as are enumerated by the Jews who had heard the Apostles speak in foreign tongues, Acts, ii. 8. 9. From what the Jews are there recorded to have said, Tertullian seems to have conceived what carries on its very face the marks of absurdity, namely, that all the nations of whom those devout Jews there make mention, were at once induced to embrace the Christian faith. It is next ob-servable, that what Tertullian here says of Christianity having in his time been professed by divers nations of the Gauls is directly contrary to the fact. In the time of Tertullian, the church of Gaul had attained to no degree of strength or size, but was quite in its infancy, and confined perhaps within the limits of one individual nation, as the inhabitants of the country themselves acknowledge. What he adds about Christ's being acknowledged in those parts of Britain to which the Roman arms had not penetrated, is still wider removed from the truth. Finally, his asserting that many unexplored nations and unknown islands and provinces had embraced Christianity, most plainly evinces that he suffered him-self to be carried away by the warmth of imagination, and did not sufficiently attend to what he was committing to paper. For how could it be possible that Tertullian should have been brought acquainted with what was done in unex-plored regions and unknown islands and provinces ? In fact, instead of feeling his way by means of certain and approved testimony, he appears, in this instance, to have become the dupe of vague and indistinct rumour.

II. **Mission of Pantænus to India.** The name of one of those,

however, who devoted themselves to the propagation of the gospel amongst the nations of the east, has been transmitted to posterity, *viz.* that of Pantænus, a man of eminent abilities, and one
by whom the cause of Christianity was, in various ways, considerably benefited.   Having applied himself with diligence to
the cultivation of letters and philosophy, and presided for a while
with distinguished credit over the Christian school at Alexandria,
he at length, either on the suggestion of his own mind, or by the
[p. 206.] command of Demetrius, his bishop, engaged in a mission to the Indians, who had about this time manifested a wish
for Christian instruction, and communicated to them that saving
knowledge of which they stood in need.   To which of the
many nations comprehended by the ancients, under the general
title of Indians, it was that Pantænus thus went, has been the
subject of dispute.   My own opinion is that this mission originated in an application made to the bishop of Alexandria by
certain Jews who were settled in Arabia Felix, and who had
been originally converted to Christianity by Bartholomew, requesting that a teacher might be sent them for the purpose of
renovating and keeping alive amongst them the true religion,
which, for want of such assistance, had gone much to decay, and
was visibly every day still further on the decline.   If this conjecture of mine be well founded, it must of necessity follow, that
those are in an error who conceive that India obtained her first
knowledge of the Gospel through Pantænus.([1])

(1) For whatever we know of the sacred legation of Pantænus to the Indians, we are indebted to Eusebius and Jerome; between whom, however, there
is some little difference of narration respecting it. By the former, in his *Hist.
Eccles.* lib. v. cap. x. p. 175. Pantænus is represented as having, on the suggestion of his own mind, undertaken a journey amongst the people of the east for
the purpose of converting them to Christianity, and to have extended his travels
even as far as the Indians. The latter, in his *Catal. Scriptor. Ecclesiast.* cap.
xxxvi. p. 107. ed. Fabric. et *Epistol.* lxxxiii. p. 656. tom. iv. opp. part ii. ed. Benedict. reports that certain delegates had been dispatched by the Indians to Alexandria, requesting of Demetrius, the bishop of that city, that a Christian instructor might be sent them; and that Demetrius, acceding to their wishes, directed
Pantænus, the prefect of the Alexandrian school to accompany those men on their
return. If then we give credit to Eusebius, we must understand Pantænus as
having voluntarily, and purely out of love towards God, undertaken the labour
of disseminating a knowledge of the gospel amongst divers of the barbarous nations of the east, including even the Indians: if on the contrary we take Jerome

for our guide, it should seem that he was sent by his bishop on a special mission to the Indians, and to none besides. Possibly it may not be very difficult to bring about a reconciliation between these two accounts. Pantænus had, probably at the instigation of his own mind, gone forth with a view to the conversion of some of the more neighbouring nations, and, perhaps, met with some success. Whilst he was thus employed, the Indian delegates, in all likelihood, arrived at Alexandria, requesting that a Christian instructor might be sent to their countrymen; and Demetrius having received the most ample testimony of his knowledge, faith, and zeal, pitched upon this same Pantænus as the most proper person to accompany them on their return. But since it is well known that the Greek and Latin writers gave the title of Indians to many of the more remote eastern nations, of whom little or nothing was known, and also occasionally made use of the term to denote the Persians, Parthians, Medes, Ethiopians, Libyans, Arabians, and others, as is not unusual with us at this day, the learned have made it a question what Indians those were to whom a knowledge of the gospel was imparted by Pantænus. Most of them imagine that the scene of his labours must have been the country of India Magna which is watered by the Indus, and which we now term Eastern India: an opinion that seems to be countenanced by Jerome, who says that Pantænus was sent to the Brachmans. *Missus est,* says he in his 83d Epistle, *in Indiam ut Christum apud Brachmanas et illius gentis philosophos prædicaret.* For Brachmans or Bramins is [p. 207.] the title by which the wise men of India Magna are distinguished to this day; but by the ancients the term Brachmanus was applied in a manner equally vague and ambiguous with that of Indians, and it appears to be not at all unlikely that Jerome might, in this instance, have no authority but his own fancy for what he said. Those illustrious scholars, Hen. Valesius, L. Holstenius, and others, have therefore rather thought that it was to the Abyssinians or Ethiopians that Pantænus went, since the appellation of Indians, (a title which they are still fond of retaining) was given also to these people by the ancients: and in addition to this, they are as it were, next door neighbours to the Egyptians, and keep up a constant commercial intercourse with them. See Basnage—*Annal. Politico-Ecclesiast.* tom. ii. p. 207. Hen. Valesius, *Adnotat. ad Socratis Histor. Eccles.* p. 13. For my own part, I can fall in with neither of these opinions; for my belief is that those Indians, who requested to have a teacher sent them by Demetrius, the bishop of Alexandria, were neither pagans nor strangers to Christianity, but Jews, who had settled in that part of Arabia, called by the Greeks and Romans Arabia Felix, and by the people of the east Hyemen: and who had previously been brought to a knowledge of Christ and his word. My reason for thinking thus is, that Jerome says, Pantænus found amongst them the Gospel of St. Matthew in Hebrew, and brought it back to Alexandria with him, and that they had received this book from Bartholomew, one of the twelve apostles, who had " preached amongst them the coming of Jesus Christ." *Catalog. Scriptor. Ecclesiast.* c. xxxvi. p. 107. It is apparent therefore that the people to whom Pantænus went, were not strangers to Christianity, as also that they were skilled in the Hebrew language, and were consequently of Jewish extraction. For since Bartholemew left with them one of the gospels written in Hebrew, it unavoidably follows, that they must have been acquainted with the Hebrew tongue. Had they been ignorant of the Hebrew, what end could it have answered to make them a present of a book in that language? It only remains then for me to show that these same Jews were inhabitants of Arabia Felix. And in this I feel no sort of difficulty whatever, in as much as it can clearly be ascertained that this part of India was the scene of Bartholomew's labours. For let any one only be at the pains of comparing together the testimony of ancient authors, respecting that India to which a knowledge of Christ and his word was first imparted by Bartholomew, and not the shadow of a doubt can remain with him, as to its having been Arabia Felix, which we well know was one of the countries included under the title of India by the ancients. See Tillemont, *in Vita Bartholomœi. Mem. Hist. Ecclesiast.* tom. i. p. 1160, 1161.

III. **Origin of the Gallic, German, and English churches.** Turning to the European provinces, we find it acknowledged by the best informed French writers, that their country, which anciently bore the name of Trans-alpine Gaul, was not blessed with the light of the gospel until this century, when a knowledge of the religion of Christ was first communicated to their rude forefathers by Pothinus, who, together with Irenæus, and certain other devout men, had travelled into Gaul from Asia. There are not wanting some, however, who would carry up the origin of the Gallic church to the apostles themselves, or their imme-
[p. 208.] diate disciples.(') From Gaul it seems probable that Christianity passed into Cis-rhenane Germany, at that time under the dominion of the Romans, and was also transferred to the opposite shores of Britain, although it is insisted on by not a few of the Germans, that their church owes its foundation to certain of the immediate companions and disciples of St. Peter and the other apostles(²); and the inhabitants of Britain would rather have us, with respect to the introduction of Christianity into their country, receive the account of Bede, who represents Lucius, an ancient king of that island, as having in this century procured some Christian teachers to be sent him from Rome by the pontiff Eleutherus.(³)

(1) The most eminent of the French writers have at different times engaged in disputes of considerable warmth, respecting the antiquity and origin of the Gallic church. There appear to be three different opinions on the subject, each of which has found its advocates.—(I.) That to which we have above given the precedence, has been defended with great ability and learning by the very celebrated Jo. Launois, in various tracts which are to be found in the first part of the second volume of the joint edition of his works. So cogent indeed are

the arguments of this illustrious writer, that his opinion has been embraced by almost every one in France who makes pretension either to superior wisdom, ingenuity, or learning. Vid. *Histoire Litteraire de la France*, tom. i. p. 223, et seq. This opinion moreover is supported by the authority of no less than three most respectable ancient historians; of whom the first is Sulpitius Severus, who, in speaking of the persecution which the Christians of Lyons and Vienne suffered, under the emperor Marcus Antoninus, (*Histor. Sacr.* lib. ii. cap. 32, p. 246.) adds, *ac tum primum inter Gallias martyria visa, ferius trans alpes Dei religione suscepta.* The next is the author of *The Acts of Saturninus*, bishop of Thoulouse, who suffered martyrdom in the third century, under the reign of the emperor Decius, a work that is generally supposed to have been written in the beginning of the fourth century. According to this writer, the churches that had been founded in France were but few and small even in the third century. Vid. Theod. Ruinart. *Acta Martyrum Sincera et Selecta*, p. 130. The third is Gregory of Tours, the parent of French history, who relates, (*Histor. Francor.* lib. i. cap. xxviii. p. 23, *et de Gloria Confessorum*, cap. xxx. p. 399, ed. Ruinart,) that under the reign of Decius there were seven men sent from Rome into France for the purpose of preaching the gospel. These seven then, it is observable, are the very ones which popular tradition pronounces to have been the companions of the apostles Paul and Peter, and amongst them is that Dionysius, the first bishop of Paris, whom the French formerly maintained to have been Dionysius the Areopagite.—(II.) By those, however, who think it of greater importance to uphold ancient notions and magnify the consequence of France, than to ascertain the truth, an origin by far more august is assigned to the Gallic church, and the apostles Peter and Paul themselves are pronounced to have been its founders. According to them, the last mentioned of these apostles traversed a considerable part of Gaul in his way into Spain; and Luke and Crescens were afterwards dispatched by him on a mission [p. 209.] to the Gauls; and the church of Paris owed its foundation to Dionysius the Areopagite, an immediate disciple of his, of whom mention is made in the Acts of the Apostles. St. Peter likewise, they say, sent his disciple Trophimus into Gaul, and St. Philip laboured in the conversion of a part of it himself. And, as if all this were not enough, they will have it, that some of the most renowned prelates of the different Gallic churches, such as Paul of Narbonne, Martial of Limoges, and Saturnine of Thoulouse, had, before their coming into France, enjoyed the benefit of the apostles' society and instruction. See the epistle of the eminent Peter de Marca, *de Evangelii in Gallia Initiis*, which Valesius has prefixed to his edition of Eusebius. It must be confessed, indeed, that the number of those who persist in maintaining the authenticity of all these particulars, is at present considerably reduced; for the fact is, that in support of a great part of them nothing better can be avouched than the testimony of obscure characters altogether unworthy of credit, or perhaps conjecture, or some vague tradition; in short, nothing but evidences of the most uncertain and unsatisfactory nature.—(III.) There are, however, to be found in France, men by no means deficient in learning, who will defend the above way of thinking with some limitation, and who, although they are ready to give up such of the above-mentioned facts as are unsupported by authority, will yet not hear of surrendering that grand citadel of ecclesiastical pre-eminence, the apostolic origin of the Gallic church. The arguments of Launois, Sirmond, and Tillemont, they will allow, place it beyond all dispute, that the celebrated Dionysius, the first bishop of Paris, concerning whose body such violent disputes have taken place between the Benedictine monks of St. Emmeran at Ratisbon, and the French monks of St. Dionysius, was not the person whom the French, from the ninth century, have believed him to have been, viz. Dionysius the Areopagite, one of St. Paul's disciples, but a very different man who flourished in the third century. They are also willing to admit that the vulgar tradition about the coming of Philip and other holy men into Gaul, is altogether undeserving of credit; and finally, that the greater part of the churches in that country which pretend to an apostolical foundation, were not in reality founded until long after the apostolic times. But the three following points they can on no account be brought to relinquish; first that the great apostle of the Gentiles in his way into Spain tarried for some time in Gaul; secondly, that Luke and Crescens were dispatched by him on a mission to the Gauls; and lastly, that so early as the second century, there had been founded in Gaul many other Christian churches besides those of Lyons and Vienne. No one that I know of has displayed greater diligence and ability in support of this last way of thinking than Gabriel Liron, a Benedictine monk of great erudition, in his Dissertation *sur l'Etablissement de la Religion Chretienne dans les Gaules;* which nearly finishes the fourth volume of a work published by him, under the title of *Singularités Historiques et Litteraires.* Paris, 1740, 8vo. It has also been defended by Dion. Sammarthanus in the preface to his *Gallia Christiana.* For my own part I must say, that neither of these ways of thinking appears to me to be in all respects well founded or unexceptionable. On the second it cannot be necessary to make any remark, since it is supported by scarcely any one of the present day, except such as are interested in upholding the credit of a [p. 210.] parcel of old stories, to which the churches are indebted for a great part of their riches. In support of the third there appear to be many things yet unestablished that may with the strictest justice be called for. Admitting it, for instance, to be certain, what in point of fact we know to be most uncertain, that St. Paul made a journey into Spain, it yet by no means follows of necessity that he must have gone through Gaul in his way thither; for it is very possible that he might have made the journey by sea. For Luke's ever having been in Gaul we have no authority but that of Epiphanius, (in *Hæres.* lib. i. § xi. p. 433.) a writer, to say no worse of him, of very indifferent credit, and by no means determinate in his way of speaking. For the word Gaul is here put by him absolutely, and we are consequently left utterly in the dark as to whether he means Trans-alpine or Cis-alpine Gaul. Dionysius Petavius indeed (*Animadvers. ad Epiphanium,* p. 90.) suspects, and not without reason, that Cis-alpine Gaul was the country meant. In proof of the mission of Crescens, the words of St. Paul, 2 Tim. iv. 10, are cited, in which the learned advocates for this legation contend, that instead of Γαλατίαν, as most copies have it, we ought to read with Epiphanius, Γαλλίαν. But even supposing that we were to yield to them in this, for our doing of which, however, nothing like a sufficient reason could readily be assigned, still here again the question would arise, as to whether it was Trans-alpine or Cis-alpine Gaul that was meant. Possibly it may be true, although it cannot be absolutely proved to be so, that in the second century there were in Gaul several churches besides those which we know to have been at that time established at Lyons and Vienne. But allowing this to be ever so certain, still it is not conclusive as to the main point in dispute, namely, whether or not the light of the gospel was first communicated to the people of Trans-alpine Gaul by the apostles themselves, and their companions and disciples. To the opinion first above noticed, *viz.* that the Gauls were not acquainted with the name of Christ prior to the arrival of Pothinus and his companions from the east, although it has very illustrious patrons on its side, there yet seems wanting some further support. The celebrated passage which we have cited from Sulpitius Severus, and concerning which such great disputes have taken place amongst the learned, can certainly authorize no further inference than this, that the Christian religion was communicated at a later period to the Gauls than to the countries of Asia and the rest of Europe. So that it amounts not to any thing like a proof that the glad tidings of Christianity had never reached the Gauls until the arrival of Pothinus, Irenæus, and their companions, in the second century. From the acts of Saturninus it is clear that the religion of Christ made but a slow progress in Gaul, and that under the reign of Decius, in the third century, there were only a few small churches scattered about here and there throughout the country, the major part of the inhabitants not having renounced idolatry even at that period. But this surely throws no obstacle whatever in the way of any one's believing that some of the apostles or their disciples had journeyed into Gaul, and that a part of that country had embraced Christianity prior to the second century. The passage referred to in Gregory of Tours, most assuredly possesses considerable force when opposed to the idle notions formerly entertained by the French respecting Dionysius the Areopagite, Trophimus, Martial, and others, as also in demonstrating the futility of the pretensions which many of the Gallic churches make to an apostolic foundation. They also prove that the number of [p. 211.] Christians in Gaul prior to the time of Decius was comparatively trifling; but all this is not showing that those are in error who contend that the way of salvation was first made known to the Gauls by one of the apostles themselves, or by men who had enjoyed the benefit of the apostles' converse and instruction. Upon the whole, when I take into consideration the unbounded zeal displayed by our Lord's apostles in the propagation of his religion, I must own I find no little difficulty in persuading myself that a province of such extent and consequence, and no farther distant from Italy, could have been altogether neglected by them, and never invited to listen to the terms of salvation propounded by their divine master. Were I to be called upon then for a summary statement of my opinion on the subject, I should say, peradventure Luke, peradventure Crescens, peradventure one even of the apostles themselves, might have taken a journey into Gaul with a view to the conversion of the natives. These primary efforts, by whomsoever made, were certainly attended with but very little success.   In the second century Pothinus, with certain companions, arriving out of Asia, experienced a more propitious reception, and succeeded in establishing a small church at Lyons.   This little assembly of Christians, however, instead of increasing, went, in the course of time, from various causes, much to decay, and the seven men who, according to Gregory of Tours, were sent from Rome into Gaul, under the reign of the emperor Decius, may be said to have found the Gallic church in a state little better than that of absolute ruin, and to have given to it, as it were, a second foundation.   With this opinion the indefatigable Tillemont nearly coincides in his *Memoires pour servir a l'Histoire de l'Eglise*, tom. iv. p. 983.

(2.) Both Irenæus and Tertullian, as we have above seen, § 1. note [1] make express mention of the German churches.   From neither of these writers, however, is the least information to be obtained as to whether these churches were founded in this or the preceding century, or any thing collected that might lead us to form a judgment of their number and size.   Even the part of Germany in which they were situated is not indicated.   This silence has afforded to the German antiquaries a very ample field for dispute.   The most learned and sagacious of them imagine, that the greater or Trans-rhenane Germany, which was very little known to the Romans, did not receive the light of the gospel in this century nor for many ages afterwards ; and therefore that the churches mentioned by Irenæus and Tertullian must have been situated in Cis-rhenane Germany, which was subject to the Roman government.   Jo. Ernest. Grabe takes exception to this opinion, in his annotations on the passage in Irenæus under consideration ; but as it appears to me on very light grounds.   For what he suggests is, that as Irenæus does not speak of Germany but of the Germanies, ἐν ταῖς Γερμανίαις, it is to be supposed that in his time there had been Christian churches established throughout the whole of Germany.   But a man of his erudition ought surely to have recollected that Irenæus might without any impropriety speak thus of Cis-rhenane Germany, which, as is well known, had been divided by the Romans into the first and second, or Superior and Inferior Germany.   Until, therefore, the opinion of the eminent men above alluded to, shall be opposed by arguments of greater force than this, its credit will remain unshaken.   Other arguments indeed have been brought forward by Jo. Nichol. ab. [p. 212.] Hontheim, in his *Historia Trevirensis Diplomatica*, tom. i. *Dissert. de Æra Episcopatus Trevirensis*, p. 10, et seq., where he lays it down that the passage in Tertullian ought to be understood as relating to that part of Eastern Germany which borders on Sarmatia and Dacia ; and the passage in Irenæus as relating to the whole of Germany. But these arguments, unless I am altogether deceived, carry no greater weight with them than that of Grabe does, and serve only to demonstrate the author's fertile and happy talent at conjecture.   Marcus Hansitzius is spoken of by him with approbation, as maintaining the same opinion in his *Germania Sacra* ; but in this I think his memory must have deceived him, for I can find nothing of the kind said by Hansitzius in the place referred to.

A greater question is as to the antiquity and origin of the German churches. The principal churches of Germany, like those of other nations, would fain carry up their foundation to the times of the apostles, and even to the apostles themselves. Amongst other things there is an old tradition, that three of St. Peter's companions, namely, Eucharius, Valerius, and Maternus, were sent by him into Belgic Gaul, and so far seconded by divine favour that they succeeded in establishing churches at Cologne, Treves, Tongres, Leige, and other places and continued in the superintendence and government of them until their deaths. Vid. Christoph. Brower. *Annales Trevirenses,* lib. ii. p. 143, et seq. *Antwerpiens.* ad d. xxix. Januarii, p. 918. But in refutation of this, those great and impartial writers, Calmet in his *Dissertation sur les Eveques de Treves,* tom. i. *Histoire de Lorraine,* part iii. iv. Bolland in his *Acta Sanctorum* Januarii, tom. ii. p. 922, et seq. Tillemont in his *Memoires pour servir a l'Histoire de l'Eglise,* tom. iv. p. 1082; and finally, Hontheim in his *Dissertatio de Æra Episcopatus Trevirensis,* tom. i. *Hist. Trevirens.* have fully shown, by arguments as conclusive as the nature of the question will admit of, that the above-mentioned sacred characters, with their associates, belong properly to the third, or rather to the beginning of the fourth century, and that the dignity of apostolic legates was gratuitously conferred upon them either through ignorance or vanity during the middle ages. To confess the truth, it appears to me extremely probable that the same persons by whom a knowledge of Christ and his gospel was in the second century communicated to the Gauls, extended the scene of their labours so far as to make the inhabitants of that part of Germany which is contiguous to Gaul, partakers of the same blessing. Gabriel Liron has, with much labour and ingenuity, endeavoured to prove the apostolical antiquity of the German churches, in his *Singularités Historiques et Litteraires,* tom. iv. p. 193, seq. But the arguments and suggestions of this learned writer, although they may induce us to refuse joining with those who go the length of positively asserting, that no apostle or apostolic legate ever set foot in Germany, and that there were no Christians in that country prior to the time of Pothinus and Irenæus, yet by no means render it clear that such success attended the labours of any apostolic missionaries in Germany as for them to collect together and establish certain churches, the presidency over which they retained during their lives, and on their deaths transferred over to others. If any of the first promulgators of Christianity [p. 213.] ever travelled into Germany, which, in the absence of all positive testimony on the subject, I will take upon me neither to affirm nor deny; it is certain that they accomplished nothing of any great moment amongst this warlike and uncultivated people, nor could any Christian churches have been established by them in that country upon any thing like a solid or permanent foundation.

(3) Previously to the reformation, Joseph of Arimathea, the Jewish senator, by whom in conjunction with Nicodemus our blessed Saviour's obsequies were performed, was commonly considered as having been the parent of the British church. The tale propagated by the monks, in support of which, however, they could advance no sort of authority whatever, was that this illustrious character and twelve other persons were dispatched by St. Philip, who had taken upon himself the instruction of the Franks, into Britain, for the purpose of diffusing a knowledge of Christianity amongst the inhabitants of that island also, and that their mission was not unattended with success; for that within a short period they were so fortunate as to make a great number of converts, and to lay the foun-

dation of the church of Glastonbury. Vid. Rapin de Thoyras, *Histoire d'Angle-terre*, tom. i. p. 84.—At present the better informed of the British do not hesitate to give up this narrative of the origin of their church as altogether a fiction; but they do not fail, at the same time, to supply its place by an account equally, nay even more august and magnificent, lest they should appear to come behind the other European churches in point of antiquity and consequence. What they assert is, that the Britons are expressly enumerated both by Eusebius and Theodoret amongst those of the Gentiles, whom these writers state to have enjoyed the benefit of receiving the faith from the mouths of the apostles themselves, and that therefore some one or other of the apostles must have travelled into Britain and resided there for some time. But since it is not a little difficult to fix on either of the apostles that were the companions of our blessed Lord, who could with the least show of probability be named as the one that took this journey into Britain, they have recourse to St. Paul, maintaining that the inhabitants of this island acquired their first knowledge of the gospel through the preaching of this great apostle of the Gentiles, who had sailed into Britain from Spain. And this conjecture or opinion they conceive to be supported by (amongst other ancient authors) Clement of Rome, who says that St. Paul travelled, ἐπὶ τὸ τέρμα τῆς δύσεως, "to the very confines of the west." To this they add, that amongst so many thousands of the Romans as passed into Britain, both during the time of Claudius and afterwards, there must no doubt have been many who professed the Christian faith. The church that was thus first established in Britain, however, they allow to have been but small, and after a little while to have wholly fallen to ruin, or at least gone in great measure to decay. They therefore consider the British church as having received, what may be termed, its principal and permanent foundation, in the *second* century, under the reign of the emperor Marcus Antoninus, and in the time of the Roman pontiff *Eleutherus*. Their opinion as to this is grounded on what is recorded by *Bede* in his Ecclesiastical History, and by others after him, as a fact not in the least to be doubted of, namely, that certain persons were, at that period, dispatched to Rome by *Lucius*, the king of Britain, requesting that some Christian teachers might be sent him; that in consequence of this application several such teachers were sent, and that by the zeal and unremitted exertions of these missionaries, the whole island was gradually converted to the Christian faith. The reader will find these different points discussed with much ingenuity, and supported with great ability and learning, by those eminent native writers: *J. Usher* in his Antiquitates Ecclesiæ Britannicæ, cap. i. p. 7. *F. Godwin* in his work [p. 214.] de Conversione Britanniæ, cap. i. p. 7. *Edward Stillingfleet* in his Antiquities of the British church, chap. i. and *William Burton* in his Animadvers. in Epist. Clement. Rom. ad Corinthios: Patrum Apostolic. tom. ii. p. 470: with whom we find not a few foreigners agreeing in opinion. Vid. *F. Spanheim*. Hist. Eccles. Maj. sæc. ii. p. 603, 604, tom. i. opp. *Rapin de Thoyras*, Histoire d'Angleterre, tom. i. p. 86 et seq. With the reader's leave I will now give my own opinion on this subject, propounding in the way of conjecture such suggestions as appear to me to have probability on their side, but adopting nothing which is not supported by the decisive testimony either of facts or of words In the first place then, as to the question of, whether or not either of the apostles themselves, or any one commissioned by them, ever took a journey into Britain with a view to the conversion of the natives; I believe it must be passed over as not to be determined, although I must confess, that probability seems to lean rather in favor of those who take the affirmative side, than of those who oppose it. St. *Paul's* voyage into Britain is most intimately connected with his journey into Spain; but with what doubts and almost insurmountable difficulties the fact of this apostle's ever having been in Spain is encumbered, is well known to every one at all conversant in these matters. The story of *Joseph of Arimathea's* being sent from Gaul into Britain by Philip, seems to have somewhat in it of truth, although corrupted and deformed through the ignorance, or arrogance, or perhaps knavery of the monks. In fact, it should seem more than probable, as to this, that what took place in Gaul and Germany happened likewise in Britain, namely, that certain devout characters, of an age by far more recent than that of the apostles, were, through one or other of the above mentioned causes, converted into apostolic missionaries. The truth of the matter I suspect to be, that the monks had collected from remote tradition and ancient documents, that some man of the name of *Joseph* had passed over from Gaul into Britain, and applied himself with success to the propagation of the Gospel there; and either from their ignorance of any other eminent Christian character of the name of Joseph, besides him of whom mention is made in the history of Christ, or from a determination to exalt the dignity of the British church, even at the expense of truth, took upon them to assert that this Joseph was none other than that illustrious Jewish senator by whom the body of our Lord was interred, and that he was sent from Gaul into Britain by the apostle Philip. In like manner, as the French converted *Dionysius*, a bishop of Paris, who flourished in the third century, into Dionysius the Areopagite, and the Germans metamorphosed Maternus, Eucharius, and Valerius, who lived in the third and fourth centuries, into primitive teachers and disciples of St. Peter, so I doubt not the British monks also, out of zeal for the honour of their church, were induced to lend a helping hand to some *Joseph*, who had in the second century crossed over to their ancestors from Gaul, and to lift him up one century higher. Being in the present day unfurnished with any positive evidence on the subject, we can only offer this in the way of surmise. A considerable degree of obscurity hangs over the history of those persons who, in the second century, accompanied Pothinus out of Asia into Gaul; possibly amongst those devout characters there might be likewise a Philip, who persuaded Joseph to undertake the journey into Britain; and whom the same monks, by way of giving a due consistency to the different parts of their tale, might raise to the dignity of an apostle. In the present day, as we before observed, [p. 215.] these things can only be guessed at; but our surmises are not mere random ones. For, not to rest upon the circumstance that the clergy of almost all the different nations of Europe have fallen into a similar error, or been guilty of the same kind of deceit, and that it would therefore be very extraordinary if those of Britain alone should not have blundered or transgressed in this respect, the account of the matter, as it has reached us, carries with it some not very obscure marks of truth. That these monks, for instance, should not have pitched upon one of the apostles, but have contented themselves with one of our Lord's friends; that of such friends Joseph should have been the one fixed on; that this their *Joseph* should not have travelled into Britain by the express command of Christ himself, or have been conveyed thither in some miraculous manner; but that on the contrary, they should allow him to have crossed over to them from Gaul, which is, in fact, admitting that Christianity had obtained for itself a footing amongst the Gauls, prior to its introduction into Britain; all these circumstances, in my opinion, seem plainly to indicate that they come not properly within the class of those who invent what is absolutely false, but were men who perverted the authentic traditions of their ancestors, so as to render them subservient to certain purposes of their own. My opinion is much the same with regard to *Lucius*, whom the more respectable of the British writers strenuously maintain to have been, not the original founder, but as it were, the second parent and amplifier of their church. That a Lucius of this description did actually exist, I have not the least doubt, but I do not believe him to have been either a Briton or a king of the Britons. The very name, which is Roman, speaks him to have been some man of eminence amongst the Romans, who were at that time masters of the island. This man probably being well disposed towards the Christian religion, or having, perhaps, already fully embraced it himself, beheld with grief the superstitions of the Britons, and with a view to its abolition, called in some Christian teachers from abroad. These his laudable intentions, we may well suppose to have been seconded by Divine Providence. I cannot, however, persuade myself to believe that he had resort to Rome for those teachers, and that they were sent over to him by Eleutherus, although this is the account which Bede gives us of the matter. Lucius had no need to send to such a distance for men qualified to instruct the Britons in the principles of Christianity, since, in the time of Eleutherus, there were resident in the neighbouring country of Gaul, particularly at Lyons and Vienne, Christians sufficiently skilled to assume the office of teachers, and burning with an holy zeal to embark in the further propagation of their faith. That Lucius should have sent to Rome for teachers, was, I suspect, altogether an invention of the monks of the seventh century, who, perceiving that the Britons were but little disposed to receive the laws and institutions of the Roman see, used every endeavour to persuade them that the British church owed its foundation to the Roman pontiffs, and that it was by the assistance of Eleutherus that Lucius, the first Christian king of Britain, brought about the conversion of his people. The information, however, which we are in possession of respecting those of the ancient Britons who had embraced Christianity prior to the arrival of Augustine, who was sent into Britain by Gregory the Great, in the sixth century, will not permit us to believe this. Had their ancestors been instructed in the principles of Christianity by teachers from Rome, most unquestionably they would have adopted the Roman mode of worship, and have entertained a veneration for the majesty, or to speak more properly, the authority of the bishop of Rome. But from the testimony of Bede, and various ancient documents that are to be found in Wilkin's Councils of Great Britain and Ireland, tom. i. p. 36, it is plain that they knew of no such character as the bishop of Rome, and could not, without great difficulty, be brought to yield [p. 216.] obedience to his mandates. In their time of celebrating Easter too, to pass over others of their observances, it appears that they were guided, not by the Roman, but the Asiatic rule; and what is particularly deserving of notice, they, like the Asiatics in the second century, maintained that the rule to which they conformed was derived from St. John. See Bede's Historiæ. Eccles. Gentis Anglorum, lib. iii. c. xxv. p. 173, edit. Chifletian. By no sort of circumstantial evidence whatever, could it, in my opinion, be more clearly proved than by the above, that it was not from any missionaries of Eleutherus, but from certain devout persons who had originally come from the east, namely, from Asia, that the ancient Britons received their instructions in the Christian discipline.

Whoever will be at the pains to connect all these things together, and to consider them with a due degree of attention, may, I rather think, not feel altogether indisposed to adopt the opinion which I myself have been led to entertain respecting the origin of the British church. It is this: if any Christian church was ever formed in Britain, either by one of the apostles themselves, or any of their disciples, which I certainly will not take upon me to deny, it could not have been a large one, and must have very soon gone to decay. Christianity, however, again recovered for itself a footing in Britain, under the reign of the emperor Marcus Antoninus, in the second century, when Eleutherus was bishop of Rome, and the Christians of Lyons and Vienne in Gaul were suffering under a most dreadful persecution from the slaves of idolatry. There happened at that time to be resident in Britain, a certain wealthy and powerful Roman of the name of *Lucius,* who had been led to entertain a respect for Christianity, and was desirous of having its principles disseminated, both amongst the native inhabitants of Britain and the Romans who were resident there. Hearing that certain devout men, who had come from Asia into Gaul, had met with considerable success in the propagation of the Gospel in this latter country, and supported with wonderful fortitude the varied train of evils to which they were exposed, he, by his authority, procured some of them to come over into Britain, and make known the true way of salvation also there. In all probability the name of the leader, or principal one of the sacred characters that thus passed over from Gaul into Britain, was *Joseph,* and that of his superior, by whose command or instigation the journey was undertaken, *Philip;* and hence arose the tale of *Joseph of Arimathea* having been sent from Gaul into Britain by the apostle *Philip.* At the time when this happened, *Eleutherus* was bishop of Rome, and occasion was hence taken by the Romish monks, who found their interests not a little concerned in making the Britons regard the Romish church in the light of a spiritual mother, to pretend that the teachers above alluded to had been sent over from Rome by the pontiff Eleutherus. Should any one, however, feel inclined rather to believe that some of the teachers from Asia, to whom the Gauls stood so much indebted for instruction, were induced either voluntarily, or from motives of personal safety, during the persecution that raged at Lyons, to cross over into Britain, and that their labours in this island were crowned with the conversion of a multitude of

18

people, the first and principal of whom was an eminent person of the name of Lucius, I shall not object to his adopting this opinion in preference to the one above suggested.

[p. 217.] IV. **Number of the Christians in this age.** It is scarcely, indeed we might say, it is not at all possible to ascertain, with any thing like precision, the proportion which the number of the Christians in this age, and more especially within the confines of the Roman empire, bore to that of those who still persisted in adhering to the heathen superstitions. Most of those by whom the subject has been adverted to in modern times have erred by running into one or other of the extremes. The number of the Christians at this period is as unquestionably over-rated by those who, not making due allowance for the tumid eloquence of some of the ancient fathers, represent it as having exceeded, or at least equalled that of the heathen worshippers,(') as it is underrated by those who contend that in this age there were nowhere to be met with, no not even in the largest and most populous cities, any Christian assemblies of importance, either in point of magnitude or respectability.(') That both are equally in an error, is manifest from the persecutions that were carried on with such fury against the Christians in this century. Had their number been any thing equal to what many would have us believe, common prudence would have withheld the emperors, magistrates, and priests, from irritating them either by proscriptions, or punishments, or rigorous severities of any kind. But on the other hand, had they been merely a trifling set of obscure, ignoble persons, they would, instead of being combated with so much eagerness and pertinacity, have been spurned at and treated with derision. Upon the whole, the conclusion that seems least liable to exception is, that the number of the Christians was in this age very considerable in such of the provinces as had been early brought to a knowledge of the truth, and continued still to cultivate and cherish it; but that nothing beyond a few small and inconsiderable assemblies of them was to be found in those districts where the light of the Gospel had been but recently made known, or if communicated at an early period, had been suffered to languish and fall into neglect.

(1) *Tertullian* is by many considered as speaking literally no more than the truth, when he urges the Romans in the following words: *Hesterni sumus, et*

vestra omnia implevimus, urbes, insulas, castella, municipia, conciliabula, castra ipsa, tribus, decurias, palatium, senatum, forum. Sola vobis relinquimus templa. Apologet. cap. xxxvii. p. 311. edit. Havereampi.   To me, however, it appears that the African orator, who seems to have been naturally inclined to exaggeration, in this instance most evidently rhetoricates in a very high degree. Were the passage to be stript of its insidious and fallacious colouring, I conceive it would be found to mean simply this : the Christians are very numerous throughout the whole Roman empire, indeed it is scarcely possible to name any department in which some of them are not to be found.

(2) The world has of late seen many writers of the most opposite characters and views assiduously coöperate in undervaluing and diminishing the churches of the second century.   Those inveterate enemies of the Christian religion, whom we style Deists, do this by way of meeting the argument which its defenders draw from the wonderful and inconceivably rapid propagation of the Gospel ; an argument which, they conceive, must completely fall [p. 218.] to the ground, could the world be brought to believe, that during the two first centuries the converts to Christianity were but few, and those chiefly of a servile and low condition.   The adversaries of episcopacy, whom we commonly term Presbyterians, take the same side with equal zeal, under the hope of proving that the charge committed to a bishop of the second century must have been comprised within a very narrow compass, and consequently that the prelates of the present day, whose superintendence, for the most part, extends over large tracts of country, are altogether a different order of men from the primitive bishops.   The pastor of a congregation of about two hundred, or at the most of six hundred persons of little or no account, (and a bishop of the second century, according to them, was nothing more) may rather be likened, say they, to a country parish priest than to a bishop of modern days.   The same thing is likewise eagerly contended for by such of our own writers as have entered the lists with the advocates for the church of Rome.   The object which these propose to themselves in so doing is, to render it evident that the vast multitude of martyrs and confessors with which the Roman calendar is crowded, must be, for the most part, fictitious ; and that the bones, which are daily brought to light from the Roman catacombs, are rather to be considered as the remains of slaves and people of the lowest order, than as reliques of Christian martyrs.   In this way do we frequently find persons of the most opposite views concur in yielding to each other a mutual support.   Wise and honest men, who take care always to temper their zeal in the cause of religion by a proper respect for truth, will readily allow that we have sufficient grounds to warrant us in making no very inconsiderable deduction from that immense host of Christians which many conceive to have existed in the second century ; but, on the other hand, they find themselves precluded by the most unexceptionable testimony of words as well as facts, (and this too deduced, not from the writings of the Christians themselves, but of men who were hostile to the Christian name,) from joining in opinion with those who maintain that, in this age, the Christian churches were but few and inconsiderable throughout the Roman empire.   To say nothing of the evidence of facts, there is the

notable testimony of an author of the greatest weight, namely, *Pliny*, the pro-prætor of Bithynia, who, in a report made by him to the emperor soon after the commencement of this century, states the province over which he presided to be so filled with Christians, that the worship of the heathen deities had nearly fallen into disuse. Epistol. lib. x. ep. xcvii. p. 821, edit. Longol· *Multi*, says he, *omnis ætatis, omnis ordinis, utriusque sexus etiam, vocantur in periculum et vocabuntur.* In this passage I would particularly recommend the words, *omnis ordinis,* to the attention of those who would willingly have us believe that the primitive churches were made up of rude and illiterate persons, slaves, old women of the lowest order, in fact, of the very dregs of the people, and that amongst the Christian converts there were none to be found of any account or dignity. Either their position must be wrong, or Pliny must have here stated an absolute falsehood. *Neque civitates tantum,* he continues, *sed vicos etiam atque agros superstitionis istius contagio pervagata est.* The whole of the province, therefore, swarmed with Christians, not merely a particular part of it. Lastly, it is plainly to be perceived from his account, that the credit of the Heathen deities had at one time been in great jeopardy, and that the number of their worshippers was exceeded by that of the Christians. This is manifest from what he states of the temples having been deserted, the sacred solemnities for a time intermitted, and the sacrifices offered to the gods reduced to a mere nothing. *Certe satis constat, prope jam desolata templa cœpisse celebrari, et* [p. 219.] *sacra solemnia diu intermissa repeti, passimque venire victimas, quarum adhuc rarissimus emptor inveniebatur.* We are reduced to the necessity then, of either believing that the report made by this circumspect and prudent writer to his imperial master was founded in fiction, or else, admitting that in the Pontic province, even so early as his time, the Heathen worshippers were far outnumbered by the Christians; at least, that the greatest part of its inhabitants had manifested a disposition to abandon the religion of their ancestors. Those who conceive that the Roman empire contained within it but few Christians at this period, think to do away the force of this testimony by saying, that in this letter to Trajan, Pliny assumes more the character of an advocate than that of an historian, and that therefore what he says is not to be understood altogether in a literal sense. Now, to this I will in candour accede, so far as to admit that Pliny was desirous of inspiring the emperor with sentiments of lenity and pity towards a set of people whom he knew to be of an harmless character, and under the influence of no evil principle, and that with this view he was led in some measure to amplify the number of the Christians; but hither surely can not be referred what he says of the temples having been before nearly deserted, the sacred rites intermitted, and the sacrifices neglected. For Trajan could have drawn no other conclusion from this than that Christianity was on the decline. In every other respect too, we find the orator quite laid aside, and things represented in plain and simple terms, without the least artificial colouring. The testimony of Pliny is confirmed by *Lucian,* to whom it is impossible to impute anything like a similarity of design. *Lucian,* in an account which he has transmitted to posterity of the life and nefarious practices of Alexander, represents this infamous impostor as complaining: Ἄθεων ἐμπεπλῆσθαι καὶ χριστιανῶν τὸν πόντον, ὃι περὶ αὐτοῦ τόλμῶσί τὰ κάκιστα βλασφημῖιι, *plenam esse Pontum Atheis et Christianis, qui audeant pessima de se maladicta spargere.* In Pseudomant, § 25, p. 232, tom. ii. opp. edit. *Gesneri.* This Alexander appears to have dreaded the perspicacity of the Christians, by whom he was surrounded, in no less a degree than that of the Epicureans, a set of men by no means of an insignificant or frivolous character, but on the contrary, intelligent and shrewd. By a particular injunction, therefore, he prohibited both the one and the other from being admitted to the secret mysterious rites which he instituted, Ἐι τις Ἄθεος, ἢ χριστιανὸς, ἤ Ἐπικύρειος, ἥκει κατάσκοπος τῶν ὀργίων, φεύγετω: l. c. § 38, p. 244. These words the illustrious translator of Lucian renders, *si quis Atheus, aut Christianus, aut Epicureus venerit, orgiorum speculator, fugito.* To me, however, it appears that we should better meet the sense of the original by rendering them, *si quis Atheus, sive Christianus sit, sive Epicureus, venerit, fugito.* The title of *Atheists* being, as it strikes me, here used by this impostor generically to denote those to whom he afterwards specifically takes exception under the two denominations of Christians and Epicureans. That the Christians as well as the Epicureans were termed *Atheists* by their adversaries is well known to every one. It redounds, however, not a little to the credit of the Christians of Pontus, that we find Alexander thus classing them with the Epicureans, a set of men on whom it was not easy to impose, either with respect to their eyes or their ears. In the present day we have many who would willingly persuade us that the primitive Christians were of such an insignificant, stupid character, as not to be capable of distinguishing miracles and prodigies from the tricks of impostors, or from some of the regular, [p. 220.] though rare operations of nature. To this Alexander, however, this cunning deceiver, who had found means to impose upon so many who were deficient neither in perception nor understanding, they appeared to be persons of a very different cast; men, in fact, endowed with a considerable share of caution and prudence, who were well capable of forming a proper estimate of miracles and prodigies, and whom all the craft and cunning of those who made it their study by tricks and deception to impose on the vulgar, could not easily delude. The fear thus manifested by Alexander of the Christians, must certainly be allowed to possess considerable weight in proving how very numerous they were in the provinces of the Roman empire; nor is it open to the same exceptions that are taken to the testimony of Pliny. Alexander cannot be charged with indulging in declamation by way of moving the passions; his complaint is dictated merely by a concern for himself and his credit with the world.

V. Causes to which the rapid propagation of Christianity is to be attributed. The astonishing progress thus made by Christianity, and the uninterrupted series of victories which it obtained over the ancient superstitions, are attributed by the writers of those days, not so much to the zeal and diligence of those who, either in conformity to what they considered as a divine call, of their own accord assumed the office of teachers, or had else been regularly appointed thereto by the bishops, as to the irresistible operation of the Deity acting through them. For, according to these authors, so energetic and powerful was the operation of divine truth, that most frequently, upon its being simply propounded, without entering into either proofs or arguments, its effects on the hearers' minds was such, that persons of every age, sex, and condition, became at once enamoured of its excellence, and eagerly rushed forward to embrace it. The astonishing fortitude and constancy likewise, they report, with which many of the Christians sustained themselves under torments of the most excruciating nature, even to the very death, inspired great multitudes of those who were spectators of their sufferings with an invincible determination to enrol themselves under the banners of a religion capable of inspiring its followers with such magnanimity of soul and such a thorough contempt for every thing temporal, whether it were good or evil.(') Finally, they represent the Deity as having bestowed on not a few of his ministers and chosen servants, such a measure of his all-powerful Spirit, that they could expel dæmons from the bodies of those that were possessed, cure diseases with a word, recall the dead to life, and do a variety of other things far beyond the reach of human power to accomplish.(²) Most certain it is that the generality of those who in this century devoted themselves to the propagation and defence of Christianity, were not possessed either of sufficient knowledge, eloquence, or authority, to be capable of effecting any thing great or remarkable without preternatural assistance. For although, as the age advanced, the study of philosophy and letters gained ground amongst the Christians in general, and [p. 221.] more particularly in Egypt, and the truths of the Gospel were embraced by some even of those who were distinguished by the title of philosophers, yet there was every where a considerable scarcity of learned and eloquent men ; and by far the greater part of the bishops and elders of the churches took to themselves credit rather than shame, for their utter ignorance of all human arts and discipline.

(1) *Tertullian*, at nearly the end of his Apology, observes, with much elegance and ingenuity, *Nec quicquam proficit exquisitior quæque crudelitas vestra, illecebra est magis sectæ. Plures efficimur, quoties metimur a vobis: Semen est sanguis Christianorum.* It is remarked also by *Justin Martyr* (in Dialog. cum.

Tryphone, p. 322. edit. Jebbianæ,) Ὅσαπερ ἄν τοιαῦτα τίνα γένηται, · σοῦτο μᾶλλον ἄλλοι πλείονες πιστοὶ καὶ Θεοσεβεῖς διὰ τοῦ ὀνόματος τοῦ Ἰησοῦ γίγνονται. *Quanto magis ejusmodi quædam in nos expediuntur tormenta, tanto alii plures fideles et veræ religionis cultores per nomen Jesu fiunt.* This he illustrates by a simile by no means inelegant: Ὁποῖον, ἐὰν ἀμπέλου τις ἐκτέμη τὰ καρποφερήσαντα μέρη, εἰς τὸ ἀναβλαστῆσαι ἑτέρους κλάδους καὶ εὐθαλεῖς καὶ καρποφόρους ἀναδίδωσι· τὸν αὐτὸν τρόπον καὶ ἐφ᾽ ἡμῶν γίνεται. *Quemadmodum enim si quis vitis excidat fructificantes partes, ut palmites quidem alios floridos et frugiferos proferat, facit : ita in nobis quoque accidit. Plantata namque a Deo et Christo Servatore vitis est ejus propulus.*

(2) That this was the case, and that those gifts of the Holy Spirit which are commonly termed miraculous, were liberally imparted by Heaven to numbers of the Christians, not only in this but likewise in the succeeding age, and more especially to those of them who devoted themselves to the propagation of the Gospel amongst the Heathen, has, on the faith of the concurrent testimony of the ancient fathers, been hitherto universally credited throughout the Christian world. Nor does it appear to me that, in our belief as to this, we can with the least propriety be said to have embraced any thing contrary to sound reason. Only let it be considered that the writers on whose testimony we rely, were all of them men of gravity and worth, who could feel no inclination to deceive, that they were in part philosophers, that in point of residence and country they were far separated from each other, that their report is not grounded upon mere hearsay, but upon what they state themselves to have witnessed with their own eyes, that they call upon God himself in the most solemn manner to attest its truth, (vid. *Origen*, contra Celsum, lib. i. p. 35. edit. Spenceri ;) and lastly, that they do not pretend to have themselves possessed the power of working miracles, but merely attribute it to others; and let me ask what reason can there possibly be assigned, that should induce us to withhold from them our implicit confidence? Some years since, however, the opposite side of the question was boldly taken up by an English author, who on other occasions had shown himself to be possessed of an excellent genius and no ordinary degree of learning; I mean *Dr. Conyers Middleton*, who, in a volume of some size, which he sent out under the title of " A free Inquiry into the miraculous Powers, &c." London, 1749, 4to. has, without ceremony, upbraided the whole Christian world with suffering themselves to be grossly imposed upon in this respect, and taken upon him to assert, that every thing which has been handed down to us by so many of the fathers, respecting the extraordinary gifts of the Spirit and the miracles of the first ages, is devoid of foundation, and utterly unworthy of credit. Those who may be desirous of learning the history of this celebrated book, and of the very acrimonious controversy to which it gave rise in Great Britain, may consult the English, French, and German literary journals, as also the confutation of the work itself, which was lately published in Germany. In this place I shall attempt [p. 222.] nothing more than by a few observations to contribute somewhat towards the illustration of this matter, which has not yet ceased to agitate the learned world, and must certainly be considered, on many accounts, as of the very highest moment. The state of the case appears to be this. The very learned author of

the Inquiry, most fully admits that the apostolic age abounded in miracles and extraordinary gifts, but denies that anything of this nature was witnessed by the world subsequently to the decease of our Lord's apostles, and hence infers, that the accounts which have reached us of the miracles wrought in the second and third centuries, are to be regarded either as the inventions of knaves, or the dreams of fools. It appears to him, moreover, that an urgent necessity exists for our coming to this conclusion, inasmuch as the principles and arguments on which the miracles of the first ages rest for support, will serve equally well to uphold the credit of the wonders pretended to have been wrought in more recent times by the saints of the Romish church : and it is consequently impossible for us effectually to assail the latter, until we can so far break through our prejudices as to give up our defence of a belief in the former. Now in all this there may perhaps be nothing to which exception can justly be taken, or that should seem to be unworthy of a man of sound sense and a Christian. For the divine origin of the Christian religion depends not at all for support on the miracles which are recorded to have been wrought in the second and third centuries. Only let it be granted that a power of altering the laws of nature was resident in Christ and his apostles, and the point is placed beyond the reach of cavil. But to any one who shall peruse Dr. Middleton's book with attention, it cannot fail to be apparent that, although his attack is ostensibly directed solely against the miracles of more recent times, yet his object was collaterally to impeach the credit of those wrought by our Lord and his apostles, and insidiously to undermine our belief of every thing to the accomplishment of which the ordinary powers of nature could not have been equal. For the arguments and mode of reasoning which he opposes to the miracles of the second and third centuries, are of such a nature as to admit of their being most readily brought to bear with equal effect on those of the first century, so that if the former fall before them, every hope must vanish of our being any longer able to support the latter. Upon perceiving, as they readily did, that such was the scheme of this ingenious but artful writer, it could not otherwise happen but that the very learned and venerable body whose province it is to watch over the interests of religion in England, should at once take the alarm, and not only make use of every effort to render the plan abortive, but also without reserve accuse its author of bad faith, and attribute to him the worst intentions. The certainty and truth of what I have here stated is sufficiently proved by the learned Doctor's very mode of argumentation, which is of such a nature that if it were to prevail [it] would greatly endanger the authority of those miracles on which the truth of the Christian religion principally rests for support. The scheme which the Doctor labors by great length of argument and an abundant display of erudition to establish, is briefly this. All the Christian writers of the first three centuries whose works have come down to us, were men possessed of no judgment or discretion, neither were they always sufficiently cautious and circumspect, but occasionally betrayed a very great proneness to superstition and credulity. Whatever therefore they may have transmitted to us respecting the miracles wrought in their days, including even those of which they state themselves to have been eye-witnesses, is to be considered in the light of mere nonsense and fable. **As** if it were certain that none but men of nice discrimination were capable of distinguishing between a true miracle and a pretended one, and that those must of necessity have always been imposed upon, who on some occasions appear to have yielded their credit on too easy terms. We could have endured it, had this eminent scholar contented himself with asserting that several of those things, which are reported to have happened in the first ages, contrary to the established order of nature, might very well be doubted of: but to attempt, by [p. 223.] a general argument like the above, open as it is to infinite exceptions, and totally destitute of any evident or necessary connection, to overthrow the united testimony of so many authors of unquestionable piety, and who, it is plain, were in many things sufficiently cautious and circumspect, indicates in my opinion, a mind replete with temerity, and disposed to strew the paths of religion with insidious difficulties and snares. Happily this illustrious writer himself appears some short time before his death, which happened in the year 1750, to have been fully convinced by the arguments of his opponents, of the weakness of his opinion. For in his last reply, a posthumous work that came out in 1751, under the title of a " Vindication of the free Inquiry into the miraculous Powers which are supposed to have subsisted in the Christian church," &c. I say in this his last literary effort, although he expresses himself in language more contentious and virulent than the occasion could possibly demand, he yet plainly acknowledges himself to be vanquished, and yields up the palm to his adversaries. For he therein disclaims ever having meant to contend that no miracles whatever were wrought in the primitive Christian church subsequently to the death of the apostles, and professes himself ready to admit, that when occasion required, God was ever ready to support the Christian cause by marks of his omnipotent power. All that he ever intended to maintain, he says, was this, that a constant and perpetual power of working miracles was never resident in the church posterior to the age of the apostles, and that therefore no credit could be due to those of the early defenders of Christianity who had arrogated to themselves such a perpetual power: in short, if I rightly comprehend the meaning of the learned author, he wished to explain himself as having never intended to assert any thing more than that amongst the teachers of the second and third centuries, there were none that possessed the power of working miracles at pleasure. But this is altogether changing the state, as they term it, of the controversy. Had the learned Doctor, when he entered on his undertaking, had nothing more in view than the establishment of this point, he might have spared himself all the pains that he took, in the first place, to write, and afterwards to defend his book. For I do not know that it ever entered into the mind of any one professing Christianity, to assert, that in the second, third, or fourth centuries there were to be found amongst the Christians, men to whom the Almighty had conceded the power of working miracles at all times and in all places, and of such a nature and as often as they might think proper. *Bella geri placuit nullos habitura triumphos.*

VI. **Human causes which contributed to forward the propagation of Christianity.** But we should do wrong to understand what is

thus recorded respecting the wonderful means by which the
Deity himself contributed towards the propagation of the Gospel, in such a way as to conceive that the cause of Christianity
was not at all indebted for its success to human counsels, labour
or studies. For without doubt the progress of divine truth was,
in no little degree, forwarded by the very wise and laudable exertions of the bishops and other pious characters in getting the
writings of the apostles, which had been collected into one volume, translated into the most popular languages, and distributed
amongst the multitude : indeed, the bare reading of these works
[p. 224.] is stated to have so affected many, as to cause them
instantly to embrace the Christian faith.(¹) The cause of Christianity derived also no inconsiderable benefit from the different
Apologies, in Greek as well as Latin, by which those learned
and eloquent writers, *Justin Martyr, Athenagoras, Quadratus, Aristides, Miltiades, Tertullian, Tatian,* and others, throughout the whole
of this century, repelled the slanders and reproaches of its fro-
ward and impetuous adversaries, and demonstrated the extreme
turpitude and folly of the popular superstitions.(²) It would be
an act of injustice moreover, were we to omit mentioning, with
due praise, the exertions of certain philosophers and men of erudition, who had embraced Christianity in various provinces of
the Roman empire, and who, from their great authority with the
people, and the facility of intercourse which they enjoyed with
the more cunning and wily enemies of religion, became highly
instrumental in causing many to turn from the paths of error
into the way of truth.

(1) Whether any one or more of the ancient translations of the sacred
volume that have reached our days, can justly be ranked amongst the literary
productions of this early period, admits of considerable doubt. It appears,
however, from very respectable authorities, that in the second century for certain, if not in the first, the books of the New Testament had been translated
into different popular languages. See Basnage *Histoire de l' Eglise,* liv. ix. cap.
i. p. 450. tom. i. How anxiously desirous, moreover, the Christians of this
age were to inform the minds of the multitude, and to lead them to Christ, by
furnishing them with translations of those writings in which the scheme of
salvation through Him is laid open, and with what industry this object was
pursued by men of every description, cannot be better understood than from
the great number of Latin translators of the sacred volume, which, according
to *Augustine,* stepped forward even in the very infancy as it were of Christianity.
For as the Latin language had been rendered familiar to a great part of the

world, and was not entirely unknown even to what were termed the barbarous nations, the Christians conceived that by their translating the books of the New Testament into this tongue, the way of truth would at once be laid open to an innumerable portion of mankind. Eager therefore to accomplish so desirable an end, they were in some instances led to form too favorable an estimate of their powers, and the task was occasionally undertaken by those who were by no means competent to its execution.—*Qui scripturas ex Hebræa lingua in Græcam verterunt*, says Augustine (*de Doctrin. Christian.* lib. ii. cap. xi. p. 19 tom. iii.) *numerari possunt, Latini autem interpretes nullo modo. Ut enim cuique primis fidei temporibus in manus venit codex Græcus et aliquantulum facultatis sibi utriusque linguæ habere videbatur, ausus est interpretari.* In this passage it is manifest, although there are some who either cannot or will not perceive it, that by *Codex Græcus* is not meant any kind of book written in the Greek language, but the *Codex Bibliorum*, or those writings which the Christians held sacred. For Augustine is not speaking of translations from the Greek [p. 225.] in general, but of versions of the Holy Scriptures. Without doubt the account he here gives is to be considered as somewhat hyperbolical: for who can bring himself readily to believe that in the infancy of Christianity the multitude of Latin translators of the sacred volume was so great as not to admit of being numbered? I conceive him therefore to have meant merely, that a considerable number of the early Christians had taken upon them the office of translating the Holy Scriptures into the Latin tongue, which was at that time one of the most popular languages. A sufficient testimony surely even this of their piety and holy zeal.—Of these various Latin translations, Augustine pronounces a decided preference to be due to one which he names *the Italic. In ipsis autem interpretationibus, Itala ceteris præferatur: nam est verborum tenacior, cum perspicuitate sententiæ.* l. c. cap. xv. p. 21. Certainly it is no small credit to a translator to confine himself closely to the words, and yet at the same time to convey with perspicuity the sense of his original. But respecting this version which Augustine names *the Italic,* a good deal of discussion has taken place amongst the learned conversant in biblical literature, and particularly in the Romish church. For they entertain no doubt, but that the version to which Augustine alludes, was the same with that which was universally received by the Latin church, prior to its adoption of the more recent translation from the Hebrew by Jerome. Wherefore they suppose it to have been made in the time of the apostles, indeed possibly by one even of the apostles themselves, and having been approved of by Christ's vicar and the successor of St. Peter, they deem it to be, in point of dignity and credit, if not superior, at least on an equal footing with the Greek text that we have of the two Testaments. To this persuasion is to be attributed the very great and very learned industry which some of the first scholars both in France and Italy have before now displayed, and still continue to display, in endeavours to bring to light and restore the reliques of this venerable version ; and indeed, if by any possibility it could be done, to recover the whole of it. For could this treasure be come at, they expect that many corruptions and other blemishes with which they will have it that the Greek and Hebrew copies of the Scriptures are at present deformed, would be happily detected and removed, and the true reading of a variety of controverted passages be established beyond dispute. The very learned Benedictine brethren of the convent of St. Maure, whose erudition reflects so much honour on France, have long been distinguished for their exertions in this way. One of them, *John Martianay*, who had before acquired no small reputation by an edition of Jerome's works and other literary undertakings, sent out at Paris in 1695, in octavo, what he considered as the genuine old Italic version of the Gospel of St. Matthew and the Epistle of St. James. A very laborious work in three large volumes folio was next published by *Pet. Sabatier* at Rheims, in 1743, under the title of *Bibliorum sacrorum Latinæ versiones antiquæ, seu vetus Italica et ceteræ, quotquot in codicibus MSS. et antiquorum libris reperiri potuerunt, quæ cum vulgata Latina et cum textu Græco comparentur.*—The most recent of those who have labored in this field is *Jos. Blanchini*, presbyter of the Oratorian Convent of St. Philip, whose *Evangeliarium quadruplex Latinæ* [p. 226.] *versionis antiquæ, seu veteris Italicæ, ex codicibus manuscriptis aureis, argenteis, purpureis, aliisque plusquam millenariæ antiquitatis*, came out in the year 1749, at Rome, in four splendid folio volumes of the largest size. It cannot be necessary that I should direct the reader's attention to any minor, or less distinguished writers, who may have either treated expressly of this subject, or casually touched on any particular point of it. Great, however, as have been the pains and erudition bestowed on this matter, they must, unless I am altogether deceived, be considered as having proved entirely fruitless and unavailing as to the object to which they were particularly directed; although, in a general point of view, the labour that has been used in investigating the Latin copies of the Scriptures may not have been entirely unproductive of advantage.—"In the first place it is assumed as a fact, by those illustrious scholars who are at present engaged in endeavours to recover the ancient Italic version, that before the time of Jerome, the whole of the church, to which the Latin language was common, made use of one and the same translation of the scriptures; which having been adopted first at Rome, and been approved of by the bishop of that city, had been communicated from thence to all the Latin churches, and under the sanction of the bishop of Rome been universally introduced into the public worship. I say this is assumed by these eminent writers, but I have not yet observed that any thing like a proof of it has ever been adduced by any one. On the contrary, I conceive it can be shown by the most irrefragable arguments, deduced not only from the writings that are extant of the ancient Fathers of the Latin church, not only from Jerome, who in the preface to his Latin version of the Four Evangelists says expressly, that the Latin translations of the sacred volume differed wonderfully from each other, and that there were *tot fere exemplaria quot codices*, not only from the most unexceptionable testimony, that the church of Milan and other churches within the confines of Italy itself made use of versions of their own which were different from the rest, but also from those very learned writers themselves, who have devoted so much time and attention to the recovery of the ancient Italic version, that the Latin churches did not all of them, either before the time of Jerome or after, make use of one and the same translation of the

Scriptures, but that the versions in use amongst them were various and dissimilar. For not to enter into an examination of any others, the versions published by Blanchini differ so very widely from each other in a great many
places, that it would be an utter violation of every sort of probability whatever, to consider them as the work of one and the same translator. In
vain does Blanchini contend that this want of harmony in his copies is to be
attributed to the carelessness of transcribers; for the points in which they differ
are, for the most part, of that nature and importance, that no want of care on
the part of the transcribers will account for their disagreement, but it must be
attributed to a diversity in the originals from whence they copied. In the next
place, these same learned characters assume, that this Italic version, which they
consider as having been common to all the Latin churches, was a work of the
first century, and that it was undertaken and perfected either by one of the apostles themselves, or at least by some companion and disciple of the apostles. But
it is to be observed in the first place, that this is a perfectly gratuitous assumption; for what evidence have they to adduce that will give any thing even like a
colour to it? And secondly, what appears entirely to have escaped their recollection, it was not until after the close of the first century that the books of the
New Testament were collected into one volume; and consequently it [p. 227.]
is impossible that any translation of these at least could have been previously
undertaken. But what nearly surpasses all belief, and most clearly evinces on
what a slippery and weak foundation the opinions of some of the most learned
men are not unfrequently built, even when they may seem to be placed beyond
the reach of controversy; I say, what is so astonishing as to be almost incredible is, that these illustrious scholars should with the utmost confidence maintain, that that particular translation which Augustine terms the Italic, and to
which he assigns the preference over every other Latin one, was that very identical version of the sacred code which they pretend to have been composed in
the first century, during the life-time of the apostles, and to have been received
and made use of by all the Latin churches after the example of that of Rome.
From whence, I pray, do these learned characters derive their information as to
this? Do they rely entirely on that passage of Augustine, which we have cited
above? For most certainly neither in Augustine, nor in any other ancient
writer, is there to be found any passage besides this, in which mention is made
of the Italic version. But surely in these words of Augustine there is nothing
which can afford, even to the most penetrating and sagacious mind, grounds for
any thing like a conclusion of this sort. From whence, therefore, have they their
information as to this? From what prime source has all that intelligence been
drawn respecting the antiquity, the excellence, the dignity, the authority of a
certain I know-not-what Italic translation, which such a number of learned men,
not only of the Romish communion, but also of other denominations of Christians, are so ready at communicating to us? From the words of Augustine, try
what we may, it is impossible to collect any thing more than this: (1.) That the
people of Africa, amongst whom he resided when he wrote, in addition to other
Latin translations of the sacred volume, were possessed of one, which by way of
distinguishing it from the rest, they termed *the Italic.* From whence, however,

it acquired this appellation, is not to be ascertained, either from Augustine or elsewhere. Possibly it might have been thus named from its having been brought from Italy into Africa; possibly from its having been the one made use of in certain of the Italian churches; with equal probability may we conjecture that it took this denomination from the country of the person by whom it was made, or from the structure, perhaps, and polish of its style. Every supposition that we may make as to this, must of necessity be obscure and uncertain. There can be no doubt, however, but that those who imagine that it was termed the Italic from the circumstance of its having been in common use throughout all the churches of Italy, conjecture ill; for it is known for certain, that the churches of Ravenna and Milan, and others of the more celebrated churches of Italy had, each of them, a peculiar and proper version of its own. (II.) From Augustine's manner of expressing himself, it is to be inferred that the translation which he terms the Italic was, in all probability, a different one from that which was used by the Roman church in the public service. For as the Roman was the principal church of the West, had this been the translation that was publicly made use of in it, Augustine would, without doubt, from motives of respect, have termed it (*Romana*) the Roman one. Augustine always entertained the greatest reverence for the Roman church, in which he considered *Apostolicæ Cathedræ principatum viguisse*, epist. xciii. tom. ii. opp. p. 69. (III.) It appears from the passage under consideration, that what is there termed by way of distinction the Italic version, was not the one made use of publicly in the African churches; for Augustine passes an encomium on it, and wishes that a preference should be given to it over every other version. A sort of recommendation for which there could certainly have been no room, had this version been already adopted in the public [p. 228.] worship. Indeed the very epithet *Italic*, which he applies to it, is an argument that it had not been so adopted: for had this translation been the one commonly used in the African churches, instead of giving it the title of *Itala*, propriety would have required him rather to term it either *nostra*, or *vulgaris*, or *publica*. *Italic* applied to anything out of Italy, necessarily implies it to be foreign. (IV.) It is clear that in the opinion of Augustine, which might be either right or wrong, (for he was certainly not possessed of sufficient skill in the learned languages to determine on the merits of a translation of the Scriptures,) this same version, whatever it may have been, was preferable to every other translation. Now, in all this, there is certainly nothing which affords the least support to what we have been so much accustomed to have told us respecting an ancient version, termed the Italic, which was common to all the Latin churches: on the contrary, it is easy to perceive therein certain things which altogether set aside and confute what we find contended for in so many books on the subject. Since then not a single passage, except this solitary one of Augustine, is to be met with in any ancient author from whence the least information can be gained on the subject, it appears to me that the labour of those who so zealously devote themselves to the recovery of this ancient Italic version, must ever of necessity prove fruitless, and that the undertaking in which they thus engage bears a very near resemblance to that of the man who endeavoured to make a collection of the verses that had been sung bv the Muses upon Helicon.   What we have above remarked, was in part noticed by that ingenious and penetrating scholar, Richard Bentley, who hath borne away the palm of criticism from all his contemporaries in Great Britain; and he was, in consequence, led to suspect that the passage in Augustine, on which alone the existence of the ancient Italic version depends for support, had been corrupted.   The way in which he proposed to correct it was, by substituting the word *illa* for *Itala*, and the pronoun *quæ*, in place of the particle *nam*.   To the propriety of this emendation, David Casley, to whom it had been communicated by Bentley, expresses his unqualified approbation in his *Catalogue of the Manuscripts in the King's library*, London, 1734, fol. except that after the word *illa*, he would add, *Latina*.   The Italic version, he, like Bentley, consigns to its proper place amongst the dreams of the learned.   According to these then the passage in question ought to run thus : *in ipsis interpretationibus illa* (or *illa Latina) præferatur quæ est verborum tenacior.*   But I must own that this alteration appears to me to have something too arbitrary and violent in it, unsupported, as it is, by the reading of any known copy of Augustine in existence.   Besides it is not called for by any necessity.   For even granting that the passage, as it stands in our copies, is correct, which I have no doubt it is, and granting also that in the time of Augustine the Christians of Africa, in addition to other Latin translations of the holy Scriptures, were possessed of one which they distinguished by the title of the Italian, or Italic version, every thing that is commonly contended for respecting this translation will still remain destitute of all support, and the labour that is consumed in endeavours to recover it may consequently be considered as entirely thrown away.

(2) It is by no means uncommon to hear the different writers of the ancient Apologies for the Christians charged uniformly with this fault, that they have exposed indeed in an admirable manner the folly of the various religions at that time prevalent in the world, and rendered strikingly manifest the falsity of those calumnies with which the Christians were oppressed, but have bestowed little or no pains in demonstrating the truth and divinity of the Christian religion.   To the generality of people it appears that more attention [p. 229.] should have been paid to the latter object than to the former, inasmuch as it required merely a demonstration of the divine origin of Christianity to overwhelm all other religions, and sink them into contempt.   But it would not be very difficult to adduce many things in reply to the accusation.   For the present we shall content ourselves with observing, that the authors of the early Apologies for Christianity, did not assume to themselves the office of teachers or masters, but came forward merely in the character of defenders. Now all that can be required of a defender to the full discharge of his duty is, to repel the calumnies wherewith the person accused is charged, and to show that he had just cause for acting in the way he did.   From the nature of their undertaking, therefore, it could only be expected of the early apologists for Christianity, that they should exonerate those who had embraced it from the reproaches cast upon them by their adversaries, and by pointing out the absurdity of the religions publicly countenanced, make it appear that there was the

greatest cause for their deserting them. The business of demonstrating the truth of that new religion, which they had adopted upon their repudiation of Paganism, was, without impropriety, left by them to its masters and teachers.

VII. **Disingenuous artifices occasionally resorted to in the propagation of Christianity.** With the greatest grief, however, we find ourselves compelled to acknowledge, that the upright and laudable exertions thus made by the wise and pious part of the Christian community, were not the only human means, which in this century were employed in promoting the propagation of the Christian faith. For by some of the weaker brethren, in their anxiety to assist God with all their might, such dishonest artifices were occasionally resorted to, as could not, under any circumstances, admit of excuse, and were utterly unworthy of that sacred cause which they were unquestionably intended to support. Perceiving, for instance, in what vast repute the poetical effusions of those ancient prophetesses, termed Sybils, were held by the Greeks and Romans, some Christian, or rather, perhaps, an association of Christians, in the reign of Antoninus Pius, composed eight books of *Sybilline Verses*, made up of prophecies respecting Christ and his kingdom, with a view to persuade the ignorant and unsuspecting, that even so far back as the time of Noah, a Sybil had foretold the coming of Christ, and the rise and progress of his church.([1]) This artifice succeeded with not a few, nay some even of the principal Christian teachers themselves were imposed upon by it ; but it eventually brought great scandal on the Christian cause, since the fraud was too palpable to escape the searching penetration of those who gloried in displaying their hostility to the Christian name.([2]) By others, who were aware that nothing could be held more sacred than the name and authority of Hermes Trismegistus were by the Egyptians, a work bearing the title of Poemander, and other books, replete with Christian principles and maxims, were sent forth into the world, with the name of this most ancient and highly venerated philosopher prefixed to them, so that deceit might, if possible, effect the conversion of those whom reason had failed to convince.([3]) Many other deceptions of this sort, to which custom has very improperly given the denomination of PIOUS frauds, are known to have been practised in this and the succeeding century. The authors of them were, in all probability, actuated by no ill intention, but this is all that can be said in their [p. 230.] favour, for their conduct in this respect was certainly most ill advised and unwarrantable. Although the greater part of those who were concerned in these forgeries on the public, undoubtedly belonged to some heretical sect or other, and particularly to that class which arrogated to itself the pompous denomination of Gnostics,(¹) I yet cannot take upon me to acquit even the most strictly orthodox from all participation in this species of criminality: for it appears from evidence superior to all exception, that a pernicious maxim, which was current in the schools not only of the Egyptians, the Platonists, and the Pythagoreans, but also of the Jews, was very early recognized by the Christians, and soon found amongst them numerous patrons, namely, that those who made it their business to deceive with a view of promoting the cause of truth, were deserving rather of commendation than censure.(²)

(1) The Sybilline verses are treated of very much at large by Jo. Albert. Fabricius, in the first vol. of his *Bibliotheca Græca*, where the reader will also find a particular account given of those writings, which were sent out into the world under the forged name of Hermes Trismegistus. The last editor of the Sybilline Oracles, was Servatius Gallæus, under whose superintendence and çare they were reprinted at Amsterdam, 1689, in 4to. corrected from ancient manuscripts, and illustrated with the comments of various authors. To this edition the reader will find added the Magian oracles, attributed to Zoroaster and others, collected together by Jo. Opsopæus, amongst which are not a few things of like Christian origin. That the Sybilline verses were forged by some Christian, with a view of prevailing the more easily on the heathen worshippers to believe the truth of the Christian religion, has been proved to demonstration, by (amongst others) David Blondell, in a French work, published at Charenton, 1649, in 4to. under the following title *Des Sybilles celebrés tant par l'Antiquité payenne, que par les saincts Peres.* Indeed we may venture to say, that with the exception of a few who are blinded by a love of antiquity, or whose mental faculties are debilitated by superstition, there is not a single man of erudition, in the present day, who entertains a different opinion. It may be observed, by the way, that Blondell's book was, after two years, republished, under a different title, namely, *Traité de la Creance des Peres touchant l'Etat des Ames apres cette vie, et de l'Origine de la Priere pour les Morts, et du Purgatoire, a l'Occasion de l'Ecrit attribué aux Sybilles.* Charenton. 1651, 4to. The fact, no doubt was, that finding purchasers were not to be attracted by the former title, the bookseller deemed it expedient to have recourse to another.

(2) From what is said by Origen, *contra Celsum*, lib. v. p. 272. edit. Spencer. as well as by Lactantius, *Institut. Divinar.* lib. iv. cap. xv. and by Constantine the Great, in c. 19. of his *Oratio ad Sanctos*, which is annexed to Eusebius, it ap-

pears that the enemies of the Christians were accustomed indignantly to up-
braid them with this fraud.

(3) That the writings at present extant under the name of Hermes, must
have been the work of some Christian author, was first pointed out by Isaac Casaubon in his *Exerc.* I. *in Baronium*, § xviii. p. 54. This has since been confirmed
by various writers, Vid. Herm. Conringius, *de Hermetica Ægyptiorum Medicina*,
[p. 231.] cap. iv. p. 46. Beausobre, *Histoire de Manicheé*, tom. ii. p. 201. Cudworth, *Intellect. System*, tom. i. p. 373, 374. edit. Mosheim. Warburton, *Divine
Legation of Moses*, vol. i. p. 442. It may be observed, however, that certain of
the learned dissent, in some degree, from this opinion, conceiving that the writings of Hermes originated with the Platonists: they suspect them, however, to
have been interpolated and corrupted by the Christians.

(4) Blondell in lib. ii. *de Sybillis*, cap. vii. p. 161. from the praises that are
continually lavished in the Sybilline verses on the country of Phrygia, is led to
conclude that the author of them was by birth a Phrygian; and since Montanus, a Christian heretic of the second century, is known to have been a native
of that region, suspects that the composition of them might be a work of his.
The Abbé de Longerue expresses his approbation of this conjecture in his Dissertation *de Tempore quo nata est Hæresis Montani*, which is to be found in
Winckler's *Sylloge Anecdotorum*, p. 255. et. seq. That the writings of Hermes
and a great part of the forged Gospels, together with various works of a similar nature, the disgraceful productions of this century, are to be attributed to
the perfidious machinations of the Gnostics, is clear beyond a question.

(5) See what I have collected in regard to this, in my Dissertation *de turbata per recentiores Platonicos Ecclesia*, § 41, et. seq.

VIII.   **State of the Christians under the reign of Trajan.**   But
whilst the circumstances above enumerated conspired most
happily to forward the cause of Christianity, the priests and
præfects of the different religions that were publicly tolerated in
the Roman empire, most strenuously exerted themselves to arrest its progress, not only by means of the foulest accusations,
calumnies, and lies, but by frequently exciting the superstitious
multitude to acts of wanton and outrageous violence.(') These
efforts of the heathen priesthood the emperors zealously seconded by various proscriptive edicts and laws, the magistrates and
presidents of provinces by subjecting the faithful followers of
Christ to punishments and tortures of the most excruciating
kind, and finally several philosophers and orators by declamation and cavil; in short, throughout the whole of this century
the Christians had to contend with an almost infinite series of
injuries and evils, and even under the very best and most mild
of the emperors that Rome ever knew, were in various districts

and provinces exposed to calamities of the most afflictive and grievous nature. At the time of Trajan's accession to the government of the empire there were neither laws nor edicts of any kind in existence against the Christians. That this was the case is clear beyond a doubt, as well from other things that might be mentioned, as from the well known epistle of Pliny to Trajan, in which he signifies to the emperor that he was altogether at a loss how to proceed with people of this description. Had any laws against the Christians been at that time in force, a man so well versed in the customs and jurisprudence of the Romans as Pliny was, must undoubtedly have been acquainted with them. The fact unquestionably was, that the laws of Nero had been repealed by the senate, and those of Domitian by his successor Nerva. So difficult, however, is it to abrogate what has [p. 232.] once acquired the force of custom, that the Christians, as often as either the priests or the populace, stirred up by superstition and priestcraft, thought proper to institute a persecution of them, continued still to be consigned over to punishment. It was this which gave occasion to Eusebius to state that under the reign of Trajan, *per singulas urbes populari motu* passim *persequutio in Christianos excitabatur.*([2]) Such a persecution took place not long after the commencement of this century in Bithynia, at the time when Pliny the Younger was president of that province, at the instigation, no doubt, of the priests.([3])

(1) Arnobius *adv. Gentes*, lib. i. p. 16. edit. Herald. *Aruspices has fabulas,* (the calumnies against the Christians) *conjectores, arioli, vates, et nunquam non vani concinnavere fanatici; qui, ne suæ artes intereant, ac ne stipes exiguas consultoribus excutiant jam raris, si quando vos velle rem venire in invidiam compererunt, negliguntur dii clamitant, atque in templis jam raritas summa est.* In regard to this passage the reader may consult what is said by Heraldus.

(2) Eusebius, *Hist. Eccles.* lib. iii. cap. 32. p. 103.

(3) We allude to the persecution treated of by Pliny in that very celebrated epistle of his to the emperor, the xcvii[th] of the 10th book. From this epistle it is manifest that Pliny himself had no wish to interfere with the Christians, but was reluctantly compelled by spies and informers to call them before him and punish them. *Interim,* says he, *in iis, qui ad me tanquam Christiani deferebantur hunc sum sequutus modum.* That these informers against the Christians were the heathen priests, is I think, clearly to be inferred from the following words: *Certe satis constat prope jam desolata templa cæpisse celebrari, et sacra solemnia diu intermissa repeti, passimque venire victimas quarum adhuc rarissimus emptor inveniebatur.* In this passage the proconsul most plainly intimates the cause of

this persecution to have been, that the temples in Bithynia were nearly abandoned, the sacred solemnities intermitted, and scarcely any victims ever presented for sacrifice. But all these things could affect none but the priests and those who had the superintendence of the sacred rites; for to these alone could it be of any material moment that the temples should be frequented and victims be brought to the altars. There can be no doubt then, but that these men had represented to Pliny, into what great jeopardy the rites of heath   ne brought, and it it is not at all unlikely that by way of giving additional force to their representations, they had stirred up the populace to clamor for the punishment of the Christians. In compliance with these applications, Pliny commanded those persons who, as he says, had been pointed out to him by an informer, to be apprehended, and found amongst them two Christian deaconesses; the presbyters, together with the bishop, having most probably either taken to flight on the breaking out of the persecution, or otherwise found means to shelter themselves from its effects. When I, moreover, compare the words of Pliny with the passage cited above from Arnobius, not a doubt remains with me but that he is to be considered as delivering, not so much his own sentiments, as those which he had collected from the mouths of the priests.

[p. 233.] IX. **Trajan's law respecting the Christians.** The attack, however, thus made on the Christians in Bithynia, eventually occasioned a restraint to be put on that immoderate fury with which it had become customary to persecute them. For it having been most clearly ascertained by Pliny, that with the exception of their dissent from the public religion, there was nothing in the principles or conduct of the followers of Christ deserving of animadversion, and it being at the same time perceived by him that their enemies in their proceedings against them had no regard whatever either to equity or clemency, he requested of the emperor Trajan, that the mode of coercing the Christians might be regulated by some certain law, intimating his own opinion to be, that on account of their great number and evident innocence, they should be treated rather with moderation than severity. In answer to this it was ordered by the emperor, that the Christians for the future should not be officiously sought after, but that if any of them should be brought before the Roman tribunals in a regular way and convicted, they should, unless they would renounce Christianity, and again embrace the public religion, be consigned over to punishment. From the first part of this regulation we may naturally infer, that the emperor did not regard the Christians with an unfavourable eye, whilst, from the latter part, it is as obviously to be collected that he was fearful of discovering too much lenity towards them, lest he should thereby exasperate the priesthood and the populace.(')

(1) It was generally believed for many centuries, that the emperor Trajan was the author of the third persecution of the Christians, and we find this very disturbance which they experienced in Bithynia under the government of Pliny, particularly adv, f~ an infinite number of books, as the commencement of such persecution. But it is scarcely possible for any thing to be farther removed from the truth than these two notions are. Trajan, so far from having given orders to persecute the Christians, exerted his authority to restrain the persecution of them, which broke out under his reign in Bithynia and other places. Without doubt he was considerably in the wrong in giving directions that persons convicted of having embraced Christianity, and refusing to return to the religion of their ancestors, should be consigned over to capital punishment; a thing for which he is sharply and eloquently rebuked by Tertullian (in *Apologet.* cap. ii.); but most unquestionably it was of the highest advantage to the Christians that he forbad any search or inquiry to be made after them. For under this arrangement the Christians might hold their secret assemblies in security, and by merely observing the dictates of common prudence, might effectually defeat all the malice of their enemies. Nor could the priests any longer take occasion, from the emptiness of the temples, and the rarity of victims, to compel the magistrates to call in question the Christians. It also supplied the magistrates with the power of silencing and putting down any popular clamour or seditions. But this illustrious act of beneficence, for which the Christians were indebted to Trajan, lost not a little of its effect, as I have before observed, by the mandate which was annexed to it for punishing such as might be convicted of being Christians, and refuse to recant; in which, as has, after Tertullian, been observed by several, the emperor disagrees with himself. For whilst, by forbidding them to be searched for or enquired after, he avows to the world that there was nothing in them pregnant with danger to the state, or in anywise deserving of punishment, he, in the next breath, by [p. 234.] ordering the execution of such as, when convicted of having embraced Christianity, might persist in professing it, pronounces them to be guilty of a crime that could scarcely be punished with too great severity. This inconsistency of Trajan with himself, may be best accounted for by supposing him to have been fearful that he might irritate the priests and the multitude, and perhaps excite popular commotions, if he should grant an absolute impunity to men labouring under so great ill will; his conduct in this respect was certainly not influenced by superstition, for had he been actuated by this principle, he would not have forbidden, but on the contrary have commanded the Christians to be sought after, with a view to avenge the insult offered by them to the gods. With regard, however, to the punishment ordered to be inflicted on obstinate Christians, another reason may be assigned. Pliny had written to him that the obstinacy of the Christians was, in his judgment, of itself, a crime deserving of death, although there appeared to be nothing improper in the religion which they refused to renounce: *neque enim dubitabam, qualecumque esset quod faterentur,*

pervicaciam certe et inflexibilem obstinationem debere puniri. The opinion thus expressed by Pliny, although unjust, and obviously unworthy of a man of his intelligence, the emperor thought proper to adopt, and the Christians were in consequence consigned over to punishment, not as men who had insulted the gods, and were inimical to the public religion, but as citizens who refused to pay obedience to the mandates of their sovereign. Whether the former or the latter of these reasons may be preferred, certain it is, that neither in Pliny's epistle nor in the decree of the emperor is there any enmity manifested towards the Christian religion, or any traces of superstition to be discovered. Those who consider the disturbance thus experienced by the Christians on the borders of the Euxine as the commencement of a general persecution of them under Trajan, seem not to be aware that from this very epistle of Pliny, as well as from other arguments, it can be made appear that the Christians had in the time of Trajan been put to trouble in various places before ever Pliny had been appointed to the government of Bithynia.

X. **Effects produced by this law of Trajan.** This decree of Trajan being registered amongst the public ordinances of the Roman empire, was the cause of many Christians' being thenceforward put to death, even under the most mild and equitable emperors. For as often as any one was to be found who would run the risk of becoming an accuser, and the person accused did not deny the crime imputed to him ; nothing further was left to the magistrate than to endeavour, by threats and torture, to subdue the constancy of the person thus convicted; which if he failed to effect, the pertinacious and obstinate delinquent was, according to this law of Trajan, to be delivered over to the executioner. Under this regulation *Simeon,* the son of Cleopas and bishop of Jerusalem, an old man of one hundred and twenty years of age, being about the year cxvi, accused by the Jews before the præfect of Syria, and persisting for several days, although put to the torture, in an absolute refusal to repudiate Christianity, was, contrary to the inclination of his judge, condemned to suffer death [p. 235.] upon the cross.(¹) In conformity to this same law likewise, *Ignatius,* the renowned bishop of Antioch, who had been accused by the priests, and was not to be moved by the threats of even the emperor himself, was in the course of the same year brought to Rome by an imperial order, and delivered over as a prey to wild beasts.(²) But what will no doubt appear to the reader particularly astonishing is, that this sufficiently harsh and inhuman law excited the discontent of such of the Christians as glowed with a more fervid zeal, on account of its lenity, inasmuch as for want of inquiry being made by the magistrate, or of some one being found to step forward as an accuser, they were often times precluded from finishing their earthly course by a glorious and triumphant sacrifice of their lives in the cause of Christ. Hence it became by no means unusual for numbers of them voluntarily to hand over their names as Christians to the Judges.([2]) This unseasonable eagerness to obtain the honours of martyrdom, however, having in the course of time become perniciously prevalent, it was at length deemed expedient to repress it by a law.

(1) Vid. *Eusebius Histor. Eccles.* lib. iii. cap. xxxii. p. 103, et seq.

(2) The *Acts of the Martyrdom of Ignatius* have been frequently published, and are to be found amongst the *Patres Apostolici*. Of the antiquity of the work there can be no doubt; it should seem, however, to have been corrupted in several places. From these Acts it appears that Trajan adhered most scrupulously to the provisions of his own law. In the first place he did not lay hands on Ignatius until the latter was regularly brought before the public tribunal by an accuser; in the next place, when the accused confessed himself guilty of the charge, he endeavoured by various arts of persuasion to prevail on him to execrate the name of Christ, and join in the worship of the Roman deities; and lastly, finding him altogether inflexible in his determination not to renounce Christianity, he adjudged him to suffer death. We also learn from these Acts that the emperor deemed it inexpedient to let this holy man suffer at Antioch, lest the fortitude which he displayed might operate to increase the veneration for his character, and also have the effect of augmenting the number of the Christians.

(3) A very remarkable instance of this kind of proceeding is mentioned by Tertullian (in *Lib. ad Scapulam*, cap. v. p. 88. opp. edit. Rigalt.) as having occurred under the reign of Hadrian. *Arrias Antoninus in Asia cum persequeretur instanter*, (i. e. according to the law of Trajan he caused all such as were accused before him and convicted, to be executed,) *omnes illus civitatis Christiani ante tribunalia ejus se manufacta obtulerunt*, (that is to say, being discontented at no one's coming forward against them as an accuser, and perceiving that the proconsul was determined strictly to abide by the emperor's injunction, and not to make any inquiry after them, they resolved to become accusers of themselves,) *cum ille, paucis duci jussis, reliquis ait:* Ω δειλοὶ ιι θέλιτι ἀποθνήσκειν, κρημνὸς ἤ Βρόχυς ἔχιτι. *O miseri, si mori vultis, nec lacus vobis desunt nec præcipitia.* The proconsul no doubt felt particularly delicate as to punishing the Christians who had thus become accusers of themselves, since it was a case that had not been provided for by the emperor: having therefore by way of terror made an example of a few, he dismissed the rest with marks of indignation and contempt.

XI **State of the Christians under the reign of Hadrian.** [p. 236.]

Although the law of which we have been speaking was not in any respect repealed or altered by the emperor Hadrian, who succeeded Trajan in the year of our Lord 117, nor had the Christians to complain of any infringement of it by the presidents or inferior magistrates; yet by the heathen priesthood means were at length discovered for enervating its force, and rendering its protection of the objects of their hatred inefficient. Finding that but few individuals could be prevailed on to take upon themselves the unthankful and perilous office of an accuser, they made it their business, on every favourable occasion to excite the lower orders of the people to join in one general disorderly clamour for the punishment of the Christians at large, or of certain individuals amongst them, whom they were taught to consider as particularly obnoxious. Amongst other opportunities that offered, they were accustomed particularly to avail themselves of those seasons when the multitude were drawn together by the exhibition of any public games or other spectacles. To general and public accusations of this sort no degree of hazard whatever was attached; whilst on the other hand it was a thing of no ordinary danger amongst the Romans to turn a deaf ear to them, or treat them with disrespect. In consequence of these tumultuary denunciations, therefore, a considerable number of Christians, at different times, met their fate, whom the magistracy would otherwise most willingly have permitted to remain unmolested.(¹) Indeed, under the reign of Hadrian it was so much the more easy for the heathen priesthood to get the multitude to unite in one general clamour for the destruction of the Christians, since, as Eusebius expressly relates, the Gnostic sects, which seem to have been made up in part of evil designing persons, and in part of madmen and fools, were at that time continually obtruding themselves on the attention of the world; and the crimes and infamous practices of which these were guilty, being indiscriminately imputed to the Christians in general, the public prejudice was in no small degree increased against the whole body of them.(²)

(1) Nothing could be more artful than this contrivance of the priests to enervate and elude the law of Trajan respecting the mode of accusing the Christians. For the presidents did not dare to regard with an inattentive ear the demands of the united commonalty, lest they might give occasion to sedition.

Moreover, it was an established privilege of the Roman people, grounded either on ancient right or custom, of the exercise of which innumerable instances are to be found in the Roman history, that whenever the commonalty were assembled at the exhibition of public games and spectacles, whether it were in the city or the provinces, they might demand what they pleased of the emperor or the presidents, and their demands thus made must be complied with. Properly this privilege belonged to the Roman people alone, whose united will possessed all the force of a law, inasmuch as the supreme majesty of the empire was supposed to be resident therein; but by little and little the same thing came to be assumed as a right by the inhabitants of most of the larger cities. When the multitude, therefore, collected together at the public games, united in one general clamour for the punishment of the Christians at large, or of certain individuals belonging to that sect, the presidents had no alternative but to comply with their demand, and sacrifice at least several innocent victims to their fury.

(2) Eusebius *Histor. Eccles.* lib. iv. cap. vii. p. 120, et. seq.

XII. **Hadrian's new law in favour of the Christians.** [p. 237.] This highly iniquitous and impious artifice of the priesthood be ing seen through by *Serenus Granianus*, the proconsul of Asia, he addressed a letter to the emperor on the subject, pointing out what an unjust and inhuman thing it was, to be every now and then shedding the blood of men convicted of no crime, merely with a view to silence the clamours of a misguided tumultuous rabble. Nor was the representation of this discerning and judicious man disregarded by his master: for an edict was soon after directed by Hadrian to *Minutius Fundanus*, the successor of Serenus, and to the other governors of provinces, forbidding them to pay attention to any such public denunciations; and signifying it to be his pleasure, that for the future no Christians should be put to death, except such as had been legitimately accused and convicted of some sort of crime.(¹) Possibly also the two masterly apologies for the Christians, that were drawn up and presented to the emperor by those pious and learned characters, *Quadratus* and *Aristides*, and of which we of the present day have unfortunately to regret the loss, might have contributed not a little to the softening of the imperial mind.(²) This lenity of Hadrian towards the Christians was looked upon by some as indicative of a disposition to favour the Christian religion, and therefore, when he subsequently caused temples without images to be erected in all the cities, a suspicion arose in the minds of many that he had it in contemplation to assign to Christ a place amongst the Deities of Rome, and meant to consecrate these edifices to his service.(³)

(1) This imperial rescript is given by Justin Martyr, in his first Apology *pro Christianis*, § 68. 69, p. 84, opp. edit. Benedict. and copied from thence by Eusebius, *Histor. Eccles.* lib. iv. cap. ix. p. 123.—That it was sent not only to Minutius, but also to the other presidents of provinces, is manifest from a remarkable passage of Melito cited by Eusebius, *Histor. Eccles.* lib. iv. cap. xxvi. p. 184, as also from an edict of Antoninus, *ad commune Asiæ*, of which we shall presently have to say more. Regarding this law of Hadrian in a general way, it appears in point of justice and clemency by far to surpass the edict of Trajan. For whereas it was directed by the latter that such Christians as obstinately refused to renounce the religion which they professed should be punished capitally, the law of Hadrian forbids any Christian to be put to death except he were convicted, according to the legal and established mode, of having transgressed the Roman laws. This seems to admit of being adduced as a proof, and indeed has been so brought forward by many, that Hadrian tolerated the Christian religion, and forbade any one to be persecuted on account of professing it. But I cannot help suspecting that this is giving the emperor credit for more lenity than it was ever his intention to display, since I observe, that even after the promulgation of this rescript, the Christians were continually put to death without having any other crime objected to them than that of their religion. Trajan had enacted, that for any one inflexibly to persevere in the [p. 238.] profession of Christianity should be a crime punishable with death, and Hadrian does not appear to have directed that this kind of perseverance should be considered in a less criminal light. I therefore do not conceive that this law of Hadrian, in its import, differed very materially from that of Trajan, but that the punishment of death continued still to be inflicted under the imperial sanction on all such Christians as were convicted of professing a contempt for the gods, and persisted in refusing to alter their opinion. *Si quis ergo accusat et ostendat quidpiam contra leges ab iis factum, tu pro gravitate delicti statue.* The form of expression is at least ambiguous, and left to the presidents the most ample power of punishing the Christians, since the worship of the gods was a thing enjoined by the laws.

(2) These apologies are treated of by Eusebius *Histor. Eccles.* lib. iv. cap. iii. with whom compare Jerome *Epist. ad Magnum Oratorem*, p. 656, tom. iv. opp. edit. Benedict. and in *Catalog. Scriptor. Eccles.*

(3) Our authority for this is Lampridius *in Vita Alexandri Severi*, cap. xliii. who after remarking that Alexander wished to have assigned Christ a place amongst the Roman deities, continues, *quod et Hadrianus cogitasse fertur, qui templa in omnibus civitatibus, sine simulacris, jusserat fieri. Quæ ille ad hoc parasse dicebatur : sed prohibitus est ab iis, qui consulentes sacra repererant, omnes Christianos futuros si id optato evenisset.* The historian in this place evidently gives us the conjecture of the multitude, which, from his own words, appears to have been grounded solely on the circumstance of Hadrian's having erected a number of temples, in none of which were placed any statues of the gods,

and which, resting on no better foundation, must have been extremely vague and uncertain. The suspicion excited by the erection of these temples could never have suggested itself, had it not been for the opinion previously entertained of the emperor's leaning towards Christianity. But from whence this opinion took its rise I am unable to say, unless it was from the equity and humanity displayed by him in his edict respecting the Christians. Probably the priests and their adherents, upon finding themselves cut off from all hopes of suppressing the Christians, might disseminate a rumour that the emperor himself was by no means ill disposed towards this new religion. But how vain and futile these conjectures were, is rendered manifest, as well by the whole tenor of his life, which was replete with instances of the grossest superstition, as by the positive testimony of Spartian (*in Vita Hadrian.* cap. xxii.) whose words are *sacra Romana diligentissime curavit; peregrina contempsit.* It may be added, that with regard to the temples erected by Hadrian without any statues of the gods, very able men have long since declared it to be their opinion, that the emperor intended to have had them dedicated to himself.

XIII. **Barchochba an enemy of the Christians.** The Christians, however, had under the reign of Hadrian to encounter a still more fierce and cruel enemy in a leader of the Jews, named *Barchochba,* or, "the son of the star," whom his infatuated countrymen regarded as the long-promised Messiah who was to restore the fallen fortunes of the house of Israel. Impatient of the injuries and contemptuous treatment which they were continually experiencing at the hands of the Romans, the Jews had once already, during the reign of Trajan, had recourse to arms for redress. The experiment entirely failed; but their wretchedness and calamities continuing still to increase, these hapless people, at the instigation, and under the conduct of the above-mentioned daring character, a man thoroughly conversant in blood and rapine, were, in the year 132, induced to hazard a [p. 239.] repetition of it.(') During the continuance of the war which he had thus excited, *Barchochba* subjected to the most cruel tortures as many of the Christians as he could get within his power, and put all such of them to death without mercy as refused, in spite of the various tortures thus inflicted on them, to abjure Christianity.(') The event of this contest, which was for a while maintained on both sides with incredible valour, was most disastrous to the Jews. An innumerable host of this ill-fated people having fallen by the sword, and Palestine being almost wholly depopulated, the dreadful scene was closed by Hadrian's ordering Jerusalem, which had begun to revive again from its ashes, to be

finally overthrown and laid waste, and causing a new city, call
ed after himself *Ælia Capitolina*, to be erected on a part of its
site([3]); at the same time debarring the Jews from every access
to such new city, as well as to any of their former sacred places
in its neighbourhood, under the severest penalties.([4])

(1) Vid. Eusebius, *Histor. Eccles.* lib. iv. cap. 6. Buxtorfius, *Lexico Talmu-
dico, voce* נכב where the reader will find every thing that is to be met with in
the Jewish writings respecting this man collected into one view.
(2) Justin Mart. *Apolog.* ii. *pro Christianis*, p. 72, edit. Paris.   Hieron. *Catalog. Script. Eccles. in Agrippa Castore.*
(3) A particular history of this new city has been given to the world by
the learned Deyling.   It is annexed to the fifth volume of his father's *Observationes Sacræ.*
(4) See amongst others, Justin Martyr, *Dialog. cum Tryphone*, p. 49. 278.
edit. Jebbian. Sulpitius Severus, *Histor. Sacr.* lib. ii. cap. xxxi. p. 245, edit.
Cleric.   Hieronymus, *Comment. in Sophoniam*, c. 2.

XIV. **State of the Christians under Antoninus Pius.** Upon the
death of Hadrian, so immediately did the aspect of affairs change,
that it seemed as if his rescript respecting the Christians had ex-
pired with him.   For scarcely had *Antoninus Pius* assumed the
government of the empire, when the Christians found themselves
assailed in various places by numerous accusers, who being
obliged by the above-mentioned edict of Hadrian to allege some
sort of crime against them, and probably finding the more equitable of the presidents disinclined to consider the bare profession
of Christianity in that light, had recourse to the expedient of
charging them with impiety or atheism.   This new attack was
met by *Justin Martyr* with an apology presented to the emperor,
in which he ably repels various other calumnies with which the
Christians were assailed, as well as completely vindicates them
against this last atrocious charge of impiety.   The effect, however, produced by this apology, was but trifling.   At length an
immediate application having been made to the emperor by several of the magistrates, for the purpose of ascertaining the extent
to which the populace, who were thus continually calling for the
blood of the Christians, were to be gratified in their demands, he
commanded them to take for their direction the law of Ha-
[p. 240.] drian, and not put any Christian to death unless it
should appear that he had committed some crime against the
state.([4])   But even this was not found sufficient to prevent those

ebullitions of popular fury which the priesthood continually made it their business to promote. For in consequence of some earthquakes which shortly after occurred in Asia, and which the priests, with their accustomed malevolence, ascribed to the displeasure of the gods at the toleration of the Christians, the multitude burst through every restraint, and heaped on these fancied authors of their calamities every species of outrage and injury. A representation of the grievous afflictions to which they were thus exposed having been submitted to the emperor by the Christians, he addressed a severe edict to the whole region of Asia, commanding, that unless the Christians should be convicted of some sort of crime, they should be discharged with impunity, and that the punishment to which, in case of conviction, they would have been subjected, should, upon their acquittal, be inflicted on their accusers.([2])

(1) This appears not only from the emperor's edict *ad commune Asiæ*, but also from the words of Melito, *apud* Euseb. *Histor. Eccles.* lib. iv. cap. xxvi. p. 148, who reminds the emperor Marcus Aurelius that his father addressed letters to the Larisseans, the Thessalonians, the Athenians, and in fact to the Greek provinces in general, forbidding them to have recourse to any tumultuary proceedings against the Christians.

(2) An imperial edict to this effect is extant in Eusebius (*Histor. Eccles.* lib. iv. cap. xiii. p. 126.) who says, that he took it from Melito's Apology for the Christians, addressed to the emperor Marcus. By certain of the learned, however, this edict has been thought not to belong to Antoninus Pius, but to his successor, Marcus Aurelius; but the reasons on which this opinion is grounded, are, unless I am altogether deceived, of no weight whatever. For to pass over the testimony of Eusebius, as well as certain particulars in the edict itself, which are not in the least applicable to Marcus, there are two things which in my opinion most clearly prove that Eusebius was not wrong in ascribing it to Antoninus Pius. In the first place, Eusebius copied it from an apology addressed by Melito to the emperor Marcus. But who can believe, if Marcus Aurelius had published such an edict respecting the punishment of the accusers of the Christians, that Melito would have deemed it necessary to write a work expressly for the purpose of exciting in him a compassion for the Christians? In the next place, those earthquakes of which the edict makes mention, and which gave occasion to the people of Asia to commence their attack on the Christians, occurred in the time of Antoninus Pius. *Adversa*, says Capitolinus, (in his Life of Antonine, cap. ix. p. 268. tom. i. *Scriptor. Hist. August.*) *ejus temporibus hæc provenerunt : Fames de qua diximus, circi ruina,* Terræ Motus, *quo Rhodiorum et* Asiæ *oppida conciderunt: quæ omnia mirifice instauravit.* But it is clear that those of the learned who attribute this edict to the emperor Mar-

cus, do so merely with a view to extenuate the afflictions which the Christians suffered under Antoninus Pius, and to make it appear as if, after the slight persecution to which they were exposed at the commencement of Antoninus' reign, the Christians had enjoyed, as it were, a perfect calm to the very end of his government. In doing this, however, they have paid a greater regard to [p. 241.] their own private opinion than to the faith of history. Notwithstanding, moreover, that the issuing of this edict by Antonine was unquestionably productive of considerable advantage to the Christian cause, and imposed a restraint on the officious forwardness of evil-disposed persons, yet the interests of Christianity would have been benefited in a much higher degree, had he repealed that law of Trajan, which awarded the punishment of death to all such Christians as should be convicted of having abandoned, and refuse to return to the religion of their ancestors. The law of Trajan was, however, suffered to remain in full force, and yet at the same time this edict of Antonine, of a nature altogether repugnant to it, was introduced into the forum. Iniquitous and cruel judges might, therefore, if they thought proper, cause both the accuser and the accused to be put to death ; the former under the edict of Antoninus Pius, the latter under that of Trajan, which none of the emperors had thought it proper to repeal. Of a case of this kind a very notable example is recorded by Eusebius in his *Ecclesiastical History*, lib. v. cap. 21. p. 189. *Apollonius*, a man respectable for his gravity and learning, was, under the reign of Commodus, accused of being a Christian. The judges forthwith condemned his accuser to have his legs broken and to be put to death : for by the edict of Antonine it was ordained, that capital punishment should be inflicted on all accusers of this sort. But by these same judges was Apollonius himself also, after that he had publicly rendered an account of the religion that he professed, and openly acknowledged himself to be a Christian, adjudged to suffer death. For by an ancient law, says Eusebius, it was enacted, that if any Christians should be once regularly brought before the public tribunal, they should on no account be dismissed with impunity, unless they would repudiate their religion. Now what other ancient law could this be that was so directly repugnant to the edict of Antonine, than the rescript of Trajan to Pliny ? By thus artfully having recourse to ancient laws that had not been expressly repealed, did the iniquity and injustice of the Roman magistrates frequently find means to deprive the Christians of every benefit to which they were entitled under enactments of a more recent date.

XV. state of the Christians under Marcus Aurelius. The security and tranquillity enjoyed by the Christians under this edict of Antonine lasted no longer than until the year clxi, when the government of the empire passed into the hands of *Marcus Aurelius Antoninus*, who from his great attachment to the Stoic system of discipline, acquired the surname of "The Philosopher." At the very commencement of this emperor's reign, the ancient practice of preferring public accusations against the Christians was vigorously resumed; and as many of the persons thus accused as acknowledged themselves to be followers of the religion of Christ, and refused to change their tenets, were delivered over to the executioner.   Upon this occasion it was that *Justin Martyr* addressed to the emperor his second apology for the Christians, a composition much resembling his former one, both as to style and argument; but which was so far from exciting in the mind of the emperor anything like lenity or compassion towards those on whose behalf it was drawn up, that after its appearance the calamities of the Christians were increased throughout the whole of the Roman empire. Nor did it appear sufficient to the emperor to free the enemies of Christianity from those restraints which his father had imposed on them: but by the publication of various edicts inimical to the Christians, he held out, as it were, an invitation or incitement to the people [p. 242.] to become their accusers.(') It appears, indeed, as well from other authorities, as particularly from the tract written by *Athenagoras* in defence of the Christians, that Marcus did not absolutely repeal the edict of his father which forbade the Christians to be put to death, unless they should be convicted of some sort of capital offence;(²) but, through the iniquity of the judges, the greatest facility was afforded to accusers in establishing any false charges which they might bring forward against the Christians; and the accused, in defiance of the laws of the empire, were, without either being regularly convicted of, or confessing themselves to have committed, any sort of crime, declared to have incurred the penalty of death.(³)

From whence this ill-will of the emperor towards the Christians proceeded, is not to be ascertained from any memorials that have reached our times.   It may, with great probability, however, be conjectured, that from the representation of the philosophers, to whose guidance he appears entirely to have surrendered himself, he was led to regard the Christians as a set of absurd, irrational, obstinate and conceited men; and therefore, upon the principles of that harsh and rigid system of moral discipline to which he was devoted, conceived it expedient rather to destroy than to tolerate them.(⁴)

(1) *Melito* in his Apology, *apud* Euseb. *Hist. Eccles.* lib. iv. cap. xxvi. **p.**

147. makes express mention of certain new edicts promulgated against the Christians in Asia, in consequence of which they were exposed to open attacks from the vilest of men, both by day and by night: and that these edicts must have been of the most harsh and severe kind is unquestionable, since *Melito* adds, that the new imperial edict, καινὸν διάταγμα, was so extremely inhuman, that the issuing of it even against barbarous enemies would not have been justifiable : ὁ μὴ δὲ κατὰ Βαρβάρων πρέπει πολεμίων. Melito, indeed, professes himself to be ignorant whether or not this edict was issued by the emperor. But this could surely be nothing more than a prudent dissimulation in him. For who would ever have been so bold as to forge imperial edicts ? Who amongst the judges could have been found sufficiently daring to give to these fictitious edicts the force of real ones ? And, with no better sanction than could be afforded by such fraudulent mandates to deprive Roman citizens of their lives and worldly possessions? The crime was of that magnitude that it could scarcely have suggested itself to the mind even of the most hardened wretch ; and to its execution so many difficulties would have been opposed, that no one but a madman could have promised himself the least success in attempting it. In enumerating, therefore, the real and actual persecutors of the Christians, we must, after recording the names of the emperors *Nero* and *Domitian,* assign the third place to that imperial philosopher, whose wisdom has not ceased to command admiration, even in the present day, the most sapient *Marcus Aurelius ;* inasmuch as he was the author of such laws against the Christians as a just and good man would never have enacted, even against a set of barbarous enemies. For the emperors that had intervened between Domitian and him, instead of exciting, had uniformly studied to repress and discountenance any persecution of the Christians. A fact with which the emperor is in no very obscure terms upbraided by Melito, although the state of the times in which he wrote obliged this apologist to speak with some reserve. It were to be wished that this edict of the emperor Marcus had reached our days, since [p. 243.] without doubt, we should have been able to gather from it the grounds of that hatred which he had conceived against the Christians. But to the primitive professors of Christianity it appeared more expedient to sink the remembrance of the laws by which the progress of their religion was opposed, than to perpetuate it. A hint, however, is supplied by one passage in Melito, which may enable us, with some degree of probability, to guess at the nature of this infamous edict. By this law of the emperor Marcus, he says, the most shameless characters, and those who were covetous of other men's property, (τῶν ἀλλοτρίων ἐρασταὶ,) were invited to turn informers against the Christians, and to hunt after them both by day and by night. Now the conclusion to which these words inevitably lead is, that in this edict there was a prospect held out to avaricious and money-loving men, of increasing their own wealth by the spoliation of others. This then being established, it seems to be highly credible, indeed almost certain, that the emperor held out pecuniary recompense as an allurement to people to become accusers of the Christians, and directed that the goods and other property of those who might be convicted of any crime, should be adjudged to the persons through whose exertions the

delinquents had been brought to justice. Such a law might not, indeed, fail to produce its designed effect on the minds of those who coveted other men's goods, but such a law was very justly characterised by Melito, when he pronounced it altogether unworthy of a good and wise emperor. It was not in this way that Nero, it was not in this way that Domitian attacked the Christians.

(2) It is clear from various documents, and from this tract of *Athenagoras* in particular, that the enemies and accusers of the Christians under the reign of Marcus, endeavoured with the utmost earnestness to fix on them three different species of crimes. 1st. The most unqualified impiety or atheism. 2dly. The celebrating of Thyestean banquets, that is, feasting on the flesh of murdered infants. 3dly. Œdipodean or incestuous sexual intercourse. Hence I think it is manifest, that it was not the will of the emperor to have the Christians put to death merely on account of their religion, but that he confirmed the law of Antoninus. For if it had been sufficient to accuse the Christians of defection from the religion of their ancestors, and manifesting a contempt for the gods of the country, as it was under the reign of Trajan, there could have been no necessity for charging them with calumnies like the above. But as the laws of the empire were particularly strict in regard to accusers, and forbade any Christian to be put to death unless convicted of some sort of crime, there was no other course left open to the malice and improbity of the enemies of Christianity but to devise certain heinous offences, and endeavour by every possible means to fix them on its professors.

(3) The history of the persecution at Lyons, which took place, as I have elsewhere shown, under the reign of this emperor, in the year clxxvii., affords a very sufficient illustration of what is here stated. This persecution had its origin in a popular tumult or contention that took place between the Christians and the heathen worshippers. During its continuance a great many of the former were cast into prison ; but owing to no one's coming forward as an accuser, and proving them to have committed some sort of crime, the hands of the magistrates were completely tied up in regard to them. By way, therefore, of obtaining an ostensibly legal sanction for the gratification of their malice, the soldiers and other enemies of the Christians prevailed, by means of threats, on certain of the servants of those whom they had apprehended, to become accusers of their masters. But what these wretches charged their masters with was not sacrilege, or a contempt for the public religion, but actual crimes, and those identical crimes too, which, under the reign of Marcus, were, by slander, attributed to the Christians, namely, the celebrating of Thyestean banquets, [p. 244.] and an incestuous sexual intercourse. To this testimony of servants against their lords, the judges gave credit, or rather pretended to give credit ; and, in defiance of the order of proceeding prescribed by the law, put the Christians to the rack ; endeavouring, by torments of various kinds, to extort from them a confession of what they were thus charged with. In vain was it that these unfortunate people persisted, with the utmost constancy, to the last, in asserting themselves innocent ; their fate had been predetermined on ; they were pronounced guilty, and were in consequence consigned over to various kinds of death. Vid. Eusebius, *Histor. Eccles.* lib. v. cap. 2. There can be no doubt but

that, in the other provinces, a nearly similar course was followed ; so as to preserve somewhat of an imposing air of justice, and make it appear as if the Christians were condemned, not for their religion, but on account of their crimes. And here we cannot but direct the reader's attention to the peculiar infelicity of the times of Marcus Aurelius, than whom a juster or more sapient emperor is supposed never to have existed ! The monarch, a prince in no respect ill inclined, gave himself up to philosophical meditation, and troubled himself but little as to the way in which the concerns of his empire might be managed. In the mean time, the magistrates taking advantage of this his indifference as to state affairs, made every thing conform itself to their will and pleasure, and scrupled not most grossly to violate those laws for which they professed themselves to entertain the highest veneration. They made no search or inquiry indeed, after the Christians, since that would have been contrary to the edict of Trajan ; they furthermore manifested their respect for the laws of the empire by not inflicting punishment on any Christian, unless accused as such ; and not only accused of being a Christian, but also proved by witnesses to have committed some heinous offence. But then, to suit their own purposes, they would, as we have seen, admit the testimony of slaves, and the veriest refuse of mankind ; and upon no better evidence than that of the vilest of mortals, would condemn men as guilty, whose constancy in protesting their innocence even torments of the most excruciating nature were found unable to subdue.

(4) It has for a long time been with me a matter of doubt whether the emperor Marcus Aurelius was so great a character as he has been esteemed for ages, and still continues to be considered by almost every one capable of forming an opinion on the subject. If our estimate of him be indeed drawn solely from those of his writings which remain, it seems to be scarcely possible that his worth should be overrated ; but if his actions be taken into the account, and brought to the test of reason, we shall find the matter wears a very different aspect. That he was a good *man*, although in no small degree a superstitious one, is what I do not in the least doubt ; but that he at all merited the title of a good *emperor* and prince, is to me a matter of question. But for the present I will pass over this, and content myself with briefly inquiring whether the condition of the Christians was not worse under the reign of this philosopher and man of genius, than it had ever been under that of any of the preceding emperors, who were strangers to philosophy. To the opinion of such of the learned as attribute the ill-will of Marcus Aurelius towards the Christians to superstition, I feel it impossible for me to subscribe. Had superstition given rise to his severity, he would, without doubt, have considered their religion alone as a sufficient reason for commanding them to be punished ; but that such was not his opinion is certain, as we have above pointed out. By far more likely is it, that his immoderate lenity, which was but little removed from utter carelessness and sloth, and which originated in that stoical evenness and serenity of mind which they denominate apathy, occasioned him to shrink from the trouble of curbing the licentiousness of evil-disposed men, and also made him look with a tranquil indifference on actions highly criminal and oppressive. To

which it may be added, that a man devoted to contemplation, and employing a considerable portion of his time in philosophical speculations, probably cared but little as to what was done in the empire, or as to the fidelity and uprightness with which the presidents and magistrates might discharge the important duties appertaining to their various offices. The conjecture, however, which, in my opinion, comes nearest to the truth, is, that the philosophers by [p. 245.] whom he was beset, and who held the Christians in detestation, instilled into his mind a wrong idea of the Christian tenets; and having to deal with a man of a credulous and easy disposition, found means to persuade him that in the worshippers of Christ an irrational, turbulent, and pernicious sect had arisen, a sect in fact, which it was on every account highly proper to repress; and in this opinion I am confirmed by a remarkable passage in the eleventh book of his work, *De Rebus ad se pertinentibus,* § iii. wherein he professes himself to entertain but an unfavorable opinion of the fortitude and contempt of death exhibited by the Christians. Marcus himself had never seen any of the Christians encounter death; and therefore, for whatever he may have reported of their behaviour under such trying circumstances, he must unquestionably have been indebted to the magistrates, and those philosophers by whom he was surrounded, and who, of course, did not fail to represent them in that light in which it was their wish for him to regard them. The words of Marcus are: "To what an admirable state must that soul have arrived which is prepared for whatever may await her—to quit her earthly abode, to be extinguished, to be dispersed, or to remain! By prepared I mean, that her readiness should proceed from the exercise of a calm, deliberate judgment, and not be the result of mere obstinacy, like that of the Christians; and that it should be manifested, not with ostentatious parade, but in a grave, considerate manner, so as to make a serious impression on the minds of other people." In this passage, the fortitude displayed by the stoics in the act of death, is compared by the emperor with the constancy of the Christians under similar circumstances. For the former he expresses a respect; of the latter he evidently speaks with contempt. Under the influence, and with the never-failing support of reason, the philosopher is represented as encountering death with a deliberate steadfastness of soul, or, in other words, as meeting death with tranquillity, because he knows that death can never be productive of evil to him; whilst the Christian, on the contrary, if we listen to the emperor Marcus, dies altogether irrationally, without any other confidence or consolation than what is supplied by a certain stubbornness and pertinacity of mind, for which no pretext is to be found either in common sense or reason. From hence it is manifest, that those who possessed the ear of the emperor had persuaded him that the Christians were a set of irrational, rude, illiterate, ignorant men, an opinion which led him naturally to conclude, that the alacrity with which they encountered death could only be the fruit of obstinacy and perverseness. Whoever they might be that instilled into the mind of the emperor such an idea of the Christians, they most certainly practised on him a very base imposition; since the Christians were possessed of weightier, and by far better reasons for meeting death without dismay, than ever the whole race of stoics had been able to supply, and in the fortitude which they displayed on quitting this earthly state, were influenced by a much sounder judgment than that by which the stoic sect were governed.   But it cannot excite our wonder that the emperor, after his mind had received the above impression, should deem it expedient to extirpate the Christians.   Dangerous, truly, must have been a sect which encouraged its votaries to encounter every sort of torment unappalled, and meet even death itself with disdain, upon no better a principle than that of a sullen, blind, irrational obstinacy.   But to proceed with the emperor's contrasted portraits.   The philosopher, we are told, encounters death with firmness and composure, unaccompanied by any tragical display : that is, unless I entirely mistake the emperor's meaning, he does not, like those who make their exit on the stage, indulge in declamation, and endeavour to gain over the minds of the spectators by an affected bombastic kind of eloquence, but preserves a magnanimous silence, and meets his fate with a [p. 246.] quiet and unshaken dignity.   Not such, says Marcus, is the conduct of the Christian ; for he, regardless of what propriety would suggest, appears to take the deaths exhibited in tragedies for his model ; and when the fatal moment arrives, expatiates at length on his hilarity, his hope, his confidence, and his contempt of death.   The emperor, no doubt, had heard that it was customary for the Christians, in the concluding act of their lives, to offer up thanksgivings to Almighty God, to commend their souls into his keeping by fervent prayer, to exhort the spectators to renounce superstition, to glorify Christ in hymns, and to do many other things of a like kind ; which could not fail to appear displeasing in the eyes of a stoic, whose leading maxims were, that it was incumbent on a wise man to maintain at all times an uniformity of aspect and demeanor ; that every disturbance of the mind was reprehensible ; and finally, that under every change of circumstances, by whatever brought about, the most perfect equability or evenness of temper was invariably to be preserved.   Under the influence of sentiments like these, it was natural for the emperor to consider the Christians as meeting death, not in a philosophical way, but rather in the style of tragic characters.   Hence, also, may we account for his being moved but little by their afflictions.   Indeed, according to the principles of the sect to which he belonged, he ought not to have known what it was to be moved at all.

XVI. **Afflictions of the Christians under the reign of Marcus.** Under no emperor, therefore, subsequently to Nero, were the Christians exposed to weightier or more numerous afflictions than they suffered during the reign of the illustrious Marcus Aurelius, whom posterity has been taught to regard as the best and wisest emperor that Rome ever saw.   Nor were there ever more *apologies* sent forth into the world on behalf of the Christians than were in his time offered to the public ; for in addition to *Justin Martyr*, of whom we have already spoken, *Melito*, bishop of Sardis, *Athenagoras*, a philosopher of Athens, *Miltiades*, *Theophilus* of Antioch, *Tatian* the Assyrian, and others whom it is unnecessary to enumerate, made it their business, in various literary productions, as well to render the innocence and piety of the Christians unquestionable, as to demonstrate the sanctity of the religion which they professed, and to expose the madness and absurdity of those other religious systems to which the world in general was so fondly attached. Of these works there are some that have reached our days, but others have perished through the ravages of time.(¹) Amongst the many who, under the reign of Marcus, were put to death for their adherence to the religion of Christ, the most distinguished were those very celebrated characters : *Justin*, the philosopher, who suffered at Rome ; and *Polycarp*, who met his fate at Smyrna. Both of these sealed their attachment to the cause of their blessed Master with their blood, in the year clxix.(²) To none, however, has posterity assigned a higher place in its estimation than to the Christians of *Lyons* and *Vienne*, who, in the year clxxvii, were in great numbers made to encounter death under various excruciating and terrific forms, in consequence of their having been falsely charged, by certain of their inferior servants or slaves, with the commission of crimes almost too shocking even to be named. The most eminent of these Gallic martyrs was *Pothynus*, the bishop and parent of the church of Lyons ; a venerable character of the age of ninety and upwards, who, not long before, had, with certain others, travelled from the east into Gaul, [p. 247.] and with great care and industry established there that Christian church or assembly which was doomed, in a particular manner, to experience the devastating fury of this very remarkable and tremendous persecution.(³)

(1) The apologies of *Miltiades* and *Melito* are those of which we have to regret the loss ; the rest are still extant.

(2) The acts of the Martyrdom of Justin Martyr and Polycarp are to be found in Ruinart's *Acta Martyrum sincera et selecta*, and in some other works. Concerning the year and month of Polycarp's death, the reader may consult a very copius and learned dissertation of the Abbé Longerue in Winckler's *Sylloge Anecdotorum*, p. 18. 25.

(3) Respecting this persecution of the Lyonese, without question the most celebrated, and in all probability the most bloody and cruel that took place in any part of the Roman empire during the reign of Marcus, there is extant in Eusebius, *Histor. Eccles.* lib. v. cap. 2. an excellent espistle from the church of Lyons to the brethren in Asia and Phrygia, which I should conceive it impossible for any one to read without emotion. The thing, as we have above

observed, although pre-determined on, was yet carried into effect under a specious show of legal formality, lest the laws of the empire should appear to have been in any respect infringed. The circumstances of the affair were briefly these: A popular tumult having been excited respecting the Christians, and many of them having, with a view to quiet the public mind, been thrown into prison, certain of their servants were prevailed upon by threats to come forward and accuse their masters of having committed very heinous offences, namely, those identical crimes which, during the reign of Marcus, had been very customarily imputed to the Christians. Having in this way established somewhat of a colourable ground whereon to act, the magistrates proceeded to inflict tortures of various kinds on the imprisoned Christians; and even went so far as to put many of them to death. The number of persons confined, however, being considerable, and one of them, a man of some consequence, named Attalus, having declared himself a Roman citizen, the president of the province seems to have felt that he had been too precipitate, and would not venture to proceed farther in the business without ascertaining the emperor's pleasure. The matter having been submitted by him to the emperor, Marcus wrote back word, that "all such as professed themselves Christians should be put to death, but that those who denied being so, should be dismissed uninjured." Under the authority of this answer, therefore, capital punishment was inflicted on all who refused to renounce Christianity; such of them as were Roman citizens being beheaded, and the rest cast for a prey to wild beasts. This rescript of the emperor to the president of Lyons seems to place his inveterate enmity towards the Christians in the clearest light imaginable; since, if respect be had solely to his words, as above cited from Eusebius, he gives exactly the same commands as Trajan did, and allows the Christians to be put to death on account of their religion alone, without anything criminal being alleged against them. But it must be confessed, that there is a difficulty in coming to any certain conclusion with regard to the sense of this rescript, since the letter of the president to the emperor is not now extant. What the president wrote, in all probability, was, that the Christians stood convicted by the testimony of a sufficient number of credible witnesses of having committed many very great crimes in their secret assemblies, but that this charge was denied by the accused with the utmost pertinacity, (at least in this way it was certainly necessary for him to write, if his object was to excuse the cruelty he had exercised upon so many of these unfortunate people) and that it had therefore become requisite for him to apply to [p. 248.] the emperor for direction as to whether the witnesses or the Christians themselves were to be belived. Supposing then the president to have written to the emperor in these or any similar terms, the imperial answer will admit of this construction: With regard to the truth of an accusation which has been substantiated according to the rules of law, we see no reason for entertaining any doubt. From such, therefore, of the persons implicated, as will not consent to abjure Christianity, we deem it proper to withhold our pardon; but should there be any who are inclined to return to the religion of their forefathers, it is our will that they should be set at liberty. At least the absence of the president's letter, so necessary to a right understanding of the emperor's answer, leaves us altogether in a state of uncertainty as to which constituted the prevailing motive with Marcus in directing the punishment of the Christians, their religion or their crimes.—With regard to the time of this persecution, the reader will find it proved in a dissertation of mine, *de Ætate Apologiæ Athenagoræ*, (*Syntagm. Dissert. ad Histor. Eccles. pertin.* vol. i. p. 315.) by irrefragable arguments, that it did not take place, as has been conjectured by certain of the learned, in the year 167, but in 177. Compare *Colonia, Histoire litteraire de la ville de Lyon*, tom. ii. Sæc. ii. p. 34. and *Baratier, de Successione Romanor, Pontiff.* p. 207. 217. That the church of Lyons, however, had been but recently established when this grievous affliction befel it, its own epistle, as preserved by Eusebius, most clearly demonstrates, for the Asiatic brethren are therein (p. 156.) told, that in the multitude of Christians who suffered on that occasion were comprehended those, by whose labour and industry chiefly the church there had been first established.

XVII. **The miracle of the Thundering Legion.** It is said, however, that some short time before his death, namely, in the year clxxiv, the sentiments of Marcus underwent a considerable change with respect to the Christians, and that in consequence of his having been very essentially benefited by them on a particular occasion, in the course of a war in which he was engaged with the Marcomanni and the Quadi, two of the bravest German nations; he was induced entirely to relieve them from every sort of penalty and hazard to which they had been previously exposed. The story is, that being so effectually surrounded on all sides by the enemy, during a season of severe and long continued drought, as not to be able to gain access to any place from whence water might be obtained, the Roman emperor and his forces were in the most imminent danger of perishing from heat and thirst. When things, however, were arrived at the last extremity, a band of Christians, who were at that time serving in Marcus's army, having earnestly cried to heaven for assistance, the Almighty was pleased at once to manifest a regard for their prayers, by causing the clouds on a sudden to pour down rain in abundance, accompanied with thunder and lightning. Reanimated by the very critical relief thus afforded them, the Romans lost not a moment in attacking their enemies, whom this alteration in the aspect of the heavens had filled with consternation and dismay, and succeeded in obtaining over them a most signal and important victory. This wonderful event made a very deep impression on the mind of the emperor, and so entirely changed his sentiments with regard to the Christians, that he publicly proclaimed to the world his conviction of their virtue and good faith towards

him, and decreed that the heaviest punishments should await all
their enemies and accusers. Such is the account given of the
matter by the early Christian writers. But it must not pass without remark, that in this narrative there are some things manifestly false ; and that, with regard to the critical fall of rain accompanied with thunder and lightning, to which the Roman army
[p. 249.] was indebted for its preservation, it possesses not the
characteristic features of a true and unquestionable miracle; but
may, without any difficulty, be accounted for upon natural
grounds, and without in the least interfering with the established
laws of divine providence.(')

(1) Concerning the thundering legion, who are reported through their prayers to have obtained from heaven a copious fall of rain, by which the emperor
Marcus and his army were extricated from a most perilous situation, at a moment when every expectation and hope of relief had entirely vanished, a controversy of no little length was some time back carried on amongst the learned ;
some contending that the event ought to be ascribed to the immediate interference of the Deity himself, who for the moment made a change in the established order of nature for the purpose of producing an amelioration in the condition of the Christians, who were living in a most wretched state of oppression
under Marcus; whilst others maintained that in what actually happened there
is nothing to be discovered which manifests anything like a deviation from the
ordinary and established laws by which the universe is governed. The arguments on either side are to be collected from a dissertation of *Daniel Laroque,*
de Legione Fulminatrice, subjoined to the *Adversaria Sacra* of Matthew Laroque,
his father, and a discourse by *Herman Witsius,* on the same subject, annexed
to his *Ægyptiaca.* Of these writers the former impugns the truth of the miracle, the latter strains every nerve to defend it. At a subsequent period some
letters passed on the subject between *Sir Peter King,* lord chancellor of Great
Britain,* and Mr. *Walter Moyle* an English gentleman of distinguished sagacity
and erudition, a Latin translation of which, accompanied with some remarks of
my own, will be found at the end of my *Syntagma Dissertationum ad disciplinas*
sanctiores pertinentium. King sides with those who maintain that Marcus and his
army were saved by a miracle; *Moyle* takes the field in support of the contrary position. As for any other authors who may have written on the subject, they do
nothing more than either merely repeat, or else endeavour, in one way or other,
to strengthen and confirm the arguments which had been previously adduced
by their above-mentioned predecessors. For my own part, I can perceive no
call for my entering much at large into this affair, and I shall therefore content
myself with stating my opinion on it in a few words. And that I may do this with
the greater regularity and precision, I will, in the first place, confine myself to

* Dr. Mosheim has here fallen into an error. Mr. Moyle's correspondent on this occasion was not
the lord chancellor King, but the *Reverend Richard King,* of Topsham in Devonshire.

a statement of such things as are, or at least ought to be, granted to either party as indisputable ; my next step shall be to point out what is evidently false : and, having divested the matter of these particulars, I will in the last place take into consideration what remains of it, and which must of necessity comprise all that can fairly and properly be made the subject of dispute.

In the first place then, it is certain that Marcus and his army were at one particular time in the course of his war with the Quadi and Marcomanni, involved in a situation beyond all comparison perilous. Marcus was better fitted to shine as a philosopher than an emperor. Intimately acquainted as he was with the maxims and discipline of the stoics, he yet appears to have been a mere novice in the military art, and through his imprudence to have given the enemy such advantages over him as nearly to involve both himself and his army in utter destruction. It is also certain that he was unexpectedly extricated from this most critical situation by means of a copious fall of rain, accompanied with thunder and lightning, and obtained the victory. It is moreover unquestionable, that not only the Christians, but also the emperor and the Romans, considered this sudden fall of rain, to which the army owed its preservation, as a preternatural event ; with this difference, however, that the former viewed it in the light of a miracle wrought by the God whom they worshipped, in answer to their prayers, whilst the latter conceived themselves to be indebted for this signal deliverance to either Jupiter or Mercury. That such was the light in which this event was [p. 250.] regarded by the Romans, is placed beyond all doubt by the united testimony of *Dion Cassius, Capitolinus, Claudian*, and *Themistius*, but still more particularly by the column erected by Marcus himself at Rome, which remains in existence at this day, and on which *Jupiter Pluvius* is represented as reinvigorating the parched and exhausted Romans by means of a plentiful rain.—That there were a number of Christians at that time serving in the imperial army, appears to be not quite so certain as the foregoing ; and there are not wanting those who expressly deny this to have been the case, on the ground that the ancient Christians are known, for the most part, to have disliked the military profession, and held wars in abhorrence. But although this may be very true in a certain degree, it is yet to be proved from various cotemporary authorities, that in this century not a few of the Christians did actually carry arms, and that the Christians in general were not such decided enemies to warfare of every kind as altogether to condemn a military life. For it can be shown that they considered such wars lawful as were necessarily entered into for the safety or defence of the empire, and had no objection to any of the brethren serving in such patriotic wars : and no one can deny but that of this description was the war carried on by Marcus against the Quadi and Marcomanni. It appears also that whenever any soldiers were led to embrace Christianity, no such thing as an abandonment of the profession of arms was imposed on them, but they were permitted to pursue that course of life to which they had previously devoted themselves. There seems, therefore, to be nothing that should oppose itself to our considering this also as certain, that amongst the soldiers of Marcus there were many Christians.—But if this admit of no doubt, it is impossible not to grant it as likewise unquestionable, that when the Roman army was reduced to such an extremity, for want of water, as to have nothing short of utter destruction before their eyes, these Christian soldiers, conformably to the dictates of the religion which they professed, addressed themselves to God in prayers for relief. The same men would doubtless attribute the unexpected fall of rain, accompanied with thunder and lightning, and the consequent discomfiture of their enemies, to the special interference of the Almighty on their behalf; would offer up their thanks to him as the author of their deliverance, and in their report of the thing to their absent brethren, would state that in consequence of their prayers to Christ, the Roman army had been extricated from a situation beyond all comparison adverse and perilous. Attending duly to this, it must be easy for any one to perceive, not only how the rumor of this miracle arose, but also how it came to be a matter of firm belief with the Christians that the Romans had been saved through the prayers of the brethren.

Having then thus dismissed what may be considered as certain, I next proceed to point out such particulars as cannot appear credible to any person conversant in history, and which the industry of some very eminent scholars of modern times has stripped of even that semblance of truth which they might formerly wear.—In the first place then, it is false, although apparently supported by the authority of Apollinaris as quoted by Eusebius, that there was a separate and entire *legion* of Christians in the Roman army. For, to pass over many other things which go completely to refute this idea, it is certain that Christianity was not, under the reign of Marcus, so far countenanced, as for it to appear credible that even a separate cohort, and much less a legion of Christians should have been tolerated in the Roman armies. Since this leading circumstance then appears to have no foundation whatever in truth, it must of necessity be false, that when every hope had vanished, this legion presented themselves in front of the army and implored the divine assistance ; it must be false, that before ever their prayers were finished, the fall of rain, accompanied with thunder and lightning took place ; and finally false, that the emperor attributed the glory of having extricated his army, to this legion, and that by way of mani-
[p. 251.] festing his sense of their estimable deserts, he conferred on them the title of *The Thundering Legion.*—The thundering legion, it has been clearly proved by Scaliger and Henry Valesius, as well as by other learned men since their time, was in existence anterior to the reign of Marcus, and could consequently never have derived its distinguishing name from this miracle. The probability is, that some Christian but little acquainted with the Roman military establishment, having heard that amongst the legions there was one distinguished by the name of the Thundering Legion, was induced hastily to conclude that this title had been given to it in consequence of the thunder with which God had on this occasion answered its prayers, and passed off what was merely a gratuitous assumption of his own, on others for the fact.—Moreover, that Marcus did not consider himself as indebted for his deliverance to the favour in which the Christians stood with heaven, is rendered indisputable by the Antoninian column at Rome, which was erected with the knowledge and consent of this emperor, and on which the preservation of the Roman army is ascribed to Jupiter. Lastly, these things being rejected as false, it becomes impossible for us to cre-

dit what is told us of letters having been issued publicly by Marcus in which the piety of the Christians is extolled, and their enemies and accusers are denounced. The epistle of Marcus to this effect, which is at this day extant, and generally to be found added to the first apology of Justin Martyr, bears on the very face of it, as is confessed even by those who in other respects support the miracle of the Thundering Legion, the most manifest marks of fraud, and seems to have been the work of some man altogether unacquainted with Roman affairs, who lived most likely in the seventh century. Mention, however, having been made of these letters of Marcus by *Tertullian.* in *Apologet.* cap. v. it has been concluded by many that such documents were actually in existence in his time, but that they afterwards perished through the ravages of time. The words of Tertullian are, *at nos e contrario edimus protectorem si literæ Marci Aurelii gravissimi imperatoris requirantur, quibus illam Germanicam sitim Christianorum forte militum precationibus impetrato imbri discussam contestatur.* But there are many things which tend to weaken and invalidate Tertullian's testimony in this instance. I pass over the word *forte* in the above passage, which has been laid hold of by learned men as a proof, either that Tertullian was not satisfied of the truth of this miracle, or else that he had never seen those letters of the emperor's; for to say nothing of what is contended for respecting the use of this particle by Tertullian, I see plainly that neither of the above points can be proved from it. The word manifestly relates, not to Tertullian, but to the emperor and his epistle, and the sense of the passage is this: that Marcus did not explicitly own or avow that the fall of rain was obtained through the supplications of his Christian soldiers, but expressed himself with some reserve, and only signified that *possibly* this great benefit might have been derived from their prayers. I also pass over the circumstance that Tertullian in another place, (*Libro ad Scapulam,* cap. iv. p. 87. ed. Rigalt.) where he similarly makes mention of this rain, obtained through the prayers of the Christians, is altogether silent as to the epistle of Marcus. But there are two things for which we have not to seek very far, which, I think, must be allowed entirely to enervate and render nugatory the testimony which Tertullian is supposed, in the above cited passage, to afford in support of these letters. The first is, that from what Tertullian has handed down to us respecting the purport of this imperial epistle, it is, unless I am most egregiously deceived, very plainly to [p. 252.] be seen that the paper which he had before him at the time of his penning that passage, was a document to which we have before had occasion to direct the reader's attention, namely, the edict *ad commune Asiæ,* issued by Antoninus Pius, whom, we well know, it has been by no means an uncommon thing for writers to confound with his successor Marcus Aurelius. For in proceeding with his statement Tertullian observes, *sicut non palam ab ejusmodi hominibus pœnam dimovit, ita alio modo palam dispersit, adjecta etiam accusatoribus damnatione et quidem tetriore.* Now the meaning of these words I take to be, first, that Marcus did not exempt the Christians from every sort of penalty to which they had been previously liable, that is, he did not absolutely interdict or prohibit their being punished; secondly, that he, however, contrived in effect to render these penalties, as it were, merely nominal; or in other words, that he wisely ordered matters so as that the judges should find it no very easy matter to bring the Christians within the lash of the law; and thirdly, that he suspended over accusers who should fail in their proof, a similar punishment to that which would have awaited the accused on conviction. It will be sufficient for me then, I conceive, to remark, that in these three respects the statement of Tertullian most aptly agrees with the edict of Antoninus Pius *ad commune Asiæ.* For by that edict the emperor did not exempt the Christians from every kind of penalty; but he ordained that no Christian should be subjected to punishment unless convicted of some sort of crime, and by this provision most certainly restricted, within very narrow limits, the power of punishing the Christians at all; and, finally, he directed that such accusers of the Christians as might fail of making good their charge against them, should be punished for their temerity. It appears to me, therefore, manifest, that Tertullian fell into the mistake of imputing to the son the edict of the father, whose name was similar; and that, having understood that Marcus and his army had experienced an unhoped for deliverance from a most perilous situation, through the prayers of the Christians, he was led to conclude, that gratitude for so signal a benefit had actuated him to the promulgation of this edict.—The second thing which renders the testimony of Tertullian, as to the epistle of Marcus, a mere nullity, is the persecution of the Christians at Lyons and Vienne, of which we have above taken notice. This persecution took place in the year clxxvii, in the third, or if you had rather, in the fourth year after the victory obtained over the Marcomanni and the Quadi. But who, let me ask, can believe that the emperor, after having, in the year clxxiv, in a public epistle, passed the highest encomium on the Christians, and declared that the heaviest of punishments should await their accusers, should all at once, in the year clxxvii, so entirely change his mind as to give them up for a sacrifice to the malice of their enemies, and enact, that all such of them as would not return to the religion of their ancestors, should undergo capital punishment?

Having disencumbered the question, then, of these particulars, the only thing that remains to be determined is, whether that fall of rain to which the Roman army owed its preservation in the Marcomannic war, is to be accounted as one of those extraordinary interpositions of divine providence which we term miracles? For if it can be ascertained that it belongs to the class of miracles, there can be no doubt but that it ought to be attributed to the prayers of the Christians who were at that time serving in the army of Marcus. Now, the question, when thus simplified, appears to me extremely easy of solution. By the unreserved assent of the learned it is now established as a maxim, that nothing can properly be considered as belonging to the class of miracles, for the occurrence of which any natural cause can be assigned. But in this fall of rain, although it might not have been expected or even hoped for, there was nothing which it exceeded the ordinary powers of nature to accomplish, nothing which of necessity required the peculiar interposition of Omnipotence. For nothing can be more common, than for the long droughts of summer to be succeeded [p. 253.] by copious falls of rain, accompanied with thunder and lightning in a degree truly terrific. Nor can it appear at all wonderful that some of the enemy should have been struck dead by the lightning, or that, in consequence thereof, their whole army should betake themselves to flight; for it was the opinion of all the German nations that every thunderbolt was commissioned of the Deity itself; and, under the influence of this persuasion, it was customary for the effects of lightning to be regarded by these people as particularly ominous.

XVIII. **State of the Christians under Commodus and Severus.** During the reign of *Commodus,* the son and immediate successor of Marcus, no very heavy or general persecution of the Christians appears to have taken place; at least nothing of this kind is recorded by any historian. There are not wanting, however, individual instances of Christians that were put to death during this period, the most remarkable of which is that of *Apollonius,* a dignified and eminent character, who, together with his accuser, underwent capital punishment at Rome.([1]) The fact was, that none of the laws which had been enacted by different emperors respecting the Christians, of which some indeed were lenient, but others most severe, having been repealed, the judges could at any time, when it might suit their humour, by straining matters a little, contrive, with an apparent show of justice, to inflict capital punishment on all such Christians as might be accused before them. Of this evil the full weight was never so sensibly experienced by the Christians as under the reign of *Septimius Severus,* the successor of Commodus. For although this emperor, upon his first assuming the government, manifested a disposition to favour the Christians, to one of whom he stood indebted for a very signal benefit;([2]) yet under cover, as it should seem, of the turbulence of the times which succeeded, the magistrates and enemies of Christianity took occasion to rekindle the flames of persecution, and to carry their oppression and cruelty to the greatest extent. By the concurrence of abundant authorities, it is rendered indisputable, that in some provinces, towards the close of this century, the Christians were exposed to such a dreadful series of calamities and sufferings as it had scarcely ever fallen to their lot to encounter before. It was the distressing view presented by these accumulated miseries of the brethren, which gave birth to that very ingenious and eloquent defence of the Christians, the *Apologeticon* of Tertullian.([3])

(1) Vid. Eusebius, *Histor. Eccles.* lib. v. cap. xxi. p. 189. Apollonius was put to death under the law of Trajan; his accuser as before noticed, under that of Antoninus Pius.

(2) Tertullian (in libro *ad Scapulum*, c. iv. p. 87, edit. Rigalt.) says, *Ipse Severus pater Antonini Christianorum memor fuit. Nam et Proculum Christianum, qui Torpacion cognominabatur, Euhodiæ procuratorem, qui eum per oleum aliquando curaverat, requisivit, et in palatio suo habuit usque ad mortem ejus: quem et Antoninus optime noverat, lacte Christiano educatus. Sed et clarissimas fæminas et clarissimos viros, Severus sciens hujus sectæ esse, non modo non læsit, verum etiam testimonio exornavit, et populo furenti in nos palam restitit.* The same writer also, in his *Apologet.* cap. v. p. 62, edit. Havercamp. [p. 254.] clearly excepts Severus out of the number of emperors that had discovered an enmity to the Christians.

(3) From the work of Tertullian it is clearly to be perceived how impiously and cruelly the Christians of that period were dealt with, before ever Severus was prevailed on to take part against them. The common people, at the instigation, no doubt, of the heathen priests, called aloud for the blood of the Christians ; the other orders did not trouble themselves about them. *Apologet.* cap. xxxv. p. 300. *Sed vulgus inquis. Ut vulgus, tamen Romani, nec ulli magis depostulatores Christianorum, quam vulgus. Plane cæteri ordines pro auctoritate religiosi ex fide, nihil hosticum de ipso senatu, de equite, de castris, de palatiis ipsis spirat.* But it should seem that some of the presidents by no means thought the Christians deserving of punishment, but exercised their cruelty on them merely with a view of obtaining popular favour ; for in c. xlix. p. 425, Tertullian presses this home upon them in the following terms : *De qua iniquitate sævitiæ non modo cæcum hoc vulgus exultat et insultat, sed et quidam vestrum quibus favor vulgi de iniquitate captatur, gloriantur, quasi non totum quod in nos potestis, nostrum sit arbitrium.* The greatest part of the magistrates, however, did not scruple to acknowledge the falsehood of the calumnies wherewith the Christians were assailed, and were ready to admit the injury that was done them ; but complained that, without a breach of various laws that stood unrepealed and in full force, it was impossible for them to turn a deaf ear to their accusers. This excuse is met by Tertullian with much address, and combated at considerable length in chapters iv, v, and vi. His exordium is as follows : *Sed quoniam, cum ad omnia occurrit veritas nostra,* (But when, by a simple exposure of the truth, we have fully refuted all those calumnies and charges that are urged against us,) *postremo legum obstruitur auctoritas adversus eam* (*i. e.* the truth) *ut aut nihil dicatur retractandum esse post leges* (*i. e.* that it would be inconsistent with Roman constancy to revoke, or deviate from, what has once been established by law,) *aut ingratis necessitas obsequii præferatur veritati,* (*i. e.* a judge, although it may be disagreeable to him, and he may perceive that the cause of truth will suffer, should yet, in his decisions, adhere strictly to the letter of the law,) *de legibus prius excurram vobiscum ut cum tutoribus legum.* Now, men who could in this way make the laws a cloak for their own injustice and cruelty, must certainly have been very worthless characters. If we except the law of Trajan, which permitted the Christians to be called in question merely on account of their religion, and directed them to be punished in case they would not renounce it, the remaining imperial laws and rescripts were rather favourable to the Christians than otherwise ; at least there was not one of them

to which a judge, if he had been so minded, might not have given a favourable interpretation. But it was necessary for these malevolent characters, these tools of the priesthood, and candidates for popular fame, to disguise their real motives under some pretext or other, and to make it appear as if they were borne out by somewhat of reason in their decisions. Such was, however, the spirit of ferocious violence with which this persecution was carried on, that even the restraint imposed by the law of Trajan with respect to making any search after the Christians, was disregarded : for they were broken in upon and apprehended in their sacred assemblies, without any accusation having been laid against them. *Quotidie,* says Tertullian, cap. vii, p. 80, *obsidemur, quotidie prodimur : in ipsis plurimum cœtibus et congregationibus nostris op-* [p. 255.] *primimur.* So far, therefore, from strictly adhering to what was dictated by the laws, these most unjust judges, in the severities which they exercised towards the Christians, did not scruple to fly directly in the teeth of the most positive injunctions. The punishments inflicted on the Christians were as cruel as the enmity borne them by their enemies was savage. The following notices of them occur in Tertullian, cap. xii. p. 125, et seq. *Crucibus et stipitibus imponitis Christianos. Ungulis craditis latera Christianorum. Cervices ponimus. Ad bestias impellimur. Ignibus urimur. In metalla damnamur. In insulas relegamur.* And in cap. xxx. p. 279, 280, we find nearly a similar enumeration. It appears also, that the common people would not unfrequently expend their fury on the Christians without the intervention of the magistrates, and run even into such extremes of malice as to dig up their dead bodies from the grave for the purpose of tearing them to pieces. Cap. xxxvii. p. 308. *Quoties etiam præteritis vobis* (the presidents) *suo jure nos inimicum vulgus invadit lapidibus et incendiis, ipsis Bacchanalium feriis : nec mortuis parcunt Christianis, quin illos de requie sepulturæ, de asylo quodam mortis jam alios, jam nec totos, avellant, dissecent, distrahant.* Now, all these things, it is observable, were done previously to the manifestation of any ill will towards the Christians on the part of the emperor, and whilst the laws that had been anciently enacted against them remained comparatively quiescent, and, as it were, superseded by others of rather a compassionate tendency. What, then, may we suppose to have taken place when Severus avowed himself the enemy of Christianity, and not only revived, in all their rigour, the ancient laws respecting it, but added to them new ones of still greater severity ?

XIX. Philosophers inimical to the Christian cause. To the flame thus prevailing in the breasts of the priests and the populace, not a little fuel was added by the writings of some of those who affected to possess a more than ordinary share of wisdom and virtue, and were distinguished by the titles of Philosophers and Orators. Of these, one of the most celebrated was a disciple of the modern Platonic school, named *Celsus,* who, towards the close of this century, attacked the Christians in a declamation teeming with invective and reproach, which, at a subsequent pe-

riod, was met by a very masterly refutation from the pen of *Origen.*(¹) At Rome likewise, nearly about the same time, the Christians were assailed by one *Crescens,* a cynic philosopher, who, according to the prevailing custom of the age, arraigned them of the grossest impiety. His attack was in a particular manner directed against Justin Martyr, who had exposed to the world the secret vices and deceptive arts of those who styled themselves philosophers ; nor was it for a moment relinquished until this very celebrated Christian father had undergone the punishment of death.(²) As cotemporary with these, it should seem that we may reckon *Fronto,* the rhetorician of Cirta in Africa, who made it his endeavour, in a studied discourse that he sent abroad into the world, to establish against the Christians that vile calumny so frequent in the mouths of the mob, of their countenancing an incestuous intercourse of the sexes.(³) Many more persons of this description, in all probability, laboured to defame the Christians; but neither their works nor their names have come down to our times.

(1) *Origen,* who, in the third century, was induced, by the advice of Ambrosius, to give to the world his well known confutation of the calumnies and [p. 256.] falsehoods of Celsus, conceived his adversary to be an Epicurean, for which, however, he seems to have had no other reason than that of there having been an Epicurean of some celebrity of the name of Celsus. But if the opinions of *Celsus* were what even Origen himself states them to have been, there can be no doubt but that he was utterly averse to the doctrines of Epicurus, and belonged to what we term the modern Platonic or Alexandrian school. The reader who wishes to see this question examined in detail, may consult my Preface to the German translation of Origen. Before the appearance, however, of any remarks of mine on the subject, it had been very learnedly shown by that eminent scholar, Pet. Wesseling, (*Probabilia,* cap. xxiii. p. 187, et seq.), that Celsus could by no means be considered as belonging to the class of the Epicureans.—We cannot close this note without observing, that abundant proof is to be collected from the weak and injurious declamation of Celsus, of the very great detriment which the cause of Christianity sustained in consequence of the corruptions introduced by the Gnostics, who, subsequently to the time of Hadrian, had attained to some degree of consequence and fame ; for the exceptionable particulars on which this malevolent adversary chiefly grounds his attack, were not recognized by those of the orthodox faith as belonging to the Christian scheme, but were merely fancied improvements that had been tacked to it by the Gnostics. Celsus, as appears from his own showing, had been chiefly conversant with men of this latter description, and fell into the error of attributing to the Christians in general, maxims which were recognized only by this particular sect.

(2) Vid. Eusebius, *Histor. Eccles.* lib. iv. cap. xvi. as also the Second Apology *pro Christianis*, of Justin himself, in which he predicts that the philosophers, and particularly Crescens, whose ignorance and corrupt morals he had made it his business to expose to the world, would endeavour by every possible means to bring about his destruction.

(3) There are two passages in *Minucius Felix* which relate to this calumniator of the Christians; from one of which we learn his country, from the other his name and mode of life. In cap. x. *Octavius*, p. 99, where he treats of the Thyestean banquets, which the Christians were accused of celebrating, he thus expresses himself: *Et de convivio notum est. Passim omnes loquuntur. Id etiam cirtensis nostri testatur oratio.* Then follows a description of these feasts, which, without doubt, was taken from the discourse of Fronto, which he had just been praising. To this passage he thus replies in the words of his *Octavius,* cap. xxxi. p. 322. *Sic de isto* (the banquet) *et tuus Fronto, non ut affirmator testimonium fecit, sed convicium ut orator aspersit.* By learned men it has been suspected, and certainly not without great appearance of reason, that this Fronto was one and the same with *Cornelius Fronto,* the rhetorician, who taught the emperor Marcus eloquence. As long as the Christian church could number within its pale none but men who were unskilled in letters and philosophy, it was regarded with a silent disdain by those amongst the Greeks and Romans who assumed to themselves the title of philosophers. But when, in the second century, certain philosophers of eminence became converts to the Christian scheme, such as Justin, Athenagoras, Pantænus, and others, without, however, renouncing either the name, garb, or mode of living of philosophers, or giving up the instruction of youth ; when, moreover, these Christianized philosophers made it their business to demonstrate in the schools the vanity of the Greek philosophy, and propounded therein a new species of philosophic dis- [p. 257.] cipline, which intimately embraced the principles of Christianity, and accommodated itself to the form of that religion which they had espoused ; and when, lastly, these same illustrious converts to Christianity made a point of exposing to the world the secret vices, the contentious squabbles, and the actual knavery of the pagan philosophic sects, the heathen philosophers perceived at once the peril of their situation, and that their credit with the world, as well as every thing else that could be dear to them, was brought into the greatest jeopardy. They therefore united with the priesthood and the populace in clamouring for the extermination of the Christians, and whilst they endeavoured, by the propagation of false accusations and calumnies, not only orally, but in their writings, to draw down destruction on the Christians at large, were particularly assiduous in directing the public vengeance against their apostate brethren who had gone over to the new religion. It was not, therefore, so much with a view to uphold what they considered to be the cause of truth, as to support their own tottering reputation, authority, and glory, and to secure to themselves the common necessaries of life, such as food and raiment, motives, in fact, of much the same kind with those which had previously excited the hostility of the priesthood, that these philosophers were induced to take the field against the Christians. This war of the philosophers against Christianity had its com-

mencement under the reign of the emperor Marcus, who was himself a philosopher, and made it his study to encourage and gratify philosophers : neither had any of the Greek and Roman philosophers, previously to this period, embraced Christianity, nor had the Christians applied themselves to the cultivation of philosophy ; indeed it was a thing which they were expressly enjoined by St. Paul to avoid. From what we have here observed, it is easily to be perceived, by any one who will exert his reason, whether there be not an apparently good foundation for the conjecture which we have above hazarded, that the philosophers were in fact the authors of the sufferings to which the Christians were exposed in the time of the emperor Marcus. At this period the jealousy of the philosophers became awakened, and a fear was excited in their breasts lest they should be despoiled of their renown, and reduced, as it were, to beggary, in consequence of the disclosures made by those of their brethren who had turned Christians. Being, therefore, able to carry every point with the emperor, and Marcus himself no doubt feeling hurt and indignant at the contempt and derision with which philosophy, considered by him as the chief good, was treated by the Christians, they found no difficulty in prevailing on him to put these people without the pale of his justice, and to permit them, in return for the insults they had offered to the honour and dignity of philosophy, to be assailed with every species of cruelty, and even deprived of their lives.

XX. **Government of the church.** Amidst these vicissitudes of fortune, the Christians applied themselves every where with an ardent and holy zeal to add to the strength and stability of their cause, and at the same time to improve it as much as possible by means of salutary laws and regulations. Over each of the larger churches, and such as were established in cities or towns of any note, there presided a teacher who bore the title of *Bishop*, and whose appointment to this office rested entirely with the people. The bishop was assisted by a council of *presbyters* or *elders*, who, in like manner, depended for their appointment on popular suffrage, and, availing himself of the aid thus furnished him, it was, in an especial degree, his duty to be ever vigilant and active in preventing the interests of religion from experiencing any detriment. To the bishop likewise it belonged to allot to each of the presbyters his proper functions and department ; and to see that, in every thing appertaining to religion and divine worship, a due respect was had to the laws and regulations which the people had enacted or otherwise sanctioned with their approbation. The *deacons* and *deaconesses* filled subordinate sta-
[p. 258.] tions in the church, and had various duties assigned to them, according as circumstances might require. The daughter churches, or lesser Christian assemblies, that through the care and

exertions of the bishop had been established in the neighbouring districts and villages, were governed by *presbyters* sent from the mother church, who, in consequence of their representing the person, and exercising, with a few exceptions, all the rights and functions of the bishop by whom they were commissioned, came to be distinguished by the title of *Chorepiscopi*, or rural bishops.—The supreme power in these equal assemblies or congregations resided in the people ; and consequently no alteration of importance, nor in fact any thing of more than ordinary moment, could be brought about or carried into effect without having recourse to a general assembly, by the suffrages and authority of which alone could the opinions and counsels of the bishop and the presbyters be rendered obligatory, and acquire the force of laws.

XXI. **Authority of the apostolic churches.** The most perfect equality prevailed amongst all the churches in point of rights and power, each of them prescribing to itself at any time, according to its own will and judgment, such laws and regulations as its circumstances appeared to demand : nor does this age supply us with a single instance of any church assuming to itself anything like a right of dominion or command over the others.(¹) An ancient custom, however, obtained of attributing to those churches which had been founded by the apostles themselves, a superior degree of honour, and a more exalted dignity ; on which account it was, for the most part, usual, when any dispute arose respecting principles or tenets, for the opinion of these churches to be asked ; as also, for those who entered into a discussion of any matters connected with religion, to refer, in support of their positions, to the voice of the *apostolic churches*.(²) We may, therefore, hence very readily perceive the reason which, in cases of doubt and controversy, caused the Christians of the west to have recourse to the church of *Rome*, those of Africa to that of *Alexandria*, and those of Asia to that of *Antioch*, for their opinion, and which also occasioned these opinions to be not unfrequently regarded in the light of laws, namely, that these churches had been planted, reared up and regulated either by the hand or under the immediate superintendence and care of some one or more of the apostles themselves.

(1) What was done by *Victor* during the controversy respecting the time

of Easter, by no means proves, as we shall presently show, that he arrogated to himself the power of making laws.

(2) If the reader will turn to Irenæus *advers. Hæres.* lib. iii. cap. iii. p. **175.** [p. 259.] ed. Massuet. and Tertullian *de Præscript. advers. Hæreticos,* cap. xxxvi. p. 245. ed. Rigalt. he will find two very notable passages, in which these illustrious writers, in their dispute with the Gnostics, make their appeal to the apostolic churches. Between these passages there is such an accordance and similitude, that I can scarcely doubt but that *Tertullian,* at the time of his writing, had Irenæus, (whom he had certainly read, as appears from his book, *contra Valentinianos,* cap. v.) before his eyes, and intentionally imitated him. The *Gnostics,* finding themselves hardly pressed by the authority of the sacred writings, endeavoured to maintain their ground by asserting that the true and genuine doctrine of Jesus Christ was not to be learnt from the writings of the apostles, for that it had never been committed to writing, but that the *apostles* had transmitted it merely by word of mouth. Their having recourse to such a miserable shift indicated plainly enough that their cause was wholly desperate : in fact, they could adduce nothing whatever in support of this ridiculous assertion ; and their opponents might therefore have contented themselves with calling upon them, as they certainly with the greatest propriety might have done, to prove what they thus alleged. *Tertullian* and *Irenæus,* however, adopted a different mode of depriving them of this subterfuge, and exposing to the world its utter falsity, namely, that of appealing to the apostolic churches. Their train of argument is this :—If it were true that the apostles had orally transmitted a docrine different from that which they committed to writing, there can be no doubt but that such doctrine would have been communicated to those churches which they themselves founded, ordained, and instructed. But it is notoriously the fact, that of all the churches which owe their foundation and institution to the apostles, and in which we know that it has been an object of main concern with their bishops, most religiously to preserve and adhere to that form of discipline which they received from their founders, there is not a single one that gives the least countenance to the fables and idle dreams of the Gnostics. We maintain, therefore, that these latter are altogether unworthy of belief when they assert, that their tenets are of an apostolic origin, being derived from the apostles through oral communication. To this reasoning the Gnostics could reply in no other way than by saying, that the churches established by the apostles had gradually departed from the maxims and tenets of their founders, and that their primitive bishops had been forcibly supplanted by others who knew nothing of the genuine apostolic discipline. Foreseeing then, that such, if any, must be their answer, *Irenæus* takes care to show that in the Roman church, which, for the sake of brevity, he takes as a fair example of the whole, the series of bishops had been continued down without interruption from the time of the apostles, and the regular succession of them been never disturbed or sullied by the intervention of any stranger or person whose principles were in any respect different from those of the apostles. From this one observation we gain considerable light as to this mode of arguing, and need no other proof of the very great error into which those of the present day fall, who take their

stand behind tradition and apostolical succession, and contend that they are justified in doing so by the example of the primitive Christian teachers. Both Irenæus and Tertullian most obviously agree in this, that they place all the apostolic churches on a precisely equal footing, and allow to each of them the same weight and authority in determining this controversy with the Gnostics. *Tertullian* is particularly explicit as to this. His words are :—*Percurre ecclesias apostolicas, apud quas ipsæ adhuc cathedræ apostolorum suis locis præsident. - - - Proxima est tibi Achaia ; habes Corinthum. Si non longe abes a Macedonia, habes Philippos, habes Thessalonicences. Si potes in Asiam tendere,* [p 260.] *habes Ephesum. Si autem Italiæ adjaces, habes Romam, unde nobis quoque auctoritas præsto est.* Tertullian, it is manifest. makes no distinction between these apostolic churches; the same authority, and the same dignity is attributed by him to all of them : the church of Rome was, in his estimation, possessed of no greater consequence, nor had it any more power to determine the dispute with the Gnostics, than that of Ephesus, Thessalonica, or Corinth. The Roman church is indeed considered by him as having been more fortunate, inasmuch as it had been blessed with the presence of Peter, Paul, and John, who poured out their blood in the cause of Christ: *Ista quam felix ecclesia! cui totam doctrinam apostoli cum sanguine suo profuderunt ; ubi Petrus passioni dominicæ adæquatur ; ubi Paulus Joannis exitu coronatur ; ubi apostolus Johannes posteaquam in oleum igneum demersus nihil passus est, in insulam relegatur.* But so far from giving countenance to the idea of a greater power with regard to determining controversies respecting religion, being possessed by the church of Rome than by that of Ephesus or any other apostolical church, he in effect gives it a direct negative. *Irenæus*, indeed, extols the church of Rome, not only on account of its good fortune, but also for other reasons of which we shall presently take more notice; but notwithstanding this, he plainly agrees with *Tertullian* as to the above point, that the power and authority of all the apostolic churches in determining the controversy that had arisen between the orthodox Christians and the Gnostics, was precisely equal. *Traditionem,* says he, *apostolorum in toto mundo manifestatam, in omni ecclesia adest respicere omnibus qui vera velint videre.*——*Etenim si recondita mysteria scissent apostoli, quæ seorsim et latenter ab reliquis perfectos docebant, his vel maxime traderent ea, quibus etiam ipsas ecclesias committebant.* Most assuredly Irenæus would not have written thus, he would not have spoken generally of all the churches that had been founded by the apostles, but have confined his reference to that of Rome alone, if either he or any other person at that time had believed that the right and power of determining controversies respecting religion was possessed by the Roman church. It is true, indeed. that he afterwards makes no mention of the other churches, but contents himself with opposing to the Gnostics the sentiments of the church of Rome alone : but it is plain. that this is not done by him from a persuasion, that to this one church alone belonged the decision of Christian controversies, but, as he openly avows. for the sake of brevity ; *sed quoniam valde longum est in hoc tali volumine omnium ecclesiarum enumerare successiones, maximæ et antiquissimæ ecclesiæ traditionem indicantes, confundimus omnes.* Tertullian and Irenæus agree also in this, that they pass over, without the slightest notice, that church, which it is natural to regard as the head and mother of all churches, and of which Christ himself was the parent and founder: I mean the *church of Jerusalem.* Tertullian, although he specifically enumerates the more celebrated of the apostolic churches, yet says not a word of that of Jerusalem. Irenæus may be considered as tacitly treating it with contempt, when he gives to the church of Rome a preference over all the others. But in this they are by no means singular, for I do not know that the church of Jerusalem, although in point of foundation superior to all the rest, is ever appealed to, or even cited, as an authority, by any of the ancient fa- [p. 261.] thers. This circumstance, however, can occasion no very great won- der to any one who is apprised, that the original and true church of Jerusalem, consisting of Jews and the descendants of Jews, who had actually seen and heard our blessed Lord himself, seceded from the remaining church under the reign of Hadrian ; and that the church which assembled in Hadrian's new city, Ælia Capitolina, and which assumed to itself the title of the church of Jerusa- lem, was altogether a distinct assembly from the ancient and original congre- gation. In these respects, then, we see that Irenæus and Tertullian are in per- fect harmony with each other ; but in what further relates to the church of *Rome,* we shall find them considerably at variance. *Irenæus* extols it on many accounts, and attributes to it a certain superiority or preëminence; but *Tertullian,* although he had read, and in other respects follows Irenæus, speaks only of the felicity or good fortune of the Roman church ; of its superiority in any other respect he appears to know nothing. The reason of this difference may, I think, be assigned without much difficulty. *Irenæus* had been at Rome, and he was, without doubt, indebted for many kindnesses to the Roman bishop, Eleutherus ; added to which, he was the bishop of a poor little church which had suffered considerably in the then recent persecution under Marcus, and stood very much in need of the counsel and assistance that were to be afforded by the great and opulent church of Rome, and its bishop. To speak in plain terms, he was no stranger to the advantages that were to be derived from the wealth and benefi- cence of the church of Rome, and he therefore made no scruple of flattering her pretensions as to a point on the accomplishment of which he knew that she was bent, namely, that of exalting herself to a superiority over the other Christian churches. But *Tertullian* was an African, and it is well known that the Afri- can church was, long after the times of which we are treating, impatient of the Roman domination, and a most strenuous asserter of the primitive Christian liberty. Therefore, although he was indebted for a considerable part of what is urged in argument by him against the Gnostics to Irenæus, as must be mani- fest to any one upon collation, he yet adopts none of the compliments that are paid by this latter writer to the Roman church ; nor does he assign to it any preëminence over the other churches, except in that superior degree of felicity which it derived from the glorious death of the apostles Peter and Paul, and the miraculous preservation of the apostle John.

But let us now see, since we have thus entered into the subject, in what consists that celebrated eulogium of Irenæus on the Roman church, which Ren. Massuetus pronounces to be a grievous stumbling block to all who have quitted the church of Rome and shaken off the yoke of the Catholic faith; which the friends of the papacy consider as the very citadel of that preëminence which the church of Rome arrogates to itself over every other church; and in explaining and commenting on which, so many great and excellent men have bestowed no little portion of labour. With the remarks of others on the subject, whether well or ill-founded, I shall not concern myself, but merely state, in as few words as possible, what, upon an impartial view of the matter, appears to me to be the truth.—After stating that in his opposition to the Gnostics, he should not adduce individually the authority and discipline of all the apostolical churches, but, for the sake of brevity, content himself with referring to the church of Rome, as exhibiting a fair example of the whole; Irenæus thus proceeds : *ad hanc enim ecclesiam*, (the church of Rome,) *propter potiorem principalitatem necesse est omnem convenire ecclesiam, hoc est, eos qui sunt undique fideles, in qua semper ab his, qui sunt undique, conservata est ea, quæ est* [p. 262.] *ab apostolis traditio.* These, then, are the words which have given rise to such subtile and laborious disquisitions. But, let them be twisted in any manner whatever, I have not the least hesitation in declaring it to be my decided opinion, that if the right which the church of Rome at this day asserts, of dictating to the other Christian churches, be founded chiefly on this passage, it stands but on a very weak and tottering foundation indeed. But, lest my judgment should appear to have been hastily formed, let it only be considered in a general way. I. That the sense in which the words of Irenæus are to be understood, is altogether obscure, and that, through either ignorance or want of skill in the Latin translator, it is impossible to comprehend, with any degree of precision, the meaning intended to be conveyed by certain terms, on the right understanding of which the intelligibility of the whole passage very materially depends. What, for instance, I would ask, are we to understand by *potior principalitas?* What meaning, again, are we to annex to the expression, *convenire ad ecclesiam Romanam?* In vain will it be for us to pretend to ascertain the sense of this passage, until the original Greek of Irenæus be recovered. II. That Irenæus is speaking of the church of Rome in the second century, a period at which it might, no doubt, with justice be asserted that all its bishops and teachers had continued steadfast in the observance of that discipline, which had been transmitted to them by the apostles Peter and Paul. To apply, therefore, what he then says, to the church of Rome in its present state, is to do much the same thing as if, in proof of the rights and power that belong to the emperors of Germany, who also bear the title of Roman emperors, we were to adduce the rights and powers that were exercised by the first emperors of the Augustan race, Octavius Augustus, Tiberius, Caligula, and Claudius. Without doubt, we should account it a very ingenious piece of pleasantry, in any man, to quote what Suetonius or Tacitus may have said respecting the authority of Augustus or Tiberius, by way of shewing what is due from the German princes to their present emperor. By the same arguments, then, as a jurist would make use of in refuting such a man, may an effectual answer be given to those who, from a passage in Irenæus, pretend to ascertain what are at present the rights and power of the Roman pontiff. III. That this is the testimony of a private individual, of one that was nothing more than the bishop of a small, insignificant church, that had been but a few years before established in Gaul, of a man, moreover, who, in his writings, has given not a few proofs of a judgment far from sound or correct, as well as of a mind evidently labouring under the shackles of prejudice. But who is there, possessed of but merely common sense and information, that would recognise in the *dicta* or precepts of any private individual, and more especially in those of an individual who had betrayed no small deficiency of judgment, and been convicted of having fallen into more than one palpable error, a standard whereby to ascertain and demonstrate the public rights of states or churches? Should there, however, be found a man so disposed, we can meet Irenæus with an authority not at all inferior to himself, either in point of judgment or of talents, namely Tertullian, who denies that the church of Rome possessed any preëminence over the rest of the churches, except it were in point of felicity or good fortune. What, therefore, the supporters of the church of Rome take upon them in this instance, to maintain, upon the authority of Irenæus, we shall assume to ourselves the liberty of denying, upon the authority of Tertullian.

Having, then, premised thus much in a general way, let us now direct our attention more particularly to the words of Irenæus. *Necesse est*, he tells us, [p. 263.] *omnem ecclesiam convenire ad ecclesiam Romanam;* and for this he assigns two reasons; the first, *propter potiorem principalitatem;* the second, *quia semper in ea conservata est apostolorum traditio.* Now it unluckily happens, that the terms in which this precept is conveyed, are such as to leave its meaning somewhat dubious. By the words *convenire ad ecclesiam Romanam,* it should seem most likely that we ought to understand *accedere ad Romanam ecclesiam,* or *consulere ecclesiam Romanam,* and that what Irenæus meant to say was this: —that it behoved all Christians, in matters of doubt, connected with religion, to resort for advice and direction to the church of Rome, (*i. e.* the church of Rome in its then state,) inasmuch as it was the most ancient and the largest of all the churches of the west, and owed its foundation to the hands of the apostles themselves. But if such be this father's meaning, and the reasons which he subjoins scarcely allow us to doubt of its being so, there is certainly nothing in it that can afford the church of Rome much support in the present day. It is not within the power even of the most subtile disputant, to make it appear that Irenæus meant that his words should be applied to the church of Rome in all subsequent ages and times. On the contrary, we have, in the latter reason which he assigns for his precept, a convincing proof that he spoke in relation only to the more ancient and early church of Rome, as it existed in his own time. The reason that he assigns why the other churches should have recourse to that of Rome, is, *quia in ea traditio apostolorum conservata est.* Now nothing can be more plain than that he here speaks merely of time past. Had he meant that the church of Rome was to be consulted and made the arbitress in all ages to come, he unquestionably would have written, *in qua traditio apostolorum conservata est, et semper conservabitur.* As to the first reason given by Irenæus, namely, *propter potiorem principalitatem,* it is altogether involved in obscurity and doubt. For *principalitas* is such an ambiguous word, and admits of being used in such a variety of senses, that, owing to the negligence of Irenæus, or his Latin translator, in not more particularly indicating what he meant by it, a degree of darkness, not easy to be dispelled, is thrown over the whole of this sentence. The conjecture that strikes me as the most plausible in regard to it, is, that by the word *principalitas*, Irenæus might mean those four honourable distinctions appertaining to the church of Rome, which he had just before enumerated, namely, magnitude, antiquity, celebrity, and apostolical origin. *Maximæ*, says he, *et antiquissimæ, et omnibus cognitæ, a gloriosissimis duobus apostolis. Petro et Paulo, fundatæ et constitutæ ecclesiæ.* In these, probably, consisted that *potior principalitas* which Irenæus attributes to the church of Rome; he never dreamt of ascertaining what would be its claims to preëminence in every future age. At least this explication of his words possesses a force and simplicity that I believe we shall in vain look for in any other. But it is time for me to put an end to this note, though materials are not wanting for extending it to a much greater length. I will, therefore, only add, that I cannot help viewing it as a thing particularly unbecoming in men of learning and talents, to pretend to say that the public rights of the universal church and the form of government prescribed for it by Christ, are to be elicited from the obscure and uncertain words of a private individual, the bishop of merely a poor little insignificant church, a good and pious man unquestionably, but one, at the same time, whose mental qualifications and endowments were certainly nothing more than of the middling order.

XXII. **Civil unity introduced amongst the Christians.** Al- [p. 264.] though, therefore, all the churches had, at the commencement of this century, various laws and institutions in common, which had been received from the apostles themselves, and were particularly careful in maintaining with each other a certain community of tenets, morals and charity ; yet each individual church which had a bishop and presbyters of its own, assumed to itself the form and rights of a little distinct republic or commonwealth; and with regard to its internal concerns, was wholly regulated by a code of laws, that, if they did not originate with, had, at least, received the sanction of the people constituting such church. This primitive liberty and independence, however, was by degrees relinquished, and it became the practice for all the minor churches within a province to form themselves into one large association, and to hold at stated seasons, much after the manner of confederate republics, a convention, in which the common interests and welfare of the whole were taken into consideration and provided for. Of the immediate authors of this arrangement we are uninformed, but it is certain that it had its origin in Greece ; and there are many things which combine to prove, that during this century it did not extend itself beyond the confines of Asia. In process of time, however, the very great advantages attending on a federation of this sort becoming apparent, other provinces were induced to follow the example of Greece, and by degrees this form of government became general throughout the whole church; so that the Christian community may be said, thenceforward, to have resembled one large commonwealth, made up, like those of Holland and Switzerland, of many minor republics. These conventions or assemblies, in which the delegates from various associated churches consulted on what was requisite to be done for the common welfare of the whole, were termed *synods* by the Greeks, and by the Latins *councils*. To the laws enacted by these deputies under the powers with which they were invested by their respective churches, the Greeks gave the name of *canons* or general rules, and by this title it also became usual for them to be distinguished by the Latins.(¹)

(1) The reader will find what I have here stated very forcibly illustrated and confirmed by Tertullian, in a very notable passage that occurs in his book, *de Jejuniis,* cap. xiii, p. 711. opp. edit. Rigalt. Tertullian is advocating the cause of the Montanists, whose tenets he had espoused, and to whom the orthodox Christians attributed it as a fault, that they had taken upon them to institute certain fasts or seasons of abstinence. The reason assigned by the regular Christians for objecting to the rules respecting fasts prescribed by the Montanists, was deduced from the nature of divine worship. God, said they, ought to be honoured and worshipped by the Christians of their own free will, not from compulsion, or by the command of another. *Denique respondetis hæc* [p. 265.] *ex arbitrio agenda, non ex imperio.* In this age, therefore, the nature and character of the true religion continued to be well understood by the generality of Christians, inasmuch as they denied it to be subject to the control of any human laws. To this argument Tertullian replies, in the first place, that the Montanists, in observing certain fasts, did not conform themselves to the ordinances of men, but to God, or the Paraclete, *i. e.* the Holy Spirit, who had enjoined those fasts by the mouths of his servants. *Plus humanæ licebit voluntati quam divinæ potestati? Ego me seculo, non Deo liberum memini; sic meum est ultro officium facere Domino, sicut indicere illius est.* He agrees, therefore, with the rest of the Christians, that religion is not to be controlled by human laws, and strenuously advocates the cause of liberty: but at the same time he insists on it that obedience is to be paid to the commands of God, as delivered by certain of his servants. To this the Antimontanist Christians readily yielded their assent. The only thing, therefore, that remained in dispute between them and Tertullian was, whether Montanus and his followers were really, as they asserted, inspired by the Holy Spirit, or not? With regard to this he replies, in the second place, that amongst the Antimontanist Christians the *bishops* had the

power of enjoining fasts, as also, in cases of great emergency, of imposing extraordinary contributions on the people. *Bene autem quod et episcopi universæ plebi mandare jejunia assolent: non dico de industria stipium conferendarum, ut vestræ capturæ est: sed interdum et ex aliqua sollicitudinis ecclesiasticæ causa.* These words are of the very first importance and authority in enabling us to ascertain the extent to which the power possessed by the bishops of the primitive church reached. Had it been possible for the bishops of this period, of their own accord, *i. e.* without the assent of the people, to do more than what is here stated, Tertullian would, most assuredly, not have failed to notice it on this occasion, when his attention was particularly directed to the rights and power which might lawfully be exercised by men over the flock of Christ. It appears, therefore, that with regard to *two* things, the bishop's sole mandate alone was sufficient. In the *first place*, he might enjoin fasts; for since everything relating to the service of God was placed immediately under the care and direction of the bishop, and fasts were considered as constituting a part of such service, it was but just that the times for observing them should be left to his appointment. The bishop, it seems, could also, in any case of emergency that called for pecuniary aid, and such cases were by no means uncommon, require of the people to make such an additional contribution, according to their means, as might enable him to meet such exigency. Concerning the bishop's power as to this, Tertullian speaks in his usual unpolished, obscure, and laconic manner; and it may, therefore, not be amiss to offer the reader some explanation of what he says on this head. It is manifest then, that under the title of *stipes* he refers to those contributions which the Christians were accustomed to make, in consequence of an admonition from the bishop. These contributions he divides into ordinary and extraordinary. The words, *ut vestræ capturæ est*, relate to those of the ordinary kind. *Captura* has here the meaning of *reditus*, (income, ability, gains.) The custom was, for every Christian ordinarily to contribute towards the common stock in a certain degree, proportionate to his means or ability. In addition to these ordinary offerings, we find a distinct mention made of certain extraordinary ones, which were called for in cases of emergency. Extraordinary expenses were not unfrequently incurred by churches in the entertainment of strangers, in relieving the sick, and those of the brethren who were languishing in captivity, and in various other ways, to the defrayment of which the free and voluntary oblations, as they were termed, of the Christians, were occasionally found unequal. The exigencies here spoken of, are in part particularized [p. 266.] by Tertullian himself *in Apologet.* cap. xxxix. p. 325. *Dispensatur,* says he, *naufragiis, et si qui in metallis, et si qui in insulis, vel in custodiis duntaxat ex causa Dei sectæ alumni confessionis suæ fiunt.* Whenever a case of this nature occurred, the bishop addressed his flock, requiring every one to contribute, not only according to his means, but in a degree proportionate to the magnitude and pressure of the occasion, so that the necessity of the church might be fully answered; and to this mandate it was customary for all to pay obedience with the utmost alacrity. The meaning, therefore, of Tertullian's words is this: "I will not speak of the very great readiness of the Christians in making the ordinary contributions required of them by the bishop; for I know that no one as to this acts from compulsion, but each person gives according to what his ability or circumstances permit. But, not unfrequently, unlooked-for accidents and emergencies occur, which demand pecuniary relief to a certain extent, and require that the ratio of contribution should be determined by the bishop: nor does any Christian, in such cases, ever hesitate in paying obedience to his commands."

In the third place, Tertullian replies, that it was customary in Greece for councils of the churches to be convened, and that therein laws were enacted and duties imposed, to which, notwithstanding that they were purely of human origin, no exception was ever taken. *Aguntur præterea per Græcias illa certis in locis concilia ex universis ecclesiis, per quæ et altiora quæque in commune tractantur, et ipsa repræsentatio totius nominis Christiani magna veneratione celebratur.* From these words it appears, (1st,) That at the close of the second century the practice of convening councils had not been adopted either in Africa, the country where Tertullian lived, or in the Latin Church, or in the East, or in Egypt, but solely in Greece, or as Tertullian expresses it, *per Græcias, i. e.* the nations both in Europe and Asia that bore the name of Greeks. (2ndly,) That these councils were in his time regarded as of mere human origin, not as having been instituted either by Christ himself or his apostles. For what he had in view was to prove that good and pious men might enjoin fasts, and prescribe other salutary regulations to the church of Christ. Since, therefore, in support of his argument, he adduces the acts of these councils, it is plain that he must have considered them as assemblies which owed their origin to mere human authority, and their acts, not in the light of oracles or dictates of the Holy Spirit, as they came to be regarded in after times, but as mere human laws and regulations. (3dly,) That even in Tertullian's time, certain places or cities had been fixed on for the assembling of these Greek councils, and that no power existed of convening them elsewhere. (4thly,) That these councils did not busy themselves about things of inferior moment, each individual church being left to determine on such matters for itself, but employed themselves in the discussion and arrangement of points of a higher and weightier nature, or such as were of general interest and importance. (5thly,) That the bishops, who were present at these councils, were merely the representatives of their respective churches; that is, that they neither assented to, nor originated anything therein in their private individual capacity, but always in the names of the churches of [p. 267.] which they were respectively the delegates. *Repræsentatio*, says Tertullian, *totius nominis Christiani celebratur.* Now *totum nomen Christianum* evidently, in this place, means, *tota ecclesia*, the whole church bearing the name of Christ. The bishops, therefore, were considered as representing, collectively, the entire associated Christian flock, and, individually, the different churches over which they respectively presided; and hence arose the veneration in which these councils were held. The opinion, that the bishops, assembled in council, officiated in the place of Christ himself, and that the very nature of their function constituted them both legislators and judges of the Christian community, had not at this time even suggested itself. Tertullian esteemed these councils worthy of the highest commendation, for he thus proceeds: *Et hoc quam dig-*

num fide auspicante congregari undique ad Christum? Vide quam bonum et quam jocundum habitare fratres in unum. He moreover adds, what is well worthy of remark, that the bishops were accustomed, before they commenced their deliberations, to petition for divine aid and assistance by prayer and fasting: *Conventus autem illi stationibus prius et jejunationibus operati, dolere cum dolentibus et ita demum congaudere gaudentibus norunt.* It appears, therefore, that ecclesiastical councils had their origin amongst the Greeks in the second century, and that their utility becoming manifest, they were gradually adopted by the church at large.—The information thus afforded by Tertullian, with respect to the origin of councils, is supported by the general history of Christian affairs; for no notice whatever occurs of any ecclesiastical councils held prior to the second century; and with regard to those holden in the course of that age, the few memorials of them that have reached us, very plainly indicate them to have been for the most part held in Greece. Towards the close of this century, the practice of holding councils of this kind passed from Greece into Palestine and Syria, as appears from Eusebius, *Histor. Eccles.* lib. v. cap. xxiii. p. 190, 191, where mention is made of councils held about the end of the second century by the bishops of Palestine and the province of Osdroëna, respecting the controversies then in agitation concerning the proper time for celebrating Easter. By certain of the learned it is also contended, that on the same occasion a council of the Italian bishops was convened at Rome by the Roman pontiff Victor. Vid. Pet. Constant. *Epist. Romanor. Pontificum,* tom. i. in Victore, § 4. p. 94. and others. In proof of this, they quote the following words of Eusebius: καὶ τῶν ἐπὶ Ρώμης δὲ ὁμοίως ἄλλη περὶ τῆ αὐτῆ ζητήματος, Ἐπίσκοπον Βίκτερα Σηλῦσα, which are thus rendered by Valesius: *alia item extat epistola synodi Romanæ, cui Victoris episcopi nomen præfixum est.* But not to rest upon the circumstance, that no mention is made of any Roman *synod* in the Greek original, the name Victor, bishop of Rome, being the only one prefixed to this epistle, puts it out of all question that it was not the letter of any *synod,* but merely of Victor himself; for synodical epistles were uniformly subscribed by all the bishops present. The only construction, therefore, of which these words of Eusebius seem properly to admit, is this: that Victor having, as was then the customary practice, consulted with the Roman presbyters, addressed, with their consent, this letter, in his own name, to the church over which he presided; which thing of [p. 268.] itself furnishes us with an argument, that the practice of many churches assembling together in council, had not at that time passed from Greece into Italy. And perhaps it may not be amiss to notice it, by the bye, that Valesius has fallen into some other mistakes with regard to the account given by Eusebius of the controversy respecting Easter, in consequence of his estimating the state of the church in the second century from its condition in after ages.

But I have not yet pointed out all that is deserving of notice with regard to this passage of Tertullian. Amongst other things, it is particularly worthy of remark, that he speaks therein of councils as having had their origin in Greece. Indeed, in no province could it have been more natural for this practice of holding councils to have arisen, than in Greece. Under a monarchical government, such as that of emperors and kings, the idea of holding councils would probably never have entered into the minds of the Christians; but in such a province as Greece was, the notion might readily enough suggest itself. The Greeks were, as we all know, divided into many minor states and republics. Amongst these petty governments an intimate association for general purposes subsisted; and for many ages, prior to the coming of Christ, it had been usual for them to hold very frequent councils, and to assemble, by their delegates or representatives, at certain places, in order to deliberate and resolve on what might best promote their common interests. The most celebrated of these assemblies was their general national council, or that of the Amphictyons, which was held at Delphi, at stated seasons of the year, in spring and autumn, and to which were referred all controversies of any considerable weight or moment, that might have arisen between any of the confederated states. Vid. *Ubbonis Emmii Grœcia vetus*, tom. iii. p. 340, et seq. *Nouveau Dictionaire Hist. Crit.* par Chaufepied, tom. i, voce *Amphictyones.* These councils were not altogether discontinued, even after Greece had been reduced into a province by the Romans. The great council of the Amphictyons, in particular, continued, with the consent of the emperors, to hold its meetings, even down to the time when Tertullian wrote, as may be seen in Pausanias. In a province so much accustomed to councils, it is no wonder that the Christians should hit upon the thought, that it might redound to the welfare of the church, if, after the example of the Greek states, and particularly of the Amphictyons, assemblies or councils of associated Christians were to meet at certain stated seasons, and deliberate respecting their common interests. Light is hence thrown on canon xxx[th] of those bearing the title " Apostolical," and which are commonly attributed to Clement of Rome, as well as on the fifth of the Nicene ones, by both of which the bishops are enjoined to assemble in council twice in the year, namely, in the spring and fall. These were the identical times at which, as we have above stated, it was usual, even so low down as the second century, for the Amphictyons to hold their meetings; and hence I think it is evident, that it was the peculiar constitution and habits of their country which led the Greek Christians to think of establishing ecclesiastical councils ; and that, in constituting assemblies of this kind, they merely availed themselves, in the cause of religion, of a measure that had long been considered as productive of very essential advantages in the state. With regard to the different points thus touched upon, I can perceive a very wide field for discussion lying open before me ; but on the present occasion I am compelled to be studious of brevity.

[p. 269.] XXIII. **Effects produced by the introduction of this civil unity.** The *associations,* however, thus introduced amongst the churches, and the *councils* to which they gave rise, although not unattended with certain benefits and advantages, were, nevertheless, productive of so great an alteration in the general state of the church, as nearly to effect the entire subversion of its ancient constitution. For, in the first place, the primitive rights of the people, in consequence of this new arrangement of things, expeperienced a considerable diminution, inasmuch as, thenceforward, none but affairs of comparatively very trifling consequence were ever made the subject of popular deliberation and adjustment; the councils of the associated churches assuming to themselves the right of discussing and regulating every thing of moment or importance, as well as of determining all questions to which any sort of weight was attached. Whence arose two sorts of ecclesiastical law, the one public or general, and thenceforward termed " Canonical," from the canons; the other private or peculiar, consisting merely of such regulations as each individual church deemed it expedient, after the ancient manner, to enact for itself.—In the next place, the dignity and authority of the bishops were very materially augmented and enlarged. In the infancy, indeed, of councils, the bishops did not scruple to acknowledge that they appeared there merely as the ministers or legates of their respective churches, and that they were, in fact, nothing more than representatives acting from instructions: but it was not long before this humble language began, by little and little, to be exchanged for a loftier tone; and they at length took upon them to assert that they were the legitimate successors of the apostles themselves, and might consequently, of their own proper authority, dictate laws to the Christian flock. To what an extent the inconveniences and evils arising out of these preposterous pretensions reached in after times, is too well known to require any particular notice in this place.—Another effect which these councils had, was to break in upon and gradually destroy that absolute and perfect equality which had reigned amongst the bishops in the primitive times. For, as it was necessary that some certain place should be fixed on for the seat of council, and that the right of convening the assembly, and presiding therein as moderator, as well as of collecting the suffrages and preserving the records of its acts, should be vested in some one or other of its members, it, for the most part, became customary to give a preference in these respects to the chief city of the province and its bishop, and hence, in process of time, sprung up the dignity and authority of " metropolitans," a title conferred by way of distinction on the bishops of principal cities. These associations of churches, situated within one and the same province, soon gave rise to the practice of many different provinces 'associating together ; and hence a still greater disparity, by degrees, introduced itself amongst the bishops. In fine, this custom of holding councils becoming at length universally prevalent, the major part of the church(¹) assumed the form of a large civil commonwealth, made up of numerous inferior republics; to the preservation of which order of things, it being found expedient that a chief or superintending prelate should be appointed for each of the three grand divisions of the earth ; and that, in addition to this, a supreme power should be lodged in the [p. 270.] hands of some one individual bishop; it was tacitly assented to(²) that a certain degree of ecclesiastical preëminence should be recognised as belonging to the bishops of Antioch, Rome, and Alexandria, the principal cities in Asia, Europe, and Africa, and that the bishop of Rome, the noblest and most opulent city in the world, should moreover take the precedence amongst these principal bishops, or, as they were afterwards styled, *patriarchs*, and also assume the primacy of the whole Christian church throughout the world.(³)

(1) I purposely express myself after this manner, since it can be made appear, from unquestionable authority, that in every part of the then known world there were certain churches, and those too of considerable magnitude and consequence, (for instance, the African church, properly so called, in Africa; the Chaldaic and Persic in Asia, and that of Britain in Europe, to pass over others that might be mentioned,) which, although they adopted the practice of holding councils, and did not keep themselves entirely aloof from all association, yet declined to make a part of that grand Christian confederation which was gradually entered into by the rest ; and were, for a long time, inflexibly tenacious of their own just liberty and independence. The churches which thus tacitly declined joining the general association, and maintained no other community with those principal prelates who were styled patriarchs, than that of religion and charity, of themselves furnish us with an effectual argument in refutation of those who ascribe the origin of this association to our blessed Lord himself, and make it to have sprung from some law of his. For had it been the command of our Saviour that his church should take the form of a large commonwealth, most assuredly no Christian assembly would have laid claim to independence, and refused to acknowledge the authority of those who were appointed to preside over the general interests of the whole body.

(2) The council of Nice, the principal one of those that are termed Œcumenical, by its sixth canon, which treats of the pre-eminence of the bishops of Rome, Antioch, and Alexandria, places it out of all question that the dignity and authority of these prelates rested, not on divine right, nor on anything in the nature of an apostolic mandate, but solely and entirely on ancient usage **or**

tacit consent. Its commencement in Latin is, *Antiqua consuetudo servetur*, in Greek, τὰ ἀρχαῖα ἔθη κρατείτω. Vid. Lud. Ell. du Pin. *de Antiqua Ecclesiæ Disciplina*, p. 19, 20.

(3) The extent of the authority and power possessed in the primitive ages by these bishops, who were thus invested with the presidency of the larger ecclesiastical confederations, may, without much difficulty, be estimated when it is considered that they were raised, by tacit consent, above their brethren merely upon the principle of supplying some external link or bond whereby the minor associations, or churches, which were all independent of each other, might be held together. What the different metropolitans were in respect of their provinces, that was a patriarch in respect of a larger portion of the world. That great thing, therefore, which we term the *Hierarchy*, and which has, most unhappily, been the cause of so many disputes and wars amongst Christians, if it be examined into with impartiality, and traced back to the first ages of the church, will be found to have taken its rise from very small and inconsiderable beginnings ; in fact, to have originally sprung from nothing more than the plan adopted by the Greek churches of moulding their ecclesiastical establishment after the model of their national civil government and councils, and that [p. 271.] it was only by degrees that it attained to that degree of consequence and stability which has enabled it, in subsequent ages, to bid defiance to all the efforts of power and art to overthrow it.

XXIV. **Comparison of the Christian with the Jewish priesthood.** By whatever advantages this new form of ecclesiastical government might be attended, they were confined exclusively to pastors of the higher order, *i. e.* the bishops who sat in these councils as the representatives of their respective churches : but much about the same time there arose and quickly gained ground in the Christian world, an opinion respecting the nature of the functions wherewith the ministers of the church were invested, which tended, in no small degree, to augment the dignity and rights of the whole sacred body. Whilst the least probability remained that Jerusalem might, at one time or other, again rear its head from the dust, the Christian teachers and elders assumed to themselves no titles or distinctions, at least none but the most modest and humble ones ;(¹) but when the fate of that once glorious city had been finally sealed by Hadrian, and not the most distant hope could any longer be entertained by the Jews of seeing their ancient government re-established, these same pastors and ministers, for the most part, conceived a wish to have it believed by their flocks that they themselves had succeeded to the rights of the Jewish priesthood. The *bishops*, therefore made it their

22

business thenceforward to inculcate the notion that they were invested with a character resembling that of the great high priest of the Jews, and were consequently possessed of all those rights which had been recognized as belonging to the Jewish pontiff. The functions of the ordinary Jewish priests were, in like manner, stated to have devolved, though under a more perfect form, on the *presbyters* of the Christian church: and, finally, the *deacons* were placed on a parallel with the *Levites* or inferior ministers of the temple. Whether the comparison thus instituted between functions altogether opposite in their nature, had its origin in art and design, or was rather the offspring of ignorance and imprudence, is a thing not now to be ascertained; of this, however, there can be no doubt, that having once been approved of and admitted to be just, it not only gave rise to a variety of errors, and introduced a greater distinction between teachers and learners than seems consonant to the spirit of the Christian discipline, but also very materially added to the rights and emoluments of the ministers and dispensers of Christ's word.(²)

(1) Ignatius, in the commencement of his epistles, styles himself θεόφορον, *deiferum,* a title assumed by him, as it should seem, in common with other bishops of his time, and importing a man commissioned to make known to the world the will and commands of the Deity.

(2) This comparison of the Jewish with the Christian sacred order, amongst other things, unquestionably gave rise to the claim of tythes and first fruits, which is certainly of higher antiquity than the time of Constantine the Great. And it seems not at all unlikely that a desire of augmenting their income, which was but slender and uncertain, might have first suggested to certain of the bishops this plan of investing the ministers of the gospel with the rights of the Jewish priesthood. That the offering of the first fruits had already, in the age of which we are treating, come to be regarded as a matter of divine [p. 272.] right, is placed, as it were, beyond all doubt by Irenæus, who in his work *contra Hæreses,* lib. iv. cap. xxxii. § 5. p. 249. represents it as having been inculcated by Christ himself in the celebration of the last supper. *Christus suis discipulis dans consilium primitias Deo offerre ex suis creaturis, non quasi indigenti, sed ut ipsi nec infructuosi nec ingrati sint, eum qui ex creatura panis est, accepit et gratias egit, dicens, Hoc est meum corpus, &c.* And in cap. xxxiv. p. 250. we are told by him, *offerre igitur oportet Deo primitias ejus creaturæ, sicut et Moses ait, non apparebis vacuus, &c.* From which passages it is manifest that the Christian teachers had already conceived the plan of bettering their condition, by calling in the authority of the Mosaic law. That tithes had not, at this time, been established, at least in the Latin church, is, I think, equally to be proved from Irenæus, who, in cap. xxxiv. p. 250. says, *Et propter hoc illi quidem*

(the Jewish priests) *decimas suorum habebant consecratas: qui autem perceperunt libertatem* (*i. e.* the Christians) *omnia quæ sunt ipsorum ad dominicos decernunt usus, hilariter et libere dantes.* It is certain, however, that in the Greek and oriental churches they began to be adopted sooner than in the Latin ones, and were rendered, I am led to think, even so early as this century, inasmuch as mention is made of them by the Greek writers of the third century, and also in the apostolical constitutions, as of a thing well known and established.

XXV. **A taste for philosophy introduced amongst the Christians.** The external change thus wrought in the constitution of the church would have been, however, far less detrimental to the interests of Christianity, had it not been accompanied by others of an internal nature, which struck at the very vitals of religion, and tended, in no small degree, to affect the credit of those sacred writings on which the entire system of Christian discipline relies for support. Of these the most considerable and important are to be attributed to a taste for the cultivation of philosophy and human learning, which, during the preceding century, if not altogether treated with neglect and contempt by the Christians, had at least been wisely kept under, and by no means permitted to blend itself with religion; but in the age of which we are now treating, burst forth on a sudden into a flame, and spread itself with the utmost rapidity throughout a considerable part of the church. This may be accounted for, in some measure, from its having been the practice of the many Greek philosophers, who, in the course of this century, were induced to embrace Christianity, not only to retain their pristine denomination, garb, and mode of living, but also to persist in recommending the study of philosophy, and initiating youth therein. In proof of this, we may, from amidst numerous other examples, adduce in particular that of *Justin*, the celebrated philosopher and martyr.(') The immediate nursery and very cradle, as it were, of Christian philosophy, must, however, be placed in the celebrated seminary which long flourished at Alexandria under the denomination of the *Catechetical School.* For the persons who presided therein, in the course of the age of which we are treating, namely, *Pantænus, Athenagoras,* and *Clement* of [p. 273.] Alexandria, not only engaged with ardour in the cultivation of philosophy themselves, but also exerted their influence in persuading those whom they were educating for the office of teachers in the church, to follow their example in this respect, and

make it their practice to associate philosophical principles with
those of religion.(²)   It is to be observed, however, that what
was termed by these philosophy, was not the discipline of any
particular sect, but a selection of such principles and maxims
from all the different philosophic systems, as appeared to be most
consentaneous to right reason, and admitted of being so tempered
and modified as to reconcile them, in a certain degree, with Christian notions and tenets.(³)

(1) That *Justin Martyr* continued to wear the philosopher's mantle subsequently to his embracing Christianity, is evident from the exordium to his dialogue with Trypho, since Trypho is there made to say that he conceived him to
be a philosopher from his garb.   Origen, in a letter preserved by Eusebius,
Histor. Eccles. lib. vi. cap. xix. states that *Heraclas*, who was afterwards bishop
of Alexandria, was accustomed, previously to his studying philosophy, to appear
cloathed after the common fashion, κοινῆ ἰσθῆτι; but that, upon his placing himself under the tuition of Ammonius, he assumed the philosopher's mantle and
continued ever after to wear it; even notwithstanding his being received into
the order of presbyters.   Ἀποδυσάμενος καὶ φιλόσοφον ἀναλαβών σχῆμα μέχρι τῆ
δεῦρο τηρῖι.   Vid. Origen. *Opp.* tom. i. p. 2. edit. Benedict. Jerome in his *Catal.
Script. Eccles.* cap. xx. p. 86. edit. Fabric. speaking of the Christian philosopher
Aristides, says, *Aristides Atheniensis, philosophus eloquentissimus et sub pristino
habitu discipulus Christi*.   There can surely be no necessity for my adducing
more instances than these.   A splendid encomium on philosophy, from the pen
of Justin Martyr, occurs at p. 5, 6. of his dialogue *cum Tryphone*, where he pronounces it to be "the chief good," μέγιστον κτῆμα, "a thing most acceptable in
the sight of God, and the only sure guide to a state of perfect felicity."   A more
ancient encomiast of philosophy is not, I believe, to be pointed out amongst the
Christian writers.   He defines philosophy, p. 12, to be ἐπιστήμη τῆ ὄντος καὶ τῆ
ἀληθῶς ἐπίγνωσις. "the science of being," (that is, of those things which are real
and immutable,) " and the knowledge of truth."   The end or object of philosophy he pronounces to be εὐδαιμονίαν, " felicity."

(2) *Pantænus* was, without doubt, the first of the Egyptian Christians that
engaged in the study of philosophy : for Origen, in that epistle of his preserved
by Eusebius, *Histor. Eccles.* lib. vi. cap. xix. p. 221. wherein he replies to those
who had imputed a love of letters and philosophy to him as a fault, defends himself under the cover of only two examples, the one ancient, the other of recent
date : the former is that of Pantænus, the latter of Heraclas, whom he represents as having been one of his fellow-students in the school of Ammonius.
Had any one amongst the Christians of Egypt engaged in the cultivation of
philosophy before Pantænus, there can be no doubt but that Origen, whom nothing whatever that had taken place in antecedent times amongst the Egyptian
Christians appears to have escaped, would, by way of more readily vindicating
[p. 274.] himself, have brought forward ealier instances of an attachment to
philosophy than even that of Pantænus.—That I should say anything of *Athe-*

nagoras appears to me altogether unnecessary, as there is extant, in addition to the apology written by him in defence of the Christians, a tract of his concerning the resurrection of the dead, which is replete with evidence of the great extent to which he engaged in the cultivation of philosophy. *Clement*, the third president of the school of Alexandria in succession from Pantænus, and whom, by way of distinction, we usually style *the Alexandrian*, has left behind him, in various things which he published, abundant proof of his partiality for philosophy, such a partiality, indeed, as appears to have exceeded all ordinary limits. Jos. Aug. Orsi, in the *Ecclesiastical History* written by him in Italian, tom. ii. p. 406. considers this Clement as the first of the Christians writers that espoused the cause of philosophy. But he is deceived ; Justin Martyr, as we have already seen, had previously stood forth as its advocate and eulogist, and undoubtedly Pantænus in his day had done the same. There can be no question, however, but that Clement is to be ranked amongst the first and principal Christian defenders and teachers of philosophic science, indeed that he may even be placed at the head of those who devoted themselves to the cultivation of philosophy with an ardour that knew no bounds, and were so blind and misguided as to engage in the hopeless attempt of producing an accommodation between the principles of philosophic science and those of the Christian religion. He, himself expressly tells us in his *Stromata*, lib. i. cap. i. p. 326. opp. that he would not hand down Christian truth pure and unmixed, but ἀναμεμιγμένην τοῖς φιλοσοφίας δόγμασι, μᾶλλον δὲ ἐγκεκαλυμμένην καὶ ἐπικεκρυμμένην, "associated with, or rather veiled by and shrouded under the precepts of philosophy." For, according to him, the rudiments or seeds of celestial wisdom communicated by Christ to the world, lay hid in the philosophy of the Greeks, after the same manner as the esculent part of a nut lies concealed within a shell. And on this ground we find him in the same book, cap. iv. p. 331. entertaining a belief that Solomon, in *Prov.* ii. 3, 4, 5, 6, 7, meant to inculcate the study of philosophy, and attributing to the cultivation of philosophy a certain efficacy in rendering men just and upright, τοῖς ὑπὸ φιλοσοφίας δεδικαιωμένοις βοήθεια θησαυρίζεται. He had before said, at p. 319, that the souls of men were fed or nourished κατὰ τὴν ἑλληνικὴν φιλοσοφίαν, " by the philosophy of the Greeks," and added the above-noticed comparison of this species of philosophy with a nut, to which he frequently has recourse, by way of expressing his opinion of the nature and value of human wisdom. For he appears to have been firmly persuaded that the essence of the Greek philosophy was sound, wholesome, and salutary, in fact, that it was perfectly consonant to the spirit of Christian wisdom, but that it was compassed about and veiled from immediate observation by a cloud of superstition and idle fictions, just in the same way as the kernel of a nut is concealed by the shell, and that we should, therefore, make it our business industriously to penetrate this exterior covering, so as to discover the true relationship between human and divine wisdom. *Stromat.* lib. vii. p. 832. cap. ii. The origin of the Greek philosophy he, without scruple, attributes to the Deity himself, whom, however, in the communication of it to the world, he conceives to have availed himself of the instrumentality of inferior agents, οὗτός ἐστιν ὁ διδοὺς καὶ τοῖς Ἕλλησι τὴν φιλοσοφίαν διὰ τῶν ὑποδεεστέρων ἀγγέλων. *Hic* (the Deity) *est, qui dat Græcis philosophiam per inferiores angelos.* To the Christian

religion he assigns a superiority over philosophy, inasmuch as the Lord reserved the promulgation of it for himself: ἀλλ' ἡ μερὶς Κυρίῳ ἡ δόξα τῶν πιστευόντων, at
[p. 275.] *opinio credentium* (the religion professed by the Christians) *pars est
Domini* (was communicated by the Lord himself.) In explaining and illustrating his opinion on this head, he is lead to intimate his perfect conviction as to
a point on which we find him pretty plainly expressing his sentiments in other
places, and in which Justin Martyr coincides with him ; namely, that before
Christ's advent philosophy was the way to eternal life, and that, therefore, no
doubt can be entertained of the Grecian sages having obtained salvation. In
his *Stromat.* lib. i. cap. vii. p. 337. lib. vi. cap. viii. p. 773. he says, that philosophy
was divinely communicated to the Greeks as a special testament or covenant,
and that it in fact constitutes the basis of that doctrine which the world has
since received from Christ: τὴν δὲ φιλοσοφίαν καὶ μᾶλλον Ἕλλησιν εἶεν διαθήκην
οἰκείαν αὐτοῖς δεδόσθαι, ὑπόβαθρον ὅσαν τῆς κατὰ Χριστὸν φιλοσοφίας. In saying this,
however, he means it to be understood that the prince of darkness, whom he
terms the inveterate cultivator of tares, had plentifully disseminated his noxious
weeds in the philosophy of Greece as well as in that of the barbarous nations.
In the same book vi. *Stromat.* cap. xvii. p. 822. et seq. he urges many things in
favour of the dignity and excellence of philosophy, amongst which the following
passage is particularly worthy of remark : Εἰκότως ἦν Ἰυδαίοις μὲν νόμος, Ἕλλησι δὲ
φιλοσοφία μέχρι τῆς παρυσίας, ἐντεῦθεν δὲ ἡ κλῆσις ἡ καθολικὴ εἰς περίστιον δικαιοσύνης
λαὸν κατὰ τὴν ἐκ πίστεως διδασκαλίαν : *merito ergo Judæis quidem lex, Græcis
autem data est philosophia usque ad adventum* (of Christ:) *ex eo autem tempore
universalis est vocatio ad peculiarem populum justitiæ per eam quæ est ex fide
doctrinam* (the Christian religion.) The sense, then, entertained by Clement of
philosophy, is very clearly to be perceived. Previously to the coming of Christ,
philosophy had, according to his opinion, been the same thing to the Greeks
that the law of Moses was to the Hebrews. Both of them were originally
derived from God, who, however, in the communication of them to mortals,
availed himself of the ministration of angels. Both of them pointed out the
road to salvation ; the former to the Greeks, the latter to the Jews. Neither
the one nor the other system of discipline could pretend to absolute perfection,
nor did either of them preserve itself free from the adulteration of human opinions. In process of time, therefore, it pleased the Deity to impart to the whole
human race a more perfect wisdom, through Jesus Christ. Neither the law of
the Jews, nor the philosophy of the Greeks, however, is to be considered as
thereby abolished, but as in part perfected, and in part disencumbered of various faulty particulars, the offspring of mere human refinement and conceit.
To any one entertaining an opinion like this, it must of necessity appear that
the leading principles of Christianity are so to be understood and interpreted as
to make them accord with the maxims and precepts of the best and wisest of the
Grecian sages.—It will readily then, I think, be granted by every one who shall
duly consider the constancy with which the prefects of the school of Alexandria,
from the time of Pantænus, persisted in recommending and inculcating the
study of philosophy, that to this school and its masters is chiefly to be ascribed
that love of philosophic speculation to which the primitive Christians were evi-

dently strangers, but which towards the close of this century began to diffuse itself gradually throughout the whole church, and insensibly to supplant that holy simplicity which characterized Christianity during the first age. For further information respecting this celebrated school at Alexandria, which, whether it was productive of most benefit or detriment to the Christian cause, would, I believe, be found hard to determine, the reader may consult the *Antiqui-* [p. 276.] *tates Academicæ* of Herm. Conringius, p. 29.; a particular dissertation on the subject, by Andr. Schmidius, prefixed by Andr. Hyperius to this book *de Catechesi;* a work written in Italian, by Aulisius, *Delle Scuole Sacre*, lib. ii. cap. i. ii. p. 5–17. and cap. xxi. p. 92; *The History of Catechisms*, in German, by Langemackius, P. I. p. 86. 122. et seq. as well as other works.

(3) *Clement of Alexandria*, who certainly holds the first place amongst the patrons of philosophy, supplies us with this definition of it; (*Stromat.* lib. i. cap. vii. p. 338. edit. Potterian.) Φιλοσοφίαν δὲ ὲ τὴν Στωικὴν λέγω, ὐδὲ τὴν Πλατωνικὴν, ἢ τὴν Ἐπικυρείον τε, καὶ Ἀριστοτελικὴν, ἀλλ᾽ ὅσα εἴρηται παρ ἑκάςη τῶν αἱρέσεων τότων καλῶς, δικαιοσύνην μετὰ ἐυσεβῆς ἐπιςήμης ἐκδιδάσκοντα τῦτο σύμπᾶν τὸ ἐκλεκτικὸν φιλοσοφίαν φημί· ὅσα δὲ ἀνθρωπίνων λογισμῶν ἀποτεμόμενοι παρεχάραξαν, ταῦτα ὐκ ἄν ποτε θεῖα εἴποιμ᾽ἄν. *Philosophiam autem dico non Stoicam, nec Platonicam, aut Epicuream et Aristotelicam, sed quæcumque ab his sectis recte dicta sunt, quæ docent justitiam cum pia scientia, hoc totum selectum dico philosophiam: cetera autem quæ ex humanis ratiocinationibus præsecta adulteraverunt, ea nunquam divina dixerim.* Now all this, without question, appears to be well and wisely said, and perfectly accords with what is laid down respecting the nature of philosophy by Justin Martyr, in his *Dial. cum Tryphone*, p. 6. et seq. But the truth is, that every one who will be at the pains to turn over the writings of Clement himself, as well as those of his very celebrated disciple Origen, and of Justin, must very readily perceive that many things were regarded by them as perfectly consentaneous to right reason and the spirit of Christianity which are, in fact, not to be reconciled with either. Notwithstanding all the desire which these good men evince to persuade us that they entertained a partiality for no particular sect, they were certainly attached to the *Eclectics*, a sect that flourished formerly in Egypt, and considered everything as indisputable which had received the sanction of that sect. Of this not a doubt can remain with any one who will take the trouble to compare Clement and Origen with Philo Judæus, one equally a disciple of the Eclectic school. This sect of the Eclectics, of which a particular account is given by Ja. Brucker in his *Historia Philosophiæ critica*, although it culled something from every sect, was yet wont to give the preference or chief authority in everything relating to the Deity, the human race, and this nether world, to Plato, than whom, it was supposed, none had retained more of the original and genuine philosophy of human nature.

XXVI. **Contentions amongst the Christians with regard to philosophy.** The rise, however, of this taste for philosophical speculation, and the ascendancy which they perceived it gradually acquiring in the minds of so many of their teachers, became a source of the most poignant regret to all such as continued steadfastly attached to that ancient and simple species of piety which had been delivered down by the Apostles and their disciples; inasmuch as they saw reason to fear that the cause of celestial truth [p. 277.] might be thereby materially injured, as in reality proved to be the case, and that divine wisdom would not long retain either its proper value or dignity in the estimation of mankind. In consequence of this the Christian church became divided into two parties, which opposed each other with the utmost warmth; the one regarding every species of human learning, and more particularly philosophy, with detestation and contempt, and enjoining the brethren to maintain the faith in all its genuine simplicity; the other contending for the utility and excellence of philosophic disquisition, and encouraging the teachers of the church to occupy themselves in demonstrating the accordance of religion with the principles of right reason.(') The issue of this dispute, which lasted for a considerable while, at length was, that victory declared itself in favour of the patrons of philosophy, and that those teachers came to be most respected who, in unfolding the doctrines of religion, called in the aid of philosophical principles and precepts.

(1) Respecting the contention between the adversaries and friends of philosophy, abundant testimonies are to be adduced, both of this and the succeeding century. Amongst those of the age now under review, there is extant in Eusebius, *Histor. Eccles.* lib. v. cap. xxviii. p. 197. a remarkable passage of an unknown author, who had written a book in opposition to the errors of Artemon, and who inveighs severely against the Artemonites for neglecting the study of the Holy Scriptures, and devoting themselves to the cultivation of philosophy and the Aristotelian logic, endeavouring to find support for their errors respecting Christ in the arts and discipline of unbelievers, *artibus ac disciplinis infidelium,* (so Valesius translates the words ταις των απιστων τεχναις), and finally studying to obscure and deprave the simple religion of the New Testament, by encumbering it with the subtle refinements of vain and impious men, τη των αθέων πανεργία (that is, as we may gather from what he before says, the rules and precepts of the Aristotelian logic). In this passage there are two things that present themselves as chiefly deserving of remark. The first is, that the men who are therein reprehended, were accustomed to scrutinize such passages of scripture as were urged against them, by the very nicest logical test: a practice which this writer hesitates not to pronounce impious and intolerable. Κἄν αυτοῖς προτείνη τις ῥητὸν γραφῆς θεικῆς, ἐξετάζουσι πότερον συνημμένον η διεζευγμένον δύναται ποιῆσαι σχῆμα συλλογισμῦ. *Quod si quis aliquem divinæ scripturæ locum eis objecerit, examinant, utrum connexum an disiunctum syllogismi genus ex eo confici possit.* The other thing that particularly

offers itself to observation in the passage we allude to is, that the class of men whose opinions and practices it combats were much devoted to the study of geometry, and applied to Christian theology that mode of teaching and demonstrating which is peculiar to geometricians: καταλίποντες δὲ τὰς ἁγίας τῦ Ͽεῦ γραφὰς, γεωμετρίαν ἐπιτηδεύουσιν, ὡς ἂν ἐκ τῆς γῆς ὄντες καὶ ἐκ τῆς γῆς λαλῶντες. *Relictis atque abjectis sacris Dei scripturis, geometriæ student, quippe qui terrestres sint et loquantur terrena.*—Ἐυκλείδης γ ὂν παρὰ τίσιν αὐτῶν φιλοπόνως γεωμετρεῖται. *Euclidis igitur geometria apud nonnullos eorum studiose excolitur.* There is, therefore, nothing done at present for which a precedent is not to be found in former times. When we find the culture of philosophy, of logic, and geometry, placed by this man amongst the crimes of heretics, it is pretty plain in [p. 278.] what degree of repute these studies were held by the generality of Christians in those days.

Many very distinct vestiges of this dispute respecting the value of philosophy and its use in theology, are to be met with in the writings of *Clement* of Alexandria, who, moreover, sometimes takes occasion to censure with sufficient acrimony those who portended great detriment to the cause of Christianity from the introduction of philosophy into the church, and called upon all the sincere professors of Christianity to revert to the ancient simplicity of the apostles. To those who read him, it will be obvious that the things which are agitated with so much eagerness in the present day, engrossed equally the attention of former ages, and that the contention between faith and reason, by which the world has been disturbed so greatly of late, is by no means a matter of recent origin. In the very outset of the work, to which he gives the title of *Stromata*, we find him undertaking the defence of philosophy. The opponents of philosophy he, in lib. i. cap. i. p. 326, divides into *two classes:* the *first* consisting of the more moderate ones, or those who contended merely that philosophy was of no use. " I am no stranger," says he, " to what is urged by some, whose ignorance leads them to see danger in every thing, namely, that our attention ought to be exclusively directed to things of the first necessity, and on which we may build our faith, and not be suffered to occupy itself in foreign and fruitless studies, such as busy and detain the mind without conducting it to any certain end." The *other class* was composed of those who were more vehement in their opposition to philosophy, contending that it was not merely useless but pernicious, and the invention of the parent of evil. " Others, however," he proceeds, " carry their hostility so far as to rank philosophy with the greatest of evils, and consider it as invented for the ruin of mankind by some malignant adversary," πρὸς τινὸς εὑρετῦ πονηρῦ, that is, as he himself explains the expression in another place, " the devil."—To the former of these he artfully replies, cap. ii. p. 327: (I.) If the inutility of philosophy were even as certain as you pretend, still it is a thing both useful and necessary that its vanity and emptiness should be demonstrated, and as this cannot be done without a knowledge of its principles, we have, even here, an argument that the study of philosophy is not without its use; εἰ καὶ ἄχρηστος ἔιη φιλοσοφία, εἰ ἐυχρηστος ἡ τῆς ἀχρηστίας βεβαίωσις, ἐυχρηστος. That I have assigned to these words their true sense is, I think, placed out of all doubt by what follows. Proceeding with his reply he observes

(II.) That even if philosophy, when regarded apart by itself, was of no use whatever, and contributed nothing towards aiding the Christian in the attainment of his grand object, yet still an acquaintance with it must be highly ornamental to the character of a Christian teacher, and by giving him a certain dignity and authority in the eyes of his auditors, must enable him, with the greater ease, to make an impression on the minds of those who were hostile to the cause of religion.—With the other class, who considered philosophy as pernicious, and nothing better than an invention of the devil himself, he disputes at much length, and, as we are bound to confess, neither unskilfully nor idly. We shall merely give the substance of a few of his arguments. (I.) In the first place, then, he contends that philosophy is not calculated to draw men away from faith or piety, as its adversaries affirmed, but was rather to be looked upon as the safeguard of religion, inasmuch as it supplied men with a fuller demonstration of faith, συγγυμνασίαν τινα πίςεως ἀποδεικτικήν. (II.) That from a collation or comparison together of such of the principles of philosophy [p. 279.] and Christianity as were inconsistent with or opposed to each other, the truth was rendered more apparent, and our stock of knowledge consequently much improved; than which nothing could be more desirable or important. (III.) That our conviction of mind must necessarily be strengthened and confirmed by our acquiring that more accurate knowledge of religion which was to be obtained through the assistance of philosophy ; βέβαιον λαμβανόντων πεῖσμα τῆς ἀληθῦς καταλήψεως. And here, by the bye, I must observe, that I cannot help wishing for a new translation of Clement by some one well skilled in the Greek language. The old one by Hervetus fails, in many places, to give us the sense of the original, and in others expresses it in a very obscure man_ ner. (IV.) That a knowledge of philosophy was requisite in order to repel and put to silence the enemies of the Christian faith, cap. iii. p. 325, since it was the practice of some of these to make sport of the truth, and represent it as replete with barbarism ; τὸ βάρβαρον ἐν παιδέια τετίμενοι : whilst others were accustomed to attack the Christians with various little teazing subtilties and jests, which, although founded in fallacy, were yet conceived with too much art to be exposed and refuted without some degree of skill. That we ought to provide ourselves, therefore, with philosophy, as a kind of defensive armour for repelling the weapons of sophistry. Cap. v. p. 331.—From these arguments we may pretty well collect the motives by which the Christian teachers of the second century were led to cultivate philosophy. There was one inducement, however, of which Clement takes no notice, but which I cannot help considering as having been a very principal one. The Christian teachers were well aware of what essential benefit it would be in promoting their cause, not only with the multitude, but also amongst men of the higher orders, could the philosophers, whose authority and estimation with the world was unbounded, be brought to embrace Christianity. With a view, therefore, of accomplishing this desirable object, they not only adopted the study of philosophy themselves, but became loud in their recommendation of it to others, declaring that the difference between Christianity and philosophy was but trifling, and consisted merely in the former being of a nature somewhat more perfect than the latter. And it is most certain that this kind of conduct was so far productive of the desired effect, as to cause not a few of the philosophers to enrol themselves under the Christian banner. Those who have perused the various works written by such of the ancient philosophers as had been induced to embrace Christianity, cannot have failed to remark, that the Christian discipline was regarded by all of them in no other light than as a certain mode of philosophising.

But to return to Clement, in other places, *Stromat.* lib. i. cap. xvii., xviii. p. 366, we find him adverting to a third opinion entertained by many Christians respecting philosophy, and which holds, as it were, a middle station between the two already noticed. This opinion was, that philosophy had been surreptitiously brought down from heaven, and communicated to mankind by those angels whom, according to the ancients, a love of pleasure had induced to rebel against God, and take to themselves wives from amongst the daughters of men. Ἔνιοι δὲ δυνάμεις τινὰς ὑποβεβηκοίας ἐμπνεῦται τὴν πᾶσαν φιλοσοφίαν ὑπειλήφασιν. *Nonnulli autem* (whom he distinguishes from those who maintain that the devil himself was the author of philosophy) *universam philosophiam quasdam potestates e cœlo delapsas inspirasse existimant.* To this opinion many of that age subscribed; amongst whom we find that *Hermias,* who was the author of a tract that has reached our days under the title of *Irrisio Philosophiæ,* and is commonly annexed to Tatian. In the exordium of his little work this writer says, δοκεῖ γάρ μοι τὴν ἀρχὴν (φιλοσοφίαν) εἰληφέναι ἀπὸ τῆς τῶν Ἀγγέλων ἀποστασίας. *Videtur mihi (philosophia) ab angelorum defectione principium repetiisse.* In proof of this he adduces the strifes and contentions of philosophers. Indeed [p. 280.] *Clement* himself appears not entirely to dissent from this opinion. Vid. *Stromat.* lib. v. p. 650. Those who thought thus respecting the origin of philosophy, could not, of course, altogether reject and condemn it, but amongst them there were not wanting some, however, who deemed it sinful for men to avail themselves of what had reached them thus surreptitiously, and through so polluted a channel. To these Clement replies, that it was indeed a very heinous crime in the fallen angels to be guilty of this theft, but that, notwithstanding the circumstance of its having been stolen, the excellence and value of the thing itself had been neither sullied nor diminished. Various other arguments, by which Clement defends the cause of philosophy, and combats those of the Christians who would fain have arrested its progress, are to be met with in his *Stromata.* Great pains are particularly taken by him in refuting such as maintained that philosophy was invented by the evil one, for the purpose of deceiving the human race and leading them astray from the truth; from whence we may infer, that this opinion was more generally received, and had taken deeper root than the rest in the minds of the multitude. To what I have above noticed I shall merely add what he urges in reply to those, who were accustomed to cast in the teeth of the advocates of philosophy the words of St. Paul in *Col.* ii. 8. admonishing the Christians to beware of being spoiled through philosophy. In the opinion of Clement, *Stromat.* lib. vi. cap. viii. p. 771, 799. St. Paul is to be considered as addressing himself in this place to the more perfect Christians, or, as he terms them, those " who had attained the very heights of Gnostic intelligence, τὸν δὲ τῇ γνωστικῇ μεταλαμβάνοντα ὕψος," and that what he meant was to caution such Christians against reverting to the philosophy of the Greeks, inasmuch as this species of philosophy was merely a kind of elementary learning, στοιχειώδη διδασκαλία, comprehending nothing more than the first rudiments of wisdom, a want of which could well be dispensed with in Christians, who had arrived at the highest degree of divine information. But all this is evidently strained, and in direct opposition to the obvious and natural sense conveyed by the words of St. Paul.

XXVII. **The school of Ammonius Saccas.** That particular scheme or mode of philosophising, which was adopted at the first by the præfects of the school of Alexandria, and a few others, did not indeed maintain its ground for any great length of time, but was by degrees considerably departed from : the spirit of philosophising, however, so far from experiencing any decline or abatement, continued to increase and diffuse itself more and more, particularly towards the close of this century, when a new sect sprung up at Alexandria under the title of "The Modern Platonists." The founder of this sect was Ammonius Saccas, a man of a subtile penetrating genius, but prone to deviate, in many things, from right reason, and too much inclined to indulge in ridiculous flights of imagination.(¹) In addition to a multitude of others who flocked to this man for instruction, his lectures were constantly attended by a great number of Christians, who were inflamed with an eager desire after knowledge, and of whom two, namely, Origen and Heraclas, became afterwards very distinguished characters, the former succeeding to the presidency of the school, the latter to that of the church of Alexandria.(²) By the Christian disciples of Ammonius, and more particularly by Origen, who in the suc-
[p. 281.] ceeding century attained to a degree of eminence scarcely credible, the doctrines which they had derived from their master were sedulously instilled into the minds of the youth with whose education they were entrusted, and by the efforts of these again, who were subsequently, for the most part, called to the ministry, the love of philosophy became pretty generally diffused throughout a considerable portion of the church.

(1) Particular celebrity attaches itself, both in sacred and literary history, to the name of *Ammonius Saccas*, a philosopher of the Alexandrian school, from whom proceeded those philosophical fanatics, the "*Modern Platonists*," who, from the third century to the sixth, lorded it with despotic sway over every other sect throughout nearly the whole of the Roman empire. That the life and actions of a man capable of effecting so great a change in the aspect

of Christianity as well as philosophy, should be, for the most part, so completely involved in obscurity as to defy elucidation, is certainly much to be regretted ; since, could we obtain a more accurate knowledge as to these, it would, no doubt, enable us, with much greater readiness, to account for many opinions and customs that sprung up amongst the Christians subsequently to his time. Whatever could be obtained on the subject from ancient authors, hath been diligently collected together and illustrated, with his usual ability, by J. Brucker, *Histor. Critic. Philosoph.* tom. ii. p. 205, et seq. who has also entered at much length into the history of the sect of which Ammonius was the founder. The reader may also consult Jo. Alb. Fabricius, *Biblioth. Græc.* lib. iv. cap. xxvi. p. 159.—Respecting the religion of Ammonius, in particular, there is considerable doubt. *Porphyry,* who had had the opportunity of hearing Plotinus, one of the principal disciples of Ammonius, says, (apud Euseb. *Histor. Eccles.* lib. vi. cap. xix. p. 220.) that he was born of Christian parents, but that, on arriving at man's estate, he went over to Paganism. *Eusebius,* however, contradicts Porphyry, and asserts that Ammonius continued stedfast in the Christian faith to the end of his life. This discordance in the testimony of Eusebius and Porphyry, as to the religion in which Ammonius ended his days, has occasioned much difference of opinion among men of erudition, some giving credit to the former, others to the latter. Those who hold with Porphyry have certainly arguments of considerable weight on their side, and feeling sensibly their force, I was some time since induced to express my conviction of the apostacy of Ammonius from Christianity. To pass over other things, who, let me ask, can easily persuade himself that the sect of the modern Platonists, than whom scarcely any set of men ever occasioned greater evils and calamities to the Christians, could possibly have been founded by a man who was actually himself a Christian ? The testimony of *Eusebius,* as to this matter, is not of the slightest weight ; for it is evident that he was misled by the name, and confounded the philosopher Ammonius with a Christian writer whose name was similar. The Ammonius to whom Eusebius alludes had, he tells us, written a variety of things : Ammonius the philosopher, we know for certain, never published any thing.—On a full review, however, of the merits of this controversy, I feel inclined to believe that Ammonius, although, for the most part, an apostate in heart, and thoroughly averse from the principles entertained by the Christians in general, yet never openly seceded from the church, but [p. 282.] disguised the real nature and tendency of his discipline. Learned men will see whether there be any weight in the reasons by which I have been led to this conjecture. (I.) When Ammonius first opened a school at Alexandria, and for a long time afterwards, he was undoubtedly, in the true sense of the word, a Christian. For many years Origen, Heraclas, and various others of the Christian youth, who had been captivated by a love of philosophy, sat under his tuition. But the teachers of the Alexandrian church would surely never have permitted these young men to select for their master a perfidious renegado. Apostates of this description were regarded in the light of impious pests ; and the most positive injunctions were given for no one to hold converse with them. This one observation alone is sufficient to detract much from the authority of Porphyry's testimony respecting the defection of Ammonius ; for, according to that, Ammonius, as soon as he was of an age to think for himself, and to comprehend the first rudiments of philosophy, renounced the profession of Christianity ; which is notoriously false. (II.) There was no necessity for Ammonius to secede from the Christian church. So far from entertaining any thing like an enmity to Christ, he held him in veneration as a person of a divine character and a teacher of celestial wisdom. What he took exception to, was the interpretation given by Christians to the maxims and precepts of the gospel. It was, therefore, very possible for him to continue amongst the Christians, and to join with them in paying every homage to Christ, but at the same time to assume the liberty of privately expounding the religion of the gospel according to the sense in which he had been led to view it himself. But it may, perhaps, be objected to me, that Ammonius, although he entertained a veneration for Christ, yet held it proper to worship the heathen deities, a thing altogether incompatible with Christian principles, and that, in the performance of this worship, therefore, he must necessarily have separated himself from the church : but this difficulty is, I think, easy to be gotten rid of by any one acquainted with what the Ammonian discipline actually was. What Ammonius enjoined was, not that these gods should be worshipped, but that they should not be treated with contempt; not that the worship of them was necessary, but that it was justifiable, decent, allowable. By the multitude, whose ruling passion is an eager appetite for bodily and sensual gratification, it was but fitting, according to the principles of the Ammonian sect, that these gods should have every sort of homage paid them, inasmuch as they were constituted by the supreme deity the guardians and dispensers of all those good things which minister to the delight of the senses; but no necessity whatever could exist for their being either invoked or worshipped by a wise man and a philosopher, whose object was the purifying of his soul, and keeping it, by means of meditation, as far as possible removed from every influence of the body. The gratifications of sense not entering into the views of the latter, he might of course, they held, omit cultivating the favour of those from whom such gratifications are to be sought, and should confine his adoration to the parent of souls alone, the Supreme Being. (III.) The disciples of Ammonius, as Porphyry declares in *Vita Plotini. c. iii.* agreed amongst themselves, in conformity, no doubt, to an injunction of their preceptor, that they would not make commonly known the more abstruse and reconlite doctrines of their master, from which resolution, however, they afterwards thought proper to recede. Ammonius himself also ever declined committing his opinions to writing, and would communicate them only by word of mouth, lest it might occasion him disturbance. But in none of his principles or maxims that have been divulged by his disciples, is there any, even the minutest thing that could possibly excite against him any ill-will, or bring him into any sort of danger amongst the heathen worshippers. [p. 283.] It appears, therefore, most likely that his motive for concealing the leading principles of his doctrine, was a fear of the light in which they would have been regarded by the Christians, amongst whom he had been born and passed the greater part of his life ; for had they once been able to discover the true nature and tendency of his doctrine, not a doubt can exist but that his excommunication would have followed as a matter of course. (IV.) The circumstance of its being positively denied by Eusebius, and, after him, by Jerome, *Catal. Scriptor. Eccles.* cap. lv. that Ammonius ever deserted Christianity, although in regard to this they may not be strictly correct, is yet an argument that his apostacy was a thing utterly unknown to these most experienced Christian writers, and not only to them but to the whole Christian world. But how, let me ask, could the public defection of so great a man and philosopher, if it had ever occurred, have failed to make a noise in the world, or altogether have escaped recollection?

(2) Origen, in an epistle preserved by Eusebius, *Histor. Eccles.* lib. vi. cap. xix. p. 221. says that Heraclas, at the time of his becoming acquainted with him, had been nearly five years under the instruction of a certain professor of philosophy. The name of this instructor he does not mention : but since he himself was taught philosophy by Ammonius, there can be no doubt but that it was to this professor he alluded. The probability is, that even at that time, the credit of Ammonius was much on the decline in Egypt, and that on that account Origen studiously avoided naming him, lest the discovery of who had been his master, might supply his adversaries with the means of exciting a still greater degree of animosity towards him.

XXVIII. **The philosophy of Ammonius.** The favourite object with Ammonius, as appears from the disputations and writings of his disciples, was that of not only bringing about a reconciliation between all the different philosophical sects, Greeks as well as barbarians,(¹) but also of producing a harmony of all religions, even of Christianity and heathenism, and prevailing on all the wise and good men of every nation to lay aside their contentions and quarrels, and unite together as one large family, the children of one common mother. With a view to the accomplishment of this end, therefore he maintained, that divine wisdom had been first brought to light and nurtured amongst the people of the east by Hermes Trismegistus, Zoroaster, and other great and sacred characters ;(²) that it was warmly espoused and cherished by Pythagoras and Plato amongst the Greeks;(³) from whom, although the other Grecian sages might appear to have dissented, yet that, with nothing more than the exercise of an ordinary degree of judgment and attention, it was very possible to make this discordance entirely vanish, and show that the only points on which these eminent characters disagreed were but of trifling moment, and that it was chiefly in their manner of expressing their sentiments that they varied.(⁴) The religion of the multitude, he also contended, went hand in hand with philosophy, and with her had shared the [p. 284.] fate of being by degrees corrupted and obscured with mere human conceits, superstition, and lies: that it ought therefore to be brought back to its original purity, by purging it of this dross, and expounding it upon philosophical principles: and that the whole which Christ had in view by coming into the world, was—to reinstate and restore to its primitive integrity, the wisdom of the ancients,—to reduce within bounds the universally prevailing dominion of superstiton,—and in part to correct, and in part to exterminate, the various errors that had found their way into the different popular religions. This great design of bringing about an union of all sects and religions, the offspring of a mind certainly not destitute of genius, but distracted by fanaticism, and scarcely at all under the dominion of reason, required, in order to its execution, not only that the most strained and unprincipled interpretations should be given to ancient sentiments, maxims, documents, and narratives, but also that the assistance of frauds and fallacies should be called in: hence we find the works which the disciples of Ammonius left behind them abounding in things of this kind; so much so indeed, that it is impossible for them ever to be viewed in any other light than as deplorable monuments of wisdom run mad.

(1) The sentiments of the sect, as to this, are clearly expressed by the emperor *Julian*, than whom it could never boast of a more illustrious member, *Oratione* VI. *contra Cynicos*, opp. p. 184. Edit. Spanhemian. Μηδεὶς ὃν ἡμῖν τὴν φιλοσοφίαν εἰς πολλὰ διαιρείτω, μηδὲ εἰς πολλὰ τεμνέτο. μᾶλλον δὲ μὴ πολλὰς ἐκ μιᾶς ποιείτω. Ὥσπερ γὰρ ἀλήθεια μία, ὕτω δὲ καὶ φιλοσοφία. *Quocirca philosophiam nobis plures in partes nemo dividat : vel potius plures ex una non faciat. Ut enim veritas una est ; ita et philosophia.* But, observes the emperor, it may be objected, in the first place, that there are a multitude of different sects. These sects, however, he replies, are merely different modes of coming at the truth, and ought to be considered in no other light than as different routes by which men may travel towards the same place. For as those who design to go to Athens, are by no means restricted to one particular road, but are at liberty to adopt different courses by sea as well as by land; so they who are in quest of the truth may pursue different modes of arriving at it. But it may be objected, secondly, he remarks, that, of those who have adopted these different modes, many have wandered out of the way and lost themselves. His answer is, that this is very true ; but let any one only be at the pains of ascertaining the courses chalked out by the respective parents or founders of these sects, and he will find them all consistent and tending to the same end, πρωτεύσαντας δὲ ἐν τῇ ἑκάστῃ τῶν διερετιῶν σκοπείτο καὶ πάντα εὑρήσει σύμφωνα. *Unius cujusque sectæ principes aspiciat ille, et quam sint omnia consentanea cognoscet.* This was the very principle adopted by

Ammonius, whose wish it was to bring all the good and wise of all nations under one and the same rule and discipline. The followers of Aristotle and of Plato, said he, may indeed differ and fall out, as may also the pholosophers of Greece and the barbarous nations; but let any one go back to the first origin of the different sects, and he will find them all consentaneous.

(2) It is plain, from the writings of *Plotinus, Proclus, Simplicius, Damascius,* and others of the Ammonian school, whose works have come down [p. 285.] to our times in sufficient number, that this sect referred the origin of all wisdom to the east, and were ever fond of citing as authorities the writings of *Hermes,* the oracles of *Zoroaster,* the verses of *Orpheus,* and I know not what other relics of the ancient philosophers of Egypt and the east. Nor do I think it by any means an improbable conjecture of some of the learned, that the writings of Hermes now extant, as well as the magic oracles, which are for the most part attributed to Zoroaster, were in fact the productions of the more recent Platonic school. Of the very great partiality entertained by this sect for the ancient philosophy of the Assyrians and Egyptians, which they contended was in every respect consentaneous to their own system of discipline, there is, amongst others, a notable testimony extant in the well-known work of Jamblicus *de Mysteriis Ægyptiorum;* the author of which in lib. i. cap. i. ii. unequivocally intimates that Pythagoras and Plato sought their philosophy from Egypt; and, to use his very words, *antiquas Mercurii columnas lectitantes philosophiam inde constituisse.* The same author, as is observed by Gale in his annotations, p. 184. although he makes Hermes the parent of all wisdom, yet, in no very obscure terms, admits that, even before his time, the Chaldeans had been in the habit of philosophising. That Ammonius himself not only instilled into the minds of his followers a veneration for this barbarous philosophy, as it was termed, but also placed the fountain of all wisdom in Upper Asia, in Chaldea, Persia, and India, is plain from what has been handed down to us by Porphyry in his Life of that eminent disciple of the Ammonian school, Plotinus, cap. iii. p. 96, 97. edit. Fabrician, vol. iv. *Biblioth Græc.* For he states him to have attained to such a degree of proficiency, under Ammonius, that he even came to the determination of further prosecuting his studies amongst the magi of Persia and India, and intended to have gone thither with the army of the emperor Gordion; Συνέχως τῶ Ἀμμωνίω παραμένοντα, τοσαύτην ἕξιν ἐν φιλοσοφία κτήσασθαι, ὡς καὶ τῆς παρὰ τοῖς Πέρσαις ἐπιτηδευομένης, πεῖραν λαβεῖν πνῦσαι καὶ τοῖς παρ᾽ Ἰνδοῖς κατορθαμένης. *Sudulus audivit* (for eleven years) *Ammonium, tantumque in philosophia profecit, ut philosophiæ insuper in qua Persæ se exercebant facere periculum affectaverit, atque etiam sapientiam precpiue apud Indos probatam prosequi constituerit.* Plotinus could certainly never have imbibed this anxious desire to acquaint himself with the maxims and tenets of the Persians and Indians, had he not heard his master extol them and declare that philosophy had been communicated to Egypt from the east. Hence too it was, that when those degenerate Christians, who are distinguished by the title of Gnostics, brought forward what they termed the oracles and writings of Zoroaster, Zostrian, and others of the eastern magi, with a view of proving that their own principles were strictly in unison with the ancient philosophy of the east, Plotinus, Porphyry, and others of the

Ammonian school, immediately made it their business to destroy the credibility of these writings, by showing that they were not the productions of those illus- trious characters to whom they were ascribed, as the reader will find related at length by Porphyry in his *Life of Plotinus*. cap. xvi. p. 118, 119. For, unques- tionably, these latter would never have troubled themselves to do this, had they [p. 286.] not earnestly wished to have it generally believed that their own doc- trine was the same with that wisdom which Zoroaster and other philosophers of the east had drawn from above, and communicated to mankind.

(3) *Ammonius* was evidently desirous of being thought a Platonist, and the title of Platonists was the denomination assumed by the whole body of his dis- ciples, as the reader may find proved from the testimony of ancient writers, by Brucker in his *History of Philosophy*, and by myself, in my dissertation *de Ec- clesia per recentiores Platonicos turbata*. It may, indeed, at first appear some- what strange that men who imagined Plato to have learnt his philosophy from the Egyptians, and the Egyptians themselves to have been indebted for their discipline to the people of the east, should have chosen to denominate them- selves after the Grecian philosopher. Why not term themselves the disciples of Hermes, or Zoroaster, whom they reverenced as the very parents of philo- sophy ? Our wonder, however, must cease when it is considered that Ammo- nius was of Grecian origin, that his auditors were Greeks, and that it was, moreover, the object of his disciples to acquire credit and obtain for themselves a reputation amongst the Greeks. From the Egyptians they, of course, had nothing to expect, inasmuch as these were always accustomed to look for in- structions to the priests and wise men of their own nation, not to Greeks : but the Greeks, attached beyond measure to every thing of their own, held, as is well known, the philosophy of what they termed barbarous nations, in the most sovereign contempt. It being a primary object, then, with Ammonius and his disciples to conciliate the favour of the Greeks, they were under the necessity of selecting for a patron some one or other of those whom the Greeks regarded as philosophers ; and amongst these they could find none whom they could adopt as such with greater propriety and convenience than Plato.

(4) The scheme thus entertained by Ammonius, of doing away all dissen- sions amongst philosophers, and making it appear that all the ancient sects, par- ticularly the Platonic and the Aristotelian, were agreed as to everything of mo- ment, is distinctly unfolded by that illustrious disciple of the Ammonian school, *Hierocles :* (*Lib. de Fato* apud *Phot. Biblioth.* cod. ccxiv. and cod. ccccli. p. 283. and 730.) and whatever writings we have extant of any of his followers, con- cur in placing this matter out of all controversy.

XXIX. **The theoretical or speculative philosophy of Ammonius.** But to descend more into particulars. Ammonius in the first place adopted the ancient and generally received principles of the Egyptians respecting the Deity, the world, the soul, providence, the power of dæmons, and the like. Agreeably, for instance, to what we well know to have been the doctrine maintained by the

Egyptian philosophers of old, he contended that every thing was a constituent part of one great whole:(') that the Deity could be severed from this universe only in imagination, or, which is the same thing, that this world had flowed from all eternity from the Deity: which is, in fact, assigning to the world an existence of equal duration with that of the Deity, although of a different kind; that all minds were equal in point of nature, but of very different degrees; that they were all, without exception, the offspring of the divine essence, and had, therefore, formerly all partaken of a state of bliss in the regions above: that most minds of the inferior order, being stimulated by a desire to enjoy [p. 287.] those pleasures which were to be derived to the senses from an alliance with matter, had descended into terrestrial bodies:(²) that every man, therefore, in addition to a sensitive and mutable soul derived from the soul of the universe, possesses, inclosed within his mortal frame, a mind unchangeable and nearly related to the Deity himself; and that hence it is the duty of a wise man to ascend in spirit to the parent of all things, and to strive by every means in his power to hold communion with him. From minds of the higher order, or, as they were termed, dæmons, the Deity had, he asserted, given to the different nations of the earth superintendents and guardians, and to the different departments of nature governors and directors. Certain of these, distinguished beyond the rest for their virtue and power, he considered as presiding over the sun, the moon, the planets, and the other stars; whilst of the remainder, to whom was entrusted the care of inferior and terrene things, many were actuated by vicious propensities; and some were so completely destitute of every virtuous and dignified principle, as even to rejoice over others' ills, and burn, as it were, with the lust of doing harm. His next care was to incorporate these principles with the Platonic discipline, a task of but little labour, inasmuch as, with the exception of but a few things, the tenets of Ammonius and those of the Athenian sage, were not distinguished from each other by any very material shades of difference.(³) In the last place he exerted every possible ingenuity and address in giving to the dogmas of the remaining sects, nay even to the fables of the ancient poets, and the history of the heathen deities, that kind of interpretation which made them appear in perfect unison with his system; and whenever he met with any thing in either of these that could by no means be brought to harmonise therewith, he rejected it as totally unfounded in reason.(')

(1) That the whole system of the Ammonian philosophy was built on that discipline which was professed by the Egyptian priests, and which they made it their boast to have derived from *Hermes,* is to be proved, as well from a variety of other things, as in particular from this, that the very same dogma on which all the wisdom of the Egyptians rested for support, constituted also the leading principle of the Ammonian school, from whence all its other maxims and tenets took their rise, *viz. that all things are from God, all things are in God, and all things are one; God and the universe constitute one whole, nor can they be separated except in imagination.* Those who are conversant in the antiquities of Egypt, well know that this dogma comprehends the whole of the secret wisdom of that nation. The reader will find this treated of at much length by the author of that discourse *de Natura Deorum,* which is attributed to *Hermes Trismegistus,* and which, from its being generally thought to have been translated into Latin by Apuleius, is commonly printed amongst the works of this latter author. He will find also the other principles which we have here enumerated, there adverted to. See moreover Euseb. *Preparat.* [p. 288.] *Evangel.* lib. iii. cap. ix. as also what is remarked by Cudworth in his *Intellectual System,* tom. i. p. 404. et seq. And that this same leading principle was most warmly espoused by Plotinus, Proclus, Simplicius, Jamblicus, and the whole herd of the Modern Platonists, is beyond a doubt; for what other than this do they say, when they assert the world to be coupled with God, and from all eternity to have emanated from God? Only let us attend to the prayer of Plotinus, the most famous of the disciples of Ammonius, offered up when he was dying, as recorded by his scholar Porphyry, in the history of his life, cap. ii. p. 94. Μέλλων δὲ τελευτᾶν - - - - εἰπὼν ὅτι σὲ ἔτι περιμένω καὶ Φήσας πειρᾶσθαι τὸν ἐν ἡμῖν θεὸν ἀνάγειν πρὸς τὸ ἐν τῷ παντὶ θεῖον. *Quum vero morti appropinquaret* - - - - - *adhuc te, inquit, expecto, atque equidem jam annitor, quod in nobis divinum est ad divinun ipsum quod viget in universo redigere.*

(2) Hence we may account for what Porphyry says of Plotinus' appearing to be, as it were, ashamed of the connection of his soul with the body ; ἐώκει μὲν ἀισχυνομένω ὅτι ἐν σώματι εἴη, *pudore quodam affici videtur, quod anima ejus in corpore esset.* Vit. Plotin. cap. i. p. 91. where observe what Fabricius has remarked on this passage.

(3) The discipline of Plato differs in many respects from the wisdom of the Egyptians ; in not a few things, however, the congruity between them is absolute and perfect. To incorporate the one with the other, therefore, could not be a work of much labour. Respecting that dogma which we have seen to be, as it were, the chief and corner-stone of the Egyptian and Ammonian philosophy, namely, that of the Deity and this universe constituting one great whole, there is no sort of accordance whatever between the system of Plato and that of the Egyptians. For Plato, as is proved beyond all controversy by his *Timæus,* although he maintained that the matter of this world is eternal, yet drew a dis-

tinction between it and God, and conceived that it was with the assent and by the will of the Deity that it had at some period been digested and reduced into form. In the hope, therefore, of being able to do away this discrepance between the Egyptian and Platonic systems of discipline, the followers of Ammonius have exerted their abilities to the utmost, and have turned and twisted the *Timæus* of Plato in every possible way, with a view to conceal its repugnance to their own tenets respecting the eternity of the world. But with all their pains they have done nothing, except it be to prove that with them the ancient dogmas of the Egyptians possessed more weight, and were held in greater esteem than the authority of Plato. As a fair specimen of the whole, we refer the reader to the commentary of Proclus on the *Timæus* of Plato.

(4) This attempt to unite the principles of every other sect and religion with those of the Egyptians, is the grand feature that distinguishes this new philosophy from the Eclectic system, which flourished at Alexandria prior to the time of Ammonius. The Eclectics sought out and adopted from every sect all such things as appeared to them to make any near approach to the truth, and rejected what they considered as having little or no foundation in reason ; but Ammonius, conceiving that not only the philosophers of Greece, but also all those of the different barbarous nations, were perfectly in unison with each other, with regard to every essential point, made it his business so to temper and expound the tenets of all these various sects, as to make it appear that they had all of them originated from one and the same source, and all tended to one and the same end.

XXX. **The moral philosophy of Ammonius.** With this [p. 289.] system of theoretical or speculative philosophy, which its author, a man of powerful talents, defended with no little portion of subtilty and address, was conjoined a course of moral discipline in the highest degree rigid and austere. On such people indeed, as were necessarily involved in the cares and concerns of this life, Ammonius did not impose precepts of much difficulty in the observance, but suffered them to live agreeably to the laws of nature and those of their country; but every one who laid claim to the character of a wise man, was strictly enjoined by him to assert the liberty of his divine and immortal part, by extricating it, as it were, from all connection with the body; the consequence of which would be, that it would, even in this life, enjoy a communion with the Deity ; and when death should disencumber it of every gross and corporeal tie, escape free and unpolluted into the arms of the first great parent of all things. With this view, he willed all such to lead a life resembling that to which Plato gives the denomination of *Orphic;*(') to abstain from wine, flesh, and every kind of food which might tend to invigorate or refresh the body; to decline marriage, to court solitude, to abstract the mind from the senses and call it off from visible objects, to strive by means of contemplation to subdue the impulses and powers of the sensitive soul; in fine, to shrink from no exertion that might tend to free the immortal spirit from all corporeal influence, and restore it to a participation of the divine nature.(²) These obligations, to which, according to the Ammonian scheme, every wise man was subject, its author, as was natural for one that had been born and educated and constantly lived amongst Christains, was accustomed to expound and recommend in a language and phraseology evidently borrowed from the Christian discipline, a practice of which many very striking instances also occur in such of the writings of his followers as are extant among us at this day.(³) In addition to this rigid system of discipline, the offspring of the peculiar tenets entertained by him respecting God and the human soul, Ammonius propounded to his followers an art fraught with less important benefits, and suited only to capacities of a refined and an exalted nature, which he termed *Theurgia*, and for which there can be no doubt but that he was indebted to the Egyptian priests. This art embraced the faculty of so consecrating and purifying, by certain secret rites, that part of the mind or soul which receives the images of corporeal things, as to render it capable of perceiving dæmons, and also of holding an intercourse with spirits or angels, and of performing, with their assistance, things admirable in themselves, and utterly beyond the powers of human nature alone to accomplish. This species of magic was not cultivated by all the philosophers of the Modern Platonic school, but only by those of the higher order, who aspired to a sort of superiority over the rest. In fact, an acquaintance with it was considered rather as ornamental than useful, and as by no means necessary in attaining to the chief good.(⁴)

[p. 290.]   (1) Plato in lib. vi. *de Legibus*, p. 626. ed. Ficin. in treating of mankind during the primæval ages, observes, amongst other things, Σαρκῶν δ'ἀπείχοντο. Ὡς ὅχ ὅσιον ὂν ἐσθίειν, ἢ δὲ τὰς τῶν θεῶν βωμὰς ἅιματι μιαίνειν. ἀλλὰ Ὀρφικοί τινὲς λεγόμενοι βίοι ἐγίγνοντο ἡμῶν τοῖς τότε, ἀψύχων μὲν ἐχόμενοι πάντων, ἐμψύχων δὲ τουναντίον πάντων ἀπεχόμενοι. *Carnibus vero abstinebant. Nam vesci carnibus et Deorum aras polluere sanguine impium videbatur. Ita Orphica quadam vita tunc vigebat. Inanimatis quippe omnibus vescebantur et ab animatis omnibus abstinebant.*

(2) More in the way of illustration, as to what we have here stated, is to be gathered from Porphyry alone, in his work περὶ ἀποχῆς, or concerning abstinence from flesh, than from all the rest of the Ammonian sect of his time put together. For, although he abounds in subtilty, he yet surpasses, in point of perspicuity, every other of the Modern Platonists, and treats not only of abstinence, but likewise of those other duties which he considered as attaching themselves to the character of a wise man. Vid. lib. i. § xxvii. et seq. p. 22–34.

(3) It has been observed long since, by men of learning, that the writings of the Modern Platonists, such as Hierocles on the golden verses of Pythagoras, Simplicius, Jamblicus, and others, are replete with Christian phrases and expressions ; and their conclusion has been, that these things were pilfered out of the sacred writings, and thus applied by the followers of Ammonius, from an anxious desire to recommend their discipline by rendering it apparently consistent with the doctrines of Christianity. With regard to this, the reader may consult a dissertation of mine, *de Studio Ethnicorum Christianos imitandi*, which is to be found amongst my other dissertations relating to ecclesiastical history. But there is certainly no occasion for our imputing to those men anything like a wicked or fraudulent intention. For who, let me ask, can feel any considerable degree of surprise at finding a system of philosophy which originated with a man like Ammonius, apparently a Christian, unfolded with a certain colouring of Christianity, and explained in terms of common use amongst Christians? The sacred writings of the Christians must have been familiar to Ammonius, even from his tender years, and his ears must have been well accustomed to their peculiar forms of speech. Besides, it is certain, that either with an artful view, or from a downright error in judgment, he encouraged the opinion that there was no difference whatever, at least none of any moment, between the system of discipline which he himself sought to establish as the true one, and that which had been propounded by Christ. Wherefore he made no scruple, when discoursing on the necessity of purifying the soul, and bringing it back to God, or in defining the nature of true virtue, to make use of Christian terms and phrases, and whatever things of this kind came from his mouth were, no doubt, treasured up with a sort of reverence by his disciples, and soon communicated throughout the whole sect.

(4) The ridiculous and empty species of science so celebrated amongst the Modern Platonists under the name of *Theurgia*, bore a very near resemblance to that kind of *magic* which was termed good or lawful, in opposition to the black or illicit magic, and was, indisputably, of Egyptian origin. Nothing indeed could be more easy than for the Egyptians, who believed that the universe was filled with good and evil dæmons, to fall into the error of imagining that there was an art, by means of which the good will of these dæmons might be obtained. The nature of this science is sufficiently explained by Augustine *de Civitate Dei*, lib. x. cap. ix. p. 187. tom. vii. opp. *Theurgiam*, says he, *Porphyrius utilem esse dicit mundandæ parti animæ, non quidem intellectuali, qua rerum intelligibilium percipitur veritas nullas habentium similitudines corporum,* [p. 291.] *sed spiritali, qua corporalium rerum capiuntur imagines. Hanc enim dicit per quasdam consecrationes Theurgicas, quas teletas vocant, idoneam fieri atque aptam*

susceptioni spirituum et angelorum et ad videndos Deos. The rational soul derived no benefit whatever from this science, and it was, therefore, very possible
for any one to be happy and blessed without understanding anything of it;
hence we may perceive the reason of its not being cultivated by the whole body
of the Platonists. *Ex quibus tamen,* continues Augustine, *Theurgicis teletis
fatetur intellectuali animæ nihil purgationis accedere, quod eam faciat idoneam ad
videndum Deum suum, perspicienda ea quæ vere sunt* (*viz.* τὰ ὄντα).————
*Denique animam rationalem —— in superna posse dicit evadere, etiamsi quod ejus
spiritale est, nulla Theurgica arte fuerit purgatum: porro autem a Theurgo
spiritalem purgari hactenus, ut non ex hoc ad immortalitatem, æternitatemque
perveniat.* These few sentences certainly offer a long and extensive field for
comment in the way of illustration; at present, however, I shall study to be
brief. According to the Modern Platonists man is possessed of a two-fold soul;
the one rational and generated of the Deity, the other sensitive and capable of
being impressed with the images of mundane things, and derived from the soul
of the corporeal world. The former of a nature imperishable and immortal, the
latter extinguishable and of merely finite duration. Each, during its continuance in the body, is inert, and devoid of light, but may, to a certain degree, be
illuminated, quickened and refined. The means by which the rational soul may
be gradually purified and illuminated, are contemplation, the practice of virtue,
constant exercitation, abstinence, and extenuation of the body. When properly
purified, it is capable, without the assistance of eyes, of seeing the Deity himself, and all those things which have a true and real existence, and becomes
united with God by the closest and most indissoluble of ties. The sensitive
soul is purified by means of certain natural remedies well known to those who
are proficients in the science termed *Theurgia;* for being generated of matter,
by matter alone can it be effected, even as corrupt bodies are to be amended by
contrivance and art, with the assistance of such powers as are contained in herbs,
precious stones, and various other things. Being thus cleansed of its impurities, this kind of soul becomes capable of perceiving dæmons and angels, and
of maintaining a familiar intercourse with them. Nor is this at all to be wondered at; for the dæmons, according to the Ammonian scheme, are clothed with
bodies of a slender and refined texture, which are invisible to mankind whilst
the senses remain in a dull, corrupt state, but become apparent and visible
when once those things are removed, by which the faculties are clogged and
rendered inert. For the same reason the celestial and rational soul, notwithstanding that it may have been purified from all contagion of the body and the
senses, and entirely cleansed from everything vicious and corrupt, can never
arrive at any knowledge of, or intercourse with dæmons. For it possesses not
the faculty of perceiving sensible things, and is therefore incapable of discerning such natures as are joined to bodies, although those bodies may be of a subtile and refined order, but erecting itself above everything corporeal, it arrives
by inexplicable means at a knowledge and intimate connection with its first
great parent.

[p. 292.]   XXXI.   **The sentiments of Ammonius respecting the dif-**

ferent popular religions. In order that the different popular religions by which a plurality of Gods was recognized, might not appear repugnant to his doctrine, Ammonius endeavoured to reduce the whole history of the heathen deities, as it had been handed down by the poets and inculcated by the priests, to somewhat of a rational system, and contended that it was altogether an allegorical exhibition of either natural or moral precepts and maxims.(') Conformably to the Christian faith, he maintained that there was one God, from whom all things had proceeded. The host of beings whom the multitude and the heathen priesthood commonly honoured with the name of gods, he would not allow to be actually gods, but merely the ministers of God, or dæmons, to whom the supreme governor of the universe had committed the superintendence and guardianship of nations, or the direction of certain parts of nature, or finally the administration and guidance of human affairs and actions.(') To these agents of Divine Providence he thought it reasonable that a certain sort of honour and worship should be paid : just as amongst men a certain degree of attention and respect is shown to the legates of kings and inferior magistrates ; but he by no means deemed it necessary that they should be addressed with the same ceremonies that were used in worshipping the Deity, much less that they should be conciliated or appeased with sacrifices and the blood of animals. According to him, none but natures that were inimical to the human race, and that delighted in sensuality, could find any gratification in the death and blood of animals. The offerings in which such natures as resembled and were allied to the Supreme Deity took pleasure, were frankincense, hymns, herbs, and things altogether innoxious. It was no other than fitting, he conceived, that prayers should be addressed to these agents of the Deity, inasmuch as to them was committed the dispensation of God's benefits and blessings ; but that prayers of this kind were to be regulated by reason and wisdom, since the good things that were placed at the disposal of these dæmons were those which concerned merely the welfare of the body, not such as might benefit the celestial and immortal spirit. It became, therefore, a wise man, he held, whose main object ought to be to improve the excellence and felicity of his mind, for the most part to pass by these inferior deities, and prefer his petitions at once to the Supreme Being.

(1) The whole Ammonian school was devoted to *allegory,* and converted the history of the heathen gods into a sort of philosophy. As a specimen, we refer the reader to Porphyrius *de Antro Nympharum apud Homer. de Styge,* and others of his smaller pieces.

(2) Paulus Orosius, *Historiar.* lib. vi. cap. i. p. 364, 365. *Quidam dum in multis Deum credunt, multos Deos indiscreto timore finxerunt. Sed hinc jam vel maxime, cum auctoritate veritatis* (that is, the Christian religion) *operante, tum ipsa etiam ratione discutiente, discessum est. Quippe cum et philosophi eorum* [p. 293.] ——— *dum intento mentis studio quærunt, scrutanturque omnia, unum Deum auctorem omnium repererunt, ad quem unum omnia referrentur; unde etiam nunc pagani, quos jam declarata veritas* (i. e. the Christian religion) *de contumacia magis, quam de ignorantia, convincit, cum a nobis discutiuntur, non se plures Deos sequi, sed sub uno Deo magno plures ministros venerari fatentur.*

XXXII. **The tenets of Ammonius respecting Christ.** With a view to render Christianity apparently consistent with his new philosophy and the ancient religion, Ammonius admitted that Christ was a great and wise character, full of the counsel and power of the Deity, an admirable *Theurgist,* and a friend to the dæmons: that the discipline which he had instituted was of a most holy nature, and had been confirmed by miracles and preternatural signs: but he denied that Christ had ever taught anything repugnant to the principles which he himself sought to establish, or that he had endeavoured to abolish the ancient popular religious rites, and the worship of the dæmons that had been appointed by the Deity to preside over nations and the different departments of nature.(¹) And that he might the more readily procure for this part of his system an acceptance with the world, he endeavoured, as far as possible, by means of strained interpretations, or rather perversions, to enlist on his side the tenets of the Christians respecting the Deity, the human soul, the world, the trinity of persons in the Godhead, good and bad angels, and the like, as well as their different maxims and precepts relating to piety and morals.(²) Such points of the Christian doctrine as it surpassed his ingenuity to render by any means subservient to his purpose, he pronounced to be unauthorised additions that had been made to the system of Christ, by ignorant and injudicious disciples. The principal articles to which he thus took exception as interpolations, were those which respected the divinity of Christ, the salvation obtained through him for the human race, the abandoning the worship of a plurality of gods, and adoring the one only Supreme Being. None of these points, he contended, had ever been inculcated by Christ himself, nor had he forbidden the paying of an honorary worship to all dæmons indiscriminately, but only to such as were of an evil nature. When in the following age this matter was brought into dispute, and the miracles of our Blessed Saviour were urged by the Christians, in proof both of his divinity and also of his having meant to explode the worship of dæmons, the philosophers of the Ammonian school maintained that several of the more eminent of the Pagan worshippers, such as Apollonius Tyanæus, Pythagoras, Euclid, Apuleius, and others, had immortalized their names by miracles equally great and splendid with those which had been wrought by Christ.([3])

(1) The reader will understand me as not meaning to deny that amongst [p. 294.] those who adopted the Ammonian discipline, there were some that were alike inimical to Christ and to the Christians. We have an illustrious instance of this in the emperor Julian, and other examples might easily be adduced from amongst the Platonists of that age. For the hatred which these persons bore to Christ and his followers, particular reasons might be assigned, which those who are versed in matters of antiquity will be at no loss in discovering: but that Ammonius himself considered Christ as entitled to the highest honour, and that his true followers, although they were the authors of most grievous injuries to the Christians, yet manifest a respect and esteem for the character of Christ himself, is placed beyond a doubt by a variety of testimonies. Propriety could not allow that a man who made it his object to bring about an union of all sects and religions, and maintained that Christ had come for the express purpose of reinstating the true and most ancient philosophy and religion of the human race, should either think or speak otherwise than honourably of this same Christ. Neither is it at all probable that the veneration for Christ, which he had imbibed, as it were, with his mother's milk, could easily have been renounced by a man who, in departing from the true and right faith, appears to have been influenced, not so much by a depraved and vicious disposition, as by too great a partiality for the Egyptian philosophy and the ardour of an exuberant imagination. The reader will probably not be displeased at my adducing some passages from ancient authors in support of what I have thus advanced. *Augustine* enters much into dispute with those philosophers of his time who professed a respect and veneration for Christ, but maintained that the Christians had not adhered to the principles of their master. Lib i. *de Consensu Evangelistarum*, tom. iii. P. II. opp. cap. vi. § xi. p. 5. *Hoc dicunt*, says he, *illi vel maxime Pagani, qui Dominum ipsum Jesum Christum culpare aut blasphemare non audent, eique tribuunt excellentissiman sapientiam, sed tamen tanquam homini: discipulos vero ejus, dicunt, magistro suo amplius tribuisse quam erat, ut eum Filium Dei dicerent, et Verbum Dei per quod facta sunt omnia, et ipsum ac Deum patrem*

unum esse: ac si qua similia sunt in apostolicis literis, quibus eum cum Patre unum Deum colendum esse didicimus : honorandum enim tamquam sapientissimum virum putant ; colendum autem tumquam Deum negant. Some little while after, § 14. cap. viii. p. 6. he gives us to understand what opinion they entertained respecting Christ's miracles, namely, that he was a Theurgist or magician of the first rank, and that he left behind him two books, comprising the principles of the Theurgic or magic art. *Ita vero isti desipiunt, ut illis libris, quos eum* (Christ) *scripsisse existimant, dicant contineri eas artes, quibus eum putant illa fecisse miracula quorum fama ubique percrebuit : quod existimando se ipsos produnt quid diligant et quid affectant.* Augustine adds that possibly books of this kind might have been written by some one under the name of Christ. Amidst much other matter it is expressly intimated by Augustine, that this reverence for Christ had been handed down to the philosophers of his time by the Platonists, and particularly by that illustrious star of the Ammonian school, Porphyry. Cap. xv. p. 8. [p. 295.] *Quid? Quod isti vani Christi laudatores et Christianæ religionis obliqui obtrectatores propterea non audent blasphemare Christum, quia quidam philosophi eorum, sicut in libris suis Porphyrius Siculus prodidit, consuluerunt deos suos quid de Christo responderent, illi autem oraculis suis Christum laudare compulsi sunt.* ——*Ac per hoc isti, ne contra deorum suorum responsa conentur, continent blasphemias a Christo, et eas in discipulos ejus effundunt.* Concerning those oracles by which the heathen deities are said to have extolled the character of our Blessed Saviour, Augustine treats more at large in lib. xix. *de Civitate Dei*, cap. xxiii. p. 428. et seq. tom. vii. opp. from Porphyry's work *de Philosophia ex Oraculis.* Amongst other things he remarks, *Dicit etiam bona philosophus iste de Christo.*—— *Denique tanquam mirabile aliquid atque incredibile prolaturus, præter opinionem, inquit, profecto quibusdam videatur esse quod dicturi sumus ; Christum enim dii piissimum pronuntiaverunt et immortalem factum, et cum bona prædicatione ejus meminerunt : Christianos vero pollutos inquit, et contaminatos et errore implicatos esse dicunt, et multis talibus adversus eos blasphemiis utuntur.* The oracle itself, of which the sense is thus given by Porphyry, I purposely omit. A Latin translation of it is to be found in Augustine, but it is not a clear one. Eusebius gives it in Greek from the above-cited work of Porphyry in his *Demonstratio Evangel.* lib. iii. cap. viii. p. 134. Another oracle, bearing in like manner honourable testimony to the character of Christ, namely, one delivered by the Milesian Apollo, is to be met with in Lactantius *Institut. Divinar.* lib. iv. cap. xiii. p. 446. Augustine conceives that these oracles were either the inventions of the enemies of Christianity, or that they were delivered by dæmons for the purpose of seducing the Christians from the true religion. *Quis ita stultus est ut non intelligat aut ab homine callido eoque Christianis inimicissimo hæc oracula fuisse conficta, aut consilio simili ab impuris dæmonibus ista fuisse responsa ; ut scilicet quoniam laudant Christum propterea veraciter credantur vituperare Christianos ; atque ita, si possint, intercludant viam salutis æternæ, in qua fit quisque Christianus.* To this opinion of Augustine, that these oracles were the inventions of the enemies of the Christians, I very readily subscribe. The philosophers, the adversaries of the Christians, as Augustine expressly states in the former-cited passage, consulted the heathen deities respecting the character of

Christ; and the priests of those deities, without doubt, returned an answer conformably to what they knew to be the opinion of the persons thus consulting
them. But it strikes me, that these philosophers were influenced by a different
motive in procuring these oracles from that which suggested itself to Augustine.
In fact, they had learnt from Ammonius, the founder of their sect, that Christ
was a character of the first eminence, and worthy of the highest praise; and
this opinion they scrupled not openly to profess. To the numerous enemies of
the Christian religion, however, their conduct in this respect was highly offensive, and particularly to the heathen priesthood, who were apprehensive that the
praises thus bestowed on Christ might injure the cause of Paganism, and would
rather have had Christ blended with the Christians in one indiscrimi- [p. 296.]
nate censure and malediction. The Platonic philosophers, therefore, with a
view to remove from themselves every sort of odium on this account, and to
prove that the opinion which they maintained respecting Christ was one that
might be justified, made inquiry of the gods as to what was to be thought of
Christ's character: and having obtained an answer, such as they desired, no
further room was left for cavil, inasmuch, as by producing the oracles, they could
at any time prove to demonstration that the opinion of the gods was on their
side. And who should pretend to call men in question for maintaining opinions
that had received the sanction of the gods?

Let us now see what other sentiments *Augustine* states to have been entertained by these philosophers respecting Christ and the Christians. They denied that it had been Christ's intention to abrogate the worship of the heathen
deities. *Veruntamen*, says he, *de Consens. Evangelistar.* lib. i. cap. xvi. p. 8. *isti
ita disputant, quod hæc eversio templorum, et damnatio sacrificiorum, et confractio
simulacrorum non per doctrinam Christi fiat, sed per discipulorum ejus, quos aliud
quam ab illo didicerunt, docuisse contendunt; ita volentes Christianam fidem,
Christum honorantes laudantesque, convellere.* On the contrary, they maintained
that Christ himself paid an honorary worship to these deities, and that it was by
their, or in other words, the dæmons' assistance he wrought his miracles, l. c.
cap. xxxvi. p. 18. *Ita enim volunt et ipsum credi, nescio quid aliud scripsisse,
quod diligunt, nihilque sensisse contra deos suos, sed eos potius magico ritu colu-
isse; et discipulos ejus non solum de illo fuisse mentitos, dicendo illum Deum, per
quem facta sunt omnia, cum aliud nihil quam homo fuerit, quamvis excellentissimæ
sapientiæ; verum etiam de diis eorum non hoc docuisse quod ab illo didicissent.*
They were ready, however, to admit that Christ had abolished the worship of
certain dæmons of the inferior order, and had enjoined men to address themselves to the deities of heaven alone, and more particularly to the Supremo
Governor of all things. That such was their opinion, Augustine proves by a
notable passage from Porphyry, of which he gives us the following translation
into Latin, in his work *de Civitate Dei*, lib. xix. cap. xxiii. § iv. p. 430. tom. vii.
opp. *Sunt* (the reader will recollect that it is Porphyry who is speaking)
*spiritus terreni minimi loco quodam malorum dæmonum potestati subjecti. Ab his
sapientes Hebræorum quorum unus iste etiam Jesus fuit; ab his ergo Hebræi dæmonibus pessimis et minoribus spiritibus vetabant religiosos et ipsis vacare prohibe-
bant: venerari autem magis cælestes deos, amplius autem venerari Deum patrem.*

Hoc autem et dii præcipiunt, et in superioribus ostendimus, quemadmodum animum advertere ad Deum monent, et illum colere ubique imperant. Verum indocti et impiæ naturæ (i. e. the Christians) *quibus vere fatum non concessit a diis dona obtinere, neque habere Jovis immortalis notionem, non audientes et deos* (i. e. those oracles which he had antecedently adduced) *et divinos viros*, (Ammonius, whom, it appears from the testimony of Hierocles *apud Phot. Biblioth.* p. 283. they were accustomed to style Θεοδίδακτος, Plotinus, whom, in like manner, they termed Θεῖος, and others who had been taught by these,) *deos quidem omnes re-* [p. 297.] *cusaverunt, prohibitos autem dæmones, et hos non odisse sed revereri, Deum autem simulantes colere, ea sola per quæ Deus adoratur, non agunt. Nam Deus quidem utpote omnium pater nullius indiget* (i. e. he delights not in sacrifices and victims), *sed nobis est bene cum eum per justitiam et castitatem aliasque virtutes adoramus, ipsam vitam precem ad ipsum facientes per imitationem et inquisitionem de ipso. Inquisitio enim purgat,* (by *inquisitio* he here means contemplation, meditation, and the abstraction of the mind from the senses ; a mind to which this kind of discipline had become familiar, was considered by the Modern Platonists as in the highest degree purified and cleansed,) *imitatio deificat affectionem ad ipsum operando.* He (Porphyry) had said a little before, *Anima* (of Christ) *aliis animabus fataliter dedit errore implicari. Propterea ergo diis exosi ——— ipse vero* (Christ) *pius et in cœlum sicut pii concessit. Itaque hunc quidem non blasphemabis, misereberis autem hominum dementiam, ex eo in eis facile præcepsque periculum.* What we hear from Porphyry, that illustrious enemy of the Christians, we may consider ourselves as hearing from Ammonius himself, and his principal disciple, Plotinus. For, as it is certain that what Plotinus taught, he had derived from Ammonius, so may we be sure, that for whatever is to be gathered from Porphyry, he himself was indebted to Plotinus.

(2) That the Modern or Ammonian Platonists made it their object, in a certain degree, to reconcile the maxims of the Egyptian and ancient Platonic philosophy with those of Christianity, must be plain to any one who shall consider the way in which Plotinus expresses his opinion respecting the existence of three principles or chief hypostases in one God; the manner in which all the philosophers of this sect speak concerning dæmons and spirits, their tenets respecting the nature of God and the human soul, and the opinions they avowed respecting the world and its origin. Most assuredly nothing can be more apparent than that all these things are so treated of and explained by them, as to make it appear that little or no difference existed between their system of discipline and Christianity. They borrow from the Christians distinctions, words, phrases, and whatever else they can, and accommodate them all to their own way of thinking. Indeed so dexterous were they at this, that we find them, according as it might best suit their purpose, at one time corrupting and debasing the Christian tenets in order to make them accord with their own opinions, whilst at another they, on the contrary, correct and amend their own principles so as to make them coincide with the maxims of Christianity. Hence it came to pass that the greater part of these Platonists, upon comparing the Christian religion with the system of Ammonius, were led to imagine that nothing could be more easy than a transition from the one to the other, and, to the great detriment

of the Christian cause, were induced to embrace Christianity without feeling it necessary to abandon scarcely any of their former principles. A memorable passage as to this occurs in Augustine's book, *de Vera Religione*, cap. iv. § vii. p. 559. tom. i. opp. *Itaque si hanc vitam illi viri nobiscum rursus agere potuissent, viderent profecto, cujus auctoritate facilius consuleretur hominibus, et paucis mutatis verbis et sententiis Christiani fierent, sicut plerique recentiorum nostrorumque temporum Platonici fecerunt.* See also his epistle to Dioscorus, ep. lxviii. [p. 298.] § xxi. & xxxiii. p. 255. 260. tom. ii. opp.

(3) It appears clearly to have been the general practice of the Platonists of the third and fourth centuries, to compare our Blessed Saviour with Apollonius Tyanæus, Pythagoras, and other philosophers who were renowned for their miracles; and that Philostratus wrote the life of Apollonius, Porphyry and Iamblicus that of Pythagoras, and other authors, most likely, those of other wise men, expressly with a view to show that amongst the worshippers of the heathen deities, there had been men distinguished for acts of a similar nature with those by which Christ had rendered himself illustrious. That such was their object, the reader will find fully proved by Gothofred Olearius, in his notes on Philostratus, and by L. Kuster in his annotations on Iamblicus and Porphyry's life of Pythagoras. Those who undertook the idle and absurd task of making this comparison, found it necessary to detract much from the honour that is due to the Saviour of the world, but they did not make it their aim to deprive his character of every sort of dignity and glory. Their object was merely to bring him down to a level with those whom they deemed to have been the wisest and best of mortals, and who bore an affinity to the immortal gods. The only things, therefore, for which they contended in this way, were these two: *First*, that the miracles of Christ do not afford any absolute or positive proof of his divinity, as the Christians maintained; inasmuch as it could be shown, that men, having no pretensions to the rank of deities, had performed things of a similarly wonderful nature; *Secondly*, that Christ could never have meant altogether to overturn and abolish the worship of dæmons, (*i. e.* the heathen deities,) or the ancient popular religions, since the most religious of the heathen worshippers had distinguished themselves by miracles, even as he. These very Lives, therefore, of the ancient philosophers, and the comparisons therein drawn between them and Christ, most plainly prove that the sect of Ammonians or that of the Modern Platonists held the character of Christ in very great honour, although they vilified and would willingly have altogether extirpated the Christians.

XXXIII. **Forced interpretation of the Scriptures.** When once this passion for philosophising had taken possession of the minds of the Egyptian teachers and certain others, and had been gradually diffused by them in various directions throughout the church, the holy and beautiful simplicity of early times very quickly disappeared, and was followed by a most remarkable and disastrous alteration in nearly the whole system of Christian discipline. This very important and deeply to be regretted change

had its commencement in the century now under review, but it
will be in the succeeding one that we shall have to mark its chief
progress.   One of the earliest evils that flowed from this immoderate attachment to philosophy, was the violence to which it
gave rise in the interpretation of the Holy Scriptures.   For,
whereas, the Christians had, from a very early period, imbibed
the notion that under the words, laws, and facts, recorded in the
sacred volume, there is a latent sense concealed, an opinion
which they appear to have derived from the Jews,(¹) no sooner
did this passion for philosophising take possession of their minds,
than they began with wonderful subtilty to press the Scriptures
[p. 299.] into their service, in support of all such principles and
maxims as appeared to them consonant to reason ; and at the
same time most wretchedly to pervert and twist every part of
those divine oracles which opposed itself to their philosophical
tenets or notions.   The greatest proficients in this pernicious
practice were those Egyptian teachers who first directed the attention of the Christians towards philosophy, namely, *Pantænus*
and *Clement.*   Their expositions of the Scriptures have not
reached our days, but it appears from such of the writings of
Clement as are at present extant, that he and Pantænus are not
to be considered as having struck out an absolutely original path
in this respect, for that in reality they were merely followers of
the celebrated Alexandrian Jew, *Philo*, whose writings they assiduously studied, and whose empty wisdom they were unhappily led to admire and to imitate.(²)

(1) In the writings of fathers, even of this century, express notice is occasionally taken of those four senses of Scripture to which the Christian expositors were for so many ages accustomed to direct the attention of their readers,
namely, the *literal*, the *allegorical*, the *tropological*, and the *anagogical.*   The
first three of these are noticed by *Justin Martyr*, (*Dial. cum Tryphone*, p. 333.
edit. Jebbian.) who, after making some remarks as to the sense attached to the
words of the sacred volume, adds, καὶ γὰρ ἐν παραβολῇ λίθον πολλαχῆ καλεῖν ἀπέ-
δειξα τὸν Χριστὸν καὶ ἐν τροπολογία Ἰακὼβ καὶ Ἰσραηλ.   *Nam per parabolam*, (that to
which Justin here applies the term *Parable*, is, by subsequent Christian writers,
denominated *Allegory*, or the allegorical sense,) *illum* (*i. e.* Isaiah) *persæpe
Christum vocare lapidem ostendi, et tropologice Jacobum et Israelem.*   Of the
anagogical sense, as they term it, whereby the scriptural accounts of things
appertaining to this life are applied to spiritual and heavenly matters, many examples are to be met with likewise in Justin, and also in Clement.   That the
early Christians derived this practice of annexing to the words of Scripture se-

veral different senses, from the Jews, no one, at present, appears in the least to dcubt. It is, moreover, to be remarked, that, although Justin, Irenæus, and the other fathers of this century, whose writings have come down to our times, are continually obtruding on us mystical and allegorical interpretations of the Scriptures, yet not one of them who dwelt without the confines of Egypt ever attempts, by means of ingenuity, to elicit from the sacred writings any of the dogmas or maxims of philosophy. By all of them the words of Scripture are made to refer to Christ and to heavenly things alone, although in a manner not altogether the most happy or judicious. This appears to me not a little extraordinary, and particularly in Justin Martyr, who certainly considered philosophy as of divine origin.

(2) Nearly all those corruptions, by which, in the second and subsequent centuries, Christianity was disfigured, and its pristine simplicity and innocence almost wholly effaced, had their origin in Egypt, and were thence communicated to the other churches. This province also gave birth to the dis- [p. 300.] commendable practice of glossing over philosophical opinions with the words of Scripture, or rather of straining scriptural phrases and expressions in support of such maxims as might appear to be dictated by reason. The first Christians who made this art their study were *Pantænus* and *Clement,* successively præfects of the catechetical school of Alexandria; men of unquestionable worth and piety, but immoderately devoted to what they deemed the true philosophy. It appears from St. Jerome, *Catal. Scriptor. Eccl.* cap. xxxvi. that many commentaries on the Holy Scriptures by *Pantænus* were formerly extant; but they have all long since fallen victims to the ravages of time. The manner, however, in which he expounded the sacred writings, may be collected from the works that are extant of his disciple and successor, *Clement* of Alexandria. One of his rules of interpretation, in particular, is preserved by Clement in his *Eclogæ ex Scripturis Prophetarum,* subjoined to his works, § lvi. p. 1002. edit. Potterian. Pantænus, it there appears, laid it down as a maxim, that the prophets, in what they uttered, spake for the most part indefinitely, using the present tense, at one and the same time, both for the future and præterite. Taking this rule of his preceptor for his guide, in expounding the words of David, Psal. xviii. 6. *Et in sole posuit tabernaculum suum,* Clement, first of all, assumes that they are to be understood as relating to Christ, and then goes on to expound the præterite *posuit* as referring both to the past time and the future; and, proceeding upon this plan, the words of David are found to admit, not merely of one, but several very extraordinary interpretations. Indeed it cannot fail to strike every one, that this rule of Pantænus is every way calculated to admit of various different senses being applied to almost every word of the sacred volume: and there cannot be a doubt but that it was invented expressly with a view of introducing the utmost latitude of interpretation in the exposition of the Holy Scriptures, so as to admit of their being accommodated, *ad libitum,* to the occurrences of past as well as future times. Let us assume merely what Pantænus assumed, namely, that the words of Scripture relating to actions or occurrences, do not refer to one particular time, but to several different periods; and it will be difficult to point out any part of the sacred volume that

24

may not be wonderfully dilated, and absolutely loaded, as it were, with a variety of senses or interpretations.—*Clement*, the disciple of Pantænus, was the author of a work of considerable length, to which he gave the title of *Hypotyposes*, and in which he is said to have given an exposition of nearly all the sacred writers, one after another. He likewise wrote a commentary on what are termed the Canonical Epistles. These works are lost; but in such of his writings as remain, we meet with sufficiently numerous examples of the manner in which he was accustomed to expound the Scriptures. To give an instance or two, by way of illustration. In his *Stromata*, lib. i. cap. xxviii. p. 426. we find it asserted, that the Mosaic laws have a four-fold sense ; τετραχῶς δὲ ἡμῖν ἐκληπτέον τὸ νόμου τὴν βόλησιν. He, however, enumerates only three of those senses : the *mystical*, the *moral*, and the *prophetical*. Every law, according to him, in the first place, represents some *sign*, that is, the words of the law are images of other things, and, in addition to their proper sense, have an improper or secondary one also attached to them. Secondly, every law comprises a *precept* for the right ordering of life. Thirdly, every law, like a *prophecy*, predicts something future. As Clement enumerates only three senses in which the law [p. 301.] is to be understood, although he speaks of four, Hervetus, his translator into Latin, conjectures that in the word τετραχῶς there is a corruption, and that, instead of it, we ought to read τριχῶς. But the learned writer has, in this respect, fallen into an error. Clement, in his enumeration, passes over the natural sense attached to the words of the law, as a thing too obvious to require pointing out, and particularizes merely the three less evident ones. For the investigating these recondite senses of the Mosaic law with effect, he deems philosophy, or the dialectic art, an highly necessary auxiliary. Διαλεκτικώτερον δὲ προσιτέον αὐτῇ, τὴν ἀκολυθίαν τῆς θείας διδασκαλίας θηρωμένοις. *Est autem valde dialectice ad legem accedendum consequentiam, (i. e.* the recondite and abstruse senses of the law,) *divinæ doctrinæ venantibus.* The tendency of these maxims, and how greatly they lean in favour of specious and philosophical explications of the law, must be manifest to every one. *Clement* also agrees with Philo Judæus in the opinion that the Greek philosophers derived all their principles from Moses. Vid. *Stromat.* lib. ii. cap. v. p. 439. Whatever, therefore, appears to him just and consonant to reason in the maxims or tenets of the philosophers, he is sure to discover laid down somewhere or other in the books of the Old Testament; and this leads him, not unfrequently, to strain and distort in a most extraordinary manner, the words of Moses and the other sacred writers, in order to make them, apparently, speak one and the same language with Plato and the rest of the philosophers of Greece.—One point which he, in particular, seeks to establish, is, that a Christian ought to cultivate philosophy and the liberal arts before he devotes himself wholly to the study of divine wisdom. The reader will, in all probability, feel his curiosity somewhat awakened on learning that this is to be proved from the history of Abraham, Sarah, and Hagar, as given by Moses. Clement's manner of doing it is this: (*Stromat.* lib. i. p. 333.) Abraham he asserts to be the image of a perfect Christian ; Sarah, the image of Christian wisdom ; and Hagar the image of philosophy or human wisdom. Abraham lived with Sarah, for a long time, in a state of connubial sterility.

The inference from this, according to Clement, is, that a Christian, as long as he confines himself to the study of divine wisdom and religion alone, will never bring forth any great or excellent fruits. Abraham, then, with the consent of Sarah, takes to him Hagar; which proves, according to Clement, that a Christian ought to embrace the wisdom of this world or philosophy, and that Sarah or divine wisdom will not withhold her consent. Lastly, Abraham, after Hagar had borne him Ismael, resumed his intercourse with Sarah, and of her begat Isaac: of this the import is, that a Christian, after having once thoroughly grounded himself in human learning and philosophy, will, if he then devotes himself to the culture of divine wisdom, be capable of propagating the race of true Christians, and of rendering essential service to the church.—*Plato* and his disciples maintained that the world was two-fold; the one *intellectual*, or only to be perceived mentally and by reason, the other *visible*, or an object of the senses. This maxim met with the approbation of *Clement:* hence he is led to contend, that Plato derived this idea of a two-fold world from Moses, and that it is to be supported on the authority of holy writ. The *intellectual* world, or that which is imperceptible to the senses, he finds alluded to in the first words of *Genesis:* "In the beginning, God created the heavens and the earth; but the earth was (ἀόρατος) invisible." And in the following words: "And God said, let there be light," &c. he, with equal facility, discovers, that a reference was intended to the *visible* or corporeal world, *Stromat.* lib. v. p. 702. et seq. [p. 302.]

This absurd art of perverting and straining the Holy Scriptures did not, however, originate with the præfects of the catechetical school of Alexandria, but was derived by them from the celebrated Alexandrian Jew, *Philo.* Clement's devotion to this writer is unbounded; him he is continually extolling, him he imitates, and from him he transcribes a variety of passages without even the changing of a word. Nor did Origen in the succeeding century, or those who followed him, act otherwise. It is not, therefore, *Origen* who ought to be termed the parent of allegories amongst the Christians, but *Philo.* Indeed this has been already very justly remarked by Photius, who observes, (in *Biblioth.* cod. cv. p. 278.) Ἐξ ἰ οἶμαι καὶ πᾶς ὁ ἀλληγορικὸς τᾶς γραφῆς ἐν τᾶ ἐκκλησίᾳ λόγος ἔσχει ἀρχὴν ἐισρυῆναι. *Et vero ab hoc arbitror omnem allegoricum Sacræ Scripturæ sermonem in ecclesiam promanasse.* This indeed is not altogether true, since many of the Jews, and in particular the Pharisees and Essenes, had indulged much in allegories before the time of Philo; but of this there can be no doubt, that the præfects of the Alexandrian school caught the idea of interpreting Scripture upon philosophical principles, or of eliciting philosophical maxims from the sacred writers by means of allegory, from Philo, and that by them it was gradually propagated amongst the Christians at large. It is also equally certain that by the writings and example of Philo, the fondness for allegories was vastly augmented and confirmed throughout the whole Christian world: and it moreover appears, that it was he who first inspired the Christians with that degree of temerity which led them, not unfrequently, to violate the faith of history, and wilfully to close their eyes against the obvious and proper sense of terms and words. The examples of this most presumptuous boldness that occur in the writings of Philo are indeed but rare: particular instances of it, however, are not wanting; as may easily be shown from Origen and others who took him for their guide, and who, manifestly, considered a great part both of the Old and New Testament as not exhibiting a representation of things that really occurred, but merely the images of moral actions. If the reader will give himself the trouble to refer to Philo *de Allegoriis Legis*, lib. iii. p. 134. he will find in the turn that is there given to the history of Joseph and Potiphar's wife, an instance which may serve to convince him that this celebrated Jew made no scruple of perverting, and even absolutely reversing the truth of sacred history whenever occasion might appear to demand it.

XXXIV. **The practice arises of expounding Christian tenets upon philosophical principles. The secret discipline.** With this evil was connected another that proved equally detrimental to the interests of Christianity. For, not content with thus perverting and straining the Holy Scriptures, in support of such philosophical tenets as they deemed just and reasonable, the Christians of the Ammonian school, with a view to illustrate, still more clearly, the perfect accordance of human with divine wisdom, and in this way the more readily to draw over philosophers to their side, proceeded to the further length of giving to the most plain and obvious maxims and precepts of the Gospel, such an exposition as might render them apparently consistent with the philosophical [p. 303.] notions and opinions which they had so unfortunately been led to espouse.(') In their manner of doing this, however, a greater degree of caution and prudence was observed by some than by others. By not a few the expositions of the Christian mysteries, which their ingenuity had thus suggested, were promulgated without reserve, and endeavours used to get them adopted by the church, as appears from the disputes that took place with Praxeas, Theodotus, Hermogenes, and Artemon. But by far the greater part, pursuing the example of the Egyptian teachers, appear to have wished, that the principles of Christianity should be unfolded and explained to the people at large, with every possible degree of plainness and simplicity, and that the more abstruse and philosophic interpretation of them should never reach the ears of the multitude, but be made known only to certain select persons of tried faith and a cultivated understanding; and not even to these through the medium of writing, but merely by word of mouth. Hence arose that more secret and sublime theology of the ancient Christians, to which we have of late been accustomed to refer, under the title of *Disciplina Ar-*

cani,(²) and which Clement of Alexandria styles γνῶσις, or *know-ledge*, but which differs from what is called *Mystical Theology*, only in name.(³)

(1) Whatever, for instance, is to be met with in Scripture respecting God the Father, the Son, and the Holy Spirit, was so expounded by these Christians as to render it consistent with the doctrine of three hypostases or natures in God, as maintained by Plato, Parmenides, and others. Clement. *Stromat.* lib. v. p. 710. Again, what is said by the sacred writers respecting the future destruction and burning of the world, was so explained by them as to make it accord with what was taught by Plato and the Stoics respecting the purification and renovation of the world by fire. Vid. Clement *Stromat.* lib. v. p. 647. 211. et seq. The restoration or resurrection of the dead was so interpreted as to accommodate it to the tenets of the Grecian sages. The different passages in holy writ that relate to the illuminating, purifying, and regenerating of the mind were, with great ingenuity, made to correspond with what was taught by most of the Egyptian and Platonic philosophers of the ancient as well as modern school respecting the philosophical death, or the separation of the rational soul from the sensitive one, and also from the influence of the body. In fact there are but few points of Christian theology, which the teachers who were inflamed with this eager desire to produce an union between Christianity and philosophy, left untouched.

(2) That the more learned of the Christians, subsequently to the second century, cultivated, in secret, an obstruse discipline of a different nature from that which they taught publicly, is well known to every one. Concerning the argument, however, or matter of this secret or mysterious discipline, its origin, and the causes which gave rise to it, there are infinite disputes. But these contentions, as is commonly the case amongst mortals, instead of elucidating, have rather tended to throw additional obscurity over a thing, of itself sufficiently intricate, and that seems, as it were, to have set illustration at defiance. [p. 304.] This has more particularly been the case since the advocates for the Papacy have endeavored to avail themselves of this secret discipline of the ancient Christians in support of their cause. To me it appears, that this obscurity might be in part removed if due attention were paid to a circumstance which seems to have been hitherto commonly overlooked, namely, that amongst the ancient Christians there existed not merely one, but several species of secret discipline, which were indeed of some affinity to each other, but between which it is necessary in regard to this question to draw a line of distinction, in order to prevent our confounding together things in themselves really different.—In the *first place*, there was a sort of secret or mysterious discipline that related to those who were enemies to the Christian religion and worshippers of false gods: but even this was of more than one kind. For *first*, there was a sort of discipline of this nature that respected all who were adverse to the Christian faith generally and without distinction. There were certain points of belief, for instance, at this time current amongst the Christians respecting the destruction that hung over the city of Rome and the empire, as well as the wars and final discomfiture

of Antichrist, the near approach of the end of the world, the millenium, and other matters, peradventure connected with these. Now if things of this kind had been promulgated without reserve amongst the multidude, there can be no doubt but that a very considerable degree of enmity and ill-will would have been excited in the minds of the Roman people towards the Christians. Great care was therefore taken to conceal everything of this nature from all except comparatively a few, of whose fidelity and secrecy there could be no apprehension. Wherefore, when Montanus and his followers, in this very century, publicly prophesied the downfall of the city and empire of Rome, it proved highly displeasing to the Christians, and they at once withdrew themselves from every sort of connection with a man who could be guilty of such imprudence. *Hoc solum*, says Tertullian, (in his *Vindiciæ Montani* which are lost, but of which this passage is preserved *apud Prædestinat.* a Jac. Sirmond. edit. lib. i. Hæres. xxvi. p. 30.) *hoc solum discrepamus* (the Montanists from other Christians) *quod secundas nuptias non recipimus et prophetiam Montani de futuro judicio non recusamus.* Now, as to the future general judgment, all Christians believed in it, and there could, therefore, have been no occasion for Montanus to prophesy anything at all about it. By *futurum judicium* in the above passage, therefore, we must understand the judgment which this man had inadvertently prophesied as awaiting the Roman empire in particular; and against this prophecy the Christians deemed it prudent to protest, lest the enmity of the Roman emperors and people, of which they had already sufficiently felt the weight, should be still further excited against them. *Another species* of secret discipline had relation to those whom the Christians were desirous of rescuing from the dominion of superstition, and initiating in the principles of Christianity. With these they found it necessary to proceed somewhat cautiously, lest, by a premature communication of the truth, their minds might receive impressions unfavourable to the Christian religion. They, therefore, observed at the first a total silence with regard to the doctrine contained in the Scripture respecting the person, merits, and functions of Christ; as well as those other mysteries, to the right comprehending of which the human mind is of itself unequal, and confined themselves wholly to such things as right reason points out concerning the Deity, the nature of man, and his duties. When these had been sufficiently inculcated and suitably received, and not before, they proceeded to points of a higher and more abstruse nature. •Respecting the practice of the early Christians in regard to this, the reader will find a notable passage in the *Apostolical Constitutions*, lib. iii. cap. v. *Patrum Apostolic.* tom. i. p. 280, 281. In either of these species of secret discipline there should seem to have been nothing at which any one of [p. 305.] an impartial and well informed mind can take any serious offence.

Entirely distinct from these there existed another species of secret discipline, which regarded Christians alone, and had respect, in part, to the *catechumens*, or those who had not as yet been received into the church, and, in part, to the regular members of the church. This discipline, so far as it regarded the catechumens, is sufficiently known. The catechumens were not admitted either to the common prayers, or to a sight of the celebration of the sacred rites ordained by Christ, or to what were termed the feasts of love; nor were they at all instructed as to the nature of these parts of divine worship, or any of the injunctions or regulations appertaining to them, until they had been regularly adopted as members of the church by baptism; and, consistently with this, the sacred preachers made it a rule to abstain from entering into any discussions immediately relating either to Baptism or the Lord's Supper, in presence of the catechumens. But this kind of discipline had certainly in it somewhat of an alien cast, and betrayed an imitation of foreign manners and customs but little laudable.—Of a much more praiseworthy nature was the practice of consulting the furtherance and advantage of weak and illiterate Christians, by directing the teachers to accommodate their discourses to the capacities of their hearers, and in popular addresses to omit all such things as were not, without difficulty, to be comprehended by persons of low and simple minds. Instructions to this effect are to be found in Origen *contra Celsum*, lib. iii. p. 143. edit. Spencer. as well as in other Christian writers. Undoubtedly nothing can be more commendable and wise than to avoid troubling weak and simple minds with things, to the right comprehension of which an ordinary degree of intelligence is by no means equal.—In addition to all these different species of secret discipline, which had relation to particular classes of men, and were regulated by certain modes and times, there remains still yet another to be mentioned, of a nature altogether different, being controlled neither by time nor place, and having respect to no class of men in particular, but, with a few exceptions, equally regarding all, as well Christians as those who were strangers to the Christian faith. This, without question, consisted of divers maxims and opinions which were cherished by the Christian teachers in private amongst themselves, and never communicated to the people at large, or even to their own immediate disciples indiscriminately, but only in secret to such of these latter as had given satisfactory proofs of their trustworthiness and taciturnity. *Clement* of Alexandria is the first writer that notices this sort of discipline; before him no mention whatever is made of it by any author. There can, therefore, be but little doubt but that it originated amongst the Christians of Egypt, and was by them communicated to the other churches. Clement represents this secret discipline, to which he gives the title of γνῶσις, as having been instituted by Christ himself. From a passage in his *Hypotyposes*, a work long since lost, which is cited by Eusebius in *Eccl. Histor.* lib. ii. cap i. p. 38. it appears that he considered this γνῶσις, or gift of knowledge, as having been conferred by our Lord, after his resurrection, on James the Just, John, and Peter, by whom it was communicated to the other apostles; and that by these this treasure was committed to the seventy disciples, of whom Barnabas was one. A similar passage to this occurs in his *Stromata*, lib. i. p. 322. in which, however, to the three apostles enumerated by Eusebius, he adds a fourth, namely, Paul, whom he also conceives to have been instructed in this secret discipline by [p. 306.] Christ himself. Nor does he discover the least hesitation in asserting, with the Gnostics, that the discipline communicated by our Blessed Saviour to mankind, was of a two-fold nature, the one calculated for the world at large, the other designed only for the wise and prudent; the former consisting of what was taught publicly to the people by Christ himself, and is to be found in the Scriptures, the latter, of certain maxims and precepts that were communicated merely by word of mouth, to a few only of the apostles. 'Ου πολλοῖς ἀπεκάλυψεν ἃ μὴ πολλῶν ἦν, λέγεις δὲ οἷς προσηκειν ἠπίσατο, τοῖς οἵοις τε ἐκδέξασθαι, καὶ τυπωθῆναι πρὸς αὐτά. *Non revelavit (Christus) multis ea quæ non erant multorum, sed paucis quibus sciebat convenire. qui et ea possent accipere et ex eis informari. Stromat.* lib. i. cap. i. p. 323. Clement makes it a matter of boast that the secret discipline thus instituted by Christ was familiar to those who had been his masters and preceptors, whom he very lavishly extols, and seems to exult not a little in having, under their tuition, enjoyed the advantage of being instructed in it himself. Apart of it, indeed, he says, had, through length of time, escaped his memory, but that the rest of it remained still fresh in his mind. He promises, moreover, that he would advert to some of the chief or leading points of this venerable knowledge in his *Stromata*, but represents himself as bound not openly to make known or explain the whole of it, lest, according to the proverb, he should put a sword in the hand of a child. Τὰ μὲν ἑκὼν παραπέμπομαι, says he, p. 324. ἐκλέγων ἐπισημόνως, φοβούμενος γράφειν, ἃ καὶ λέγειν ἐφυλαξάμεν. *Nonnulla quidem consulto prætermitto, scienter delectum faciens, timens scribere, quæ etiam cavi dicere.* In another place, *viz.* p. 327. he says, Στρωματεῖς κρυπτεῖν ἐντέχνως τὰ τῆς γνώσεως βόλονται σπέρματα *Libri mei Stromatum volunt artificiose celare semina cognitionis.* To any one who might be at a loss to account for his declining to make publicly known, and in a great measure altogether concealing, a species of knowledge, confessedly of the highest importance and value, he replies, (cap. iii. p. 328) that it was not to be comprehended, except by minds that had been thoroughly purged and delivered from the dominion of the passions, that there would, moreover, be a danger in it, lest occasion might be given to contentious persons for cavilling and insult. "Οτι μέγας ὁ κίνδυνος, τὸν ἀπόρρητον ὡς ἀληθῶς τῆς ὄντως φιλοσοφίας λόγον ἐξορχήσασθαι τοῖς ἀφειδῶς πάντα μὲν ἀντιλέγειν ἐθέλουσιν "ἐκ ἐν δίκῃ, πάντα δὲ ὀνόματα καὶ ῥήματα ἀποὀρίπτουσιν ἀ̓αυῶς κοσμίως. *Quia magnum est periculum vere arcanam veræ philosophiæ rationem iis propalare, qui profuse quidem ac petulanter, sed non jure, volunt contra omnes dicere, omnia autem nomina et verba turpiter ac indecore ejaculantur.* See also lib. ii. p. 432. et seq. Many other passages of this kind are to be met with in Clement, by any one who will be at the trouble of diligently exploring his *Stromata.*—What those maxims and principles were which *Clement* conceived himself to be precluded from communicating to the world at large, cannot long remain a secret to any diligent and attentive reader of his works. There cannot be the smallest question but that they were philosophical explications of the Christian tenets respecting the Trinity, the soul, the world, the future resurrection of the body, Christ, the life to come, and other things of a like abstruse nature, which had in them somewhat that admitted of being expounded upon philosophical principles. They also, no doubt, consisted of cer- [p. 307.] tain mystical and allegorical interpretations of the divine oracles, calculated to support those philosophical expositions of the Christian principles and tenets. For since, as we have above seen, he expressly intimates that he would, in his *Stromata*, unfold a part of that secret wisdom which was designed only for the few, but that in doing this he would not so far throw off all reserve, as to render himself universally intelligible; and since we find him, in the course of the above-mentined work, continually giving to the more excellent and important truths contained in the sacred volume, such an interpretation as tends to open a wide field for conjecture, and also comparing, not openly, but in a concise and half obscure way, the Christian tenets with the maxims of the philosophers, I am willing to resign every pretension to penetration, if it be not clearly to be perceived of what nature that sublime knowledge respecting divine matters must have been, of which he makes such a mystery. Nor was there any other species of secret knowledge besides this possessed by his principal disciple, *Origen*, who, although he was anxious to make the Christian religion conform itself, in almost every respect, to the rule of his philosophy, had yet the wisdom to propound his opinions with prudence and caution, and to avoid a full and explicit discovery of them.

What *Clement* says respecting the *divine origin* of this discipline is, unquestionably, a mere fiction, devised either by him or some other admirer of philosophy, with a view to silence the importunate remonstrances of those friends to Christian simplicity who, mindful of St. Paul's injunction, were continually protesting against any attempt to blend philosophy with the religion of the gospel. To Clement such sanctified deceptions and pious inventions appeared not at all unwarrantable; indeed, there can be no doubt, but that they were countenanced by all such of the Christian teachers as were of the Egyptian or Modern Platonic school. Why James, and John, and Peter, should have been, in particular, fixed upon as the apostles whom Christ selected as the most worthy of having this recondite wisdom communicated to them by word of mouth, is very easily to be perceived. For these were the three disciples whom our Blessed Saviour took apart with him up into the mountain when he was about to be transfigured, Matt. xvii. 1. Luke, ix. 28. To represent them, therefore, as having in a particular manner been favoured with an insight into all mysteries, appeared to be but consistent and proper.—In reality there can be no doubt but that Clement, and most probably also his masters, whose authority he frequently adduces, learnt the mode of blending philosophy with religion from Philo; and the secret discipline, or the practice of cautiously concealing their philosophical explications of the Scriptures and the principles of Christianity, from the Egyptians as well as from Philo. The thing, in fact, is not altogether dissembled by Clement, who frequently compares his secret discipline with the heathen mysteries and the interior and recondite wisdom of the philosophers, and defends it by a reference to both of these. But the matter must be clear, beyond a question, to any one who shall peruse the writings of Philo with attention; since he in many places equally extols the secret discipline, and, for the most part, speaks of it in the same terms, and defends it by the same reasons and arguments as Clement. Nor is the recondite discipline of Philo of a different nature from Clement's; on the contrary it corresponds with it in every respect. Vid. *Philo*, in lib. *de Cherubim*, p. 144, 145. [p. 308.] *de Sacrificiis*, p. 139. lib. *de Plantatione Noë*, p. 231. et passim. Being, in lib. iii. *Allegor. Legum*, p. 131. about to give an explication of the words of Sarah, in *Genesis*, xxi. 6. " God hath made me to laugh," he thus bespeaks the atten-

tion of those who were initiated in the secret discipline, Ἀναπετάσαντες τὰ ὦτα, οἱ μύςαι, παραδέξασθε τελετὰς ἱεςωτάτας. *Itaque quotquot estis initiati, expansis auribus accipite mysteria sacratissima.* After this preamble he presents the reader with a philosophical explication of these words of Sarah, which cannot be said to be altogether an obscure one, but, at the same time, it is by no means clear or perspicuous: in short, you may plainly perceive that what he aims at is, not to make himself understood generally, but only by such as had been initiated in the secret discipline or philosophical religion. In this he is imitated exactly by *Clement.* In his book lib. *de Cherubim,* p. 146, 147. edit. Anglic. p. 115. ed. Paris, Philo undertakes to explain, from the Mosaic history, the manner in which virtue is generated, and how, of itself, it generates other virtues. For first of all he thus gravely repulses the profane: Ἀκοὺς ἐπιφραξάτωσαν δεισιδάιμονες τὰς ἑαυτῶν ἢ μεταστήτωσαν. *Superstitiosi vel discedant vel obturent aures suas.* Τελετὰς γὰρ ἀναδιδάσκομεν θείας τὰς τελετῶν ἀξίως τῶν ἱεςωτάτων μύστας *divina enim mysteria tradimus his, qui talibus sacris digne initiati sunt.* ――――
Ἐκείνως δὲ ὀκ ἱεροφαντήσομεν κατεσχημένοις ἀνιάτω κακῶ, τύφω ῥημάτων κὰι ὀνομάτων γλισχρότητι, και τερθρείαις ἐθῶν. *Illos autem haudquaquam ad hæc sacra admittimus, qui tenentur morbo insanabili, fastu verborum et nominum fuco, et morum præstigiis.* Numerous passages similar to these are to be found in Clement. The explication and demonstration drawn from Moses, to which this pompous exordium is a prelude, is, indeed, upon the whole, not unintelligible; its entire force and signification, however, is not to be comprehended except by the initiated in the mysteries of the Philonian philosophy; and to all such a very earnest and particular injunction is addressed by Philo at the conclusion of his Institutes, requiring them on no account to make the vulgar partakers of their knowledge. It will be enough for me to give merely a translation of his words. "Having then, O ye initiated! through the channel of purified organs, acquired a knowledge of these things, let them sink deep into your minds as holy mysteries, not to be revealed to the profane. Bury them within your bosoms, and preserve them as a treasure; a treasure consisting, not of corruptible things, such as silver and gold, but of the fairest and most valuable portion of true wealth, namely, a knowledge of God and of virtue, and of the offspring that is generated of them both. Whenever ye chance to meet with any one else of the initiated, beseech him with the most earnest intreaties not to conceal from you any mystery that he may have more recently discovered, and leave him not until you shall have obtained from him the most intimate insight into it." In his book, *de Sacrificiis Abelis et Caini,* p. 173. tom. i. opp., he, with astonishing subtilty, deduces from *Gen.* xviii. 6, where Sarah is said have "made ready quickly three measures of fine meal, and baked cakes thereof upon the hearth," a support for the principle which he frequently takes occasion to inculcate of the existence of three powers in the Deity; and having done so, he here likewise, by way of conclusion, makes a point of remarking that neither this nor any other mystery ought to be generally made known: μηδενὶ προχείρως ἐκλαλῆ τὰ θεῖα μυςήρια, ταμιευομένη δ'αὐτὰ κὰι ἐχεμυθοῦσα ἐν ἀποῤῥήτω φυλάττη. *Anima divina mysteria nemini proloquatur facile; sed servans ea recondita reticeat et in secreto servet.* No detriment, I am persuaded, can ensue from my declining to

notice at large the remarks on this and similar passages that have been published by Thomas Mangey, the late editor of Philo, since they afford [p. 309.]
but little assistance to a reader who is desirous of penetrating into the causes
and reason of things.—It may, however, be worthy of notice in this place, that
Philo makes the principle of the existence of three powers in the Deity, concerning which there has been amongst men of the first eminence such a diversity of opinion and conjecture, a part of the secret discipline. Hence it is that
we never find him either openly propounding or attempting any explication of
it, but, on the contrary, always speaking of it in such ambiguous terms as serve
only to involve it in obscurity. Nor does he at all times observe one and the
same mode in treating of it, but pursues a very different method in some places
from what he does in others. In regard to this, see what I have said in my
notes on Cudworth's *Intellectual System*, tom. i. p. 640, as well as what has
been most learnedly remarked both in respect to this and other passages of
Philo, by that eminent scholar and most successful emulator of illustrious predecessors, Jô. Bened. Carpzovius, in his *Exercitationes in Epist. ad Hebræos ex
Philone Prolegom.* p. cxxxv. et seq. In my opinion, therefore, it must ever
prove a mere waste of time and pains to attempt any explication of the trinity
of *Philo*, or to ascertain in particular his notions respecting the nature of what
he terms the *Logos* or *Word*. The wary Jew is particularly cautious of committing himself with regard to these things, and evidently wishes to excite rather than to gratify a thirst for a more intimate insight into them. I speak from
experience; no interpretation that can be devised or thought of is readily to be
reconciled with all the different passages respecting these mysteries, that occur
in his works; indeed, such is the discordance of these passages, that they appear even totally repugnant to each other. In this way it was but befitting for
a man to proceed when treating of the secret or mysterious discipline. Ἄδεται,
says he, in his book *de Sacrificiis Abelis et Caini*, tom. i. p. 189, where, with a
very cautious and delicate hand, he touches on some of its leading points,
Ἄδεται δὲ τὶς καὶ τοιῦτος ὡς ἐν ἀπορρήτοις λόγος, ὃν ἀκοαῖς πρεσβυτέρων παρακατίτεσθαι
χρὴ νεωτέρων ὦτα ἐπιφράξαντας. *Celebratur et alia, quæ tamen ad mysteria,*
(*i. e.* the secret discipline) *pertinet sententia, deponenda penes aures seniorum, ob-
turatis juniorum auribus.* On the present occasion I cannot but feel that it
would be wrong in me to detain the reader with what else might be adduced
from Philo on this subject: a word or two more, therefore, and I have done.
Philo, without doubt, imitated the Egyptians; *Clement*, as unquestionably, followed the example of Philo; and *Origen* trod clearly in the footsteps of both.
The more recent Christian teachers, for the most part, formed themselves upon
the model of this latter father. The secret discipline of *Philo* consisted in the
application of philosophic principles to religion and the sacred writings; nor
was that of *Clement* ever thought to differ from it, except by those who had not
sufficiently informed themselves on the subject. The reader will understand
me in what I have said above as not meaning to attribute the absolute invention
of this discipline to *Philo:* for we know that long before his time it had been
the practice of several Jews to expound and illustrate Moses from the writings
of Plato and other Greek philosophers: but of this, I think, there can be **no**

doubt, that Clement and the other Egyptian teachers by whom this discipline was first introduced into the Christian church, were indebted for their acquaintance with it entirely to Philo.   Wonderful, indeed, is it to contemplate the influence and authority which this Alexandrian Jew had at one time acquired [p. 310.] amongst the Christians.   We may even go the length of saying that, without Philo, the writings of those whom we term " the Fathers" would, in many respects, be frequently altogether unintelligible.

(3) The *secret discipline* was of a more comprehensive nature than the mystical theology, inasmuch as it embraced the whole of the philosophical theology that sprung up in Egypt in the second century, and gradually found its way from thence to other nations. What we find termed *mystical theology* appears to have comprised the best and noblest part of this secret discipline; I mean that which respects life and morals, the purifying of the soul, and exalting it above every object of sense. For it is well known, that the true and genuine Mystics adopted, as the very basis and ground-work of their discipline, those principles respecting the Deity, the world, the soul, and the nature of man, which the Christians had borrowed from the Egyptian and Modern Platonic philosophy, and were accustomed, from this century downwards, to communicate merely to a select number of auditors.

XXXV. **Moral theology assumes a two-fold character.** As the love of philosophy originated amongst the Christians, a two-fold interpretation of those principles by which the intellect is instructed in the way of salvation, the one public, and accommodated to vulgar minds, the other secret, and intelligible only to capacities of the higher order ; so likewise did it occasion a two-fold form to be assumed by that wisdom which, in a more particular manner, respects life and morals; the one suited to the multitude, who incline to society and suffer themselves to be involved in the cares and concerns of this life ; the other calculated for such as, aspiring after a higher degree of sanctity and a more intimate communion with the Deity, turn their backs on the business, noise, and bustle of the world. It is true, indeed, that even at an early period, when the Christians were as yet strangers to philosophy, there were to be found amongst them persons who, by abstaining from those things which gratify the senses, such as marriage, flesh, wine, and the more solid kinds of food, and by neglecting every culture or attention to the body, sought to disengage and purify their minds from all inordinate desires and affections, and thus to consecrate themselves entirely to God :(') but upon the introduction of the Egyptian and Platonic philosophy, this simple mode of life was reduced into the form of an art, and interwoven with such maxims respecting the Deity, the human soul, and the nature of man, as were thought most consonant to reason. All such Christians, for instance, as aspired to a degree of sanctity beyond the vulgar, were enjoined, by means of contemplation, sobriety, continence, mortifications of the body, solitude, and the like, to separate, as far as possible, that soul which was the offspring of the eternal reason of the Deity, from the sensitive soul, as well as from every sort of bodily influence, so that they might, even in this life, be united to and enjoy the most intimate communion with the Supreme Parent of souls; and upon the dissolution of the body, their minds being thoroughly disencumbered of every [p. 311.] sordid and debasing tie, might regain, without impediment, their proper stations in the regions above. To this source is to be ascribed the rise of the *Mystics,* a denomination of men that first made their appearance amongst the philosophising Christians of Egypt, in the course of this century, and gradually spread themselves throughout the Christian church.(²) Hither, also, may we refer the origin of *Monks, Hermits,* and *Cœnobites,* whose rules and institutions are uniformly grounded upon the principle of delivering the immortal spirit from the oppression under which it groans in being connected with the body, of purifying it from the corruptions of sense, and of rendering it fit to be admitted into the presence of the Deity in the realms of everlasting light and life.(³)

(1) That amongst the early Christians there were some who professed a more strict and severe course of life than others, and not only debarred themselves of lawful gratifications and indulgences, but also broke down the strength and vigour of their animal frame by frequent fastings and other rigorous practices, is placed out of all doubt by numerous testimonies. It is also well known that these persons were commonly termed "*Ascetics,*" from the verb ἀσκἴω, which means to train or prepare one's self for a combat. See, amongst many other authorities, Deyling, *Exerc. de Ascetis Veterum,* subjoined to the third book of his *Observationes Sacræ;* and Bingham's *Antiquities of the Christian Church,* vol. iii. p. 3. et seq. What gave rise to this sort of people, and at what time they first made their appearance, is not equally clear. To me it appears that those Ascetics (for they were not at all of one and the same description, neither did they all observe the same rules) I say, it strikes me that those Ascetics who declined marriage and preferred a life of celibacy, without, however, rejecting any other of the comforts and conveniences of life, must have been the most ancient of any; and that persons of this description were to be found even in the very infancy of Christianity. For we know that what is said by Christ himself in *Matt.* xix. 12. respecting those who make themselves eunuchs for the kingdom

of heaven's sake, as well as what St. Paul says in 1 *Corinth.* vii. 7. 25. et seq. 33. respecting the preference due to celibacy, was by most so understood from the first as to cause it generally to be believed that unmarried persons were happier, more perfect, and more acceptable to God than others. Hence there was always to be found amongst the Christians no small number of persons who deemed it expedient to avoid marriage. Let us hear the celebrated Christian philosopher of this century, *Athenagoras,* in *Apolog. pro Christianis,* cap. xxviii. p. 129. ed. Oxon. "Ευροις δ'άν πολλὸς τῶν παρ ἡμῖν κὰι ἄνδρις κὰι γυναῖκας καταγηράσκοντας ἀγάμυς, ἐλπιδι τῦ μᾶλλον συνέσεσθαι τῷ Θεῷ. *Invenias autem multos ex nostris in utroque sexu, qui in cœlibatu consenescant, quod ita Deo se conjunctiores futuros sperent.* And to the same purport Tertullian, *de Cultu Feminar.* lib. ii. p. 179. cap. ix. ed. Rigalt. *Non enim et multi ita faciunt, et se spadonatui obsignant propter regnum Dei tam fortem et utique permissam voluptatem sponte ponentes?* Those Ascetics, who either abstained from flesh and wine, or else mortified their bodies by frequent fastings, or devoted themselves to a course of severe and laborious discipline, by way of counteracting all vicious propensities and perturbations of the mind, are, unquestionably, of more recent origin, and cannot, I think, be placed higher than [p. 312.] the age of which we are now treating. On these, also, we find commendation bestowed by the writers of this century; but they are always placed beneath those who were emphatically termed ἐγκρατεῖς "the *continent,*" in opposition to the "incontinent;" that is, they are always placed after those who had renounced marriage. *Quid enim,* says Tertullian, (de *velandis Virginibus,* cap. iii. p. 194.) *si et incontinentes dicant se a continentibus scandalizari (i. e.* supposing those who are married should complain of being scandalized by those who have professed celibacy) *continentia revocanda est?* Add to which what is to be found in DuFresne's *Glossary,* tom. ii. p. 1020. sub voc. *Continentes.* Without doubt we may conclude that Christ himself and St. Paul were considered as having expressly recommended celibacy, but that with regard to an abstinence from flesh and wine, fastings and the like, they had left behind them no particular injunctions: that the latter, therefore, although perhaps in themselves both proper and laudable, were nevertheless regarded as of merely human institution, whilst the former appeared to possess the character of a divine recommendation. Tertullian in one part of his treatise *de Cultu Fœminarum,* lib. ii. cap. ix. p. 179. makes mention of both these species of Ascetics, but in such a way as plainly to show that in point of dignity and sanctity, he gave a decided preference to the *continent,* or those whom he terms " Voluntary Eunuchs." For after having spoken of these latter, he goes on thus :—*Numquid non aliqui ipsam Dei creaturam sibi interdicunt, abstinentes vino et animalibus esculentis, quorum fructus nulli periculo aut sollicitudini adjacent, sed humilitatem animæ suæ in victus quoque castigatione Deo immolant?* To any one who will duly weigh the force of these words, and compare them with what goes before, it cannot fail to be apparent that Tertullian was far from placing the Abstinent on a level with the Continent, or those who renounced marriage.—The opinion, pretty generally entertained by the learned, that these Ascetics of the early ages were accustomed to distinguish themselves from other Christians by their dress, and that in particular, by way of pointing themselves out as philosophers, they adopted the mantle or cloak, appears to me to require the support of stronger and more positive testimony than any one has hitherto been able to adduce in its favour. I am ready to allow, indeed, that such of them as made pretensions to a greater degree of strictness either in point of continence or abstinence, might affect to make this known by the quality or colour of their garb: But that the Ascetics of the early ages, as a body of men, distinguished themselves by any peculiar dress, or that the philosopher's cloak or mantle, in particular, was ever considered as appropriate to them, is what I cannot, by any means, bring myself to believe. The testimonies that are usually brought forward in support of the above opinion are either of more recent date than the first three centuries, or else relate merely to those philosophers, who, notwithstanding their conversion to Christianity, retained this pristine garb, that is, the mantle or cloak: of which practice the reader will recollect me to have noticed some examples a few pages back. And I really must enter my protest against any such unwarrantable deduction as this,—that because those who were philosophers before they embraced the Christian faith, remained so still notwithstanding their conversion to Christianity, and continued as before to invest themselves with a cloak or mantle by way of distinction, it is incumbent on us to believe that all the Christian Ascetics assumed this cloak or philosophical dress likewise. If, however, some [p. 313.] certain individuals of the Ascetics, by way of manifesting to the world the kind of life to which they had devoted themselves, did actually assume the philosophic cloak, which I beg to be understood as by no means intending to deny, there cannot be a doubt but that they did so purely out of imitation of the heathen sages, and by way of pointing out to the Greeks and Romans, that amongst the Christians also were to be found philosophers.

(2) It was not until long after the light of Christianity had risen on the world, that the terms " mystical theology" and " *Mystics* " were ever heard of. The things themselves, however, to which these names came afterwards to be applied, are by far more ancient than the Christian church. Long antecedent to the coming of Christ, there were to be found, not only amongst the Egyptians, but also amongst the Jews, who copied after the Egyptians, (as is placed out of all question by the *Essenes* and *Therapeutæ*,) as well as in other nations, certain persons who made it their study, by means of fasting, labour, contemplation, and other afflictive exercises, to deliver their rational souls, which they considered as the offspring of the Deity unhappily confined within corporeal prisons, from the bonds of the flesh and the senses, and to restore them to an uninterrupted communion with their God and parent. This discipline arose out of that ancient *philosophy* of the Egyptians, which considered all things as having proceeded from God, and regarded the rational souls of the human race as more noble particles of the divine nature. When the Modern Platonic school made that philosophy, in a certain degree, its own, its disciples were also incited to the adoption of this system of bodily mortification. Neither, as has long since been remarked, is there any other tendency in what is laid down by Plato himself respecting the origin of minds, and of their fall into earthly bodies. *Philo,* whom we have already so often cited, will here again furnish us with

considerable light. The tenets of this very celebrated Jew, (whose opinions were for a while held in much more esteem than they deserved by the Christians,) respecting the soul, were, in fact, a compound or medley of the Egyptian, Platonic, and Mosaic principles. In the first place, he lays it down, that in man there are *two souls;* the one rational and generated of the Word, the other sensitive : *de Allegor. Legis*, lib. i. p. 51, 54, 57. tom. i. opp. The former or rational mind he regards as a portion of the Deity, that is, according to the Egyptians, a part of the most refined and supreme æther, and that conformably to the Mosaic account, this had been imparted to man by the breath of God; in which it is to be remarked that he differs from Plato. Vid. *Allegor. Legis*, lib. iii. p. 119. The latter or sensitive soul he considers as impelled and animated by the divine mind, *Allegor. Legis*. lib. i. p. 51 and 54. The rational soul, according to him, is the seat of abstract notions; whilst the sensitive soul is occupied solely by the images of things that are objects of the senses : *de Mundi Opificio*, p. 41. et seq. tom. i. ed. Anglic. I pass over a variety of things which, for the most part, border too nearly on excessive refinement, and are not laid down with sufficient perspicuity. Proceeding on principles like these, he inculcates a doctrine altogether similar to that taught by the Mystics; namely, that the celestial and rational soul should erect itself above every object of the senses,—that it should seek, by means of contemplation, to separate itself from the body,—that, mindful of its divine origin, it should be constantly aspiring to communion with its parent, and that it should endeavour, by every possible means, to undermine and weaken the power and influence of the body and the senses. To a soul once exalted above empty and corporeal things, he holds forth a promise of divine illumination and pleasure incredible.—It may not be [p. 314.] amiss, perhaps, to confirm what I have thus stated by a specimen or two, in order that the votaries of mysticism may be brought acquainted with the sources from whence those principles, in which they so much delight, are drawn. Let us then hear with what pomp and poetical colouring *Philo* describes the ascent of the soul to God, *de Mund. Opificio*, p. 16. tom. i. opp.

Ψυχὴ πᾶσαν τὴν αἰσθητὴν ἐσίαν ὑπερκύψας ἐνταῦθα ἐφίπται τῆς νοητῆς καὶ ὧν εἶδεν ἐνταῦθα αἰσθητῶν, ἐν ἐκείνη τὰ παραδείγματα καὶ τὰς ἰδέας θεασάμενος, ὑπερβάλλοντα κάλλη, μέθη νηφαλίω κατασχεθεὶς, ὥσπερ οἱ κορυβαντιῶντες, ἐνθυσία, ἐτέρω γεμίσθεὶς ἱμέρω καὶ πόθω βελτίονος. *Anima emergens supra omnem sensibilem essentiam demum intelligibilis desiderio corripitur,* (we have here, obviously, what is termed by the Mystics, the *"purgation,"* next follows their *" illumination,"*) *illic conspicata exemplaria, ideasque rerum quas hic vidit sensibilium, eximias illas pulchritudines,* (a coincidence with the Platonic philosophy is here observable,) *ebrietate quadam sobria capta, tamquam Corybantes lymphatur alio plena amore longe meliore.* This high measure of felicity is crowned by a conjunction with the Parent Deity of all things : ὑφ' ὃ πρὸς τὴν ἄκραν ἀψίδα παραπεμφθεὶς τῶν νοητῶν ἐπ' αὐτὸν ἰέναι δοκεῖ τὸν μέγαν βασιλέα. Γλιχομένω δ' ἰδεῖν, θεῖν φωτὸς ἄκρατοι καὶ ἄμιγεις αὐγαὶ χειμάρρω τρόπον ἐκχέονται, ὡς ταῖς μαρμαρυγαῖς τὸ τῆς διανοίας ὄμμα σκοτοδινίαν. *A quo ad summum fastigium adducta rerum intelligibilium, ad ipsum magnum regem videtur tendere ; tum vero in videndi cupidam purissimus ac merissimus divinæ lucis radius more torrentis effunditur, ita ut ad eum splendorem caliget mentis oculus.* Surely the reader will believe that he has been listening to the Coryphæus of the Mystics, *Dionysus,* or to some *Henry Suso,* or to some other similar character. In his *Allegor. Legis.* lib. i. p. 59, 60. he divides souls into two classes, " the *Confessing*" (ἐξομολογυμένυς), and " the *Labouring*" (ἐργαζομένυς). The " confessing souls " are those which, being freed from all contagion of the body, as well as divested of all cogitation and emotion, and exalted above every object of the senses, have given themselves up entirely to God, and maintain themselves in the most perfect state of quietism. Ὅταν γὰρ ἐκβῆ ὁ νῦς ἑαυτῦ καὶ ἑαυτὸν ἀνενέγκη Θεῶ - - - - τηνικᾶυτα ὁμολογίαν τὴν πρὸς τὸν ὄντα ποιεῖται. Now, in what author, I would ask, shall we find language better agreeing with the pompous declamation of the Mystics, or more aptly coinciding with their discipline ? *Quum mens extra semetipsam excesserit, Deoque seipsum obtulerit — — — — tunc confessionem edit erga eum qui solus vere est.* But let us proceed :— ἑὼς δὲ ἀυτὸν ὑποτίθηται ὡς ἀιτίον τινος, μάκξαν ἀρίσηκε τῦ παραχαξεῖν Θεῶ καὶ ὁμολογεῖν ἀυτῶ. *Quamdiu vero anima se causam rei cujuspiam existimat* (that is, so long as the soul itself thinks, or reflects, or exercises a will of its own) *multum abest quin confiteatur, cedatque Deo.* But even all this is not sufficient: for he will not allow even that cessation of the soul from every kind of action or exertion, which he enjoins, and which is the object or end of the mystic life, to be the work of the soul, but will have it to be the operation of the Deity. The rational soul, he maintains, to be a portion of the Deity, and that it is therefore by the innate, or rather implanted power of God in her, that she is enabled to cast off the bonds of the flesh and the sensitive soul, and to compose herself to a state of the most perfect quietism. Κὰι γὰρ ἀυτὸ τῦτο [p. 315.] τὸ ἐξομολογεῖσθαι νοητέον, ὁτι ἔργον ἐστὶ ὀχὶ τῆς ψυχῆς, ἀλλὰ τῦ φαίνοντος ἀυτῆ Θεῦ τὸ ἐυχάξιστον. *Nam et ipsa confessio debet intelligi non animæ opus, sed Dei qui eam hanc gratitudinem docet.* The " *labouring souls* " of Philo are those which endeavour, by a constant exercise of thought, reflection, and judgment, to arrive at virtue ; and strive to counteract all vicious propensities and perturbations, by means of reading, meditation, and prayer : and concerning these he subsequently discourses much at large.—Let us now endeavour briefly to ascertain from his *Allegor. Legis.* lib. i. p. 64, 65. what his doctrine was respecting the *body.* The very perfection of true wisdom he pronounces to consist in alienating one's self from the body and its concupiscence. Under the denomination of the body, however, he immediately gives us to understand that he means to include the *senses,* also, of the body, nay, even the very *voice* itself; so that he should seem to enjoin a man desirous of attaining to a state of virtue, not only to mortify the senses, but also to forego the use of his tongue and voice. Σχεδὸν γὰρ σεςίας ἔργον τῦτ' ἐστὶν, ἀλλοτριῦσθαι πρὸς τὸ σῶμα, καὶ τας ἐπιθυμίας ἀυτῦ ἐις δ'ἀπολᾶυσιν κακίας, ἢ μόνον δεῖ πῶς ἔχειν τὸν νῦν, ἀλλὰ καὶ την αἴσθησιν, κὰι τὸν λόγον, καὶ τὸ σῶμα. This subject is pursued by him at much length, and he cites in support of his doctrine even Moses himself, with whom he maintains that Heraclitus is in perfect unison. Lastly, he asserts that the soul, during its continuance in the body, lies, as it were, buried in a sepulchre, and partakes in no degree of life, until after its separation from

25

vitiated and inert matter. Ψυχῆς ὡς ἂν ἐν σήματι τῷ σώματι ἐντετομϐευμένης· ἐι δὲ ἀποϑάνοιμεν τῆς ψυχῆς ζώσης τὸν ἰδίον βίον καὶ ἀπελλαγμένης κακᾶ καὶ νεκρᾶ τῷ συνδέτν σώματος. *Anima corpori insepulta est tamquam monumento : quod si mortui fuerimus,* (the soul being delivered from the body,) *tum demum anima vivit vitam propriam, et a colligato sibi corpore, quod malum et mortuum est, liberatam.* In short, it would be easy for any one, who might be so inclined, to collect from the writings of Philo an entire body of mystical theology, corresponding even to minuteness, with the system of Dionysius and the other Mystics of more recent times. I cannot, therefore, help feeling somewhat surprised that Arnold Poiret and others should, in their catalogue of mystic writers, have omitted to insert the name of this Jew, than whom, certainly, there is not a more ancient mystical author extant amongst us, and from whom, it should seem, that the philosophising Christians drew the greatest part of their mystic discipline.

The principles and maxims, then, of which we have been speaking, having, in the course of this century, insinuated themselves into the minds of the Egyptian Christians, and their teachers and instructors beginning also to acquire a strong relish for the writings of Philo, there sprung up suddenly a two-fold species of piety and virtue, the one popular and public, the other mysterious and secret; as also a two-fold order of Christians, the one consisting of " *Operants,*" or those who engaged in the labours and business of life ; the other of " *Quiescents,*" or those who endeavoured, by means of frequent meditation, corporeal mortifications, silence, solitude, debilitating of the senses, and the like, to deliver the soul from the prison of the body, and unite it to the parent or fountain of all minds. Of each of these species of discipline, very obvious traces are to be discovered in the writings of *Clement* of Alexandria and *Justin* [p. 316.] *Martyr,* which have as yet, however, been adverted to but by a few, and by some even of these been wrongly interpreted. By *Christ. Thomasius,* for instance, an author who, on other occasions, has proved himself to be a man of erudition, as well as by some others, an accusation was, not many years back, preferred against Justin Martyr and other Christian teachers of this and the succeeding century, on the ground of their having been guilty of a most base and ridiculous sophism in maintaining that Christ, or the Word, was in all the Grecian philosophers, and more especially in Socrates, and that through this *Christ,* or Interior *Word,* these men had attained unto everlasting salvation. Vid. *Observat. Halens. Latin.* tom. ii. observ. VII. § xxx. p. 108. et seq. It is certain, however, that these persons have rather betrayed their own ignorance of ancient matters, than convicted either Justin or his associates of any thing like misrepresentation. The reasoning of Justin, according to Platonic principles, which he and other Christians of those times had been led to espouse, was perfectly correct, nor did he, as has been insinuated, by a kind of amphibology, impose either on himself or others, but cherished precisely the same opinion respecting an indwelling *Christ,* and an Interior *Word,* as is entertained by the Mystics of modern times. According to these Christian disciples of Plato and Philo Judæus, *Christ* is the same in God that *reason* is in man. Believing, therefore, as they did, that all minds or souls originally were parts of, and sprung from the *Logos*, or Divine Reason, an opinion which they had derived partly from the Egyptians, and in part from Plato, it could not but follow that they should consider *Christ* as dwelling in the minds of all men, and as operating and acting in all who followed the dictates of right reason. With regard to the consequences attendant on this, I have not, at present, room to enter into any discussion of them.

In dismissing this subject, however, I cannot help directing the reader's attention, in a particular manner, to the wonderful influence which country and climate have on men's morals, modes of life, and opinions. The notion of all minds having sprung from God, and that they were to be brought back to a state of the most perfect quiescence in the bosom of this their first great parent by means of contemplation, and corporeal mortifications, originated in regions where men's bodies are oppressed and exsiccated by the solar heat, and was communicated from thence to other nations. In those countries, the immoderately fervid state of the atmosphere renders men averse to labour or action of any kind; and causes them to place their supreme felicity in rest, in contemplation, in a cessation from every kind of action of mind as well as of body. As it was impossible for them then to regard the Deity in any other light than as superlatively happy, they were naturally led to believe that God himself acted in no way whatever, but committed the government of the universe to dæmons or genii, and preserved himself in a state of perfect quiescence, ease, and contemplation. Hence proceeded those tenets of the orientals,—of God being like a light of the most pure and serene nature,—of the world and its inhabitants being committed to the care and guardianship of dæmons,—of the absolute inaction and quietism of the Supreme Being,—of the tranquil procession of all things from the Deity, without any decree or exertion on his part, and the like. So prone are mortals, in forming their notions of the Deity, to have too much respect for what passes within their own bosoms, and to make the contracted scale of their own senses a standard whereby to estimate the feelings and felicity of Omnipotence. Again, believing, as the people of those countries did, that the minds of men, like all other things, had emanated from God, and were partakers of the divine nature, it was but consentaneous that they should [p. 317.] place the felicity of these also, and the very height of religion, in contemplation and stillness, and should both point out the way of attaining to that tranquillity, and also pronounce those to be the happiest, and most like to God, who secluded themselves from the society of men, and, turning their backs on the concerns of this world, passed their days in a state of most sacred inaction and holy ease. These opinions, when they came to be blended with Christianity, gave rise to a multitude of solitary and gloomy characters, who were at first chiefly confined to Egypt, but whose example, inasmuch as it carried with it a great appearance of sanctity, was quickly followed by great numbers in other nations. By the inhabitants of regions where the cold strings the nerves, and invigorates men's bodies so as to give them a propensity to action and labour, a very different notion of the Deity had been formed, and consequently their conceptions of mental happiness by no means corresponded with those entertained in more genial climates. Instead of a God delighting only in quiet and repose, we here find a

Deity all business and activity. *Mystical theology*, therefore, the offspring of a burning climate and a slothful race of mortals, found, upon its introduction into Europe from the East, an abundance of admirers and eulogists, but no very great number of disciples who exemplified its precepts in their lives. In point both of morals and institutions there was always a very material difference between our monks and mystics and those of Egypt, India, Syria, and Arabia. Men born under skies like ours, are strangers to that apathy and inertness which constitute, as it were, the very soul of the mystic discipline. Indeed of this wonderful influence of climate we are furnished with an illustration even in the provinces of Europe alone. For, confining ourselves merely to this quarter of the globe, we shall find that, in districts exposed to the rays of a fervid sun, the votaries and friends of Mysticism are numerous, whilst in countries of a moderate or frigid temperature there are to be met with but very few, if any.

(3) That there was a difference between the *monks* and the *Ascetics* of the first ages, has of late been very generally insisted on, and, in my opinion, on very sufficient grounds. According to my view of the subject, there was certainly not only a difference, but a very great difference, between them. I am bound to confess, however, that it appears to me no less certain that the monks were derived from the Ascetics. As long as the Ascetic regimen consisted merely in continence, and an abstinence from sensual gratifications and indulgences, and was unfettered by any of the precepts of the Egyptian philosophy, there was nothing to prevent men professing it from continuing in society, and residing in the midst of their kindred and their families: but when that regimen assumed a different aspect, when it came to be reduced into a system, and connected with the philosophical doctrines respecting the nature of the soul, and of bodies; when the Ascetics adopted the belief, that every endeavour was to be used to set free the divine spark that lay imprisoned within the body,—to subdue the influence of the senses,—to separate the mind from sense, and restore it to its first original,—to blot from it all sensual images, and repress in it every tendency to perturbation; when they came to regard Quietism as constituting the supreme good,—when their doctrines, I say, had once assumed this character, it was but natural for them to renounce the society of men, and devote themselves to a life of seclusion and solitude. For they surely could have found nothing more difficult than, amidst the noise of worldly occupations and the frequent interruptions of friends and acquaintance, to regulate their lives according to these principles, *i. e.* to purify the mind, to repress the senses, and to maintain a tranquillity unruffled by any sort of cogitation or emotion whatever. These principles, which [p. 318.] the *Ascetics* in Egypt first imbibed from the mouths and writings of their teachers towards the close of this century, were by far more widely diffused in the succeeding one, owing to a love for the Egyptian, or, if the reader would rather, the Alexandrian and Ammonian philosophy becoming every day more general amongst the African and Asiatic Christians. About this period, therefore, we find the *Ascetics* beginning to withdraw themselves from cities and the society of men, and retiring into solitudes and deserts, and hence they acquired the title of " *monks,*" *i. e.* solitary persons. Vid. Cassian, *Collation.* xviii. cap. v. p. 517. opp. The reader will not, however, understand me as

meaning to deny that there had been, even at an earlier period, some few who, by way of arriving at a higher degree of sanctity, had renounced every intercourse with men, and spent their lives in retirement and seclusion from the world: for there are many circumstances which tend to induce in us a belief that such was actually the case. But of this there can be no doubt, that until the Christians began to entertain a partiality for that pernicious species of philosophy to which we have so often adverted, it was by no means deemed necessary to forego all intercourse with the world, to attain to even the very highest degrees of sanctity, and that by far the greater part of the Ascetics never did segregate themselves from the families to which they belonged. When at length the Ascetics, by way of more readily delivering the imprisoned soul from the bondage of the body and the senses, and rendering it capable of perceiving and holding communion with the Deity, were led to separate themselves from all commerce with the world, they by degrees adopted the plan of forming themselves into societies or colleges, and having agreed on a rule of life correspondent with their tenets, each society chose for itself a governor, director, or superintendant, to whom the rest of the collective body might look up for example, advice, and encouragement. Hence the origin of monasteries and abbeys.—But there were some to whom even this kind of social intercourse, limited as it was, appeared incompatible with the grand design of liberating and composing the immortal mind. To them there appeared to be danger lest a community of labours and prayers, nay, even the very seeing and holding converse with the brotherhood might awaken the mind to various cogitations and emotions, and thus prevent it from arriving at a state of quiet and repose. They, therefore, withdrew into deserts and caverns, and there devoted themselves to a life of severity and mortification, a life, in fact, estranged from every kind of human solace and convenience, and hence they come to be termed " *Anchorites* " or " *Hermits.*"—I will confirm what I have thus said respecting the causes which occasioned the Ascetics to withdraw from the world and become monks, by the testimony of *Cassian*, as to the end or purpose of the monastic life, which must, in the present instance, be allowed to possess the greatest weight, inasmuch as it conveys the sentiments of some of the immediate successors of these first Christian monks. For it is well known that *Cassian* drew what he records respecting monastic affairs and institutions from the monks of Egypt, with whom he was particularly conversant. Thus then in *Collation* ix. ch. ii. p. 360. he introduces the illustrious Egyptian Abbot, Isaac, as expressing himself: *Omnis monachi finis, cordisque perfectio ad jugem atque indisruptam orationis perseverantiam tendit, et quantum humanæ fragilitati conceditur, ad immobilem tranquillitatem mentis ac perpetuam nititur puritatem. Ob quam possidendam, omnem tam laborem corporis, quam contritionem spiritus indefesse* [p. 319.] *quærimus et jugiter exercemus, et est inter alterutrum reciproca quædam inseparabilisque conjunctio.* And in chap. iii. *Ab omni discursu atque evagatione lubrica animus inhibendus, ut ita paulatim ad contemplationem Dei ac spiritualis intuitus incipiat sublimari.* In Collation i. which is entitled *de Monachi intentione*, we find this subject treated of at much length by another Egyptian abbot of the name of Moses, who, in chap. iv. p. 219. states, amongst other things, that, *finis professionis monachorum est regnum Dei, sed destinatio eorum est illam cordis purificationem quæ ad visionem Dei ducat.* This he, in chap. viii. p. 221. illustrates by the example of Martha and Mary, affirming that a monk ought *a contemplatione ascendere ad illud quod dicitur unum, id est, Dei solius intuitum, ut etiam sanctorum actus et ministeria mirifica supergressus, solius Dei jam pulchritudine scientiaque pascatur.*—Monks, or Mystics, were, therefore, the offspring of that secret moral discipline of the Christians which was built upon the Egyptian philosophical tenets respecting the Deity, the world, the soul, and the nature of man ; and may be placed much on a level with the Essenes and Therapeutæ of the Jews. Some faint vestiges of this are discoverable, even at the present hour, in the minds and institutions of the monks of Syria, Egypt, and Greece ; of which, did I not feel myself called upon to bring this note to a speedy conclusion, I could readily adduce very abundant proof. The European monks of our times, on the contrary, appear to have altogether lost every idea of the causes that gave birth to the mode of life which they profess, and scarcely retain any semblance, or even shadow of primitive manners or regulations. In this, however, there is nothing that should occasion any great surprise. Mystical theology and its offspring, the monastic life, are the fruit of an ardent sun and a parching climate, and, consequently, not at all calculated to arrive at any degree of maturity in our part of the world. It has uniformly happened, therefore, to all the various orders of monks that have at different times been established under skies so temperate as ours, that, within a short period, they experience no very trifling abatement of their primitive fervor, and suffer the precepts and institutions of their founders to become, as it were, a mere dead letter.

XXXVI. **Alteration in the form of Divine worship.** Religion having thus, in both its branches, the speculative as well as the practical, assumed a two-fold character, the one public or common, the other private or mysterious, it was not long before a distinction of a similar kind took place also in the Christian discipline, and form of Divine worship. For observing that in Egypt, as well as in other countries, the heathen worshippers, in addition to their public religious ceremonies, to which every one was admitted without distinction, had certain secret and most sacred rites, to which they gave the name of *"mysteries,"* and at the celebration of which none, except persons of the most approved faith and discretion, were permitted to be present, the Alexandrian Christians first, and after them others, were beguiled into a notion that they could not do better than make the Christian discipline accommodate itself to this model. The multitude professing Christianity were therefore divided by them into the [p. 320.] *"profane,"* or those who were not as yet admitted to the mysteries, and the *"initiated,"* or faithful and perfect. To the former belonged the *"catechumens,"* or those that had indeed enrolled themselves under the Christian banner, but had never been regularly received into the fellowship of Christ's flock by the sacrament of baptism; as also those who, for some transgression or offence had been expelled from communion with the Faithful. The latter, who were properly termed *"the church,"* consisted of all such as had been regularly admitted into the Christian community by baptism, and had never forfeited their privileges, as well as of those who, having by some misconduct incurred the penalty of excommunication, had, upon their repentance, been again received into the bosom of the church. It became, moreover, customary, even in this century, more especially in Egypt and the neighbouring provinces, for persons desirous of being admitted into either of these classes, to be previously exercised and examined, we may even say tormented, for a great length of time, with a variety of ceremonies, for the most part nearly allied to those that were observed in preparing people for a sight of the heathen mysteries. Upon the same principle, a two-fold form was given to Divine worship, the one general and open to the people at large, the other special and concealed from all, except the faithful or initiated. To the latter belonged the common prayers, baptism, the *agapæ* or love-feasts, and the Lord's Supper; and as none were permitted to be present at these *"mysteries,"* as they were termed, save those whose admission into the fellowship of the church was perfect and complete, so likewise was it expected that, as a matter of duty, the most sacred silence should be observed in regard to everything connected with the celebration of them, and nothing whatever relating thereto be committed to the ears of the profane. From this constitution of things it came to pass, not only that many terms and phrases made use of in the heathen mysteries were transferred and applied to different parts of the Christian worship, particularly to the sacraments of baptism and the Lord's Supper,(¹) but that, in not a few instances, the sacred rites of the church were contaminated by the introduction of various pagan forms and ceremonies.(²)

(1) Instances in abundance, of terms and phrases applied after this manner, are to be found in *Clement* of Alexandria alone, who seems, as it were, to pride himself in placing the rites of Christianity on a parallel with the heathen mys-

teries, and in applying to the former certain terms and modes of expression deduced from the latter. Possibly we may not do wrong in referring to this source the application of the term " *Symbolum*" to those professions of faith which were made use of to distinguish the Christians from the rest of the world. The signs or watch-words communicated to those who were admissible to the mysteries, in proof of their fraternization, and that they might be readily distinguished from impostors, were, it is well known, termed "*Symbola.*" The oriental Christians, also, of this age, were accustomed to compare baptism with that lustration with which it was the practice to consecrate, in a certain [p. 321.] degree, those who were about to be initiated in the mysteries; and the profession of faith, delivered at the font, with the watch-word, or sign, communicated to the candidates for admission to the secret rights of heathenism : on which account it was usual for this profession of faith to be solemnly delivered in the very act of baptism to every one admitted into the church. Indeed, in its operation the profession of faith, to which we allude, was by no means dissimilar to the sign of mystical initiation amongst the heathen. For as, by means of the latter, those who had been admitted to a participation of the mysteries, were to be distinguished from the profane, so likewise, did that sum of the Christian religion, which newly baptized persons received at the font, serve as a mark whereby to know the true faithful, not only from heathen worshippers, but also from the catechumens. To any one allowing to this a due measure of attention, I think it will not appear improbable, that the term "*Symbol*" was one of those things that were adopted by the Christians from the discipline of the heathen mysteries. Nothing, certainly, is more common than for two things having several points of resemblance, to come in the course of time to be distinguished by one and the same title.

(2) A subject highly favourable, as it should seem, to the display of literary talent, and, certainly, every way worthy of the attention of a scholar well versed in matters of antiquity, has long offered itself to the public in the rites derived by the Christians, from the discipline of the mysteries. As yet, however, it has never been regularly taken up by any one. Until this be done, evidence sufficiently manifest and positive, as to the fact of the adoption of heathen forms and ceremonies by the Christians, is to be collected from the following authors as well as others ; *viz.* Is. Casaubon. *Exerc.* XVI. *in Annal. Baron.* p. 388. Ia. Tollius, *Insignib. Itineris Italici ; Not.* p. 151, 163. Anton. van Dale, *Diss. in Antiquit. et Marmora,* diss. I. p. 1. 2. Pet. King, *Hist. Apost. Creed,* cap. i. § xvi. p. 8. 15. 23. Ez. Spanheim, *Remarques sur les Empereurs de Julien,* p. 133. 134. 138. 434. et seq. Edm. Merill, *Observat.* lib. iii. cap. iii. David Clarkson, *Discours sur les Liturgies,* p. 36. 42, 43.—Should any one inquire what causes could possibly have led the Christian teachers to adopt the rights of paganism, I answer, that in all probability, their only motive was an anxious desire to enlarge the bounds of the church. The rites, themselves, certainly possessed no very particular recommendation in point of grandeur or dignity ; but a hope might very naturally be entertained, that the heathen worshippers, upon finding somewhat of an accordance to subsist between the religion in which they had been bred up, and Christianity, as to externals, might the more readily be pre-

vailed on to dismiss their prejudices and embrace the latter. The end proposed in this case was, in itself, certainly of the most pure and upright nature, and may, therefore, justly be entitled to our praise ; but it must, at the same time, be acknowledged, that the means made use of for attaining it were not equally unexceptionable and praiseworthy.

XXXVII. **Christian writers.** As by far a greater number of learned and philosophical characters were converted to Christianity in the course of this century than during the preceding one, it is not to be wondered at, that this period should also have had to boast of many more authors who consecrated their talents to the service of the true religion and the edification of the brethren. Numerous, however, as the Christian writers of this age were, but few can be named whose works have escaped the ravages of time. Of those who wrote in Greek there are [p. 322.] three of distinguished eminence, namely, *Irenæus, Justin Martyr,* and *Clement* of Alexandria; men whom, allowing for the times in which they lived, we certainly cannot otherwise regard than as learned, eloquent, and gifted with no contemptible degree of genius and talent. The first of these having passed from Asia Minor into Gaul, was primarily made a presbyter, and afterwards bishop, of a small church which had in this century been founded at Lyons. Of his writings in support of the Christian faith, which were not a few, none besides his *five books against heresies* have come down to our time; and indeed these (with the exception of the first) have reached us merely through the medium of a wretchedly barbarous and obscure Latin translation.(') The second, who was finally led to embrace Christianity after having tried almost every philosophical sect, published, amongst many other works, *two Apologies for the Christians,* addressed to the emperors Antoninus Pius, and Marcus Aurelius, which are not undeservedly held in very high estimation.(²) Both of these suffered martyrdom in the cause of Christ; the latter at Rome under the reign of the emperor Marcus, the former at Lyons during the persecution of Severus.—The third, a presbyter of the church of Alexandria, and præfect of the Christian school established in that city, was a man of various reading, and particularly well versed in the literature of ancient Greece. Of the numerous works in behalf of Christianity that are ascribed to him, we possess merely his *Stromata. Pedagogue,* and *Exhortation to the Greeks.* Unfortunately his attachment to philosophy was such as to lead him into many and very great errors.(³) To these three are to be added *Theophilus,* bishop of Antioch, whose *three books to Autolycus,* in defence of the verity and dignity of the Christian religion, are still extant. *Tatian,* an Assyrian philosopher and orator, of whose numerous writings we possess no other than an *Oration addressed to the Gentiles* of his time, but which will not be found undeserving of perusal, even in the present day; and finally *Athenagoras,* a philosopher of no mean rank, and præfect of the Christian school of Alexandria, whose *Apology for the Christians,* and *Treatise concerning the Resurrection,* have both of them happily escaped the ravages of time.(⁴)

Of the Christian *Latin writers* of this century none of any name or value have reached our days except *Tertullian,* who was originally a lawyer, but afterwards became a presbyter of the church of Carthage. Much of ingenuity and acumen undoubtedly discovers itself in the various treatises of this author now extant, which are written partly in defence of the Christian religion against its enemies and corrupters; and partly with a view to the reformation of men's morals, and the lighting up within their bosoms a spirit of genuine godliness and piety; but they are all of them composed in a style, not only tumid and bombastic, but [p. 323.] beyond all measure obscure. The opinions, moreover, which they exhibit, are harsh, oftentimes uncertain, and not less foreign from reason than from the sacred writings. In fine, they plainly indicate him to have been a man of a credulous turn of mind, much addicted to severity, and possessed of more subtilty than solid learning.(⁵)

(1) Two very splendid editions of the books of Irenæus *adversus Haereses,* were given to the world soon after the commencement of the eighteenth century. The one by the learned Io. Ernest. *Grabe,* Oxon. 1702, fol. the other by Ren. *Massuet,* a Benedictine of the congregation of St. Maur. Lutet. Paris. 1710. fol. To the last are prefixed very ample dissertations by the editor, in which a variety of things relating to Irenæus and the sects whose principles he combats are brought under examination and illustrated. By both of these, however, a wide field has been left open to any future editor of Iranæus. Many are the passages that still require the hand of a sagacious emendator, and many are the passages that still invite the attention of an erudite and able expositor. Each of the above-named editors hath fallen into numerous errors even with regard to the very distinction of words.

(2) An edition of the works of Justin, the philosopher and martyr, (we purposely omit noticing any editions of particular tracts of his, such as his *two Apologies* and his *Dialogue with Trypho*) was published at London in the year 1722. fol. by Styan *Thirlby*, an ingenious writer, but who has omitted every thing that has been improperly attributed to Justin. This edition has never been held in much estimation. A more ample one was published at Paris, 1742, fol. by Prudentius *Maranus*, a Benedictine monk, who has included every thing that goes under the name of Justin, and enriched the whole with copious notes, and some long dissertations of his own. To Justin, moreover, are added the following minor Greek writers of this century, viz. *Tatian, Athenagoras, Theophilus*, of Antioch, and *Hermias*, the author of a little book holding up the Greek philosophers to ridicule, and to which he gave the title of *Irrisio*. The diligence of Prudentius in collecting various readings and passages of ancient writers, entitles him certainly to commendation; but he is by no means happy in his judgment of the opinions of Justin and others of the fathers, or in his proposed corrections of the errors of transcribers.

(3) A very excellent and beautiful edition of Clemens Alexandrinus was published by Archbishop *Potter*, Oxon. 1715, fol. The world, however, has been taught to look for a better and more ample one, to the French Benedictines.

Potter, a man of very great ability, and particularly well skilled in Greek literature, has certainly, in an eminent degree, deserved well of Clement. For he has discovered a peculiar felicity in the restoration of a great number of passages, and aptly illustrated many others by quotations from ancient authors. Owing, however, to a weakness of sight, and the pressure of matters of the first moment, it was not permitted to this illustrious character to do all that, under different circumstances, he might have accomplished. The Latin translation, therefore, still remains incorrect, and in many parts we have still to lament a want of light and perspicuity. Very great difficulty is oftentimes to be encountered in developing Clement's meaning, it being frequently involved in much obscurity, and founded upon maxims or principles, at present, but little known: neither is it by any means an easy matter, on many occasions, to perceive the order and concatenation of his thoughts.

(4) An edition of *Theophilus*, separately corrected and illustrated was [p. 324.] published by Io. Christ. *Wolf*, Hamb. 1724, 8vo. The remains of this Christian writer were again given to the world, with additional annotations and various readings, by Prudentius Maranus, at the end of his edition of Justin Martyr. *Tatian* was published separately by William *Worth*, Oxon. 1700. 8vo.; and *Athenagoras* by Edw. *Dechair*, Oxon. 1706, 8vo.; both enriched with various annotations of learned men. Nothing, certainly, can be more beautiful than these two editions, in point of external form, but of their internal merit we are constrained to speak with some reserve; for whether regard be had to the words themselves, or to the sense intended to be conveyed by them, there was certainly abundant room afforded for bringing forward these authors to much greater advantage.

(5) Of all the editions of Tertullian's works, that of Nic. Rigaltius, Paris,

1641, fol. may be deemed the best.   The one published by Ph. Priorius, Paris, 1663, fol. is indeed more enriched with annotations of the learned, but not better or more correct.   The two editions which have subsequently issued from the Venetian press, are, in point of beauty and elegance, far behind those of Paris: nor is their fidelity always to be relied on.   An edition of this very obscure writer, at once comprehensive, accurate, and sufficiently illustrated, has long been a desideratum with the students of ecclesiastical antiquities.   Such an one has, at different times, been promised to the world, by men of very eminent abilities, and amongst the rest, by the Benedictine fraternity, but, unless I am altogether deceived, the learned will never be gratified with such an edition of Tertullian as they would wish to possess.   For not to notice the obsolete and unusual terms which he, on some occasions, seems studiously to go out of the way for, and equally passing over a variety of phrases connected with jurisprudence, and of which it is scarcely to be hoped that any one should give us any satisfactory explanation at the present day, his thoughts are, in innumerable in stances, expressed in a way so concise, so obscure, and so ambiguous, that we are left in a state of utter uncertainty as to what it is that he means.

XXXVIII. **Rise and propagation of Christian sects.   Judaizing Christians.** Amidst this mixture of prosperous and untoward circumstances, and these endeavours, on the part of certain teachers, to render letters and philosophy instrumental in giving additional stability and recommendation to the cause of Christianity, the church most unhappily became divided into various factions and sects, which had for their authors and leaders a set of men who wished rather to take their own wisdom for a standard than to be guided by the words of Christ and his apostles.   The first dissension of this nature that took place occurred amongst the Christians of Palestine under the reign of the emperor *Hadrian.* For when Jerusalem, which had begun in some measure to revive from its ashes, was finally razed to the foundation by this emperor, and the whole Jewish nation were rendered subject to laws of the most rigorous cast, the greatest part of the Christians inhabiting Palestine renounced the law of Moses, to which they [p. 325.] had before paid obedience, and placed themselves under the guidance of a leader named *Marcus,* who was not a Jew, but a stranger, and whom they appear to have selected for the express purpose of manifesting that they meant to have nothing in common with the Jews.   Filled with indignation at this proceeding of their brethren, the rest of the Jewish converts, who still retained an immoderate attachment to the law of Moses, withdrew into that part of Palestine which is distinguished by the name of

Perœa, and there established a peculiar church of their own, in which the ceremonial law was retained in all its ancient dignity. This church, which could, unquestionably, have been but a small one, never attained to any degree of celebrity, but, after having maintained its ground in Palestine for some centuries, began, not long after the age of Constantine the Great, to go back, and gradually dwindled away into nothing.(')

(1) A very notable passage relating to this matter, occurs in *Sulpitius Severus, Histor. Sacr.* lib. ii. cap. xxxi. p. 245. *Et quia Christiani (i. e.* those living in Palestine) *ex Judæis potissimum putabantur (namque tum Hierosolymæ non nisi ex circumcisione habebat ecclesia sacerdotem) militum cohortem custodias in perpetuum agitare jussit, quæ Judæos omnes Hierosolymæ aditu arceret. Quod quidem Christianæ fidei proficiebat : quia tum pæne omnes Christum Deum sub legis observatione credebant. Nimirum id Domino ordinante, dispositum, ut legis servitus a libertate fidei atque ecclesiæ tolleretur. Ita tum primum Marcus ex gentibus apud Hierosolymam episcopus fuit.* Although this passage of *Sulpitius* is neither so lucid nor so regular as might be wished, it yet clearly points out the origin of that church, which held, that by becoming Christians men did not exonerate themselves from the necessity of observing the law of Moses. For it appears from it ; (I.) That the Christians of Jewish extraction, residing within the confines of Palestine, as long as any hope remained that Jerusalem might recover from its first overthrow, were accustomed to unite an observance of the Mosaic ritual with the worship of Christ. (II.) That the greatest part of these Christians were, under the reign of *Hadrian,* when every hope of seeing Jerusalem revive was extinguished, induced to repudiate the law of Moses, and chose one *Marcus,* a stranger, for their bishop. This, unquestionably, they did under an apprehension that if they appointed a bishop of Hebrew origin he might be induced, from an innate attachment to the law of his forefathers' to attempt the gradual restoration of those ceremonies which they had come to the determination of for ever renouncing. (III.) That the reason which induced these Christians to renounce the law of Moses was the severity of the emperor *Hadrian,* who had surrounded with a military guard the space on which the city of Jerusalem formerly stood, and prohibited the whole race of Jews from having any access thereto. With regard to this point, indeed, Sulpitius is less perspicuous and luculent than could be wished, and is altogether on the reserve as to many things on which it would have been more judicious in him to have spoken out. Upon the whole, however, we can pretty well ascertain what his meaning is, and without much difficulty supply those particulars in respect of which he is deficient.—The Christians residing in Palestine, so long as they continued to observe the law of Moses, were looked upon by the Romans as Jews; and certainly not altogether without reason. When Hadrian, [p. 326.] therefore, had prohibited the Jews from all access to the spot whereon Jerusalem had formerly stood, these Christians found themselves equally interdicted from any approach thereto. But it seems that these latter felt particularly un-

easy under this restraint, and were most anxiously desirous to free themselves from it. They therefore renounced altogether the ceremonies of the Mosaic law, and lest the Romans might doubt of their sincerity, they committed the government of their church to one who was not a Jew but a stranger. Having thus openly divorced themselves from every connection with the Jewish law, they were permitted by the Romans to have free access to that district from whence the Jews were altogether excluded. All these things, it must be admitted, may, with a moderate degree of attention, be collected from *Sulpitius*, notwithstanding the very great degree of negligence with which he writes.

But we shall now proceed to make some inquiry as to a point on which this author is altogether silent; namely, as to what cause could possibly have excited in these Christians so very strong a desire to have access to the site of Jerusalem, that sooner than not obtain this object of their wishes, they were led to abandon their paternal law and rites, and subject themselves to a man who was not a Jew? Is it to be believed that superstition could have stimulated them to all this? Could they have been prompted by a wish to feed and refresh their minds with a view of those places in which our Blessed Saviour had passed his life, and risen again from the dead? Could they have been actuated by the belief, which was at one time so very general amongst the Christians, and which continues to be entertained by not a few even in the present day, that it constitutes not the meanest part of religion and piety to visit sacred places? But it is absolutely incredible that men possessing such a strength of mind as to repudiate the religious ceremonies of their ancestors, which had been adhered to for ages with the utmost scrupulosity, and to commit the superintendence of their sacred rights and religion to a foreigner, should, at the same time, have been so weak and superstitious as to be incapable of enduring the thought of being excluded from those places which Christ, whilst here below, had honoured by his presence. If such were their character, it might well be said, that in their breasts superstition had been opposed to superstition, and that the greater, contrary to all probability, had fallen before the lesser one. There must, unquestionably, therefore, have been some other reason which induced these Christians to consider the liberty of having free access to the site of Jerusalem, as of greater moment than an adherence to their paternal ceremonies and institutions, and not to hesitate at purchasing this privilege by an utter renunciation of the Mosaic law. Nor do I conceive that much labour or difficulty will be encountered in ascertaining what this reason was. At no very great distance from the spot whereon Jerusalem formerly stood, the emperor *Hadrian* had constructed a new city bearing the name of *Ælia Capitolina*, and which had been endowed by him with very considerable privileges. Into this new colony the Christians, who had fled for refuge to the insignificant little town of Pella, and its neighbourhood, and were daily experiencing great deprivations and inconvenience, felt an anxious desire to be admitted. But the emperor had peremptorily excluded all the Jewish nation from this, his newly-built city; and as the Christians who adhered to the law of Moses, were apparently not distinguishable from Jews, this prohibition was, of course, considered as extending likewise to them. Feeling it, then, of the first importance to their well-being, to procure for themselves the liberty of removing, with their effects, into the city of Ælia, and of being admitted to the rights of citizenship there, a considerable number of these Christians came to the resolution of [p. 327.] formally renouncing all obedience to the law of Moses. The immediate author of this measure was, in all likelihood, that very *Marcus* whom they appointed as their bishop: a man whose name evidently speaks him to have been a Roman, and who, doubtless, was not unknown to those of his nation that had the chief command in Palestine, and might possibly have been related to some officer of eminence there. Perceiving, therefore, one of their own nation placed at the head of the Christians, the Roman præfects dismissed at once all apprehension of their exciting disturbance in the newly-established colony, and from this time ceased to regard them as Jews. In consequence of this favourable alteration in the sentiments of the Romans towards them, the Christians found themselves no longer debarred from the liberty of settling in the newly-founded city, but were, without scruple, admitted to a participation of its privileges, which were of the most valuable and important nature.—In what we have thus suggested, there is nothing whatever difficult of belief, and it must certainly be allowed to receive a sanction of no little weight, from what we find expressly recorded by Epiphanius, *de Ponderibus et Mensuris,* § xv. p. 171. that the Christians, upon their renouncing the law of Moses, were suffered to remove from Pella to Jerusalem. By Jerusalem, we must understand the emperor Hadrian's new city, which, posterior to the time of Constantine the Great, insensibly lost the name of Ælia Capitolina, and acquired that of Jerusalem. Vid. Henr. Valesius, *Adnot. ad Eusebium,* p. 61. But even if no memorial of this were extant, no room whatever could be afforded for controversy. For it is indisputably certain that, from the time of Hadrian, there existed a Christian church of celebrity at Ælia, and that the prelates, who were commonly termed bishops of Jerusalem, were, in point of fact, bishops of Ælia. I must beg the reader, however, not to understand me as meaning that the Christians of Palestine, in renouncing the law of Moses, were influenced solely by a wish to obtain the liberty of removing into the city of Ælia. Without doubt, that Marcus, at whose instance they were prevailed on to renounce the law of Moses, made it appear to them, by irrefragable arguments, that the authority and dignity of the Mosaic ritual had been abolished by the coming of the Messiah. By men, however, who had been accustomed, even from their tenderest years, to regard the law of Moses with the highest degree of veneration, his arguments would have been received with less effect had they not been seconded by a prospect of being admitted to a share in the privileges of Ælia, and of thus obtaining a deliverance from the oppressions, and numerous other evils to which the Jews were at this period subjected ; or if the second and complete subversion of Jerusalem by Hadrian, had not extinguished every hope of seeing the temple rebuilt, and the Jewish nation reinstated in the privilege of worshipping God on that spot, after its accustomed manner.

Sulpitius does not add that this remarkable defection from the observances of their forefathers, was not general amongst the Christians of Judæa, but that a part of them still remained invincibly attached to the Mosaic law, and withdrew from every intercourse with those of their brethren who had renounced it. Indeed, there was no occasion for his noticing this, inasmuch as the thing was notorious. Nothing, in fact, can be better attested, than that there existed in Palestine *two* Christian churches, by the one of which, an observance of the Mosaic law was retained, and by the other disregarded. This division amongst [p. 328.] the Christians of Jewish origen, did not take place before the time of *Hadrian*, for it can be ascertained, that previously to his reign, the Christians of Palestine were unanimous in an adherence to the ceremonious observances of their forefathers. There can be no doubt, therefore, but that this separation originated, in the major part of them, having been prevailed on by Marcus to renounce the Mosaic ritual, by way of getting rid of the numerous inconveniences to which they were exposed, and procuring for themselves a reception, as citizens, into the newly-founded colony of Ælia Capitolina.

XXXIX. **The Nazarenes and Ebionites.** Insignificant, however, as these Judaizing Christians, comparatively, were in point of numbers, unanimity was not to be met with amongst them; for they were divided into two sects differing widely from each other in their tenets respecting Christ, and the necessity of obedience to the law, and possibly as to various other matters of opinion. Of these the one, namely, that of the *Nazarenes,* is not considered by ancient Christian writers as coming within the class of heretics; but the other, that of the *Ebionites,* is uniformly reckoned in the catalogue of those sects whose principles strike at the very fundamentals of the Christian faith. Neither of them adopted those accounts of our Blessed Savour's life which were held sacred by other Christians, but each had a peculiar gospel of its own, differing in severel respects from that which we regard as genuine.(') By the *Nazarenes,*(') our Blessed Saviour was considered, not only as having been generated of a virgin, but also as partaking, in a certain degree, of the divine nature.(') The rites instituted by Moses, they regarded as still necessary to be observed by all Christians of the Hebrew race, but they did not exact a conformity to the Jewish law from such as were of a different origin: neither did they consider the additions that had been made to the Mosaic ritual at different times, by certain masters and doctors of the law, as deserving of any sort of respect, but treated them as things that ought to be either abolished or at least suffered to sink into oblivion.(')

(1) That the gospel of the *Nazarenes* was not the same with that of the *Ebionites,* is most clearly manifest from the few notices respecting each of

them, that are to be met with in ancient writers. Vid. Jo. Albert. Fabricius, *Cod. Apocryph. Nov. Test.* tom. i. p. 355. et seq. In the gospel of the Ebionites, for instance, to pass over other things, the first two chapters of St. Matthew were omitted, whereas, it appears from St. Jerome, that these chapters formed a part of the gospel of the Nazarenes. The reader will find this subject more particularly adverted to in my *Vindiciæ Antiquæ Christianorum Disciplinæ contra Tolandi Nazarenum*, sect. i. cap. v. p. 112. Setting aside the actual difference of their tenets, this one fact is sufficient to prove that the Ebionites and Nazarenes were two separate and distinct sects.

(2) *Epiphanius* is the first who ranks the *Nazarenes* in the class of heretics. By more ancient writers, the *Ebionites* are considered as of that description, but not the Nazarenes. The reason of this, I suspect, to have been, that the Christians, previously to the time of Constantine the Great, although they might regard the *Nazarenes* as brethren, laboring under a degree of error, yet [p. 329.] never considered them as corrupters of the Christian faith: nor will this appear extraordinary to those who are in the least conversant with Christian antiquities. For the tenets of the Nazarenes respecting Christ, were, by far, more just and correct than those of the Ebionites, and, although they would have deemed it inexcusable in themselves, to neglect the ceremonial observances of the law of Moses, they yet, by no means, exacted an obedience to the Jewish ritual from those who were not of the Hebrew race. But Jews of this description, who were contented with observing the law themselves, and sought not to impose it on others, were, in the second and third centuries, looked upon as genuine Christians, and deemed not unworthy of the name of brethren. This is clearly intimated by Justin Martyr, *Dial. cum Tryph.* p. 136. edit. Jebbian. For being interrogated by Trypho, in his disputation with him, whether those Jews who, notwithstanding that they had embraced the Christian faith, continued steadfast in their observance of the law of Moses, could obtain salvation? he thus replies: λέγω ὅτι σωθήσεται τοιοῦτος, ἐὰν μὴ τὸς ἄλλυς ἀνθρώπυς ἐκπαντὸς πείθειν ἀγωνίζηται ταῦτα αὐτῷ φυλάσσειν, λέγων ἡ σωθήσεσθαι αὐτὸς, ἐὰν μὴ ταῦτα φυλάξωσιν. *Ego quidem salvatum talem iri aio, qui alios homines in sententiam suam adducere annisus non fuerit, non servatum eos iri affirmans nisi eadem,* (the law,) *secum servarerint.* Many more things of this kind are to be found in Justin's dialogue; but at the same time, he does not dissemble that there were some who were less liberal in their determination of this point.—But, possibly, it may be objected by some that the *Nazarenes* were anciently included under the name of *Ebionites :* nor is this objection altogether destitute of colour. For it is certain, that the writers of the second and third centuries occasionally made use of the term *Ebionites,* in a much more comprehensive sense than we find it bearing in works of a more recent date. In fact, it should seem that, at that early period, the denomination of Ebionites was applied indiscriminately to all such Jews, as notwithstanding their conversion to Christianity, continued to observe the law of Moses. Vid. Origen *contra Celsum,* lib. iii. opp. tom. ii. p. 385. Hence it comes to pass, that we find the Ebionites of those times distributed into two classes, the orthodox, and the heretical; into those who believed our Blessed Saviour

to have been born of a virgin, and those who denied this. Vid. Origen *contra Cels.* lib. v. tom. ii. opp. p. 625. Eusebius, *Histor. Eccles.* lib. iii. cap. xvii. p. 99. Theodoret, *Fabul. Hæretic,* § ii. cap. i. p. 219. et. seq. But when I take into consideration what is said by Irenæus, and others, on the subject of the Ebionites, I cannot help giving the preference to the opinion which I have first above stated respecting them.

The term *Nazarene,* moreover, with these men, had precisely the same import as that of *Christian* has with us. For being Jews, and speaking only the Hebrew language, they found a difficulty in naturalizing the word *Christianus,* which is of Greek origin, and therefore substituted *Nazaræus,* a term bearing equal relation to our Saviour Christ, in its room. St. Matthew in his Gospel, chap. ii. 23. states it as a prediction of the prophets of the Old Testament, that the Messiah should be called a Nazarene. Under the sanction of this authority then, these Judaizing Christians thought themselves warranted in assuming the title of Nazarenes, just in the same way as the Greek converts had taken the denomination of Christians from the Redeemer's title of Χριϛὸς. Either term alike indicates the disciples or followers of that Messiah, who had been [p. 330.] promised of old to the Jewish nation. Hence we may collect the sense in which we ought to understand what Epiphanius has recorded respecting the Nazarenes. *Hæres.* xxix. § vi. ὅτε Χριϛιανὸς ἑαυτὸς ἐπονόμασαν, ἀλλὰ Ναζωραῖυς. *Nolunt Christiani vocari, sed Nazaræi.* Being Jews, they felt a repugnance to adopt a Greek denomination, but selected a Hebrew term of similar import and significance, and one that appeared to them of an equally honourable nature, since it was no uncommon thing for our Lord to be styled a Nazarene; and instances had occurred even of his having applied this appellation to himself. In this, certainly, there was nothing whatever that could reasonably be imputed to them as a fault.

(3) What the precise opinion entertained by the *Nazarenes,* respecting Christ, was, is not altogether clear. Many of our most eminent scholars, such as Grotius, Vossius, Spencer, and Huet, conceive them to have been altogether exempt from error in their notions on this subject, and that their belief was in no respect different from ours as to the union of two natures in Christ, the one human, the other divine. By no one has this orthodoxy of the Nazarenes been vindicated with greater learning and ability than by Mich. *Lequien,* in his *Adnot. ad Damascen.* tom. i. p. 82, 83. as well as in a particular dissertation *de Nazarenis et corum Fide,* which is the seventh of those that he has annexed to his edition of Damascene's works. Nothing whatever has been suffered to escape his diligence that could possibly aid in demonstrating that the Nazarenes' belief respecting Christ was equally correct with our own. But none of all the proofs which he adduces from ancient authors can be said so far to establish the fact as to leave no room for doubt. Manifest, indeed, it is, that the Nazarenes regarded our Blessed Lord as of a higher and more exalted nature than a mere man: and that they looked upon him as having been begotten of a virgin by the omnipotent will of the Deity, and admitted him to be, in a certain sense, the Son of God, endowed with divine power. But whether they believed him to have had an existence prior to Mary, and that God and man were united in

his person, admits of very considerable doubt. In fact, the sense of all the passages that have been brought forward by men of erudition, with a view to establish this, is very uncertain and equivocal. On the contrary, there are some passages in ancient authors which appear to furnish sufficient proof of the Nazarenes having denied the divinity of Christ. See, for example, Origen's discourse, *de Duobus Cæcis*, tom. i. opp. p. 427. edit. Huet.

(4) That the *Nazarenes* were averse to the rites and institutions which had been added to the Mosaic precepts by the Pharisees and interpreters of the law; and that they considered nothing as obligatory except the genuine commands of the great Hebrew legislator, is abundantly manifest from the testimony of St. Jerome, who had not only read their books, but lived on terms of familarity with them. Vid. *Com. in Esaiam*, tom. ii. opp. p. 34. and 106. But whether they considered the law of Moses as of general obligation, or as binding on the Jews exclusively, remains as yet a question with the learned. For my own part, I feel not the least hesitation in declaring my assent to the opinion, that the Nazarenes believed the Mosaic law to be obligatory on no other Christians than those who were descendants of the stock of Abraham. And a principal reason with me for acceding to this opinion is, that St. Jerome, who was intimately acquainted with their principles and tenets, represents them as having entertained the highest veneration for *St. Paul*, and as having assigned him a distinguished place amongst those whom they regarded as teachers of celestial truth. Hieron, *Com. in Esaiam*, tom. ii. p. 35. For how could it be possible that the great apostle of the Gentiles, who laboured with such zeal in proving that the law of Moses ought not to retain its ancient force and authority, should have been commended and held in high esti- [p. 331.] mation by men who considered obedience to that law as indispensable in every one who would arrive at salvation? Not a doubt can exist but that the *Ebionites*, who would willingly have imposed an observance of the Mosaic law on the Christians in general, execrated St. Paul as an impious impugner of that law. This argument is of greater strength and weight than to be shaken by certain *dicta* of St. Augustine or others, that by a forced interpretation may be made to militate against it.

XL. The Ebionites. The *Ebionites*, who derived their name either from some man, or from some particular fact or opinion,(') were a sect of a much worse description than that of the Nazarenes. For in the first place, although they held our Saviour Jesus Christ in great veneration as a divine legate or prophet, they would not admit that any miraculous circumstances attended his birth, but maintained that he was the natural son of Joseph and Mary, begotten according to that law by which all other mortals are produced. In the next place they not only observed the Mosaic law of ceremonies in all particulars themselves, but also insisted on its being requisite for every one who would obtain

favour with God, to do the like. St. Paul, therefore, who had so
strenuously exerted himself in demonstrating that no necessity
existed for conforming to the Mosaic ritual, it may easily be believed, found but little favour with them. Lastly, they refused to
give up even the superstitious appendages which had been added
to the institutions of Moses by the Pharisees and doctors of the
law.([2])

(1) *Tertullian* , and, after him, many other ancient Christian writers derive
the appellation of " *Ebionites*" from some man. Vid. Jo. Albert. *Fabricius,
Adnot. ad. Philastrum de Heres.* p. 81. et seq. Neither is there any difficulty
in believing that some Jew of the name of *Ebion* might have been the author
of those tenets by which the Ebionites were distinguished from other Christians of the Hebrew race. But, inasmuch as *Origen, Philocal.* cap. i. p. 17.
who is followed by Eusebius, *Hist. Eccles.* lib. iii. cap. xxvii. p. 99. states this
sect to have acquired the title of " *Ebionites*," or " *paupers*," from the low and
abject sentiments which they entertained respecting Christ; and the same *Origen*, in another place, *contra Celsum*, lib. ii. p. 56. accounts for the name from
their attachment to the indigent and insufficient law of Moses; and lastly, since
the Ebionites themselves, as is observed by *Epiphanius, Hæres.* xxx. § xvii. p.
141. considered the name to have had an allusion to the *poverty* and neediness
of their ancestors, certain of the learned have conceived that more credit is due
to these opinions than to the former one, although they at the same time betray an utter ignorance as to which of these latter is most to be relied on.
Were it to be left to me to determine this point, I should at once give the
preference to the opinion of the Ebionites themselves; for nothing can be more
certain than that by far the greatest number of those Christians of Jerusalem,
from whom the Ebionites were descended, were involved in a state of *indi-
gence ;* nor is it at all unlikely, that this their poverty might have been cast in
[p. 332.] their teeth by the rest of their brethren, and finally have given rise to
a taunting, ignominious appellation. Origen and Eusebius, as may be gathered
even from the inconsistency of the former, in his explication of this name, convey no information that can be depended on, as to the origin of the term
Ebionites, but merely give us their own interpretation of the word, or point out
how aptly it appears to reconcile itself with the tenets of the sect. But as this
question respecting the origin of the term Ebionites is, in fact, of no very great
importance, I prefer leaving it undetermined, to engaging in any controversy
on the subject.

(2) In the statement which I here submit to the reader respecting the
Ebionites, I am borne out, in several particulars expressly, and as to others in
no very obscure terms, by *Irenæus* and the best Christian writers of the early
ages. With regard to the last circumstance noticed, namely, that of their having retained, in addition to the rites prescribed by Moses, the superstitious observances and practices introduced by the Pharisees, in opposition to the Nazarenes, by whom these innovations were utterly lopped off and discarded, it

may, indeed, appear to a cursory examiner of the authors above alluded to, to admit of some doubt. An attentive consideration, however, of the following words of *Irenæus* will, I think, place the matter out of all dispute. *Et circumciduntur ac perseverant in his consuetudinibus, quæ sunt secundum legem et Judaico charactere vitæ.* Lib. i. *adv. Hæres.* cap. xxvi. p. 105. et seq. Irenæus here obviously makes a distinction between an observance of the precepts of the law and the Jewish mode or character of life, and represents the Ebionites as conforming no less to the one than the other. But as to this Jewish character, or mode of life, distinct from the precepts of the law of Moses, what else can it mean than that rule of life and morals which had been imposed on the necks of the Jewish multitude by their masters and doctors, as a sort of secondary law?—What Irenæus adds of their having worshipped the city of Jerusalem as the immediate residence of the Deity, I consider as indisputably false and injurious. For it was never held lawful for the Jews to worship, even in the slightest degree, anything except the one true and living God. What gave occasion to this calumny was their custom of turning always towards the site of Jerusalem when they offered up their prayers. Prior to the war of Hadrian there can be no doubt but that the Jews were accustomed to resort, for the purpose of prayer, to the spot whereon the temple had formerly stood, in order that they might conform themselves, as far as possible, to the custom of their forefathers, and the ancient religious discipline of their nation. But even this miserable consolation was wrested from them by Hadrian, who, by a severe edict, forbade any Jew to approach Jerusalem, and surrounded the whole area of the temple and the holy city with a military guard. Nothing more was left then to this afflicted people, so fondly attached to the practices of their ancestors, than, when engaged in prayer, to turn their faces towards the spot where once had stood their city and their temple.

Epiphanius, Hæres. xxx. in treating of the Ebionites, attributes to them many other errors than those above enumerated, amongst which are to be found several, not only of a silly, but of the very grossest nature. He, however, takes care to apprise his readers, § iii. p. 127. and § xiv. p. 141. that his remarks respect the *Sampsæans* and the *Elcesaites* as well as the Ebionites, and that the primitive *Ebionites* were entire strangers to any such heretical opinions. It would be wrong, therefore, to blend those doctrines with the tenets of the Ebionites.

XLI. Sects generated of the oriental philosophy. From [p. 333.] the insignificant and obscure sects which we have thus enumerated, unsupported as they were by any considerable degree either of talents or authority, the Christian church experienced comparatively but little detriment. By far the greater part of the ill-will and malignity which it had to encounter from without, as well as of the discord and dissensions by which it was internally distracted and disturbed, is undoubtedly to be attributed to those who were for expounding the religion of Christ upon the principles of the oriental *philosophy*. During the first century these men can scarcely be said to have emerged from obscurity: they lived unnoticed, and the converts that they made were but few; but under the reign of *Hadrian*, the apostles, and the principal of their disciples being dead, they began to take courage, and by degrees succeeded in forming numerous congregations of their followers in various of the provinces; and indeed did not rest satisfied with merely instituting these associations, but left no means unessayed that might contribute either to their reputation, their stability, or their increase.(') Under the banners of these new sects great numbers of Christians, who had previously entertained none but sound opinions, were tempted to enrol themselves, being seduced, in part by a fanatical kind of eloquence that characterised many of their leaders, in part by the very great show of piety exhibited by others, and in part by the prospect of being countenanced in living more at their ease and sinning without controul. A no less disastrous evil attending the rise of the Gnostics was, that both the Jews and the heathens, considering the disgraceful maxims and tenets of these sectaries as the genuine principles of Christianity, were led to regard the religion of the Gospel with increasing hatred and contempt: so that the Christian teachers were thenceforward necessarily compelled to employ a considerable portion of the time allotted to the establishment and propagation of the faith, in repressing the progress of Gnosticism, and in exposing, through the medium of writings and disputations, the insane pretensions and principles maintained by its abettors.(²)

(1) Several of the more early Christian writers have left it on record, that under the reign of Hadrian, when the Apostles were all dead, the Gnostic sects, that had previously languished in obscurity, began to emerge from their concealment; and that by the exertions which they used in gaining proselytes, and establishing congregations of their followers, the cause of genuine Christianity was most sadly disturbed and impeded. Vid. Clemens Alex. lib. vii. *Stromat.* cap. xvii. p. 898. et seq. Cyprian. *Epist.* lxxv. p. 144. ed. Baluzian. Hegesippus apud Euseb. *Hist. Eccl.* lib. iii. cap. xxxii. p. 104. and lib. iv. cap. xxii. p. 142. although as to the sense of this latter passage the learned are not exactly agreed. The admission of this testimony is unavoidable, inasmuch as we meet with nothing in other writers at all repugnant to it, and the origin of none of the Gnostic sects, except that of the Cerinthians, can be traced higher than to the age of Hadrian.

(2) The *Greeks and Romans*, who were strangers to the genuine principles

of Christianity, erroneously conceived that the maxims and tenets of the Gnostics were those of the Christians at large. Many of these maxims and tenets, however, were not only foolish and ridiculous, but fundamentally vile and disgraceful, and hence it came to pass, that the Christians were looked [p. 334.] upon either as persons devoid of reason, and worthy only to be held in derision, or else as a set of unprincipled wretches that could not be treated with too much severity. The testimony of many of the ancient fathers might be cited as to this, but I shall content myself with adducing only one passage out of *Irenæus, adrers. Hæres.* lib. i. cap. xxiv. *ad detractionem divini ecclesiæ nominis, quemadmodum et gentes, a Satana præmissi sunt,* (he is speaking of the *Carpocratians,* a Gnostic sect of infamous memory,) *uti secundum alium modum, quæ sunt illorum audientes homines, et putantes omnes nos tales esse, avertant aures suas a præconio veritatis, aut, et videntes, quæ sunt illorum, omnes nos blasphement, in nullo eis communicantes, neque in doctrina, neque in moribus,neque in quotidiana conversatione. Sed vitam quidem luxuriosam, sententiam impiam* (habentes) *ad velamen malitiæ ipsorum nomine* (Christianorum) *abutuntur.* The case was much the same with the *Jews,* who had settled amongst the Greeks and Romans without the confines of Palestine. For many of these who were at first far from being equally prejudiced against Christianity with the rest of their brethren, upon hearing the Gnostics maintain that the God of the Hebrews and of the Old Testament was a different being from the True and Supreme God,—that nothing like divine authority or dignity could properly be attributed either to Moses or his law,—that the God of the Jews was indeed an angel endowed with vast power, but devoid of clemency and wisdom, and a slave to the lust of dominion,—that the resurrection of the dead was undeserving of belief,—that matter was intrinsically corrupt, and, consequently, all bodies inherently vicious and depraved, I say, upon hearing the Gnostics avow not only these but various other principles and maxims diametrically opposite to the religious tenets of the Jews; and hastily running away with the idea that such was the way in which Christ had instructed his disciples to think and believe, they were led to regard the Christian religion with every possible degree of hatred and disgust.

XLII. **Gnostic sects.** This business of arresting the progress of Gnosticism amongst the multitude, became every day a concern of still wider extent, and attended with increasing difficulties, in consequence of the numerous dissensions, disputes, and seperations that were continually taking place amongst the votaries of the oriental philosophy. For notwithstanding all of those who looked upon the Creator of the world as a different being from the Deity, may be considered as having commenced their career upon nearly one and the same set of principles, yet they had proceeded but a little way when, as many of them as preferred following their own judgment rather than any other man's,

struck off into different paths, and not only gave to the philosophy which they had espoused a diversity of modification in itself,
but also introduced variations in the manner of reconciling and
connecting it with the Christian religion. Hence were generated
[p. 335.] disagreements, disputations, and controversies, which
soon gave rise to factions, parties, and sects that were continually
at strife with each other. It is by no means easy to determine as
to the number of these sects. There seems, indeed, to be but
little hazard in our considering them as having been less numerous than they are represented by ancient authors; but at the same
time it is certain, that the greatest discord prevailed amongst the
Gnostics, and that the sects generated by this discord were not a
few.(¹) Owing to the inconsistency and obscurity of ancient authors, we find ourselves equally in the dark as to the precise time
when either of these sects individually was formed, or the circumstances that attended its rise: but since it is certain that all of
them, which attained to any degree of consequence or celebrity,
were in a flourishing state so early as the *middle* of this century,
it is not to be doubted but that the principal of them must have
been instituted not long subsequent to its commencement.

(1) It seems not at all improbable that the ancient Christian teachers, in
consequence of their not observing a due degree of caution in distinguishing
between the Gnostic sects might multiply them without reason. Each sect,
most likely, was at the first known by a variety of names; one perhaps derived
from the place where it originated, another from its founder, and another again
from some particular tenet or leading principle: and it is certainly very possible
that from their either not sufficiently attending to this circumstance, or perhaps
being entirely unacquainted with it, those who made it their business to oppose
these sects might fall into the error of representing them as much more numerous than they actually were. It should seem, also, that certain of these sects
were known by different names in different parts of the world; by one, for instance, in Syria, by another in Egypt, and by a third, possibly, to some of the
other provinces: a portion of this or that particular sect, moreover, it is probable might acquire a peculiar denomination from some eminent teacher to
whom they might have attached themselves. Men, by far more sagacious than
the ancient Christian pastors were, have been frequently imposed upon in matters of this kind, and been led to believe in the existence of a much greater
number of sects than ever had any being. Even modern ecclesiastical history
supplies us with a remarkable instance in illustration of this in the case of the
Anabaptists.

XLIII. **The Elcesaites.** In bringing some of the principal of these sects under review, we find our attention first called towards the *Elcesaites,* whose founder, according to Epiphanius, was a Jew named *Elxai,* who, under the reign of *Trajan,* so successfully ingratiated himself with a Jewish sect, named the *Ossens,* as to make converts of them all, and prevail on them, in a body, to adopt his errors. This man, although a Jew, and of course a worshipper of the one only true God, yet contrived to blend much of the superstitions of the east with the religion of his forefathers; and, amongst other things, protested altogether against the use of *sacrifices;* contending that the offering up of victims to the Deity was a practice to which the patriarchs of old were utter strangers. This circumstance, considering that in other respects he manifested a reverence for Moses, and adhered strictly to the Jewish ritual, seems to indicate his having belonged to the [p. 336.] sect of the *Essenes,* who pretended that the law of Moses ought not to be taken literally, but that there was a recondite system of morality concealed beneath its precepts. It is, however, not by any mean certain, as even Epiphanius himself allows, that the Elcesaites were a Christian sect. Elxai, it is true, in a book which Epiphanius had seen, speaks in a general way of Christ, and bestows on him very high encomiums; but nothing whatever is added from whence it can be ascertained whether or not he meant, under that title, to speak of Jesus of Nazareth. This certainly is not characteristic of a Christian; and I, therefore, for my own part, entertain not the least doubt but that the Elcesaites were a Jewish sect, and some branch of the Essenes.(')

(1) Epiphanius, *Hæres.* xix. § iii. p. 41. Eusebius, *Hist. Eccles.* lib. vi. c. xxxviii. p. 234. Theodoret. *Fabul. Hæret.* lib. ii. c. vii. p. 221. et seq.

XLIV. **The philosophy of Saturninus.** If the Elcesaites then be considered as not coming properly within the description of a Christian sect, we are certainly bound, in marshalling the leaders of the different Gnostic factions, to assign the first place to *Saturninus* of Antioch, whom the early Christian writers represent as having been a disciple of the Samaritan *Menander:* a circumstance which, though it cannot well be believed, must yet be allowed to possess no inconsiderable weight as an argument in favour of the antiquity of this sect.(') This man, previously to his becoming a Christian, belonged to that class of philosophers who believed that, in addition to the Deity, of whom they pretended that no one had any knowledge, there had existed from all eternity a material principle intrinsically evil and corrupt, over which presided a certain governor or prince. This world, and the first parents of the human race, he supposed to have been created by seven angels, without the knowledge of the Supreme Deity. These seven spirits, there can be no doubt, were the same with those powerful genii begotten of God, whom the people of the east conceived to reside in and rule over the seven planets or moveable stars; for that such were the founders of this nether world, was an opinion entertained by various others of the Gnostics. The fabric of the world, when completed, did not appear displeasing in the sight of the Almighty, wherefore he breathed into man, who as yet was endowed with nothing beyond mere animal life, a rational soul; and having divided the newly-created world into seven districts, he permitted the seven angels by whom it had been fashioned, to assume the dominion thereof, reserving, however, to himself a supreme and irresistable command over the whole. One of these angels, Saturninus held to be the ruler of [p. 337.] the Hebrew nation, the being that brought them up out of the land of Egypt by the hand of Moses, and afterwards gave them a law, and whom the Jews, therefore, not knowing anything of the Supreme Deity, ignorantly paid their adoration to as God. To *Satan*, or the ruler who presided over matter, this creation of the world and the human race was in the highest degree displeasing; wherefore, being stimulated by hatred and emulation, he contrived to introduce upon earth, in opposition to the human beings on whom the Deity had bestowed a rational and virtuously disposed soul, another race of men, created by himself out of matter, and endowed with a malignant and irrational soul like his own.(²) Hence was generated that astonishing difference which is found to exist between the inhabitants of the earth; of whom some are of a sound and virtuously disposed mind, others of a radically vicious character, inclining to every thing that is evil. The former derived their body from the founders of this world, their soul from the Supreme Deity; the latter derived both body and soul from Satan, the governor of matter.(³) That all these things were devised by way of accounting for the existence of natural as well as moral evil, must be obvious to every one.

(1) If *Saturninus* had been a disciple of *Menander*, propriety would have required that his sect should have been referred to the *first* century: and amongst the learned there have not been wanting several, as Le Clerc and others, who, upon this single ground alone, have been actually induced to refer it to that age. But in this instance too hasty and implicit a reliance has certainly been placed on those ancient writers who represent Saturninus as having been educated under Menander. For first, the discipline of Menander differs most materially from that which Saturninus professed; and in the next place, Menander, as I have above shown, cannot, with the least propriety, be considered as coming within the description of a Christian heretic. Much rather, therefore, may we credit the testimony of Eusebius, *Hist. Eccl.* lib. iv. cap. vii. and Theodoret. *Fabular. Hæretic.* lib. i. cap. ii. p. 193. by both of whom Saturninus is expressly represented as having flourished under the reign of the Emperor *Hadrian.*

(2) The principal ancient writers that have treated of the discipline of Saturninus are Irenæus, *adv. Hæres.* lib. i. cap. xxiv. Tertullian, *de Præscript. contra Hæret.* cap. xlvi. Theodoret. *Fabular. Hæret.* lib. i. c. ii. Eusebius, *Histor. Eccles.* lib. iv. cap. vii. Epiphanius, *Hæres.* xxiii. p. 62. and Augustine. *in lib. de Hæresib.* c. iii.: but by none of these has the subject been handled otherwise than in a confused, concise, and obscure manner. The consequence of this has been, that whenever modern writers have attempted to extract an account of the philosophy and religion of this Syrian from any of the authors above-mentioned, they have been sure to fall into errors, and conjure up for themselves difficulties where none in reality exist. Those errors and difficulties I have made it a part of my business to correct and overcome, as far as the obscurity of ancient authors, and their irregular mode of narration would permit: and I will here lay before the reader a statement of those particulars in which I have found reason to differ from the commonly received opinion.

(I.) That *Saturninus* assigned to the corrupt material principle, which he considered as having been coëternal with the Deity, a peculiar prince or governor, is no where expressly stated by any of the ancient authors; from what they have left us on record, however, respecting his *Satan*, we may, I think, fairly collect as much. Saturninus taught, as must clearly be perceived by [p. 338.] any one who shall attentively consider what is said of him by Irenæus, that Satan, upon discovering the human beings that had been formed by the creators of the world, and endowed with a rational soul by the Supreme Deity, went to work and created, out of matter, a man of a corrupt and opposite character. This Satan, Irenæus terms the " *Angel* inimical to the creators of the world," but more particularly " to the God of the Hebrews." But, certainly, his very work bespeaks him to have been something greater and more powerful than an angel. The creators of the world were angels, but they possessed not the power of imparting to the human beings whom they had formed a rational soul. The men of their creation breathed and crawled about upon the face of the earth like worms, and had it not been for the commiseration of the Supreme Being, they never would have possessed that spark of life, a rational soul. But the power of *Satan* was such, that he could bestow on the man whom he created an actual soul, a soul, perverse it is true, and naturally inclined to what is evil, but indisputably intellectual or rational. The ancient writers indeed do not expressly state this, but it is an inference which admits of no controversy. For wicked men, who are descended from that original man whom Satan created, are unquestionably endowed with a soul as much as good men, although it be a soul that naturally inclines them to evil. But this soul they certainly cannot have received from God, the fountain of nothing but what is good, and they therefore must have been indebted for it to Satan, their father. The Satan of Saturninus then, although an evil being, must have been equal in power to the Supreme Deity, and alike capable of animating bodies with a rational soul.

From these premises it follows, that we must believe Saturninus to have attributed to his *Satan* an independent existence coëval with that of the Deity, and likewise the command or controul of matter from all eternity. It is, moreover, to be supposed, that the soul with which Satan inspired the man that he had formed, was taken by him from the soul of matter. Wherefore, it should seem most likely, that Saturninus agreed with some others of the Gnostics in believing matter to be animated.

(II.) That the Diety was not displeased with the world that had been created by the seven angels, is another circumstance as to which ancient authors are silent, but which may fairly be inferred from his having imparted to the men formed by these same angels a rational mind or soul. Having rendered the inhabitants of the world capable of living well and happily therein, it is impossible that the world itself should have appeared displeasing in his sight. Although, therefore, the world had been created without the knowledge of the Deity, yet, when it was perfected, he beheld it with approbation, and deemed it worthy of having its existence continued for a certain time.

(III.) That Saturninus considered the Deity as having placed this world under the government of those who had framed it, reserving to himself, however, the supreme dominion, and likewise the worship of mankind, is clear from what he taught respecting the defection of the founders of the world from God. If there had been no previous obligation or subjection, there could have been no desertion of duty or rebellion. Those of the learned are deceived, therefore, who represent Saturninus as having maintained that the founders of [p. 339.] the world were originally evil beings; an error into which many have fallen with regard to the discipline of various others of the Gnostic sects. The spiritual beings noticed by Saturninus are of three descriptions; the Supreme Deity, the angels who created the world, and Satan, the prince or Governor of matter. The Supreme *Deity* he considered as essentially good, the Chief Good; the prince of matter, as essentially evil; the creators of the world, the rulers or governors of the seven moveable stars, as neither essentially good like the Deity, nor evil like Satan, but holding, as it were, a middle kind of character, that is, being endowed with free will, they were at liberty to follow either good or evil.

(IV.) That *Satan*, or the prince of matter, was enraged with the founders of the world, and privily counteracted the designs of them and the Supreme Deity, by creating a depraved and malignant race of men, we find noticed by ancient writers; but as to the cause of his indignation and hatred, they are wholly silent, leaving this, like almost every other part of the discipline of Saturninus, but very imperfectly described. It will be no very difficult matter, however, to supply the deficiency in this instance from conjecture. Those seven angels, in their formation of the world, and replenishing it with inhabitants, had invaded the province of Satan, and drawn away matter from his dominion. Filled with indignation, as it was natural for him to be, at this, he, out of opposition, introduced upon earth a race of men of his own forming, by whom those who had been created by the angels might be continually vexed and tormented.

(3) Irenæus states expressly in lib. i. cap. xxiv. that *Saturninus* was the first of the Gnostics that divided mankind into two classes, the one naturally good, the other evil. The fact was, that he despaired of being able to account for all the evil in the world from matter alone, and therefore had recourse to the expedient of supposing all whose propensities appeared to be radically vicious, to have been inspired with a wicked soul, and that the prince of matter had created this race of men and breathed into them a soul similar to his own—a soul naturally inclined to every thing evil and depraved—in order to prevent his being altogether excluded from any dominion over the world. But with regard to the tenets of Saturninus, respecting the formation of the first men, Irenæus, like other ancient authors, speaks very indistinctly. He says, in a general way, *duo genera hominum plasmata ab angelis dicit.* Learned men have been hence led to conclude, that Saturninus conceived the founders of the world to have created bad as well as good men, and that, therefore, they must have been of an evil nature themselves. But to an attentive reader it must be obvious that he did not conceive wicked men to have derived their origin from the same parents as had produced the good, but that they were the children of Satan.

XLV. The Saturninian system of theology. Upon his conversion to Christianity, *Saturninus* made it his endeavour to produce, as far as possible, a congruity between the religion that he had thus espoused and his former philosophical opinions. The way he took was to pretend that the founders and governors of the world had, after a certain period, rebelled against the Supreme Deity.(') That in consequence of this, *Christ*, the Son of God, had descended from above and taken upon him a body, not indeed a true or real body composed of depraved matter, but merely the shadow or resemblance of one. That the cause or purpose for which [p. 340.] Christ came into the world, was, that he might overthrow, not only the dominion of the founders of the world, but also that of Satan, or the prince of matter, and his satellites: he was, moreover, to destroy those ministers of Satan, the men of his creation; and finally to liberate and bring back to God the good men, in

whom existed a divine soul.(²) The moral discipline prescribed
by Saturninus to his followers was rigid and austere. Regarding
matter as inherently corrupt, and the body, therefore, as the seat
of all vices, he enjoined an abstinence from wine, flesh, and every
aliment that might tend to recruit or invigorate the corporeal
frame; so that the body, being extenuated and brought low, the
mind might, with the greater readiness and alacrity, perceive and
worship the Supreme Deity. He was also averse to marriage,
inasmuch as its object was the propagation of bodies.(³) In what
way, or by what authorities Saturninus supported his tenets and
doctrine, we are altogether uninformed. It appears however that
the code of the Old Testament, which we know to have been held
in reverence by the Gnostics, was rejected by him, on the ground
of its having been compiled in part by the creators of the world,
and in part by the prince of matter, or Satan.

(1) Respecting this sedition of the founders of the world, which Saturninus
represented as the cause of Christ's advent, Irenæus thus expresses himself:
Et propter hoc quod dissolvere voluerint patrem ejus (of Christ) *omnes principes*
(of the world), *advenisse Christum ad destructionem Judæorum Dei, &c.* At the
first sight, certainly, this may appear particularly obscure; but it will not long
embarrass any one who is acquainted with the discipline of the Gnostics. The
creators of the world, being elated with pride, conceived a wish to be themselves considered as gods by the human race, and, in consequence of this, became desirous of extinguishing all knowledge and worship of the Most High
amongst men. By *Patrem Christi dissolvere,* therefore, Irenæus means arro-
gating to themselves that which was due to God alone, and extinguishing in
men's minds all knowledge of the Supreme Father: The orthodox Christians
and the Gnostics were in perfect agreement as to this, that the worship of a
plurality of gods, which, at the time of Christ's appearance, prevailed nearly
throughout the world, had been introduced by a set of proud, spiritual beings,
unjustly covetous of divine honours; and that the gods, therefore, whom the
nations worshipped, had a real existence, and were, in fact, evil dæmons. But
there was this difference between the Gnostics and other Christians, that the
former reckoned the God of the Jews as one of those apostate spirits who were
desirous of withdrawing men from the worship of the true and Supreme God ;
and conceived that the creators of the world, whom they distinguished from the
Supreme Deity, were the principal authors of this grievous iniquity; whereas
the latter believed that certain evil angels, who had themselves previously rebelled against the true God and only Creator of the world, and every thing in
it, and who, in consequence of such their rebellion, were suffering under a
[p. 341.] severe, but well-merited punishment, had instigated men to withhold
their worship from the true and Supreme God, and bestow it on natures hateful in his sight.

(2) This view of the Saturninian discipline, it must be acknowledged, is mutilated and defective in almost all its parts; but the fault must rest with the ancient writers, who have not left us the means of rendering it more perfect. A few things, however, may be added, as obviously deducible from the tenets above noticed.—As Saturninus would not admit that Christ took upon him a real body, he must, of necessity, have denied his having been seized and ill-treated by the Jews, his having suffered on the cross, and also his resurrection from the dead. His belief must therefore have been, either that some other person underwent capital punishment in Christ's stead, or that it was merely some semblance or shadow of Christ that appeared on the cross.—The object of Christ's advent, according to Saturninus, was, that he might restore to man-kind the knowledge of the Supreme Deity, which they had unfortunately lost. It is evident, therefore, that he had no idea of an *expiation* of sins through Christ, but conceived, according to the leading principle of Gnosticism, that γνῶσις, as it was termed, or a knowledge of the Supreme Father of the universe, and a thorough contempt for the false gods that were worshipped by the world at large, were alone sufficient to the obtaining of salvation.—None of the human race, however, he contended, could attain to a knowledge of the Deity, but those on whom the Supreme Being had conferred a divine soul. The far greater part of mankind, therefore, having, according to him, been endowed by Satan with an iniquitous mind, were, of course, incapable of deriving any bene-fit from Christ.—Those who received Christ were the good; and the minds of these being illuminated with a knowledge of the true God, reverted, on the dis-solution of the body, to the celestial Father, the body itself returning to matter from whence it had been first taken. Those who rejected Christ were the wicked; and these Saturninus considered as destined to perish altogether; the body itself being resolved into matter, and the evil soul which animated the body returning to the soul of matter from whence it was originally taken. None of the Gnostics, it may be remarked, seem to have been aware of any other end for which Christ came into the world, than that he might overthrow idolatry, and revive amongst the human race a knowledge of the true God.

(3) Irenæus does not say that all the followers of Saturninus abstained from animal food, but merely that many of them did so, and that not a few weak persons were vastly captivated by this sort of self-denial. It appears, then, that Saturninus either left his disciples at liberty to abstain from animal food or not, according to their pleasure, or that he did not prescribe a course of discipline equally harsh and severe to all. Of the two, the latter strikes me as the most probable. His followers, I should conceive, were arranged much in the way that was afterwards adopted by Manes and others, *i. e.* divided into disciples of the first and second class. The latter, not aspiring to any very superior degree of sanctity and virtue, although they never exceeded the bounds of sobriety and moderation, yet made use of the same kinds of bodily aliment as other men; but the former, being anxious to dispel those clouds with which the mind was subject to be enveloped from its connection with the body, and to arrive at a clearer knowledge of the Deity, allowed themselves no sort of bodily sustenance, except of the most slender kind.—After this manner,

also, ought we, I think, to understand what is said by ancient writers of the Saturninians having been prohibited from marrying. For, although Irenæus [p. 342.] states these men to have looked upon marriage and generation as of Satanic origin, from whence it necessarily follows that they must have regarded all sexual intercourse as absolutely unlawful, it is with difficulty I can bring myself to believe that Saturninus allowed none of his disciples to marry. All leaders of sects make it their principal object to collect together as many followers as possible. But sects, whose leading principle it is to subdue, and even stifle altogether, the instincts of nature, can never become numerous or extensive, but after existing for a while in a low, dwindled state, are sure to fall to decay. With a view to prevent this, otherwise inevitable consequence, the founders of those sects, whose moral discipline was particularly rigid and austere, were accustomed, for the most part, to exact an implicit conformity to their rules, merely from such as were meant to stand forth as an example to others; the rest were left much at liberty to consult their own natural inclinations. The Saturninian sect appears never to have extended itself beyond the confines of Syria; it should also seem to have been but of short duration.

XLVI. **The philosophy of Basilides.** Nearly about the same time that Syria, and more particularly its chief city, Antioch, was infested and disturbed by the wild theories of Saturninus, an Alexandrian philosopher of a similar genius, named *Basilides,* was endeavouring to introduce amongst his countrymen and the inhabitants of the various provinces of Egypt another form of religion, differing widely from the principles entertained by the Christians at large.(') His system took for its basis certain points which, in common with Saturninus and the rest of those who were addicted to the oriental philosophy, he assumed as indisputable; namely, that there had eternally existed a *Deity* of the very highest excellence; of a nature, in fact, beyond all human conception: that *matter* had also an eternal existence; that it was animated, and intrinsically corrupt; and from these premises it necessarily followed that the frame or machine of this world could not have been the work of the Deity, inasmuch as he was totally estranged from every thing evil.(') The nature of the Deity, however, together with the origin of this world, and of the human race, was explained by him after a more diffuse and subtile manner than by Saturninus, in consequence of his calling in the assistance of the Egyptian philosophy. His doctrine was, that the Deity had, long before the foundation of the world, begotten of himself seven natures of the most exalted kind; or, as the Gnostics termed them, *Æons,* who, together with the Deity, from whom they proceeded, constitute a perfect and supremely blessed *Ogdo-ad*.([2]) Of these *Æons* two of the feminine sex, if any conclusion is to be drawn from their names, *viz. Sophia* and *Dynamis,* or *Wisdom* and *Power,* generated of themselves certain princes or angels of the first order. These latter having founded for themselves an habitation or heaven wherein to dwell, begat certain other angels of an order somewhat inferior to their own; who, in like manner, having constructed an heaven for themselves, became the parents of a third order of angels. These fabrications of heavens [p. 343.] and generations of angels, were by degrees multiplied to such an extent that they at length came to correspond with the number of the days in the year, no less than three hundred and sixty-five heavens, and as many different classes of angels, having been successively called into existence.([4]) All these heavens were supposed to be under the dominion of a Supreme Lord, to whom Basilides gave the name of *"Abraxas;"* a title that should seem to have comprehended under it little more of mystery than this, that the Greek letters of which it is composed, if taken as numerals, will be found to express the number of the Basilidian heavens, *viz.* 365.([5]) The last, or three hundred and sixty-fifth of these heavens, being situated immediately on the confines of eternal matter, the prince of those angels whose dwelling this nether heaven was, conceived the idea of digesting the confused mass that thus lay near him, and of forming it into a world, and replenishing it with inhabitants. This design he, with the assistance of the minor angels that were resident with him, at length carried into effect: but whether with or without the knowledge of the Supreme Deity is uncertain. Of this, however, we are left in no doubt, that Basilides did not conceive the form of this world and of mankind to have been first devised by these angels themselves, but that they worked after a model with which they had been supplied by *Sophia,* or *Wisdom,* one of the *Æons*.([6]) The first of the human race, in addition to a body composed of matter, were possessed of a sensitive and concupiscent soul derived from the soul of the world. To this, through the benevolence of the Deity, was subsequently added an intelligent and rational soul, whose powers, however, were much impeded and diminished by that brutal soul which had been derived from matter.([7]) The angels who framed this world apportioned the government of it and its inhabitants amongst themselves in such a way as that each nation or people might have its peculiar president or ruler. The chief of these angels was represented as having made choice of the Jewish nation for himself, and given it a law by the mouth of his servant Moses.

A rule of life and action was also prescribed to the various other nations of the earth by the angels to whose guardianship and government they had been respectively assigned. Finally, with a view to the preservation of the rational souls, or those that were of a kindred to the Divine Nature, the Supreme Deity had, according to Basilides, at various times sent to the different nations of the world legates and prophets from himself, who, by their exhortations and instruction, might prevent those souls from sinking altogether into a state of brutal insensibility.(ᵃ) The souls that were attentive and paid obedience to the calls of these divine missionaries, were, upon the dissolution of the material body, received up into the regions of felicity; but those which rejected the proffered benevolence were constrained to migrate into other bodies, either of men or brute animals, and there to take up their residence until they should become qualified for reascending to their pristine blissful abodes.(ᵒ)

[p. 344.] (1) *Basilides* and his sect are treated of by all those ancient authors that have written on heresies, and whom we have above referred to when speaking of Saturninus. But since most of them merely copy, and not unfrequently incorrectly, from *Irenæus*, we shall direct our attention principally to him. It may not be amiss, however, occasionally to turn to those authors who, in treating of other matters, have here and there incidentally adverted to Basilides or his tenets, the principal of whom is *Clement* of Alexandria, who had read the books written by Basilides and his son Isidore, and in his *Stromata* cites many passages from them in the very words of the authors themselves. For Basilides himself wrote four and twenty books of commentaries on the gospel; and his son left behind him exhortations, moral precepts, and a variety of other things. None of these works, it is to be regretted, are at this day extant. We have also to lament the loss of a copious confutation of the above-mentioned work of Basilides by Agrippa Castor, a very celebrated and erudite Christian writer of this century. From the passages cited out of the books of Basilides by Clement, it is easily to be perceived that the man was neither destitute of gravity, nor of an appearance of great piety towards God: For he writes in a very decorous and religious style. His manner of diction, however, is obscure and out of the common track, so that there is occasionally a difficulty in getting at his meaning. Nor is his adversary, *Clement*, in many instances, at all more intelligible. Indeed, he not unfrequently is so unfortunate as to involve the maxims which he assails in still greater obscurity, and seems to enter the lists against things which he does not sufficiently understand.—Turning to more modern writers, in addition to what is to be met with in the ordinary ecclesiastical historians, and the *Dissertationes in Irenæum* of Ren. Massuetus, it will be found that great care and industry have been exerted in digesting and illustrating the tenets of Basilides by *Isaac Beausobre*, in his *History of the Manichees*, vol. ii. p. 8. et seq. Basilides is ranked by this writer amongst the precursors of *Manes;* and not improperly so, in my opinion, if by the title of "precursor" we are to understand one who builds his discipline on the same foundation, and consequently has many tenets in common. Beausobre, however, in other respects unquestionably a man of the first eminence, may well be complained of in this, that although he cannot deny Basilides to have entertained errors of the most flagrant nature, he yet consumes much time in exculpating him, and setting him off to advantage. The labour, however, is, in not a few instances, altogether thrown away.—Basilides flourished nearly at the same period with Saturninus, that is, under the reign of *Hadrian,* and died, according to the *Chronicle* of St. Jerome, at Alexandria, about the time that Barchochcba, the pretended Messiah of the Jews, was endeavouring to bring about a revolution in Palestine. The ancient Christian writers who, without a shadow of reason, feign to themselves a regular succession of heretics, similar to that of the Grecian philosophers, represent Basilides also, as having been a disciple of Menander the Samaritan; but what we have remarked above respecting Menander, must, we conceive, be sufficient to prove this altogether unfounded.

(2) From what is handed down to us by ancient writers respecting the tenets of Basilides, there is nothing to be collected that can authorize us in concluding that, like the rest of the Gnostics, he considered matter as being under the dominion of a ruler or prince peculiar to itself, or that he believed in the existence of angels naturally inclined to evil. For everything [p. 345.] that has occurred respecting the world and the human race he apparently refers to three causes alone, namely, (I.) The Supreme Deity, of whom it is impossible to form any adequate conception; (II.) Depraved matter; and (III.) The creators of this world.

(3) *Irenæus* mentions *six Æons* only, as having been recognized by Basilides, viz. the *Deity* himself, or the *Father*, *Nus*, *Logos*, *Phronesis*, *Sophia*, and *Dynamis*. But *Clement* of Alexandria, *Stromat.* lib. iv. p. 637. adds *two more*, *Justitia* and *Pax*, and expressly states that Basilides held the divine family to be composed of *eight* individuals.—In regard to this subject two questions suggest themselves. First whether these *Æons* are to be considered as *persons* truly and really distinct from each other? or whether they ought not rather to be regarded as merely *virtues* or attributes of the Supreme Being, and that it was in thought or imagination alone that Basilides separated them from the Deity, and gave them the form of persons? The *latter opinion* is espoused by Ren. Massuetus, *Dissert. in Irenæum*, I. p. 38. and Isaac Beausobre, *Hist. de Manichee*, tom. ii. p. 6, 7. as well as by some others. And without doubt it appears to be, in a certain degree, favored by the names which Basili-

des gives to the Æons, inasmuch as they are those by which certain of the virtues or attributes of intelligence and will are denoted. There is a circumstance, however, which I am free to own, draws me over entirely to the other of these opinions, and that is, that the *Æon* next in point of rank to the Father, namely, *Nus,* cannot possibly be regarded in any other light than as a *distinct person.* For this *Nus* is represented as the son of the Supreme Father, and as descending to this world for the purpose of liberating captive minds. Such then as he is, who holds the chief station in this divine family, must unquestionably all those who follow him be; nor can any reason whatever be assigned for our thinking otherwise of them, except it be what we have above noticed respecting their names; from whence, however, no conclusion on the subject can properly be drawn, since it is certain that many of the Gnostics whose Æons it is impossible for us to regard in any other light than as real persons, distinct from each other, and from the Supreme Deity, gave to such of their Æons names of a similar nature and description with those above enumerated.—The second question is, whether the *Æons* of Basilides, like those of Valentine and others of the Gnostics, were of different *sexes,* and whether they were conceived to have intermarried with each other? Referring to their names we find some of them masculine, others feminine: but there are not so many masculine as feminine names in his catalogue ; neither does Irenæus or Clement, or any other ancient author represent Basilides as teaching anything respecting the marriages of his Æons; which certainly seems to indicate his having entertained notions less gross, as to this point, than some others of the Gnostics. But from acceding to this opinion we find ourselves recalled by *Clement,* who, after giving us the tenets of Basilides respecting the origin of the world in his own words, subjoins this, moreover, as one of his principles; Ὅσα ἐκ συζυγίας προέρχεται, πληρώματα ἐστιν· ὅσα δὲ ἀπὸ ἑνὸς, εἰκόνες. *Quæcumque ex conjugatione procedunt, pleromata sunt : quæcumque autem ab uno, imagines sunt.* Stromat. lib. iv. p. 603. In this passage *pleroma* must be understood to have the same meaning with *Æon.* This is evident from the words of Basilides himself, as quoted by Clement just before, where we find him expressly making use of the term αἰών. For as by a figure of rhetoric, those natures which inhabit eternity are denominated [p. 346.] *Æons,* so also those who dwell with the Deity in the Pleroma, or place of his peculiar residence are termed *Pleromata.* Basilides, therefore must be understood as saying that an *Æon* could be generated in no other way than as the human race are, namely, ἐκ συζυγίας, from an intercourse of the sexes. But if this was his doctrine, it is clear that his discipline could not have materially differed from that of the rest of the Gnostics; and that the account given of it by ancient writers is far from being perfect or complete.

(4) That such was the doctrine of Basilides, has, I believe, hitherto been universally credited on the faith of Irenæus, who explicitly enough tells us that it was so, *adv. Hæres.* lib. i. cap. xxiv. Nor do I myself entertain the least doubt of the thing, inasmuch as I know that other notions very nearly resembling these ridiculous fancies were cherished by the Egyptians, amongst whom Basilides was born and educated. *Beausobre,* however, in his *Histoire de Manichee,* tom. ii. p. 9. will have it to be impossible that Basilides could have been

so utterly absurd and irrational as seriously to maintain the existence of three hundred and sixty-five heavens, and an equal number of angelic orders. But in justification of his incredulity he can allege no other reasons than these:—The opinion is in itself childish and absurd:—it could therefore never have entered into the mind of Basilides. Basilides was an astronomer:—but it is incredible that any astronomer should have believed in such a multitude of heavens:—the thing, therefore, could not have been believed by Basilides. Now that reasons such as these should, for a moment, have had any weight with a man of quick capacity, is to me a matter of astonishment; for nothing surely can be more devoid of force; and if they be once admitted, the greatest part of what ancient writers have handed down to us respecting the Gnostics must, of necessity, be rejected as unworthy of belief. Great indeed might have been the force of these arguments had Basilides been a wise man and a skilful astronomer: but so far from this having been the case, it is admitted, even by those who wish the best to him, that he was a man of weak judgment, and fettered, in no trifling degree, by the trammels of superstition. But to what purpose should we multiply words? If his dogmas respecting the number of the heavens stood unsupported by any circumstance else, it would be placed beyond the reach of controversy by the name of *"Abraxas"* alone, which he gives to the Supreme Lord of those heavens, and which contains within itself precisely the number 365.

(5) That the name *" Abraxas"* or *" Abrasax,"* for it is spelt in both ways, was considered by Baslides as a sacred word, and was applied by him to a certain nature of the most exalted order, admits not of the least doubt. But what this nature was, as also what was the origin and meaning of this appellation, is a matter of much obscurity, and one that has consequently given rise to a great variety of conjectures and disputations amongst the learned. *Irenæus,* from whom all the rest appear to have borrowed what information they convey respecting this controverted word, touches on it but very briefly, lib. i. c. xxiv. § 7. *Esse autem,* says he, *principem illorum* (of the 365 heavens)—'ΑϐϱάξαϚ, *et propter hoc* ccclxv. *numeros habere in se.* From these words two things are to be collected. *First,* that the Supreme Lord of the heavens had this title applied to him by Basilides: and *Secondly,* that his reason for so applying it was, that if the letters of which it is composed be taken as numerals, or in an arithmetical sense, they exhibit the number 365, and therefore, in a certain degree, express the function and dignity of the Supreme Lord of all the heavens. It is not, however, stated by Irenæus, and I would wish the reader particularly to attend to this, nor by any other ancient Greek or Latin author, that this [p. 347.] name was invented or first thought on by Basilides. The *second* point which we gather from Irenæus, inasmuch as it receives the strongest confirmation from the very word itself, which, in reality, if the letters composing it, be taken as numerals, will be found to express the number 365, appears to be admitted with scarcely any exception by the learned of the present day; and although there are not wanting eminent men who think that this word was looked upon as possessing some other power besides its numeral force, and who have endeavoured by a reference to the ancient Egyptian and Greek languages, or in

some other way to ascertain what it was, they have never yet been able to bring forward anything bearing the least semblance of truth or respectability, in support of their opinions. See Bern. de Montfaucon. *Palæograph. Græc.* lib. ii. cap. viii. Basnage, *Histoire des Juifs,* tom. iii. p. 700. Paul. Ernest. Jablonsky, *de Nominis Abraxas Significatione,* which last the reader will find in the *Miscellan. Nov. Lipsiens.* tom. viii. § xi. p. 88. et seq. Let us then content ourselves with that which is apparent, and not waste our time in searching after things that, in all probability, we shall never discover.—With regard to the point first above alluded to as deducible from the words of Irenæus, we find it giving rise to great diversity of opinion amongst men of the most eminent abilities, by whom a very learned warfare has been carried on as to who that prince or Supreme Lord of the heavens was, to whom Basilides gave the name of Abraxas. Those ancient writers who lived nearest to the time of Irenæus assert that by the term *Abraxas* was meant the Supreme Deity; and to this the greater part of more modern authors, without hesitation, assent. But the writers of ancient times, as well as those of modern days, who give this interpretation to the words of Irenæus, manifestly run into the error of expounding the di-cipline of Basilides upon orthodox principles. With Christians of the true faith, the creator and ruler of the heavens is one and the same with the Supreme Deity; but the opinion of Basilides was of a very different complexion. According to him, the three hundred and sixty-five heavens were neither framed by the Supreme Deity, nor were they at all subject to his dominion or controul. His belief was, that the angels were the fabricators of the heavens, and that the government of these celestial abodes rested with those who had thus framed them. Besides, there is another thing which deprives this ancient opinion of all weight or authority. Basilides maintained that the Supreme Deity had no name, and would never countenance his being spoken of under any other title than that of "*the Father.*" We have the express testimony of Irenæus as to this, who states that the Supreme Deity was styled by Basilides, *innatus et innominatus Pater.* He must, therefore, have been inconsistent with himself had he, after this, given to the Deity any specific title. Another opinion was started in the last age by John Chifflet who, in his *Comment. ad Gemmas Basilidianas,* p. 58. contends that by the title Abraxas was signified the *sun,* who completes his annual circuit in three hundred and sixty-five days. This opinion has been adopted by several of our later writers of the first reputation, and amongst others, by the very learned Isaac Beausobre, who, in his *History of the Manichees,* tom. ii. p. 51. has, with great ability and learning, brought forward various new arguments and reasons in its support. But in ad-
[p. 348.] dition to not a few other things, in which these arguments are defective it is particularly deserving of remark that they assume it for a fact, but fail altogether in proving, that Basilides regarded the *sun* as the prince or supreme lord of all the heavens. For my own part, after having considered everything that has been handed down to us respecting the tenets of Basilides, with the greatest possible attention, I can find nothing whatever that should afford the least grounds for our even suspecting, that he might conceive the sun to be the residence of that great angel whose empire he supposed to extend over all the

heavens. *Beausobre*, in all probability, perceiving this, endeavours indeed to make the discipline of Basilides wear a very different aspect from that which it exhibits as described by Irenæus and others, and contends that the idle conceit of a continued series of 365 heavens belongs to Irenæus and not to Basilides. But, as I have remarked above, he does this without any evidence or authority; and, after all, gains little or nothing by it in support of his hypothesis respecting the title Abraxas. For it may still continue to be required that the fact of Basilides having attributed to the sun the government or dominion of the skies, and of his having in consequence thereof considered this grand luminary, or some all-powerful genius residing therein, as deserving of the most distinguished, not to say divine honours, should be proved to us, not by Abraxean or Basilidian gems, that is, not by ænigmatical sculptures of which we have as yet received no explanation that can be depended on, but by passages from ancient authors. That eminent scholar, Paul. Ernest. *Jablonsky*, however, has thought fit, upon the whole, to espouse this opinion. though not without exercising his genius upon it, and endeavouring to make it accommodate itself, in some measure, to the religion of the gospel, lest it should seem too extravagant for a Christian man to entertain. See his very learned dissertation *de Significatione Nominis Abraxas*, printed in the *Miscellanea Lipsiens. Nov.* vol. vii. He conceives that Abraxas meant the sun, and thinks that although this is not expressly stated by the ancient Christian fathers, yet that they occasionally gave obscure intimations of it. § ix. Basilides, according to him, transferred this title to *Christ*, who in the sacred writings is compared to the sun, and, *Malach.* iv. 2. is termed the Sun of Righteousness. Abraxas, therefore, was the name of Christ himself, and Basilides, in thus applying it, meant to instruct his followers that the long and anxiously expected Sun of Righteousness had appeared, and that grateful and acceptable year of the Lord, spoken of by Isaiah the prophet, lxi. 2. was begun. It would give me pleasure could I perceive that these things were as clear and well-founded as they are ingenious and pious. But the fact is, that there are many things assumed by this illustrious writer as established, which appear to me to be by no means placed beyond the reach of controversy. He assumes, for instance, that Basilides ascribed a divine authority to the books of the Old Testament; which certainly was not the case, if any faith whatever is to be placed in ancient writers:—that the name Abraxas was first invented by Basilides: but no such thing is to be met with anywhere on record;—that those gems on which the name of Abraxas is to be found, and which are commonly termed Basilidian gems, were all of them of the manufacture of Basilides; a thing that appears to me altogether incredible;—that from these gems something certain and definitive may be collected; but which unquestionably admits of very considerable doubt.—In short, not only these, but a variety of other things are assumed by him, to which no one the least conversant in matters of antiquity can easily be brought to yield his assent; indeed, ingenuously to confess the truth, his whole hypothesis appears to me to carry with it an air of darkness and ambiguity, and to be by no means easy of comprehension. For my own part, laying aside all conceits and conjectures, however [p. 349.] much they may be distinguished by erudition or acumen, I think that as to this point *Irenæus* alone is deserving of attention, and that it may be clearly enough collected from him who this Abraxas was that makes such a conspicuous figure in the Basilidian discipline. According to Irenæus this title was given by Basilides to the prince or supreme governor of all the heavens. Undoubtedly then this *Abraxas* could have been none other than the first and greatest of the angels that were generated of *Sophia* and *Dynamis ;* he who, together with his associates, founded that first of the heavens which, in point of formation, took precedence of all the rest. His rule or government naturally extended itself over all the heavens that were subsequently formed, for he was the father of the angels that framed them, and, of course, had much the same kind of reverence paid him by these his progeny as was manifested for the Deity, by the Æons resident with him in the pleroma. He was, therefore, deservedly styled *Princeps Cælorum,* the prince or supreme lord of the heavens : and the discipline of Basilides recognizes no other prince of the heavens besides him. The name *Abraxas,* which comprises the number 365, was peculiarly applicable to him, inasmuch as it was he alone that orignated the whole 365 heavens ; of which none would have existed had he not framed the first and highest of them, and likewise begotten that inferior order of angels by whom the second heaven was made.

A great abundance of ancient *gems,* bearing, in addition to divers other figures of Egyptian invention, the name or title of *Abraxas,* is at this day extant, and more of them continue to be every now and then discovered in various parts of Egypt. In addition to what is to be met with in other authors who have incidentally adverted to the subject, the reader will find a considerable number of specimens of these gems exhibited by J. *Macarius* in a treatise of his expressly dedicated to their illustration, and which was enlarged and published by J. *Chifflet,* Antwerp, 1657, 4to. under the following title, *Abraxas, seu de Gemmis Basilidianis Disquisitio,* as well as by Bern. de *Montfaucon Palæograph. Græc.* lib. ii. cap. viii.—Relying upon what is stated by Irenæus and other ancient authors, that the title Abraxas was held sacred by the Basilidian sect, the learned have been almost unanimous in considering all these gems as of the manufacture of Basilides and his followers, and that they were distributed to his disciples in the place of *amulets* to guard them against poisons, witchcraft, and such-like ills : and hence among students of antiquity it has been usual to distinguish them by the title of Basilidian gems. *Beausobre,* however, in his *Histoire de Manichée,* vol. ii. p. 51. has with much strength of genius entered the lists against this prevailing opinion, contending, that from the words and figures engraven on these gems, it is clear that, instead of being ascribed to persons possessing the least tincture of Christianity, they ought rather to be considered as the productions of men utterly unacquainted with the true religion, and the slaves of a most base and degrading superstition. With not a few the force of his arguments has prevailed : but amongst these we are not at liberty to reckon the eminently learned *Jablonsky,* who, in his dissertation already noticed, labours hard to overthrow Beausobre's reasoning, and to uphold the common opinion respecting the Christian, and more particularly the Basilidian origin of these gems. The fact is, that unless these gems be regarded as of Christian orgin, Jablonsky's interpretation of the word Abraxas must inevitably fall to the ground. According to my view of the subject it seems impossible to deny Beausobre this much, that no inconsiderable portion of these gems are of a nature that will not admit of our believing them to [p. 350.] have come from the hands of any Christian workman, although, unquestionably, some of them exhibit certain marks or signs that may be considered as having somewhat of a distant reference to the Christian religion. For by far the greater portion of them carry on their face the insignia of the Egyptian religion, and are evidently the offspring of a superstition too gross to enslave the mind even of an half Christian. In my opinion, therefore, *Basilides* did not first devise or invent the title of *Abraxas*, but borrowed it, as he did a variety of other things, from the discipline of the Egyptian priests: nor is there, as I have already above observed, any ancient writer whatever that attributes the invention of this title to Basilides. Now let us only for a moment suppose, that *Abraxas* was a title by which the Egyptians were accustomed, long before the rise of Christianity, to designate the ruler or chief of those dæmons or angels whom they believed to preside over the heavens and the stars, and we shall have no further to seek, either as to the nature or design of these gems, or the reason of their being inscribed with this name. It was an ancient opinion of the Egyptians that the *dæmons* who rule over the heavens and the stars, possess also no little degree of influence over human affairs, and that amongst them there are some who delight in the evils of the human race, and make it their study, either of themselves, or through the instrumentality of agents, to afflict mankind with diseases or other grievous ills. With a view then to defend themselves against these enemies and torturers, and to secure both body and mind from the calamities which evil spirits of this kind might meditate against them, these deluded people were accustomed to inscribe on gems the name of that dæmon whom they supposed to have the supreme command over all the heavens and their rulers, together with some additional letters or figures which they supposed to possess great virtues, and to hang these gems as amulets about their necks. Their notion was, (indeed the superstition is not even yet obliterated amongst the vulgar of the east,) that the evil demons, upon beholding the terrific name of their supreme lord and ruler, accompanied with the above-mentioned mysterious words and figures, would find themselves incapable of working any harm to the person wearing this defence, and would consequently take to flight. Basilides, who was an Egyptian, transplanted this opinion, and the practice consequent upon it, into his system, with this difference only, that rejecting such figures or words as were profane, and would have been a scandal and disgrace to the religion he had adopted, he, in their room, annexed to the title of Abraxas certain others more suitable to the Christian character.

(6) *Basilides* did not, like the other Gnostics, consider the architect of this world to be evil in his nature ; but appears rather to have thought very highly of him, terming him, according to Clement, "the prophet and image of the True God ;" to whom *Sophia* or *Wisdom*, that is one of the *Æons*, communicated the model of the world and of the human race. *Stromat.* lib. iv. p. 603. Nearly all the Gnostics, indeed, were agreed in this, that the founder or founders of

this world did not themselves devise the fashion thereof, or of mankind, but in the formation of both, had before their eyes that model of the world and of the human race which exists with God in the pleroma. In truth, it was impossible for *Basilides*, consistently with his tenets, to think otherwise than well of the Creator of the world, inasmuch as he deduced the origin of such creator through two *Æons* from the Deity himself, and consequently must have admitted of his bearing somewhat of an affinity or relationship to the divine nature. This creator of the world was not, however, considered by him as good after the same manner that God is good ; namely, as being altogether incapable of meditating, [p. 351.] or even conceiving any thing evil ; but rather as possessing a middle kind of nature, and endowed with a freedom of will that might be turned either to a good or a bad account. From the Supreme Being nothing evil could proceed, from matter nothing good. But the angels who formed the world out of matter, or who were supposed to administer and govern it, had an equal power of inclining themselves either way, to good or to evil. This was the opinion of all the Gnostics, who believed that the creator of the world, or as they termed him, *Demiurgus,* was not originally of an evil nature ; a circumstance that at once accounts for our finding *Demiurgus* extolled and spoken of in the most exalted terms by persons who in the next breath represent him as the author and cause of much mischief and calamity. The fact was, that they regarded him as a being of an excellent nature, but at the same time as one that had made an ill use of his liberty.

(7) Almost all the Gnostic sects considered man as possessed of *two souls ;* the *one* brutal, and endowed merely with a perceptive libidinous faculty ; the *other* rational, and gifted with wisdom and intelligence : the latter divine in its origin, the former earthly and derived from the soul of matter. Nor were different sentiments on the subject entertained by *Basilides*, of whom Clement expressly says, Δύο γὰρ δὴ ψυχὰς ὑποτίθεται καὶ ὗτος ἐν ἡμῖν. *Is ergo duas quoque in nobis ponit animas.* *Stromat.* lib. ii. p. 448. His son *Isidore* also wrote a particular treatise περὶ προσφυὸς ψυχῆς, *de Anima adnata,* that is concerning the soul which *coalesces*, or, as it were, *unites* itself in one with the rational soul, the · concupiscent soul that is continually leading astray the intelligent soul with which it is associated in the body. From this work of *Isidore's* Clement quotes several passages.—To the question, however, of how it came to pass that a portion of the divine nature, a soul of reason and intelligence, should be condemned to a residence in this loathsome vitiated body ? the Gnostics do not return an uniform answer. Of what might be the opinion of *Basilides* as to this, the learned profess themselves to be altogether ignorant. But to me it appears that all uncertainty on the subject is removed by *Clement*, who had read the books of Basilides, and who, after giving a long quotation from him, adds as follows; Ἀλλὰ τῶ Βασιλείδη ἡ ὑπόθεσις προαμαρτήσασαν φησὶ τὴν ψυχὴν ἐν ἑτέρῳ βίῳ τὴν κόλασιν ὑπομένει ἐντᾶυϑα. *Sed Basilidis hypothesis dicit, animam, quæ prius peccaverat in alia vita, hic pati supplicium.* *Stromat.* lib. iv. p. 600. At the first I entertained some doubt as to whether these words referred to the souls of all mankind, or to those of martyrs alone. For the passage preceding them relates to martyrs only. But the words of Clement that immediately

follow, entirely remove this doubt, and render it evident that we ought to understand the passage as referring to the souls of the whole human race. The souls of men he divides into two classes; (1.) "The elect," or those of martyrs; (II.) "The common," or those of the ordinary description. The former he represents as receiving an honorary punishment in martyrdom, the latter as undergoing the punishment due to their offences. It is evident, therefore, I think, after what manner Basilides accounted for the association of divine souls with gross material bodies. The greater part of these souls had been guilty of some grievous transgression in the regions above, and had consequently rendered themselves obnoxious to punishment. When the founder of this world, therefore, had created the human race endowed with nothing more than merely a sensitive soul, the Deity caused those other souls to take up their [p. 352.] abode, for a season, in men's bodies, by way of expiating their offence, and rendering themselves worthy of being restored to their former estate. And in this the Deity acted conformably to his goodness. For since these souls had, by their transgression, incurred an exclusion from the celestial regions, and rendered it impossible that they should ever be again received there without having made expiation, a way was pointed out to them, in the maintenance of a continual conflict with matter and the temptations of the sensitive soul, by which they might wipe away the remembrance of their offence, and once more cleanse themselves from every impurity and stain.

(8) The Basilidians pretended to be in the possession of the oracular communications of certain of these legates and prophets that had been sent by the Deity to the human race before Christ's advent. The prophecies of *Cham*, for instance, which are mentioned by Clement, *Stromat.* lib. vi. p. 642. the discourses of *Barcabba* and *Barcophus*, noticed by Eusebius, *Histor. Eccles.* lib. iv. c. vii. p. 120. and other writings of a like description. All of these were forgeries, no doubt, but yet I think they must have been of some antiquity.

(9) *Origen* is my authority for stating Basilides to have believed in the migration of disobedient souls on the dissolution of the corporeal frame, into new bodies, either of men or brute animals. See his *Comm. in Matth.* tom. xxviii. p. 136, as also *in Rom.* v. p. 530, edit. Huetian. The principle also strictly accords with his other tenets respecting the human soul.

XLVII. **The Basilidian system of theology.** When Basilides, overpowered by the divine lustre of Christianity, had been induced to enrol himself amongst the number of its votaries, he made it his study to bend and interpret its principles in such a way as that they might appear rather to support than to militate against these his philosophical tenets. The cause of Christ's advent he maintained to be the defection of the founders and governors of this world from the Supreme Deity, the contentions and wars amongst themselves, in which they were continually engaged, and the consequent utter depravity and miserable situation of the whole human race. Those eminently powerful *genii*, he asserted, who both created and govern the world, being endowed with the most perfect freedom of will, as to the choice of either good or evil, inclined by degrees to the latter, and endeavoured to root out and obliterate all knowledge of the true God, with a view to get themselves regarded and worshipped by mankind as gods in his stead. They then engaged in wars amongst themselves, each one striving to extend the sphere of his own power.(¹) The president or ruler of the Jewish nation, in particular, the chief angel of the whole, aimed at nothing short of universal sovereignty, his efforts being directed to the entire subjugation of his associates, and the various regions of the earth over which they respectively resided. The consequences produced by this perturbed state of things were, that the true religion sunk into oblivion, men resigned themselves wholly to the dominion of depraved appetites and lusts, and every part of the earth groaned under an [p. 353.] accumulation of calamities, crimes, and wretchedness. Touched with compassion on beholding souls of a divine origin involved in so much misery and distress, the Supreme Deity directed his *Son*, that is *Nus,* the first of the seven *Æons* begotten of himself, to descend on earth for the purpose of putting an end to the dominion of these presiding angels, particularly that of their superlatively proud and arrogant chief whom the Jewish nation had learnt to venerate as a God. Having accomplished this, he was to revive amongst men the long lost knowledge of his father, and teach them to subdue the force of those turbulent and irregular appetites which war against the soul. Taking upon himself, therefore, the form and semblance of a man, but without assuming a real body, the son made his appearance amongst the Jews, and entered on the duties of the function that had thus been assigned him by his father, confirming the truth of his doctrine by miracles of the most stupendous nature. Enraged at this invasion of his dominion, the god of the Jews caused Christ to be apprehended and condemned to suffer death; but the latter, not being cloathed with a real body of his own, adopted that of *Simon* the Cyrenian, who had been compelled to bear his cross, and transferred his form to Simon; so that instead of Christ it was Simon the Cyrenian whom the Jews crucified.(²) The souls that paid obedience to the precepts and injunctions thus communicated to them from above, might expect, upon the dissolution of the body, to regain their original seats in the blissful mansions above; but those who neglected availing themselves of the proffered instruction, were destined to migrate into other bodies, either of men or brute animals, until their impurities should be wholly purged away. As for the *body,* a mass of corrupt and vitiated matter, no hope was to be entertained of its being ever restored to life again. Of the books of the Old Testament, which he conceived to have been composed, in part, by command of the prince of the Jewish nation, and in part at the instance of the other angels, Basilides could not, of course, have made any great account. What the books of the New Testament might be, of which he approved, is not at present known.

He wrote a long explanatory comment indeed on the gospel, but whether the gospel, which he thus took upon him to expound, was one of those which we recognize as genuine, or a different one, is not altogether certain.(²)

(1) To us of the present day, all this may appear very silly and ridiculous; but it was not viewed in this light by the oriental nations and the Egyptians, from whom Basilides borrowed a considerable part of his system. An opinion had, from very remote antiquity, prevailed amongst the nations of the east, and was adopted by the Jews, that this world was governed by *angels,* and that each nation or people had its presiding or *ruling angel.* Whatever, therefore, might happen to any particular region, either of a fortunate or a disastrous nature, was attributed not so much to the earthly sovereign or prince of that region as to its angelic guardian and governor: the former, in every thing which he might do, whether good or evil, being considered as acting under the immediate incitement or instigation of the latter. Hence, when kings and nations went to war with each other, the angels presiding over those nations were [p. 354.] conceived to be the authors of such wars. For these celestial rulers were supposed to burn with a desire of extending the limits of their dominion and acquiring an increase of power, and, with that view, to infuse into the minds of kings and nations a disposition to make war on other states. It is easy, then, to perceive in what sense we ought to understand what is taught by so many of the Gnostics respecting the angels occasioning disturbance in mundane affairs, stirring up wars amongst mankind, and bringing down a variety of afflictions and calamities on the human race.

(2) In exhibiting a view of the tenets of Basilides respecting *Christ,* I have followed the example of every other writer of ecclesiastical history that I have seen, and taken for my guide *Irenæus.* I must, however, confess that it is exceedingly difficult, I had almost said impossible, to reconcile Irenæus's account with what Clement of Alexandria says respecting the Basilidian institutes, and

the quotations which he gives us from the writings of Basilides himself. This was first noticed, I believe, by Ren. Massuetus, *Dissert. in Irenæum*, p. 61. But this author prefers the authority of Irenæus to that of Clement, and endeavours to give such an interpretation to the words of the former as would do away the above-noticed want of harmony between the two. In this, however, he is unquestionably wrong, since it is evident that in every thing respecting Basilides, *Clement*, who had actually perused the writings of the man himself, and who, being an Egyptian, had had the opportunity of witnessing on the spot the rites and observances of the Basilidian sect, which had its origin in Egypt, must be much more deserving of attention than Irenæus, who resided in Gaul, and must necessarily have obtained what information he might possess on the subject merely at second hand. *Beausobre*, with more propriety, in his *Hist. de Manichée*, vol. ii. p. 24, et. seq. deemed it best to turn his back entirely on Irenæus, and in eliciting the sentiments of Basilides respecting Christ, to depend wholly on what is to be met with on the subject in Clement.— *Clement*, it may first be observed, adduces (*Stromat.* lib. iv. p. 600.) a passage from the writings of Basilides, in which he denies that *Christ* was without spot or stain, and intimates in no very obscure terms, that by his sufferings and death he merely made atonement to divine justice for his own proper sins. *Basilides* was one who detracted much from the sanctity and pre-eminence of the martyrs, who were extolled and venerated beyond measure by the Christians of his time, contending that the sufferings and evils which they endured, were inflicted on them by the just judgment of God, on account of sins which they had committed either in the course of their lives here below, or else, before their coming into this world, in the regions above. To this error the orthodox Christians opposed the example of our Saviour, who, although he was in the highest degree holy and immaculate, was yet exposed to inexpressible sufferings, and underwent even death itself. By way, then, of getting rid of the force of this argument, Basilides had the temerity to assert that Christ, inasmuch as he was a man, could not have been immaculate or a stranger to every thing sinful. Ἐι μὲν τοι σφοδρότερον ἐκβιάσοιο τὸν λόγον, ἐρῶ, ἄνθρωπον, ὄντιν᾽ ἄν ὀνομάσης, ἄνθρωπον εἶναι δίκαιον τε τὸν Θεόν. Καθαρὸς γὰρ οὐδεὶς, ὥσπερ εἶπε τις, ἀπὸ ῥύπυ. *Quod si vero me vehementius urgeas, dicam, quemcunque hominem nominaveris, esse hominem, justum autem Deum. Nullus enim est mundus, ut ille dicit, a sorde.* Basilides, we may observe, expresses himself with some caution, and with a view to avoid exciting ill-will, forbears making any direct mention of Christ by name. But *Clement*, who was in possession of his writings, says that he is treating ἀντικρὺς περὶ τῦ κυρίυ— [p. 355.] —"openly of our Lord," and after some further remarks, adds, that such a man was deserving of the title of "atheist," inasmuch as he deified the devil, (θείαζων μὲν τὸν διάβολον) and had the audacity to term our Lord a man obnoxious to sin, (ἄνθρωπον ἁμαρτήτικον). In making this accusation, however, *Clement* suffered himself to be carried into extremes, and has, in consequence, given to the tenets of Basilides a much darker colouring than belongs to them. Basilides never thought of deifying the devil, or any thing like it. He maintained, indeed, that the founder or creator of this world was of divine origin; but this being was not, according to his tenets, the same with the devil, as Clement rashly persuaded himself, but a nature of the most exalted kind, although one that had somewhat deviated from the right path.—But if Basilides held that Christ himself, inasmuch as he was a man, could not be immaculate, how can that be true which *Irenæus* reports of his having maintained that Christ assumed merely the *semblance* or shadow of a body, and that *Simon*, the Cyrenian, was crucified by the Roman soldiers in his stead? To offend God by sinning, and to undergo the penalty of sin, a being must necessarily be clothed with a real body. The argument deduced from this passage of Basilides is seconded by what Clement says (*Stromat.* lib. i. p. 408.) of the Basilidians having been accustomed annually to commemorate the baptism of Christ with great devotion on the fifteenth day of the month termed by the Egyptians *Tubi*, which answers to the ninth or tenth of our January. No being could have undergone lustration or ablution by water but one invested with a real body. If Basilides therefore believed Christ to have been actually baptized by John in the waters of Jordan, it follows, of necessity, that his opinion must have been misrepresented by those who tell us that he maintained Christ to have taken on himself merely the *semblance* of a body. On these grounds it should seem that the commonly received opinion as to the tenets of Basilides, in regard to the point under consideration, must be given up.—Basilides, like others of the Gnostics, made a distinction between *Jesus* and *Christ*. *Jesus* he accounted to have been a mortal, born according to the ordinary course of nature, a man of great sanctity, but yet not free altogether from sin. *Christ* he regarded as one of the *Æons*, that is, the chief of those immutable natures that had been begotten of God himself. Piety having led the upright man Jesus to submit himself to the baptism of John, Christ by the divine command, descended into him from the regions above. When this same Jesus was seized on by the Jews and condemned to undergo capital punishment, Christ departed out of him, and returned again into heaven, leaving Jesus at the mercy of his enemies, who put him to death by crucifixion. In all probability *Irenæus* might transfer to Basilides a dogma peculiar to some other Gnostic sect, or attribute to the whole Basilidian sect and its founder, an erroneous supposition entertained by merely a few of its members; or finally, be misled by authorities that were not to be depended on.—Although I am persuaded that the case must be nearly as I have here stated it, I yet cannot help acknowledging that I was a long time held in doubt as to whether the two passages above cited from *Clement* were of sufficient weight to overthrow the authority of Irenæus, supported as it is by the consent of all ancient writers. For, to any one who shall attentively consider the words of Basilides as quoted by Clement, it may very naturally occur that possibly Clement might be [p. 356.] mistaken in his application of this passage to our Blessed Lord, inasmuch as Christ's name is not mentioned therein. That a day, indeed, should have been annually kept sacred by the Basilidians in commemoration of the baptism of Christ, has nothing in it absolutely irreconcilable with the account given by Irenæus For since some of the Gnostics maintained that Christ, in appearance, was nailed to the cross, died, and rose again from the dead, it is very possible Basilides might have believed that the spectators were imposed on by a similar illusion in regard to his baptism.—But my doubts were all removed, and I at once gave *Irenæus* entirely up, upon my meeting a third passage in *Clement*, superior to the two above noticed, and of a nature that renders it utterly incapable of being reconciled with the tenets of Basilides, as stated by Irenæus. For in his *Stroma'a*, lib. i. p. 408. Clement has expressly left it on record that the Basilidians had disputes among themselves as to the particular day on which Christ died. All, indeed, were agreed that his death took place in the sixteenth year of the reign of the emperor Tiberius ; but as to the particular day, some contended that it was on the 25th of the Egyptian month *Phamenoth*, others that it was on the 19th of the month *Pharmuth*, and others again that it was on the 25th of this latter month. *Clement* adds that there were some among the Basilidians who believed Christ to have been born on the 24th or 25th of the month *Pharmuth*. But how, let me ask, could there have been any disputes as to the particular day of our Blessed Saviour's birth or death amongst people who denied that Christ had ever been born or died at all? How could such people have maintained that Simon, the Cyrenian, underwent the punishment ordained by the Jews for our Lord? If what Irenæus states respecting the tenets of the Basilidians be correct, their disputes would have been as to the particular day of Simon's death ; respecting the day of the death of Christ no dispute could possibly have taken place amongst men who believed him never to have died at all.

But in what way soever this ought to be understood, the doctrine which *Irenæus* states to have been taught in the Basilidian school is clear beyond a question ; namely, " that it behoves men not to confess him who was actually crucified, but him who came in the form of man, and was supposed to have been crucified. . . . If any one confess him that was actually crucified, he is yet a servant, and in bondage to those (angels) by whom the bodies of men were created ; but whosoever shall deny him is freed from their dominion :"—Basilides made a distinction between the man *Jesus* and the *Æon*, the *Son* of the Supreme God, the *Christ* that descended into Jesus at the time of his baptism by John. When the Jews laid hold on *Jesus, Christ* withdrew himself from him, and left the man alone to encounter their fury. It was the man Jesus alone, therefore, divested entirely of the divinity, whom the Romans caused to expire on the cross. Wherefore, according to Basilides, it was wrong to place one's trust in him who was actually crucified, who was merely for a time the earthly tabernacle or abode of the Son of God, and who, when suspended on the cross, had nothing whatever of the divine nature remaining in him ; but right reason required that salvation and happiness should be sought for in none other than that *Christ*, by whose power alone the man *Jesus* had accomplished the various miracles that he wrought. A full and complete knowledge of the tenets of Basilides respecting the Saviour of the human race, is what we have not the means of obtaining ; but what his opinion was of the cause for which Christ came into the world is [p. 357.] sufficiently apparent. *Christ*, he maintained, did not come for the purpose of expiating by his sufferings and death the transgressions of the human race, and making satisfaction to the divine justice in man's stead : for he immediately took his departure out of *Jesus*, when the latter was about to undergo the punishment of death : and as to what *Jesus* underwent, he, as we have already seen, was deemed to have made atonement thereby merely for his own proper offences, not the sins of others; for, being a polluted mortal himself, it was impossible that he could become a propitiatory sacrifice for other transgressors. The only reason, therefore, according to Basilides, for which *Christ* came into the world, and for a time joined himself to the man Jesus was, that he might overthrow the dominion of the founders of this world, and particularly that of the God of the Jews, and by restoring to mankind the long-lost knowledge of the Supreme Deity, prevail on them to forsake the worship of those beings who falsely styled themselves gods; that he might moreover excite in men's minds such a determined opposition to those lusts which are generated of the body and the sensitive soul, as would eventually free them from all impurity, and thus qualify them, upon the dissolution of the corporeal frame, for re-ascending to the blissful regions above, from whence they originally sprang.

(3) *Origen* expressly says that *Basilides* had a proper *gospel of his own.* *Com. in Luc.* p. 210. edit. Huetian. But as this is not imputed to him by Clement, or any other ancient writer, I consider it as false. That the gospel, however, which he made use of, was in some respects different from ours, is what I can easily bring myself to believe. *St. Jerome* (*Proem. Comm. ad Titum*) states, that of St. Paul's *Epistles*, those addressed to *Timothy* and *Titus* were rejected by Basilides; nor is there any difficulty in crediting this. The first of the Epistles to the *Corinthians* I collect to have been approved of by him from the passage cited by Clement. *Stromat.* lib. iii. p. 509. But what I think more particularly deserving of remark as to this point is, that Basilides did not pretend that his tenets could be substantiated solely from those sacred writings which are in the hands of the Christians at large, but intimated that he had been beholden for them in part to other sources. A part, he said, he had learnt from the mouth of *Glaucias,* whom he described as having been the interpreter (ἑρμηνέα) of *St. Peter,* meaning, as I suppose, one who was master of the sentiments or opinions communicated privately by St. Peter to certain select disciples, whilst another part had been derived immediately from *St. Matthias.* Vid. Clemens Alexandr. *Stromat.* lib. vii. p. 898. 900.—His doctrine, therefore, like that of most others of the Gnostics, was, that the discipline propounded by Christ was of a two-fold nature; the one simple, popular, public, and to be collected from the writings of the New Testament; the other sublime and secret, received from our Saviour's lips by his apostles, and transmitted by them, not in writing, but merely by word of mouth, to certain disciples of known and approved fidelity.

XLVIII. **The moral doctrine of Basilides.** The moral discipline prescribed by Basilides, although founded, in some degree, in superstition, and supported rather by vain and empty subtleties than any true or solid principles, yet held out no encouragement to the irregular appetites and vices of mankind. The soul, he maintained, was possessed of a sufficient power or energy to overcome every incitement to evil, internal as well as external; and consequently that no man could become wicked except through [p. 358.] his own fault. God, he asserted, would forgive no other offences but those which had been unknowingly and unwillingly committed, and considered even a propension or leaning towards any sin, in one and the same light with the actual commission of such sin. All this is so obviously repugnant to a licentious course of life and action, that it is impossible for us to place any faith in the accounts of those ancient authors who represent Basilides as having countenanced the utmost laxity of manners amongst his followers.(¹) The unfavourable suspicions that were entertained by many respecting the nature of his moral discipline, appear to have been excited in part by the infamous lives led by some of his disciples,(²) and in part by the objectionable opinions which he maintained in regard to the lawfulness of concealing one's religion, of denying Christ in times of peril, of partaking of the flesh of victims offered to idols, of disparaging the estimation and authority of the martyrs, and peradventure as to various other points.(³) The Basilidian sect flourished for a considerable time, and had not become altogether extinct even so late as the fourth century.

(1) Irenæus, St. Jerome, Epiphanius, and other ancient writers, represent Basilides as having granted to his followers the most perfect liberty of doing whatever they might list. They, in fact, state him to have recognised no distinction whatever between good and bad actions. But to this accusation we are prevented from giving credit by the passages cited from the writings of Basilides himself, as well as from those of his son Isidore, by Clement of Alexandria, in which the points of moral doctrine above adverted to, as well as others of a similar nature, are propounded in direct and express terms. Points like these could never have been maintained by one who gave the rein to every natural appetite, and indulged his followers in the practice of all kinds of iniquity. See Clemens Alexandr. *Stromat.* lib. iv. p. 600. where we have the words of *Basilides* himself expressly declaring that " he who would commit adultery is an adulterer, although opportunity may have failed him ; he who would not scruple to commit murder a murderer, although his hands may never have been imbrued in human blood ;" which corresponds exactly with the doctrine delivered by Christ. See also lib. iv. p. 634. where he asserts that God will pardon no sins without punishment, " except such as may have been committed involuntarily or through ignorance," which, indeed, is pronounced too harsh and severe, even by Clement himself. Finally, in lib. ii. p. 488. we have the words of his son *Isidore*, severely rebuking those who, with a view of palliating their sins, say, " I found myself irresistibly compelled to do so and so ;—in what I have done I have not acted willingly, I was seduced into it." Men, he adds, by the assistance of the rational part, (that is the immortal soul of

divine origin,) have it in their power, and ought to subdue the inferior creature (that is, the brutal sensitive soul).

(2) Clemens Alexandrinus, in his *Stromata*, lib. iii. p. 510. describes the Basilidians, who were resident at Alexandria in his time, as being very debauched and dissolute in their manners. Some of them appeared to think that, having attained to the utmost summit of virtuous perfection, no further restraint on their appetites was necessary : others considered themselves as elected to salvation, and deemed it impossible for them, by any sort of transgres-ion, to fall from that state of felicity. But *Clement*, as became an honest man and a lover of truth, adds, that these reprobate Basilidians gave a very wrong interpretation to the precepts of their masters, and opposes to [p. 359.] them the very words of Basilides. Οἱ προπάτορες, says he, τῶν δογμάτων ὁ ταῦτα ἀυτοῖς πράττειν συγχαρῦσιν. *Inventores sive patres dogmatum quæ probant, non potestatem illis fecerunt talia perpetrandi.* Clement, therefore, although inimical to the Basilidian sect, yet found himself compelled in justice to acknowledge that neither in the writings of Basilides, nor in those of his son Isidore, was there anything whatever that should countenance men in a sinful course of life, and that the dissolute conduct of the disciples could, in no shape, be charged on the doctrine or precepts of the master.

(3) Nothing whatever excited a greater dislike to Basilides amongst the orthodox Christians than the sentiments entertained by him respecting the *martyrs.* By the unanimous voice of the Christian church, the martyrs were exalted to the right hand of the Majesty on high, and pronounced worthy of having almost divine honours paid to them ; but, according to *Basilides*, their merits were, by no means, of a transcendant nature ; neither ought any greater reverence to be paid to their memory than to that of other pious persons.—The ancient writers, indeed, who treat of the doctrine of Basilides, are not strictly in union with each other, neither do they all attribute to it the same degree of turpitude ; but in this they are all agreed, that it was every way calculated to enfeeble and corrupt the minds of Christians, and seduce them from that fidelity and allegiance which they owed to their Divine Master. Nor can any one doubt of this, who shall attentively consider even those extracts alone from the writings of Basilides, which are to be met with in Clement of Alexandria. The opinion entertained by him respecting the martyrs was connected, as must readily be perceived by any one who will compare together what is said by ancient writers respecting the morals and conduct of the Basilidians, with *another* and still more grievous *error*, namely, that it was lawful for Christians, not only to conceal and disguise their religion, but also, in case of life or fortune being brought into danger, even to deny and abjure the very name of Christ. The Basilidian doctrine, as to this point, is given us in the following terms by Irenæus, (*adv. Hæres.* lib. i. cap. xxiv. p. 102.) with whom other ancient authors agree : *Sicut Filium* (that is Christ, who for a certain time joined himself to the man Jesus) *incognitum omnibus esse, sic et ipsos a nemine oportere cognosci.* - - - *Quapropter et parati sunt ad negationem* (Christi) *qui tales sunt, immo magis ne pati quidem propter nomen* (Christi) *possunt, cum sint omnibus similes* (that is, because they live just in the same way as the heathen worshippers, and

conform themselves in every respect to the manners of the people amongst whom they happen to reside). That men of a selfish turn of mind should readily have embraced this error, in those perilous times when the Christians were daily made to undergo punishments of the most horrible nature, and frequently had to meet death under all its terrific forms, cannot in the least be wondered at; and we are certain that it found acceptance with many, particularly the Gnostics. Nor were the Basilidians unsupplied with somewhat of a specious and imposing argument, whereby to colour and extenuate this perfidious kind of conduct. For since they denied that Christ, the son of the Supreme Deity, ever actually coalesced in one and the same person with the man Jesus, and maintained that it was the man Jesus alone (Christ having quitted him) who suffered upon the cross, they might, without falsehood, affirm that they did not worship as the Deity, or the offspring of the Deity, him whom the Romans, at the instigation of the Jews, put to death, neither did they rely on him for salvation. Nay, they might have gone the length of adding, that they considered *Jesus* who was crucified as a sinner, [p. 360.] who had merited the grievous punishment that he underwent; for that such was their opinion is manifest from the words of Basilides, which we have quoted above. And that they were accustomed, in defence of their conduct, to have recourse to some such quibbling as this, is plainly to be collected from Irenæus, who represents them as maintaining that "men ought not to confess him who was actually crucified," (*i. e.* the man Jesus, out of whom Christ had departed previously to his being affixed to the cross,) " but him who came in the form of man, and was supposed to have been crucified." Men professing sentiments like these might well remain safe and secure in the very midst of the enemies of Christianity, who had no idea, as appears from Pliny, that any Christian would revile Christ crucified. The distinction thus made between Christ and Jesus was a thing of which they entertained not the least conception.—The Basilidians, then, were particularly anxious, by every means in their power, to avoid being confounded with those Christians who were denounced by the Roman laws. This led them to do as well as submit to several things from which all true Christians would have recoiled with horror. One of these undoubtedly was that of being *present* at the pagan sacrifices, and partaking of the meats offered to false gods. Ancient writers cast this in their teeth with all imaginable rancour, but are entirely silent as to the motive; which may, however, readily be conceived from what we have noticed above. All true Christians made it a point, conformably to the injunction of St. Paul, never to be present at any of the sacrifices or religious feasts of the heathens, and considered it as an abomination to touch meats that had been offered to the pagan deities, circumstances which rendered their detection at all times extremely easy. The Basilidians, therefore, who made security their study, had recourse to an opposite line of conduct, and neither scrupled to mingle with the heathen worshippers in their sacrifices, nor to feast with them afterwards in their temples on the remnants of the victims. If life or safety required it, they were also ready boldly to avow that they had nothing to do with Christ, meaning, in this case, the *man* that was actually crucified, not the true *Christ*, whom they supposed to have descended from above, and, after sojourning here on earth for a while, to have again returned to his Father's abode. By means of this their perfidious dissimulation they succeeded, according to ancient authors, in escaping the persecutions which befel the other Christians; and we, consequently, find *no martyrs* of the Basilidian sect. The Basilidians, in fact, were not in the least ambitious of martyrdom. This being cast in their teeth by the other Christians, who were accustomed to place no little part of their felicity and glory in the number of their martyrs, and to consider an eagerness after martyrdom as a characteristic feature of the true church, Basilides and his son retorted by assailing the credit of the martyrs, and maintaining that those Christians acted very unadvisedly who either professed a wish to pour out their own blood in the cause of Christ, or contended that a greater degree of sanctity and honour ought to be ascribed to the martyrs than to other Christians. By way of supporting himself in this opinion, he assumed it for a fact, as appears from his own words, as cited by Clement, *Stromat.* lib. iv. p. 600. that the evils which men suffer in this life are nothing more than the punishment of offences committed by the soul either during its residence in the body, or in a previous state of exis- [p. 361.] tence. God being all just, he said, it was impossible that he should suffer an innocent and unoffending person to undergo pain and affliction; and we were, therefore, of necessity compelled to believe that men must, by their transgressions, have merited whatever calamities we may see befall them. This then being assumed, his conclusion was, that, so far from attaching any peculiar degree of sanctity to the character of those Christians who were punished and put to death by the Romans on account of their religion, we should rather consider them as belonging to the class of those who, either in this life or in a previous state of existence, had grievously offended the Deity by their trangressions. In defence of this opinion he went, as we have above seen, the length of asserting that even Jesus of Nazareth himself, in whose body Christ the Son of the Deity for a while took up his abode, in being crucified underwent merely the punishment due to his own proper offences. The horror excited, even by the bare mention of this doctrine, in the minds of those Christians whose discipline was founded on the sacred writings, occasioned the author of it to be viewed by them in the most unfavourable light. By Basilides himself, however, the principle was not considered as unjustifiable or injurious to the Deity, inasmuch as, according to his foolish way of thinking, a distinction existed between Christ the Son of God and the man Jesus, Christ having been a compound of two persons, the one human, the other divine. That sentiments like these, differing so widely from what were commonly entertained, and apparently calculated to do away every kind of piety towards God, should have caused the Christians in general to think unfavourably of the whole moral discipline of Basilides, cannot in the least be wondered at, although it was certainly in great part far from being of that dissolute and unseemly character which was commonly attributed to it. Considerable grounds for suspicion were likewise afforded by the depraved and perverse lives led by many of the Basilidians, who, by an abuse of the precepts of their master, endeavored to justify themselves in all manner of iniquity.

XLIX. The system of Carpocrates. Whatever might be the errors and depravity of Saturninus and Basilides, Alexandria produced, nearly about the same time, in the person of *Carpocrates*, a character by far worse than either of these two, nay, a very monster of a man, if faith is to be placed in those accounts of his tenets and doctrine which are given us by ancient as well as more recent authors. To confess the truth, however, the more ancient writers have not only left us a very lame and unintelligible account of the Carpocratian system of discipline, but appear to have failed in arriving at any thing like a perfect comprehension of it themselves; nay, in some respects to have actually misrepresented it; whilst, at the same time, in regard to other particulars, they themselves seem to have been much misunderstood by more recent authors.(¹) The *philosophy* of Carpocrates respecting the Deity, the world, and the nature of man, differed but little from the sentiments entertained on these subjects by the rest of those whom we commonly term Gnostics. He believed, for instance, that there existed a Deity supreme over every thing, and, in point of nature, infinitely beyond the reach of all human conprehension;—that of this Deity had been generated certain *Æons* or immortal and immutable natures;—that *matter* was eternal, and that it was the fountain or source of every thing evil and pernicious. He further held that the *world* had been founded by angels who, in point of nature, were far inferior to the Supreme [p. 362.] Being;—that the rational *souls* of men had been sent down from the regions above into terrene bodies, as into a sort of prison;(²)—that the founders of this world, after extinguishing amongst mankind every knowledge of the true and Supreme Deity, had arrogated to themselves the title and honours of gods, and endeavoured by every means to prevent the souls imprisoned in bodies of matter from understanding that there was any nature of a more excellent or perfect kind;—that considerable assistance was afforded to them in this matter by a certain angel, malignant in his very nature; that is, the *devil;* whose study it is to draw over mankind from the true God to the prince of this world;—that the souls who are so unfortunate as to be thus seduced by this evil angel, upon their being released by death from one body, are constrained to migrate into another, whilst such as successfully resist his wiles, and those of the founders of this world, ascend, on the dissolution of the body, to God the parent of all souls. All this has nothing in it at all incredible, and sufficiently accords with those principles on which the whole Gnostic philosophy was built.

(1) For the religion of Carpocrates our leading authority is *Irenæus*, who, in c. xxv. of his first book *advers. Hæres.* enters into the nature of it at much length, but in a manner by no means either comprehensive, distinct, or perspicuous. Respecting his moral discipline some few particulars are given us by *Clement* of Alexandria, *Stromat.* lib. iii. p. 511. et seq. that appear to be deserving of credit, inasmuch as they were extracted from a book written by *Epiphanes* the son of Carpocrates, *de Justitia Dei.* What other particulars we find recorded by Epiphanius, Tertullian, Theodoret, and other hæresiologists, are partly transcribed from Irenæus, and in part collected from vulgar report; neither do they altogether accord with each other. It is utterly out of the power of any one, therefore, to exhibit anything like a correct and complete view of the Carpocratian system of religion in all its parts. Many things are wholly omitted by Irenæus, which it is impossible for us to supply, even in the way of conjecture, and on others he barely touches in a transient manner, without troubling himself to give us either comment or explanation.

(2) What the sentiments of Carpocrates were respecting the soul is very obscure and uncertain. Of this, indeed, we are pretty well assured, that he considered the souls of men as of divine origin, and as having been sent down from above into these earthly bodies as into a prison; but as to what kind of nature he might attribute to them, or to what cause he might ascribe their being thus consigned to terrene bodies, we have no ground sufficient to warrant even a conjecture. There is, however, a passage cited by Clement of Alexandria (*Stromat.* lib. iii. p. 513.) from the book written by *Epiphanes* the son of Carpocrates, *de Justitia Dei,* from whence it appears that the latter conceived the souls of men to have had their appetites and instincts implanted in them by the Deity himself, not only those of an harmless or an indifferent nature, but such likewise as are unlawful and prohibited. Hence it is apparent, not only that his opinion respecting the original nature of the soul was a very extraordinary one, and vastly different from that entertained by the rest of the Gnostics, but also that he did not, like others of the Gnostics, conceive man to have been endowed with two souls, the one merely sensitive, concupiscent, and [p. 363.] deduced from matter, the other rational, and free from every disorderly appetite.

L. **The Carpocratian theology.** Ancient authors, however, leave us entirely in the dark as to the mode in which Carpocrates endeavoured to make the Christian religion accommodate itself to these principles. The doctrine he taught is commonly reported to have been that Jesus was begotten of Joseph and Mary, according to the ordinary law of nature; and that he was superior

to the rest of mortals in no other respect than that of having a
more excellent soul residing within him, and being endowed by
the Deity with certain qualities and virtues by means whereof
he was enabled to overcome the power of the founders of this
world.   But there is not wanting abundant cause for suspicion
that, as to this, his tenets have been misrepresented; and that, in
point of fact, he, like other Gnostics, made a distinction between
the man Jesus and Christ, considering the latter as one of the
Æons, and son of the Supreme Deity.(') With regard to the
cause, however, for which Christ was sent down by his Father to
mankind, it is impossible, if his other tenets be duly considered,
that Carpocrates could have believed it to have been any other
than that he might abolish the worship of a plurality of gods : or
to speak after the manner of the Gnostics, put an end to the dominion of the founders of this world ; and after having excited in
the souls that had long been languishing under the dominion of
superstition, a wish to know and worship the Supreme Deity,
might point out to them the way in which this knowledge of the
True God would enable them to triumph over the wiles of the
devil, as well as the power of the founders of this world, and
qualify them for re-ascending, on the dissolution of the body, to
their original stations in the realms of light.

(1) All the writers of ecclesiastical history agree in declaring that by none
of the Gnostics was the character of our Blessed Saviour held in so little respect
as by Carpocrates.   *Christ*, if we may give credit to their statement, was considered by Carpocrates as having been a *mere man*, begotten of Joseph and Mary
according to that law by which all other mortals are produced ; but a mind of
greater strength and dignity than usual having accidentally fallen to his lot, the
Deity was pleased, in addition, to confer on him divers virtues to which other
men were strangers, and commission him to enlighten the human race, and withdraw them from the worship of the founders of this world.   That such were his
sentiments they are led to believe from the following words of Irenæus : *Jesum
autem* (dicit Carpocrates) *e Josepho natum, et cum similis reliquis hominibus fuerit, distasse a reliquis secundum id, quod anima ejus firma et munda cum esset,
commemorata fuerit quæ visa essent sibi in ea circumlatione, quæ fuisset ingenito
Deo.*   According to this, Carpocrates believed that the soul of Jesus, previously
to its connection with the body, existed just in the same way as all other
[p. 364.] souls, with the Deity in the regions above, but that, on its being sent
to occupy a body here below, it did not, like other souls, lose all remembrance
of what it had known and understood in its former state, but, having once obtained a clear perception of the truth, took care never again to lose sight of it,

and consequently maintained for itself a superiority over other minds. This doctrine manifestly savours of Platonism, and the discipline of the Oriental philosophers. For *Plato*, as is well known, held that a knowledge of the truth is implanted in the soul by nature, but that, upon its junction with the body, this knowledge is obscured, and an entire forgetfulness of every thing past takes place. Under the influence of this opinion, he maintained, that to inquire and gain knowledge is nothing more than to renew or recover the memory of things that had been before known but forgotten. When such a soul, as Carpocrates conceived Christ's to have been, became united to the material body begotten of Joseph, it could not otherwise happen but that a man of an extraordinary and preëminent nature should be thereby constituted.—Of the association of any third or divine nature with the body and soul of Jesus no mention occurs in these words of Irenæus; wherefore very learned men have been led to conclude that Carpocrates believed Jesus to have been a man composed of a mortal body and an immortal soul, and nothing more. This opinion appears to be corroborated by several things which are subsequently recorded by Irenæus. In the first place, we find it stated by him that certain of the Carpocratians were so arrogant as to assert that they themselves were equal to Jesus, (*ut se Jesu dicant similes,*) others so mad as absolutely to maintain that they were superior to him, (*fortiores eo esse,*) inasmuch as they had received souls of the same degree and order as Christ's. But could it be possible, let me ask, for any thing peculiarly great or divine to be attributed to Christ by persons who were so sottishly vain as to imagine that they themselves were equal or even superior to him?—It is, in the next place, stated by Irenæus that the Carpocratians had painted likenesses of Christ, as well as other representations of him, which they crowned, and held up to veneration in company with those of the philosophers Pythagoras, Plato, and Aristotle. When interrogated as to the way in which they had obtained these likenesses, they replied, that a portraiture of Christ had been painted by the command of Pilate. These things certainly seem to prove that Christ was considered by the Carpocratians merely in the light of a philosopher, and was placed by them on a level with Plato, Pythagoras, and the rest. But upon pursuing the thread of Irenæus's discourse, it appears to me that both ancient and modern writers have neglected to bestow a due degree of attention on his words, and in consequence thereof have failed in arriving at a just conclusion respecting the opinion which Carpocrates entertained of Christ; for which, however, some excuse is certainly to be found in the brevity and obscurity of the writer's style. What I would remark is, that immediately after the words cited at the commencement of this note, Irenæus goes on thus: *Et propter hoc ab eo* (the Supremo Deity) *missam esse ei* (the soul of Jesus) *virtutem uti mundi Fabricatores effugere posset, et per omnes transgressa et in omnibus liberata adscenderet ad eum.* Now allowing their due weight to these words, I cannot help feeling strongly inclined to believe that Carpocrates thought no less respectfully of Christ than Basilides and other Gnostics, and held that one of the divine Æons, (for the Gnostics term these *virtues,* in Greek *δυνάμεις,*) descended into the man [p. 365.] Jesus, who, on account of the superior excellence of his soul, was, beyond all other mortals, deserving of such honour, at the commencement of his ministry, and continued with him during his progress; but that upon his being seized and condemned to suffer death, this *Æon* departed out of him, and reäscended to the regions above. This, at the least, is evident, that Carpocrates recognized in Jesus *three* distinct parts: 1. a *body* begotten in the course of nature; 2. a *soul* sent down from the immediate residence of the Deity for the purpose of being associated with this body; and, 3. a *virtue* divinely communicated to this soul on account of its superior excellence; which *virtue*, in all probability, ought to be accounted as one and the same with that *Christ* whom the leaders of the various Gnostic factions pretended to distinguish from the man Jesus. With regard, therefore, to what is reported by Irenæus as to some of this sect having accounted themselves equal to Jesus, and the whole of them having placed him no higher than on a level with the philosophers, it must be considered as not referring to *the virtue* which for a time resided in Jesus, or to Christ the Son of the Deity, but merely to the man Jesus taken in the abstract.—This explication of the tenets of the Carpocratians respecting Christ, derives no little confirmation from what Irenæus says of their having taught that souls were saved " through *faith*," i. e. in Christ, " and *Charity.*" For if the sentiments entertained by Carpocrates respecting Christ were what they are commonly represented to have been, it is impossible to annex any sense or meaning to these words. How could *faith* in a mere man be held up as the means of bringing any one to salvation? Certain of this sect, we are told, made it a matter of boast that they were possessed of souls in no respect inferior to the soul of Jesus; nay, some even went so far as to assert that they were endowed with souls superior to that of Jesus. Both, therefore, must have felt persuaded that they possessed within themselves the same power of successfully combating the founders of this world as Jesus Christ did. But if a faith in Jesus Christ, supposing them to have considered him merely as an eminent man, could, in their opinion, have led to salvation, surely they must have believed that a faith in those men, who were equal or even superior to Jesus Christ, would be attended with equally beneficial consequences. But this would have been contradicting themselves, inasmuch as it would have been admitting that a faith in Christ was not absolutely necessary to salvation. But if Carpocrates made a *distinction* between Christ and the man Jesus, as I think he did, we may readily perceive in what sense he might say " that salvation was obtained through faith in Christ." In such case there can be no doubt but that his meaning must have been that a faith in that *Virtue*, or *Æon*, the Son of the Supreme Deity, who animated and governed the man Jesus in the execution of his divine commission here on earth, would obtain from the Father celestial happiness for all such souls as might be possessed of it.—What we have thus suggested will receive also considerable illustration and support from the following words of Irenæus, if properly attended to: *Jesu autem dicunt* (i. e. the Carpocratians) *animam in Judæorum consuetudine nutritam contempsisse eos* (the founders of this world) *et propter hoc virtutes accepisse, per quas evacuavit quæ fuerunt in pœnis passiones, quæ inerant hominibus.* Commentators, as is not unusual with them, have passed these words of Irenæus over without remark, although they certainly call for attention and explanation far beyond many others on which an abundance of

pains has been bestowed.   For any illustration of this passage, therefore, we
are driven to depend wholly on ourselves.   It may be remarked, then, [p. 366.]
(I.) that Irenæus here represents Carpocrates as having taught " that the soul of
Jesus contemned the fabricators of this world," or those angels who made this
world, and hold dominion over it: which is much the same thing as if he had
said, that Jesus did not worship those gods whom the nations of the earth held
in reverence, but confined his adoration to the only True and Supreme Deity.
(II.) It is added as the reason why the soul of Jesus entertained a contempt for
the founders of this world,—*quod Judæorum consuetudine nutrita esset :* that is,
the Jews held the gods of the nations in contempt, and worshipped only one
Deity, therefore Jesus, who was born and educated amongst the Jews, was led
to do the like.   I shall not stay to remark that what is thus stated corresponds
but ill with the account which Irenæus just before gives us of the Carpocratian
tenets respecting the virtue and fortitude naturally belonging to the soul of
Jesus, or that it reflects but little honour on the character of Jesus: but I cannot pass over this, that if the doctrine of Carpocrates be rightly conveyed in
these words, he must have excluded the God of the Jews from the number of
the angels who framed this world, and regarded him as the Supreme Deity;
which, if it were true, would separate him widely indeed from all others of the
Gnostics. For, if the soul of Jesus, in worshipping one God alone, and treating
with contempt the founders of this world, imitated the example of the Jewish
people, it follows, of necessity, that the Jews could not have worshipped the
founders of the world, but must have confined themselves to the service of the
one Supreme God.   But it is impossible to believe that Carpocrates could have
thought thus honourably of the Jews and their religion.   For, not to notice
other things, we have in Clement of Alexandria a very striking passage cited
from Epiphanes, the son of Carpocrates, in which he derides the Jewish law,
and openly contends that the best part of it is nonsensical and childish. *Stromat.* lib. iii. p. 514.   Either Irenæus, therefore, must have been guilty of an
error, or the Latin translator must have much misrepresented his meaning. (III.)
Irenæus points out the reward which, according to the Carpocratians, the Deity
conferred on the soul of Jesus on account of the contempt thus shown by him
for the founders of the world; *viz. Virtutes per quas evacuavit quæ fuerunt in
pœnis passiones quæ inerant hominibus.* The last three words are unintelligible,
and may, therefore, be considered as having been somehow or other corrupted;
but the meaning intended to be conveyed by the others is clear enough: namely,
that the Deity communicated to the soul of Jesus certain virtues or powers by
means whereof it might *evacuate*, that is, triumph over, the pains and afflictions to
which his body was exposed. Carpocrates, therefore, believed that Jesus in reality
underwent torments and death, but that in consequence of the virtue divinely
communicated to him he was insensible of their severity and power. As to the
particular way in which he conceived this to have been brought about, whether, for
instance, he imagined Jesus to have been deprived by the Deity of all sensation,
or whether he conceived the Deity to have inspired Jesus with a fortitude and
elevation of mind superior to every evil that could be inflicted on him, we are
not competent to speak. We should evidently do wrong, however, were we to

confound these virtues by which Jesus was enabled to triumph over the pains of the cross, with that one great *virtue*, which resided in him during the time that he lived at liberty and wrought his miracles amongst the Jews. The latter he was understood to have possessed previously to his being seized on and crucified, with the former he was not supposed to have been endowed until in the very act of contending with torments and death. These things considered, we may conclude Carpocrates to have taught that that great virtue, which had its residence in Jesus during the time of his teaching and working miracles amongst [p. 367.] the Jews, departed out of him when he was about to suffer: but that the Deity did not leave him comfortless, but supplied him with such other succours from above as effectually prevented his soul from sinking under the weight of those manifold and grevious injuries and sufferings to which his corporeal frame was exposed.

LI. **The moral discipline of Carpocrates.** All ancient writers concur in representing the moral discipline of Carpocrates as in the highest degree vile and pernicious, and the lives led by his followers as having consequently been gross, libidinous, and filthy in the extreme. Nor can we altogether withhold our credit from this: for it is certain that he countenanced a community of women, and inculcated several other things which had a manifest tendency to encourage men in various wicked and flagitious practices. There are not wanting, however, circumstances which incline us to believe that the inferences deduced from his tenets have not been in every instance correct, and that the turpitude of certain of his maxims was tempered and corrected by doctrine of a very different character and tendency contained in others.(') Nor can I easily bring myself to believe what is handed down to us respecting a place amongst the gods having been assigned to his son Epiphanes by the inhabitants of the city of Sama, in the island of Cephalonia.(²) Like the rest of the Gnostics, he asserted that his tenets and doctrine were founded on the secret discipline communicated by Christ to a few only of his followers. Hence it is clear that he could have attached but little weight or authority to the sacred writings. He did not, however, reject them entirely, but seems in particular to have approved of the gospel according to St. Matthew.(³)

(1) Nothing can possibly be conceived more infamous and gross than the moral doctrine of Carpocrates was, if any faith is to be placed in the accounts given us of it by all ancient writers. According to them he maintained: (I.) That there is nothing naturally evil in itself, but that all distinction between

good and bad actions exists merely in human opinion and laws; and consequently, that every one, in a moral point of view, is perfectly at liberty to do as
he may like. (II.) That women, and every thing else belonging to this world,
ought to be common, for that it was the will of God that all men should possess an equal right in every thing. (III.) That the road to everlasting felicity
lay open to those souls alone who devoted themselves to the perpetration of
every vile and flagitious action which it was possible for the heart of man to
conceive. I pass over certain things less heinous and disgusting, inasmuch as
every thing that can be deemed impious and detestable is certainly comprehended in the above. Conformably to these principles, it is said to have been
customary for the Carpocratians, in their nocturnal assemblies, to extinguish
the light and engage in a promiscuous libidinous intercourse. Clem. Alex.
Stromat. lib. iii. p. 514. Of the above, that which I have noticed in the third
place, I conceive to be a mere calumny, which had its origin probably in some
tenet or other not sufficiently understood. For can any one possibly believe that
a man who regarded the Deity as just, good, and beneficent; who conceived
men's souls to be the offspring of this Deity; and who entertained a reverence
for Christ; can any one, I say, for a moment persuade himself that a man of
this description (and that Carpocrates was such an one is evident from the passages cited by Clement of Alexandria out of the writings of his son Epiphanes)
should have maintained that none but souls contaminated by every species of
iniquity, and as it were glutted with sensual indulgence, would ever find their
way back to the Deity, the fountain of all good? Equally void of any [p. 368.]
solid foundation do I consider what is told us respecting the nocturnal orgies of
his disciples. For this opinion I shall presently assign certain reasons that I
rather think the reader will consider as carrying with them some weight.—As
to the *first* and *second* of the tenets above noticed, they are avowed without reserve by *Epiphanes*, the son and most strenuous defender of Carpocrates and
his opinions, from whose book *de Justitia Dei*, Clement of Alexandria (*Stromat.*
lib. iii. p. 512. et seq.) gives us some long quotations, in which it is endeavoured,
by various arguments, to prove that many things are by human laws pronounced
to be evil, which, in point of fact, have nothing whatever of evil or iniquity belonging to them. The Deity, it is boldly affirmed by this writer, designed every
good thing which he bestowed on mortals, to be used and enjoyed by them in
common. Mankind, by their laws, however, have destroyed this communion of
use, and introduced a separate property in things. Human laws, therefore, he
maintains, are repugnant to the divine will. These maxims are evidently inculcated by him with a reference to matrimony, and what are termed men's goods:
for he says expressly, that women, according to the divine law, ought to be
common, and that the same principle applies to fruits, corn, and animals; and
that it is merely of human ordination that those who assert their right to the
enjoyment of these things, in common are termed adulterers and thieves. This
passage is followed by another even worse. For he pronounces the law "Thou
shalt not covet," to be absolutely ridiculous, inasmuch as the desires and appetites of the soul were implanted in it by the Deity; and still more ridiculous,
he says, is the addition of the Jewish legislator, "Thou shalt not covet thy

neighbour's goods;" for it was impossible that the Deity, who implanted desires in the soul, could have commanded that these desires should be subdued and extinguished. But the most ridiculous thing of all he pronounces to be that injunction of the same legislator, "Thou shalt not covet thy neighbour's wife;" for there can be no doubt but that the Deity designed all women to be common. These things certainly admit of no palliation whatever; and it should, therefore, seem to be established beyond a question by the words of Carpocrates himself, or at least those of his son, that nothing whatever was considered by him as unlawful, but that theft, fornication, adultery, &c. although prohibited by human laws, were, in his opinion, consentaneous to the divine will. Which opinion is even still more impious than that which is attributed to him by the early Christian writers: *viz.* "That all actions are in their nature indifferent, and that it is by human laws alone that certain of them are pronounced to be evil." For whoever maintains that the lusts and appetites by which mankind are disturbed, were implanted in their minds by the Deity himself, and that the actions to which men are prompted by such lusts and appetites, are consentaneous to the divine will, must of necessity hold that theft, fornication, robbery, adultery, &c. are to be regarded as good works. Hence, then, we may perceive that it was not, altogether, without grounds or reason that some were led to assert, that Carpocrates believed heaven to be accessible to such souls only as had in this life devoted themselves to the perpetration of every species of crime and iniquity. My belief, however, is that the man did not propound the above principles to his disciples at large, but only to certain select and confidential ones. A teacher, who, like Carpocrates, maintained that our blessed Saviour's doctrine was of a two-fold description, the one popular, the other secret, would naturally have recourse to a similar method of instruction, and address himself to the multitude after a different manner from that which he adopted with regard to his friends and intimates. The atrocity and impiety of his opinions and doctrine, however, are in no degree extenuated by this.

Notwithstanding all these things, however, I cannot help confessing myself strongly inclined to believe, that the wickedness and depravity of Carpocrates [p. 369.] could never have been so preposterously absurd and loathsome as is commonly imagined, but that, to the tenets above noticed, which are undoubtedly of the most vile and abominable nature, there must have been subjoined others, calculated, in a certain degree, to correct their turpitude and counteract their poison. Every one acquainted with human affairs must well know that if certain parts of various systems of discipline were to be separated from the rest, and considered by themselves, they would assume, not only an absurd, but an altogether impious and execrable character; but let them only be restored to their proper situation, and again connected with those things from which they were disjoined, and most of their deformity will at once disappear. Ancient writers bring us acquainted with but a very small portion of the Carpocratian philosophy and religion, and even this is exhibited by them in a very loose and disorderly manner. Could we obtain a view of the entire body, with all its various joints and sinews, it is very possible that the things which now produce affright, and fill us with a certain degree of horror, might, I will not say put on an unexceptionable and attractive appearance, for that certainly is not within the reach of possibility, but assume somewhat of a less hideous and disgusting aspect. In truth, it exceeds my powers of comprehension to understand how a man who, to pass over other things, believed the Deity to be, in every sense, perfection itself, who referred the seeds of all iniquity to matter, who considered immortal souls during their residence in the body to be confined, as it were, within a prison, who maintained that the Deity was anxious for the deliverance and salvation of these souls, and that Christ had pointed out to them the way of extricating themselves from the darkness of matter; how such a man, I say, could look upon *virtue* as merely an empty sound, and believe that every one was at liberty to follow the dictates of his lusts and appetites. Still more incomprehensible does this become to me when I perceive, what is apparent, even from the passages cited out of the writings of his son, that the man thus held up to us as such a monster of iniquity, was in full possession of his reason. Then, we have the testimony of Irenæus expressly stating Carpocrates to have taught that men were to be saved through faith and charity, διὰ πίστεως καὶ ἀγάπης σώζεσθαι. Now a man who entertains this opinion, let him expound it in what manner he may, must certainly condemn any injuries done to others, and require that his followers should cultivate some sort of acquaintance with both justice and virtue, which is in direct opposition to the dogma generally attributed to Carpocrates, "that no actions are naturally evil in themselves, and that the distinction between good and bad actions exists merely in human laws and opinions." For if future felicity is to be acquired by the exercise of love and good offices towards others, it necessarily follows that there must be some divine law in existence commanding us to abstain from every thing that may injure our fellow creatures, and to do those things that may contribute to their welfare. Lastly, it strikes me as particularly deserving of remark, that the same Irenæus who exhibits the Carpocratians in such an unfavourable point of view as to other things, stands forward as their patron and defender against those who reproached them with the commission of crimes and offences of the deepest dye; and says that he could by no means give credit to the rumours that were prevalent of their iniquities; καὶ εἰ μὲν πράσσεται παρ᾽ αὐτοῖς τὰ ἄθεα καὶ ἐκθεσμα, καὶ ἀπειρημένα, ἐγὼ οὐκ ἂν πιστεύσαιμι. *Et si quidem fiant hæc apud eos quæ sunt irreligiosa, et injusta, et vetita, ego nequaquam credam.* Surely this may be accounted testimony of no small weight, coming as it does from one who was in other respects their most hostile adversary. Possibly the doctrine of Carpocrates might be this,—that the distinction between good and bad actions had no existence but in human laws, but at the same time that in the present corrupt and perverse state of things such laws were proper and necessary.

(2) Clement of Alexandria, (*Stromat.* lib. iii. p. 511.) relates that [p. 370.] *Epiphanes*, the son of Carpocrates of Alexandria, by a Cephalonian woman, a young man of vast attainments and promise, but who died at the age of seventeen, had a place assigned him amongst the gods by the inhabitants of the city of Sama, in the island of Cephalonia, and that divine honours were annually paid to him in that city, where were to be seen a magnificent temple, altar, &c. erected to his memory. The same account, somewhat amplified, is to be met

with in Epiphanius, *Hœres.* xxxii. p. 210. and 211.—But it should seem that this narrative is altogether of one and the same cast, and equally undeserving of credit with that of Justin Martyr, respecting the apotheosis of *Simon Magus,* and the statue erected to his memory by the Romans. For who can believe that the people of Sama, who were polytheists, and addicted to the superstitions of the Greeks, could have acted such a strangely inconsistent part, as to assign a place amongst their gods, and annually pay divine honours to a young man who was a Christian, or at least a worshipper of Christ, and who held in detestation the gods of the Gentiles, whom, in common with his father, he believed to be a set of proud, malignant angels, the authors of this world, and the present calamitous state of things in it? Then again, why confer these honours on Epiphanes, any more than on his father?—or his mother, who was a Cephalonian, a woman of the country? In fact, I suspect that, as in the case of Simon, so likewise in this of Epiphanes, an affinity between words and names has, owing to a want of caution in the first Christians, given rise to a most egregious error. Those who are conversant with the Greek language, well know that the word Ἐπιφανίων was a term very frequently made use of in the Grecian rites; and that it was common for the Greek writers to denominate the appearance of any particular deity ἐπιφάνεια. The festivals instituted in commemoration of such divine manifestations or appearances were also termed ἐπιφάνια. It strikes me, therefore, as highly probable, that it might have been customary for the people of Sama to refer to some festival or other of this kind under the title of ἐπιφάνεια, and that certain Christians of Egypt, accidentally sojourning in that city, but entirely unacquainted with the customs, religion, and names of the Greeks, being caught by the sound of the word, and recollecting that *Epiphanes,* the son of Carpocrates of Alexandria, had a Cephalonian woman for his mother, hastily ran away with the idea, that this Ἐπιφάνια was a festival instituted by the people of Sama, in honour of that Epiphanes. On their return to Alexandria, it was natural for them to recount what they had thus witnessed, and, as they thought, well understood: and hence, I take it, arose the *fable* of the apotheosis of Epiphanes, and the expensive honours that were annually paid to his memory by the people of Sama.

(3) Irenæus tells us that the Carpocratians, in their writing, (συγγράμμασιν,) stated that their tenets and doctrine were communicated by Jesus in a secret, mysterious manner, to his apostles, with an injunction that they should make these things known only to certain select and confidential persons. Most of the *Gnostics* were accustomed to shelter themselves behind a tale of this sort, by way of getting rid of anything that might be urged against them out of the books of the New Testament. The apostolic writings, they asserted, contained merely the ordinary religion of Christ, or that which was suited to the capacities of the multitude, a thing totally different to the sublime and recondite Christian discipline. Eventually, however, the very means which they thus took to forward their own cause, and depreciate the authority of the Sacred [p. 371.] Writings, were productive of consequences directly the reverse. For, by admitting, as they did, that the books of the New Testament were the writings of Christ's apostles, and at the same time denying that their own tenets were

derived from this source, they, in fact, supplied their adversaries with two very powerful arguments in support of the genuine Christian faith. Since Carpocrates, then, pretended to have derived his system of discipline from the secret communications of Christ to his apostles, we may naturally conclude that he held the books of the New Testament very cheap, and considered them as calculated merely for the multitude. As Irenæus, however, states him in support of his opinion respecting the transmigration of souls, to have adduced the words of St. Matthew, chap. v. ver. 25, 26. there seems to be reason for believing that he approved of the writings of that evangelist.

LII. **The system of Valentine.** In fecundity of genius, however, extent of travels, reputation, number of disciples, and various other respects, the heretics whom we have just been commemorating were left at an infinite distance behind by *Valentine*, who, like them, was born in Egypt, but having at the commencement of this century originated a new system of discipline, and met with no little success in the propagation of it amongst his countrymen, was induced to transfer his abode to Rome.(¹) In this city and its neighbourhood he prevailed on such a number of Christians to embrace his corrupt opinions, that the church became alarmed, and, after having been twice excommunicated without effect, he was at length absolutely and finally expelled from her bosom as a desperate and incorrigible heretic. Forsaking Italy, therefore, he withdrew to the island of *Cyprus,* where, laying aside all dissimulation, he became the parent of a sect, which in point of form and external observances differed in no material degree from other Christian assemblies; but in opinions and tenets retained scarcely any resemblance to them whatever. From this spot the sect soon widely diffused itself throughout Asia, Africa, and Europe. *Valentine,* it should seem probable, ended his days in Cyprus, somewhat about the middle of this century. It is reported that the idea of instituting a new sect first suggested itself to him in consequence of his having been disappointed in the attainment of the bishopric of I know not what city, and that his conduct ought rather to be ascribed to ambition than to error: but the history of his fortunes seems to give a complete contradiction to this.(²)

(1) Of all the Gnostic sects, not one, with the exception of the Manichees, has more engaged the attention of ancient writers, in describing its tenets and discipline, than that of the Valentinians. Not to notice the more recent writers of the third, fourth, and fifth centuries, such as Epiphanius, Theodoret, Augus-

tine, and others, who have either regularly or incidentally been led to treat of this sect and its tenets, we find, on recurring to the writers of the second century, the æra of its origination, Irenæus devoting the first seven chapters of his work, *Adversus Hæreses*, to a comprehensive review of its discipline ; Tertullian [p. 372.] not only attacking its principles in a particular treatise, but also inveighing warmly against them in his book *de Præscript. adv. Hæret.* as well as in various other parts of his writings; and Clement of Alexandria very frequently adverting to them in his *Stromata*, for the purpose of exposing their fallacy, and bringing them into discredit. Notwithstanding this, however, it would be easy to point out many things in the Valentinian system of discipline, which are but partially intelligible, and in regard to which we cannot but wish for further information. The most natural conclusion is, that as to some particulars, the knowledge which these writers themselves had acquired was but very imperfect, although as to others our ignorance, no doubt, may arise from their not having expressed themselves with a sufficient degree of perspicuity and precision.—There can be no doubt but that the Valentinian sect was of more recent origin than those of which we have already given an account, for it is pretty plainly to be collected from the testimony of ancient authors, that it had no regular existence until after Valentine had quitted Italy, and taken up his residence in the island of Cyprus; which unquestionably did not take place until about the middle of this century. Previously to this, Valentine, although he differed in opinion materially from other Christians, and met with no little success in the propagation of his errors, yet maintained communion with the church, and was willing to pass for one of its members. That form of religion, however, which he considered as the true and genuine one, must have suggested itself to him at a much earlier period, inasmuch as he had taught it in Egypt and at Rome, many years prior to his excommunication and expulsion from the church.—According to Clement of Alexandria, *Stromat.* lib. vii. p. 898. he was supposed to have been a pupil of *Theodas*, the disciple of St. Paul. If this be true, he must have lived in the *first century,* and attained to a great age. The interpretation given to the words of Clement as to this, by almost every writer who has adverted to them, is, that Valentine made it a matter of boast that his discipline was founded on principles privately imparted by St. Paul. Nor does it appear to me at all unlikely, that this might be what Clement intended to convey. For it was the custom of the Gnostics, who could not but admit that their opinions were at variance with the sacred writings, to shelter themselves behind certain secret communications from Christ and his apostles. I think it but right, however, to observe, that we have no express statement in Clement to the above effect. All that he says is simply this, that there were persons who represented Valentine as having been a disciple of Theodas. As to the authors of this rumour he is silent.

(2) Tertullian, in his discourse *contra Valentinum,* cap. iv. informs us that Valentine aspired to a bishopric, a station for which his genius and eloquence appeared eminently to qualify him, but that the preference was given to a martyr, or more rightly a confessor ; and that, filled with indignation at this, he became an opponent of the genuine religion, and set about establishing a new

sect. Now as to the first part of this statement, namely, that Valentine was disappointed in the hope of being promoted to a bishopric, there is nothing in it at all difficult of belief; but the latter part of it must undoubtedly be false, if what Tertullian himself and other ancient writers report respecting the fortunes of this man be true. For Tertullian, in his book *de Præscriptione Hæreticorum*, cap. xxx. p. 242. expressly represents him as for a long time practising dissimulation, and studiously glossing over his erroneous doctrines, not only during his residence in Egypt, but also afterwards at Rome; which plainly proves that nothing could be farther from his intention than that of establishing an heretical sect. The same writer says that, led away by too great a desire after knowledge, and an unbounded curiosity, he by degrees forsook the [p. 373.] high road of truth, and laboured in disseminating his erroneous principles amongst the Christians at Rome. On this account he was twice subjected to a temporary excommunication, and as often received again into the bosom of the church, but it being found that no faith whatever was to be placed in his promises, for that he constantly recurred to his old habits, and the propagation of his heretical opinions, he was at length excluded, without hope of return, from every sort of association or intercourse with the faithful. From all this, it is manifest that he felt an unwillingness to be divorced from the church, and consequently could have entertained no thoughts of establishing a separate sect. For surely a man who, on two occasions, exerted himself to the utmost to obtain re-admission into the church, after having been excommunicated, and with a view thereto twice entered into an engagement to amend his opinions and conduct, could have felt no disposition whatever to become the parent of a sect, but must have been anxious to retain his connexion with the faithful. When at length, however, his utter expulsion from the church was irrevocably sealed by a public decree, we find him withdrawing to the island of Cyprus, and there laying the foundation of a particular sect. It was not, therefore, the disappointment of his hopes with regard to a bishopric, but the severity of the Roman church, that made Valentine a sectary, and led him to secede with his disciples from the regular Christian Fold. I rather suspect, then, that Tertullian must have blended together two things entirely unconnected with each other, and confounded the cause of Valentine's journey to Rome with the cause of his separation from the church. The true history of the matter, in all probability, is this: Valentine had been led to cherish the expectation of succeeding to the bishopric of some church in his native country, *Egypt.* It was an ancient and established rule, however, amongst the Christians, that whenever any persons coming within the description of *confessors* were to be met with amongst the members of a church, they should on a vacancy be promoted to the bishopric of such church in preference to all other, yea, even more learned candidates. A confessor, then, probably presented himself in the church to the presidency over which Valentine had aspired, and the hopes and expectations of the latter consequently terminated in grievous disappointment. Filled with vexation and disgust at his want of success, he bade adieu to his native country, and travelled to *Rome.* During his abode in the capital of Italy, so far was he from meditating the formation of a sect, or any thing detrimental to the church, that he rather studied, by means of his eloquence and reputation for learning, to open a way for himself to its offices and honours. Finding himself, however, here again deceived in his expectations, and the Roman church having, in consequence of his pertinacity in error, expelled him from her bosom without hope of return, he withdrew into the island of Cyprus, and there became the parent and patron of the sect which goes under his name.

LIII. The Valentinian Æons. The leading principles of the Valentinian system of discipline corresponded with those of the various other *Gnostic* sects ;(¹) nor did its founder attempt to disguise this, but was well contented that himself and his followers should be styled Gnostics. Being endowed by nature, however, with a genius most surprisingly prolific, he boldly ventured forth beyond the limits within which the rest of this tribe had deemed it expedient to confine themselves, and dilating on such topics as had been previously noticed by them merely in a general way, distributed them into parts, and, with the assistance of an inexhaustible imagination, endeavoured to fill up the intervals in such a way as effectually to meet the numerous difficulties with which he knew they were beset.(²)   First, in the *Pleroma*, or that immense space re-[p. 374.] fulgent with unclouded light, which the Gnostics considered as the immediate habitation of the Deity, he placed *thirty Æons*, or natures of the highest dignity, of whom the one half were *males*, the other *females*. These, again, he divided into *three orders* of different degrees of excellence and power : an *Ogdoad*, a *Decad*, and a *Duodecad*. The *Ogdoad*, which possessed in many respects a superiority over the rest, and contained within it the causes and reasons of all things, he represented as made up of two *Tetrads*. The first of these Tetrads he stated to consist of the Deity himself, whom he termed *Bythus* and *Propator*, and his spouse, *Ennoia* (*Thought*), who was also occasionally styled *Sigè* (*Silence*), together with their immediate offspring, *Nus* (*Mind*), and *Aletheia* (*Truth*). The second, which was somewhat inferior in point of dignity to the first, he represented as being composed of *Logos* (the *Word*), and *Zoë* (*Life*), *Anthropos* (*Man*), and *Ecclesia* (the *Church*). Of these latter four, he conceived the first two to have been generated of *Nus* and *Aletheia*, and in process of time to have become the parents of the second pair. The *Decad*, which followed next in succession to the *Ogdoad*, he considered as owing its existence, in the first instance, to *Logos* and *Zoë*.

From these sprung *Bythius* and *Mixis*, who, in their turn, begat *Ageratos* and *Henosis*, from the union of whom again were produced *Autophyes* and *Hedone*, of whom were generated *Acinetos* and *Syncrases*, whose offspring, *Monogenes* and *Macaria*, terminated the Decad. For in these *Æons* the generative power was supposed gradually to diminish until it became quite extinct. From *Anthropos* and *Ecclesia*, the other branch of the second Tetrad, sprung that order or class of the celestial family to which the title of *Duodecad* was given, in consequence of its being composed of *twelve Æons*, the one half males, the other females. The first two of these were *Paracletos* and *Pistis*, of whose offspring, *Patricos* and *Elpis*, were generated *Metricos* and *Agape*. By the union of these latter again were produced *Ainos* and *Synesis*, of whom were begotten *Ecclesiasticos* and *Macariotes*, with whose offspring, *Theletos* and *Sophia*, who proved unfruitful, the Duodecad terminates.—To these *thirty Æons* were added *four others* of a singular and extraordinary nature, to whom no female associates were assigned. Of these, the first, who was styled *Horus,* being placed by his parents, *Bythus* and *Sigè,* at the extreme limits of the *Pleroma,* kept a continual guard over its boundaries, and restrained the inferior *æons,* lest possibly, being stimulated by an ambitious curiosity, they might be tempted to overleap their proper barrier, and be swallowed up in that immense ocean by which the *Pleroma* was supposed to be surrounded. Next after *Horus* came *Christos* (*Christ*), and *Pneuma agion* (the *Holy Spirit*), two unassociated *æons,* whom *Bythus,* the father of all, through the channel of *Monogenes,* called into existence for the purpose of instructing and confining within the line of duty such other *æons* as might be found wavering, or in any degree disposed to deviate therefrom. The last of this numerous spiritual family was *Jesus,* a most noble *æon,* produced by the united act [p. 375.] of all the other *æons,* endowed by them with every gift and faculty of the most exalted kind, and constantly encompassed with a mighty host of angels as a guard.—In this long and tiresome fable, it is scarcely possible to believe that there can be anything contained at all savouring either of wit, wisdom, or ingenuity: and all the pains which have hitherto been bestowed in endeavouring to reconcile these intricate reveries of a disordered brain with reason and truth, can only be regarded in the light of so much labour entirely thrown away.(')

(1) From what *source* the Valentinian religion and philosophy were derived, has been made the theme of much ingenious disputation by the learned of modern days, since the time that Jo. Franc. *Buddeus,* in his dissertation *de Hæresi Valentiniana,* annexed to his *Introductio ad Historiam Philospohiæ Hebræorum,* pronounced both the one and the other to have originated in the *Cabbala,* or philosophy of the Hebrews. Ancient authors, for the most part, conceived the Valentinian system to have been a child of the *Platonic school;* but if we abstract from it a few things, which certainly bear an affinity to some of the Platonic tenets, the remainder will be found to differ so essentially from the philosophy of the ancient academy, that without violence no sort of reconciliation can be produced between them. Much less are those to be attended to, who represent Valentine as having endeavoured to imitate and improve upon the *theogonies* and *cosmogonies* of *Hesiod* and other ancient Grecian, Phœnician, and Egyptian poets. That there is a vast difference between those ancient *theogonies* and the Valentinian philosophy respecting the Deity and this world, must readily be perceived by any one who will be at the pains of comparing them together.— With regard to its having been derived from the *Cabbala,* it must certainly be admitted that, in the system of Valentine, there are some things bearing no very distant resemblance to the maxims delivered down by the ancient Jewish masters; but, at the same time, there are in it other things in abundance of a diametrically opposite character. Besides, it is my belief that, for the rudiments of that discipline which the doctors of the *Cabbala* profess, the Jews were indebted to the Oriental philosophers. Those who coincide with the English prelate, G. *Hooper,* in referring the Valentinian fictions to an Egyptian origin, find themselves equally embarrassed with the rest when they come to enter into particulars.—In my opinion, the class to which Valentine ought to be referred is not so involved in obscurity but that it may be pointed out without any very great difficulty. By all the ancient writers he is reckoned amongst the *Gnostics;* and his system possesses all those features by which the Gnostic discipline is peculiarly characterized, such as a *Pleroma, Bythus, Æons, Sophia, Demiurgus,* and the like. Without doubt, then, the first elements of the system which he originated were drawn from the *Oriental philosophy.* To these he added not a few conceits of his own, and after a new mode digested, expounded, amplified, and brought into connection various things which had been treated of by others merely in a confused, obscure, brief, and desultory manner. This could not have proved any difficult task to one whom all writers concur in representing as a man of the most fertile imagination and unbounded fancy. In what respects, however, Valentine was beholden altogether to the Gnostic discipline, or for what particulars he was indebted principally to his own invention, the Gnostic tenets furnishing him merely with a general outline, it is impossible for any one at this day to determine with anything like precision.

(2) The difference between Valentine and the various other leaders of Gnos-
[p. 376.] tic sects, will be found to consist chiefly in what I am now about to

point out. Most of the latter appear to have been in the habit of philosophizing long previous to their embracing Christianity. Their endeavours, therefore, were directed to make the Christian religion accommodate itself to the philosophic system of which they approved. With *Valentine*, on the contrary, a profession of the Christian faith seems to have preceded the study of philosophy; the consequence of which was, that in his system philosophy was made wholly subservient to Christianity, and certain parts of the former, which appeared not easily to admit of a reconciliation with the principles of the latter, were altogether thrown into the shade. The greater part of the *words* which he makes use of in unfolding his opinions, are taken from the books of the New Testament. This circumstance, according to my judgment, plainly declares that these books, together with the Christian religion, must have been received and approved of by him before he set about constituting a regular discipline of his own. Certainly, many of his *Æons* would not have had *Christian names* given to them, but others of a very different character, had Valentine, previously to his embracing Christianity, been in the habit of philosophizing in the same way as the rest of the Gnostics did respecting the Deity and the origin of all things. Another argument as to this point is, I think, to be drawn from the *reasons* (in themselves truly ridiculous, most assuredly, and proving to demonstration the man's extravagance and folly, but nevertheless deduced from the books of the New Testament) which he adduces in support of various parts of his discipline. Being questioned, for instance, as to how he came to know that there were exactly *thirty* Æons, neither more nor less, he answers, that he drew his conclusion as to this from the *thirty years* of Christ's life which were suffered to elapse previously to his entering on his ministry. Irenæus *contra Hæres.* lib. i. c. 1. § 3. p. 7. In the adoption of this number he, with great, but very childish subtlety, attempts still further to justify himself from our blessed Saviour's parable respecting the labourers sent by the householder into the vineyard. Matthew xx. First, he contends that by the *hours* at which the labourers were hired we ought to understand *Æons*; and then reckoning up those hours, he, with the utmost confidence, asserts that nothing whatever can be clearer than that the number of the Æons must be *thirty*; for if *one*, and *three*, and *six*, and *nine*, and *eleven* be added together, they will be found to yield a total of *thirty*. What can be more obvious? His *duodecad* he defends on the ground that Christ, when he was twelve years of age, disputed with the Jewish doctors in the temple, and that twelve was the number of our Lord's apostles. Irenæus, l. i. c. 3. p. 14. Many arguments of a similar description might, with a very moderate degree of labour, be collected from Irenæus and other writers.—Now all these things, unless I am much mistaken, obviously indicate a man desirous of adjusting and determining various philosophical precepts which he had accidentally picked up, by the test of *scripture*, not one labouring to make the principles of Christianity conform to certain rules and maxims of philosophy in which he had been previously grounded. I am induced therefore to believe that *Valentine*, after embracing the Christian faith, in all its genuine simplicity, accidentally fell in with some man or other addicted to the Gnostic philosophy, and that, being captivated with its nonsensical theories, he conceived the resolution of comparing them with the sacred writings, expecting that, with the assistance of scripture, he might be able to expound them in a way more accurate and consentaneous to religion than had hitherto been pursued by the Gnostics. The *result* of this undertaking was, [p. 377.] that he became the author of a new kind of philosophical religion, differing not so much in words and terms as in the disposition and connection of the things themselves from others that had preceded it. The terms *Pleroma* and *Æons*, for instance, were obviously derived from his instructor in the *Gnostic way* of philosophizing; but in expounding the nature of the former, and determining the number of the latter, he, after consulting the sacred writings, struck out into a path entirely his own.

(3) Amongst men distinguished for their learning there have not been wanting some who, possessing the rational faculty in an eminent degree themselves, are unwilling to believe that *Valentine* could have been wholly destitute of it, and have therefore endeavoured to hit upon some means or other for interpreting his principles and tenets in such a way as might at least give them the appearance of being partly founded in truth. The strange and unaccustomed kind of *language*, they say, to which he had recourse, threw such a veil of obscurity over his tenets and doctrines as the ancient fathers found themselves utterly unable to penetrate; but only let this veil be removed by a skillful and sagacious hand, and the things themselves, rather than the representation of those things, be brought under review, and there will appear to be much less disagreement between the Valentinian tenets and opinions and those of the Christians in general, than has been commonly imagined. Vid. Camp. Vitring. *Observat. Sacr.* l. i. c. 2. p. 138. et seq. Souverain, *Platonisme devoilé*, cap. viii. p. 68. Isaac de Beausobre, *Histoire de Manicheé*, v. i. p. 548. 551. 582. 588. et seq. Ja. Basnage, *Histoire des Juifs*, tom. iii. p. 729. and amongst the first, Pet. Faydit, *Eclaircissemens sur l'Histoire Eccles. des deux premieres Siecles*, p. 12. *et Alteration du Dogme Theologique par la Philosophie d'Aristote*, p. 186, 365. et seq. where he intimates himself to have in contemplation *An Apology for Valentine.*—The reader will understand me as by no means wishing to discommend such attempts, which seem to speak highly in favour of the sagacity, equity, and prudence of their authors; neither does the circumstance of their having been made, occasion in me any great surprise. For it cannot be denied but that here and there certain sparks of the truth appear to gleam forth from amidst the Valentinian dross; and we are certain that the early Christian fathers, in numberless instances, were not sufficiently on their guard against mistaking and misrepresenting the tenets which they undertook to combat. It seems to me, however, that I am fully warranted in going the length of saying this much, that if *Valentine* himself could arise out of his grave, he would reject the good offices of these his ingenious and erudite defenders. For we have his own confession, that the discipline which he taught was altogether at variance with the religion professed by the greater part of the Christians of his day. He also denied that his principles and tenets were to be supported from the holy *Scriptures* as they were then read, and as they are read by us at present, and boasted that they were in great measure founded on the *secret* communications of Christ and his apostles, and certain writings of St. Matthias. From all these things, then, it is

manifest that it must be acting in direct opposition to what would be his wishes, were he alive, for any one to maintain that the only difference between his tenets and those of his opponents consists merely in words, and the manner in which they have been handed down to us. Besides, amongst those advocates for Valentine, there is not to be found one who will pretend to deny that in his system of discipline, not a few things present themselves which are altogether inexplicable, and some so utterly stupid and absurd as to afford no ground whatever for excuse. A circumstance which, unless I am much mistaken, is of itself sufficient to prove what a waste of time and pains it is for persons to employ themselves in endeavouring to purge such a system of its dross, and give it a new complexion. For we find it confessed, that the enigmatical parts present an insurmountable obstacle to our arriving at any certain conclusion with regard to such parts as are more intelligible; and, surely, the absurdities with which it abounds, inasmuch as they leave us in no doubt as to the man's extra- [p. 378.] vagance and folly, must be allowed to place it beyond a question, that Valentine could not have been such a character as to merit that any wise man should become either his defender or apologist. How, I would ask, can that be sound or wholesome, which is interwoven and incorporated with what is erroneous and absurd?—or that be consentaneous to reason, which depends on principles and opinions that set all reason at defiance? By way of illustration, let us take, for example, the *thirty Æons* of the Valentinian system, and the mode in which they are connected with each other. Those of the learned who have undertaken to advocate the cause of Valentine, suggest, with more or less confidence, that by these *Æons* we ought not to understand real *persons* existing separately from the Deity; for that all this heresiarch had in view, was to distinguish between certain notions and *ideas*, by assigning to them particular names, and clothing them with the form and character of persons. This *celestial family of Æons*, begotten of the Deity himself, is, they say, to be regarded in somewhat of a metaphysical light, as exhibiting the succession, series, and connection of the *virtues* and actions of the Supreme Being. For nothing can be more common than for those who would wish to speak perspicuously of things altogether abstracted from sense to have recourse to a *personification* of their ideas. But this opinion, although it may for a moment carry with it a specious and imposing air, will, on examination, be found to have nothing either of weight or probability attached to it. For as Valentine was confessedly a *Gnostic*, and the *Æons* of all the other Gnostics were conceived to be, not merely feigned or imaginary, but real *persons*, it is most natural to conclude that the Valentinian Æons were regarded as beings of a like description. Again, if we proceed to apply this exposition to the Valentinian discipline, it may indeed be possible for us, though not without difficulty, to make it in some degree accord with the *first four pair* of Æons; but let us attempt to move one step farther on, and we are immediately encountered by resistance, all the Æons thenceforward, by the actions and affections which are attributed to them, tacitly declaring it to be utterly impossible that they could ever have been intended to represent notions or ideas of the Divine *virtues* and actions. (1.) These Æons, as we shall presently see, were supposed to have been filled with *envy* at the glory with which *Nus*, the most exalted of them, was invested; a circumstance, as it strikes me, incontestably proving that both he and they could have been considered in no other light than as real *persons.* For in what way a divine virtue or action could be filled with envy, or sicken at another's exaltation, is certainly not within the reach of any ordinary degree of comprehension. (2.) All these Æons were ambitious of mentally *comprehending* the magnitude of their first parent, the Supreme Deity. (3.) An attempt to gratify this inordinate ambition brought the last of them, who was inferior to the rest in point of virtue, into the greatest peril. (4.) *Christ* and the *Holy Spirit* were generated of the Deity for the purpose of repressing, in the other Æons, this most dangerous wish of attaining to a knowledge of the Divine Nature, and preventing them from yielding to its impulses. (5.) Edified and invigorated by these instructors, the Æons, who had previously occupied themselves wholly in contemplating the majesty of the first great Parent, directed their attention to a different object, and by an union of their energies produced *Jesus,* with a host of angels for his guard, a nature constituted, as one may say, of the very marrow of all the Æons. (6.) This *generation* of Jesus, exhausted, as it were, those powers with which they previously superabounded; for they are represented as afterwards keeping a due restraint on themselves, and not indulging in their former inordinate desire of attaining to a comprehension of the Deity. (7.) On the borders of the *Pleroma* was placed *Horus,* a most powerful Æon, whose province it was to take care lest any of his brethren, under the influence of some sudden impulse, [p. 379.] might be tempted to overleap the boundaries of their celestial abode. Now all these things are obviously of such a nature as to preclude every possibility of their being attributed to any other than *beings* endowed with intellect and will, and existing by themselves really and truly, distinct, not only from the Deity, but from each other. *Valentine* must, therefore, either have been out of his senses, and not have known what he meant himself, or he must have believed his Æons to have been real *persons,* the offspring of the Deity, and have regarded the *Pleroma,* as he termed it, in the light of a kingdom divided into as many provinces as there were pairs of Æons, each having two rulers peculiar to itself, the one a male, the other a female. I can perceive it, however, to be very possible that the notion may suggest itself to some, and in fact I believe it has so suggested itself, that these *Æons* were similar to the *Ideas* which Plato is said to have feigned to himself, and which many of his disciples certainly did feign to themselves, namely, natures really existing in the Deity as living *exemplars* or images of mundane things. Without doubt, Valentine, if respect be had to the names of merely some of his Æons, may appear to have had somewhat of this kind in contemplation; but, when examined throughout, the names of others will be found altogether irreconcilable with this supposition. Nor does it strike me that his cause would derive any considerable degree of support from this interpretation, even supposing it to be in every respect well founded; for what are those Platonic *Ideas* but persons?

LIV. **The Valentinian theology.** These *Æons,* although of divine origin, were yet supposed to be liable to the same passions and perturbations of mind as distract the human race.(¹)   All of them, for instance, are represented as being filled with envy at the distinguished felicity enjoyed by *Nus,* the chief son of the Deity, who alone was adequate to the full comprehension of his father's greatness, and all of them described as animated with the most ardent desire of attaining to a similar degree of knowledge, not one of them believing it beyond the reach of his capacity to arrive at a just conception of the transcendent majesty and excellence of the first great Parent.   Inflamed beyond measure with this desire of fully comprehending the nature of the Supreme Deity, *Sophia,* or *Wisdom,* the youngest, and consequently the weakest of the *Æons,* became at length so agitated and perturbed, that, had she not been prevented by *Horus,* the guardian of the celestial boundaries, she would have overleaped the limits of the *Pleroma,* and plunged headlong into the vast ocean of matter that lay beyond it.(²)   This violent commotion, however, was productive of an effect which it was utterly out of the power of *Horus* to prevent, namely, that *Sophia* was delivered of a daughter styled *Achamoth,* who, being expelled from the *Pleroma,* was immersed in the rude and chaotic mass of unformed matter which lay without it.   With a view to prevent the other branches of his family from incurring any similar risk, *Bythus,* or the Supreme Being, by means of *Nus,* produced two new *Æons, Christ* and the *Holy Spirit;* of whom the former had it in command to instruct the celestial family that the immense greatness of the Deity could be comprehended only by *Nus,* or the First Begotten; whilst the latter was to exhort and persuade the *Æons* [p. 380.] to subdue, as far as possible, every irregular commotion of mind, and to make it their object to celebrate and worship their first great Parent with a tranquil spirit.   Calmed and enlightened by the admonitions of these instructors and guides, the *Æons* unanimously resolved to give a different direction to their energies, and, uniting together their powers, produced, with the approbation, and in honour of the Supreme Father, the being styled *Jesus,* the most illustrious Star of the Pleroma.

(1) This imperfection in the *Æons,* or Divine Natures, will excite but little surprise if it be considered that the *Deity* himself was regarded by all descriptions of the Gnostics, and particularly by the Valentinians, in a very different light from that in which he was viewed by every other denomination of Chris-

tians, and that they did not allow even this first great Author of all things to be possessed of any thing beyond a limited degree of intelligence and power. Most assuredly the *knowledge* of the Deity could not, according to them, have been very extensive, since he was incapable of foreseeing what would be the fate of the Æons generated of himself, and took no means to provide for their safety and tranquillity until his eyes were opened by the vastly perilous attempt of the Æon *Sophia*. That they believed him to possess merely a circumscribed *power*, is equally evident from his being represented as unable to prevent the occurrence of many things contrary to his will without the limits of the *Pleroma*, or to obstruct the institution of a new order of things to the origination of which he could not but have been inimical. The parturition of *Sophia*, we are told, was unquestionably highly displeasing to the Deity. The consequences of that parturition, then, such as the formation of matter, the birth of *Demiurgus*, the fabrication of the world, and the like, could never have been acceptable in his sight. Whatever things were done, therefore, without the limits of the *Pleroma*, appear to have been accomplished without his approbation, and may, consequently, be adduced as so many proofs of his infirmity or want of power. The Deity of the Gnostics was also destitute of various *other qualities*, which right reason as well as the sacred writings point out as belonging to the Supreme Being. If such, then, were the ideas entertained by the Valentinians and the whole tribe of the Gnostics respecting the first great Parent of all things, who can feel in any degree surprised that his offspring should have been regarded by those pretenders to superior wisdom as agitated by blind and unruly affections, and pining away under the influence of envy and inordinate curiosity?

(2) In the Greek of Irenæus it is εἰς τὴν ὅλην ἰσίαν, which is rendered by the old Latin translator *in universam substantiam*. But it is evident that this is the same as τὴν τῶ ὅλυ ἰσίαν, *universitatis rerum materiam*. Without side the Pleroma was situated, according to Valentine, the immense mass of matter. He did not, however, as we shall presently see, conceive it to be possessed of either motion, form, or a generative power.

LV. **The Valentinian theology.** Scarcely were the internal peace and tranquillity of the celestial commonwealth thus re-established, when commotions of the most violent kind began to take place without its limits ; commotions which eventually occasioned the formation of this world, and the generation of the human race. *Achamoth*, the daughter of the Æon *Sophia*, upon being expelled from the Pleroma, lay at the first in a very miserable state, being utterly destitute of either form, figure, or light. Touched with her calamitous situation, *Christ*, who, as we have seen, was invested with the function of a governor and instructor of the Æons, in conjunction with the *Holy Spirit*, imparted to her somewhat of form, intelligence, and rationality. Aroused and stimulated by the assistance thus given her, *Achamoth* made a nearer advance to the Pleroma, and endeavoured to obtain for herself a larger portion of light. In her attempts at this, however, she found herself sedulously opposed by *Horus*, the ever-watchful guardian of the borders of the Pleroma; a circum- [p. 381.] stance which threw her into the most violent perturbations, and overwhelmed her, as it were, with apprehension and anxiety. At one time, giving way to despondency, she would be dissolved in tears; at another, recollecting the light of which she had obtained a glimpse, her countenance would be illuminated with smiles. These different affections had a very wonderful influence on the barren and shapeless mass of matter with which she was surrounded, and eventually gave birth to the various elements of the universe. From the irresistible desire with which she was inflamed of obtaining further light, arose " *The Soul of the World,*" " *The Soul of Demiurgus,*" and the like; from her anxiety and sorrow, all other things. All *liquid* matter had its origin in her tears, all *lucid* matter in her smiles, all the *elements* of the world in her sorrows and despondency.(¹) All the component parts of the world were therefore now supplied; but there was still wanting an architect who might reduce them into order, and knit them together in one grand whole. Addressing herself in supplication, therefore, to *Christ, Achamoth* obtained the favour of having *Jesus,* or the Saviour, sent to her, surrounded with his host of angels. With this assistance she produced three substances, the *material,* the *animal,* and the *spiritual;* on one of which, namely, the animal, she bestowed the gift of *Form,* a boon rejected by the other two; and hence sprung *Demiurgus,* the Founder and Governor of all things.(²)

(1) Valentine should seem from this to have regarded *Achamoth*, or, as she was at other times styled, *Enthymesis*, as the parent of *matter*, which, in point of fact, was nothing more or less than referring the origin of matter to the Deity himself. For *Achamoth*, the parent of matter, was the daughter of Sophia; and this latter was derived of the Deity, being the last of the Æons. Valentine, therefore, did not assert the existence of *two* eternal principles, the Deity and Matter; but conceived all matter to have been, in point of fact, derived from the Deity, although with the intervention of divers generations. Such is the exposition that has been given of the tenets of *Valentine* on this head by several very eminent scholars; and it must be confessed that in doing so they appear to have some support from the testimony of ancient writers. I cannot, however, say that this, by any means, accords with the judgment which I myself have

been led to form on the subject. The doctrine of Valentine, it is my belief, was, that *matter* had existed without the limits of the Pleroma for an infinite period prior to Achamoth's birth, but in a confused and unformed state, entirely destitute of motion, and every other quality. For, as we have already observed just above from Irenæus, and could, if it were necessary, confirm, by the testimony of Tertullian and other ancient writers, Valentine placed without the limits of the Pleroma τὴν ὅλην, or τῦ ὅλυ ἐσίαν, *substantiam universam* or *universi*, " the universal *substance*," or " the substance of the universe." Now by this name no one, surely, will pretend to say that he could have meant empty *space*, for the very name itself entirely precludes such a supposition; and if he did not mean space, it appears to me impossible that he could have meant any thing else but *matter*. Whatever, therefore, is related by ancient authors respecting the offspring born of Achamoth without the limits of Pleroma, ought to be understood as indicating merely those mutations or changes which her perturbations pro-
[p. 3S2.] duced in matter which had previously lain in a state of absolute quiescence, and destitute of every quality. Her *tears* did not generate the liquid matter, but merely occasioned a part of matter, which had previously existed in a solid state, to deliquesce and separate itself from the rest. Her *smiles* did not produce the pellucid matter, but merely caused a portion of matter, which had previously been opaque and absolutely impervious, to become luminous and transparent. Her *sorrow* did not call into existence air, water, fire, and earth, but merely caused such commotions in a part of matter, that all these elements were produced from it. In short, *Enthymesis*, or *Achamoth*, might be looked upon, with regard to a few things, as the author of certain *modifications*, and she might likewise be considered as having communicated divers *qualities* to matter in general; but she certainly, in my opinion, could never have been regarded by Valentine as the parent of matter itself.

(2) This fable is recounted at much greater length by Irenæus, Tertullian, and other ancient writers. To me, however, it appeared unnecessary to lay before the reader any thing more than a sketch of its leading features ; or, if I may so speak, I deemed it sufficient to exhibit a general view of the different acts, without entering into the minutiæ of each scene in detail.

LVI. **The Valentinian tenets respecting the creation.** *Demiurgus* being thus generated of animal matter, undertook, without delay, the formation of the corporeal universe, a work in which he was privately assisted in part by *Jesus,* or the Saviour, and in part by his mother *Achamoth.* The course he pursued was, in the first place, to *separate* the animal matter from the material. Of the former, or the animal portion, he then formed certain celestial bodies, particularly *seven heavens*, by which, it is easy to perceive, were meant seven *planets* or wandering stars, which constituted places of residence for, and were governed by an equal number of the most powerful spirits or angels.(') The supreme heaven

Demiurgus reserved to himself, and assigned to his mother that space which separates the Pleroma from the world. The *material* portion, in consequence of its having originated from a three-fold source, namely, the apprehension, the sorrow, and the anxiety of *Achamoth*, was of a three-fold nature, and, under the plastic hand of *Demiurgus*, gave birth to three distinct genera of things. From that which was the fruit of *Achamoth's* apprehension or *fear*, were produced the various descriptions of animals; from the off-spring of her *sorrow* the evil angels, of whom the principal one, that is, the *devil*, had his habitation in the air below *Demiurgus;* and from that which had flowed from her *anxiety*, the elements of the world, all of which had been tempered with fire. *Man* was compounded by *Demiurgus* of both substances, the material and the animal, and enveloped by him with an external, sensible *body*, as with a tunic or mantle. To these two constituent parts of man, a portion of the spiritual or celestial substance was add-ed by *Achamoth*, the mother of *Demiurgus,* but entirely without the knowledge of her son. The outward corporeal frame of each individual man, therefore, was said, by ancient authors, to com-prise, as it were, *three* men: 1st, The *material* man, who was in-capable of salvation; 2dly, The *animal* man, who might be either saved or lost; and, 3dly, The *spiritual* man, who could never perish, having been generated of the celestial or divine sub-stance.(²)

(1) We may here discover evident traces of the nonsensical dreams [p. 383.] of the Egyptians respecting *seven animated planets*, or moveable stars, pos-sessing the governance and direction of the corporeal universe. The idea was adopted by most of the Gnostics, especially by such as had received their edu-cation in Egypt.

(2) The particulars here stated are not, it must be confessed, handed down to us by ancient writers in a manner so determinate, full, and perspicuous as might be wished. By no one, however, who will be at the pains of comparing with each other all the different branches of the Valentinian system of disci-pline, can any difficulty be experienced in comprehending what it was that these authors in reality meant to convey. *Man*, according to Valentine, was com-posed of a *twofold body*, the one internal, the other external; as likewise of a *twofold* soul. The internal body consisted of fluid matter; the external one, which he speaks of as a tunic enveloping the one within, was framed of matter that had remained dense and concrete. The latter was perceptible by the senses, the former not. This *twofold body* Irenæus and other ancient writers denomi-nate *the material man;* but whether in the Valentinian sense, or merely accord-ing to their own understanding of the matter, I am unable to determine. Dis-

solution inevitably awaited this *material man*, or, more properly speaking, this corporeal frame of the man, after which it would be again absorbed in the grand mass of matter from whence it had been originally taken. For the Valentinians, like all the other Gnostic sects, were constrained by the nature of their principles to deny every possibility of a future *resurrection* of the body. Of the *twofold soul* possessed by man, according to the Valentinian theory, the one was taken by Demiurgus from the *animal substance* or matter, that is, as is sufficiently evident, from the more subtile and ethereal species of matter, or that of which the *soul of the world* was constituted and likewise the heavens framed. This soul is that which contains within it the *vital* principle, as also the faculties of *sense* and *perception*, and was by ancient writers termed *the animal man*. The ultimate fate of this soul might be either perdition or salvation. This is to be understood thus : if the sensitive soul should forsake the worship of Demiurgus and his associates, and, turning itself to the Supreme Deity, should resist every unlawful appetite, and submit its faculties to the direction of the rational soul, which is the same thing as placing itself under the dominion of right reason, it would in time coalesce, to a certain degree, with the rational or celestial soul, and in this way obtain for itself immortality. Should this same soul, however, pursue an opposite course, and, spurning at the dominion of the rational soul, prefer continuing under the government of the senses, it would, on the dissolution of the body, return to the soul of the world, or that more subtile species of matter from whence it was originally taken. The *other soul*, or that which was conferred upon man by *Achamoth*, and which ancient writers denominate *the spiritual man*, is the *rational* mind, which, from its very nature is *immortal*, having been taken from the divine substance of which the Æons consist. That this soul should perish must be impossible, since it would be the very height of absurdity to suppose any part of the *divine essence* obnoxious to decay; wherefore, at some time or other, either sooner or later, it must of necessity *ascend* to the regions above, not indeed to the Pleroma itself, where none but natures of the highest and most perfect order reside, but to that vast region of space inhabited by its mother Achamoth.—In these his tenets respecting man, *Valentine* differed widely from the rest of the Gnostics, provided the sentiments of these latter have not been curtailed or abridged by ancient authors, but been handed down to us whole and entire.—As to the reason that induced *Achamoth* to add [p. 384.] to the sensitive soul another of a better and more noble description, *viz.* a rational one, it appears to me very easily to be discovered. *Achamoth* was naturally inclined to favour the *sensitive* soul, inasmuch as it was her own offspring, and consequently felt desirous, if by any means the thing could be brought about, to accomplish its salvation. Hence she was induced to give it, for an associate or *companion*, a particle of the divine essence, or a celestial soul, hoping, that by means of this alliance, the sensitive soul might be corrected, and, in addition thereto, be imbued with a knowledge of the Supreme Deity. In support and confirmation of this part of his discipline, there can be no doubt but that *Valentine* availed himself of all those passages that are to be met with in St. Paul's epistles respecting appetite opposing itself to reason, and the contentions between the *flesh* and the *spirit*.

LVII. **The Valentinian tenets respecting Christ.** The Founder of the world, having perfected the work which he had undertaken, became at length so puffed up with arrogance and pride as to imagine that he himself was the only true God, and in consequence thereof, to arrogate to himself, by the mouths of divers prophets which he dispatched to the Jewish people, the honours due to the Supreme Deity. His example, as to this, being followed by his associates, the presidents or rulers of the celestial orbs, as well as by the minor angels, who were invested with dominion over the different parts of the universe, every knowledge of the real and only Supreme God was gradually obliterated from the minds of the human race, the generality of mortals resigning themselves wholly to the empire of their lusts, and turning a deaf ear to all the suggestions of reason.(') With a view to the extrication of mankind from this deplorable state, *Christ,* who was compounded both of the animal and the spiritual substance, and was furnished, moreover, with a sensitive body, (composed, however, of ethereal matter,) descended from the regions above to this nether world, passing through the body of *Mary,* without contamination, as water does through a conduit. Upon the baptism of this celestial guest by *John,* in the waters of Jordan, *Jesus,* an Æon of the highest order, descended on him in the form of a dove.(²) The divine man, thus constituted, immediately commenced, by means of discourses, miracles, and denunciations, a most vigorous attack on the tyranny of the founder of this world and his associates, whilst, at the same time, he re-instated mankind in the knowledge of the Supreme Deity, and instructed them as to the mode of bringing into subjection that soul which is the seat of sensual appetite and all our irregular desires. Enraged at these proceedings, the *Founder of the World* caused Christ to be apprehended and crucified. Previously, however, to his undergoing this punishment, not only the Divine *Jesus,* the Son of the Deity, but also the *rational soul* with which he had been animated, took their departure out of him and fled away. It was his *sensitive soul* alone, therefore, that in conjunction with his æthereal body was affixed to the cross. Those mortals, who in obedience to the precepts of Christ, should renounce the worship of all false gods, the God of the Jews not excepted, and confining their adoration to the Supreme Father alone, should make [p. 385.]

30

the *sensitive* and concupiscent soul submit itself to the castigation and emendatory discipline of right reason, would obtain salvation for their souls of both descriptions, which, on the dissolution of the body, would be transferred to the regions of unbounded space adjoining the *Pleroma*, and there be made partakers of everlasting joy and felicity. The *sensitive* souls of those, on the contrary, who should pursue an opposite course, and spurning at the controul of the *rational* soul, should persevere in upholding the cause of superstition, had no prospect whatever held out to them, but that of everlasting *perdition.*(³) When all those parts of the Divine nature, constituting what were termed celestial souls, should be delivered from the bondage of matter, and cleansed from all impurity, *Achamoth* would, it was asserted, pass into the *Pleroma*, and there be united with *Jesus* as with a husband; whilst *Demiurgus* would proceed to take up his abode in those regions of space contiguous to the Pleroma, which had previously been the habitation of his mother. The *spiritual* or celestial souls, at the same time taking leave of the *sensitive* souls, their former companions, would, in like manner, ascend into the *Pleroma*, and for the future be associated with the angels: whilst the *sensitive* souls, or those of inferior order, would continue to experience the highest degree of felicity in the region without the Pleroma, under the dominion of *Demiurgus*. Finally, the *fire* that had been originally distributed throughout every part of the universe, would burst forth from its concealment, and involving the whole machine of the world in flame, produce its utter destruction.(⁴) That *Valentine* should have encouraged, or even countenanced in his followers any thing like moral *depravity,* or a sinful and flagitious course of life, is altogether impossible; since his injunctions were that the inferior soul of man should always be made to yield obedience to the one that was superior, or, in other words, to right reason. We, at the same time, however, feel no difficulty whatever in so far giving credit to Irenæus, and other ancient writers, as to believe that certain of his disciples and followers might have led a very disgraceful course of life, and endeavoured, by a perversion of the precepts of their master, to supply themselves with an excuse for plunging into vice and every species of iniquity.(⁵)

(1) These particulars are but very obscurely handed down by Irenæus and

others. By calling in, however, the assistance of the various Gnostic systems, and collating the different parts of the Valentinian scheme with each other, we have been enabled, as we trust, to throw some little additional light on the subject, and to place it in such a point of view as may bring the reader acquainted with the true nature and internal economy of Valentinianism in all its branches.

(2) As to the opinion entertained by Valentine respecting *Christ*, or the Saviour, we are left, by the early Christian writers, as much in the dark as we are with regard to the Valentinian tenets respecting *man*. The Saviour, they say, was represented by Valentine as consisting of *four* parts : a spiritual part, an animal part, a corporeal part, and, finally, a celestial part, or the real Saviour, which, assuming the form of a dove, descended upon Christ at his baptism. Now to this partition, which, by the bye, I believe not to have originated with *Valentine*, but to have been purely the invention of *Irenæus*, it may perhaps be scarcely worth the while to take any formal exception : but it is certainly far from being well conceived, and adapts itself but awkwardly to the subject. The Valentinian *Saviour*, like the Saviour recognized by all other Christians, was constituted of an union of the *Son of God* with *man*, but he differed materially from the Saviour of other Christians in this, that he consisted of *two persons*, of whom the *divine* one continued with that which was *human* merely for a few years, in order that the important legation to mankind might be fulfilled, and [p. 386.] took his departure when the latter was about to undergo capital punishment. The *human* person, or man, should seem to have been looked upon as in a great measure resembling other men ; for we find a two-fold soul ascribed to it, the one *divine* or rational, which is termed by ancient writers the *spiritual part of Christ*, the other *sensitive*, precipient, the seat of appetites and aversions, and which is styled by authors of antiquity the *animal part of Christ*. With this two-fold soul they likewise conjoined a *body*. In the nature of its body, however, this human person differed very considerably from other mortals. For, in the first place, this its body was not twofold as the bodies of other men were held to be, the one *internal* and fluid, the other *external* and dense or solid, but merely a single, uncompounded corporeal frame. Again, this body was not composed of *terrene matter*, but of that which was subtile and ethereal, although visible or perceptible by the senses. For had Christ been clothed with a corporeal frame resembling ours, it would, according to the Valentinian scheme, have been possible that, yielding to the contagious influence of the body, he might have inclined to the sensitive or concupiscent soul, and stirred it up to contend for dominion with the divine or rational soul. In that *human* person, or man, with whom *Jesus* the Son of God, one of the most exalted of the *Æons*, consented to unite himself, it was but fitting that nothing should be contained which might oppose itself to right reason, but that every motion, every propensity and desire should be subject entirely to the dictates of the celestial mind. Wherefore he was not furnished with a terrene body, but adorned with one of pure *æthereal* or celestial mould. Hence, also, in the last place, this human person was of necessity held by the Valentinians to have acquired nothing whatever from the Virgin Mary, but to have passed through her womb as water through

a *conduit.* For had he adopted any, even the minutest particle from the body of Mary, it might, like leaven, have corrupted the whole mass, and generated in the sensitive soul, a propensity inimical to right reason ; matter being considered by the Gnostics as the source or foundation of all our vices and depraved inclinations. As to the notions entertained by the Valentinians, respecting the *Son of God;* who, for a while, united himself to this very extraordinary and admirable human person, it is not necessary that I should say much: suffice it to observe, that although they regarded him as a Being of a very high and excellent nature, their ideas of him fell far short of those which Christians in general entertain of the Son of God. They consider him, it is true, as an *Æon* of the most exalted rank, begotten of the essence of the Deity, but neither in nature, degree, or power, is he placed by them on an *equal* footing with the father.— From the particulars which I have thus enumerated, it must, I think, be strikingly apparent, how widely the Valentinian tenets, respecting the person of *Christ,* differ from ours. Upon the seizure and condemnation of Christ by the Jews, the Valentinians held, that not only the *son* of the Deity, or that Æon which had resided within him, took his departure, but also *one* of the souls by which he had been animated, namely, the *rational* or celestial one. It was the *sensitive* soul alone, they believed, that in conjunction with the æthereal body was affixed to the cross. From this, however, it is apparent that the Valentinians must have conceived Christ to have *actually* suffered and died.

(3) Great as was the difference of opinion between the Valentinians and other Christians with regard to the person of Christ, it was equalled by their discrepance in sentiment respecting his *function,* and the cause for which he died. For *Valentine* did not believe that the sins of mankind had been *expiated* by the [p. 387.] sufferings and death of Christ; neither did he believe that the Son of God, or even the rational soul of the man Christ, had been at all affected by such sufferings and death. According to him, the only purpose for which the glorious *Æon,* termed *Jesus,* came into the world was, that he might *offer terms* of salvation to those souls in which is seated the faculty of sense and volition. The *terms* were, that they should forsake the worship of all false gods, the God of the Jews, or founder of the world, not excepted, and, devoting themselves to the Supreme and only true God, render, according to the example of Christ, all their propensities and desires subject to the controul of the rational or celestial mind. All that the Valentinians, therefore, ascribe to Christ, was his having communicated a *knowledge* of the true God to our benighted race, and taught, by his precepts and example, that our desires were to be placed under the dominion of reason.

(4) The *Valentinian fable,* in its termination, corresponds exactly with that of the *Manichæans.* A perfect agreement between them is also discoverable in not a few other particulars. This one circumstance alone is sufficient to place it beyond all controversy that the *Gnostic* discipline was, in a great measure, derived from the tenets of the *Oriental* philosophers respecting the origin of evil. By not only Valentine, however, but others of the Gnostics, there was blended with those Oriental maxims no small portion of the idle conceits and physical opinions of the *Egyptians.* The general tendency of the Oriental, the

Gnostic, and the Manichæan schemes is to inculcate, that this *world* was framed out of rude and vitiated matter, without the knowledge or consent of the Supreme Deity, and that, either through accident or design, no inconsiderable portion of the *divine or celestial substance* was incorporated therewith. That the Deity is constantly endeavouring, by the assistance of right reason, gradually to detach this portion of himself, or of the divine substance, and more particularly such part of it as is imprisoned within the bodies of the human race, from depraved matter, and once more to restore it to its origin in the realms of light. During the time necessarily required for the accomplishment of this object, he patiently tolerates the existence of this universe, or machine of the world, and may even be said, in a certain degree, to employ his power in upolding it. For such is the nature of its construction, that it nourishes within its bosom the seeds of its own destruction, *i. e.* an active and vigorous combustible principle diffused throughout its whole frame, and which, unless it were kept in subjection by the Deity, would soon put an end to the world and everything belonging to it. When all the souls of men, however, and every particle of the divine essence, shall have obtained a deliverance from matter, the Deity will no longer prevent this slumbering *fire* from bursting forth, but suffer it to issue from its caverns and recesses, and involve the whole corporeal universe in flames and destruction. This doctrine may have been exhibited by different sects under a variety of forms, some more subtile, others more homely and gross, some again more simple, others more refined and ingenious; but the sum and substance of the matter itself will be found to be in all the same.

(5) Much has been handed down to us by Irenæus, lib. i. c. vi. and much by other ancient authors, respecting the wickedness and crimes of the *Valentinians;* whom they represent as having maintained that everything was lawful for them, inasmuch as they had attained to the highest degree of divine knowledge, and as having freely indulged in the violation of every law, divine as well as human. By no ancient writer, however, is *Valentine himself* charged with anything of this kind, nor do we any where find a depravity of morals attributed to the sect at large. The accusation of Irenæus extends merely to certain of the Valentinians. Hence, I think it is evident that Valentine could not have countenanced his disciples in a vicious course of life; but that certain of his followers, by giving a different interpretation to the precepts of their master from what he ever intended, endeavoured to make them a cloak for their iniquities. [p. 388.] This might very easily occur. As it was the opinion of many of the Christians, that let a man only be possessed of faith and he might sin as much as he liked, so is it highly credible that certain of the Valentinians might maintain that, when once a person had abstracted the soul from the body, and attained to that intimate knowledge of the true God which they styled γνῶσις, he could in no shape whatever be affected by the actions of the body. Into this grievous error they were, indeed, the more likely to fall, from their disbelief of the future resurrection of men's bodies. The Valentinian *discipline* itself, so far from countenancing men in a sinful wicked course of life, expressly inculcated that the way to eternal happiness lay open only to those souls who, after the example of Christ, should render all their propensities and desires subject to the celes-

tial and imperishable soul, or, in other words, to right reason. Irenæus, and others who have written after him, I know very well, relate that Valentine recognized three descriptions or classes of men : σωματικοὶ, or the *corporeal;* ψυχικοί, or the *animal;* and πνευματικοὶ, or the *spiritual.* The *corporeal* men, are the heathen or the worshippers of false gods; the *spiritual* men, the Valentinians or Gnostics; and the *animal* men, all other Christians. Of these, the *first* must of necessity perish; the *second,* by an equal necessity, must be saved; the *last* are capable of being either saved or involved in perdition. That the *spiritual* men should busy themselves at all as to good works, is perfectly unnecessary, since it is impossible that they should perish. The *animal* men are under the necessity of cultivating piety. The *corporeal* men, inasmuch as they are entirely destitute of hope, may consider themselves as absolved from every law. Now, if such had been the doctrine taught by Valentine, it would certainly have been holding out an invitation to the greater part of the human race to indulge in every species of iniquity, and granting to his followers, in particular, the license of doing whatever they might list. But the tenets which we thus find ascribed to Valentine, by Irenæus and other ancient writers, are manifestly *repugnant* to various parts of the Valentinian discipline; and it is, moreover, certain that Valentine considered *all men* to be by nature *equal;* all endowed with a two-fold soul, and the gate of salvation as irrevocably closed against none. I, therefore, entertain not the least doubt but that these ancient authors understood his sentiments but very imperfectly, or else were, on some account or other, induced designedly to misrepresent them. That mankind were distributed by Valentine into *three classes,* the animal, the spiritual, and the corporeal, is what I by no means pretend to question; but he certainly never did think, nor was it possible he should think, that the *corporeal* class were destitute of souls, and of necessity doomed to perdition. What he meant to say was doubtless this, that amongst men of the corporeal class, or the worshippers of false gods, the body commonly usurps the dominion, and stifles every energy and power of the soul. As long, then, as they should continue in that state, nothing was to be hoped for by them upon the dissolution of the body; for if they died under such circumstances, the sensitive soul would perish, and the rational one, being incapable of death, would be transferred into another corporeal frame. After a similar manner ought we to understand what he says of men of the *animal* class; for his doctrine was, not that these were destitute of a rational soul, but that the sensitive and concupiscent soul had in them obtained the mastery, so as to prevent the celestial soul from executing its office. They were, therefore, according to him, nearer to salvation than those of the corpo- [p. 389.] real class, who referred every thing to the body, and totally neglected the soul. The class to which he gave the title of *spiritual* consisted of those in whom that particle of the divine essence, the celestial mind, the seat of reason and of wisdom, enjoys the preëminence, and holds in subjection not only the body, but also that other soul by which the body is acted upon and influenced. These must of necessity be saved, inasmuch as they resemble Christ, and conduct themselves agreeably to his example.—I have been obliged to speak the less distinctly respecting the difference in the *two-fold soul,* with which Valentine considered man as having been endowed, in consequence of ancient authors having omitted to mark this difference with sufficient precision. This much, however, is clearly to be perceived, that one was considered as being by nature *immortal;* the other as not being immortal by nature, but capable of becoming so upon yielding due obedience to the superior soul. It is also apparent that the former was looked upon as formed of the *divine substance,* or that whereof the Deity himself consists; the latter as constituted of the more noble part of matter, or such as was made use of in the framing of the heavens. We are not, however, able to speak with equal confidence as to the nature or extent of the *virtues* or powers which each was supposed to possess. Valentine, it is true, represents the superior soul as the immediate seat or residence of rationality and wisdom; but, at the same time, he places a certain sort of *reason* also in the inferior soul. For he enjoins this latter to attend to the dictates and direction of the superior soul, a thing that, without reason and intelligence, it must have been utterly incapable of doing. It had also the power of either obeying or resisting the superior soul, and must consequently, in addition to reason, have been endowed with *liberty* or freedom of will, a thing not possessed by the superior soul. These, as well as various other particulars of the Valentinian discipline, admit not in the present day of an explication altogether satisfactory, inasmuch as ancient writers are silent as to many things of essential importance to a right understanding of the subject, whilst they, at the same time, pervert other things, and not unfrequently give us, as the genuine tenets of Valentine, what are merely inferences or deductions drawn by themselves. Finally, in their account of this man's doctrines and opinions, everything like method or order is beyond all measure disregarded; and various things, which ought to have been associated together and brought into one view, are disunited and kept far apart.

LVIII. **Inferior sects that owed their origin to the Valentinian school.** From the Valentinian school are said to have issued not a few founders of other sects, who, retaining the fundamental principles of their master's discipline, endeavoured, either by certain partial emendations or by a new exposition and arrangement, to improve upon the original plan, and communicate to it a more specious and imposing air. It should seem, however, not at all unlikely that the same thing which occurred in the case of *Simon Magus* again took place with regard to *Valentine;* namely, that every one who professed sentiments bearing the least affinity or resemblance to his opinions was at once, without farther evidence, accounted to be of the number of his disciples. Amongst those who are thus reported to have derived the first rudiments of their discipline from Valentine, we may first mention *Ptolemy,* the founder of the sect of the *Ptolemaites,* a man of ingenuity and eloquence, who differed widely from the general body of the Valentinians in his tenets respecting the Æons, as well as in regard to some other points. His *Æons* are not only differently named and arranged from those of his reputed preceptor, but he appears likewise to have considered them merely in the light of divine *attributes* or virtues.(') Far different were the sentiments of *Secundus,* who is commemorated by Irenæus as a very distinguished [p. 390.] disciple of the Valentinian school. According to him, the *Æons* were real substances or *persons,* and, what is particularly deserving of remark, he placed at the head of them two principles, *light* and *darkness,* a circumstance which plainly proves him to have borrowed more from the *Oriental* philosophy than his master had done, and also indicates in him somewhat of an inclination to the discipline of the *Manichees.*(²) A third disciple of the Valentinian school, not at all inferior to these in point of fame, indeed, rather their superior, was *Heracleon,* an author whom we find Clement of Alexandria and Origen repeatedly citing, for the purpose of exposing and confuting his errors. Whether Heracleon dissented in reality from Valentine, or merely in words and phrases, and if there was really a difference between them, in what such difference consisted, and what were the peculiar opinions or tenets of the former, are points which, in the present day, it will be found far from easy to determine.(³)

(1) Respecting *Ptolemy,* in addition to Irenæus, Tertullian, (*Lib. contr. Valent.* c. iv. p. 290.) Augustine, and others, I would recommend the reader particularly to consult Epiphanius, *Hæres.* XXXIII. p. 216. 222. who gives us a letter of his to a woman named Flora, which was afterwards published more correctly by J. Ernest. Grabe, in his *Spicilegium Patrum et Hæreticorum,* tom. ii. p. 69. In this letter he communicates without reserve his sentiments respecting the *law* of Moses, declaring it, in his opinion, not to have been derived from the Supreme Deity; but to have been framed in part by the Jewish doctors, in part by Moses, and in part by Demiurgus, or the founder of this world. This opinion respecting the origin of the law of Moses, it has not been unusual for learned men to consider as peculiar to *Ptolemy;* but as to this, they are unquestionably in an error. That the Jewish law did not owe its origin to the Supreme Being, was an article of common belief throughout the whole *Gnostic* school, although the leaders of the different sects into which it branched might differ somewhat in the mode of expressing their sentiments on the subject. Even *Valentine* himself did not think otherwise.

(2) Vid. Irenæus, lib. i. cap. xi. Epiphanius, *Hæres.* xxxi. Augustine, *de Hæres.* cap. xii. It is certain that much difference of opinion subsisted between *Ptolemy* and *Secundus* as to the nature of the Æons, the one considering them

as merely modes or *virtues* of the Divine nature, the other as real substances or *persons;* and each contending that his own sentiments on the subject corresponded with those which had been entertained by their master. Respecting the nature and true grounds of this dispute, one might readily engage in much learned disquisition; but, as there is no necessity for it, I shall content myself merely with observing, that from this controversy *Valentine* appears to have been a man of some genius, certainly; but, at the same time, one of a weak indecisive mind, who, indeed, propounded many new opinions, but left the greater part of them so ill defined as to afford matter for continual disputes amongst his disciples.

(3) Vid. J. Ernest. Grabe, *Spicileg. Patrum et Hæreticor.* tom. ii. p. 82. et seq.

LIX. **Marcus and Colarbasus.** Amongst the disciples of Valentine, we find ancient authors agree also in reckoning (though on what authority is uncertain) one *Marcus,* the founder of the sect of the Marcosians, and a *Colarbasus,* who was some how or other connected with this Marcus, either as an associate, a pupil, [p. 391.] or a preceptor. Of *Colarbasus* not much is handed down to us by either Irenæus or any other writer. What little they do say of him almost entirely respects his tenets concerning the *Æons,* whom, it appears, he distributed, named, and associated in a very different way from Valentine. To enter further, therefore, into the history of this man's opinions, would be only a waste of words. Concerning *Marcus,* however, many things are left us on record, particularly by Irenæus. Of these some may easily be reconciled with the principles of the Valentinian discipline, but others are entirely new, and at the same time exceedingly obscure, so much so, indeed, as scarcely to admit of explication.—Amongst other notable attainments and exploits, he is said to have discovered very profound mysteries in the Greek letters, to have studied magic, worked miracles by the assistance of demons, debauched women, instilled into his followers the vilest of principles, and compiled a code of the most puerile and absurd institutions. In the heavy catalogue of accusations thus brought against him, some particulars were no doubt well founded, others wholly fictitious, and some deduced from a misapprehension or a wrong interpretation of his opinions. To draw the proper line of distinction between the one and the other of these might not, perhaps, be altogether beyond the power of a person intimately conversant with the Gnostic discipline; but it would be a work replete with labour and fatigue. Contemplating the history of this man with every possible degree of candour, and even rejecting as spurious every part of what are stated to have been the Marcosian tenets, except such things as could not possibly have been feigned, it will, nevertheless, be found impossible to form a more lenient judgment of *Marcus* than this: That he was a man of the Jewish persuasion, in all probability neither wicked nor impious, but, at the same time, one who exercised his mental powers only to make himself ridiculous, and who, having his brain bewildered with Oriental, Egyptian, and Jewish extravagancies, converted the universal religion, which he pretended to profess, into a system of the most egregious nonsense and deformity.(¹)

(1) Respecting the tenets of *Marcus*, and the sect of the *Marcosians*, founded by him, which, extending itself through various regions, particularly *Gaul*, imposed on many of the more plain and simple of the Christians, Irenæus treats much at large, (*Adv. Hæres.* lib. i. cap. xiv. et seq.) although in a very immethodical, unconnected manner. The subject has also been taken up after him by others. Of these tenets we need only direct our attention to such as it was utterly impossible that either Irenæus or any other author should have feigned, to be convinced that the man must have been disordered in his brain, indeed, entirely out of his wits. The evidence of this is, in fact, so glaringly obvious, that we can only wonder it should ever have entered into the heads of learned men to exercise their genius in endeavouring to reclaim and purify so incorrigible and hopeless a subject. By way of *specimen*, we will present the reader with the Marcosian tenets respecting the force and power of the *Greek letters*, as they are given us by Irenæus, nearly in the very words of Marcus himself. ταῦτ' ἂν (the reader will understand that these are the words of one of the Supreme *Æons*, whom Marcus represents as having been sent to him in the form of a woman) ταῦτ' ἂν τὰ παρ' ὑμῖν εἴκοσι τέσσαρα γράμματα ἀπορροίας ὑπάρχειν γίνωσκε τῶν τριῶν δυνάμεων εἰκονικὰς, τῶν περιεχυτῶν τὸν ἄλον τῶν ἄνω στοιχείων τὸν ἀριθμόν· τὰ μὲν γὰρ ἄφωνα γράμματα ἐννέα νόμισον εἶναι τῆ πατρὸς καὶ τῆς ἀληθείας, διὰ τὸ ἀφώνους αὐτοὺς εἶναι, τυτέσιν ἀῤῥήτους καὶ ἀνεκλαλήτους· τὰ δὲ ἡμίφωνα ὀκτὼ, ὄντα τῆ λόγω καὶ τῆς ζωῆς, διὰ τὸ μέσα ἅσπερ ὑπάρχειν τῶν τέ ἀφώνων καὶ τῶν φωνηέντων· καὶ ἀναδέχεσθαι τῶν μὲν ὕπερθεν τὴν ἀπόρροιαν, τῶν δ'ὑπὲρ αὐτὴν τὴν ἀναφοράν· τὰ δὲ φωνήεντα καὶ αὐτὰ ἑπτὰ ὄντα τῆ ἀνθρώπῳ καὶ τῆς ἐκκλησίας, ἐπεὶ διὰ τοῦ ἀνθρώπῳ φωνὴ περιελθῖτα ἐμόρφωσε τὰ ὅλα. ὁ γὰρ ἦχος τῆς φωνῆς μορφὴν αὐτᾶς περιετοίησεν. *Has igitur, quæ apud nos sunt, viginti quatuor litteræ, emanationes esse intellige trium virtutum imaginales, earum quæ continent universum, quæ sunt sursum elementorum* [p. 392.] *numerum. Mutas enim litteras novem puta esse patris et veritatis, quoniam sine voce sint, id est, inenarrabiles et ineloquibiles. Semivocales autem cum sint octo, Logi esse et Zoës, quoniam quasi mediæ sint inter mutas et vocales, et recipere eorum quidem quæ supersint emanationem, eorum vero quæ subsint elevationem. Vocales autem et ipsas septem esse, anthropi et ecclesiæ, quoniam per anthropum vox progrediens formavit omnia. Sonus enim vocis formam eis cir-*

cumdedit. Irenæus, lib. i. cap. xiv. § 5. p. 70. Communications, similarly sub-tile, and even still more ridiculous and obscure, respecting the force and pro-perties of the Greek letters, and their accordance with divine matters, both pre-cede and follow the above. That it should ever have entered into the mind of Irenæus, or any other person, to have invented things like these, and ascribed them to Marcus, by way of bringing him into discredit, is not to be believed. They are, in fact, taken from his writings, and given in his own words. Now, can any one, let me ask, who is himself in possession of his senses, for a mo-ment regard these sublime mysteries as the offspring of a sound and rational mind?—But I will add *another specimen*, which must, I think, place it beyond all question, that *Marcus* and his followers altogether turned their backs on every principle of true wisdom, and were devoted to the silly conceits and ex-travagancies of the Egyptians. In Irenæus are to be found certain *prayers*, which the Marcosians dictated to dying people, to be recited when, in their journey to the celestial regions, they came to pass through the provinces of *Demiurgus* and his associates. Iren. lib. i. cap. xxi. § 3. p. 97. In these prayers also, there is no room to suspect any thing like fraud or misapprehension. If the sense or meaning of them be attended to, they will be found to have a near resemblance to those of a similar kind in use with the *Ophites*, which are preserved by Ori-gen in his work *contra Celsum*, although they certainly differ from them some-what in words. They are, moreover, of such a description as to preclude every idea of their having been invented by any adversary of the Marcosian sect. It was the opinion, then, of the Marcosians, as well as of the Ophites and others of the Gnostics, and derived by them, as I conceive, from the Egyptians, that the *souls* of the good and virtuous, upon taking leave of the body, and proceed-ing to the mansions above, had to pass through the celestial orbs, and the planets or wandering stars, which were under the dominion of *Demiurgus* and other most powerful *Genii*, who were completely adverse to this passage of souls through their domains, and particularly anxious to arrest their progress. The efforts of these invidious tyrants, however, might, it was believed, by means of certain words and phrases, be so far rendered abortive as to prevent their im-peding souls in their ascent to the Deity; and it was of course considered as expedient that dying persons should provide themselves with prayers and for-mulæ of this description : τότυς δὲ τὰς περὶ τὸν Δημιεργὸν ἀκίυσαντας, (we give the words of Irenæus) σφόδρα ταραχθῆναι, καὶ καταγνῶναι αὐτῶν τῆς ῥίζης, καὶ τοὺς γένυς τῆς μητρός· αὐτόν δὲ πορευθῆναι εἰς τὰ ἴδια ῥίψαντα τὸν δεσμὸν αὐτῶ, τυτέσι τὴν ψυχὴν· *Hæc autem eos qui circa Demiurgum sunt audientes, valde con-turbari, et reprehendere suam radicem, et genus matris: ipsos autem* (the souls which had taken their leave of the body), *abire in sua, projicientes nodos ipsorum, id est, animam,* meaning the sensitive soul itself, or what of the sensitive soul these celestial souls might have brought with them from the body. For any one to attempt to explain away the utter inanity and absurdity of things like these, appears to me a most miserable abuse both of learning and talents.—I would not, however, be understood as denying that some things with [p. 393.] which the Marcosian sect is reproached by Irenæus and others, might either be misunderstood by ignorant people unacquainted with the force of the words and terms made use of, or unfairly represented by heedless and malevolent spectators, to whom every thing appeared vile and flagitious that was unusual with the Christians; amongst which I reckon what is reported respecting the sorcery and delusive tricks, or if the reader had rather, the religious fallacies of Marcus, which appear to me unworthy of the least credit, inasmuch as it is to be supported by no kind of argument, and may be invalidated on several grounds. Whatever Irenæus has transmitted to us respecting things of this sort, appears to have been collected from the testimony of certain women, who might have easily been imposed upon, and under the hope of obtaining for themselves a more ready re-admission into the congregation of the faithful, whom for a while they had deserted, might possibly have been induced to embellish their narration in a way not exactly corresponding with the truth. It is said, for example, that in the celebration of the Lord's Supper, Marcus was accustomed, either by means of magic or some sort of juggling, to *tinge* the wine in the chalice with a red or purple colour. ποτήρια οἴνῳ κεκραμένα (says Irenæus, lib. i. cap. xiii. p. 60.) προσποιούμενος, εὐχαριςεῖν, καὶ ἐπὶ πλέον ἐκτείνων τὸν λόγον τῆς ἐπικλήσεως, πορφύρεα καὶ ἐρυθρὰ ἀναφαίνεσθαι ποιεῖ· ὡς δοκεῖν τὸν ἀπὸ τῶν ὑπὲρ τὰ ὅλα χάριν τὸ αἷμα τὸ ἑαυτῆς εὐζειν ἐν τῷ ἐκείνῳ ποτηρίῳ διὰ τῆς ἐπικλήσεως αὐτυ. *Pro calice vino misto, fingens se gratias agere, et multum producens verba invocationis purpureus et rubicundus calix ut appareat facit, ita ut videatur gratia ab iis qui sunt supra omnia* (i. e. the Æons) *sanguinem suum in illius calicem per ejus invocationem stillare.* Now, with regard to this, learned men have denied, and, as I think, rightly, that for the accomplishment of a thing of this sort, any recourse to magic could be necessary. They suspect, nevertheless, that Marcus must, in some way or other, have deluded the eyes of the beholders. But, for my own part, I have not the least doubt but that, in this case, a very innocent practice, and one that originated from a good design, has been exposed to unmerited reproach through the mistake of some spectator who was unacquainted with the Marcosian discipline. The custom with this sect, no doubt, was, that the chalice should be filled first with *white* wine, probably by way of representing, by a sort of figure, the purity and sanctity of Christ's blood. In the act of consecration, however, it was the usage for the priest to mingle a portion of *red* wine with the white, so as to make the contents of the chalice in some sort resemble blood, and thereby excite in the minds of those present, a more lively recollection of the Redeemer's sacrifice. Possibly it might happen, that this mingling of the red wine with the white by the priest, might escape the observation of certain persons who chanced to be occasional witnesses of the public worship of the Marcosians, and that upon perceiving red wine distributed in the cup, without being aware that any other than white wine had been poured into it, they were led to conclude that this change must have been wrought by the assistance of some evil spirit, and to represent the matter in this light to others. Who is there that can be ignorant of the multitude of errors to which mistakes of this kind gave rise? My opinion is precisely the same with regard to the other miracle which is subsequently related by Irenæus.—On the table, around which it was customary for the Marcosians to assemble, when celebrating the Lord's supper, was placed a cup of much larger size than the chalice out of which the communicants drank. Into this larger cup it was the usage for the priest to pour what little portion of the wine might be left by the communicants in the chalice, or smaller cup; and the consequence, we are told, was, that these few drops became on a sudden so amplified, as to fill such larger vessel, even to overflowing, with liquor of an ensanguined colour. Irenæus recounts this as one of the *prodigies*, or, if the reader had rather, one of the *frauds* of Marcus; for I must own that his words admit of being taken [p. 394.] in either sense: κὰι τοιαῦτά τινα ἐιπὼν, κὰι ἐξοισρήσας τὸν ταλαίπωρον θαυματοποιὸς ἀνεφάνη, τῦ μεγάλυ πληρωθέντος ἐκ τῦ μικρῦ ποταρίν ὡστι κὰι ὑπεριχχεῖσθαι ἐξ ἀυτῆ. *Dein cum talia quædam dixit, et infelicem illam (mulierem) ad insaniam adegit, tum mirabilia facere videtur, majore calice minore ita ut (poculum) redundaret impleto.* But it is easily to be collected, even from the words of *Irenæus* himself, by any one who shall duly attend to them, although it must be acknowledged that his manner of expressing himself in this passage is very confused and obscure, that no trick or deception was actually practised in this case, and that the idea of the thing's having been accomplished by any fraudulent or preternatural operation, in all probability originated with certain ignorant or heedless and prejudiced spectators. With the Marcosians it was not the custom for several to partake in succession of one cup, as is the practise with other Christians, but a separate portion of wine was given to each person by the priest. When any one did not drink the whole of what was thus handed to him, the remainder was poured into a larger cup that stood on the table; and the chalice was replenished with a fresh quantity of wine for the person next in rotation. Whatever was left in the smaller cup being thus constantly emptied into the larger one, the latter, of course, in time, became full; nor can I bring myself to believe that this sect could have been so stupid and silly as to regard a thing of such necessary occurrence in the light of a miracle. What I suspect is, that certain occasional *spectators* of the Marcosian rites, observing the wine to increase in the larger cup, which had been placed on the table empty, without perceiving the actual cause by which such increase was produced, were hastily induced to imagine that it was either accomplished by the assistance of some evil demon, or otherwise brought about by some subtle kind of fraud.

LX. **Bardesanes.** Ancient writers are also agreed in reckoning, as the disciples of Valentine, (in addition to others, whom we deem it unnecessary to notice, inasmuch as they are scarcely known even by name at this day,) those two very celebrated characters, *Bardesanes* and *Tatian*, from both of whom the cause of Christianity derived no inconsiderable degree of benefit, although each of them became the parent of a new sect, and patronized several very important errors. In this, however, it is manifest that the authors to whom we allude must have laboured under a mistake, since the doctrine of Bardesanes, as well as that of Tatian, is very considerably removed from the Valentinian prin-

ciples and discipline. Each had a manifest leaning to the Oriental opinions which were cherished by the Gnostics respecting the
origin of all things, and more particularly evil; but by neither
was the plan of the Gnostics adhered to in endeavouring to produce an accommodation between those tenets and the principles
of Christianity. *Bardesanes*, who was born of Christian parents at
Edessa, in Mesopotamia, and appears to have been a man of very
considerable talents and erudition, had, by his writings, acquired
for himself no little degree of reputation under the reigns of the
emperors Marcus Antoninus and Lucius Verus; but, having unluckily been induced to espouse the Oriental (or, as ancient writers term them, Valentinian) notions respecting the existence of
two principles, he devoted himself for a while to the propagation
of an erroneous doctrine; and, being possessed of great subtilty
[p. 395.] and address, succeeded in gaining over numerous converts, from whence sprung the sect of the *Bardesanists* that flourished in *Syria* and the neighbouring regions.(') After some time,
indeed, he again embraced the orthodox faith, and became the
determined opponent of certain of those errors of which he had
formerly been the distinguished patron and defender; but the
poison which he had imbibed was never thoroughly eradicated
from his mind,(²) nor was he ever capable of healing the cruel
wound which his conduct had given to the interests of Christianity. His doctrine was, that all things had originated from
two principles: the one good, *i. e.* the *Deity;* the other evil, *viz.* the
Prince and Governor of matter, which he held to be eternal and
intrinsically corrupt. The formation of the world, and the creation of mankind, he ascribed to the supreme and superlatively
excellent Deity; but a world of an infinitely better constitution
than the one which we at present inhabit, and mankind of a nature
vastly superior to that of the human race at this day.(³) The
primitive world, according to Bardesanes, was entirely free from
every species of evil; and *man,* as he came from the hands of his
Maker, was compounded of a celestial mind joined to an aërial or
highly subtilized body. When the Prince or Governor of matter, however, had succeeded in seducing the innocent soul into
sin, the Deity permitted him to go the further length of enveloping man with a dense and cumbrous body, composed of depraved
matter; and, by way of punishing the human race for their de-

fection, allowed this author of all evil to mar the fair face of the world, and despoil it of the greatest part of its beauty.(*) Hence the perpetual contention between reason and appetite, by which mankind are tormented in the present day; for the gross and corrupt material body with which man became thus invested is ever impelling the soul to acts of iniquity and sin. For the purpose of putting an end to this calamitous state of things, *Jesu*, according to this heresiarch, descended from the mansions above and assumed a corporeal frame; a frame, however, not at all resembling the bodies with which the human race are enveloped, but of a celestial and ethereal nature. It was, therefore, in appearance merely that this heavenly guest was brought forth, or that he ate, suffered, and underwent death; for that in reality he neither was born, nor did he die.(*) The doctrine which he represented Jesus as having taught, was that the souls of men should yield in nothing to the influence of the body, but be constantly striving to release themselves from the chains of vitiated matter. On the dissolution of the material body, the souls who had availed themselves of the instruction thus afforded them, would, he held, ascend, invested with their original bodies of ethereal mould, into the presence of the Supreme Deity; whilst the terrene and external body itself, which had, in fact, been the prison of the soul, and the origin or fountain of all its transgressions, would, he supposed, again be absorbed in the vast material mass from whence it had been taken, without the least hope of reviviscence or a future resurrection.

(1) Of *Bardesanes* we find frequent mention made by ancient writers. His history is particularly entered into by (amongst others Eusebius, *H. r. Eccles.* lib. iv. c. 30. p. 151. Epiphanius, *Hæres.* lvi. p. 476. Theodoret, *H. e. Fab. Hær.* lib. i. cap. 22. p. 208. Augustine *de Hæresibus,* cap. xxxv. See also the *Chronicon Edessenum* apud Jos. Simon. Assemann. *Biblioth. Orient. Vaticana,* p. 396.) tom. i. p. 389. et. seq. Various extracts from his writings are also to be met with in Eusebius *de Præparat. Evangelica,* Porphyry *de Abstinentia,* and the works of other ancient authors, which leave us in no doubt as to his genius and abilities. The nature of his discipline is by no one more clearly explained than by Origen, *Dialog. contra Marcionitas,* sect. iii. p. 70. et. seq. edit. Wetsten. From all these different sources, however, it is impossible for any one to obtain any thing like a full and complete history of the life of Bardesanes, or a perfect and satisfactory conception of his philosophy and religion. By more modern writers, therefore, who have undertaken to illustrate the history of this heresiarch and his tenets (the most distinguished of whom, in addition to *Tillemont,*

a very laborious and accurate writer, certainly, but one by no means deserving of the very high degree of reputation which he enjoys, and *Assemann,* to whom I have just above referred, are Fred. *Strunzius* in his *Historia Bardesanis et Bardesanistarum,* published at Wittenburg in 4to. and Isaac *Beausobre* in his *Histoire de Manichée,* vol. ii. p. 128.), we find several things left involved in obscurity, and much of uncertain conjecture intermixed with real history.—Respecting the *origin* of the lapse of Bardesanes, a different account is given by *Eusebius* from what we meet with in *Epiphanius.* By the former, Bardesanes is represented as having been addicted to the Valentinian tenets previously to his embracing the orthodox faith, whereas the latter states him to have first of all cherished the true faith, and then to have been seduced into error by the Valentinians. If, as is most probable, Bardesanes was born of Christian parents, the account given by Epiphanius is certainly the one best entitled to credit, and I have, therefore, without scruple, adopted it.

(2) This is expressly stated by Eusebius, *Histor. Eccles.* lib. iv. cap. 30. and might, if it were necessary, be confirmed by the testimony of other writers. *Bardesanes* in fact discarded whatever was so obviously repugnant to the principles of Christianity as not to admit of any thing like a reconciliation therewith, such, for instance, as the Valentinian tenets respecting an evil principle, the eternity of matter, the body of Christ, the return of our mortal frames to matter without any hope of a future resurrection to life, and the like; but as to the notion of sin having owed its origin to matter, and various other opinions which he had before been led to espouse, he retained them to the last, and availed himself of their assistance in expounding a part of the Christian religion.

(3) This notion respecting the origin of the world and of mankind most decisively separates Bardesanes from Valentine and every other Gnostic leader, by all of whom the world was considered as having been framed, in opposition to the will of the Deity, by a being to whom they gave the title of Demiurgus.

(4) It may not be amiss to apprize the reader that I cannot pretend to vouch the authority of ancient writers for every thing that I have here stated. *In none* of these authors, for instance, is there to be found any thing respecting a *primitive* world created by God, and a posterior world corrupted through the machinations of the Prince or Governor of matter; but *they all* speak as if Bardesanes had imagined the universe, as it is at present constituted, to have been the work of the Supreme Deity, and consequently that the world, as we now behold it, differs in no respect from the world as it existed prior to the lapse or transgression of souls. Again, they appear to intimate it as his belief, that men, in consequence of their disobedience, were, by way of punishment, invested by the Deity himself with depraved and vitiated material bodies.—But I will venture to assert, that unless we would make Bardesanes inconsistent with himself, [p. 397.] it is impossible to attribute to him sentiments like the above. For how could any man, who considered the Deity as exempt from every species of evil, and, at the same time, regarded matter, not only as intrinsically corrupt, but also as subject to the dominion of an evil ruler, how, let me ask, could any .

man, viewing things in this light, have believed that the all-good Deity would either have invaded the vile and contaminated province of his adversary and enemy, or moved a finger in giving arrangement or distribution to vitiated matter, or, lastly, have placed souls, generated of himself, in a region so thoroughly devoted to iniquity? By no kind of sophistry could acts like these have been reconciled with a nature decidedly hostile to every thing evil. Bardesanes, therefore, must either have recognized a primitive world, the workmanship of the Deity, in contradistinction to a latter one that had been corrupted by the author of all evil, or he must have believed in the existence of a paradise beyond the confines of this world, and conceived the universe which we inhabit, to have been framed by the Prince or Governor of matter in humble imitation of such paradise. In the second place, how could it be possible for a man, who was obviously anxious to exempt the Deity from every imputation of evil, to have believed that this all-perfect Being was induced, in consequence of the fall of the human race, to clothe them with a vitiated body, composed of matter that was under the dominion of his adversary, and teeming with every corrupt and depraved appetite? Can that Being be deemed in an absolute sense good, who is the author or cause of sinful or evil conduct in others? I have no doubt, therefore, but that, in expounding the doctrine of Bardesanes respecting the conjunction of the body with the soul, there must have been something or other omitted by Origen and the rest of the ancient writers. According to the opinion which I have been led to form on the subject, Bardesanes must have held either that the Deity, in consequence of man's having sinned, and thus rendered himself subject to the dominion of the malicious ruler of matter, would not interfere to prevent the latter from encumbering the human race with bodies formed of clay; or else that mankind had, in an unguarded moment, through the machinations of the Author of all evil, been so far beguiled, or rather besotted, as to fall in love with the bodies which he presented to them, and assume them of their own accord.

(5) The opinion thus entertained by Bardesanes respecting the celestial or ethereal nature of Christ's body, must, unless I am much mistaken, have been the only reason that induced ancient writers to class him with the Valentinians, with whom he held scarcely any thing else in common.

LXI. Tatian.

Tatian, who was a native of Assyria, and a man of considerable learning and talents, having, according to his own account,(') from a perusal of the sacred writings, been led to entertain a favourable opinion of Christianity, betook himself to Rome, and there assiduously laboured in cultivating a more intimate acquaintance with its nature and principles under the tuition of the celebrated *Justin Martyr*. The latter having been called upon to lay down his life in the cause of his Divine master, *Tatian* at first opened a school in the city of Rome, but at length was induced to return to his native country, where, either on the insti-

31

gation of his own mind, (for he was naturally of an austere disposition,) or, by the persuasion of others, he was led to embrace the tenets of those who, in expounding the principles of Christianity, called in the assistance of the *Oriental* philosophic notions respecting the Deity, matter, the world, and the human soul. The exact form of the religion which he invented, or otherwise [p. 398.] adopted, is not to be collected from any ancient writer.(')
Of this much, indeed, we are certain, that it must have possessed somewhat of the Valentinian cast, since, besides ascribing great honour to the *Æons*, we find that it recognized a distinction between the founder of the world and the Supreme Deity, and disclaimed the notion of Christ's having assumed a real body.(')
There can, therefore, be no difficulty in accounting for the circumstance of Tatian's having been regarded by many as a disciple of the Valentinian school. It is, however, equally certain, that as well in other things as in the precepts which relate to morality, the disagreement that existed between the system of *Tatian* and that of *Valentine* was far from being either trifling or inconsiderable. *Matter*, for instance, being considered by the former as intrinsically evil, and the bodies of men consequently as not having been framed by the Deity, but as so many prisons of celestial souls, he willed his followers to abstain from propagating their species, and likewise from everything that might conduce either to the strengthening or recreation of their corporeal fabric; in other words, he commanded his disciples to avoid wedlock, to forego the use of animal food as well as of wine, and, leading a solitary life, to content themselves with a very moderate quantity of the most slight and meagre sustenance. To *such* an excess, indeed, were his regulations with regard to abstinence carried, that even in the celebration of the Lord's supper, he enjoined the use of water instead of wine.(') This severe and melancholy system of discipline procured for his followers, of whom Tatian had soon to boast of great numbers in Syria, the people of which country naturally lean to an austerity of manners, and subsequently in other regions, the denominations of *Encratites*, or "the Continent;" *Hydroparastates*, or "Water Drinkers;" *Apotactites*, or "Renuntiants" of this world's goods, and the like; although it was by no means unusual for them to be termed, in reference to the author of their sect, *Tatianites*, or *Tatianists*. A species of piety that wears

an austere and rigid aspect being sure to make a considerable impression on the minds of people in general, it is not to be wondered at that this sect should have maintained its ground in various countries so low down as the fourth century, or, indeed, even later.(⁵)

(1) In his oration "to the Greeks," which has escaped the fate of his other writings, and remains extant at this day. Although not entirely free from errors, it is a discourse replete with various erudition, and written in a style by no means deficient in polish. It is commonly to be found annexed to the works of Justin Martyr, and was in 1700 published separately at Oxford, in 8vo., accompanied with various annotations, by an English student of the name of Worth.

(2) Besides Irenæus, Epiphanius, and others, who have written expressly on the subject of the early Christian sects and heresies, there are many, who, in treating on other topics, have incidentally been led to make mention of Tatian: from none, however, can he be said to have received that measure of attention to which a man of his eminence was certainly entitled.

(3) Vid. Clemens Alexand. *Stromat.* lib. iii. p. 460, *and Excerpt. ex Philosoph. Orient.* p. 806, Epiphanius, *Hæres.* xlvi. cap. i. p. 391. Origen in *Lib. de Oratione* cap. xiii. p. 77. Edit. Oxon. Hieron. *Comm. in Galat.* vi. p. 200. &c.

(4) A dislike to *wine* should seem to have prevailed amongst the philosophers of the East from a very remote period, and more particularly [p. 399.] amongst such of them as believed in a two-fold origin of things, by whom we find it commonly termed the blood of the Devil, or evil principle. See what has been collected on the subject by Paul Ernest Jablonsky, in his *Pantheon Ægyptiorum*, part i. p. 131. In prohibiting the use of wine, therefore, to his followers, *Mahommed* does not appear to have originated any new or difficult law, but merely revived and sanctioned with his authority an ancient regulation of the Arabs, the Persians, the Syrians, and other oriental nations. We may, hence, too, easily account for that detestation of wine by which almost all the Gnostics of Asiatic origin, and, at a subsequent period, the Manichæans were characterized.

(5) Vid. Jos. Simon. Assemanni, *Biblioth. Oriental.* Clement. Vatican. tom. i. p. 93. Assemann, who was himself a Syrian, and well acquainted with the temper and habits of his countrymen, very justly remarks, that the naturally rigid and austere disposition of the Syrians tended greatly to favour the extension of this sect.

LXII. **The Ophites.** That I should enter into a history of the smaller and more obscure of the Gnostic sects, of which a numerous catalogue might easily be collected from ancient writers, will not, I take it for granted, be thought necessary ; for, besides that nothing of any moment respecting them is to be met with on record, it should seem that ancient authors fell into the error of considering, as separate and distinct sects, what were merely members or branches of other sects; to say nothing of the occasion that was afforded for the mistaken multiplication of sects, by the practice that appears to have prevailed of frequently giving to an individual sect a great variety of denominations.(') I cannot, however, omit taking notice of the *Ophites,* a sorry, infatuated set of men, on whose tenets Irenæus and other ancient writers have bestowed a much greater degree of attention than on those of many other sects. With regard to the first rise of this sect, there are various considerations which will not permit us to doubt of its having had its *origin* amongst the Jews, or of its having existed long prior to the age of Christ. Struck with the magnitude and splendour of our blessed Saviour's miracles, a part of the Ophites were induced to acknowledge his divine authority, reserving to themselves, nevertheless, the liberty of making the religion which he promulgated conform itself to certain principles which they had previously adopted from the Egyptian and Oriental philosophy. The remainder of the sect, however, continued to cherish their ancient superstitions, and execrated the name of Christ in common with other Jews. Hence arose two descriptions of the *Ophites,* the one *Jewish,* the other *Christian.* The tenets of the latter embraced most of those vain fancies which were cherished by the other Gnostics of Egyptian origin, respecting the Æons; the eternity of matter; the creation of the world without the approbation or knowledge of the supreme Deity; the imprisonment, as it were, of souls within the body; the directors or rulers of the seven planets, or wandering stars; the tyranny exercised by *Demiurgus,* whom they termed *Jaldaboth,* and his associates, over celestial minds; the progress of souls ascending to the [p. 400.] Deity through the seven celestial orbs, and the means which *Sophia,* or *Achamoth,* had in contemplation for delivering them from the power of Demiurgus: they also held that *Christ* had descended from above, and joined himself to the most just and holy man, *Jesus,* for the purpose of overthrowing the dominion of the architect of this world; but that, upon the seizure of Jesus by the Jews, Christ withdrew himself, and returned to his station in the celestial regions. The difference, therefore, between these Ophites and the other Gnostics of Egyptian origin, as to things of any material moment, was but small. They had, however, one tenet peculiar to themselves, and to which they owed the appellation of *Ophites,* namely, that the serpent by whom our first parents were beguiled was not an enemy, but a friend to the human race; and that it was either Christ himself, or *Sophia,* who, under the disguise of a serpent's form, wished to overthrow the councils of the architect of this world, or *Jaldaboth,* and to accomplish the salvation of mankind. Under the influence of this strange persuasion, they are said to have nourished a number of living *serpents,* and paid them a sort of honorary worship.(²)

(1) It would be very possible for any one who might feel so disposed, to collect from the works of ancient writers, a sufficiently extensive catalogue of Gnostic sects, that are represented as not coming within the description of any of those to which we have above adverted. Mention in particular is made of the followers of *Cassian,* the *Docetes,* the *Severians,* the *Apostolics,* the *Adamites,* who are said to have aimed at reviving the manners by which mankind were characterized in a state of primitive innocence; the *Cainites,* who are reported to have held in reverence Cain, Corah, Dathan, the inhabitants of Sodom, and Judas Iscariot; the *Abelites,* who are represented as having allowed marriage, but at the same time discountenanced the procreation of children; the *Sethians,* who regarded Seth as the Christ; the *Florinians,* a sect that owed its origin to Florinus and Blastus, two Valentinians, who had their residence at Rome, and various others of different denominations. Of any thing that remains on record, however, respecting these sects, it would be but a waste of time to take notice, inasmuch as their history is in part very obscure, in part devoid of every thing like certainty, and in part utterly unworthy of being related. Besides, it is incredible that the Gnostic tribe could ever have been split into such a multitude of sects and factions, although it is not to be denied but that its tenets were well calculated to give rise to a great diversity of opinions. It is my belief, therefore, that the variety of names by which it was not uncommon for an individual sect to be distinguished, one, perhaps, having a reference to some distinguishing tenet, another to its founder, another to some particular place or the like, occasionally led people into the error of imagining that there existed so many separate and distinct sects. The error, for instance, that is ascribed to the Docetes, respecting the body of Christ, was not properly the error of one sect, but was common to a great portion of the Gnostic tribe, and I, therefore, have no doubt, but that those who were termed Docetes by some, had a different denomination given to them by others: whence it happened that what was merely one individual sect, was regarded by uninformed people as two. The sect of the *Ophites,* or Serpentinians, was founded by one Euphrates; in all probability, therefore, although they were styled by some *Ophites,* yet others gave them the title of Euphratices, and those who were ignorant of this might con- [p. 401.] sider the latter as a distinct sect from the former. By Epiphanius and others, the Gnostics are represented as an individual sect, distinct from the Valentinians, the Carpocratians, the Basilidians, and the rest: and yet it is notorious at

this day, that all these latter arrogated to themselves the title of Gnostics, as a badge of superior wisdom. I intentionally pass over some other things that might be noticed as opposed to our believing the heretical sects to have been so numerous as ancient authors represent.

(2) For a more particular discusssion of the history and tenets of this sect, as far as they are at present to be collected from ancient writers, the reader is referred to a German work of mine, written expressly on the subject, and printed at Helmstadt, 1746, in quarto.

LXIII. **Cerdo and Marcion.** Nearly about the same time that the Roman church was infested by the depraved opinions of Valentine, its tranquillity was further disturbed by the dissemination within its bosom of another system of heretical discipline that owed its origin to one *Cerdo,* a native of Syria; a system which, if we can depend on ancient authors for having given it to us entire, was certainly shorter, more simple, and, consequently, easier to be understood than that of Valentine, but built upon the same principles, and teeming with similar depravities.[1] With Cerdo was associated *Marcion,* the son of a bishop of Pontus, a man of genius and learning, as well as of distinguished gravity and moderation, who had, at an earlier period, when he resided in Asia, manifested his dissent from the established tenets of the church, and thereby, as it should seem, rendered himself an object of public censure.[2] On his arrival at Rome, *Marcion* appears, for a while, to have disguised his real sentiments with regard. to religion, under the hope of being able to obtain for himself some situation of dignity in the church ; but having, in an unguarded moment, been led to disclose so much of the nature of his tenets as effectually to cut himself off from every expectation of this kind, (for he was so imprudent as, in familiar conversation with some of the Roman presbyters, to speak contemptuously of the books of the Old Testament, and the God of the Hebrews,) he at once threw off the mask, and, openly associating himself with *Cerdo,* devoted the remainder of his days to the establishment of a new sect in Italy, and various other provinces through which he travelled.[3] So eminently successful was he in the accomplishment of this object, that he left behind him a most numerous tribe of followers in almost every region of the earth, who, in spite of every effort that was made to subdue them, continued to maintain their ground down to the *fifth,* nay, even to the *sixth* century.[4] Of his disciples, *Lucan* or *Lucian, Severus, Blastes,* and others, but more particularly *Apelles*, are said, in some respects to have corrected the errors of their master, in others to have aggravated them, and to have become the authors of various new sects; but the accounts give nof them by different writers, possess but little consistency, and seem not at all calculated to stand the test of severe examination.

(1) Respecting this *Cerdo*, whom almost all ancient writers concur [p. 402.] in representing as the preceptor of Marcion, but who, with greater propriety perhaps, might have been termed by them Marcion's friend and associate, but very little is to be met with on record. We know, indeed, that he was by birth a Syrian, and that he lived and taught at Rome about the middle of this century; but as to every thing else respecting him, we are left altogether in the dark, or in a state of the greatest uncertainty. With regard to the life and fortunes of *Marcion*, not much more that can be relied upon, has been handed down to posterity. By most of the ancient writers, however, the tenets of both have been either professedly or incidentally brought under review. In addition to what is to be met with on the subject in *Irenæus*, (who takes continual occasion for displaying his decided hostility to the principles of Marcion,) *Epiphanius*, *Theodoret*, and other heresiologists, we find most of the early fathers whose works have reached our times, adverting to various of the Marcionite tenets, for the purpose of expressing their detestation of them. Were we to be called upon for a reference to those writers from whom most information is to be obtained with regard to the discipline of Marcion, we should assign the first place to *Tertullian*, whose five books against this heresiarch we deem worthy of perusal, although written in a very tumid and embarassed style, to say nothing of the poem against Marcion, extending likewise to five books, which is commonly attributed to *Tertullian*, and annexed to his works, although by many thought unworthy of his pen, and ascribed to some other author; and in the next place we should direct the reader to that dialogue against Marcion which is commonly, although, as some suppose, falsely attributed to *Origen*, and was published separately in Greek and Latin, by J. Rudolph Wetstein, Basil, 1674, 4to. From neither of these, however, must the reader expect to obtain a regular and complete view of the system of Marcion in all its parts: what they give us is merely a sketch of its leading features, or rather an exhibition of such parts as are distinguished for their deformity, without any kind of order or connection. Of more modern writers, Isaac *Beausobre* has bestowed great pains in developing the true principles and nature of the Marcionite discipline, in his *Histoire de Manichée*, tom. ii. p. 69, et seq. although in a way that occasionally savours too much of his propensity to hunt after excuses and apologies for heretics. Of Tillemont, Massuet, and others, I say nothing: all these run into the opposite extreme, being too ready to give credit to every thing which ancient writers have left on record respecting Marcion and his preceptor.

(2) *Epiphanius*, (*Hæres.* xlii.) relates that *Marcion* was at first distinguished for the severity of his morals, and led a solitary life, but that becoming the vic-

tim of illicit passion, he seduced a young woman, and was in consequence thereof excommunicated by his father the bishop; that finding it impossible to obtain the forgiveness of his parent upon any terms, he fled to Rome, and endeavoured, by the most urgent solicitations, to prevail on the presbyters, by whom the Roman church was at that time governed, Hyginus being dead, to receive him into the communion of the faithful; but that these presbyters constantly declined complying with his request, on the ground that it was not permitted them to do so without the consent of the bishop by whom he had been excommunicated, (and in this particular, certainly, the statement is perfectly in unison with what we know to have been the ancient discipline; for in primitive times it was an invariable rule, that no one who had been expelled from communion with the faithful, should be again received into the bosom of the church, without the knowledge and consent of the bishop by whom he had been excom-
[p. 403.] municated,) and that *Marcion*, therefore, inflamed with indignation, associated himself with *Cerdo*, who was at that time busied in disseminating his erroneous doctrines at Rome. With the exception of Beausobre, implicit credit has been given to this by almost every writer subsequent to Epiphanius; and the statement, considered merely in itself, has certainly nothing at all incredible in it. There are certain circumstances, however, which, when they come to be taken into the account, will not permit us to regard the matter as placed altogether beyond the reach of controversy. In the first place, all the ancient writers who treat of the history and opinions of Marcion, appear to have been quite uninformed as to what is thus related by Epiphanius, except the uncertain author of the Appendix to Tertullian's book *de Praescriptionibus advers. Hæreticos*; and the authority of Epiphanius is certainly, as every one knows, not of such weight as that his testimony singly should be allowed to overbalance the silence of every other ancient writer. And in the next place it is worthy of remark, as has been observed by several of the learned, that *Marcion* during his residence in Asia, before ever he had visited Rome, appears to have given disturbance to the church by his tenets; (Vid. Dion. Petavius *Not. ad. Epiphan. Heres.* xxii. Jos. Sim. Asseman, *Biblioth. Oriental.* Clement. Vatican. tom. i. p. 389. Jo. Pearson, *Vindic. Ignatian.* p. ii. cap. viii. p. 372. Anton Pagi *Critica in Baronium,* tom. i. ad ann. 144. sect. 3.) which renders it extremely probable that the true reason of his being excommunicated by his father was, not his illicit amours, but his heretical doctrines. And in my opinion it would be no very unhappy conjecture were it to be suggested that the meaning of *Epiphanius* had been misapprehended, a literal interpretation having inadvertently been given to what this author had never intended to have been received in any other than a figurative sense, and that by the virgin whom Marcion is represented as having seduced, we ought to understand merely the Church, whose purity he had sullied by the dissemination of unsound opinions. The ancient fathers were, it is well known, very frequently wont to compare the church to a virgin, and to treat the institution of a new sect as a violation of maiden purity. It is also by no means impossible, that the transgression of which it appears from Tertullian (*de Præscript.* cap. xxx.) and others, that Apelles, the disciple of Marcion was guilty, might mistakenly have been imputed to his master.

(3) According to Epiphanius, *Marcion* inquired of the Roman presbyters in what sense we ought to understand what is said by our blessed Saviour in Luke v. 36. of not putting new wine into old bottles, or sewing an new piece upon a old garment. The presbyters appear to have explained the meaning of Christ's words, as well as they were able, but I am bound to confess, in a way that does them but little credit, either on the score of learning or penetration. Dissatisfied with their answer, Marcion is represented as having avowed his belief, that by those words it was Christ's intention to intimate, that the books of the *Old Testament* were superseded by his authority, and that those of the New Testament were, not to be considered as having any connection with them.

(4) Tertullian in his *Præscript. adv. Hæret.* cap. xxx. p. 242. says, that *Marcion* was twice excommunicated from the Roman church, and that it was intended to have yielded to his intreaties, and received him back again even the third time, provided he would undeceive those whom he had corrupted with his errors, and bring them back with him into the bosom of the church, but that death overtook him before he could accomplish this, and that he consequently died excommunicate. Irenæus has recorded much the same thing of *Cerdo;* and learned men have therefore been led to conclude, that Tertullian has in this instance fallen into an error, and imputed that to *Marcion* which properly belonged to *Cerdo.* Vid. Tillemont *Memoires pour servir a l' Histoire de* [p. 404.] *l'Englise,* tom. ii. p. ii. p. 514. et seq. The thing is certainly not of such moment as to countenance us in devoting any time to its investigation.

LXIV. **The system of Marcion.** Ancient writers vary considerably in their exposition of the discipline of Marcion. Their disagreement, however, is not so great as to prevent us from ascertaining, in a general way, what were his sentiments respecting the origin of all things, and the nature of Jesus Christ, whom he considered as having come into the world for the purpose of saving souls. In the first place, he, after the example of the Oriental philosophers, figured to himself *two* primary principles, from whence all things had proceeded: the *one* devoid of every thing evil, the *other* destitute of every kind of good; the former, the *Prince of Light;* the latter, the lord or governor *of matter and darkness.* Of these two deities, the best and most powerful not only begat of himself a number of immortal and immutable natures of different orders and degrees, but also laid the foundations of the superior or celestial world in which the stars hold their course. The *Creator* of this nether world and its inhabitants, he represented as holding a middle station between those two primary beings, considering him as an angel of divine origin, endowed with the most extensive powers, who had formed this visible universe and the human race out of corrupt and shapeless matter, against the consent of its prince or ruler, mingling, however, therewith a considerable portion of celestial or æthereal matter, and uniting with the vitiated and mortal body a soul divine in its origin, and endowed with rationality.(¹)   This founder of the world was, according to Marcion, that Being whom the *Jews* worshipped as the Supreme Deity ; the same that commissioned Moses, and gave to the Hebrew nation, through him, a law; a law not indeed positively evil, but imperfect, and suited to men who were ignorant of the Supreme Deity, and paid greater obedience to their own sensual appetites and inclinations than to the dictates of right reason.   Between this parent of the material world, and the two above-mentioned eternal principles of all things, the chief point of difference appears to have been, that the former was looked upon as being neither positively good, nor yet as absolutely evil, but of a nature partaking of both, or, as Marcion expressed it, he was *just*.(²)   For, by means of punishments and calamities, which the good Deity was from his nature incapable of inflicting, this middle Being took vengeance on all those who neglected his laws, whilst, on the other hand, he, with blessings and rewards, which it was not in the nature of the evil Deity to [p. 405.] confer, remunerated those who acted uprightly, and led a life agreeable to his commandments.   Between him and the Lord or Governor of matter there was perpetual war ; for, since in the creation of the world and the replenishing of it with inhabitants, he had invaded the province of this Prince of darkness, the latter, out of revenge, set himself to work with every possible degree of care and diligence, to seduce mankind from their allegiance to their maker, and bring them into subjection to himself.   Those souls who suffered themselves to be led astray by the counsels of this deceiver, and paid obedience to his mandates, would, according to Marcion, on the dissolution of the body, be sent by the God of the Jews, the founder and legislator of the world, into a place of wo, where they would suffer inexpressible torments; whilst those who, in spite of every artifice, remained steady in their allegiance to their Creator, would, after death, be transferred into the regions of unbounded felicity and joy.(³)

(1) None of the ancient writers furnish us with a complete view of the system of Marcion. Its external form may in some sort be collected from them,

but as to its interior arrangement we are left wholly in the dark. Upon comparing together early authorities, we, in spite of their great disagreement with each other, are pretty well able to ascertain what were its leading features, but as to any of its minor parts, or the way in which the whole might be knit together, we have nothing to guide us beyond conjecture. Conjecture, however, may in this case be exercised with greater confidence than in some others, since the religion of Marcion bears a very strong resemblance to the discipline of the *Manichees*, with regard to which we possess much fuller information. *Marcion*, no doubt, was provided with a long story respecting the origin of this visible world, of a similar nature to that with which Manes furnished his followers; but ancient writers give us merely a summary of it, and content themselves with stating him to have maintained, that the world was framed of evil matter, by an angel of the first order, whom, by way of distinction, he denominated the Deity, or god of the world. As the Marcionites, however, did not pretend to deny but that there were many things good in this visible world, which could not have been derived from the kingdom of the evil principle, and since they moreover admitted that mankind were possessed of a divine soul, a soul bearing an affinity to the supreme Deity, we are of necessity constrained to regard them as believing, like the Manicheans, that a portion of celestial matter had been mingled with that which was naturally evil, and the bodies of men endowed with heavenly souls derived from the habitation of the supreme Being. This much I have thought fit to add by way of supplement to what is to be met with in ancient authors. At present I see no occasion for farther remark.

(2) There can be no doubt but that the many ancient, as well as modern writers, who represent Marcion as having taught that the founder of the world was by nature evil, have been guilty of an error. Origen, Tertullian, and numerous other authorities, might be cited in proof of his having considered the *architect of this universe*, as a being entirely distinct from both the good and the evil deity. The Supreme God, the Lord and governor of light, he regarded as in the strictest sense good, so as to be absolutely incapable of harbouring an evil thought or intention; nay, so infinitely benevolent as not to be able to punish, even his enemies. The prince, or ruler of darkness and matter, he believed to be positively evil, an utter stranger to every sort of good, and destitute of the power of blessing, even his friends. The *founder of the world*, he esteemed as neither good nor evil, but as being what he termed *just*, [p. 406.] that is, being invested with the power of either blessing or chastising, he consigned his enemies over to punishment, and remunerated his friends. *Origen Dial. contra Marcionit.* p. 48. edit. Wetsten. ἡ ἦν μέση ἀρχὴ ὑπηκόυσι τῷ ἀγαθῷ ἄνεσιν διδῶση, ὑπηκόυσι δὲ τῷ πονήρῳ θλίψιν δίδωσι. *Medium principium* (i. e. the founder of the world, whom he considered as holding a middle station between the good and the evil deity) *quietem præbet illis qui obediunt bono, pœnas autem infligit illis qui parent malo principio.* To which may be added what is said by Clement of Alexandria, *Stromat.* lib. iii. p. 425.—Οἱ ἀπὸ Μαρκίωνος φύσιν κακὴν - - - - ἐκ δικαίῳ γενομένην δημιοργήν. *Marcionis sectatores dicunt naturam rerum factam esse a conditore seu Demiurgo qui justus est.* More as to this will be found in Beausobre's *Histoire de Manichée*, vol. ii. p. 89, et seq.

(3) I have above expressed myself nearly in the words of the ancient writers. I will now endeavour, in the way of explanation, to supply what, not only they, but more recent authors have omitted. The *Creator of the world* was, according to Marcion, the same with the God and legislator of the *Jews*. They, therefore, who obeyed him, were Jews either by birth or conversion, and observed the law of Moses. His adversaries were the Gentiles, who, rejecting the God of the Jews, paid their adoration to a multitude of false deities. For the *gods*, whom the heathens worshipped, Marcion, like most of the ancient Christian teachers, regarded as wicked angels, or ministers of the evil principle, the lord or governor of darkness. Whoever then paid divine honours to these, he of course regarded as the subjects of the evil principle, the ruler of matter. In short, the sum of what Marcion wished to inculcate, appears to have been this, that the Jews exclusively would be saved, inasmuch as they continued stedfast in their obedience to the founder of the world, but that perdition would be the lot of all the heathen nations, in consequence of their yielding themselves servants to the evil deity.

LXV. **The tenets of Marcion respecting Christ.** With a view to put an end to this war of the evil principle with the founder of the world, and, at the same time, to recall the souls that lay imprisoned within material bodies back to their true origin, the supreme and all-benevolent Deity, according to this heresiarch, sent down to the Jews a most excellent nature, nearly resembling himself, namely, his son *Jesus Christ,* investing him with no sort of body or material clothing, but merely with such a *semblance* or likeness of a body as might render him visible to human eyes.(')
The *son,* with a view to obtain for himself a more ready attention from the people to whom he was thus commissioned, *pretended* that he was the Christ, of whom their ancient prophets had sung, and demonstrated the truth of his legation by a variety of miraculous acts.(') With respect to the nature of Christ's functions, Marcion held that he, in the first place, had it in command to revive amongst mankind the *knowledge* and worship of the supreme and only true God, and to overthrow, not only the *kingdom* of the Prince of Darkness, which had its foundation in, [p. 407.] and was upheld by superstition, but also the government and dominion of the founder of this world, or the God of the Jews; and, in the next place, he was to supply the souls endowed with reason with instruction as to the means whereby they might cleanse themselves from the contagion of the body and of matter, and render themselves worthy of attaining to everlasting felicity

in the realms of light.—Such being the objects of his mission, he was at once assailed with the united strength of the *Prince* of Darkness and the *founder* of this world.   The latter, in particular, perceiving that no respect whatever was paid by Jesus to his law, and that his subjects were incited to sedition, procured him to be apprehended by his servants, and condemned to undergo the punishment of death; not being in the least aware that the person with whom he had to deal was the son of the supreme Deity.   His expectations, however, were completely disappointed; for, as Jesus was not invested with a real body, it was impossible that he could be subjected to punishment, or die.   *Christ*, however, permitted his imaginary body to be apparently punished, and deprived of life, by way of impressing on the minds of mortals, that the vile and corrupt body wherewith they are clothed, ought to be deemed unworthy of the least consideration by a wise and religious man.(²)—Having executed his commission, here on earth, the Son of God, according to Marcion, descended into the infernal regions, and set at liberty all those souls whom the founder of the world had there condemned to the flames, in consequence of their having manifested a contempt for his law.(³)— The *rule of life* prescribed by Marcion to his followers, is acknowledged, even by his adversaries, to have been severe in the extreme.   Impressed with the belief that the soul was constantly in the greatest danger of being enervated and corrupted, through the influence of the material body by which it was enveloped, he particularly inculcated the necessity of bringing the latter into subjection, and recommended to his followers to avoid marriage. He also willed them to spurn the delights of sense, and content themselves with diet of a meagre, attenuating nature, such as bread, water, herbs, pulse, and fish.(⁴)

(1) Ancient writers are far from being either consistent or perspicuous, in their exposition of the tenets of Marcion respecting the Son of God.   Such particulars relating to this subject as are expressly handed down to us by the majority of those fathers, who, in point of weight and antiquity, are best entitled to credit, or which may fairly be deduced from their writings, in the way of inference, the reader will find given above.   From these it is perfectly clear, that Marcion would not allow that the Saviour of the world was clothed with a real body, or took upon him our nature ; but whether he believed him to have been invested with merely the shadow or *resemblance* of a body, or with a body composed of refined *ethereal matter*, appears to admit of some doubt.   Each of these

opinions has its abettors.—Another point that may be said to admit of being
contested, with little advantage in point of argument on either side, is, wnether
Marcion believed the Son of God to have made his appearance amongst the
Jews on a sudden, under the form or likeness of a perfect man, or conceived
him to have been apparently *born* of a virgin, in like manner as he believed him
in appearance, and according to the opinion of mankind, to have died ?

(2) Marcion was ready to admit, that the ancient Jewish prophets, whose
writings are comprised in the code of the Old Testament, had held forth the
[p. 408.] promise of a *Messiah*, or deliverer to the Hebrew nation : nor did he
pretend to doubt, as is manifest from a passage of Tertullian, which we shall
presently bring forward, but that this Messiah would, at some time or other,
actually make his appearance, and in a certain degree restore the fallen fortunes
of the house of Israel.   But he positively *denied*, that our blessed Saviour was
such Messiah : and, indeed, according to his tenets, it was impossible for him
to act otherwise.   For since it was his belief, that the God whom the Jews
worshipped, was merely the founder of this world, and not the supreme or superlatively excellent Deity, it could not but follow, that he should have regarded
the ancient Jewish *prophets* as the legates merely of this creator of the universe, and not of the Supreme Being ; and likewise have conceived, that the
Messiah, whose advent they predicted, would not be one and the same with the
Son of the Most High, whom he believed to have made his appearance in Jesus,
with a view to the salvation of men's souls.   For it was not to be imagined,
that the Lord of everlasting light, or the Supreme Deity, would commission
the servants of the architect of this world, a being so vastly inferior to himself,
to announce the advent of his son.   It, however, militated in no trifling degree
against this opinion, that the Son of God actually professed himself to be that
Christ or Messiah, whose coming had been predicted by the prophets of the
Old Testament.   For, notwithstanding that *Marcion* had a proper gospel of his
own, differing considerably from ours, and maintained that such particulars in
the history of Christ as were in opposition to his tenets, ought to be rejected as
spurious interpolations, he had not the hardihood to call in question such a glaring
fact, as that of our blessed Saviour's having, throughout the whole course of his
ministry amongst the Jews, maintained that he was that Messiah whom their
prophets had taught them to expect.   By way of removing this obstacle, therefore, *Marcion* asserted that our Saviour had, in this instance, practised a *deception* on the Jews, and falsely personated their promised Messiah, by way of
obtaining from them a more favourable reception and hearing.   *Constituit Marcion*, says Tertullian, (*contr. Marc.* lib. iii. cap. xv.) *alium esse Christum qui
Tiberianis temporibus a Deo quondam ignoto* (i. e. the good principle) *revelatus
sit in salutem ominum Gentium, alium qui a Deo creatore* (i. e. the God of the
Jews, whom he termed Just) *in restitutionem Judaici status sit destinatus quan-
doque venturus. - - - sed quomodo inquit* (Marcion) *irreperet* (Jesus, or the Son
of God) *in Judæorum fidem, nisi per solemne apud eos' et familiare nomen*
(namely that of Christ).   Now, one who could believe that the Son of God
himself had recourse to fraud and lying, for the purpose of insinuating himself
with the Jews, must necessarily have conceived that every species of fallacy

was allowable which might contribute towards advancing the truth, and I am therefore induced to think, that ancient writers are deserving of credit in what they state as to Marcion's having vitiated, mutilated, and in divers respects altered, the books of the New Testament.

(3) What I here state respecting the *motive* for Christ's undergoing a feigned death, is merely a conjecture of my own. Marcion indisputably denied that Christ in reality either suffered or died; but, at the same time, he affirmed that his imaginary or apparent death was attended with salutary consequences to the human race. For we find *Megethus*, a Marcionite, represented by Origen, *Dial. contr. Marcion.* sect. ii. p. 53. as thus speaking: ὁ δημιυργὸς ἰδὼν τὸν ἀγαθὸν λύοντα αὐτῷ τὸν νόμον ἐπεβόλευσεν αὐτῷ, μὴ εἰδὼς, ὅτι ὁ [p. 409.] θάνατος τῆ ἀγαθῆ σωτηρία ἀνθρώπων ἐγίνετο. *Conditor* (*i. e.* the Founder of the world, or God of the Jews) *ubi animadvertit bonum illum* (*i. e.* Jesus, the Son of the good Deity) *legem suam* (*viz.* the law of Moses) *violare, struxit ei insidias, nescius boni hujus* (*i. e.* Jesus) *mortem hominum salutem esse.* Now, to me it appears quite impossible to divine any other kind of salutary consequences that could be derived by the human race from the feigned death of Jesus, than what I have above pointed out. Jesus Christ, by apparently giving himself over to death, meant to impress on mankind that neither the body, nor the dissolution of the body, deserves a moment's concern, and that, for the sake of the soul, even violent hands might be laid on the body, inasmuch as it was a mere machine, composed of depraved matter, the very fæces, as it were, of the malignant Deity. Hence all the Marcionites, as we find recorded by the whole body of ancient fathers, so far from fearing, or seeking to avoid death, were anxious to encounter it; nor were they ever surpassed by any other sect, either in the number or the courage of their martyrs.

(4) Marcion held that Jesus, after having executed the commission with which he was charged to mankind, descended to the infernal regions, and brought up with him from thence the souls of all the *sinners* of whom mention is made in the books of the Old Testament, such as Cain, the Sodomites, Corah, Dathan, and Abiram, whilst he left behind him the souls of all the *just*, such as Abel, Noah, and Abraham. See Irenæus, lib. i. cap. 29., Epiphanius, and others. Many, it is true, would have this to be a mere story invented by his enemies; but they labour under an error. From the very nature of Marcion's discipline, it was impossible that he should have believed otherwise. According to him, the *sinners* recorded in the writings of the Old Testament, had not incurred the displeasure of the Supreme Deity, but offended merely the Founder of this world, or the God of the Jews. Christ, therefore, having come into the world for the express purpose of putting an end to the dominion of this latter being, it was but just that he should set at liberty those who were suffering punishment for their disobedience to his laws. On the other hand, it was his opinion that the *saints* of the Old Testament had never made it their study to please the Supreme Deity, but merely the architect of this world; wherefore there could be no reason whatever for Christ's having anything to do with them. Besides, these latter were not in a state of suffering or unhappiness, but were receiving the reward of their obedience to the Parent of the world and his commandments.

(5) That Marcion prescribed to his followers a rigid and austere course of life, and that it was the practice of his disciples therefore to reject every kind of worldly gratification, and pass their lives in a state of continence, penury, and bodily affliction, so as to render the arrival of their last hour an object of desire rather than of fear, is admitted by all the ancient Christian writers.—I think it right, however, in this place, to repeat an observation that I have already made above, namely, that the accounts which are handed down to us by ancient authors, of the rigid and severe system of moral discipline by which certain of the Gnostic and other sects were characterized, are not to be understood as applying indiscriminately to all the individuals of which such sects were composed, but in an especial manner to the priests and such select disciples as might be ambitious of attaining to a more than ordinary degree of sanctity. For the founders of these sects were naturally anxious for their increase and propagation ; and being fully aware that the rigid course of moral discipline which they prescribed must, if generally adopted, tend in great measure to defeat this object, took care so to temper their injunctions as that the multitude should be at [p. 410.] liberty to live after the manner of other people, the more rigid precepts having a reference merely to the public instructors and such as were more than ordinarily studious of securing ther own salvation.

To conclude: It cannot fail to be readily perceived by every one who shall investigate, with attention, the account here given of the sects that are usually classed under the general title of Gnostics, that the chief point of difference between them rested in this, that some of them recognized the ancient oriental dogma respecting the existence of two principles in its full extent, whilst others abridged it somewhat, and supplied the place of what they thus cut off with visionary fancies drawn from other quarters. In the following respects they appear to have been all of one mind, namely,—that in a ldition to the Deity, *matter*, the root and cause of every thing evil and depraved, had existed from all eternity ;—that this corrupt matter had not been reduced into order by the Supreme and all-benevolent Deity, but by a nature of a far inferior rank ;—that the founder of the world, therefore, and the Deity, were beings between whom no sort of relationship whatever existed ;—that the *bodies* of mankind owed their formation to the founder of the world, but that their *souls* were the offspring of the Deity ;—that the former, therefore, would return to matter without the least hope of revivification, whilst the latter, provided they threw off the yoke of the founder of this world, would ascend to the Deity, or at least to that region which lies immediately contiguous to the habitation of the Deity. Those, mor_over, who were natives of *Syria* and Asia assigned to matter a peculiar *prince* or governor whom they believed to have been self-existent, or to have sprung from matter itself; in other words, they believed in the existence of an evil principle as well as a good one. This prince of matter, however, they considered as a distinct being from the founder of the world. To those of the Gnostics who had been bred up in *Egypt*, such as Basilides, Valentine, and others, this prince or governor of matter was entirely unknown; but they in their turn, encumbered the oriental doctrine with various whimsical conceits, of Egyptian origin, respecting the heavens, the stars, the descent and ascent of souls, the princes or rulers of the wandering stars, the eternal forms of all things existing in the Pleroma, as well as several other matters to which the Asiatics seem not altogether to have yielded their assent.

LXVI. **The heresy of Montanus.** The various commotions which thus arose out of the endeavour to bring about an accommodation between the Oriental philosophy and the Christian religion, although in themselves sufficiently afflictive, may be said to have prevailed rather without the confines of the church, and to have interfered but little with its internal state. By far more baneful and pernicious in their consequences, to the welfare of the Christian cause, were those disagreements and dissensions which, not long after, sprung up within the very bosom of the church itself, and amongst Christians who, in respect to the sum and substance of religion, were entirely agreed. Of this species of dissensions, the first entitled to notice is that which *Montanus*, under the reign of Marcus Aurelius, about the middle of this century, originated at *Pepuza*, an obscure, insignificant little village in Phrygia.(') This heresiarch, a man of low origin, and, as it should seem, not naturally inclined to evil, but of a [p. 411.] melancholic disposition and infirm judgment, in consequence of some morbid affection of the mind, became so disordered in his imagination as to conceive that the Holy Spirit, the *Paraclete*, or Comforter, by whom the apostles of our blessed Saviour had been animated, had, by divine appointment, descended upon him for the purpose of foretelling things of the greatest moment that were about to happen, and promulgating a better and more perfect discipline of life and morals than that which had been built upon the apostolic mandates.(²) Teeming, therefore, with this fancied inspiration, and bursting through every kind of rational restraint, he poured forth a multitude of *prophecies*, in which the Roman territory and government were threatened with calamities of the most grievous nature; and a severer rule of life and action was prescribed to mortals in the very words, as it was pretended, of the Deity himself.—At the first, he so far succeeded as to prevail on many to believe that he was in reality the character which he wished to pass for, and to win over to his party, amongst several others of no mean rank, two opulent women named *Priscilla* and *Maximilla*, who, with others of his disciples, pretending, like their master, to the gift of prophecy, diffused his opinions within a short time throughout Asia, Africa, and some portion of Europe.(³) When people's minds, however, began in some degree to recover from the effect of this first impression, and these recently-divulged prophecies came to be scrutinized with proper calmness and attention, the imposture became apparent, and the *bishops* of Asia, after discussing the subject in certain of their councils, adopted the resolution of expelling Montanus, together with his friends and associates, from every sort of connection with the faithful.　The example thus set by the Asiatic prelates was gradually followed by the other Christian bishops, so that the excommunication of the Montanists became at length universal. Cut off, therefore, from all intercourse with the general body of Christians, these heretics formed themselves into a peculiar church, the chief president over which had his residence at Pepuza, in Phrygia.　This *sect* continued to flourish down to the *fifth* century, when it experienced some annoyance from imperial edicts;(⁴) and the list of its members was ennobled by not a few names, distinguished both for learning and genius, amongst which none claims a higher rank in point of celebrity than that of *Tertullian,* a man of great eminence, certainly, but beyond all measure rigid and austere, who, in several books written by him expressly on the subject, advocates, with considerable firmness and spirit, the cause of the sect under whose banners he had been induced to enlist.(⁵)

(1) Respecting the tenets of Montanus and his followers, we are supplied with sufficient information, as well by the extracts, from certain books no longer in existence, which are given us by Eusebius in his *Ecclesiastical History,* lib. v. c. 16. et seq. as from what is left on record by other historians of ancient sects, and more particularly *Tertullian,* who has devoted a series of books to the defence of the Montanists and their tenets.　My opinion, however, is, that in as far as it relates to this sect, the testimony of this latter writer is not to be received without caution ; for to pass over the fact, that we are quite in a state of uncertainty as to which of his books were written prior to his becoming a [p. 412.] Montanist, and which after, I am altogether deceived if he does not frequently, as is the general practice of advocates, give a certain sort of colouring to the doctrines of his master, and exhibit rather what he wished Montanus to have maintained, than what Montanus actually did maintain.—Abundantly supplied, however, as we are with information as to the tenets and opinions of Montanus, there is a certain degree of confusion and obscurity which rests over the history of this heresiarch and his followers, nor can it, in the absence of all

authentic memorials, be readily reduced into any kind of order. Learned men have disputed, and seem likely, to the end of time, to maintain disputes as to the exact *period* of the rise of this faction in Phrygia. Above I have followed the conjecture that appears to be supported, and not without reason, by the major part of those who have turned their attention to the subject. It is, however, far from being approved of by all. Jo. Phil. Baratier (in his book *de Successione Romanor. Pontificum*, p. 135 et seq.) contends at much length, that we ought to refer the rise of this sect to the year cxxvi. The Abbè de Longerue, (whose dissertation *de Tempore quo Montani Hæresis nata est*, is to be found in Winkler's *Sylloge Anecdotorum*, p. 254,) endeavours to prove that it sprang up under the reign of Antonius Pius about the year cxl. J. Le Clerc, (in his *Historia Ecclesiastica duor. prim. Sæculor.* p. 676,) places its origin under the year clvii. The calculations of other writers have produced different results; but between these the discordance has not been less, so that in spite of every endeavour to reconcile them, recourse must necessarily be had to conjecture at last.—Amongst more recent writers I have not met with one who has not either condemned or vindicated Montanus to excess. Those who represent him as an execrable mortal; a compound of deception, vice, and every species of iniquity; a wretch imbued with the vilest notions respecting religion, a very bond-servant to the devil, and terminate their invective by stating him and Maximilla to have been guilty of self-murder, may certainly urge the authority of ancient writers on their side; but then they are such writers as are little to be depended upon, and this account of Montanus may therefore well be considered as in no slight degree overcharged.—On the other hand, those who hold him up as a pattern of sanctity and virtue, a man divinely inspired, and enduring persecution for righteousness sake; one who, with the exception of a few trifling errors, the aberrations of an ingenuous mind, had nothing whatever to be desired in him; who, in short, would have us believe that the ancient Christians, by whom Montanus was excommunicated, were, as to every thing essential, of the same way of thinking with himself, and, in the severities which they exercised towards him, were influenced entirely by prejudice and passion, most assuredly carry their vindication of him to an extent which the truth will not justify. —That Montanus was not actuated by a wicked mind, but was an ignorant simple man, but little acquainted with the genuine principles of religion and piety, and that a certain degree of mental imbecility, conjoined with a melancholic disposition, at length drove him out of his senses, is what I feel no difficulty in believing; but that he was a martyr to his sanctity, and attempted nothing amiss, or that he was not out of his wits, are points to which I am certain it will never be in my power to yield my assent. Great ingenuity and no less eloquence have been lately displayed in an attempt to dispel the obscurity that envelopes the tenets of Montanus by Theophilus *Wernsdorf*, a man distinguished for his learning, and eminently skilled in matters of antiquity, whose *Commentatio de Montanistis Sæculi II. vulgo creditis Hæreticis*, published at Dantzic, 1751, 4to. reached me while I was engaged on this note. He is the advocate of Montanus, and maintains that the ancient Christians could have had but little if any cause for condemning him. The difference of opinion between us is not so great as to prevent me from acknowledging that this learned writer has handsomely executed the task which he undertook.

[p. 413]   (2) The ancient writers, whom the greater part of the more recent ones implicitly follow, represent Montanus as having so egregiously violated common sense as to maintain that he was actually the *Paraclete*, or Holy Ghost itself. But I strongly suspect that, in this instance, the words of these authors do not put us exactly in possession of their real sentiments, which, no doubt were correct. None of them, unless I am altogether deceived, could have meant to say that Montanus conceived himself to be the very person of the *Paraclete*, or that his body was animated by the Holy Spirit in the place of a soul; for to have believed this he must have been inconsistent with himself, and the most silly of mortals. These writers, then, could only have meant that Montanus endeavoured to persuade the people that the *Paraclete spake through him*, and that the prophecies which he uttered were not of his own conception, but dictated by the Paraclete; and in this they were perfectly correct, for such was certainly his doctrine. The ambiguity and indistinctness with which both ancient and modern writers have expressed themselves on this subject is to be ascribed solely to the obscurity of *Tertullian*, who very frequently terms Montanus *The Paraclete*, and whose words and manner of expression these authors were led to make their own.—What I have said of the man's labouring under some morbid affection of the mind stands in need, I think, of no justification; for since the innocence and austerity of his life absolves him from every suspicion of evil design, and the enormities that we find occasionally reported of him are undeserving of any sort of credit; since, moreover, the notion entertained by certain of the early Christian writers, that both his body and soul had been taken possession of by the devil, carries with it not the smallest semblance of truth, indeed is altogether contradicted by the very prophecies which he uttered, there remains, as it strikes me, no other conclusion to which we can arrive than this, that he was a man disordered both in body and mind; unless, perhaps, some should be willing rather to suspect him of having practised a pious fraud.

(3) In addition to others distinguished for their virtue and sanctity it appears that even the bishop of Rome, whom most writers suppose to have been *Victor*, was for a while induced to regard Montanus in the light of a prophet divinely inspired, and that it was *Praxeas* who awakened him from this delusion. Vid. Tillemont *Memoires pour servir a l' Histoire de l' Eglise*, tom. ii. p. iii. p. 124. et seq.

(4) That the sect of the Montanists had not become extinct even so low down as the *fifth* century, is evident from the imperial edicts relating to it that are extant in the *Codex Theodosianus*, tom. vi. We there find the Montanists denounced by a law of *Honorius*, under the year 398. p. 168. as also by another severe edict of the same emperor, promulgated A. D. 407. (p. 177.) where they are termed *Phrygians* and *Priscillianists*, from *Priscilla*, one of the female converts to Montanism, and associated with the Manichees. Under the following year 408. (p. 182.) we find the *Priscillianists* again denounced by a fresh edict; and two years after, viz. A. D. 410. (p. 186.) under the titles of *Montanists* and *Priscillianists*, they are still further proscribed by the emperor *Theodosius* the

Younger. In the year 415, (p. 200.) another rigid law was enacted against the *Montanists;* and finally, in the year 423 (p. 202.) we find them made the objects of a penal enactment under the titles of *Phrygians* and *Pepuzites,* which latter appellation they acquired from the little town of Phrygia, from whence the sect had originally sprung. The frequent repetition of laws like these, proves plainly that numerous branches of this sect were in existence even so late as the *fifth* century.

(5) In embracing Montanism, *Tertullian* appears to have been less actuated by a cool and discriminating judgment than by self-love, or a wish to promote the growth of certain opinions to which he was immoderately attached. [p. 414.] Most of the principles of moral discipline propounded by Montanus, so far from being either new or unheard of amongst the Christians, had been actually adopted by several of them before his time. Of this number was *Tertullian,* a man of a morose and saturnine disposition, to whom the moral discipline of the Christians in general had long appeared by far too indulgent and relaxed. Upon finding, therefore, that Montanus was an advocate for the principles which he considered as true and just, he at once, without ever seeing or hearing the man, pronounced that he must have been inspired of the Holy Ghost. The object of this good father's patronage was, in fact, not so much Montanus as himself and his own opinions.

LXVII. **The errors of Montanus.** With regard to the leading and generally-received notions of the Christians on the subject of religion, *Montanus* attempted no innovations of any moment;(') nor were his moral precepts altogether new and unheard of, or of such a nature as to appear intolerable in the eyes of the Christians. For in the age in which he flourished there were not wanting, even amongst the more orthodox Christians, certain who publicly avowed their approbation of most of those points which constituted the leading features of the discipline which he inculcated: such as, that fasts ought to be multiplied and protracted; that second marriages were unbecoming in persons professing the religion of Christ; that the church ought not to extend its pardon to persons guilty of the more grievous sins; that all decoration of the body ought to be disregarded; that for women to array themselves in costly attire was repugnant to the injunctions of the apostles Paul and Peter; that the study of letters and philosophy tended rather to injure than promote the cause of religion and piety; that virgins ought to wear veils, lest they might awaken impure desires in persons beholding them; that it was not allowable for Christians in times of persecution to betray anything like timidity, or to adopt a prudential line of conduct; and, consequently, that it was incompatible with genuine Christian fortitude for persons, at such seasons, to endeavour to save themselves by flight, to redeem their lives by money, or to hold their meetings for the purposes of worship by stealth or in a private manner.   Neither was any sort of stigma considered as attaching itself to those who defended such opinions, nor does it appear that they were on that account deemed the less worthy of being continued in communion with the faithful; indeed, by many they were even highly commended, and by others were looked upon with an increased degree of respect and veneration.(²)—Notwithstanding, however, that the shades of difference between the doctrine of Montanus and that of other Christians as to most points were but trifling, very sufficient cause existed for expelling him from all communion with the faithful.   For those things which had been merely propounded by others in a spirit of meekness, and without any detriment to Christian harmony and liberty, were arrogantly brought forward by him as oracles dictated by the Holy Spirit for the benefit of the universal church; whence it necessarily followed, that he must have regarded all those who refused to place implicit confidence in him and his fe[p. 415.] male associates as contemners of the Holy Spirit, and considered himself and his followers as constituting the only true church.   This one circumstance of itself, without doubt, virtually separated him from the church, and amply justified the Catholic Christians in refusing any longer to hold communion with him and his associates.(³)   In the *prophecies,* moreover, which were uttered by this heresiarch and his female companions, there was a tone which might well induce the Christians at large to avoid maintaining any sort of intercourse with him ; for, since he announced the most disastrous fortunes as awaiting the human race, there was certainly reason to apprehend that the Christians, if they continued in association with him, might come to be regarded as enemies to the commonwealth.(⁴)

(1) Neither *Montanus* nor his female disciples in their prophecies made any scruple of touching upon the principal dogmas of Christianity ; nay, they occasionally avowed them, and entered the lists as their defenders against those who would have corrupted them.   *Tertullian,* in his book *de Resurrectione,* cap. lxiii. p. 429. represents Montanus and his male and female disciples, whom he designates by the titles of *Servi et Ancillæ Dei,* as having stood forth in defence

of the doctrine of the Resurrection against the Gnostics, and also as having, *per novam prophetiam de Paracleto inundantem,* removed many of the difficulties with which, not only this article of faith, but others were encumbered. *Cujus (prophetiæ,)* he continues, *si hauseris fontes, nullam poteris sitire doctrinam, nullus te ardor exuret quæstionum, Resurrectionem quoque carnis usquequaque potando refrigerabis.* In the same book, cap. xi. p. 386, he adduces a fragment of one of the prophecies of *Priscilla,* in which she particularly reprehends those who opposed the doctrine of a future resurrection of the body. *Nemo tam carnaliter vivit quam qui negant carnis resurrectionem. . . . De quibus luculenter et Paracletus per prophetidem Priscam : Carnes sunt et carnem oderunt.* Disputing against Praxeas, *Tertullian* asserts that the Paraclete recognized three persons in the Godhead, and that he himself had been much assisted by the prophecies of the Paraclete, in attaining to a right comprehension of this dogma. *Protulit,* says he, (in *Lib. contra Praxeam,* cap. xiii.) *Deus Sermonem, quemadmodum etiam Paracletus (i. e. Montanus) docet, sicut radix fruticem, et fons flurium, et fax radium.* And after some intermediate observations, he thus proceeds: *Nos qui et tempora et caussas Scripturarum per Dei gratiam inspicimus, maxime Paracleti* (the Holy Spirit speaking, as he believed, through Montanus) *non hominum discipuli, duos quidem definimus, Patrem et Filium, et jam tres cum Spiritu Sancto . . . duos tamen Dominos et duos Deos numquam ex ore nostro proferimus.* It is plain, therefore, that Montanus must have discussed some of the most weighty points of religion, and resolved them in a manner sufficiently subtile and refined. In handling these topics, however, he appears to have studiously avoided bringing forward any thing materially differing from the generally received opinions. St. Jerome, indeed, Epist. xxxvii. *ad Marcellam,* tom. iv. Opp. p. 64. edit. Benedict. accuses the Montanists of Sabellianism, [p. 416.] *illi Sabellii dogma sectantes, Trinitatem in unius Personæ angustias cogunt.* But how little faith is to be placed in this accusation, must be apparent from the words of Tertullian, above cited, in which he most expressly declares the Paraclete, as he terms Montanus, to have recognized *three persons* in the Godhead. If I may take credit to myself for any penetration, the charge thus brought forward by St. Jerome was a most invidious and unwarranted consectary deduced from the circumstance of Montanus having arrogated to himself the person of the Paraclete, and asserted that the Deity himself spake through him. For from this, his adversaries, as appears from Epiphanius, *Hæres.* xlviii. § ii. p. 412. tom. i. Opp. were led to conclude that he wished to pass himself for the Deity; and a person who had been so mad as to have entertained such a wish, might certainly have appeared to his enemies, as desirous of abolishing all distinction of persons in the Godhead, and compressing the Deity *in unius personæ angustias,* namely, his own.—In thus exonerating Montanus from the imputation of having violated the leading principles of Christianity, the reader must not understand me, however, as meaning to insinuate that his errors were but of a light or trivial nature. For on the contrary, it is certain that he entertained very injurious, and not only injurious, but highly dangerous sentiments, respecting the moral discipline propounded by Christ and his apostles; a circumstance of itself sufficient to warrant his being excluded from the number of the orthodox Christians, and classed among heretics.—He taught, for instance, that the *moral law* was left by the Son of God and his apostles, in an imperfect or rude and immature state, and that he himself was commissioned by the Holy Ghost to fill up and bring to perfection what Christ had thus left jejune and incomplete. This dogma, *Tertullian*, the most distinguished of all the followers of Montanus, hesitates not to propound in the most undisguised terms, in various parts of his writings, although, as to other things, he occasionally has recourse to subterfuge, and endeavours, in some degree, to qualify the opinions of his master. Let us hear how he speaks in his book *de Velandis Virginibus*, cap. i. p. 192. which may be taken as a fair specimen of the whole. *Justitia*, (i. e. the moral law,) *primo fuit in rudimentis, natura Deum metuens, dehinc per legem et prophetas promovit in infantiam, dehinc per evangelium efferbuit in juventutem, nunc per Paracletum* (Montanus) *componitur in maturitatem. Hic erit solus a Christo*, (i. e. after Christ) *magister et dicendus et verendus*. Can any thing possibly be more evident? Montanus conceived that there was as much difference between the moral discipline enjoined by Moses and the prophets in the words of God, and that which was propounded by Christ, as there is between an infant and a young man, and that between the moral law of Christ and that prescribed by the Holy Ghost through himself, there existed as great an inequality, as there is between a youth and a man arrived at maturity.—In another place, *de Monogamia*, cap. xiv. p. 686. Tertullian expresses himself after the following manner: *Regnavit duritia cordis usque ad Christum, regnaverit et infirmitas carnis usque ad Paracletum*. It was his opinion, therefore, that Christ made an allowance for the infirmity of our flesh, and only contended against hardness of heart; but that Montanus, [p. 417.] by the command of the Deity, assailed also the infirmity of the flesh. Now this was certainly an *essential error*, and involved within it other errors of a like noxious nature, and equally subversive of the true principles of religion. The importance of this error is not diminished, but rather increased, by the consideration that the additions made by Montanus to the moral discipline enjoined by our blessed Saviour, consisted merely of certain precepts of light moment relating to fasts, second marriages, the veiling of virgins, and other particulars, respecting external demeanour. For since Tertullian would willingly have us believe that, by the promulgation of these precepts, Montanus, or the Holy Spirit through him, had brought the moral law to maturity, or, in other terms, given the finishing hand to that which was before imperfect, it is plain that he must have considered external actions, modes, and institutions, and those too of rather a minute and trifling nature, as constituting the most material part of religion and piety; an opinion equally intolerable and pernicious with the former. Jesus Christ and his apostles have left it in command, that we should love the Lord our God beyond every thing, and our fellow mortals as ourselves. Now these injunctions, according to Montanus, were indeed very good, but at the same time merely juvenile ones, and calculated only for the Christian world during its minority; whereas the additions made to them by Montanus himself respecting fast-days, virgins wearing veils, the avoiding second marriages, and the like, carried the moral law to an infinitely higher degree of dignity and perfection, and rendered it suitable to the Christian commonwealth when advanced to the age of manhood and perfection. The sum and substance of the moral law, therefore, it necessarily followed, was to be looked upon as contained in these minute and insignificant regulations. The latter of these errors was not, as far as can be ascertained at the present day, ever openly attributed to Montanus by his adversaries, but he was properly charged by them with the former, as with one of the most grievous nature. Nor have I the least doubt but that it was this error chiefly that occasioned him to be regarded in the light of an impostor, and produced the excommunication both of him and his followers.— An ancient writer, whose catalogue of Heresies is annexed to Tertullian's book *de Præscript. Hæreticorum*, represents (in cap. lii. p. 254.) the Montanists as holding *Paracletum plura in Montano dixisse, quam Christum in Evangelio protulisse, nec tantum plura, sed etiam meliora atque majora.* And in this he certainly does them no injury whatever. For *Tertullian*, whose testimony necessarily carries with it peculiar weight, as coming from one who must have been intimately acquainted with the opinions of his sect, intimates this very thing in the words which we have above cited. The discipline of Christ is represented as bearing merely a juvenile character; that of Montanus one of masculine vigour and maturity. Who, then, can entertain a doubt but that the latter must have been deemed to have propounded greater and better things than the former? Those who are intrusted with the education of youth, over whom reason in general possesses but little influence, take care to accommodate their precepts to the infirmity of their charge; but greater and better things are brought forward by those to whom is committed the institution of persons arrived at man's estate, and whose unruly appetites have been brought into some sort of subjection.—St. *Jerome* (Epist. xxxvii. tom. iv. Opp. p. 64.) attributes to Montanus the same error, but exaggerates and amplifies it beyond all measure. *Deum voluisse in Veteri Testamento per Moysen et prophetas salvare mundum, sed quia non potuit explere, corpus sumpsisse de virgine, et in Christo, sub specie filii prædicantem mortem obiisse pro nobis. Et quia per duos gradus mundum salvare nequi-* [p. 418.] *verit, ad extremum per Spiritum Sanctum in Montanum, Priscam et Maximillam, descendisse: et plenitudinem quam Paulus non habuerit . . . habuisse Montanum.* In this, certainly, there is somewhat of truth, but it is coupled with one or two things that have no foundation whatever in fact. No grounds, for instance, exist for charging Montanus with entertaining the Sabellian dogma of one person in the Deity acting under the different characters of Father, Son, and Holy Spirit; a thing altogether foreign from his mind; and the doctrine he inculcated respecting a change and gradual improvement in moral discipline is invidiously transferred to the catholic religion, and the mode of obtaining everlasting salvation.—The conclusion to which, I think, equity would direct us, is, that Montanus and his associates were not aware of all the evils with which the great and dangerous error into which they fell was pregnant, and I am, therefore, unwilling to have him charged with all its consequences. The error, however, was in itself of the most grievous nature, and the accusers of Montanus appear to have well understood its enormity, a circumstance that must be allowed fully to justify their severity.

(2) Montanus asserted that it was the *design* of the Holy Spirit or Paraclete,

through his means, to render perfect the system of *moral discipline* which Christ had left incomplete. The improvements, however, which he suggested as necessary to be made in the Christian code, had not any direct or immediate relation to the amendment of the *interior* man, or the furtherance of real and substantial *piety*, but primarily had respect merely to the reclaiming of Christians to a greater degree of strictness and gravity in their *external* demeanour. The most material of his precepts I have enumerated above; of which, however, it may not be improper to remark there are *three*, namely, those respecting the neglect of *dress*, the impropriety of female *ornaments*, and a contempt for *letters* and philosophy, which are not expressly attributed to *Montanus* by ancient writers, but which, inasmuch as they are warmly contended for by *Tertullian*, the most distinguished of his followers, might, I thought, with every degree of probability, be reckoned amongst the number of his institutes. The rest are indisputably his.—In the first place, then, he wished to introduce amongst Christians a greater frequency of *fasting* than had been customary. Other Christians, for instance, had contented themselves with celebrating only one solemn fast in the year, namely, the *Antepaschal* one; but *Montanus* enjoined his followers to observe *two* additional weeks, with the exception of the Saturdays and Sundays, as seasons of abstinence, that is, not absolutely to decline at such times taking any sustenance at all, but to content themselves with food of an arid, meagre nature, and to drink nothing therewith but water. The manner in which these additional yearly fasts, each of which consisted of five days, were observed, occasioned them to be termed *Xerophagiæ*. Montanus was also an advocate for the multiplication of *private fasts;* he did not, however, fix these at any particular number, but left every one at liberty to consult his own inclination, contenting himself with merely inculcating, in a general way, that frequent fasting was of wonderful efficacy in appeasing the Deity, as well as in healing the mind, and fortifying it against those evils to which Christians must of necessity be exposed. A more *rigid* celebration of those fasts, which they observed in common with other Christians, was likewise enjoined by this heresiarch to his followers. For whereas the Christians in general were accustomed, during the grand yearly antepaschal fast, to take some sort of refreshment after sunset, Montanus ordained that those of his sect should pursue a different mode, and not only at this season, but also during any private fasts which they might think fit to impose [p. 419.] on themselves, retire to rest supperless. The weekly fasts that were observed by the Christians of those times, *viz.* the fourth and sixth days, or, as we term them, Wednesdays and Fridays, were commonly considered as terminating at the ninth hour, or, according to modern computation, at three o'clock in the afternoon; but Montanus would not allow of their being brought to such an early conclusion, and insisted on it that they should be prolonged until the evening.—Of *second marriages*, which were considered by this heresiarch as unlawful, I say nothing. That St. Paul had given his sanction to them he did not pretend to deny, but contended that the *Paraclete* had, through him, revoked the license that had been granted by the apostle.—Against Christians guilty of any of the more *grievous* sins, such as adultery, murder, and idolatry, equal severity was not exercised by all the churches. By most of them pardon was usually granted for the first offence to adulterers, but murderers and idolaters were always irrevocably excommunicated. *Montanus*, however, asserted it to be the command of the Holy Spirit, that persons polluted by either of the three enormous sins above-mentioned, should be expelled from the church absolutely, without any hope of return. Of the hope of obtaining forgiveness from God he did not pretend to deprive those people, but he insisted on it that the church ought, on no account, to be reconciled to them, lest, in so doing, its clemency might encourage a disposition to sin.—In most churches it was customary for the widows and wives to go *veiled;* not so the virgins. *Montanus* enjoined that these latter also should wear veils.—In times of persecution it had been not unusual for Christians either to redeem their lives of the heathen magistrates with *money*, or, if they deemed this not justifiable, to consult their safety by flight. Against resorting to either of those expedients *Montanus* protested in the strongest terms, and exhorted the followers of Christ not to be put to flight by the threats of their enemies, but to meet them manfully, and with disdain.

Montanus, however, is not to be considered as the first author of these various precepts, but rather as having enforced what had been originally propounded by others. For as the early Christians differed in opinion as to many other things, so likewise were they far from being agreed as to the external services that were to be rendered to the Deity; and in the second century there existed, if it may be permitted us so to speak, *two moral systems,* whereof the *more moderate* and lenient one permitted Christians to follow the ordinary course of life in as far as it was not repugnant to, or militated against the divine commands; but the *more rigid* and severe one sought not only to separate the followers of Christ from the rest of mankind in their manners, their garments, their discourse, and the whole regimen of their lives, but also to impose on them many more burthens, and to involve them in greater difficulties and dangers than were attached to the commands either of our blessed Lord or his apostles. With the exception of a very few things, the *latter* of these systems may be said to have worn almost the same aspect with that which was inculcated by *Montanus* and his associates.—The Christians, therefore, it appears, took no exceptions to the precepts of Montanus, nor could they, with the least propriety, have done so; for they not only tolerated principles similar to his in others, but even highly commended them. But this they could by no means bring themselves to bear with, that an individual should take upon him to pronounce those things to be of the *first necessity,* which were by others deemed merely good and useful; and to obtrude on the brethren his own opinions as new *commands* of the Holy Spirit supplementary to the system of morals promulgated by Christ; [p. 420.] whence it inevitably followed, that all who would not adopt them should be regarded as contemners of the Holy Spirit. All the regulations which Montanus was desirous of introducing amongst the Chrstians, are manifestly in themselves of a light and trifling kind; but, in his opinion, they were excellent and of the last importance; in fact, every way worthy of being propounded to the human race as coming directly from the Holy Spirit himself. The less, however, the dignity attached to commands which any one may be willing to have us receive as dictated by the Holy Ghost, the greater the crime of him who would impose on the brethren such minute and trifling observances.   *Tertullian*, indeed, in some places, seems to express himself as if Montanus did not consider his precepts as possessed of any virtue or efficacy in the attainment of salvation, and regarded the communications made by the Holy Spirit to mankind, through him, in the light rather of admonition and *advice* than of laws and commands; but he does this only in places where he is seeking to throw all the blame of dissension and discord on his adversaries, or endeavouring to gain patrons and friends for himself and his associates.   In others, where he assumes the character of the disputant, and undertakes the defence of Montanus, he, in no very obscure terms intimates, that those who refused to comply with the injunctions of his preceptor, or rather of the Paraclete, speaking through his preceptor, deprived themselves of very material assistance in obtaining everlasting salvation.   And that the genuine sentiments of Montanus are given us in these last-mentioned passages, is placed beyond a doubt by numerous testimonies.   By way of showing that I do not state this without some sort of foundation, I will adduce one passage, in which he evidently holds out that, by means of fasts, *expiation* might be made for that sin of our first parents which hath contaminated all their posterity; than which it is scarcely possible to devise anything more foreign to the principles and spirit of Christianity.   *Porro*, says he, (in *Lib. de Jejuniis*, cap. iii. p. 705. edit. Rigalt.) *cum et ipse jejunium mandet . . quis jam dubitabit omnium erga victum macerationum hanc fuisse rationem, qua rursus interdicto cibo et observato præcepto, primordiale jam delictum expiaretur, ut homo per eamdem materiam causæ Deo satisfaciat, per quam offenderat, id est per cibi interdictionem, atque ita salutem æmulo modo re-accenderet inedia, sicut extinxerat sagina, pro unico illicito plura licita contemnens.*   In fact, *Tertullian* is not sufficiently consistent with himself, but, as is not uncommon with persons possessing a genius above controul, inclines at this time one way, and at that time another, according to circumstances.

(3) The opinion of the age in which he lived would not allow of its being imputed to Montanus as a crime, that he assumed the character of a *prophet.* A persuasion continued to prevail amongst the Christians of those times, that the spirit of *prophecy* had not become altogether extinct, and there were then in existence divers persons who were recognized by the Christians under the character of divine legates.   What produced the separation between *Montanus* and the Catholic Christians was, that these latter felt assured within themselves, by certain arguments and reasons, that he was not *commissioned of God*, but of [p. 421.] the Devil.   This opinion of theirs was grounded chiefly on the three following considerations : 1. That his prophetic effusions were delivered in an ecstasy, that is, as I conceive, he professed himself to utter these commands of the Most High, under the influence of an irresistible impulse, without being in the least degree conscious himself of what it was he said. 2. That he introduced the Deity himself as speaking. 3. That he promulgated, as coming immediately from God, *laws* that were partly new, and nowhere to be met with in the sacred writings, and, in part, contradictory to the institutions of Christ and his apostles. Of these arguments, the two former ones might, unless I am much mistaken, be confuted and completely gotten rid of, but the last is of the

greatest weight, and can by no means be overthrown, although *Tertullian*, with a zeal that may well excite our pity, labours strongly in diminishing its force. *Novitatem igitur*, says he, (in *Lib. de Jejuniis*, cap. i. p. 701.) *objectant de cujus inlicito præscribant: aut hæresim judicandam, si humana præsumptio est, aut pseudo-prophetiam pronuntiandam, si spiritualis indictio est. - - - Certe in Evangelio illos dies jejuniis determinatos putant, in quibus ablatus est sponsus, et hos esse jam solos legitimos jejuniorum Christianorum, abolitis legalibus et propheticis vetustatibus. - - - Differenter jejunandum ex arbitrio, non ex imperio novæ disciplinæ, pro temporibus et caussis uniuscujusque. - - Sic et Apostolos observasse, &c.* To which add what is said by him in his book *de Monogamia*, cap. i. p. 673. where he clearly intimates it to be a point in dispute between the Catholies and Montanists ; *An capiat Paracletum aliquid tale docuisse, quod aut novum deputari possit adversus Catholicam traditionem, aut onerosum adversus levem sarcinam Domini.* No one, surely, let him boast what he may of being commissioned of God to promulgate a more holy and perfect system of moral discipline than was prescribed by our blessed Saviour and his apostles, unless he at the same time bring forward something that may assist our faith, or contribute towards the further purification of our minds, can have the least pretensions to be ranked amongst the number of divinely-inspired teachers or prophets. By the adversaries of Montanus, indeed, somewhat more has been built upon this argument than can, in point of fairness, be deduced from it, for it certainly by no means warranted the conclusion that Montanus was inspired of the Devil. The argument itself, however, is in no degree affected by this error, but was possessed of the same force in that age as it has at present. *Montanus*, on the other hand, most strenuously contended, that the Deity himself, or the *Paraclete*, spake through him, and was loud in his reproach of all those who refused him their support. The only true *church*, he asserted, consisted of himself and his followers ; the rest were, without exception, condemned by him as spurious. An ancient writer, cited by Eusebius (*Histor. Eccles.* lib. v. cap. xvi. p. 181), says, τὴν δὲ καθόλυ καὶ πᾶσαν τὴν ὑπὸ τὸν οὐρανὸν ἐκκλησίαν βλασφημεῖν διδάσκοντος τῦ ἀπηυθαδισμένυ πνεύματος, ὅτι μήτε τιμην μήτε πάροδον εἰς αὐτὴν τὸ ψευδοπροφητικὸν ἐλάμβανε πνεῦμα. *Universam vero, quæ per orbem terrarum sparsa est, ecclesiam, idem ille arrogantissimus spiritus maledictis appetere eos docebat, eo quod nec honorem nec aditum ullum ad ipsam pseudo-propheticus spiritus aperiret.* And beyond all doubt, this statement is entitled to the highest credit ; for unless Montanus would have been inconsistent with himself, it was necessary for him boldly to assert that all such churches as opposed him [p. 422.] were at enmity with the Holy Spirit, and alienated from God. *Themison*, in like manner, who ranks not as the last of his adherents, is charged by Apollonius, *apud Euseb.* l. c. cap. xviii. p. 185. with having, in the Catholic epistle that he wrote, spoken blasphemously of our Lord and his apostles, (*viz.* by asserting that the moral discipline which they had inculcated was imperfect,) and also of the holy church : βλασφημῆσαι δὲ εἰς τὸν κύριον καὶ τὺς Ἀποστόλυς καὶ τὴν ἁγίαν ἐκκλησίαν. Hence *Montanus* (as is also intimated by Apollonius, *apud Euseb.* l. c. cap. xviii. p. 184. and confirmed by the testimony of other authors), was led to give *Pepuza* and *Tymium*, the two little towns of Phrygia, where he and his associates resided, the title of *Jerusalem, i. e.* the only true church, with a view to gather together there men from all parts. *Tertullian* is not at all more mild or lenient than these, although, as I have above noticed, he occasionally seems desirous of paving the way towards an accommodation; for he takes every opportunity of loading all such Christians as differed from Montanus with contumely, and constantly applies to them the title *Psychici, i. e.* men destitute of the Holy Spirit; whilst he terms those who sided with that heresiarch, *Spirituales*, and the only Holy. *Penes nos autem*, (says he, in *lib. de Monogamia*, cap. i. p. 673.) *quos spiritales merito dici facit agnitio spiritalium charismatum, continentia tam religiosa est.* - - - *Sed Psychicis non recipientibus spiritum ea quæ sunt spiritus non placent.* What need I add that (in his book *de Pudicitia*, cap. xxi. p. 744.) he, without the least circumlocution, denies *any church* in opposition to *Montanus* to be the true one? *Quid nunc et ad ecclesiam et quidem tuam Psychice?* - - - *Ecclesia proprie et principaliter ipse est spiritus, in quo est Trinitas unius Divinitatis, Pater et Filius et Spiritus Sanctus;* where we may observe, by the bye, the grounds on which Montanus and his followers came to be charged with *Sabellianism.* For Tertullian speaks as if he believed all the three persons of the divine nature to be only that *one* which animated Montanus. *Et ideo ecclesia quidem delicta condonabit, sed ecclesia spiritus (i. e.* of Montanus), *per spiritalem hominem, non ecclesia numerus episcoporum.*—From what we have thus adduced it is manifest, that instead of the Catholic Christians expelling Montanus from the church, the separation rather originated with him, and that he withdrew himself from a church that he could not consider as the true spouse of Christ. And, indeed, the Montanists themselves confessed that the origin of the division was not to be imputed to the Catholic Christians, but that they themselves first seceded, refusing any longer to hold communion with what Tertullian terms *Psychica et carnalis ecclesia.* Epiphanius *Hæres.* xlviii. cap. xii. p. 413. λέγυσι διὰ χαρίσματα ἀφεσάναι τῆς ἰκκλησίας. *Jactant se ob cœlestia dona (i. e.* the Prophecies of Montanus which the Catholic Christians rejected) *ab ecclesia discessisse.* And the same author twice recognises this as a true representation of the case in the introduction to his history of this sect, remarking, in cap. i. p. 402, 403, that the Montanists separated themselves (ἀπέσχισαν δὲ ἑαυτὰς), from the church; and a little while after that ἐξέθησαν ἐκ τῶν ἁγίων, [p. 423.] they withdrew themselves from the fold of the saints.—All sort of communion being renounced, and war publicly declared by *Montanus* against the church, the *bishops* of Asia retaliated by disclaiming, in solemn convocation, all further connection with a man, whose hostility to the church was, by his own declaration, thus placed beyond a question. And to what other conclusion, I pray, could this affair have led? Between a man who, professing himself to be a legate of the Most High, declares war against all such as may venture to call in question his commission, and those who not only call in question such his commission, but also think themselves justified in regarding that man as a false prophet, and one of the agents of the devil, what sort of communion, either of offices or religion, can, for a moment, possibly be maintained?—I have entered the more fully into this subject for the purpose of showing what a wrong estimate, respecting the schism of Montanus, has been formed by such of the learned as attribute the whole blame of discord and division, on this occasion, to the Catholic Christians. That the conduct of these latter was in no degree reprehensible, is what I do not take upon me to assert; but this much, certainly, is apparent, that *Montanus* originated the quarrel, and that the Catholic Christians had abundant cause for condemning a man who had not only imbibed the most pernicious opinions, but had also been the author of a schism or separation in the church.

(4) At the *time* when Montanus prophesied, namely, under the reign of the emperor *Marcus Aurelius* the philosopher, the affairs of the Christians were everywhere, as we have above shown, involved in the utmost *peril*. It became, therefore, a matter of the very first importance to them to be strictly on their guard, lest, in anything which they might say, teach, or do, they might lay themselves open to misrepresentation, or furnish the Romans with any pretext for accusation or complaint. But that imprudent, or rather insane man, *Montanus*, predicted, without reserve, a variety of things in the highest degree obnoxious to the Romans; such, for instance, as the *overthrow* of their city and empire; the destruction that awaited the world; wars, plagues, and calamities of divers kinds, that might speedily be expected, as well as the tremendous advent of *Antichrist;* concerning which things, whoever dared to utter any prophecies, were always considered by the Romans as enemies to the state, and consequently made to undergo capital punishment. *Tertullian*, in his apology for Montanus, a work that unfortunately has perished, reduces the whole matter in dispute between his master and other Christians under *two* general heads, namely, "second *marriages*," and "the future *judgment*." His words are preserved in the ancient work edited by J. Sirmond, Paris, 1645, 8vo. that goes under the title of *Prædestinatus*, lib. i. cap. xxv. p. 30. *Hoc solum discrepamus, quod secundas nuptias non recipimus, et prophetiam Montani de futuro judicio non recusamus.* It is to be observed that *Tertullian* here makes light of the controversy between Montanus and the church, as was customary with him whenever he conceived that it might tend to promote his purpose; but on this we shall not stay at present to make any remark. All that we would wish to impress on the reader's attention is, that it is clear from these words that *Montanus* had, amongst other things, predicted somewhat respecting a future judgment, and that this prophecy of his was held most sacred, and had more than ordinary weight attached to it by his followers; but that it was marked with the most decided disapprobation by the Catholic Christians. It would be idle in any one to pretend to refer this prediction to the last *general* judgment of the world and the human race; for as to this there was the most perfect accordance between Montanus and all other Christians. Indeed, it was impossible that the Christians should make it a matter of accusation against Montanus, that he predicted the near approach of the last judgment: for it was at that time a point of common belief with the whole church, that the final consummation [p. 424.] of all things was at hand. We are bound to conclude, therefore, that Montanus predicted the approach of some *particular judgment*, (*i. e.* some calamities and evils not far remote) of which the Christians knew that they could not join with him in prophesying, without involving themselves in the utmost peril. But what

else could this be than the judgment that awaited the Roman empire? **The** temerity of this man, unless I am altogether deceived, was such, that he announced the most signal punishments as about to fall on the Romans, the enemies of the Christian faith, and predicted, at no very distant period, the final overthrow of the whole empire.—That other Christians, as to this, entertained a belief similar to his, namely, that our blessed Saviour would speedily avenge the blood of his slaughtered servants on the Romans, and overturn their government, is what I very well know. But of this their belief they made a secret, referring it to the *Disciplina Arcani,* or that kind of knowledge which it was deemed expedient to cherish in silence, and entrusted only to a few of approved stability and faith, inasmuch as they were well assured, that any disclosure or promulgation of it could not be made without exposing their fortunes to the utmost jeopardy and hazard. And in this place I will content myself with referring merely to those prophecies respecting the dreadful calamities which awaited the Roman empire, that are set down as received from the mouths of the Christians by the author of *Philopatris* (a work commonly ascribed to Lucian :) vid. *Luciani Opera,* tom. iii. p. 613. et seq. edit. Reizian. Hence we are furnished with an easy interpretation of the words of an ancient writer, cited by Eusebius, *Hist. Eccles.* lib. v. cap. xvi. p. 180, and of which the learned have hitherto confessed themselves utterly unable to elicit the meaning. He says that *Montanus* foretold things that were to come, παρὰ τὸ κατὰ παράδοσιν καὶ κατὰ διαδοχὴν ἄνωθεν τῆς ἐκκλησίας, ἔθος, *præter morem atque institutum Ecclesiæ a majoribus traditum et continua deinceps successione propagatum;* which is as much as to say, that it was the ancient and invariable *usage* of the church, cautiously to abstain from divulging or making public mention of any tenets or prophecies that might tend to excite animosity against the Christians, or bring them into danger; such, for instance, as those which respected the coming of Antichrist, the overthrow of the Roman empire, or any other impending evils or calamities. But *Montanus* broke through this custom, and proclaimed to the world what had never before been communicated to any, except confidential ears. And in this most hazardous line of conduct, the females who had espoused the cause of Montanus should seem to have been by no means backward in following the example of their master; for *Maximilla* predicted πολέμους καὶ ἀκαταστασίας, "*wars and tumults,*" as awaiting the Roman empire, (Euseb. l. c. p. 182,) and that, after her death, no more prophetesses would arise, but people might look for συντέλεια τῆ αἰῶνος, "*the consummation of all things.*" These prophecies, supposing that nothing else offensive or objectionable had been brought forward by Montanus and his associates, must surely of themselves have justified all such Christians as had the welfare of the church at heart, in excluding these bold and incautious men from their society. The sect of the Montanists, as they themselves boast, and the ancient fathers do not pretend to deny, abounded in *martyrs.* It should seem, however, not at all improbable, that most of these might have fallen martyrs to their own *imprudence* and *temerity* rather than in the cause of Christ, and been put to death by the Roman magistrates as conspirators against the commonwealth.

LXVIII. **Praxeas.** Amongst the adversaries of [p. 425.] Montanus, none held a more distinguished place than *Praxeas*, a man of no mean reputation in the church, inasmuch as he had, on an occasion that involved his life in the utmost peril, manfully avowed his faith in Christ before a heathen tribunal, and on the same account undergone an imprisonment of no inconsiderable duration.(¹) Having at a subsequent period, however, been led to engage zealously in the task of combating the erroneous doctrines of others, he unfortunately fell into an *error* himself respecting the Divine Nature and the Saviour of the human race, not at all less grievous than those with which he had undertaken to contend; for, by means of various arguments supported by passages drawn from the holy scriptures, he endeavoured to do away *all distinction* between the Father, the Son, and the Holy Spirit; and maintained that it was not some one divine Person, but the *Father*, the sole Creator of all things, that united himself with human nature in the person of Christ. Hence his followers came to be termed *Monarchians* and *Patripassians*.(²) Being detected in this error, and publicly accused thereof at Rome, he put on the appearance of concession, and in a recantation, which he wrote and published, professed his entire acquiescence in the catholic sentiments respecting the Divine Nature. Upon passing over afterwards into Africa, however, he again stood forth the avowed patron of the doctrine which he had abjured at Rome, and sought and obtained many adherents from amongst the people. It does not, however, appear that he became the parent of a particular sect.

(1) For whatever can with any degree of certainty be offered in the way of history respecting *Praxeas*, we are of necessity indebted wholly to the treatise written in confutation of his doctrine by *Tertullian*, a work by no means deficient either in learning or address, but obscure in the extreme, and vehement beyond all measure; a work, in fact, written by a man who was an enemy not only to the Praxean doctrine, but also to the author of that doctrine, inasmuch as he had been the chief instrument in prevailing on the bishop of Rome, who had at first lent a favourable ear to Montanus and his prophecies, and whom learned men conceive to have been *Victor*, to change sides and go over to his adversaries. This offence against his master kindled such wrath in the bosom of *Tertullian*, that he sets no bounds whatever to his reprehension, and occasionally breaks out into an abusive strain altogether unbecoming the Christian character.—In contemplating the nature of Praxeas's *error*, I have been led to *suspect*, and, I think, not without reason, that such error might have had its origin in his hostility to Montanus. *Montanus*, as appears from Tertullian, had, in his oracles,

treated of the dogma of the existence of three persons in the divine nature, and studiously inculcated a true and real distinction between the Father, the Son, and the Holy Spirit. Vid. Tertullian *contra Praxeam*, c. xiii. p. 644. *Nos*, says he, *maxime Paracleti, non hominum discipuli, duos quidem definimus, Patrem et Filium, et jam tres cum Spirito Sancto, secundum rationem œconomiæ, quæ facit numerum.* And in the same book, cap. ii. p. 635. Tertullian avows himself, by means of the Paraclete, (*i. e.* Montanus,) whom he terms *deductor omnis verita-* [p. 426.] *tis*, to have been better instructed in the dogma respecting God the Father, the Son, and the Holy Spirit; that is, he had received from the mouth of the Paraclete a fuller and clearer knowledge of that dogma. *Praxeas*, then, the decided opponent of Montanus as to most other things, being in all probability determined to have nothing whatever in common with such a man, and expecting, perhaps, that it might place his adversary in a still more invidious light, came, as I suspect, to the resolution of resisting him on this ground also, and, in opposition to the dogma of Montanus, recognizing a Trinity of Persons in the Godhead, sent forth his own dogma asserting the *absolute individuality of the Deity.* An infinity of examples might be adduced of men whom the very love of truth itself has plunged into error.

(2) Tertullian's book against Praxeas is unquestionably of a very sufficient length, but, at the same time, it is not so explicit as to bring us thoroughly acquainted with the opinions of the man whom it is its object to confute. Of this, indeed, it leaves us in no doubt, that *Praxeas* denied a *distinction* of persons in the Divine Nature, we mean, any *real* distinction between the Father, the Son, and the Holy Spirit, and contended for what is termed by Tertullian the *Monarchy* of God. In fact, it should seem that he considered those who recognized any *real* distinction between the Father, the Son, and the Holy Spirit, as maintaining the existence of *three* Gods. After what manner, however, Praxeas expounded those passages of Scripture which relate to the Son and the Holy Spirit, and contrived to make them accord with his tenets, is far from being equally perspicuous. From certain passages in Tertullian's work, it should seem to have been the opinion of this heresiarch that, by the terms Father, Son, and Holy Spirit, three *modes* of existence, as well as agency of the Divine Nature, were indicated, and that the Deity, when existing and operating in *Christ*, after a new and unaccustomed manner, assumed the title of Son, but that, when residing and acting in holy and pious persons, it was his will to be denominated the *Holy Spirit.* *Post tempus*, says Tertullian, when speaking the sentiments of his adversary, cap. ii. p. 634. *pater natus et pater passus ; ipse Deus, Dominus omnipotens, Jesus Christus prædicatur.* And shortly after, cap. iii. p. 635. *Unicum Deum non alias putat credendum, quam si ipsum, eumdemque et Patrem et Filium et Spiritum Sanctum dicat. . . . . Numerum et dispositionem Trinitatis divisionem præsumunt Trinitatis. . . . Itaque duos et tres jam jactitant a nobis prædicari, se vero unius Dei cultores præsumunt, quasi non et unitas irrationaliter collecta, hæresim faciat, et Trinitas rationaliter expensa veritatem constituat. Monarchiam* (inquiunt) *tenemus*, cap. v. p. 637.—But to pass on to more explicit proofs, in chap. x. p. 680. Tertullian thus expresses the sentiments of the Monarchians : *Neque Pater idem et Filius ut sint ambo unus et utrumque alter, quod*

vanissimi isti Monarchiani volunt. Ipse se, inquiunt, Filium sibi fecit. Indeed, that there was nothing repugnant or absurd in this opinion, they pretended to demonstrate by the example of a virgin's bringing forth without having known man. *Ergo, inquiunt, difficile non fuit Deo, ipsum se et Patrum et Filium facere, adversus traditam formam rebus humanis. Nam et sterilem parere contra naturam difficile Deo non fuit, sicut nec virginem.* Now these things, unless I am altogether deceived, can be understood after no other manner than this: [p. 427.] The Deity, who is, in the strictest sense of the word, *One*, put on in some sort a different form, and assumed a different mode of existing and acting, when, joining himself to Christ, he took the name of a Son, and, under that character, conveyed instruction to the human race. *Deus fecit se sibi Filium;* for, being possessed of infinite power, he can easily vary his essence at pleasure. The very passages of the New Testament, moreover, by which Praxeas endeavoured to uphold his dogmas, seem to demonstrate that it ought to be expounded in the way that I have pointed out. *Sed*, says Tertullian, cap. xx. p. 651, *argumentationibus eorum adhuc retundendis opera præbenda est. . . . . Nam sicut in veteribus nihil aliud tenent quam, ego Deus, et alius præter me non est, ita in Evangelio responsionem Domini ad Philippum tuentur; ego et Pater unum sumus; et, qui me viderit, videt et Patrem; et ego in Patre et Pater in me. His tribus capitulis totum instrumentum utriusque testamenti volunt cedere;* which words, whoever shall adduce, by way of doing away all distinction between the Father and the Son, must necessarily hold that there is no difference whatever between the Father and the Son, except the mode or form of existing and acting.

But this interpretation of the Praxean dogma is *opposed* by certain other passages in Tertullian, wherein he expressly intimates it to have been the opinion of his adversary, that the title of *Son*, as given to Christ, ought not to be considered as the name of the Deity residing in Christ, but of his *human nature;* that the Deity himself, who is termed the Father, united to himself the Man Christ; and that this same *Man* was denominated the *Son of God*, in consequence of his having been begotten by the Deity of the Virgin Mary; a way of thinking not at all to be reconciled with his having taught, that what was divine in Christ was a certain form or mode of the Divine Nature to which the Deity gave the title of *Son*, by way of distinguishing it from that other form or mode which is termed *the Father*. Let us hear Tertullian himself, cap. xxvii. p. 659, *undique obducti distinctione Patris et Filii* (that is, borne down and overwhelmed by the words of the sacred volume, in which express distinction is made between the Father and the Son) *quam, manente conjunctione, disponimus ut solis et radii, et fontis et fluvii, per individuum tamen numerum duorum et trium; aliter eam ad suam nihilominus sententiam interpretari conantur ut æque in una persona utrumque distinguant, Patrem et Filium, dicentes Filium carnem esse, id est, Hominem, id est, Jesum; Patrem autem Spiritum,* (meaning the soul, if I mistake not,) *id est, Deum, id est, Christum. Et qui unum eumdemque contendunt Patrem et Filium, jam incipiunt dividere illos potius quam unare. Si enim alius est Jesus, alius Christus, alius erit Filius, alius Pater, quia Filius Jesus, et Pater Christus. Talem Monarchiam apud Valentinum fortassis didicerunt, duos facere Jesum et Christum.* Agreeably to this opinion, Praxeas maintained

Patrem passum esse in Christo, or, as he preferred expressing it, *compassum esse cum Filio,* or, with the Man Jesus. Tertullian, cap. xxix. p. 662. observes, [p. 428.] *Ergo nec compassus est Pater Filio; sic enim directam blasphemiam in Patrem vereti, diminui eam hoc modo sperant, concedentes jam Patrem et Filium duos esse; si Filius quidem patitur, Pater vero compatitur. Stulti et in hoc. Quid est enim compati quam cum alio pati? . . . Times dicere passibilem quem dicis compassibilem.*—From which passage, by-the-bye, it is apparent how the followers of Praxeas came to be termed *Patripassians,* as also, that, by this appellation, no sort of injury was done them, as certain of the learned have supposed. Those who deny that the title of *Patripassians* could with propriety be assigned to them, do so under the impression that these people believed the Father, Son, and Holy Spirit to be three *forms* or *modes* of the divine nature, which, it is plain, must be at the least very uncertain, from what we have above remarked. In addition, then, to those remarks, if this title be taken into the account, I think not a doubt can well be entertained, but that the *latter* of the two expositions above given of the Praxean dogma must be the right one.—We may, therefore, consider Praxeas as having maintained, I. That the Deity is, in the strictest sense, an *individual* Being, altogether uncompounded and *indivisible.* II. That this Being is, in holy writ, termed the Father. III. That this same individual Being *formed for himself a son* in the Man Jesus. IV. That he coalesced, in one Person, with such Man, his Son. V. That when this Man, his Son, suffered, he, the *Father, suffered with him.* VI. That whenever our Saviour, therefore, is termed the *Son of God,* this title must be considered as applying merely to his *human nature.*—What the opinion of Praxeas was respecting the *Holy Spirit,* is no where expressly pointed out by Tertullian. It may readily, however, be conceived, from the nature of his discipline, that he must have regarded it as a sort of *ray* or *virtue* of the Father, *i. e.* the Deity. Whether Tertullian, moreover, who, as we have seen, gives two different expositions of the Praxean dogma, did not at the first sufficiently comprehend its nature and force, and was too precipitate in applying to the Divine Nature the saying of the Monarchians, *Deus ipse se sibi Filium fecit;* or whether the Monarchians, upon finding themselves driven, as it were, into a corner by the multitude of passages in holy writ, in which a clear distinction is made between the Father and the Son, forsook their former opinion, and had recourse to that other which acquired for them the denomination of Patripassians, must of necessity be left undetermined.

But now *another question* suggests itself. Since it is certain that Praxeas did not consider the *eternal Son of God,* or any mode of the Divine Nature under the name of a Son, to have been resident in the Man Christ, but believed the *whole Father,* or the Deity, to have taken up his abode in the Son of God, that is, in the *Man* formed by God, in *what way* are we to understand what he says of the association of the Father with the Man Jesus? Did he, by the title of the Father, mean to be understood as designating the very *Person* of the Father or Deity, or merely a certain *power* or efficiency, as some term it, of God the Father? Almost every one leans to the *former* opinion, and, I think, not without reason, if any faith is to be placed in Tertullian, who is the only author from whom any information, as to this dogma of Praxeas, is to be derived in the present day;

for, in a variety of passages, this writer represents his adversary as having maintained that the *Father* was *born*, and *suffered* on the cross; nay, he ad- [p. 429.]
duces the Monarchians themselves as in a certain degree ackowledging this, inasmuch as they pronounced the Father to have suffered together with the Son;
an idea which, if I am possessed of the least penetration, the followers of
Praxeas could never have entertained, had they imagined that it was merely a
certain *power* or virtue of the Father that was present in the Son. For how
could a certain divine *power* or efficiency, communicated to the Son for a time,
have *suffered* and been crucified with him?—Mich. Le *Quien*, however, the
learned editor of Damascene's works, would rather have us believe *Praxeam
censuisse Dominum Jesum sola Deitatis efficientia imbutum fuisse, non autem esse
personam Patris, quæ in Deitate et humanitate substitisset ut Pater proprie passus
et crucifixus diceretur.* Adnot. ad Damascen. *Lib. de Hæresibus,* tom. i. p. 90.
In support of this interpretation, however, the learned writer adduces nothing
but that one passage of Tertullian, cap. xxvii. p. 659, just above cited, in which
he represents the Monarchians as maintaining *Patrem esse spiritum Jesu, id est,
Deum.* But how, from this passage, anything like that which he takes to be the
true exposition of the Praxean dogma is to be supported, I must confess myself
utterly at a loss to comprehend. The learned Pet. *Wesseling,* therefore, found
but little difficulty in overthrowing this new interpretation of the Monarchian
tenets, and upholding the ancient one by numerous citations from Tertullian.
See his *Probabilia,* cap. xxvi. p. 223, et seq. Franeq. 1731, 8vo.—My own sentiments, as to this matter, are already given. If Tertullian is deserving of attention, the dogma of the Monarchians admits of no other interpretation than what
has commonly been given to it, and which the reader will find specified above.
I would be far, however, from dissembling, that it may be a matter of some
doubt how far Tertullian, whose treatise against Praxeas was obviously the production of a mind hostile, perturbed, and boiling with indignation, is to be relied
upon for having given us an ingenuous, ample, and faithful exposition of the
opinions of his adversary.—By accident, I met with a notable passage in Justin
Martyr, *Dial. cum Tryphone,* p. 371, 372, edit. Jebbian. in which he observes, that
amongst the Christians of his time there were some who maintained, that the word
of God, or the Son, was merely a certain *power* or *virtue* of the Father, and which
could in no wise be separated from the Father; as the light of the sun upon the earth
is not to be disunited from that which shines in the heavens; that such divine
virtue had manifested itself in many different ways, and hence had acquired a
variety of names, being sometimes termed an Angel, sometimes a Glory, at
other times a man, and, at others the Word; that God emitted this *virtue* at his
will, and again at his will recalled it: γινώσκω τινὰς φάσκειν τὴν δύναμιν τὴν
παρὰ τῦ πατρὸς τῶν ὅλων φανεῖσαν - - - - ἄγγελον καλεῖσθαι ἐν τῇ πρὸς ἀνθρώπυς
πρόσδω. *Scio esse qui dicant virtutem a Patre rerum ominum provenientem, An-
gelum vocari cum ad homines progreditur : δόξαν δὲ ἐπειδὴ ἐν φαντασίᾳ φαίνεται.
Gloriam vero, cum in visione quadam exhibetur. ἄνδρα δὲ ποτὲ καὶ ἄνθρωπον
καλεῖσθαι ἐπειδὴ ἐν μορφαῖς τοιαύταις φαίνεται. Virum autem et hominem no-
minari quando in formis ejusmodi* (namely, in the form of a man, or a human
being) *conspicitur. καὶ λόγον καλῦσιν, ἐπειδὰ καὶ τὰς τῦ πατρὸς ὁμιλίας φέρει*

[p. 430.] τοῖς ἀνθρώποις. *Verbum appellari eam, quod patris sermones ad homines perferat.* ἀχώρισον τῦ πατρὸς ταύτην τὴν δύναμιν ὑπάρχειν, ὄντερ πρότον τὸ τῦ ἡλίυ φῶς ἐπὶ γῆς ἔιναι ἀχώρισον ὄντος τῦ ἡλίυ ἐν τῶ ὄρανῶ. *Virtutem autem illam a patre nullo modo disjungi posse, quemadmodum solis lux in terris a sole qui in cœlo est segregari nequit.* Ὁ πατὴρ, ὅταν Βέλνται, δύναμιν αὐτῦ προπιδᾶν ποιῖι. καὶ ὅταν Βέλνται, πάλιν ἀναςέλλει ἐις ἑαυτὸν. *Pater cum vult, efficit ut hæc ejus virtus prosiliat, et cum vult, eamdem ad seipsum retrahit.* Now, those who taught a doctrine like this, must necessarily have denied all real distinction of *persons* in the divine nature, and believed the divine nature of Christ to have been merely a *virtue* or *ray* sent forth for a while from the eternal light of the Father. To this description of Christians it is not impossible that *Praxeas* might belong, and that having, with a view in some measure to disguise his tenets, expounded them differently at different times, *Tertullian* was prevented from attaining to anything like an exact or precise knowledge of them.

LXIX. **Theodotus and Artemon.** Just about the same period, or some short time before, the Catholic doctrine respecting Christ and the existence of three persons in the divine nature was assailed after a different manner by one *Theodotus,* who had passed over to Rome from Constantinople, and practised the art of a tanner, but was, notwithstanding, a man of no mean proficiency in letters.(') This heresiarch denied altogether the *divinity* of Christ, refusing to acknowledge in him any other kind of personal excellence than that of his corporeal frame having been divinely begotten.(²) The same doctrine is said to have been maintained at Rome, either some short time before, or else within a little while after Theodotus, by one *Artemas* or *Artemon,* from whom the *Artemonites* took their denomination.(³) Towards the close of the century *Theodotus* was condemned by the Roman bishop *Victor;* and it should seem not unlikely that *Artemon* and his disciples were excommunicated by the same prelate.—The notices that have reached us respecting these sects, both of which should seem to have quickly disappeared, are but scanty. The circumstance of all others most deserving of attention in respect to them is, that the Theodotians and Artemonites are said to have set a great value on *philosophy* and *geometry,* indeed more than well comported with a proper respect for religion and the sacred writings.(⁴) In truth, the principal fruit derived from the introduction of a taste for the Grecian philosophy amongst the Christians was, that by the application of its precepts to the *mysteries* of religion birth was given to a variety of opinions and disputes respecting the manner in which these latter ought to be understood.

(1) Respecting Theodotus and Artemon, there is a long quotation given by Eusebius in his *Ecclesiastical History*, lib. v. cap. xxviii. from an ancient writer whose name is not mentioned. But neither from this, nor from Epiphanius, nor Theodoret, nor any other of the ancient hæresiologists, can we obtain a [p. 431.] full and satisfactory account of these men and their opinions.

(2) *Theodotus*, as is related much at large by Epiphanius, *Hæres.* liv. cap. i. ii. iii. p. 464, et seq. and in a shorter way by Tertullian, Augustine, and Philaster, being called in question at Constantinople on account of his religion, *abjured* his faith in Christ, and when he was sharply reproached with this by the Christians of Rome, to which city he had fled for refuge, he, by the excuse which he offered, plunged still deeper into sin. For he denied himself to have committed any offence at all against God, inasmuch as *Christ*, whom he had denied, was nothing more than a *mere man*. That this account should have been invented, there is no reason whatever for believing. We are not, however, furnished by it with anything like a perspicuous or satisfactory view of this heresiarch's sentiments respecting Christ; nor are the ancient writers agreed in their exposition of his tenets on this subject. *Epiphanius* states him to have maintained, that Jesus was begotten according to the same law by which all other mortals are produced, namely, of the seed of man. But the ancient author of the *Catalogue of Heretics*, annexed to Tertullian's prescriptions, and with whom Theodoret agrees, says, that *Theodotus* did indeed regard Christ as a mere man, but, then, as a man that had been *begotten* of a virgin *by the Holy Spirit*. And to this testimony learned men are disposed to give more credit than to Epiphanius, a writer of no great weight, and far from being correct in his account of heretical opinions. But if the inference be just, to which learned men have been led by the ancient author of the *Little Labyrinth*, a work written in opposition to the Theodotians and Artemonites, and from which a citation is given by Eusebius, *Hist. Eccles.* lib. v. cap. 28, namely, that the doctrine of Artemon was the same with that of Theodotus, the correctness of even this last statement will admit of being called in question. For not to notice that there are not wanting those who conceive the opinions of Artemon to have corresponded with those of Paul of Samosata or Arius, we are told by *Gennadius*, of Marseilles, *de Dogmat. Ecclesiast.* cap. iii. p. 4. edit. Elmenhorst. that Artemon held, *Christum divinitatis initium nascendo accepisse*. He did not, therefore, deny Christ to be God and man, but conceived him to have been styled God in consequence of God's having associated himself with the man Christ from the very commencement of his existence; which opinion more nearly corresponds with that which, as we have above shown, was entertained by *Praxeas*, than with that which is commonly attributed to Theodotus. Artemon's opinion, we mean, was, that a certain divine *power*, not a person, united itself to the man Christ, who was born of a virgin, and that, in consequence of this association of the divinity with the human nature of Christ, he who was a *man* was, in the sacred writings, also termed *God*, and might be styled God. But, to confess the truth, it appears to me to be much less certain than is commonly imagined, that *Theodotus* and *Artemon* entertained one and the same opinion respecting Christ. *Theodoret* clearly makes a distinction between the Theodotians and the Artemonites; and although the

author of the *Little Labyrinth*, as quoted by Eusebius, associates them together in his work, and directs his arguments against them jointly, it is yet far from [p. 432.] being clear that there were no points of dissension between them. This much, certainly, they had in common, that they denied all *real distinction* of persons in the Godhead, and consequently would not admit that a divine *person* had united himself with *Christ*. Wherefore, they might well be encountered in one and the same work, and with one and the same set of arguments. But a community of sentiments, as to these particulars, by no means rendered it impossible that they should differ in their opinions respecting Christ.

(3) Whether it was *Theodotus* or *Artemon* that first disturbed the church by the propagation of an erroneous doctrine, is one of those subjects on which the learned are divided, with scarcely any preponderance of argument on either side. The reader, if he please, may pass over a question so uncertain and minute; but should any one wish to know and weigh the arguments that are adduced on either side, he may have recourse to *Wesseling*, who, in his *Probabilia*, cap. xxi. p. 172–180, having diligently pondered the whole of them, coincides with those who consider *Theodotus* as having preceded *Artemon*.

(4) With regard to this, there is given us by Eusebius, *Histor. Eccles.* lib. v. cap. xxviii. p. 197, et seq. a passage from an ancient writer, which is well deserving of attention, although the reprehension it conveys may be thought, perhaps, somewhat too severe.

LXX. **Hermogenes.** A station in point of time somewhat prior to these last-mentioned corrupters of the Catholic doctrine respecting the divine nature and the Saviour of the human race, appears to belong to *Hermogenes,* a painter by profession, but at the same time a man of subtile genius, and a *philosopher,* whom we find denounced by *Tertullian* as a heretic of the first class, although he seems never to have become the parent of any particular sect, but to have passed the whole of his days in undisturbed communion with the church.(') Hermogenes was a corrupter of the catholic doctrine respecting the *origin* of the world. For since he considered *matter* as the source or fountain of all evil, he felt it incumbent on him to deny that the Deity had created matter out of nothing.—This involved him in the necessity of maintaining, that the matter of which God formed the world was *eternal,* although subject to his power.(²) Under the denomination of the world, he included not only corporeal substances but *mind* and *spirit,* which he considered as having been in like manner produced by the Deity from vicious and eternal matter.(³) As to any other points of Christian belief, he appears to have attempted no innovation whatever.(⁴)

(1) Amongst the works of *Tertullian* that are extant, there is a vehement philippic of his against Hermogenes, possessing some degree of merit, it is true, in point of ingenuity and eloquence, but written in a style at once difficult and obscure. In this work, Tertullian encounters merely the *tenets* of Hermogenes respecting *matter* and the origin of the *world.* The opinion of the latter concerning the nature of the *soul*, had been attacked by him in another book, now lost, which he notices in his Treatise *de Anima*, cap. i. as intituled *de Censu Animæ.* In this contention with Hermogenes, *Tertullian* is remarkably *abusive*, although he does not pretend to deny that his adversary was a [p. 433.] man of genius, eloquence, and sound understanding as to the leading principles and tenets of the Christian religion; which will appear the more surprising to those who are aware that the Christians, in the age of which we are treating, were accustomed to deal more mildly with those who considered *matter* as having existed with the Deity from all eternity, and the world as having been compounded thereof. But it was not so much his errors as his *morals*, which were quite in opposition to the discipline of Montanus, that rendered Hermogenes hateful in the eyes of Tertullian, who, as every one knows, was an ardent *Montanist.* For he had often times been married, a thing held impious by Montanus, and, in the exercise of his profession, had disregarded the rigid rules laid down by this preceptor. *Præterea*, says Tertullian, cap. i. p. 265, *pingit illicite, nubit assidue; legem Dei in libidinem defendit, in artem contemnit. . . . totus adulter et prædicationis et carnis. Siquidem et nubentium contagio foetet.*

(2) Hermogenes was not led to deny that matter had been created out of nothing by the all-powerful will of the Deity, in consequence of a belief that the thing was altogether *impossible*, but from his taking it for granted that *matter* was the sole fountain of every thing vicious and *evil*.—For he is brought forward by *Tertullian*, at the commencement of his book, as arguing after the following manner: If God made matter, he made it either of himself, or out of nothing. Either of these suppositions is absurd. If God made matter of himself, he could not have been a simple, indivisible, immutable being.—If he created it out of nothing, he could not have been good, or superlatively excellent. For matter is intrinsically vicious and corrupt. *Proinde*, (we give Tertullian's very words,) *ex nihilo non potuisse eum facere*, (i. e. matter,) *sic contendit, bonum et optimum definiens dominum, qui bona atque optima tam velit facere quam sit.* Hisconclusion, therefore, was, that no *alternative* was left us but to believe, that matter was *coëral* with the Deity, having existed together with him from all eternity. From this mode of reasoning, it is manifest that Hermogenes considered the production of matter as, to use the language of philosophers, *physically possible*, but as every way unworthy of the Deity, and therefore *morally impossible*, and that this his opinion was founded on the persuasion, that matter was the seat and origin of every thing evil.—Since the error, then, of Hermogenes, respecting the fabrication of the world from eternal matter, proceeded entirely from this opinion respecting the origin of evil, *Tertullian* ought to have made the cause or origin of evil the chief ground of his contention with him, and to have shown that evil was derived, not from matter, but from other sources. This being once proved, the erroneous notion of Hermogenes respect-

ing the creation of the world must of necessity have fallen to the ground. But omitting every thing of this sort, Tertullian at once commences a furious attack on the dogma of his adversary respecting the eternity of matter; that is, he passes over in silence the root and principle of the error, and contents himself with attacking merely a consectary deducible from it.—To this observation, we may add another no less necessary to the right understanding of the doctrine of Hermogenes. Although he considered matter as coëval with the Deity, he nevertheless maintained that the Deity had from all eternity *ruled* over it, and held it in subjection, a circumstance which renders his opinion much more [p. 434.] tolerable than that of certain others, who either assigned to matter, which they believed to be eternal, a peculiar ruler distinct from the Deity, or else contended that, before the foundation of the world, the Deity and matter had no connection whatever.—That the opinion of Hermogenes was really such as I here state it to have been, is placed out of all dispute by one of the arguments which he brings forward in proof of the eternity of matter. The *argument* I allude to is this: God hath been Lord from all eternity ; therefore, from all eternity there must have existed matter subject to his dominion. But let us hear the exposition which *Tertullian* himself gives us of this argument, cap. iii. p. 866 : *Adjicit et aliud. Deum semper Deum etiam Dominum fuisse, numquam non Deum. Nullo porro modo potuisse illum semper Dominum haberi, sicut et semper Deum, si non fuisset aliquid retro semper, cujus semper Dominus haberetur : fuisse itaque materiam semper Deo Domino.*

(3) It is certain, from what is said by Tertullian in his book *de Anima*, cap. i. and other testimonies, that Hermogenes did not attribute a more noble origin to men's *souls* than to their bodies. No doubt, he might conceive that matter of a more *subtile* kind was used by the Deity in the formation of souls, but still he did not deny them to have been composed of matter. And to me the *reason* easily suggests itself, why Hermogenes should have thought thus. Perceiving that souls were subject to depraved propensities and appetites, and, at the same time, being fully persuaded that every thing evil and vicious was generated of matter, and had its residence in matter, he could *not* but conclude that the souls of men, no less than their bodies, were framed or composed of matter. Whether he entertained the same opinion respecting the good *angels*, is not to be known at this day. But that he conceived the *evil angels*, together with their leader or chief, to have been formed out of matter, and that they would, at a future day, again be resolved into matter, is recorded by Theodoret, *Fabular. Hæret.* lib. 1. cap. xix. p. 207. tom. iv. opp. In what way he contrived to reconcile these principles with the tenets of the Christians at large, respecting the *immortality of the soul,* the angels, and other things, it might possibly be in our power to ascertain, were we in possession of the book written against him by Tertullian, *de Censu Animæ.*

(4) *Tertullian,* although he was most intimately acquainted with the tenets of Hermogenes, and regarded him with an implacable hatred, yet never once accuses him of entertaining any other errors than those above noticed respecting *matter,* the *creation* of the world, and the nature of *souls.* What is of still greater importance, this vehement writer acknowledges, in express terms, that

the dogma of his adversary respecting *Christ*, the corner-stone of all religion, was sound and orthodox. *Christum*, says he, cap. i. p. 265, *Dominum non alium, videtur aliter cognoscere* (that is, he appears to entertain a belief respecting Christ similar to that of other Christians) *alium tamen facit, quem aliter cognoscit; (i. e.* what he professes respecting Christ, however, in words, he enervates and renders of no avail by his opinions,) *immo totum quod est Deus aufert, nolens illum ex nihilo universa fecisse. A Christianis enim conversus ad philosophos,* . . . . *sumpsit a stoicis materiam cum Domino ponere, quæ ipsa semper fuerit, neque nata, neque facta, nec initium habens omnino, nec finem, ex qua Dominus omnia postea fecerit.* These charges, in fact, although most invidiously [p. 435.] brought forward, instead of criminating the person against whom they are adduced, serve clearly to demonstrate his innocence. And I, therefore, cannot agree with those of the learned who suppose that *Hermogenes*, whom *Clement* of Alexandria, in his *Eclogæ Propheticæ*, § lvi. p. 1002, reports to have taught that Christ deposited his body in the sun, was one and the same with the painter of whom we have been treating, who contended for the eternity of matter, although, in support of this their opinion, they may urge the authority of Theodoret. That *Hermogenes* also, against whom *Theophilus* of Antioch, and *Origen*, are stated by Theodoret to have written, I take to have been a different man from him to whom our attention has been directed. Possibly amongst the Valentinians, or some others of the Gnostics, there might have been a man of this name that attained to some degree of celebrity, in consequence of his broaching certain new opinions.

LXXI. **Controversy respecting the Pascal observances.** In addition to these numerous and great disputes, involving the very essentials of religion, there arose towards the close of this century, between the Christians of Asia Minor and those of other parts, particularly such as were of the Roman church, a violent contention respecting a matter that related merely to the form of religion or divine worship; a thing, in itself, truly of light moment, but in the opinion of the disputants, of very great importance. The affair was this. The *Asiatic* Christians were accustomed to celebrate their passover, that is the Pascal feast which it was, at this time, usual with the Christians to observe in commemoration of the institution of the Lord's Supper and the subsequent death of the Redeemer, on the *fourteenth day* of the *first Jewish month;* that is to say, at the same time when the *Jews* ate their Pascal lamb; occasioning thereby an interruption in the fast of the great week. This custom they stated themselves to have derived from the apostles *Philip* and *John*, as well as from many other characters of the very first eminence. But the *rest of the Christians*, as well in Asia as in Europe and Africa, deemed it irreligious to terminate the fast of the great week before the day devoted to the commemoration of our Saviour's return to life, and therefore deferred the celebration of their passover, or pascal feast, until the night immediately preceding the anniversary of Christ's resurrection from the dead. And for their acting thus, the *Roman Christians*, in particular, alleged the authority of the apostles *Paul* and *Peter.*—This difference gave birth to another of still greater moment. For as the Asiatic Christians always commemorated our Lord's return to life on the *third day* after their partaking of the Pascal supper, it was a circumstance liable to occur, and the which, no doubt, frequently did occur, that they kept the anniversary of Christ's *resurrection*, which afterwards acquired, and continues still to retain the denomination of *Pascha* or *Easter*, on a different day from the first day of the week, or [p. 436.] that which is commonly termed *Sunday;* whereas the other Christians, as well those of the East as of the West, made it a rule to hold their annual celebration of our blessed Saviour's triumph over the grave on no other day than that on which it actually occurred, namely, on the *first day* of the week.(')

(1) Ancient writers, at the head of whom we may place Eusebius, *Hist. Eccles.* lib. v. cap. xxiii. are very negligent and obscure in the accounts they give us of the nature and causes of this great controversy respecting the time of keeping Easter, which had nearly been productive of a most deplorable schism. Hence the whole class of more recent authors, who have treated of the subject, and none more than those who, in estimating the force and meaning of ancient terms, have permitted themselves to be led away by modern notions, and are not over-burthened with information, as to the manners and customs of early times, have, in their explanation of it, fallen into various errors, and been by no means happy in unfolding the true grounds of the dispute.—The *common opinion* is, that the Asiatic Christians were reprehended by the rest for celebrating the anniversary of our Lord's resurrection at the same time that the Jews were accustomed to eat their passover. But this is altogether a *mistake,* and a thing with which they are never once reproached by any ancient authors. And, indeed, to be convinced how little foundation there could be for such an idea, we need only ask ourselves what,—I will not say reason, but semblance or shadow of a reason, could possibly have induced these Christians to commemorate the resurrection of our Lord at the time of his having been put to death? Most certain it is, that Christ's return to life did not take place on the fourteenth day, when the Jews, agreeably to the injunctions of their law, are accustomed to celebrate their passover, but two days afterwards, at the least, that is to say, on the *sixteenth*, or perhaps even so late as the seventeenth day. Nor were the Asiatic Christians ignorant of this; nor did they pretend to deny it. What, then,

could possibly have impelled them to be guilty of such an egregious incongruity, as to determine that the grand annual celebration of Christ's resurrection should be observed on the *fourteenth* day of the month, a day on which they were well apprised that such resurrection did not take place? There are extant, moreover, in an epistle written by *Polycrates*, the bishop of Ephesus, in defence of the Asiatic custom, and which is in part preserved by Eusebius, *Hist. Eccles.* lib. v. cap. xxiv. I say, there are extant in this epistle certain passages, from which it is clear that no dispute whatever existed as to the time of celebrating the anniversary of the resurrection. *Polycrates* says, that he and the rest of the Asiatic bishops, in keeping the passover on the fourteenth day of the month, conformed themselves to the Gospel, the common rule of faith and religion to Christians; ἐτήρησαν τὴν ἡμέραν τῆς τεσσαρεσκαιδεκάτης τῶ πάσχα κατὰ τὸ Ἐυαγγέλιον, μηδὲν παρεκβαίνοντες, ἀλλὰ κατὰ τὸν κανόνα τῆς πίστεως ἀκολυθῦντες. *Servarunt* (those holy men) *diem Paschæ quarta decima luna juxta evangelium, nihil omnino variantes, sed regulam fidei constanter sequentes.* In the sequel *Polycrates* again appeals to the Holy Scriptures, and, relying on their authority, concludes his disputation in the words of the apostles, *Acts,* v. 29. [p. 437.] "We ought to obey God rather than men." The Asiatics, therefore, we see, contended that they conformed to the example of Christ, as propounded in the Gospel. Nor did their adversaries pretend to deny that the Gospel, and the example of Christ, as held forth in the Gospel, were in favour of the Asiatic rule. What they contended for was, that in things of this sort, there was no necessity for closely and literally adhering to the rule of the Gospel, or the example of Christ, as exhibited in the Gospel. If, said they, (as appears from the *Ecclesiastical History* of Socrates Scholasticus, lib. v. cap. xxii.) the days and months, when Christ did any particular thing are not, in the least, to be deviated from by those who would imitate his example, it is necessary that none of those circumstances should be omitted, with which his celebration of the passover was accompanied; "it ought, therefore, to be eaten in an upper chamber," &c. Now, what are we to gather from all this? Do we find it stated in the Gospel, that Christ arose from the dead on the fourteenth day of the month, or that this was the day set apart for the commemoration of that event? Did Christ, when he partook of the paschal supper with his disciples, celebrate the festival of his resurrection? Nothing of this kind, as every one well knows, is to be met with in our Lord's history. It is plain, then, that what the *Asiatics* contended for must have been this, that the day on which they were accustomed to hold their paschal feast, was the same with that on which it appears from the Gospel that Christ, whose example it is incumbent on all Christians to follow, celebrated the passover with his disciples. The dispute, therefore, between them and the rest of the Christians, had no relation to the day of Christ's *resurrection* from the dead, but respected the holding of a *paschal supper,* similar to that which was celebrated by Christ with his disciples a short time previous to his crucifixion.—This *common error,* respecting the feast of Christ's resurrection having been celebrated by the Asiatic Christians on the same day that the Jews ate their passover, arose out of a mistaken interpretation of the word *Pascha.* Since the time of the Council of Nice this term has, for the most part, been considered as indicating that day on which our blessed Saviour arose from the dead, and on which it is usual for us to commemorate this his triumph over death and the grave. But by the more early Christians, previous to the Council of Nice, another meaning was annexed to it, it being made use of by them to designate the *day* on which *Christ celebrated the passover,* and was offered up on the cross, the true paschal lamb, for the sins of the human race. Of its bearing this signification, numerous *examples* might be adduced, but I will content myself with merely giving two, by way of convincing those who are but moderately informed on the subject of Christian antiquities, that I am not without authority for what I thus state. The *first* I shall take from *Tertullian,* the most celebrated Latin writer of this century, who, in his book, *de Oratione,* cap. xiv. p. 155. Opp. expresses himself in the following terms: *Sic et die Paschæ, quo communis et quasi publica jejunii Religio est, merito deponimus osculum, nihil curantes de occultando quod cum omnibus faciamus.* Now, who does not perceive that by the word *Pascha,* we here ought to understand the day on which the Christians were accustomed to commemorate our blessed Saviour's death? For, on this day it was the universal practice, throughout the whole Christian church, to fast; whereas, on the anniversary of Christ's *resurrection,* every kind [p. 438.] of fasting was inhibited. In another place, *viz.* in his book *de Jejuniis,* cap. xiv. p. 712. Tertullian terms the whole *week,* which the Christians commonly styled the *great,* or *the holy* week, *Pascha.* *Quamquam vos etiam sabbatum si quando continuatis, numquam nisi in Pascha,* (that is, on the Sabbath of that week in which the paschal feast is celebrated in commemoration of Christ's death and sufferings) *jejunandum putatis.* By other writers, also, we find the word *pascha* used in this latter sense. To the example of this very ancient Latin author, I subjoin that of a Greek writer of much more recent date, namely, the author of the *Chronicon Paschale,* edited amongst the Byzantine historians, by Rader, and Du Cange; whence, it appears, that even long subsequent to the Council of Nice, the ancient notion attached to the term *Pascha* had not become entirely extinct. This author, at p. 8. of the Parisian edition of his work, by Du Cange, most clearly applies the term *Pascha* to a different day from that whereon the anniversary of Christ's resurrection is kept, and which we term *Pascha,* or Easter, and indicates by this word the day dedicated to the annual commemoration of our blessed Saviour's *death.* In memory of Christ, the true paschal lamb, says he, κατ' ἑκαστὸν ἐνιαυτὸν ἡ τῦ Θεῦ ἐκκλησία τὴν ἀγίαν τῦ πάσχα ἑορτὴν ἐπιτελεῖ, ἀπλανῶς τηρῦσα τῆς ιδ' τῦ πρώτυ μηνὸς τῆς σελένης. *Quotannis ecclesia Dei sanctum paschatis festum celebrat, recte observata* xiv. *primi mensis Lunæ.* Καὶ εἰ μὲν εὑρεθείη αὕτη - - - - ἐν ἡμέρᾳ κυριακῆ τὴν ἀγίαν τῆς ἐκ νεκρῶν ἀναστάσεως Χριστῦ τῦ Θεῦ ἡμῶν ἑορτὴν ἄγει. *Hac vero* (the fourteenth day of the month) *inventa, sequenti Dominica sanctum Christi Dei nostri ex mortuis resurrectioni festum peragit.* Many more passages of a similar kind might be cited from this chronicle, but I pass them over as unnecessary. I will add, however, a notable passage from the epistle written by the Emperor *Constantine the Great,* to the bishops who could not attend the Council of Nice, and which is preserved by Theodoret, *Hist. Eccles.* lib. i. cap. ix. p. 627. The extract will be found to apply more immediately to the subject before us, and places it out of all dispute, that the controversy between the Asiatic and other Christians, respecting the paschal season, had no reference whatever to the day of Christ's resurrection, but to that of his sufferings and *death.* Περὶ τῆς says the Emperor, ἁγιωτάτης τῆ πάσχα ἡμέρας γενομένης ζητήσεως ἰδοξε κοινῇ γνώμη καλῶς ἔχειν, ἐπὶ μιᾶς ἡμέρας πάντας τὸς ἀπανταχῦ ἐπιτελεῖν. *De sanctissimo Die Paschæ quum lis exorta esset* (this was one and the same controversy with that of which we are now treating, for after having lain dormant, it was renewed at the time of the Council of Nice, and was finally set at rest by a decree of that assembly) *optimum factu communi sententia* (of the Nicene fathers) *visum est, uno eodemque tempore hunc omnes ubique gentium celebrare.* In what sense it was meant that the term *Pascha* should be understood in this passage, is shortly after rendered manifest by the emperor himself, in the following words: ἐξέsι γὰρ τῦ ἐκείνων ἴθυς ἀπoβληθέντος ἀληθεσίερα τάξει, ἣν ἐν καιρῶ τῆς τῦ παθὸς ἡμέρας περὶ τῦ παρόντος ἐφυλάξαμεν, καὶ ἐπὶ τὸς μέλλοντας αἰῶνας τὴν τῆς ἐπιτηρήσεως ταύτης συμπλήρωσιν ἐγγίνεσθαι. *Fas enim est rejecta illorum* (the Jews) *consuetudine, veriore instituto, quod circa diem passionis hactenus tenuimus, ejusdem observationis usum ad futura sæcula propagari.* By *Pascha,* therefore, the subject of their disputation, it is plain, was meant, ἡμέρα τῦ παθὸς, the day of our Lord's *passion.* Not being aware of this ancient signification of the word *Pascha,* more recent writers, when they read of the Asiatic Christians [p. 439.] having been involved in a controversy with those of Rome respecting the paschal feast, were hastily led to persuade themselves that the Asiatic Christians celebrated the anniversary of Christ's *resurrection* on the same day on which the Jews ate their *Passover;* understanding the word *Pascha* according to its more recent sense, and never adverting to the possibility of its having, in earlier times, borne a different one.—The merit of first discovering this, however, does not properly belong to me. The person who, first of any, as far as my information reaches, discovered that the common notion in regard to this celebrated controversy respecting the paschal season was erroneous, was that illustrious member of the order of Jesuits so distinguished for his writings, the father *Gabriel Daniel.* See his *Dissertation de la Discipline des quartodecimans pour la Celebration de la paque,* in the third volume of his *Recueil de divers ouvrages Philosophiques, Theologiques, et Historiques.*—*Paris,* 1724, in 4to. p. 473-506. The same thing, if I well remember, is also noticed by Pet. *Faydit,* in his notes to a sermon preached on the feast of St. Polycarp.* This error was, moreover, subsequently adverted to in a *Programma* propounded in the University of Gottingen on Easter-day, by that very profound and ingenious scholar Christoph. Aug. *Heumann,* who seems not in the least to have been aware of its having been previously detected by other people. *Whiston,* too, in the Memoirs of his Life and Writings, Lond. 1749, 8vo. tom. ii. p. 601, complains that no one appeared to be acquainted with the true grounds and cause of this Paschal controversy, and acknowledges that he himself was for a long time involved in similar ignorance; but adds, that in his three Tracts, London, 1742, 8vo. he had unfolded the true

---

* In a subsequent publication, Dr. *Mosheim* took an opportunity of stating that his memory had in this instance proved unfaithful, and that, on a re-perusal of *Faydit's* book, he found himself under the necessity of retracting the compliment which he had here paid to that writer's penetration.

nature of it from original authorities. Of these several works, I regret to say that I have neither just at this moment within my reach, except that of *Daniel*, who, although he certainly discovers much information and judgment as to several particulars, yet, in regard to many others, has not, as it appears to me, attained exactly to a true state of the question. I will, therefore, myself make trial how far it may be possible to place the nature of this very obscure controversy in a just and perspicuous point of view.

(I.) The *early Christians* retaining, as they did, not a few of the Jewish rites and ceremonies, were accustomed, after the manner of the Jews, to partake on a certain day of a *Paschal supper*, and eat together a Paschal lamb. This has been demonstrated from various authorities by Hen. *Dodwell*, in his work *on the Use of Frankincense in the Church*. At present, I shall not occupy myself in regularly repeating such demonstration, inasmuch as the truth of the thing will be rendered apparent by various circumstances, to which it will be necessary for me to advert in the course of this discussion. This *custom* maintained its ground both in the eastern and the western church for many ages. Amongst the *Oriental* Christians, the Armenians, the Copts, and others, it prevails even at this day. By the Christians of the *West* it has been gradually relinquished; some obvious traces of it, however, are still to be discerned even in Christian Europe. The principal difference, in fact, is, that amongst the European Christians the celebration of this sacred repast, which used formerly to take place in the churches, or other places of public assembly, is now confined within the walls of private houses.—This *repast* the early Christians were accustomed to distinguish [p. 440.] by the Jewish denomination of *Pascha*, and, certainly, not without some show of reason; for, in point of external form, it corresponded very nearly with the *Pascha*, or passover of the Jews. The repast itself was undoubtedly of Jewish origin, and might, therefore, well continue to be distinguished by the ancient Jewish appellation. In the causes or reasons for celebrating this repast, the Christians and Jews were widely separated from each other.

(II.) The causes or *reasons* by which the Christians were actuated in the celebration of this paschal feast are not beyond the reach of discovery. In the *first* place, they held themselves bound to follow the *example* of our blessed Saviour, who, previously to his laying down his life for the salvation of the human race, celebrated the passover with his disciples, and had thereby, as they thought, given his sanction to this Jewish rite, and, in a manner, commended the observance of it to his disciples; *secondly*, it appeared to them that the remembrance of the *holy supper*, which our blessed Saviour instituted after his celebration of the passover, might be best preserved in this way. Nor can there be any doubt but that they closed this their paschal feast with the celebration of the Lord's supper; *lastly*, believing, as they did, on the authority of St. Paul, 1 Cor. v. 7, that the Paschal lamb of the Jews was a *type* or figure of Christ's being offered up for the sins of mankind, it appeared to them that there could be no better way of commemorating the Redeemer's sacrifice, and bringing it, as it were, immediately before their eyes, than by celebrating that figurative representation of it which God himself had prescribed. This idea, moreover, of Christ's death having been prefigured in the slaughter of the Paschal lamb, and the fruits of his death by the Paschal feast, being deeply rooted in the minds of the early Christians, occasioned them, as we have above shown by examples, to term the day devoted to the commemoration of our Saviour's *death* the Paschal day.

(III.) The Christians of Asia Minor were accustomed to celebrate this sacred feast, commemorative of the institution of the Lord's supper, and the death of Jesus Christ, at the same *time* when the Jews ate their Paschal lamb, namely, on the evening of the *fourteenth day* of the first month. For, as is clear from the words of *Polycrates*, bishop of Ephesus, which we just above cited from Eusebius, they considered the *example* of Christ as possessing the force of a *law;* and, as is equally manifest, they did not conceive our Saviour to have anticipated the passover, as is believed by many at this day, and particularly by the Greeks, but that the Paschal lamb was eaten by him and his disciples precisely on the same day on which the Jews, conformably to the directions of the Mosaic ritual, were ever accustomed to eat theirs. Let us hear, as to this, *Epiphanius,* who, although he is very obscure in his explication of the opinion of the *Quarta-decimans,* as those were termed who celebrated their Paschal feast at the same time with the Jews, yet intimates perspicuously enough, that the matter in dispute between them and the other Christians respected the time of eating the Paschal lamb. In *Hæres. L. Quarta-decim.* § ii. p. 420, he expresses himself after the following manner: πρῶτον γὰρ ἐν τῇ τεσσαρεσκαιδεκάτῃ τὸ πάσχα ἄγυσι, χρείαν ἔχυσι τὸ πρόβατον λαβεῖν ἀπὸ δεκάτης, κὺι τηρεῖν αὐτὸ ἕως τεσσαρεσκαιδεκάτης. - - ἐὰν δὲ πρὸς ἐσπέραν τυθῇ τὸ πασχα ἢ αὐτη τεσσαρεσκαιδεκάτη ἐπιφώσκυσα ἐξ διατελεῖ ἡμέρας ἐν τῇ νηςεία. *Primum enim si (Quarta-decimani) Pascha die* xiv. *celebrant, necesse est ut Agnum jam die decimo* [p. 441.] *adducant, atque ad diem decimum quartum (vivum) custodiant. Quod si ad Vesperam Pascha fuerit immolatum quod* xiv. *die illucescente geritur, sex dies jejunio tribuendi sunt.* In these words of Epiphanius there are some things which defy explanation, and *Petavius* himself, by the Latin translation which he has given us of them, and which is in part erroneous, and in part imperfect, has tacitly acknowledged that he was unable to comprehend altogether what it was that Epiphanius meant to convey.—I will, however, endeavour to separate what is clear and apparent from what must of necessity remain involved in obscurity.—*First,* then, it is manifest that the dispute with the Quarta-decimans was respecting the *Paschal feast* and the *Paschal lamb,* not the day for commemorating the resurrection of our blessed Saviour from the dead. For in this passage the word *Pascha,* in the first instance, evidently means the Paschal feast, and, in the second, the Paschal lamb. *Secondly,* it is clear that the Quarta-decimans, like the Jews, ate their Paschal lamb on the *fourteenth day* of the month. *Thirdly.* it is apparent that they took home this lamb, in order to its undergoing the requisite preparation, so early as the *tenth day. Fourthly,* it is obvious that they kept this lamb alive until the *fourteenth* day. *Fifthly,* it is plain that they *slew this lamb,* with certain ceremonies, no doubt, on the evening of the *fourteenth* day. Whence it follows, *Sixthly,* that they solemnly *feasted* on this lamb on the night following this evening. We shall presently see that the adversaries of the

Quarta-decimans did not disagree with them respecting this *supper* itself, but as to the *time* of celebrating it.

(IV.) By this Paschal *feast*, which the Asiatic Christians were accustomed to celebrate at the same time with the Jews, an interruption took place in that strict and solemn *fast* which the other Christians made it a rule inviolably to observe throughout the whole of the great or holy *week*. Immediately after the celebration of this feast, however, it was the practice of the Quarta-decimans to *resume* their fasting, and continue it until the day appropriated to the commemoration of our Saviour's *return* to life. The reader will find this recorded by Epiphanius in *Hæres.* lxx. *Audianorum,* § xi. p. 823. The *Audians,* in their celebration of the Paschal feast, were accustomed to follow the example of the Asiatic Christians or Quarta-decimans, and justified their practice by alleging that, in the *Apostolical Constitutions,* (a work different from the one that has reached our days under that title, and at present considered as irrecoverably lost,) the Apostles had expressly enjoined that, in celebrating their Paschal rites, the Christians were to observe the same *time* with the Jews. *Epiphanius* labours hard to deprive them of this argument; and, amongst other things with which he encounters them, adduces the following passage from the same Constitutions: λέγουσι οἱ αὐτοὶ Ἀπόστολοι, ὅτι ὅταν ἐκεῖνοι ἐυωχῶνται, ὑμεῖς τηςεύοντες ὑπὲρ αὐτῶν πενθεῖτε, ὅτι ἐν τῇ ἡμέρᾳ τῆς ἑορτῆς τὸν χριστὸν ἐςαύρωσαν. Καὶ ὅταν αὐτοὶ πενθῶσι τὰ ἄζυμα ἐσίοντες ἐν πικρίσιν, ὑμεῖς ἐυωχεῖσθε. *Iidem Apostoli* (in the Constitutions which ye quote as favouring your practice) *præcipiunt, Dum epulantur illi* (the Jews), *vos jejunantes pro illis lugete, quoniam Festo illo die Christum in Crucem sustulerunt. Cumque illi lugentes azymis et lactucis agrestibus vescentur, vos epulamini.* The Christians are here enjoined by the Apostles to celebrate [p. 442.] the passover with the Jews, and thereupon they are told to feast and rejoice at the time when the Jews were sorrowfully eating their unleavened bread and bitter herbs, and, on the contrary, to mourn and fast on the day that the Jews rejoiced on account of their having put Christ to death. *Petavius,* the erudite translator of Epiphanius, avows himself unable to comprehend the meaning of the Apostles in this. But, from what we have observed above, there is as much light thrown upon this apostolical injunction as is necessary. The Christians who agreed with the Jews as to the time of celebrating the Passover, held with joy and gladness their Paschal feast, in commemoration of the institution of the Lord's supper, on the same night that the Jews fed on bitter herbs and unleavened bread; but on the following day, when the Jews gave themselves up to rejoicing, these Christians returned again to fasting, humiliation, and tears, inasmuch as it was on that day that their Lord and Master Christ had been put to death on the cross.

(V.) On the *third day following the fourteenth* of the month, the Asiatic Christians always celebrated the anniversary of Christ's *resurrection* from the dead. For since, as we are informed by Polycrates, they made it a point to follow as exactly as possible the example of Christ, and the rule of the Gospel; and it appeared, from the testimony of the evangelists, that Christ arose from the dead on the *third* day after the Jewish passover, consistency required that they should fix on this day for the annual commemoration of that glorious event. This practice, however, gave rise to another *difference* between them and other Christians. For it was the custom with the latter never to keep the feast of the *resurrection* on any other than the *first day of the week*, or, as we term it, *Sunday*; whereas the former, we mean the *Asiatic* Christians, very frequently celebrated Christ's triumph over death and the grave on one or other of the ordinary week days. For, as the *fourteenth* day of the month did not always fall on one and the same day of the week, and they always commemorated our blessed Saviour's return to life on the *third day after* the fourteenth, it of course happened that such commemoration took place with them in one year on a *Monday*, in the next, perhaps on a *Tuesday*, and in a third on a *Wednesday*, and so on. When the *fourteenth day* of the month, for instance, fell on a Tuesday, these Asiatic Christians kept the feast of the resurrection on the *Thursday* following; or, supposing it to fall on a Wednesday, their feast took place on the *Friday* after. Hence the Roman prelate *Victor*, and those who took part with him, decreed, ὡς ἄν μὴ δὲ ἐν ἄλλῃ ποτὲ τῆς κυριακῆς ἡμέρᾳ τὸ τῆς ἐκ νεκρῶν ἀναςάςεως ἐπιτελοῖτο τῷ Κυρίῳ μυςήριον. Καὶ ὅπως ἐν ταύτῃ μόνῃ τῶν κατὰ τὸ Πάσχα νηςειῶν φυλλαττοίμεθα τὰς ἐπιλύςεις. *Ne videlicet ullo alio quam Dominico Die mysterium resurrectionis Domini unquam celebretur; utque eo duntaxat die Jejuniorum Paschæ terminum observemus.* Eusebius, *Histor. Eccles.* lib. v. cap. xxiii. p. 190. It is plain, therefore, that the Asiatic Christians must frequently have celebrated *The mystery of the Resurrection of Christ* on a different day from Sunday: for, had they, in the celebration of this mystery, conformed to the practice of other Christians, there would have been no necessity for this regulation. In these words of *Eusebius*, however, it is observable that a clear distinction is made between the day of the mystery of Christ's *resurrection* and what is termed [p. 443.] *Pascha*, that is, the season devoted to the commemoration of his *death* and passion. In the observance of *Pascha*, that is, the commemoration of Christ's sufferings and *death*, the Asiatic Christians, as to time, agreed precisely with the rest: the only thing in which they differed was, that whereas the latter *fasted* without intermission throughout the whole of the season, the Asiatics indulged themselves with a temporary relaxation on the fourteenth day. The mystery of Christ's resurrection, however, was not always celebrated by them on the *Sunday*, as was the uniform practice of all other Christians, but occasionally on other days of the week, agreeably to what we have above remarked. This difference was certainly of greater moment, and, to confess the truth, one less easily to be endured than the other. For to celebrate the festival of Christ's resurrection on a different day of the week from that whereon he actually arose, must have appeared repugnant not only to the faith of history, but to ancient custom and Christian decency.

(VI.) The Christians dwelling without the confines of Asia, deemed it irreligious to terminate the Paschal *fast* before the festival of the resurrection; and, as altogether unbecoming and disgraceful in Christians, to hold out any ostensible connection between their *paschal lamb*, so widely differing in its purpose and design from that of the Jews, and the Jewish passover. They, therefore, *deferred their Paschal feast* until the night preceding the festival of our Saviour's resurrection, and connected the commemoration of the institution of the Lord's

supper with that of Christ's triumph over death and the grave. Let us hear as
to this *Epiphanius, in Hæres.* l. *Quartadecimanorum,* § iii. p. 421, ἡ ἀγία Θεῦ
ἐκκλησία - - - κέχρηται ἤ μόνον τεσσαρεσκαιδεκάτη, ἀλλὰ καὶ τῆ ἑβδομάδι - -
ἵνα κατὰ τὰ ὑπὸ τῦ κυρίυ γενόμενα κατὰ τὸ πρωτότυπὸν, ἔιη ἀνάςασις τε καὶ ἐυαχία.
*Ecclesia sancta Dei - - - non solum decimam quartam diem sed etiam hebdomada
observat - - - ut ad eorum exemplar quæ sunt a Domino gesta Resurrectio epulæ-
que celebrentur.* And after some intervening remarks, he continues, Φέρομεν δὲ
ἐπὶ τὴν ἀγίαν κυριακὴν τὸ τέλος τῆς συμτοραώσεως· λαμβάνομεν δὲ τὸ πρόβατον ἀπὸ
δεκάτης, ὄνομα τῦ Ἰησῦ ἐπιγνόντες διὰ τὸ Ἰῶτα, ἵνα μὴ λάθη ἡμᾶς μηδὲν τῶν
κατὰ τὴν ἀλήθειαν πασᾶν τῆς ζωτικῆς ταύτης τῦ πάσχα τῆς ἐκκλησιαςικῆς
πραγματείας. *In sanctum Dominicam religiosissimi temporis finem conjicimus :
sed agnum jam tum a decimo die sumimus quoniam in Iota littera Jesu nomen
agnoscimus, ne quid omnino diligentiam nostram effugiat, quod ad ecclesiasticam
salutaris paschæ celebrationem pertinere videatur.* Now, we will not spend our
time in endeavoring to dispel the obscurity in which this passage also of Epiphanius is involved, but direct our attention merely to such things as stand in
no need of elucidation. In the *first* place, then, it is to be remarked, that the
adversaries of the Asiatic Christians celebrated a *paschal feast* just as these
Christians themselves did. *Secondly,* that they *conjoined this feast* with the festival of our Lord's resurrection. *Thirdly,* that as to this matter they, no less
than the Asiatics, persuaded themselves that they followed the *example* of
Jesus Christ; but in what way they could possibly have made this appear is not
very easy to comprehend. *Fourthly,* that by this *feast,* which they celebrated
in the night preceding the day devoted to the commemoration of our Lord's
resurrection, they closed their paschal season, or that most holy period of time
which was annually set apart for the solemn commemoration of Christ's suffer-
[p. 444.] ings and death. This *feast,* therefore, constituted no part of the commemoration of the resurrection, but was the grand *concluding act* of the preceding
paschal season. The night being elapsed, these Christians commenced with
the dawning day their celebration of the anniversary of Christ's triumph over
death and the grave. *Fifthly,* it appears that the *paschal* lamb, of which they
partook on the night preceding the feast of the resurrection, was selected and
put under a course of preparation on the *tenth day* of the month ; a circumstance corresponding precisely with the practice of the Asiatics. For this *Epiphanius* gives us a far-fetched reason derived from the letter I, which is the first
in the name of Jesus. The force of this reason, however, may be comprehended
without difficulty. The letter *Iota* was made use of by the Greeks to denote
the number ten. These Christians then, if any faith is to be placed in the
statement given by Epiphanius, reasoned after this manner; the *name* of *Jesus*
begins with the letter I ; but the letter I denotes the number *ten* ; that lamb,
therefore, which is the shadow or emblem of Jesus, who was sacrificed for our
sins, ought to be selected from the flock, and brought to the house of the high
priest on the *tenth day.* This mode of reasoning was certainly by no means
foreign to the genius or disposition of the early Christians, who, like the Cab-
balist Jews, conceived great mysteries to be involved in certain numbers. I
must confess, however, that I do not believe this to have been the true origin

of the custom, but rather suspect *Epiphanius* to have followed, in this instance, merely the suggestions of his own fancy. The *lamb* thus separated from the flock on the tenth day, and in a certain degree consecrated, was not immediately slain, but seems to have been kept alive until the evening next preceding the feast of the resurrection. *Sixthly*, it appears that these adversaries of the Asiatic Christians gave to the whole of the season which they devoted to the commemoration of Christ's sufferings and death, and more particularly to that feast with which they concluded it, the denomination of *Pascha*. This is manifest from the last words of Epiphanius.

(VII.) These things, then, being duly weighed and ascertained, it is, I think, plainly to be perceived in what respects the Asiatic Christians or Quarta-decimans *differed* from the rest. Their disagreement was *not*, as the learned father *Daniel* imagined, respecting the proper season or day for commemorating Christ's *death*: for it was no less the practice of the Christians in general than of the Asiatics to consider as peculiarly solemn and sacred, that day on which Christ made atonement by his *death* for the sins of the human race: and even as to the *very* day itself, no difference of opinion whatever existed between them and the Asiatics; παρατηρόμεϑα, says Epiphanius, *Hæres.* L. i. §iii. p. 421. μὲν τὴν τεσσαρεσκαιδεκάτην. *Et nos quartam illam decimam diem* (which is held sacred by the Quarta-decimans) *religiose servamus*. Neither did the *time* for celebrating the feast of our Lord's resurrection constitute the principal or leading point in dispute between them, but the *time* for holding the paschal supper. The dispute, in fact, embraced the *three* following questions: *First*, whether it was proper to begin the day devoted to the commemoration of Christ's sufferings and death with the paschal supper, and thereby break in upon the sacred and solemn *fast* of the day? The Christians of Asia Minor asserted the propriety of this usage, the other Christians denied it. *Secondly*, whether it was becoming, in the disciples and followers of Christ, to eat their paschal lamb at the same *time* when the *Jews*, his most inveterate and rancorous enemies, ate theirs? The Asiatic Christians contended that it was; the other Christians that it was not. *Thirdly*, [p. 445.] whether it was proper to celebrate the feast of our blessed Saviour's *resurrection* always on the *third* day *after the fourteenth* day of the month on which he was put to death? The Asiatic Christians maintained that it was; the others, that it was not; these latter insisting that as it was on the *first day of the week* that Christ actually arose from the dead, no other day than this ought to be appropriated to the commemoration of that stupendous and unparalleled event.

LXXII. **Termination of the Paschal Controversy.** In the course of this century attempts were not unfrequently made to put an end to this dissension, which was found by sad experience to yield repeated occasion for unchristian-like wranglings and the most intricate and acrimonious disputes.([1]) Under the reign of *Antoninus Pius*, in particular, about the middle of this century, a serious discussion of the affair took place at Rome between *Anicetus*, the bishop of that city, and *Polycarp*, the celebrated bishop of Smyrna.(²) But by no arguments whatever could the Christians of Asia be prevailed on to abandon their practice, which they considered as having been handed down to them by the apostle *St. John.* Impatient, therefore, of their pertinacity, it was towards the close of this century determined by *Victor,* bishop of Rome, that these Asiatics should be dealt with after a more peremptory manner, and be compelled by certain laws and decrees to conform themselves to the rule observed by the greatest part of the Christian community. In this resolution he was supported by the voice of several councils that were called together in various provinces on the subject; and under the cover of their sanction, he addressed to the Asiatic bishops an imperious epistle, admonishing them no longer to persist in differing from other Christians as to their pascal observances.(³) Finding, however, that they were not in this way to be moved, but that they boldly addressed letters to the Roman church by *Polycrates,* bishop of Ephesus, in justification of their ancient practice, *Victor* proceeded to the further length of *excluding* them from his communion, or, in other words, he pronounced them altogether unworthy of being any longer considered by him and his church in the light of brethren.(⁴) This imprudent step might have been productive of the most serious detriment to the interests of Christianity, had not *Irenæus,* bishop of Lyons, in Gaul, interfered, and, although differing himself in opinion from the Asiatics, written letters to the bishop of Rome and the other prelates, pointing out, in the most forcible terms, the injustice of depriving of their rights, and pronouncing unworthy of the name of Christians, brethren, whose sentiments, with regard to religion itself, were strictly correct, and against whom no other matter of offence could be alleged than a diversity as to certain external rites and observances. The *Asiatics* also, in a long epistle which they circulated throughout the Christian world, took care to remove from themselves every suspicion of an attempt to corrupt the Catholic religion. A sort of *compromise,* therefore, took place with regard to those ritual differences, each party retaining its own peculiar opinions and usages, until the holding of the *council of Nice,* in the fourth century, when the custom of the Asiatics was altogether abolished.

(1) The reader may consult as to this Epiphanius in *Hæres. Audia-* [p. 446.] *norum,* lxx. § ix. p. 821.

(2) See Eusebius, *Histor. Eccles.* lib. iv. cap. xiv. p. 127, and lib. v. cap. xxiv. p. 193. In fact, it is to this author that we are indebted for nearly the whole of what is here related.

(3) *Polycrates,* in his Epistle to the Roman church, *apud* Euseb. *Hist. Eccles.* lib. v. cap. xxiv. p. 192, says, ὁ πτύρομαι ἐπὶ τοῖς καταπλησσομένοις. *Nihil moveor iis quæ nobis ad formidinem intentantur.* These words plainly prove that *Victor* did not pursue a moderate and amicable course with his Asiatic brethren, but had recourse to *threats,* and wished to have impressed their minds with fear.

(4) Eusebius, *Histor. Eccles.* lib. v. cap. xxiv. p. 192, says, Βίκτωρ ἀθρόως τᾶς Ασίας πάσης ἅμα ταῖς ὁμόραις ἐκκλησίαις τᾶς παροικίας ἀποτέμνειν ὡς ἑτεροδοξότας τῆς κοινῆς ἑνώσεως πειρᾶται, καὶ σηλιτεύει γε διὰ γραμμάτων ἀκοινωνήτους ἄρδην πάντας τὸς ἐκεῖσε ἀνακηρύττων ἀδελφός. Of these words *Valesius* gives us the following translation: *Victor omnis Asiæ vicinarumque Provinciarum Ecclesias, tamquam contraria rectæ Fidei sentientes, a Communione abscindere conatur, datisque litteris universos qui illic erant fratres proscribit, et ab unitate ecclesiæ prorsus alienos esse pronuntiat.* From the word πειρᾶται, which Eusebius makes use of, this learned writer thought himself justified in concluding that *Victor* did not in reality *exclude* the Asiatics from all communion with the faithful, but merely *wished,* or attempted so to exclude them, and that this his attempt was frustrated by the interference of *Irenæus.* This interpretation is approved of by many of the friends to the papacy, who seem to imagine that the temerity of *Victor* is thereby somewhat extenuated. *Others* would contend that at least this much must be granted them, that the words of Eusebius are ambiguous, and that we are consequently left in a state of obscurity, as to whether *Victor actually* excommunicated the Asiatics, or merely *wished* and endeavoured to have them excommunicated. By the greater part, however, not only of Protestant, but Roman Catholic writers, it has long been considered, that what is subsequently said by Eusebius of Victor's having, by letters, excluded the Asiatics from his communion, relieves his preceding words from every sort of obscurity, and makes it apparent, that the Roman prelate did not content himself with merely willing the thing, but *actually* carried his threats into execution. But *to me* it appears, that even these, although their ideas on the subject are more correct than those of *Valesius* and his followers, have not exactly caught the meaning of Eusebius. The historian, unless I am altogether deceived, is speaking of *two designs* which *Victor* had in view, the *one* of which was merely conceived, the *other* carried into effect. *Victor* both wished and endeavoured to bring about the *expulsion* of the Asiatics from all *communion with the Catholic church,* as corrupters of the true religion; but in this he failed of success: for the other bishops would neither conform themselves to his will, nor imitate his example. What, therefore, he could accomplish without the concurrence of the other bishops, that he did; that is to say, he by letter *expelled* the Asiatics from all *communion with the church of Rome,* over which he presided. The latter words of Eusebius are badly rendered by Valesius, and through this faulty

translation, support has been afforded to a common error in regard to what was done by Victor on this occasion, to which I shall presently advert. The [p. 447.] Greek words, ἀνακηρύττων ἀκοινωνήτους are rendered into Latin by Valesius thus, *ab unitate ecclesiæ prorsus alienos esse pronuntiat.* But this by no means corresponds with the Greek original, in which nothing whatever is said of alienation, *ab unitate ecclesiæ.* The translation ought to have ran, *a communione suæ alienos pronuntiabat.* The words of this eminent scholar, however, are strictly in unison with the *common opinion* of both Roman Catholics and Protestants, who are all unanimous in considering *Victor* as having, by his letters, deprived the Asiatic brethren of every sort of communion with the whole Christian church; in fact, as having on this occasion asserted the same powers with regard to excommunication, as were exercised by his successors posterior to the age of Charlemagne. The Protestants, in particular, call upon us to mark in this case the *first specimen* of the arrogant and domineering spirit of the bishop of Rome, the first example of anti-christian excommunication. But these worthy men laboured under an error, and formed their judgment of a matter of antiquity from the practice of more recent times. In the age in which *Victor* lived, the *power* of the bishop of Rome had not attained to such an height as to enable him to cut off from communion with the *church at large* all those of whose opinions or practices he might see reason to disapprove. The very history of the Paschal controversy now before us, places this out of all dispute. For, had the bishop of Rome possessed the right and power of cutting off whom he pleased from all communion with the church at large, neither *Irenæus* nor the rest of the bishops would have *dared* to oppose his will, but must have bowed with submission to whatever he might have thought proper to determine. Every bishop, however, possessed the power of excluding all such as he might consider to be the advocates of grievous errors, or as the corrupters of religion, from all communion *with himself and the church over which he presided,* or, in other words, he might declare them *unworthy* of being considered any longer as *brethren.* This power, indeed, is possessed by the teachers of the church even at this day. Victor, then, exercised this common right with which every bishop was invested, and by letters made known to the other churches that he had excluded the Christians of Asia Minor, on account of their pertinacity in defending their ancient practice, from all communion with himself and the church of *Rome,* expecting, in all probability, that the other bishops might be induced to follow his example, and, in like manner, renounce all connection with these Asiatics. But in this he was deceived: ἀλλ᾽ ὐ πᾶσι γε τοῖς ἐπισκόποις ταῦτ᾽ ἠρέσκετο, says Eusebius, *Histor. Eccles.* lib. v. cap. xxiv. p. 192, *Verum non omnibus hæc placebant Episcopis.* The rest of the bishops declined following the example of the Roman prelate in a line of conduct so very dangerous and imprudent. There can be no doubt, however, but that they would have followed his example, indeed, whether willing or not, they *must* have followed it, if in this age the doors of the church might have been closed against men by the mere *will* of the Roman bishop. The conduct of *Victor,* therefore, on this occasion, although distinguished by temerity and imprudence, does yet not wear so dark an aspect as is commonly imagined, neither could it have been attended with consequences of such extensive importance as those would have us believe who hold it up as the first abuse of excommunication. The fact is, that they who treat the matter in this way are guilty of an abuse with regard to the term *excommunication.* Victor did not (according to the sense in which the term is at present understood) *excommunicate* the Asiatics, but merely declared that he, and the members of the church over which he presided, must cease to consider them in the light of *brethren* until they should consent to renounce their objectionable practices.

END OF THE FIRST VOLUME.

No. of pages of Text,	520
No. of pages of Prefaces, Contents, &c.,	22
No. of pages in Volume,	561

DATE DUE

GAYLORD			PRINTED IN U.S.A.

CPSIA information can be obtained at www.ICGtesting.com
Printed in the USA
LVOW10s1716150915

454265LV00020B/1458/P

3 4711 00225 2999

9 781313 725675